D1604456

Foundations of
Deductive Databases
and Logic Programming

To Rita
for her love and support

Foundations of Deductive Databases and Logic Programming

Contributors

Krzysztof R. Apt
Francois Bancilhon
Howard A. Blair
Upen S. Chakravarthy
Maarten H. van Emden
John Grant
Lawrence J. Henschen
Tomasz Imielinski
Paris C. Kanellakis
Robert Kowalski
Jean-Louis Lassez
Vladimir Lifschitz
Michael J. Maher
Sanjay Manchanda
Kim Marriott
Jack Minker

Lee Naish
Hyung-sik Park
Teodor C. Przymusinski
Raghu Ramakrishnan
Kotagiri Ramamohanarao
Fariba Sadri
Yehoshua Sagiv
John C. Shepherdson
Elizabeth A. Sonenberg
Peter Szeredi
James A. Thom
Rodney W. Topor
Allen Van Gelder
Adrian Walker
David S. Warren

Edited by Jack Minker
Department of Computer Science
University of Maryland and
Institute for Advanced Computer Studies

MORGAN KAUFMANN PUBLISHERS, INC.
95 First Street
Los Altos California 94022

Editor and President   *Michael B. Morgan*
Production Manager   *Jennifer Ballentine*
Production Assistants   *Todd R. Armstrong and P.J. Schemenaur*
Design   *Michael Rogondino*
Composition   *E / F Typographic Lab*
Index   *Foxon-Maddocks Associates*

Library of Congress Cataloging-in-Publication Data

Foundations of deductive databases and logic programming / edited by
   Jack Minker.
   p. cm.
   Bibliography: p.
   Includes indexes.
   ISBN 0-934613-40-0
   1. Deductive data bases. 2. Logic programming. I. Minker, Jack.
   QA76.9.D32F68   1987
   006.3—dc19   87-33870
                                                                      CIP

Morgan Kaufmann Publishers, Inc.
95 First Street, Los Altos, CA 94022
© 1988 by Morgan Kaufmann Publishers, Inc.
All rights reserved.
Printed in the United States
ISBN 0-934613-40-0

92   91   90   89   88   5   4   3   2   1

Contents

Introduction

Jack Minker

Department of Computer Science and
Institute for Advanced Computer Studies
University of Maryland
College Park, MD

Background

The fields of deductive databases and logic programming are intimately re-lated. Theoretical developments in one area have impacted on the other. This is not surprising as both subjects are an outgrowth of work in automated theorem proving. Much exciting research is being conducted in both of these areas. However, the research in each area is presented at conferences where the two groups do not generally intersect. Research in deductive databases is beginning to appear in database conferences and database journals, while research in logic programming appears in artificial intelligence conferences, logic programming conferences, and logic programming journals. The only workshop devoted ex-clusively toward both areas was organized in 1977 by Jean-Marie Nicolas and Hervé Gallaire in Toulouse, France. The book *Logic and Databases*, edited by Hervé Gallaire and Jack Minker [1978], contained refereed and revised ver-sions of some of the papers that were presented at that workshop. The book was influential in having interested researchers in the deductive approach to databases. Although there have been some workshops devoted toward similar areas since 1977, there was no one workshop that was devoted toward the sub-ject of deductive databases and logic programming.

Logic programming is an outgrowth of work in automated theorem prov-ing. In 1965, J. Alan Robinson introduced a single method of inference for first-order logic, termed the resolution principle. It is a refutation method; that

1

is, one starts with a set of clauses and performs inferences until one discovers a contradiction. If the set with which one starts is unsatisfiable, the resolution principle is guaranteed to find a contradiction. If it is not, it may never terminate. The resolution principle works on arbitrary clauses in first-order logic, where a clause is of the form,

$$P_1, P_2, \ldots, P_m \leftarrow Q_1, Q_2, \ldots, Q_n,$$

where the P_i, $i = 1, \ldots, m$ and the Q_j, $j = 1, \ldots, n$ are atomic formulae, which may contain function symbols, constants, and variables. All variables in a clause are assumed to be universally quantified. Any closed first-order formula may be transformed to clausal form (Chang and Lee [1973]). The set of atoms to the left of the arrow is referred to as the head of the clause and the set of atoms in the right hand side is referred to as the body of the clause. A clause has both a declarative and a procedural (or problem solving) reading. The declarative reading is that for all values of the variables in the clause, P_1 or P_2 or...P_m is true if Q_1 and Q_2 and...Q_n are true. The procedural (problem solving) reading is that for all values of the variables in the clause, to solve P_1 or P_2 or...or P_m, Q_1 and Q_2 and...and Q_n have to be solved.

In dealing with arbitrary clauses, many variants of the resolution principle have been proposed (Chang and Lee [1973], Loveland [1978]). One of the variants is termed linear resolution, developed by Loveland [1978]. Kowalski and Kuehner [1971] refined linear resolution and developed an inference system termed SL resolution which, like linear resolution, is complete and sound. The underlying idea in SL resolution is to be able to select a single literal in a clause and to use only the literal selected to unify with against other clauses. Not all literals in a clause may be selected for unification. Only the most recently introduced literals may be used. SL resolution does not decrease the computational complexity associated with theorem proving in the presence of arbitrary clauses. In general, there are three parts to SL resolution: *extension* of a clause by resolution with a clause from the given set of clauses, termed input resolution, *factoring* a clause, and *ancestry resolution*, resolving a clause with an ancestor of a clause. In contrast to linear resolution, one need only select a single literal in a clause on which to perform resolution. The literal selected must be from the most recently introduced literals into the resolvent of a clause.

Theoretical foundations of logic programming have been under development since the early 1970s, when Kowalski [1974] proposed the concept of logic programming and Colmerauer (Roussel [1975]) and his students implemented the first version of PROLOG. Both Kowalski and Colmerauer noted that a subset of first-order logic, Horn clauses, was adequate for a programming language. A Horn clause is a clause in which $m \leq 1$ and $n \geq 0$. The restriction to Horn clauses drastically decreases the complexity of finding solutions to problems. Hill [1974] demonstrated that a modification to SL resolution was complete and sound for Horn clauses. He termed the inference system LUSH (linear resolution with unrestricted selection function based on Horn clauses). Neither factorization of a clause nor ancestry resolution is needed for LUSH resolution. Furthermore, the selection restriction of SL resolution is no longer needed, and one can select an arbitrary literal in the clause on which to resolve. LUSH resolution was renamed by Apt and van Emden [1982] to be SLD resolution (*SL* resolution for *D*efinite clauses). This inference system is used in implementations of the PROLOG language.

Theoretical foundations of logic programming received a major impetus from the work of van Emden and Kowalski [1976] who described the semantics of logic programming and related it to conventional language concepts. In particular, they noted that the use of Horn clauses led to a unique minimal model. That is, the intersection of all Herbrand models of a program that consists of Horn clauses is a model. They showed also that logic programs have a closure operator over the Herbrand Base. Apt, Blair, and Walker in their chapter in this book show how to extend the closure operator to obtain a declarative semantics for extended Horn clauses in stratified programs that permit negative atoms in the body of a clause.

When dealing with Horn clauses, one cannot prove statements about negative atoms that do not appear in a program. Indeed, Horn logic programs only permit clauses in the program that are definite. That is, they have exactly one positive atom in a program clause. Within PROLOG, one treats negation as the failure to find a positive solution to an atom. Theories about negation were proposed by Reiter, the Closed World Assumption [1978b], and by Clark [1978], who related negation to the introduction of only if statements. Clark proved the soundness of the inference system SLDNF (SLD resolution plus the Negation-as-Failure rule) for extended Horn clauses, provided the negation-as-failure rule was only used on ground atoms. An extended Horn clause permits negative atoms in the body of a clause. Apt and van Emden [1982] provided a framework of fixpoint techniques in which to formulate the problems of soundness and completeness that are now standard. Lassez and Maher [1984] established the soundness and completeness of fair SLD-resolution for computing finite failure. The completeness of SLDNF for Horn clauses under the same conditions as Clark's was proved by Jaffar, Lassez, and Lloyd [1983]. An overview of these issues is presented in Jaffar, Lassez, and Maher, and the book written by Lloyd [1984], *Foundations of Logic Programming*, presents a theoretical treatment of logic programming and contains the details of the proofs.

The area of deductive databases was an outgrowth of work by Green and Raphael [1968a, 1968b] in 1968. They were the first to recognize the importance of work by Robinson [1965] on deduction and to apply it to the field of databases. Green [1969] in his thesis, also presaged work in logic programming. In the area of foundations of deductive databases, Reiter [1978, 1984] has written several important papers describing theories of databases and how they generalize conventional relational databases. He developed the concept of a Closed World Assumption (CWA) that treats negation in deductive databases. He has shown also how deductive databases can handle concepts such as some aspect of null values and indefinite data, that could not be handled in conventional relational databases. In a series of papers, Lloyd and Topor (Lloyd and Topor [1985, 1986], Topor [1984]) have developed a theoretical basis for deductive databases. They also show how to implement their generalization in a logic programming language such as PROLOG. The generalization refers to general Horn clause theories, where a general Horn clause is a formula of the form, A ←W, where A is an atom and W is a typed first-order formula.

Work in the above areas has been restricted to theories in which there is a single conclusion in a clause (or extended clause). To handle non-Horn theories, Minker [1982] developed the concept of a Generalized Closed World Assumption (GCWA). He provides both a model theoretic and a proof theoretic definition of the GCWA and proves that the same answers are obtained in both approaches. It extends Reiter's Closed World Assumption that applies to Horn deductive databases.

A comprehensive survey of the field of deductive databases as of 1984 is given by Gallaire, Minker, and Nicolas [1984]. Their survey contains an extensive bibliography on the subject. A historical perspective of thirty years of work in deductive databases and its relationships to logic programming and automated theorem proving, starting from work in 1957, was written by Minker [1987]. This paper provides also an extensive bibliography on deductive databases and contains references to the early work in this field.

Workshop on Foundations of Deductive Databases and Logic Programming

Because of the above developments, in 1985 I thought that the time was ripe to hold a workshop devoted primarily toward the subject of foundations of deductive databases and logic programming. The purpose of the workshop was to provide a common forum for leading researchers in both fields. The primary emphasis of the workshop was toward theoretical foundations in both fields. Whereas no conferences or workshops were oriented toward theoretical aspects of these subjects, there are numerous conferences devoted to applications.

In addition to bringing together leading researchers, I thought that it would be important to attract more researchers to these areas both in terms of faculty and students. In particular, I wanted to influence graduate students to enter into this exciting area of research.

It was with the above objectives that I solicited funds from the National Science Foundation (NSF) to support the workshop. The NSF awarded me a grant to be utilized to provide partial support for travel and subsistence for participants, faculty, and students to attend the workshop and for preprints of the workshop. The workshop, entitled Workshop on Foundations of Deductive Databases and Logic Programming, was held August 18-22, 1986, in Washington, DC. In addition, support for my time and efforts was provided jointly by the University of Maryland Department of Computer Science and Institute for Advanced Computing Studies (UMIACS). UMIACS also provided financial support for the meeting, reception, and a dinner in honor of the authors and assigned Mrs. Johanna Weinstein to work with me on the arrangements and general organization of the workshop. I could not have organized the workshop without her invaluable assistance. John Grant, of Towson State University, was a constant source of ideas and assistance in organizing the workshop.

The preprints that appeared in the *Proceedings of the Workshop on the Foundations of Deductive Databases and Logic Programming* (Minker [1986]) were, in many cases, preliminary papers. The authors made them available for the workshop participants. There was no attempt to referee or edit the papers as I wanted to have research ideas presented that were in progress. The papers that appear in this book have been drawn from that workshop. Each paper has been reviewed by at least three experts drawn both from the workshop attendees and from others who were expert in the particular subject but did not attend the workshop.

Overview of Book

The papers that appear in this book extend the theoretical developments outlined above. I have subdivided the articles into three major parts:

1. *Part I—Negation and Stratified Databases*

2. *Part II—Fundamental Issues in Deductive Databases and Implementation*

3. *Part III—Unification and Logic Programs*

The first part of the book, *Negation and Stratified Databases*, is devoted to the important problem of negation in deductive databases and logic programming. As noted in the background material, there are a number of approaches that have been developed for negation. It has been known that problems arise for certain classes of axioms. The concept of a stratified database identifies one of the problems as the case where a negated atom appears in the body of a clause. In this case, to avoid problems, it must be possible to order the database clauses, as described below. The first chapter in this part provides an overview of the problem of negation, while subsequent chapters describe the accomplishments that have been made in negation and stratification.

This part of the book starts with a comprehensive survey by Shepherdson in Chapter 1 on negation and stratified databases. Shepherdson describes the major developments that have taken place and summarizes previous developments as well as those reported at the workshop and in this book. He discusses the various results that have been obtained and their relationships to one another. It would be useful for the reader to review this chapter before reading the other chapters in this part of the book.

In Chapter 2, Apt, Blair, and Walker introduce the important concept of a stratified database in which one deals with extended or general clauses that have negated atoms in the body of a clause. A database that consists of a set of clauses is *stratified* if the clauses can be partitioned into ordered sets of clauses such that if a negated atom appears in the body of a clause in a partition, then the definition of the atom appears in a previous partition, and if a positive atom appears in the body of a clause, then its definition appears either in the same partition or in a previous partition. They develop a fixpoint theory of nonmonotonic operators and apply it to provide a declarative meaning of a general program. They prove also the consistency of Clark's [1978] completed model database for stratified programs and clarify some previously reported problems with negation in logic programming.

Van Gelder, in Chapter 3, independently developed the concept of stratified programs. He showed that general logic programs with the so-called bounded term size property and freedom from recursive negation (i.e., the program is stratified) are "completely classified" by what he refers to as tight semantics in which every atom in the Herbrand base of the program either succeeds or fails.

Lifschitz, in Chapter 4, using the concept of prioritized circumscription, obtains results with respect to the semantics and minimal model of stratified programs. The concept of circumscription was introduced by McCarthy [1980] in the context of artificial intelligence and common-sense reasoning. Circumscription is a method of minimizing predicates to exclude concepts that are not explicitly stated in the theory. It is of interest to see that work in artificial intelligence relates to work in deductive databases and logic programming.

In Chapter 5, Przymusinski then extends the notion of stratified logic programs to deductive databases that allow negative premises and disjunctive consequents (i.e., they are general non-Horn logic programs). He introduces the concepts of a *locally stratifiable database* and of a *perfect model* of a database and shows that the set of perfect models provides an appropriate semantics for such a database. In addition, he shows the relationships between prioritized circumscription and stratified databases.

The paper by Topor and Sonenberg, Chapter 6, rounds out this area. They study a class of "domain independent" databases: ones for which the set of correct answers to a query is independent of the domains of variables in database clauses. They prove that every *allowed* stratified database is domain independent and that every domain independent stratified database has an equivalent allowed database.

For related work in stratified databases, see papers by Naqvi [1986], who also independently developed the concept of a stratified database, and by Chandra and Harel [1982, 1985], who also discussed stratification but in a slightly different context. For other relationships of circumscription to deductive databases, see papers by Minker and Perlis [1984a, 1985], by Lifschitz [1986] and by Reiter [1982].

Part II—Fundamental Issues in Deductive Databases and Implementations deals with fundamental issues in deductive databases, of both a theoretical and a practical nature. Implementations of large systems will be required before one can say that deductive databases have fully matured. There are a number of fundamental issues that must be resolved before this may become a reality. Some of the issues addressed in this book are the use of semantic information to optimize deductive search, the development of informative answers to queries, updating integrity constraints, deleting data, handling recursive axioms in the theory, and accessing data and axioms efficiently.

The first chapter of this part, Chapter 7, by Chakravarthy, Grant, and Minker, provides the foundations for incorporating integrity constraints with axioms to achieve general program clauses. The incorporation of integrity constraints permits semantic optimization to be performed on queries, as integrity constraints provide semantic information regarding a database. The approach permits queries to be terminated that violate the constraints, may introduce selection or join conditions into a query, or may obviate the need for a join condition. The addition of this type of information also can be used to provide intelligent response to users when queries either succeed or fail, as described by Gal and Minker [1987].

Imielinski, in Chapter 8, proposes that instead of performing all deductions during query run-time, there is a variety of situations in which it should suffice to respond to the user by specifying an axiom as an answer. If this is not satisfactory, the user can always force further deduction to take place. Imielinski argues that a general axiom provides more ''intelligent'' answers to a user than the detailed answer that consists of the tuples that satisfy the query. In addition, it saves searches of the database. The approach by Imielinski can, in principle, be combined with the results described in the previous chapter.

The problem of updating, deleting, and checking integrity constraints is discussed by Kowalski and Sadri in Chapter 9. They propose an extension to SLDNF for checking constraints in deductive databases and show that their inference system is as complete as SLDNF. They achieve the effect of the simplification methods of a number of investigators whose work they describe. In addition, they handle the problem of updating data when facts or general rules are input or when data is deleted. In both cases, care must be taken as the addition of new facts may cause other facts to be entered and the deletion of a fact may cause other facts to be deleted.

Another approach to database updates is given in Chapter 10 by Manchanda and Warren. They present a logical semantics for database updates based on dynamic logic (Harel [1979]). They present a language for writing update programs, called DLP (Dynamic Logic Programming). Update programs may be logic programs with negation, augmented with simple update operations. DLP supports data definition, view definition, querying, updating, and general computing. They show that very simple view transformations on a view definition can be used to obtain correct view update translators for the view.

Henschen and Park, in Chapter 11, consider the case where the theory is non-Horn. They provide results with respect to computing yes/no answers to queries posed over non-Horn databases. Negation is handled by the use of the Generalized Closed World Assumption of Minker [1982]. For other work on non-Horn clauses see Grant and Minker [1986] and Przymusinski [1986].

Recursive axioms in logic programs and deductive databases have caused problems with respect to termination. There have been a number of papers written that propose solutions to this problem. Bancilhon and Ramakrishnan survey these developments in Chapter 12. In addition, they describe a mathematical model by which the various approaches may be compared. They also provide detailed results applying the model to the various algorithms that have been proposed. The significance of the work is that they have identified some of the important factors that influence the algorithms and demonstrate their utility.

The implementation of deductive databases has been restricted, primarily, to those in which the facts and deductive rules reside entirely in core memory. If deductive databases are to become a reality, the problem of large databases must be addressed. In Chapter 13, Thom, Ramamohanarao, and Naish develop what they call a superjoin algorithm, based on a hash coding scheme, to retrieve data from remote devices. The algorithm is described first in terms of relational databases, and then they outline how the approach may be extended to deductive databases by compiling the axioms (or unfolding the axioms), provided that the axioms are free of recursion. This idea was proposed originally by Reiter [1978a]. The paper briefly touches on the case of recursion. Their objective is to include their work as part of NU-PROLOG (Naish [1985]).

Part III—Unification and Logic Programming constitutes the last part of the book. A number of topics are treated. A comprehensive survey is presented of theoretical results concerning logic programs and parallel complexity. Additional work presented in this part is on optimizing DATALOG (function-free Horn clause) programs, unification, equivalence of logic programs, and transforming programs to convert AND-control in logic programs to OR-control.

In Chapter 14, Kanellakis surveys logic programming and parallel complexity. The problems addressed are related to query optimization for deductive databases and to fast parallel execution of primitive operations in logic programming such as fixpoint operators, term unification, and term matching. There are many computational issues in logic programming and deductive databases. The chapter provides both the detailed results and many open problems that exist.

The concepts of unification and most general unifier are fundamental in automated theorem proving, logic programming, and deductive databases. In Chapter 15, Lassez, Maher, and Marriott trace the roots of the unification algorithm to Herbrand. They show that the notion of most general unifier and its properties are open to different interpretations. They present the alternatives, clarify the relationships, and provide new results and a comprehensive theory of unification.

Maher, in Chapter 16, provides a systematic treatment of the relative strengths of various formulations of equivalence of logic programs. These formulations arise from different formal semantics that exist for logic programs. The relative strength of various methods is examined. The work relates to verification and correctness of programs.

DATALOG programs, that is, PROLOG programs without function symbols, are considered by Sagiv in Chapter 17. It is known that the equivalence problem for DATALOG programs is undecidable (see the chapter by Kanellakis). Two programs are equivalent if they produce the same result for all possible assignments of relations to the extensional predicates. Sagiv shows that the problem of whether two DATALOG programs are uniformly equivalent is decidable. Two programs are uniformly equivalent if they produce the same result for all possible assignments of initial relations to all the predicates. In addition, he provides an algorithm to remove redundant parts from a DATALOG program. By a redundant part of a program, he means either a redundant rule or a redundant atom in the body of a rule. Doing so can only decrease the time needed to evaluate a query as it reduces the number of join operations.

In the last chapter, Chapter 18, van Emden and Szeredi discuss converting AND-control of logic programs into OR-control of logic programs. They achieve this by the well-known method of unfolding followed by folding. They illustrate how this may be accomplished and supply the required OR-control, resulting in a program that can be run by a standard PROLOG interpreter.

Future Directions

In addition to providing foundational results in deductive databases and logic programming, the research described in the book leaves open a number of problems. We shall touch upon a few of them in this section.

Part I—Negation and Stratified Databases addressed the problem of negation. Shepherdson provided a thorough discussion of how negation has been treated in alternative theories and presents the major results that are known. He demonstrates that the Closed World Assumption is computationally not practical, while negation as failure has a practical implementation. Research is needed to close the gap between these two areas. To some extent, the concept of stratification as developed by Apt, Blair, and Walker, and by Van Gelder moves in this direction. Can more be done in this area or has stratification closed as much of the gap as possible? Where does local stratification fit into this picture, as described by Przymusinski? See the chapter by Apt, Blair, and Walker for open problems and conjectures concerning stratification.

Implementation of an efficient query-answering procedure for stratified programs is needed. In the case of programs that are function-free, one is dealing predominantly with databases. Bottom-up techniques used in databases, combined with top-down search, are likely to be useful and have to be developed. Is there a variant of SLDNF that can be utilized to answer queries? Przymusinski provides one such procedure that must be evaluated to determine its effectiveness.

Shepherdson notes that a number of concepts have not been treated, such as the case where it is known that certain facts are unknown. He discusses several ways in which this may be accomplished and speculates on the use of other logics. Will this be necessary, or will variants of first-order theories be the direction in which one should proceed? Indeed, there are alternative theories that can be developed, such as ones which treat null values or other indefinite data. Theoretical results are required in these areas.

Przymusinski treats the problem of non-Horn clauses and stratification. However, he does not provide a fixpoint theory that extends the work of Apt, Blair, and Walker, who treat extended Horn theories in which the body of a clause may have negated atoms. Since Przymusinski shows that in some cases there is a minimal model, one would expect the existence of a fixpoint. Initial results may be found in unpublished papers by Ross and Topor [1987] and by Minker and Rajasekar [1987]. Methods to verify local stratifiability of a database have yet to be developed and present an open problem.

It has been known that artificial intelligence, logic programming, and deductive databases are interconnected in the area of nonmonotonic and default reasoning. Both Reiter [1982] and Minker and Perlis [1984a, 1985] have shown that circumscription, as developed by McCarthy [1980], is related to these fields. Lifschitz and Przymusinski further make this relationship. Stronger relationships should be developed among the three fields of artificial intelligence, deductive database, and logic programming. It is clear that all three are intimately related to logic.

Topor and Sonenberg describe domain independent databases and provide several open problems in this area. The reader should refer to their paper.

Part II—Fundamental Issues in Deductive Databases and Implementations deals with a number of topics in deductive databases. Unlike the material in Part 1 in which the papers were related, the papers are on alternative topics. Chakravarthy, Minker, and Grant discuss how one can incorporate semantic information in the form of integrity constraints to the deductive search process. How does one extend their results to incorporate non-Horn clauses as part of the integrity constraints, recursive axioms both in the theory and in the integrity constraints, and negative atoms both in the theory and in the integrity constraints? It also remains to be seen how their work can be implemented efficiently. As noted above, their work can be utilized to obtain intelligent and cooperative answers for users. How can this work be integrated with the approach taken by Imielinski who describes how one may obtain intelligent answers through the theory alone and without integrity constraints? It will also be of interest to extend the results of Imielinski to classes of axioms other than the set investigated in his paper.

Kowalski and Sadri provide a mechanism to test integrity constraints and to update databases. They use a modification to SLDNF which is as complete as SLDNF. A point of interest is how efficient the approach is. Whereas they use first-order logic in their approach, Manchanda and Warren describe a language based on dynamic logic to update and delete data from deductive databases. It will be of interest to determine how efficient an implementation may be achieved by their method and its relationships to the work of Kowalski and Sadri.

Non-Horn clauses introduce problems with respect to computation. Henschen and Park consider this problem. They develop an algorithm to obtain Yes/No answers to queries in the presence of non-Horn clauses. The problem of recursion is not treated adequately in their paper and extensions are required. Other approaches have been developed to answer queries concerning non-Horn clauses that can handle arbitrary queries (Grant and Minker [1986], Przymusinski [1986], and Yahya and Henschen [1985]). Unfortunately these methods are inefficient. Can more efficient methods be developed? Can approximations be made to answers that correspond in a sense to linear approximations or higher order approximations when dealing with non-linear systems?

Handling recursive axioms are important. It has been shown that bottom-up methods can be developed that are effective. Bancilhon and Ramakrishnan have developed a model to permit the evaluation of alternative methods proposed to handle recursion. The experiments that they have done provide convincing arguments of the merit of the approach. However, they test only a few general classes of problems. Will the same results pertain when other sets of axioms are used? Are there other strategies to recursion that avoid infinite recursion? Are they likely to yield improvements over current methods? Kanellakis describes work where it can be determined when recursion terminates. He calls this bounded recursion, lists references to the literature and the results that have been obtained. It will also be of interest to study the behavior of general logic programs which contain function symbols.

The superjoin algorithm of Thom, Ramamohanarao, and Naish requires testing on large sets of data and axioms to determine its effectiveness. In addition, their paper provides only a brief sketch as to how one may handle recursive axioms. Additional work will be required here. It will also be of interest to combine the method of Chakravarthy, Minker, and Grant to include the use of semantic information in the use of large deductive databases.

Part III—Unification and Logic Programs deals with the analysis of logic programming algorithms, unification, and transformations associated with logic programming. With respect to elementary unification, the study by Lassez, Maher, and Marriott is so complete and thorough that it is difficult to see if any open questions remain. On the other hand, Kanellakis provides an extensive list of open problems that still exist in logic programming and parallel complexity. The reader is referred to that paper for details.

The effectiveness of the work by Maher for automatic program generation and verification needs to be determined. It appears also that the method can be utilized to determine the extent to which one can translate between two presumably different theories.

The application of the Sagiv algorithm to actual DATALOG programs will be of interest. Is it worthwhile to do the work required to transform the code? It would appear to be the case as the transformations are performed in high speed memory, while the retrieval is accomplished using data on peripheral devices. The extension of the methods to transform general logic programs remains a research problem.

The van Emden and Szeredi paper discusses transforming AND-control to OR-control programs. It will be of interest to apply the methodology described to existing parallel logic programming systems to be able to evaluate its utility.

Summary

It is clear from the chapters in this book that research in deductive databases and logic programming is intimately related. We have tried to describe both the contributions that have been made and research directions needed. As may be seen from the work described in Chapter 4, by Lifschitz, the research also impacts the field of artificial intelligence in the areas of nonmonotonic and default reasoning. Foundational results described in this book have the potential of permitting artificial intelligence systems to be developed based on theoretical results rather than on ad hoc programs. It is important that this occurs, as science makes progress when there are sound theoretical developments that can be used as a basis for describing the real world.

Although there have been many foundational results described in the various chapters, there remain a large number of theoretical issues that are as yet unsolved. We have sketched several such open problems in the previous section. These open problems are based on the chapters of this book and are not intended to be complete. Deductive databases and logic programming are fields that are developing rapidly, both in practice and in theory. The chapters to follow contribute significantly to these areas. Work that has come out of the workshop has already made an impact on research in deductive databases as may be seen by the following references (see Apt and Pugin [1987], Beeri and Ramakrishnan [1987], and Lassez, McAloon, and Port [1986]). The contributions made by the chapters of the book are a tribute both to the authors and to the referees who critiqued and caused extensive revisions to be made to each paper.

The material in the book can be used as the basis of a graduate course seminar in deductive databases. Students should have an appropriate background in the two fields of deductive databases and logic programming before attempting to read the book. A background in deductive databases can be achieved by familiarity with material in the book edited by Gallaire and Minker [1978], reading the survey article by Gallaire, Minker, and Nicolas [1984], the historical perspective paper by Minker [1987], and by reading references described in those sources. Background in logic programming may be obtained by familiarity with PROLOG, as obtained in books by either Sterling and Shapiro [1986], or Clocksin and Mellish [1984], and in texts by Kowalski [1979] and Lloyd [1984]. The book by Lloyd provides important material for understanding the research described in Part 1 of the book.

Acknowledgments

The list of referees are contained in the section, Referees, of this book. Every paper in the book was improved by the referee process. I am indebted to the referees for their hard and tireless work. I am especially indebted to Jean-Louis Lassez who was the editor in charge of determining whether or not the paper that I co-authored should appear in the book. He and Michael Maher made valuable suggestions on the sequencing of papers for the book and for the remarks that appear in this introduction. Not all papers presented at the workshop appear in this book. Some of the authors were unable to revise their papers to meet our time schedule. I greatly appreciate the comments of my students, Yuan Liu, Jorge Lobo, and especially Arcot Rajasekar who made valuable comments concerning the above material. John Grant also provided useful comments to me concerning these introductory remarks. I also greatly appreciate the support given to me by the National Science Foundation under grant number DCR-8602676 that permitted me to conduct the workshop described above that has led to this book. I would also like to express my appreciation to Larry Davis, Director of the University of Maryland Institute for Advanced Study, for supporting the workshop and providing me with clerical support for this book and to Victor Basili, Chairman of the Department of Computer Science, for his support.

References

1. Apt, K. R. and Emden, M. H. van [1982] Contributions to the Theory of Logic Programming, in *JACM* **29**, 841–862.

2. Apt, K. and Pugin, J. M. [1987] Maintenance of Stratified Databases Viewed as a Belief Revision System, *Proc. of the Sixth ACM SIGACT News-SIGMOD-SIGART Symposium on Principles of Database Systems*, San Diego, CA, 136–145.

3. Beeri, C. and Ramakrishnan, R. [1987] On the Power of Magic, *Proc. Principles of Database Systems*, San Diego, CA.

4. Chandra, A. and Harel, D. [1982] Structure and Complexity of Relational Queries, *Journal of Computer System Sciences* **25**, 99–128.

5. Chandra, A. and Harel, D. [1985] Horn Clause Queries and Generalizations, *Journal of Logic Programming* **2**(1):1–15.

6. Chang, C. L. and Lee, R. C. T. [1973] *Symbolic Logic and Mechanical Theorem Proving*, Academic Press, New York.

7. Clark, K. L. [1978] Negation as Failure, in *Logic and Data Bases* (H. Gallaire and J. Minker, Eds.), Plenum Press, New York, 293–322.

8. Clocksin, W. F. and Mellish, C. S. [1984] *Programming in Prolog*, Springer-Verlag.

9. Emden, M. H. van and Kowalski, R. A. [1976] The Semantics of Predicate Logic as a Programming Language, in *JACM* **23**, 733–742.

10. Gal, A. and Minker, J. [1987] Greater Cooperation Between Databases and User: Integrity Constraints Provide an Answer, *Proc. 2nd International Workshop on Natural Understanding and Logic Programming*, Vancouver, BC, Canada.

11. Gallaire, H. and Minker, J. [1978] *Logic and Databases*, Plenum Press, New York.

12. Gallaire, H., Minker, J., and Nicolas, J.-M. [1984] Logic and Databases: A Deductive Approach, *ACM Computing Surveys* **16**(2):153–185.

13. Grant, J. and Minker, J. [1986] Answering Queries in Indefinite Databases and the Null Value Problem, in *Advances in Computing Research* (P. Kanellakis, Ed.), 247–267.

14. Green, C. C. [1969] The Application of Theorem Proving to Question-Answering Systems, Tech. Rep. CS 138, PhD, Computer Science Department, Stanford University, ARPA Order No. 457, RADC F30602-69-C-0056.

15. Green, C. C. and Raphael, B. [1968] The Use of Theorem-Proving Techniques in Question-Answering Systems, *Proc. 23rd National Conference ACM*, Washington, DC.

16. Green, C. C. and Raphael, B. [1968] Research In Intelligent Question Answering Systems, *Proc. ACM 23rd National Conference*, NJ, 169–181.

17. Harel, D. [1979] First-Order Dynamic Logic, in *Lecture Notes in Computer Science*, Springer-Verlag.

18. Hill, R. [1974] LUSH Resolution and Its Completeness, DCL Memo No. 78, School of Artificial Intelligence.

19. Jaffar, J., Lassez, J., and Lloyd, J. W. [1983] Completeness of the Negation as Failure Rule, in *Proceedings Eighth International Joint Conference on Artificial Intelligence*, Karlsruhe, West Germany, 500–506.

20. Kowalski, R. A. [1974] Predicate Logic as a Programming Language, *Proc. IFIP 4*, Amsterdam, 569–574.

21. Kowalski, R. A. [1979] *Logic for Problem Solving*, Elsevier North Holland, NY.

22. Kowalski, R. A. and Kuehner, D. [1971] Linear Resolution with Selection Function, in *Artificial Intelligence* **2**, 227–260.

23. Lassez, C., McAloon, K., and Port, G. [1986] Stratification as a Tool for Interactive Knowledge Base Management, RC 12355 (55416), IBM T. J. Watson Research Center, Yorktown Heights, NY.

24. Lassez, J. and Maher, M. J. [1984] Closure and Fairness in the Semantics of Programming Logic, *Theoretical Computer Science* **29**, 167–184.

25. Lifschitz, V. [1986] Pointwise Circumscription: Preliminary Report, *Proc. AAAI*, Philadelphia, PA, 406–410.

26. Lloyd, J. W. [1984] *Foundations of Logic Programming*, Springer-Verlag, Germany.

27. Lloyd, J. W. and Topor, R. W. [1985] A Basis for Deductive Databases Systems, *Journal of Logic Programming* **2**(2):93–109.

28. Lloyd, J. W. and Topor, R. W. [1986] A Basis for Deductive Database Systems II, *Journal of Logic Programming* **3**(1):55–67.

29. Loveland, D. W. [1978] *Automated Theorem Proving: A Logical Basis*, North-Holland, NY.

30. McCarthy, J. [1980] Circumscription-A Form of Non-Monotonic Reasoning, *Artificial Intelligence* **13**(1 and 2):27–39.

31. Minker, J. [1982] On Indefinite Databases and the Closed World Assumption, in *Lecture Notes in Computer Science* **138**, Springer-Verlag, 292–308.

32. Minker, J. [1986] *Proc. of Workshop on Foundations of Deductive Databases and Logic Programming*.

33. Minker, J. [1987] Perspectives in Deductive Databases, Tech. Rep.1799, University of Maryland, College Park, MD, to appear in *J. Logic Programming*.

34. Minker, J. and Perlis, D.[1984a] Protected Circumscription, *Proc. Workshop on Non-Monotonic Reasoning*, New Paltz, NY, 337–343.

35. Minker, J. and Perlis, D. [1984b] Applications of Protected Circumscription, *Proc. Conference on Automated Deduction*, Napa, CA.

36. Minker, J. and Perlis, D. [1985] Computing Protected Circumscription, *Journal of Logic Programming* **2**(4):235–249.

37. Minker, J. and Rajasekar, A. [1987] A Fixpoint Semantics for Non-Horn Logic Programs, UMIACS Tech. Rep. 8724, Computer Science Center Technical Report 1869, University of Maryland, College Park, MD.

38. Naish, L. [1985] Negation and Quantifiers in NU-Prolog, Technical report 85/13, University of Melbourne.

39. Naqvi, S. A. [1986] A Logic for Negation in Database Systems, in *Proc. of Workshop on Foundations of Deductive Databases and Logic Programming*, (J. Minker, Ed.), Washington, DC, 378–387.

40. Przymusinski, T. [1986] A Query Answering Algorithm for Circumscriptive Theories, *Proc. of the ACM SIGART International Symposium on Methodologies for Intelligent Systems*, Knoxville, TN, 85–93.

41. Reiter, R. [1978a] Deductive Question-Answering on Relational Data Bases, in *Logic and Data Bases*, (H. Gallaire and J. Minker, Eds.), Plenum Press, New York, 149–177.

42. Reiter, R. [1978b] On Closed World Data Bases, in *Logic and Data Bases*, (H. Gallaire and J. Minker, Eds.), Plenum Press, New York, 55–76.

43. Reiter, R. [1982] Circumscription Implies Predicate Completion (Sometimes), *Proc. Amer. Assoc. for Art.Intell. National Conference*, Pittsburgh, PA, 418–420.

44. Reiter, R. [1984] Towards a Logical Reconstruction of Relational Database Theory, in *On Conceptual Modelling*, (M. L. Brodie, J. L. Mylopoulos, and J. W. Schmit, Eds.), Springer-Verlag, New York, 163–189.

45. Robinson, J. A. [1965] A Machine-Oriented Logic Based on the Resolution Principle, *J.ACM* **12**(1).

46. Ross, K. A. and Topor, R. W. [1987] Inferring Negative Information from Disjunctive Databases, Technical Report 87/1, University of Melbourne.

47. Roussel, P. [1975] PROLOG: Manuel de Reference et d'Utilisation, Group d' Intelligence Artificielle, Marseilles, France.

48. Sterling, L. and Shapiro, E. [1986] *The Art of Prolog*, MIT Press.

49. Topor, R. W. [1984] Making PROLOG More Expressive, *Journal of Logic Programming* **1**(3):225–240.

50. Yahya, A. and Henschen, L. J. [1985] Deduction in Non-Horn Databases, in *J. Automated Reasoning* **1**, 141–160.

I

NEGATION AND STRATIFIED DATABASES

1

Negation in Logic Programming

John C. Shepherdson
Mathematics Department
University of Bristol, England

Abstract

A survey of treatments of negation in logic programming. The following aspects are discussed: elimination of negation by renaming, definite Horn programs and queries, the relation between the closed world assumption and the completed data base, and their relation to negation as failure, negation as failure for definite Horn programs, special classes of program for which negation as failure coincides with classical negation applied to the completed data base or closed world assumption, semantics for negation in terms of special classes of models, semantics for negation as failure in terms of 3-valued logic.

Introduction

To a logician the ideal solution to the problems of incorporating negation into logic programming would seem to be to permit the full use of classical negation in programs and queries and to couple this with an automatic theorem prover which is sound and complete for full first order logic (with equality). There are two reasons why this solution has not been widely adopted. One is that it is very time-consuming; the other is that in many situations, e.g., data base queries, some other sort of negation, "negation by failure," is more useful. So most of the work on negation in logic programming has started from the other end, trying to graft some kind of negation onto the very efficient

SLD-resolution used in PROLOG. The most general kind of program clause usually considered is

$$A \leftarrow L_1, L_2, ..., L_m.$$

where A is an atom and $L_1, ..., L_m$ are literals. This is indeed very general. Almost every clause can be written in this form. The only ones that cannot are the negative clauses

$$\leftarrow A_1, A_2, ..., A_m$$

where $A_1, ..., A_m$ are atoms. But one would expect this to make a profound difference to the ability to use negation since an interpretation in which all predicates are true of everything is a model for any program containing no negative clauses. The only way to express totally negative information is by negative clauses.

As well as this deficiency in the ability to express negation, the use of SLD-resolution, in which only positive literals can be matched (with the heads of program clauses) leads to incompleteness in the proof procedure. For example from the program

$$A \leftarrow B$$
$$A \leftarrow \neg B$$

and the goal

$$\leftarrow A$$

it is not possible to derive the empty clause without using also a rule allowing

$$\leftarrow \neg B, L_1, ..., L_m$$

to be rewritten as

$$B \leftarrow L_1, ..., L_m.$$

Such a rewriting rule would make resolution much less efficient because it would introduce more possible derivation steps.

To a logician these shortcomings make this appear to be an unpromising framework in which to deal with negation. This is certainly true if, when one writes down a data base or program, prog, and asks a query, one is asking

```
"Is 'prog  →  query' valid in classical first
    order logic?"
```

But although this declarative view of a program may be the ultimate ideal of logic programming, it is not the way most logic programmers operate today. They tend to think of prog as being a program, a procedure to be executed using SLD-resolution and negation as failure. If they want a logical statement to express the meaning of prog, they are prepared to use some completely different statement prog′, such as the Clark completion of prog. And the question they want to ask about the query may not be

```
"Is 'prog  →  query' valid, i.e., true in all
    models"
```

but

```
"Is 'prog  →  query' true in all models of a certain
    kind (e.g., Herbrand, minimal Herbrand)."
```

For example most people who write:

```
      num(0)  ←
   num(s(x))  ←  num(x)
pair(g(x,y))  ←  num(x), num(y),
```

do not intend to consider all models of these sentences, where the set of numbers (objects x satisfying num(x)) can be any set containing 0 and closed under the function s, and the set of pairs (objects z satisfying pair (z)) can be any set containing g(x,y) for all numbers x, y. They most likely intend that the set of numbers should contain only $0, s(0), ss(0), \ldots$, and that the set of pairs should contain only objects of the form $g(s^m(0), s^n(0))$.

There are three well known (declarative) semantics for logic programming, which in this example all achieve these effects. One is the least fixpoint model, another is the closed world assumption, and the third is the completed data base.

The least fixpoint model is the Herbrand model obtained by starting with the empty set and closing under the operation of adding all ground atoms that are the heads of ground instances of program clauses whose bodies have already been included.

The closed world assumption corresponds to the Herbrand model in which a ground atom is taken to be false if it is not a logical consequence of the program.

The completed database is obtained by assuming that the clauses of the program (or database) were intended as, to quote Clark [1978], its inventor, "just the if-halves of a set of if-and-only-if definitions of the data base relations" and that what was implied in our example was:

$$\text{num}(y) \ \longleftrightarrow \ y = 0 \ \lor \ \exists x (y = s(x) \ \land \ \text{num}(x))$$
$$\text{pair}(z) \ \longleftrightarrow \ \exists x \exists y (z = g(x, y) \ \land \ \text{num}(x) \ \land \ \text{num}(y)).$$

If we also restrict to Herbrand models (i.e., use the Herbrand base of the original program), then we again get the "intended" model above.

There is also a well known syntax (or procedural or operational semantics or proof procedure) that in this example is both sound and complete with respect to the above semantics, namely the result of adding negation as failure to SLD-resolution. (We shall follow Lloyd [1984] and call this SLDNF-resolution rather than "a query evaluation procedure," as in Clark [1978] or "a QEP" as in Shepherdson [1984, 1985].) Indeed this proof procedure, with its ease of implementation, seems to have arisen about the same time as some of the above semantics.

For more general programs, the correspondence between these four concepts is no longer so close and a large part of this survey is taken up with the relations between them.

There are several aspects of negation in logic programming that are not dealt with in this survey which the reader may wish to pursue: programs using equality theory (Jaffar and Lassez [1984, 1986]), negation as inconsistency (Gabbay and Sergot [1986]), N-PROLOG (an extension of PROLOG allowing implications in the bodies of clauses; Gabbay [1985]), and a modal logic interpretation of negation as failure (Gabbay [1986]).

Even if the practicing logic programmer does not regard the written text of the program as its declarative meaning, we feel that in order to be true to the basic aims of logic programming two fundamental principles should be observed.

1. The semantics of negation should be clear and easily intelligible. That is, the naive programmer should be able to understand the full meaning of what he writes.

2. The syntax should be computable. That is, at least in theory, an automatic proof procedure should exist. Indeed if the only reason for abandoning the clear and well-known concept of classical negation is the inefficiency of its implementations, we might not unreasonably ask for a complete proof procedure to be feasibly implementable.

We shall measure all the kinds of negation discussed against these principles and point out when they fall short.

Before dealing with semantics for negation as failure, we dispose of three special cases where full classical negation can easily be implemented.

Elimination of Negation by Renaming

If there are no occurrences in the program of $p(t_1,...,t_n)$ for any terms $t_1,...,t_n$, then negative literals $\neg p(u_1,...,u_n)$ can be made positive by introducing a new predicate $\text{nonp}(x_1,...,x_n)$ for $\neg p(x_1,...,x_n)$. This was considered by Meltzer [1983]. A well known example of it is in Kowalski [1979] where the statements

> Every fungus is a mushroom or a toadstool,
> No boletus is a mushroom.

are made into Horn clauses by introducing the predicate "nonmushrooms":

> $\text{toadstool}(x) \leftarrow \text{fungus}(x), \text{nonmushroom}(x)$
> $\text{nonmushroom}(x) \leftarrow \text{boletus}(x).$

This trick obviously works also when there are positive occurrences of $p(t_1,...,t_n)$ provided none of these can be unified with any of the negative ones. With each of the types of program and query we deal with later one should associate the more general types reducible to it by renaming.

Lewis [1978] gives an efficient algorithm for determining whether a set of clauses can be transformed by predicate renaming into a set of Horn clauses.

Definite Horn Programs with General Queries

There is no problem in allowing queries containing negation if the program consists entirely of definite Horn clauses. There is no need to add any rule for negation; SLD-resolution is complete for classical negation, for a query containing a negative literal cannot succeed, and it should not, because it cannot be a logical consequence of the program since that has a model in which all predicates are true of everything.

{Note that for queries containing negation, this remains true (i.e., that SLD-resolution is complete) for general programs made up of clauses as above with positive heads but arbitrary bodies. But for positive queries, SLD-resolution may then be incomplete, as the example above shows:– program A ← B, A ← ¬B, query A i.e. goal ← A.}[1]

General Horn Programs and Queries

Sakai and Miyachi [1983] have shown that it is very easy to extend PROLOG by allowing programs to contain negative Horn clauses and allowing goal clauses to be either negative or definite Horn clauses. So a program is now any set of Horn clauses, and a query is any conjunction containing at most one negative literal, the corresponding goal clause being any Horn clause, i.e., one containing at most one positive literal. This depends on the well-known fact that if a set of Horn clauses is inconsistent, so is some subset containing just one negative clause. The query procedure is as follows:

First check the program for consistency by taking its positive part, i.e., the set of definite clauses in it, and querying this in turn with the negations of the negative program clauses (i.e., taking each of these negative clauses as a goal). If any of these queries succeed, i.e., if any of these goals allows the derivation of the empty clause, then the program is inconsistent and every query succeeds.

If the program is found to be consistent, then proceed as follows:

If the query consists entirely of positive literals then discard any negative program clauses and test the query in the usual way with the positive part of the program. If the query contains a (single) negative literal, then its negation can be written as a definite Horn clause G. If there are no negative program clauses just fail the query immediately because, as in the last subsection, a negative query cannot be a consequence of a positive program. Otherwise add G to the positive part of the program and query in turn each of the negations of the negative program clauses (i.e., use each of these clauses in turn as a goal). The only unusual feature is that answers to the query are, in general, no longer of the familiar definite form, i.e., expressible by a single substitution. Instead, every time G is used within one derivation of the empty clause, the value substitution is stored as one of the disjuncts of an indefinite answer substitution.

{Note that if the program contains negative Horn clauses, for this procedure to work the query must be the negation of a Horn clause and cannot, as in the

---

[1]We use the word *query* in the following sense: When you present a query Q to a program P you are asking whether P → Q is valid (or, in later sections, true according to some other semantics). When using SLD-resolution you determine this by adding the *goal* ¬Q to P and trying to derive a contradiction in the form of the empty clause. So our notation is at variance with the widespread use of the word query in logic programming where the query Q is written ← Q; in our view this is the negation of the query, i.e., the goal.

last subsection, be an arbitrary conjunction of literals. For example the program

$$A \leftarrow B$$
$$\leftarrow A$$

with the query $\neg A \wedge \neg B$, i.e., the goal

$$\leftarrow \quad \neg A, \quad \neg B$$

is equivalent to the first example in the last subsection (program $A \leftarrow B$, $A \leftarrow \neg B$, goal $\leftarrow A$).}

This case of general Horn clauses is also treated by Gallier and Raatz in [1986a] and extended to include equality in [1986b].

Fixpoint Models

Let P be a general program in the sense of Lloyd, i.e., a finite set of clauses of the form

$$A \leftarrow L_1, L_2, \ldots, L_m,$$

where A is an atom and $L_1, L_2, \ldots, L_m$ are literals. As usual we identify a Herbrand interpretation with the subset of the Herbrand base B_P consisting of those ground atoms that are true in it. Associated with the program P is the operator T_P which maps a subset I of B_P into the subset $T_P(I)$ comprising all those ground atoms A for which there exists a ground instance

$$A \leftarrow L_1, L_2, \ldots, L_m,$$

of a clause of P with all of $L_1, L_2, \ldots, L_m$ true in I. So $T_P(I)$ is the set of immediate consequences of I, i.e., those which can be obtained by applying a rule from P once only.

Clearly

I is a model for P iff $T_P(I) \subseteq I$.

If P is composed of definite Horn clauses then T_P is a monotonic and continuous operator and has a least fixpoint $lfp(T_P)$ which is obtainable as $T_P \uparrow \omega$, the result of iterating T_P ω times. This is obviously the least Herbrand model of P. If the clauses of P can be regarded, as in the example with num and pair above, as recursive definitions of the predicates in their heads, it is the model which corresponds to these recursive definitions.

In general, however, T_P is not monotonic and may not have fixpoints. For example, if P is $q \leftarrow \neg q, \neg r$ then $T_P(\phi) = \{q\}$ but $T_P(\{q\}) = \phi$; there is no fixpoint of T_P and no least Herbrand model—there are two *minimal* Herbrand models $\{q\}$, $\{r\}$ (i.e., models with no proper submodel), but their intersection is not a model.

Although all that is required for I to be a model of P is that $T_P(I) \subseteq I$ i.e., that I is a *pre-fixpoint* of T_P, fixpoint models have a special interest, particularly in the context in which negation is usually considered in database theory and logic programming, where positive ground literals are assumed false unless they can be supported in some way by the program. Apt, Blair, and Walker [1988] formalize this notion by saying that an interpretation I is *supported* if for each ground atom A which is true in I there is a ground instance.

$$A \leftarrow L_1, L_2, \ldots, L_m,$$

of a clause of P such that $L_1, L_2, \ldots, L_m$ are true in I. Then

I is supported iff $T_P(I) \supseteq I$.

So

I is a supported model of P iff it is a fixpoint of T_P, i.e., $T_P(I) = I$.

It should be noted that the operator T_P depends not only on the logical content of the program P, but also on the way it is written. For example $p \leftarrow \neg q$ and $q \leftarrow \neg p$ give rise to different T_P. This is true even when P consists of definite Horn clauses because adding the tautology $p \leftarrow p$ changes T_P.

The above results on definite Horn clauses can be extended to include negative Horn clauses as well if we introduce a new ground atom f (false), write a negative Horn clause in the form

$$f \leftarrow A_1, \ldots, A_m$$

and add to the conditions for I to be a model of P that it should not contain f.

Fixpoint models enter into the discussion again in several later sections.

The Closed World Assumption

Reiter's *closed world assumption* [1978] is based on the idea that the program contains all the positive information about the objects in the domain and that any positive ground literal that is not implied by the program is false. This can be axiomatized by adjoining to the program P the set of axioms ext(P) given by:

$$\text{ext(P)} = \{ \neg A : A \text{ is a positive ground literal and } P \not\models A \}.$$

Note that since this is defined in terms of non-provability we must not be surprised if we leave the world of computable proof procedures and violate our principle II above. We shall see shortly that this can happen even when P is a definite Horn clause program.

It is also implicit that we restrict to *term* models. (These are called Herbrand models in the usual logic programming case where P consists of clauses or, more generally, universal sentences; but we also want to consider the case where P consists of arbitrary first order formulae, in which case the word "Herbrand" would be more appropriately attached to term models in the language extended to include the Skolem functions needed to express P in universal form.) To axiomatize that restriction we add the
equality axioms EA:

$$x = x$$
$$x = y \;\rightarrow\; y = x$$
$$x = y \wedge y = z \;\rightarrow\; x = z$$
$$x_1 = y_1 \wedge \ldots \wedge x_n = y_n \rightarrow [p(x_1, \ldots, x_n) \leftrightarrow p(y_1, \ldots, y_n)],$$

for each predicate p

$$x_1 = y_1 \wedge \ldots \wedge x_n = y_n \rightarrow [f(x_1, \ldots, x_n) = f(y_1, \ldots, y_n)],$$

for each function f,
freeness axioms FA:

$$f(x_1, \ldots, x_n) \neq g(y_1, \ldots, y_m)$$

for each pair f, g of distinct functions,

$$f(x_1, \ldots, x_n) = f(y_1, \ldots, y_n) \;\rightarrow\; x_1 = y_1 \wedge \ldots \wedge x_n = y_n$$

for each function f and

$$t(x) \neq x$$

for each term t(x) different from x in which x occurs.

The freeness axioms express that we are restricting to free interpretations where, as Kunen [1987] puts it, "no objects are equal unless they are required to be equal by logic." He calls the theory consisting of the usual axioms of predicate logic together with EA and FA, Clark's Equational Theory (CET). The last axiom, $t(x) \neq x$, is somewhat different from the rest; we shall call it the *occur axiom*.

Finally we add the

domain closure axiom DCA:

$$x = t_1 \vee x = t_2 \vee \ldots.$$

where $t_1, t_2, \ldots$ are all the ground terms.

If there are functions this is an infinite disjunction. For this reason a weaker finite disjunction is used for some purposes, e.g., by Lloyd and Topor [1985]:

weak domain closure axiom WDCA

$$\exists y_1 \ldots \exists y_n (x = f_1(y_1, \ldots, y_n)) \vee \ldots \vee \exists y_1 \ldots y_m (x = f_j(y_1, \ldots, y_m)),$$

where $f_1, \ldots, f_j$ are all the functions.

(Constants are treated as 0-ary functions throughout.)

To facilitate comparison with the completed database we shall adopt a similar notation to that used by Lloyd for the latter and write

$$\mathrm{cwa}(P) = P \cup \mathrm{ext}(P) \cup \mathrm{EA} \cup \mathrm{FA} \cup \mathrm{DCA}.$$

Note that

when cwa(P) is consistent it is categorical,

i.e., it determines a unique model, because $\mathrm{EA} \cup \mathrm{FA} \cup \mathrm{DCA}$ restricts the domain to the ground terms, and $P \cup \mathrm{ext}(P)$ determines the truth values of all ground literals.

Let us first confirm the unpalatable fact, pointed out by Apt, Blair, and Walker [1988], that when there are functions any semantics like this based on a complete theory that adds no new positive facts can give rise to a non-computable syntax.

(When there are no functions, there is a decision procedure for programs made up of any finite set of clauses, for we are in the well-known Bernays-Schoenfinkel case ($\forall \exists$ for validity, $\exists \forall$ for satisfiability), and it is easily seen that there is also a decision method for discovering whether a clause is a consequence of cwa(P), since the set of ground terms is finite. But there may not be a feasible one, for Plaisted [1984] has shown that for clauses with at most three literals any decision method for the Bernays-Schoenfinkel case takes non-deterministic exponential time in the worst case (even for three literal Horn clauses it takes deterministic exponential time). And if one is using resolution there is the depressing result of Haken [1985] that even for propositional clauses resolution takes exponential time.)

The point is that, as Tarnlund [1977] has shown, for each recursively enumerable set W, there is a definite Horn clause program P with constant 0, function s and predicate p such that, for all natural numbers n

$$P \models p(s^n(0)) \quad \text{iff } n \in W.$$

Now no new positive facts can be proved from cwa(P), i.e.,

$$cwa(P) \models A \text{ implies } P \models A, \text{ for all ground atoms } A,$$

provided cwa(P) is consistent, which it is for such P. Since cwa(P) is complete, i.e., implies either A or $\neg A$ for each ground atom A it follows that

$$cwa(P) \models \neg p(s^n(0)) \quad \text{iff } n \notin W,$$

so if W is chosen non-recursive the set of consequences of cwa(P) will not be recursively enumerable.

If the reason for abandoning classical negation was because the proof procedure was too complex it would be a poor exchange to replace it with one that was not even computable. But presumably when the closed world assumption is used, it does correspond to reality, so that one should be grateful that it is possible to deal with it at all in first order logic and take comfort in the fact that human mathematicians cannot have a proof procedure either. Perhaps one should look for axioms or axiom schemes that might produce a slightly less incomplete proof procedure. No doubt Voda [1986] has something like this in mind when he argues that induction axioms are more useful than classical negation.

Note that the non-existence of a proof procedure for cwa(P) is not due to the infinitary disjunction DCA (though we shall see in the next section that if the intended program contains existential quantifiers then just restricting to Herbrand models can have this effect). Here it is due solely to the non-recursive enumerability of the axiom set ext(P); the axioms EA $\cup$ FA $\cup$ DCA are not involved in the deduction of $\neg p(s^n(0))$. Indeed it is worth clarifying the role of the axioms involving equality.

In the usual logic programming situation these axioms are irrelevant:

THEOREM 1

If P consists of universal sentences, if Q is an existential sentence and the equality predicate occurs in neither P nor Q, then

$$\text{cwa (P)} \models \text{Q iff P} \cup \text{ext (P)} \models \text{Q}.$$

Proof: If P $\cup$ ext(P) $\not\models$ Q then P $\cup$ ext(P) $\cup$ $\neg$Q is satisfiable. But all these axioms are universal and do not contain equality so by the usual Skolem[2] argument they have a Herbrand model. This also satisfies EA $\cup$ FA $\cup$ DCA. ∎

An immediate consequence of Theorem 1 is:

COROLLARY 1

If P consists of universal sentences and equality does not occur in it then

$$\text{cwa (P)} \text{ is consistent iff P} \cup \text{ext (P)} \text{ is consistent.} \ ∎$$

So for both of these results the domain closure axiom DCA is irrelevant and can be replaced by the weak domain closure axiom WDCA. For general queries this is no longer true; the full strength of the domain closure axiom may be required:

EXAMPLE 1

There is a definite Horn program P and a query Q such that cwa(P) $\models$ Q but wcwa(P) $\not\models$ Q, where wcwa(P) is obtained from cwa(P) by replacing DCA by WDCA.

```
Take P as
    even (0)  ←
    even (s (s (x)))  ←  even (x),
    Q as
    ∀x (even (x)  ∨  even (s (x))).
```

All models of P whose domain is the Herbrand universe $\{0, s(0), s^2(0), \dots\}$ satisfy Q, but wcwa(P) has a model consisting of this standard model together with a copy of the integers in which nothing is deemed to be even. ∎

---

[2]Martin Davis admits in [1983], p. 10, footnote 27, that he was the one who was guilty of talking about Herbrand's theorem and the Herbrand universe when the result in question was first established by Skolem. Herbrand would not appreciate the attribution, for although he undoubtedly knew the theorem, he would have considered it non-constructive and meaningless. His theorem was a much deeper constructive result. But it is probably too late now to talk of the Skolem universe.

Finally we note that the occur axiom, OA,t(x) $\neq$ x is redundant if DCA is used, i.e.,

EA $\cup$ FA $\cup$ DCA $\;\longrightarrow\;$ OA.

This is not true if DCA is replaced by WDCA; e.g., with constants 0,s, the formula s(x) $\neq$ x is not provable from EA $\cup$ FA $\cup$ WDCA, for this has a model consisting of the natural numbers together with an element ω such that s(ω) = ω.

The closed world assumption, as well as possibly having no computable proof procedure, is often considered to be too strong a presumption in favor of negative information. And if there is indefinite knowledge about ground atoms, then cwa(P) is inconsistent; e.g., if P is

p $\leftarrow$ $\neg$ q

where p,q are 0-ary predicates (propositional constants), then

ext(P) = $\{\neg p, \neg q\}$

so P $\cup$ ext(P) is inconsistent. This condition is actually necessary and sufficient for the inconsistency of cwa(P):

THEOREM 2

If P consists of universal sentences and equality does not occur in it, then cwa(P) is consistent iff for all ground atoms $A_1,\ldots,A_r$,

$$P \models A_1 \vee \ldots \vee A_r \text{ implies } P \models A_i \text{ for some } i = 1, \ldots, r.$$

Proof: If P $\not\models$ A_i for all i = 1,...,r then $\neg A_1,\ldots, \neg A_r$ all belong to ext(P) so if P $\models$ ($A_1 \vee \ldots A_r$) then P $\cup$ ext(P) is inconsistent, hence cwa(P) is inconsistent.

Conversely if cwa(P) is inconsistent, then by Corollary 1 so is P $\cup$ ext(P), hence so is some finite subset of it. So there exist $\neg A_1,\ldots, \neg A_r$ in ext(P) such that P $\cup \{ \neg A_1,\ldots, \neg A_r \}$ is inconsistent, i.e.,

$$P \models (A_1 \vee \ldots \vee A_r). \quad \blacksquare$$

Indefinite information about non-ground literals need not imply the inconsistency of the closed world assumption as the program P of Ex. 8 of Shepherdson [1984] shows:

p (x) $\leftarrow$ $\neg$ q (x)
p (a)
q (b) .

However the consistency of the closed world assumption for certain extensions of P does imply that P is equivalent to a definite Horn clause program. As Hodges [1985] has pointed out, this follows from a model-theoretic theorem of Maltsev:

THEOREM 3
If P is a set of first order sentences such that for each set S of ground atoms (possibly involving new constants) cwa(P ∪ S) is consistent, then P is equivalent to a set of definite Horn clauses.

Proof: See below, after Theorem 5. ∎

Note that, as the preceding example shows, the result is no longer true if the phrase "possibly involving new constants" is omitted. This example also shows that the consistency of the closed world assumption depends on the underlying language; for that program P, cwa(P) is consistent if the set of ground terms, the "Herbrand universe," is the usual one determined by P, i.e., {a,b}; but if it is enlarged to {a,b,c} then cwa(P) becomes inconsistent. This ambiguity does not arise in the familiar case when P is a set of Horn clauses because then (Theorem 6 below) cwa(P) is consistent iff P is consistent, which clearly does not depend on what Herbrand universe is considered.

The theorem of Maltsev referred to here was, of course, not expressed in terms of the closed world assumption but in terms of free algebras. Makowsky [1986] gives a very full discussion of the relevance of the model-theoretic properties of Horn clauses to logic programming and in particular gives model-theoretic properties equivalent to the consistency of the closed world assumption. The most important of these is:

THEOREM 4
If P is a set of first order sentences then a term structure M is a model for cwa(P) iff it is a *generic* term model of P, i.e., for all ground atoms A,

$$M \models A \text{ iff } P \models A$$

i.e., A is true in M iff it is true in all models of P.

Proof: By saying that M is a term structure (or in the usual LP terminology, Herbrand structure) we mean that its domain is the set of ground terms and that it interprets equality as identity. So it satisfies EA ∪ FA ∪ DCA. It satisfies the remainder of cwa(P), i.e., P ∪ ext(P) iff it is a model of P and if $P \not\models A$ implies $M \not\models A$. ∎

This notion of a generic model is analogous to that of a free algebra; just as a free group is one in which an equation is true only if it is true in all groups, i.e., is a consequence of the axioms of group theory, so a generic model of P is one in which a ground atom is true only if it is true in all models of P, i.e., is a consequence of P. So it is a unique most economical model of P in which a ground atom is true iff it has to be. If we identify a term model as usual with the subset of the base (set of ground atoms) which are true in it, then it is literally the smallest term model (but note Remark 2 below).

It is also obviously equivalent to being an initial term model for P, i.e., one from which there is a unique homomorphism to any other model of P.

REMARK 1

The genericity of a generic term model extends from ground atoms to existential quantifications of conjunctions of atoms, i.e., if s is a sentence of the form

$$\exists x_1 \ldots x_n (A_1(x_1 \ldots x_n) \wedge \ldots \wedge A_r(x_1 \ldots x_n))$$

where $A_1(x_1,\ldots,x_n),\ldots,A_r(x_1,\ldots,x_n)$ are atoms, then if M is a generic term model,

$$M \models s \quad \text{iff} \quad P \models s.$$

Proof: Straightforward. ■

So a positive query of the usual purely existential form is true in M iff it is a consequence of P. It is, however, not true that a correct answer substitution for the query in M is correct in all models; e.g., if P is

```
p(0)
p(s(x)),
```

then the identity substitution is a correct answer to the query p(x) in any Herbrand model, but is not a correct answer substitution in the usual sense, for $\forall x p(x)$ is not a consequence of P.

REMARK 2

Being a generic term model is not in general equivalent to being a term model which is generic for *term* models, i.e., such that

$$M \models A \quad \text{iff} \quad A \text{ is true in all term models of P.} \qquad (*)$$

This is equivalent to being a least term model of P, i.e., one contained in all other term models. However, if P consists of universal sentences, the two concepts are equivalent.

Proof: Take P to be $\forall x \exists y p(x,y)$ with $\{a\}$ as the set of ground terms. Then the term model with $p(a,a)$ true satisfies (*) because $p(a,a)$ is true in all term models of P, but it is obviously not true in all models of P. Condition (*) is obviously equivalent to saying that M is a least term model of P. If P consists of universal sentences, the usual Skolem argument shows that if A is true in all term (i.e., Herbrand) models of P, it is true in all models of P. ∎

We shall derive Theorem 3 from the slightly more general Theorem 5 below, which was first proved by Mahr and Makowsky [1983]. However their proof relied on a theorem of Maltsev whose statement was slightly incorrect. A complete self-contained proof appears in Makowsky [1986]. It goes via the well known model-theoretic characterisation of universal Horn theories as those whose set of models is closed under products and substructures. Although this is a very simple and important property from the point of view of model theory, it seems to us to be of no great importance in logic programming, so we give a direct elementary proof.

THEOREM 5

Let P be a set of first order sentences such that, for each set S of ground atoms (possibly involving new constants), if $P \cup S$ is consistent then $cwa(P \cup S)$ is consistent, relative to any extension of the language by new constants. Then P is equivalent to a set of Horn clauses, which, by the compactness theorem, may be taken to be finite if P is finite.

Proof: Let P_h be the set of universal Horn sentences, (i.e, Horn clauses, considered, as usual, to be universally quantified) which are consequences of P. It is clearly enough to show that every model M for P_h is a model for P. To do this extend the language by adding a new constant for each element of M. Take S to be the set of ground atoms in the extended language which are true in M. Then for each ground atom A we have

$$P \cup S \models A \text{ iff } M \models A. \tag{1}$$

For if $M \models A$ then A belongs to S, so $P \cup S \models A$. Conversely if $P \cup S \models A$ then, for some finite subset $\{S_1,...,S_n\}$ of S,

$$P \cup \{S_1, \ldots, S_n\} \models A,$$

so

$$P \models (S_1 \wedge \ldots \wedge S_n \rightarrow A).$$

Let $S'_1,...,S'_n,A'$ be the result of replacing all new constants in $S_1,...,S_n,A$ by new variables. Then, using $\forall$ to denote universal closure,

$$P \models \forall (S'_1 \wedge \ldots \wedge S'_n \rightarrow A').$$

But $\forall (S'_1 \wedge \ldots \wedge S'_n \rightarrow A')$ is a universal Horn sentence so this shows it belongs to P_h, hence it is true in M, hence so is

$$S_1 \wedge \ldots \wedge S_n \rightarrow A,$$

and since $S_1, \ldots, S_n$ are true in M it follows that A is true in M. This part of the argument also works with **f** (false) instead of A and shows that $P \cup S$ is consistent. By hypothesis cwa($P \cup S$) is consistent, so by Theorem 4 it has a term model M_o in which for all ground atoms A,

$$M_o \models A \text{ iff } P \cup S \models A$$

So, by (1), M is the same as M_o, hence is a model for P. ∎

Proof of Theorem 3: By Theorem 5, P is equivalent to a set of Horn clauses. If this set contained a negative Horn clause

$$\leftarrow A_1(x_1, \ldots, x_n), \ldots, A_r(x_1, \ldots, x_n)$$

then taking new constants $c_1, \ldots, c_n$ and letting S be $\{A_1(c_1, \ldots, c_n), \ldots, A_r(c_1, \ldots, c_n)\}$ would make $P \cup S$ inconsistent hence cwa($P \cup S$) inconsistent contrary to hypothesis. ∎

The converse of Theorem 5 can be stated a little more strongly in that new function symbols as well as new constants may be added:

THEOREM 6
If P is a set of Horn clauses and S is any set of ground atoms (possibly involving new constants and function symbols) and $P \cup S$ is consistent then cwa($P \cup S$) is consistent relative to any extension of the Herbrand universe by new constants and function symbols.

Proof: $P \cup S$ is a set of Horn clauses so the result follows from the result of Reiter [1978]. ∎

THEOREM 7
If P is a consistent set of Horn clauses then cwa(P) is consistent relative to any extension of the Herbrand universe.

Proof: Take the Herbrand structure M such that, for ground atoms A,

$$M \models A \text{ iff } P \models A.$$

This certainly satisfies $\{\neg A: P \not\models A\}$ so we have only to check that it satisfies P. Each ground instance

$$B \leftarrow A_1, \ldots, A_r \quad (\text{or} \leftarrow A_1, \ldots, A_r)$$

of a clause of P is true in M, because if $M \models A_1,\ldots,A_r$ then $P \models A_1,\ldots,A_r$ so $P \models B$ (or $P \models \mathbf{f}$, which is ruled out by the consistency of P), so $M \models B$. ∎

Since every set of definite Horn clauses is consistent (the whole Herbrand base is a model for it) we have:

THEOREM 8
If P is a set of definite Horn clauses and S is any set of ground atoms (possibly involving new constants and function symbols) then cwa(P ∪ S) is consistent relative to any extension of the Herbrand universe. ∎

(These results and the other results of Makowsky [1986] are valid for first order languages with equality. In that case the equality axioms become part of the logic and the freeness axioms are dropped from the closed world assumption and in the definition of a term model. A situation can then arise where P has an initial model but not an initial term model. For example, if P is

$$\forall x \exists y \, p(x, y)$$
$$y = y_1 \leftarrow p(x, y), p(x, y_1),$$

with $\{0\}$ as the set of ground terms, the only term model is $\{p(0,0)\}$ which is not initial, but the natural numbers with $p(x,y)$ interpreted as ''y is the successor of x'' is an initial model. In this case P is asserting that p is the graph of a one argument function s, and if you introduce that instead, i.e., take P to be the empty set of axioms over the Herbrand universe $\{0, s(0), s^2(0), \ldots\}$, then the natural numbers model becomes an initial Herbrand model. Makowsky shows, in his Theorem 5.9, that this example is typical, that P ∪ S has an initial model model for each set S of ground atoms iff P is equivalent to a ''partially functional $\forall \exists$-Horn theory.'' What this amounts to is that P only fails to be a universal Horn theory because certain functions have been represented by their graphs (as relations) and that by introducing these functions in a natural way you can obtain an equivalent theory which is universal Horn. In this paper we are confining ourselves to the case where the equality predicate is not one of the atomic predicates, and it is easily seen that in this case if P (or P ∪ S) has an initial model, it has an initial term model.)

Hodges and Makowsky both claim that Theorems 3 and 5 set limitations on the extension of logic programming beyond Horn clauses.

Hodges [1985] draws from Theorem 3 the

SAD COROLLARY
There is no possible extension of strict PROLOG which is first order and logically pure. ■

By logically pure he means that logically equivalent programs should always yield the same answers to queries.

Similarly Makowsky [1986] says:

> We have shown that universal Horn theories are exactly the framework in which the notion of a generic example can be applied. This should prevent other researchers from trying to generalise Logic Programming or the semantics for abstract data types to larger classes of first order formulas as done in Carvalho et al. [1980]. If it has to be generalised then the direction chosen by R. M. Burstall and J. A. Goguen [1984] seems to be much more appropriate.

I would agree that the possession of a generic model, in which a ground atom is true iff it has to be, i.e., iff it is true in all models, is a very attractive property and means that for some purposes (e.g., when considering positive consequences) you can behave as though this was the only model. But you have to pay a very high price for this very desirable situation; as every logician using PROLOG soon realizes, Horn clause logic is a small fragment of first order logic. Makowsky suggests that this is the limit of logic programs which admit a procedural interpretation, implying that the existence of a unique generic model is essential for this. I do not see why this is necessary, for it is the very essence of computing that some procedures give ''yes'' or ''no'' answers and others give no answer at all, corresponding to incomplete information, or not enough information to pin down a unique interpretation. Again, the closed world assumption is very natural for some programs concerned with databases, but it is considered by most logic programmers to be too drastic. To require the closed world assumption to be consistent for all extensions by new facts seems to be appropriate only for programs dealing with databases of the simplest kind. Most logic programmers feel the need to go beyond pure Horn clauses and are willing to consider other forms of default reasoning, e.g., Clark's completed data base, or Minker's generalized closed world assumption. Instead of accepting only a generic or least Herbrand model they are willing to consider minimal or ''supported'' or ''natural'' models. As far as ''negation as failure'' is concerned, pure Horn clause logic is undoubtedly one of the few cases where its semantics is clear and completely acceptable, but there again logic programmers are constantly trying to extend its use and to provide alternative semantics in terms of wider clauses of models as above or, like Kunen [1987] in terms of 3-valued logic.

It is worth noting also that these nice properties of Horn clauses all depend on an asymmetry in the treatment of positive and negative information: in the closed world assumption a ground atom is supposed false unless it can be proved true; in a generic model it is ground atoms (not their negations) that are true iff they are true in all models; and in a homomorphism, it is the basic relations (not their negations) whose truth is preserved.

(Sato [1982] considers a negative closed world assumption, where ground atoms are considered to be true if they cannot be proved false. However, he shifts his ground from requiring "proved" to mean "a logical consequence of P," which would give the exact dual of the usual closed world assumption, to something like "derivable by the negation as failure rule." The former is rather drastic. For example if P is a definite Horn clause program it gives the Herbrand model with everything true. The latter has some connection with Fitting's 3-valued semantics.)

So I do not think these negative conclusions should be taken too seriously. To be fair, Hodges and Makowsky in subsequent passages retreat a little from their extreme statements. Hodges suggests devious ways of avoiding his Sad Corollary and Makowsky says:

> The reader should not misunderstand our point: we do not claim that one has to restrict oneself to Horn formulas when dealing with logic programming or data bases. We only propose an explanatory paradigm; If there are reasons that the existence of initial models ... is crucial for the activity one has in mind then the restriction to Horn formulas is necessary.

He has certainly established this, and for the semantics of abstract data types, where initial models do seem to be of crucial importance (and usually easily obtainable), he is probably right to advocate limitation to Horn formulas.

Finally we note the possibility that one might want to apply the closed world assumption to most predicates but to protect others from it, where it is known that the information is incomplete. For reference to this notion of protected data see Minker and Perlis [1985].

The Completed Database

From now on we shall use the word *program* to denote a set of clauses of the form

$$A \leftarrow L_1, \ldots, L_m$$

where A is an atom and $L_1, \ldots, L_m$ are literals (not containing the predicate $=$). This is what Lloyd [1984] calls a general program. (In the new edition he will call it a normal program.)

(Lloyd and Topor [1985] have shown that many of the results can be generalized to the case where $L_1,...,L_m$ are arbitrary formulas of first order logic. This is done by translating a program P of this more general kind into a program P' of clauses of the usual form where $L_1,...,L_m$ are literals. For details see the new edition of Lloyd [1984]. But note that although Lloyd and Topor's translation of P into P' makes comp(P') equivalent to comp(P) (as far as the original predicates of P are concerned), it does not make P' equivalent to P. On the other hand the translation obtained by Skolemization preserves P but not comp(P). So both methods distort the relationship between P and comp(P).)

To form the completed data base, or completion, comp(P) of such a program each clause

$$p\,(t_1, \ldots, t_n) \;\leftarrow\; L_1, \ldots, L_m$$

in which the predicate p appears in the head, is rewritten in *general form* as

$$p\,(x_1, \ldots, x_n) \leftarrow \exists y_1 \ldots \exists y_p\,(x_1 = t_1 \land \ldots \land x_n = t_n \land L_1 \land \ldots \land L_m)$$

where $x_1,...,x_n$ are new variables and $y_1,...,y_p$ the variables of the original clause. We assume there are only finitely many clauses. If their general forms are

$$p\,(x_1, \ldots, x_n) \;\leftarrow\; E_1$$
$$\cdots$$
$$p\,(x_1, \ldots, x_n) \;\leftarrow\; E_j$$

then the *completed definition* of p is

$$p\,(x_1, \ldots, x_n) \;\leftrightarrow\; E_1 \lor \ldots \lor E_j.$$

(The empty disjunction is taken to be false, so if $j = 0$ this may be written $\neg p(x_1,...,x_n)$.)

The *completion*, comp(P), of P is now defined to be the collection of completed definitions for each predicate in P together with what was called CET in the last section, i.e., EA $\cup$ FA, the equality and freeness axioms.

Clearly

$$\text{comp}\,(P) \;\models\; P.$$

Usually comp(P) is stronger than P, and can easily be inconsistent, e.g., if P is $p \leftarrow \neg p$.

It is often argued that in everyday language when one writes P one really intends to assert comp(P), that when one says

"I'll go if my wife does, and I'll go if any of her friends do."

what one really means is that

"I'll go iff my wife or one of her friends does."

This may very well be true, and one of the aims of high level programming languages is to stay as close to ordinary discourse as possible. But this is definitely not one of the features of everyday logic that I would like to see imported into programming languages. Having spent years trying to teach mathematics students to distinguish between "if" and "iff," I am dismayed at the prospect of them using a programming language where they are forced to confuse them. In the interests of WYSISYM (What you say is what you mean) logic programming, I think that if this is the semantics that PROLOG intends, then the PROLOG manuals should at least explain that

$$p(x):- q(x)$$
$$p(x):- r(x) \qquad\qquad (1)$$

does not mean

$$p(x) \leftarrow q(x)$$
$$p(x) \leftarrow r(x)$$

but

$$p(x) \leftrightarrow (q(x) \lor r(x)). \qquad\qquad (2)$$

Or better still, you should actually write (2); if the form (1) is useful as an intermediate form, then the machine should produce it automatically.

The step from P to comp(P) is certainly a step away from the clarity aimed at in ideal logic programming, where the declarative meaning of the program should be apparent from the text of the program as written. Although in simple cases comp(P) may be what most people have in mind when they write P, it is not easy to foresee the effect of forming comp(P) when P contains "recursive" clauses with the same predicate occurring on both sides of the implication sign, or clauses involving mutual recursion, e.g., $p(s(x)) \leftarrow q(x), q(s(y)) \leftarrow p(y)$. Those who doubt this should consider that, using the method of Lloyd and Topor above, given any first order formula ϕ it is possible to find a program P such that comp(P) is a conservative extension of ϕ (together with the equality and freeness axioms) (i.e., the logical consequence of comp(P) involving only the language of φ are the same as those of φ ∪ EA ∪ FA). So comp(P) can be essentially any formula of first order logic. This can even be achieved with P having clauses only of the simple form A ← ¬B where A,B are atoms. In fairness it should be added that similar mental acrobatics may be involved in appreciating the significance of the closed world assumption or fixed point models or any of the other semantics proposed for negation as failure. Referring to our Principle I of the introduction, these semantics may satisfy the requirement of being clear in the sense of mathematically precise, but they are not, at least not in all cases, easily intelligible. As far as Principle II is concerned, comp(P) emerges with flying colors; the set of consequences of comp(P) is clearly recursively enumerable (but (Theorem 13 below) the set of sentences true in all *Herbrand* models of comp(P) may not be).

Despite this step back into obscurity, it is becoming increasingly common to regard the completed database as giving the appropriate semantics for logic programming; i.e., to say that when one writes a program P and asks a query Q one is not asking

"Is Q a logical consequence of P?"

but

"Is Q a logical consequence of comp(P)?"

Indeed some writers do not even mention this, but take it for granted that this is what the reader will understand.

The fixed point models and the models of cwa(P) already discussed are restricted to being Herbrand models. This is not the case for comp(P). However some people do consider this restriction to be appropriate so it is important to be clear about what is meant by a Herbrand model of comp(P) because this has existential quantifiers and the equality symbols "=" in it, and it contains the freeness axioms.

EXAMPLE 2
Let the program P be:

$$p(f(y)) \leftarrow p(y)$$
$$q(a) \leftarrow p(y)$$

comp(P) is

$$p(x) \leftrightarrow \exists y (x = f(y) \land p(y))$$
$$q(x) \leftrightarrow (x = a \land \exists y\, p(t)).$$

Lloyd [1984] says that

> comp(P) $\cup$ {q(a)} does not have a Herbrand model.

This is true if the Herbrand universe is to be that of P, i.e.,

$$\{a, f(a), f^2(a), \ldots\}$$

for we want

$$\exists y p(y) \text{ but } \neg p(a), \neg p(f(a)), \neg p(f^2(a)), \ldots .$$

But, according to the general theorem of Skolem-Herbrand, it does have a Herbrand model (provided "=" is not forced to be identity) over the universe you get by introducing function symbols to get rid of the existential quantifiers. A Skolemized clausal form of comp(P) $\cup$ {q(a)} is equivalent to EA $\cup$ FA together with

$$p(f(y)) \leftarrow p(y)$$
$$p(x) \rightarrow x = f(g(x)) \wedge p(g(x))$$
$$q(a)$$
$$p(c)$$
$$q(x) \rightarrow x = a$$

which has a model over the new Herbrand universe, which is built up from a,c by applying f,g. One such model has

$$q(x) \quad \text{true for } x = a$$
$$p(x) \quad \text{true for } x = t(c) \quad \text{i.e., all terms involving } c,$$

and = as the equivalence relation with t(c) = f(g(t(c))) for all terms t(c) involving c. (This doesn't violate the axiom t(x) $\neq$ x of FA because that applies only to "old" functions, i.e., $f^r(x) \neq x$.) ∎

There are three reasons for this apparent conflict with the Skolem-Herbrand theorem which appears to say that if a sentence has a model, it has a Herbrand model. Given a language L, we define what in logic programming is called the Herbrand universe U_L for L as the set of all ground terms which can be formed out of the constants and functions in L (adding a constant if L has no constants). A Herbrand interpretation for L is one whose domain is U_L with constants assigned to themselves and an n-ary function symbol f assigned to the mapping $(t_1, \ldots, t_n) \mapsto f(t_1, \ldots, t_n)$. When we wish to indicate the dependence on L we shall call this a Herbrand(L) interpretation. So it is a free interpretation with equality assigned to identity. The Skolem-Herbrand theorem says that if a universal sentence ϕ of L has a model it has one which differs from a Herbrand model only by having equality assigned to a congruence relation on U_L. Let us call this a Herbrand/quotient model. And if ϕ does not contain the equality symbol this congruence relation can be taken to be identity, i.e., the model can be a Herbrand model. This is the typical situation in Wysiwym logic programming. There the program P is a conjunction of a finite set of clauses which are implicitly universally quantified, the query Q is an existential sentence and neither P nor Q contains the equality symbol. So the sentence being tested for validity is P $\rightarrow$ Q and the sentence being tested for satisfiability is the negation of this, i.e., the sentence P $\wedge$ $\neg$Q, which is universal and does contain the equality symbol. In this case the theorem tells us that nothing is changed by restriction to Herbrand over any language containing the symbols in P and Q. If Q is true in all Herbrand models of P, then it is true in all models of P.

The first chance of conflict arises if the sentence being tested for satisfiability is not a universal sentence, e.g., if P is not purely universal and Q is not purely existential. Then the result is only generally true over languages which also contain Skolem functions that enable the existential quantifiers from P $\wedge$ $\neg$Q to be eliminated. As Example 2 shows, even if P is definite Horn, its completion comp(P) may contain existential quantifiers. So if you are asking whether comp(P) $\rightarrow$ Q is valid, even for existential Q, then restriction to Herbrand models over the language of P and Q is a genuine restriction.

The second chance of conflict arises if the sentence ϕ being tested for satisfiability contains the equality symbol. And as Example 2 illustrates, the equality symbol is usually essentially involved in comp(P) even when it does not occur in P. In this case the result is weakened to: "If ϕ has a model it has a Herbrand/quotient model over any language which contains Skolem functions for ϕ."

The third chance of conflict in the case of comp(P) arises because this contains the freeness axioms FA, which depend on the language L. Let us denote by FA(L) the freeness axioms for L, i.e., the axioms

$$f(x_1, \ldots, x_n) \neq g(x_1, \ldots, x_m)$$

for each pair f,g of distinct functions of L,

$$f(x_1, \ldots, x_n) = f(y_1, \ldots, y_n) \rightarrow x_1 = y_1 \wedge \ldots \wedge x_n = y_n$$

for each function f of L, and

$$t(x) \neq x$$

for each term t(x) of L different from x in which x occurs. In order to get a "Herbrand" model for comp(P) $\wedge$ q(a) in Example 2, it is not enough to allow equality to be interpreted by some congruence relation and to require that the Herbrand universe contains Skolem functions for comp(P). You also need some of these Skolem functions to be new, i.e., not subject to the freeness axioms. In fact you want $\exists y p(y)$ to be true so you need a term t such that p(t) is true. But however large the original language L was, the freeness axioms FA(L) and the definition of p in comp(P) i.e.,

$$p(x) \;\longleftrightarrow\; \exists y (x = f(y) \land p(y))$$

imply that p(t) is false, for all terms t of L. For t is of the form $f^r(t_1)$ where t_1 has an outer function symbol different from f and the definition of p implies

$$p(f^r(t_1)) \;\longrightarrow\; p(f^{r-1}(t_1)) \;\ldots\; \longrightarrow p(t_1),$$

but the freeness axioms imply $t_1 \neq f(y)$, so the definition of p implies $\neg p(t_1)$, hence $\neg p(t)$.

Those who talk about Herbrand models of comp(P) usually mean free models whose domain is the Herbrand universe for the language containing only the constants and functions appearing in P. We shall denote this language by L_P and call these *Herbrand(L_P) models* in future. It will be tacitly assumed that queries are restricted to the language L_P. However some writers suppose that the language L is given in advance, and may contain constants and functions not in P. An extreme example of this is Kunen [1987], who uses a standard "universal" language KU which has for each n infinitely many n-place function symbols. There are arguments in favor of each point of view. The Herbrand universe of P contains all the terms that are involved in the description of P, and Kunen's Herbrand universe contains infinitely many irrelevant terms. On the other hand it gives more stable results. We have already seen in the last section that the consistency of cwa(P) may depend on the language; similar shifts occur with comp(P). For example if you take the program P:

$$p(0)$$
$$p(s(x)) \;\longleftarrow\; p(x)$$

then $\forall x p(x)$ is true in all Herbrand(L_P) models of comp(P). But if you form P' by adding the assertion q(a) to P then $\forall x p(x)$ is false in all Herbrand($L_{P'}$) models of comp(P'), because comp(P') implies $\neg p(a)$. So if your semantics for P is "truth in all Herbrand(L_P) models of comp(P)" it does in Kunen's words (private communication) "seem a bit strange; PROLOG logic *is* non-monotonic, but we do not expect a truth value to switch from true to false upon the addition to the database of a statement in a completely disjoint language." (The query $\forall x p(x)$ here is not of the usual existential form. That can be arranged at the cost of using a non-Horn clause program P, by adding the clauses

$$r \leftarrow \neg s$$
$$s \leftarrow \neg p (x)$$

to P. Now r will be true in all Herbrand(L_p) models of comp(P) but false in all Herbrand($L_{p'}$) models of comp(P') when P' is obtained as above by adjoining q(a) to P.) Perhaps the best point of view, for those who think it is appropriate to restrict to some sort of Herbrand model, is between the two: That you do have in mind some fixed Herbrand universe for each program P, but it is not necessarily determined by the function symbols actually applying in P. This is the point of view we adopt. We do not need to say what the language is except in those cases where it affects the result, in which case we shall be particularly interested in the extreme cases of the languages L_p and KU.

(Actually the freeness axioms which are responsible for some of these peculiarities of comp(P) also prohibit its use in many applications, since they forbid equations such as john = spouse(mary). To deal with that one needs a system which allows the equality relation in clauses, e.g., Jaffar, Lassez, and Maher [1984a,1986a] which is beyond the scope of this paper.)

We sum up the properties of Example 2 in:

THEOREM 9
There is a definite Horn clause program P and a ground atom A such that whatever language L is used for P and comp(P), the sentence $\neg$A is true in all Herbrand(L) models of comp(P) but not in all models of comp(P). ∎

As we saw, to get a model of comp(P) in which $\neg$A is false you must enlarge the Herbrand universe and also take a quotient model, assigning equality to a congruence relation.

When considering Herbrand models of the program P itself the language used becomes relevant if arbitrary queries are allowed.

THEOREM 10
There is a definite Horn clause program P and a query Q which is true in all Herbrand (L_p) models of P but not in all Herbrand models of P.

Proof: Example 1 will do. You can get a Herbrand model of P in which Q is false by using a language with Skolem functions for P $\wedge$ $\neg$Q, i.e., a new constant c. Then take even(c), even (s(c)) both false. ∎

However, for the purely existential queries customary in logic programming the Skolem-Herbrand theorem gives:

THEOREM 11

If P is universal and Q is existential and neither contain the equality symbol, then Q is true in all models of P iff it is true in all Herbrand(L_p) models of P. ■

So the restriction to Herbrand(L_p) models is a genuine restriction when considering arbitrary queries relative to P or even ground queries relative to comp(P).

Note that this restriction can be axiomatized (if you allow infinitary axioms; Example 1 shows you can't replace DCA by WDCA) by adding EA ∪ FA ∪ DCA to P or DCA to comp(P). Apt and van Emden [1982], Fitting [1985], and Kunen [1987] have warned that in general this restriction to models with a fixed infinite domain destroys the computability of the proof procedure, i.e., violates our Principle II. This is familiar from arithmetic. If you write down the axioms $s(x) \neq 0$, $s(x) \rightarrow x = y$ and the recursive definitions of + and ×, then the set of sentences true in all models of these is the set of first order consequences and is recursively enumerable. But the set of sentences true in models with domain the natural numbers is the set of true sentences of arithmetic which is not recursively enumerable.

This argument can be reproduced in Horn clause logic.

THEOREM 12

There is a definite Horn clause program P such that the set of sentences which are true in all Herbrand(L_p) models of P is not recursively enumerable.

Proof: Take a recursive relation R(m,n) such that $\forall n R(m,n)$ is not recursively enumerable. Then take a definite Horn clause program P such that

$$P \models r(s^m(0), s^n(0)) \quad \text{iff} \quad R(m,n) \text{ holds.}$$

The Herbrand universe of P is $\{0, s(0), s^2(0), \dots\}$ so $\forall y\ r(s^m(0), y)$ is true in all Herbrand(L_p) models of P iff for all n, $r(s^m(0), s^n(0))$ is true in all Herbrand(L_p) models of P, i.e., iff $\forall n\ R(m,n)$ holds. ■

What we have shown is that by restricting to the Herbrand universe of P, the quantifiers in the query are converted into natural number quantifiers. So the argument shows that the set of Herbrand(L_p) consequences of P can be of any level in the arithmetic hierarchy. And if you start with a universal recursive relation (e.g., corresponding to a universal Turing machine), you can do this in a uniform way and push the level up to hyperarithmetic.

However, the set of sentences (not containing =) true in all Herbrand(KU) models of P *is* recursively enumerable because it coincides with the set of sentences true in all models of P. For if P ∧ ¬Q has a model it has, since it does not contain =, a Herbrand model over the language obtained by extending the language of P by adding Skolem functions for $\neg Q$, hence also over Kunen's language, which can be regarded as an extension of this.

THEOREM 13

There is a definite Horn clause program P such that the set of negative ground literals $\neg A$ which are true in all Herbrand models of comp(P) is not recursively enumerable.

Proof: Take R as in the last proof but now take a definite Horn clause program P_0 such that

$$P_0 \models \bar{r}(s^m(0), s^n(0)) \quad \text{iff} \quad \neg R(m, n) \text{ holds.}$$

This can be written so that

$$\text{comp}(P_0) \models \neg\bar{r}(s^m(0), s^n(0)) \quad \text{iff} \quad R(m, n) \text{ holds.}$$

Form P by adding to P_0 a new unary predicate u and a clause

$$u(x) \leftarrow \bar{r}(x, y).$$

The completed definition of u is

$$u(x) \leftrightarrow \exists y \bar{r}(x, y),$$

so $\neg u(s^m(0))$ is true in all Herbrand(L_P) models of comp(P) iff for all n, $\neg\bar{r}(s^m(0), s^n(0))$ is true in all Herbrand(L_P) models, i.e., iff $\forall m \, R(m, n)$. ∎

In contrast to Theorem 12, this result is true whatever language is used in forming the Herbrand universe, since we can arrange for comp(P) to imply $\neg\bar{r}(x, t)$ for terms t not of the form $s^n(0)$.

"Not recursively enumerable" can be replaced by Π_1^1-complete; see Blair [1982]. And for a general program you can use positive ground literals as queries instead of negative ones, for you can construct the universal quantifier inside comp(P) by adding a clause $v(x) \leftarrow \neg u(x)$. (This is not possible for definite Horn programs because then, by Theorem 14, if a positive ground literal is true in all Herbrand(L_P) models of comp(P), it is true in the least fixed point model of P (and comp(P)) hence by Theorems 8 and 4 and Remark 2, it is true in all models of P, hence in all models of comp(P). So the set of positive literals true in all Herbrand(L_P) models is the same as the set of positive literals true in all models of comp(P), which is recursively enumerable.)

There is a very neat fixpoint characterization of the Herbrand models of comp(P) in terms of the operator T_P defined in section 5:

THEOREM 14

The Herbrand models of comp(P) are the fixpoints of T_P.

Proof: Note that the result is true whatever language is used for P and comp(P). This is almost obvious in view of our remark above in the section on fixpoint models that an interpretation I is a fixpoint of T_P iff it is a supported model of P, since "supported" is equivalent to satisfying the "only-if halves" of the completed definitions of the predicates in P. Apt and van Emden [1982] gave a proof for the case where P consists of definite Horn clauses and Apt, Blair, and Walker [1988] noticed that the proof (e.g., Lloyd [1984], Prop.14.3, pp.72–73) works equally well for general programs. ■

If P is a definite Horn clause program then comp(P) adds no new positive information, i.e.,:

THEOREM 15

If P is a definite Horn clause program and Q is a positive sentence, i.e., one built up using only $\wedge$, $\vee$, $\forall$, $\exists$, then

```
comp (P) ⊨ Q implies P ⊨ Q.
```

In particular this is true if Q is a ground atom.

Proof: Suppose P $\not\models$ Q. Then P $\wedge$ $\neg$Q is satisfiable. Extend the original language L to a language L$'$ containing Skolem functions which put $\neg$Q into Skolem form $\forall$ $\neg$Q$'$ where Q$'$ is a positive quantifier free formula. Now P $\wedge$ $\neg$Q$'$ has a Herbrand model M. This contains the least Herbrand model M_1 = lfp(T_P) of P which by Theorem 14 is also a model for comp(P). (This is comp(P) as defined using the language L$'$, i.e., containing the equality and freeness axioms appropriate to L$'$, but since these contain the corresponding axioms for L, M is a model for the original comp(P) defined in the language L.) Since Q$'$ is positive and $\forall$ $\neg$Q$'$ is true in M it is also true in M_1, for all ground atoms false in M are false in M_1. So $\neg$Q is true in M_1, so comp(P) $\not\models$ Q. ■

Since the language KU of Kunen has the new Skolem functions needed for $\neg$ Q this argument proves

COROLLARY 2
The hypothesis comp(P) ⊨ Q of Theorem 15 can be replaced by the apparently weaker hypothesis

        Q is true in all Herbrand(KU) models of comp(P). ∎

It is convenient to note here:

THEOREM 16
If P is a definite Horn clause program and Q is a conjunction of literals then

    P ⊨ ∃Q implies P ⊨ Qθ for some ground substitution θ

Proof: We may suppose all literals in Q are positive for otherwise, as noted in the introduction, the result is true vacuously because P ⊭ ∃Q. If P ⊨ ∃Q then ∃Q is true in all models of P, in particular in lfp(T_p). Since this is a Herbrand model, Q must be satisfied by ground terms, i.e., there is a ground substitution θ such that Qθ is true in lfp(T_p). But Qθ is a conjunction of ground atoms and lfp(T_p) is a generic Herbrand model so Qθ is true in all models of P, i.e., P ⊨ Qθ. ∎

THEOREM 17
If P is definite Horn then comp(P) is consistent.

Proof: In the section on fixpoint models it was shown that a definite Horn program has a least fixpoint model. By Theorem 14 this is a model for comp(P). ∎

Other classes of programs P for which comp(P) is consistent, e.g., hierarchic, stratified, are given in later sections, and it is shown that the 3-valued analogue of comp(P) is always consistent. But the general problem of deciding, given P, whether comp(P) is consistent, is, as expected, undecidable:

THEOREM 18
The problem of deciding whether comp(P) is consistent is recursively undecidable.

Proof: By the method of Lloyd and Topor referred to above, given any first order sentence φ construct a program P such that comp(P) is a conservative extension of φ together with the equality and freeness axioms. A method of deciding the consistency of comp(P) would give a method of deciding the satisfiability of φ. ∎

The Relation between the Closed World Assumption and the Completed Database

The closed world assumption, cwa(P), and the completed database, comp(P), are superficially similar. They are both examples of reasoning by default, assuming that if some positive piece of information cannot be proved in a certain way from P, then it is not true. But for cwa(P), the notion of proof involved is that of full first order logic, whereas for comp(P), it is "using one of the program clauses whose head matches the given atom." At first sight this is a narrower notion of proof so that more ground atoms should be false under comp(P) than under cwa(P), i.e., cwa(P) should be a consequence of comp(P). But it is not so simple because comp(P) actually adds, in the "only if" halves of the completed definition of a predicate p, new universal statements which can be used to prove things about predicates other than p. Also cwa(P) includes the domain closure axiom which restricts to Herbrand models, and this is not included in comp(P), though it is often tacitly supposed to be. In fact when cwa(P) and comp(P) are compatible, it is cwa(P) which implies comp(P) because cwa(P) is categorical.

EXAMPLE 3
For the program P:

$$p \leftarrow \neg p,$$

cwa(P) is consistent but comp(P) is not. ∎

EXAMPLE 4
For the program P:

$$q \leftarrow \neg p,$$

comp(P) is consistent but cwa(P) is not. ∎

EXAMPLE 5
For the program P:

```
p ← q
q ← ¬p
q ← q,
comp (P) and cwa (P) are both consistent but they are
         incompatible, i.e.,
comp (P) ∪ cwa (P) is inconsistent.
```

Note that the domain closure axiom is not involved here. ∎

Since some people confuse the closed world assumption and completed database it is of interest to give conditions for their compatibility:

THEOREM 19
comp(P) $\cup$ cwa(P) is consistent iff

1. comp(P) is consistent, and

2. for all ground atoms $A_1,...,A_r$

    $$\text{comp (P)} \cup \text{DCA} \models (A_1 \vee ... \vee A_r) \text{ implies P} \models A_i$$
    $$\text{for some } i = 1, ... r.$$

Proof: If 2) is false, i.e., $P \not\models A_i$ for $i = 1,...r$ but comp(P) $\cup$ DCA $\models A_1 \vee$ ... $\vee A_r$, then comp(P) $\cup$ cwa(P) is inconsistent, for all of $\neg A_1,..., \neg A_r$ belong to cwa(P).

Conversely if comp(P) is consistent but comp(P) $\cup$ cwa(P) is not, then there exist $A_1,...,A_r$ such that, for $i = 1,...,r$, $P \not\models A_i$ and $\{\neg A,..., \neg A_r\} \cup$ comp(P) $\cup$ DCA is inconsistent.
This implies

$$\text{comp (P)} \cup \text{DCA} \models (A_1 \vee ... \vee A_r). \quad \blacksquare$$

Adding DCA to comp(P) here amounts to restriction to Herbrand models. There is a corresponding result with DCA omitted from the hypothesis and DCA left out of cwa(P); similarly if DCA is replaced by WDCA. One might hope to simplify condition 2) if the consistency of cwa(P) was added to the conditions, but the natural conjecture that one could take $r = 1$, i.e., that sufficient conditions for consistency of comp(P) $\cup$ cwa(P) are consistency of comp(P), consistency of cwa(P) and that

$$\text{comp (P)} \cup \text{DCA} \models A \text{ implies P} \not\models A,$$

is false, as the following example shows

$$
\begin{aligned}
p &\leftarrow p_1 \\
p &\leftarrow p_2 \\
p &\leftarrow p_3 \\
p_1 &\leftarrow p_1 \\
p_2 &\leftarrow p_2 \\
p_3 &\leftarrow \neg p.
\end{aligned}
$$

THEOREM 20
If P is definite Horn, then comp(P) $\cup$ cwa(P) is consistent.

Proof: If P is definite Horn, it has a least fixpoint model which is also a least Herbrand model, so by Theorems 14, 4, and Remark 2, it is a model for comp(P) ∪ cwa(P). ∎

It may also be of interest to consider the effect of applying the closed world assumption on top of the completed database, i.e., cwa(comp(P)). (There is nothing to be gained by doing it the other way around for cwa(P) is categorical, and since it contains negative clauses, it is not quite clear what its completion should be—probably comp(P) ∪ cwa(P).)

THEOREM 21

cwa (comp (P)) ⊆ cwa (P) ∪ comp (P) .

Proof: Using A as a variable ranging over ground atoms,

cwa(comp(P)) = comp(P) ∪ EA ∪ FA ∪ DCA ∪ {¬ A: comp(P) $\not\models$ A}
comp(P) ∪ cwa(P) = comp(P) ∪ EA ∪ FA ∪ DCA ∪ {¬ A: P $\not\models$ A},
and P $\models$ A implies comp(P) $\models$ A. ∎

THEOREM 22
cwa(comp(P)) can be properly contained in cwa(P) ∪ comp(P), in fact can be consistent when the latter is not.

Proof: Example 4. ∎

THEOREM 23
cwa(comp(P)) is equivalent to cwa(P) ∪ comp(P) iff for all ground atoms A,

comp (P) $\models$ A implies P $\models$ A

i.e., when comp(P) gives no new information about ground atoms.

Proof: See proof of Theorem 21. ∎

THEOREM 24
If cwa(P) ∪ comp(P) is consistent then cwa(comp(P)) is equivalent to it.

Proof: Condition 2 of Theorem 19 implies the condition of Theorem 23. ∎

COROLLARY 3
If P is definite Horn then cwa(P) ∪ comp(P) is the same as cwa(comp(P)).

Proof: Theorems 15 and 23. ∎

Negation as Failure

By "negation as failure" or SLDNF-resolution, we mean the result of adding negation as failure to SLD-resolution, i.e., the query evaluation procedure described in Clark [1978], where a negative literal is selected only if it is a ground literal $\neg A$. The next step is then to query A; if A succeeds, then the evaluation of $\neg A$ fails; if A fails on every evaluation path then, $\neg A$ succeeds. Since by König's lemma the evaluation tree is then finite, this is usually called *finite failure* to distinguish it from the situation where the evaluation tree has no successful path but has infinite paths. *Queries are now restricted to the usual existential form*

$$\exists x_1 \ldots \exists x_k (L_1 \wedge \ldots \wedge L_i), \text{ abbreviated to } \exists (L_1 \wedge \ldots \wedge L_i)$$

where $L_1, \ldots, L_i$ are positive or negative literals. The negation of this, $\leftarrow L_1, \ldots, L_i$, is presented as a goal clause. If Q succeeds the answer θ given by the evaluation path is the resultant substitution for the variables of Q. If every evaluation path ends with fail then the answer is false.

The different evaluation paths correspond to the different program clauses whose head matches the chosen literal. Different query evaluation procedures result from different rules for selecting the literal to be resolved on. Shepherdson [1984, 1985] followed Clark in calling these selection rules but here we follow Lloyd [1984] and call them *computation rules*. (PROLOG's computation rule is to select the leftmost literal and its search rule is a depth first search trying the program clauses in the order in which they are written.) We shall not be concerned with search rules; we shall state results in terms of properties of the full evaluation tree, e.g., "all branches end in fail," "some branch ends in success." But we do need to consider computation rules, since we no longer have the nice property that all such rules are equivalent, as they are for definite Horn clause programs.

Most PROLOG implementations are unsound because they allow negation as failure to be used on non-ground literals. We do not allow this; i.e., all computation rules used are supposed to be *safe* in the sense of Lloyd [1984]. But even if the above procedure is correctly applied, the fact that non-ground negative literals cannot be dealt with (which is inherent in any free variable treatment, since $\forall x \, \neg P(x)$ is not the same as $\neg \forall x P(x)$ i.e. $\exists x \, \neg P(x)$, which is our meaning in queries) leads to some disturbing incompleteness in the proof procedure.

EXAMPLE 6

A query may not succeed even though some ground instance of it does, contrary to the logical principle.

$$p(a) \rightarrow \exists x p(x).$$

Proof: Take the program to be

$$p(x) \leftarrow \neg r(x).$$

Then the query p(a) succeeds but p(x) (meaning $\exists x p(x)$) does not; it flounders, i.e., all evaluation paths terminate in a goal consisting entirely of non-ground negative literals, to which no rule is applicable. ∎

EXAMPLE 7
A query $L_1 \wedge L_2$ may succeed although L_1 does not succeed under any *computation* rule, contrary to the logical principle

$$L_1 \wedge L_2 \rightarrow L_1.$$

Proof: Take the program

$$p(x) \leftarrow \neg q(x)$$
$$r(a).$$

The query p(x) $\wedge$ r(x) succeeds but p(x) flounders. ∎

There is no escape here by considering a logic that is weaker than classical logic, for these principles are surely true in any logic which might conceivably be useful. It is possible to devise criteria for disallowing queries like this but they may depend on the computation rule used, as well as some property of the program, and may turn out to be undecidable.

However, it is not a question here of the procedure giving a wrong answer, just of failing to give an answer to a query, when it does give an answer to a query which trivially implies the given one.

The practical logic programmer may not be disturbed by this or by any other form of incompleteness because it may well be insignificant compared with the incompleteness forced by the limitations of time and space imposed by any implementation on a real machine. But it is as well to be aware of the theoretical limitations and to realize that for queries involving negation one cannot expect completeness unless they are grounded.

Negation as failure is so easy to implement and so widely used that it is worth trying to find an appropriate semantics. It is clear that this cannot be expressed in terms of the classical logical content of the original program P, for q ← ¬p and p ← ¬q give different results (in the first p fails and q succeeds and vice-versa for the second). These are not intuitionistically equivalent but the program q ← ¬p, p ← p is equivalent to q ← ¬p in intuitionist or any conceivable logic, yet it gives a different result—everything loops, nothing succeeds or fails. This could be regarded as an extreme form of incompleteness but it is undesirable, and contrary to the ideal of logic programming, that the behavior of the program should depend on the way it is written rather than on its logical content. So one must look for a semantics in terms of some other expression derived in some systematic way from P. This is usually taken to be comp(P) after Clark's discovery [1978] that negation as failure is sound with respect to comp(P): It is certainly not sound with respect to P, as the first example above shows. Note that the logical difficulties just referred to vanish if we take Clark's completion, comp(P), to be the intended program, for the three programs above have three different completions.

THEOREM 25
(Soundness of negation as failure with respect to [wrt] the completion.) Let P be a (general) program and Q a conjunction of literals, with free variables $x_1,...,x_n$. Apply SLDNF-resolution to P with Q as the query.
Then

1.   if Q fails then comp(P) $\models \neg \exists x_1... \exists x_n Q$

2.   if Q succeeds with answer θ then comp(P) $\models Q\theta$.

Proof: Clark [1978], pp.305–312 or Lloyd [1984], pp.79–80. ∎

COROLLARY 4
(Intuitionistic soundness) Theorem 25 can be strengthened by replacing the classical consequence relation $\models$ by the intuitionistic derivability relation $\vdash_I$.

Proof: Shepherdson [1985]. ∎

Classical soundness holds also for the closed world assumption, cwa(P).

THEOREM 26
(Soundness of negation as failure wrt the *closed world assumption*.) As in Theorem 25 with comp(P) replaced by cwa(P).

Proof: Shepherdson [1984]. ∎

We saw in the last section that comp(P) and cwa(P) could be very different, so because negation as failure is sound with respect to both of them means that it must sometimes be very incomplete with respect to either of them. What meaning should we tell the naive programmer to have in mind when he writes the program?

The result of SLDNF-resolution can also depend on the computation rule, for example, given the program

$$p \leftarrow \neg q$$
$$p \leftarrow p$$

and the query

$$\neg q \wedge p$$

it returns success if the rule is always to choose the first literal, but loops if it is always to choose the last literal. So some rules are more incomplete than others. Shepherdson [1984, 1985] showed that there are maximal computation rules R_m such that if a query succeeds with answer θ under any rule it does so under R_m, and if it fails under any rule it fails under R_m, but it is not clear whether there are any recursive maximal rules.

A query such as $\neg p(x) \wedge q(y)$ which has a variable occurring in a negative literal which does not also occur in a positive literal cannot possibly succeed (although it can fail if $q(y)$ fails) because there is no way $\neg p(x)$ can be grounded, and it cannot be eliminated until it is grounded. Let us say, as in Shepherdson [1985] (possibly following Clark [1978]),

> a query is *weakly allowed* if every variable in a negative literal also occurs in a positive literal.

Then if we restrict ourselves to weakly allowed queries, we shall avoid some of the obvious incompleteness due to the fact that non-ground negative literals cannot be handled. This can be formally defined as follows:

> a query *flounders* if some evaluation path ends in a goal containing only non-ground negative literals.

In general the condition of being weakly allowed is not sufficient to prevent a query floundering (e.g., program $p(x) \leftarrow \neg q(x)$, query $p(x)$) but under some commonly occurring conditions on the program it does (Shepherdson [1985], Theorem 3.5):

If the body of each program clause is a weakly allowed query, and every variable in the head also appears in the body, then a weakly allowed query cannot flounder.

A stronger interpretation of what Clark [1978], p.317, meant by an allowed query is

> A query is *allowed* if none of its positive literals flounders and every variable in a negative literal also occurs in a positive literal, all of whose success branches ground it.

This is not a necessary condition for not floundering (e.g., if (p(a) fails then p(a) & ¬q(x) does not flounder) but is sufficient (Shepherdson [1985], Theorem 3.3). Unfortunately whether a query is allowed or flounders depends on the computation rule and is *probably* undecidable for some programs (Borger [1987]). The notion of weakly allowed, although not always sufficient to ensure not floundering, has the great advantage of being independent of the computation rule and decidable on sight.

Negation as Failure for Definite Horn Clause Programs

For definite Horn programs there are some completeness results for negation as failure with respect to the completed database. Denote the existential quantification of Q by ∃Q.

THEOREM 27
Let P be a definite Horn program and let Q be a conjunction of atoms. Then using SLDNF-resolution,

1.   Q succeeds with answer including θ under all computation rules iff comp(P) $\vdash$ Qθ (iff comp(P) $\vdash_I$ Qθ iff P $\models$ Qθ iff P $\vdash_I$ Qθ),

2.   Q succeeds under all computation rules iff comp(P) $\models$ ∃Q,

3.   Q fails under every fair computation rule iff comp(P) $\models$ ¬∃Q.

A *fair* computational rule (Lassez and Maher [1984]) is one where on each infinite evaluation path every literal in the goal is eventually chosen. The "leftmost literal" rule of PROLOG is not fair but could be made fair by putting the new literals introduced by unification at the right-hand end. To see that (iii) does not holdtifor all rules, take the program p(x) ← p(x), q(a) and the query p(a) ∧ q(b) with the PROLOG rule.

Proof:

1.   Here negation as failure is not involved. The results follow from Theorem 15, the completeness of SLD-resolution for positive queries (Lloyd [1984], Theorem 9.5, p. 47), and the fact that the soundness of SLD-resolution holds intuitionistically (check Lloyd [1984], Theorem 7.1, pp. 38–39), i.e. that,

    if Q succeeds with answer including θ then P $\vdash_I$ Qθ.

    The chain of inference is

    ```
    (comp(P) ⊨ Qθ) ⇒ (P ⊨ Qθ) ⇒
            (Q succeeds with answer including θ)
        ⇒ (P ⊢I Qθ) ⇒ (comp(P) ⊢I Qθ)
        ⇒ (comp(P) ⊨ Qθ).
    ```

2.   Follows from (1) and Theorem 16.

3.   The soundness half of (3) is Theorem 25 (1), the completeness is due to Jaffar, Lassez, and Lloyd [1983], and appears in Lloyd [1984] as Theorem 16.1, pp. 82–83. ∎

Although following Jaffar, Lassez, and Lloyd, we have called this a completeness result for negation as failure, it has nothing to do with the use of the negation as failure rule in a computation. Since the query and the program clauses are all totally positive, the rule of negation as failure is never invoked in the computation. The only thing the result has to do with negation is that it tells us when a positive query fails under ordinary SLD-resolution, namely (provided a fair rule is used) when its negation is a consequence of comp(P).

Unfortunately the above completeness results only apply in full to positive queries, where the negation as failure rule is not invoked at all. If we pass to existential queries of the form

$$\exists (A_1 \wedge \ldots \wedge A_r \wedge \quad \neg B_1 \wedge \ldots \wedge \quad \neg B_s)$$

none of them holds; we shall see that they fail even for queries of a more restricted form. And it should be noted that even here the use of the negation is minimal. Since P is supposed to consist of definite Horn clauses, the only negations that occur are those in the original query, and the negation as failure rule is not used iteratively, but only at the end, to declare a grounded $\neg B_j\theta$ a success or failure according to whether $B_j\theta$ fails or succeeds using ordinary SLD-resolution for positive clauses and queries. Nevertheless, we do need to use it at least once, for a non-positive query, so we can only expect completeness if we use a fair computation rule. So the appropriate definitions of completeness corresponding to those of Theorem 27 are that SLDNF-resolution is

1. θ-complete for Q if for all substitutions θ,
     comp(P) $\models Q\theta$ implies   Q succeeds with answer including θ,

2. $\exists$-complete for Q if
     comp(P) $\models \exists Q$ implies   Q succeeds,

3. $\neg$-complete for Q if
     comp(P) $\models \neg \exists Q$ implies   Q fails,

in each case the conclusion must hold using SLDNF-resolution with all fair computation rules.

Theorem 27 says that SLDNF-resolution is complete in all three senses for queries which are conjunctions of positive literals. However, for queries containing negation:

THEOREM 28
For definite Horn programs SLDNF-resolution is

1. θ-complete for all allowed queries but not for all weakly allowed queries,

2. ∃-complete for all ground queries but not for all allowed queries,

3. ¬-complete for all purely negative ground queries but not for all ground queries.

Proof: The positive results follow easily from Theorem 27 and the fact that if comp(P) implies a disjunction of ground atoms, it implies one of them, which follows from Theorems 15, 2, and 8 or, more directly, from the existence of the least fixed point model. Counter-examples are:

1. Program $p(x) \leftarrow$,   query $p(x) \wedge \neg q(x)$.

2. Program $p(a) \leftarrow$, $p(f(a)) \leftarrow p(f(a))$,   query $p(x) \wedge \neg p(f(x))$.

3. Program $p \leftarrow p$,   query $p \wedge \neg p$. ∎

   Since SLDNF-resolution is also sound with respect to the intuitionistic consequence relation $\vdash_I$ (Corollary 3), the positive results here hold also for the intuitionistic completeness notions obtained by replacing $\models$ by $\vdash_I$. Indeed they show that the classical and intuitionistic consequence relations coincide in these cases. In cases (1) and (3), the counter-examples given serve to give the negative results also for the intuitionistic case. In case (2), the intuitionistic notion of ∃-completeness coincides with that of θ-completeness because ∃Q is an intuitionistic consequence of comp(P) only if some Q is. It might be fairer to say that what one really has is intuitionistic completeness, and since one has intuitionistic soundness as well, one only gets classical completeness ''by accident'' when the classical and intuitionistic consequence relations coincide. That they do at all here is because P contains no negative literals. The reason why classical completeness fails in the counter-example to (2) above is that the query has classically the indefinite answer x = a or x = f(a), but it does not have any definite answer; and SLDNF-resolution can only give definite answers. The same is true of intuitionistic logic; you cannot prove A ∨ B unless you can prove A or prove B. Classically here

$$(p(a) \wedge \neg p(f(a))) \vee (p(f(a)) \wedge \neg p(f(f(a))))$$

is a consequence of this program, but not intuitionistically, since the program does not give us enough information to prove either of the separate disjuncts.
   Finally it should be emphasized, in the interests of Wysiwym, that these completeness results relate to comp(P) (of course they also hold with respect to P, but SLDNF-resolution is not sound with respect to P). They certainly do not apply to cwa(P)—and could not, for as shown in the section on the closed world assumption, there are definite Horn clause programs P for which the set

of negative ground literals that are consequences of cwa(P) is not recursively enumerable.

Since the operator T_P is monotonic for a definite Horn clause program P, it not only has a least fixpoint lfp(T_P) but also a greatest fixpoint gfp(T_P), the union of all fixpoints. By Theorem 14 this is the greatest Herbrand model of comp(P). So the *Herbrand rule* of Lloyd [1984], p. 85, to infer $\neg$A, for a ground atom A, if A is false in all Herbrand models of comp(P), allows $\neg$A to be inferred if A belongs to the complement (wrt the Herbrand base B_P) of gfp(T_P). Theorem 9 shows that this is a larger set than that of the atoms A that are false in all models of comp(P), i.e., those for which comp(P) $\models \neg$A. But it is smaller than the set of those that are false under the closed world assumption, i.e., for which P $\not\models$ A; that set is the complement of lfp(T_P). Part (3) of Theorem 27 gives a neat characterization of the set of A for which comp(P) $\models$ $\neg$A; it is the set of all atoms all which fail under fair computation rules. In Lloyd [1984], pp. 66–67, or Lassez and Maher [1984], this "fair SLD finite failure set" is shown to coincide with the "SLD finite failure set," i.e., the set of atoms that fail under some computation rule and also with the "finite failure set" defined as the complement of $T_P{\downarrow}\omega$. (The descending ordinal powers $T_P{\downarrow}\alpha$ of T_P are defined by $T_P{\downarrow}0 = B_P$, $T_P{\downarrow}(\alpha + 1) = T_P(T_P{\downarrow}\alpha)$, $T_P{\downarrow}\alpha = \bigcap_{\beta<\alpha} T_P{\downarrow}\beta$ for α a limit ordinal. The greatest fixed point gfp(T_P) is equal to $T_P{\downarrow}\alpha$ for some ordinal α; the above example shows that α may be greater than ω.) For a fuller description of these relationships, see Lloyd [1984], pp. 86–87, from which Figure 1 is taken.

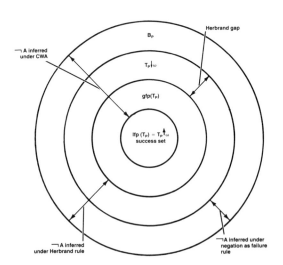

Figure 1: Relationship between the Various Rules

Jaffar, Lassez, and Maher [1984] have pointed out another characterization of the set of ground atoms A which are false in all Herbrand models of comp(P). They call it the "ground finite failure set," the set of all A for which all ground derivations are failed finitely. What this means is that you replace P by its set P_g of ground instances and consider SLD-derivations from P_g. A ground atom A is said to finitely fail if all branches of its derivation tree end in failure after a finite number of steps. What distinguishes this from ordinary finite failure, and makes it non-computable, is that there may now be infinitely many clauses of P_g with a given head, so that the derivation tree can have infinitely many branches from each node, so that König's lemma fails, and although each branch of the tree is finite, there may be no upper bound on their length and the whole tree may be infinite. The difference between this ground finite failure set and the finite failure set, i.e., between the set of A which are false in all Herbrand models of comp(P) and those which are false in all models of comp(P), i.e., $T_P \downarrow \omega - gfp(T_P)$, is called the Herbrand gap. If this gap is empty, there is some duality between success and finite failure, least fixed point and greatest fixed point, upward and downward iteration of T_P. (This duality is dealt with in some detail in Jaffar, Lassez, and Maher [1986].) And the set of A which are false in all Herbrand models of comp(P) is the same as the set which are false in all models, so is computable. This is obviously desirable if one is interested only in the Herbrand models, which appears often to be the case. So Jaffar and Stuckey [1986] suggested that all "decent" programs should satisfy $T_P \downarrow \omega = gfp(T_P)$. They called such programs canonical and showed that every definite Horn program is in a sense equivalent to a canonical program. Another natural condition is that comp(P) should have exactly one Herbrand model, i.e., that $lfp(T_P) = gfp(T_P)$. Example 2 has this property but is not canonical; p $\rightarrow$ p is canonical but does not have this property. A program satisfying both of these conditions, i.e., $T_P \uparrow \omega = T_P \downarrow \omega$ is called determinate. This means that negation as failure is complete with respect to cwa(P) as well as to comp(P). It means that not only is there just one Herbrand model but also the intersection of any model with the Herbrand base is uniquely determined, in other words, comp(P) is ground categorical; for each ground atom A either comp(P) $\models$ A or comp(P) $\models \neg$A. Blair [1987] shows that all recursive relations are computable by determinate programs. He also shows that the problems of deciding whether a program has any of these properties are highly non-recursive.

It is interesting to look at definite Horn programs in the light of Makowsky's notion of generic model which we introduced in connection with the closed world assumption. A generic model for P is a model M in which, for ground atoms A,

$$M \models A \text{ iff } P \models A,$$

A is true in M iff it is true in all models of P. (We saw that in general this is stronger than being true in all Herbrand models of P but that it is the same if P consists of universal sentences, which is the case here.) We saw in Theorems 4 and 8 that a definite Horn clause program has a generic Herbrand model that is the least Herbrand model $lfp(T_P)$. Since many logic programmers, when they write down a program P, actually intend comp(P), it is fortunate that $lfp(T_P)$ is also a generic Herbrand model for that, i.e.,

$$lfp(T_P) \models A \text{ iff comp}(P) \models A.$$

This follows from Theorems 14 and 15.

Since we are now considering negation, let us look at the dual notion—let us call it n-generic—where we replace ground atoms by their negations, i.e., let us say a n-generic model for P is a model M where, for all ground atoms A,

$$M \models \neg A \text{ iff } P \models \neg A.$$

This is not very interesting when P is a definite Horn clause program. There is such a model, indeed a Herbrand one, but it consists of the whole Herbrand base B_P because the set of A for which A is false in all models of P, or even all Herbrand models of P, is empty. But when we consider models for comp(P), we find there is a n-generic model for comp(P), i.e., a model M such that each A is false in M iff it is false in all models of comp(P). This is not, in general, a Herbrand model, however, but its intersection with the Herbrand base is $T_P{\downarrow}\omega$. To prove this we must show that the set of axioms

$$\text{comp}(P) \cup \{A: \text{comp}(P) \not\models \neg A\}$$

is consistent. By the compactness theorem, this fails only if for some finite set $A_1,\ldots,A_r$ of ground atoms

$$\text{comp}(P) \models \neg(A_1 \wedge \ldots \wedge A_r) \text{ but}$$
$$\text{for } i = 1,\ldots,r \text{ comp}(P) \not\models \neg A_i.$$

Theorem 27 (3) shows this is impossible, for if comp(P) $\models \neg(A_1 \wedge \ldots \wedge A_r)$ then the ground query $A_1 \wedge \ldots \wedge A_r$ fails under every fair computation rule, hence some A_i fails under some fair computation rule, hence comp(P) $\models \neg A_i$ by soundness Theorem 25 (1). There is also a Herbrand model M for comp(P) which is "Herbrand n-generic," i.e., such that

A is false in M iff A is false in all Herbrand models of comp(P).

Indeed it is obvious from the remarks above that gfp(T_P) is such a model. It follows from the above that comp(P) has a n-generic Herbrand model iff $T_P \mid \omega = $ gfp(T_P), i.e., iff it is canonical.

Programs for which Negation as Failure Is Complete wrt the Completed Database

In view of the popularity of the use of negation as failure, and the view that it is really comp(P) you are talking about, it is useful to know classes of programs for which negation as failure is complete, for classical negation, relative to comp(P).

The completeness results in the last subsection for definite Horn programs were mainly limited to positive queries. The limitations of SLDNF-resolution resulting from the lack of quantifiers and ways of dealing with them mean that the largest class of queries we could hope to get completeness for is the class of weakly allowed queries, since a query that is not weakly allowed cannot succeed. The largest class for which one might expect to get completeness is the class of allowed queries. Conditions on the program which yield this were given in Clark [1978].

Let us say a query has the finite tree property if its evaluation tree is finite and each branch ends in success or failure. If, in addition, all successful branches result in full instantiation, we say it has the finite grounded tree property. Since we are talking throughout this section about SLDNF-resolution we shall often take this for granted, as we have just done. We say SLDNF-resolution is complete for a query Q if it is, according to the definitions of the last subsection, θ-complete, $\exists$-complete and $\neg$-complete for Q. Since we know it is sound with respect to comp(P) this means that, for such a query, SLDNF-resolution gives exactly the same results as classical logic applied to comp(P).

LEMMA 1

If comp(P) is consistent, then SLDNF-resolution is complete for queries with the finite tree property.

Proof: The result for $\exists$-completeness and $\neg$-completeness is an immediate consequence of the consistency of comp(P) and of the soundness of SLDNF-resolution with respect to comp(P). (Note that the condition that comp(P) be consistent, which is obviously necessary, was omitted from the statement of this result in Shepherdson [1985], Theorem 5.2.)

For θ-completeness we use Theorem 3 of Clark [1978], that if $\theta_1, \dots, \theta_j$ are all the answers given by the evaluation paths that end in success then

$$\text{comp}(P) \models (\theta \longleftrightarrow \hat{\theta}_1 \vee \hat{\theta} \vee \dots \vee \hat{\theta}_j),$$

where $\hat{\theta}$, the 'general form of the answer θ' is

$$\exists (x_1 = e_1 \lor {}_\land \cdot \lor {}_{\land i} = e_i)$$

where

$$\theta = \{x_1/e_1, \ldots, x_i/e_i\}.$$

It follows that if comp(P) $\models$ Qθ then one of $\theta_1,\ldots,\theta_j$ must include θ. ∎

This basic result is not very useful by itself since it is not easy to decide whether a query has this property. We proceed to give simple conditions on the program which ensure this for allowed queries.

LEMMA 2

If for each predicate p the query $p(x_1,\ldots,x_n)$ has the finite tree property, if every ground atomic query succeeds or fails and the computation rule is fair, then every query has a finite evaluation tree.

Proof: Shepherdson [1985], Theorem 5.5, following Clark [1978], p. 318, who inadvertently omitted the condition that every ground atomic query succeeds or fails. If the query is not an allowed query some of the branches of the tree may end in flounders. ∎

THEOREM 29

Under the conditions of Lemma 1, SLDNF-resolution is complete for allowed queries. If "finite tree" is strengthened to "finite grounded tree," it is complete for weakly allowed queries. Also every allowed (weakly allowed) query succeeds or fails.

Proof: Shepherdson [1985], Corollary 5.6, again following Clark [1978]. ∎

These conditions are still not easily testable, so we follow Clark in giving simple conditions which imply them.

A program satisfies the *hierarchical condition* if its predicates can be assigned to *levels* so that in each clause

$$p(t_1, \ldots, t_k) \leftarrow L_1 \land \cdots \land L_m$$

about an ith level predicate p, the predicates occurring in $L_1,\ldots,L_m$ are of level less than i.

This prevents any evaluation tree having infinite branches, because a unification step replaces a literal by lower level literals.

A program satisfies the *allowability condition* if the body of each clause is an allowed query.

THEOREM 30

If the program satisfies the hierarchical condition, and the allowability condition for all computation rules, then SLDNF-resolution is complete for allowed queries under all computation rules, and all allowed queries either succeed or fail.

Proof: Clark [1978], Theorem 4, or, more fully, Shepherdson [1985], Theorem 6.1. ■

Since allowability depends on the computation rule and is not easy to check, it is worth stating a result for weak allowability. This needs an extra hypothesis, that every variable which occurs in the head of a program clause appears in the body. This can be combined with weak allowability and succinctly expressed in the terminology of Lloyd and Topor [1986]:

A *program is allowed* if every variable occurring in a clause occurs in a positive literal of the body of the clause.

THEOREM 31

If the program satisfies the hierarchical condition and is allowed, then SLDNF-resolution is complete for weakly allowed queries under all computation rules. Every such query succeeds or fails, and every answer substitution grounds all variables in the query.

Proof: Shepherdson [1985], Theorem 6.12. The remark about grounding is due to Lloyd and Topor [1986], Proposition 1; it is a consequence of the condition that every variable in the head of a clause appears in the body, for the only way such a variable can disappear is by being grounded in a step that unifies a goal literal with the head of a unit clause, and the above condition implies that the head of a unit clause is ground. ■

This is the best possible completeness result and the condition on the program can be checked on sight, but it is very restrictive. It forbids any kind of recursive definition, and although it admits most of the natural ways of defining new predicates in terms of previously defined ones, it does not allow definitions of the form $p(x) \leftarrow$ or $p(s(x)) \leftarrow$. The reason is that then a weakly allowed query $p(x) \wedge \neg q(x)$ would lose its "cover" and go into $\neg q(x)$, which flounders. As noted in Shepherdson [1985], such definitions can be allowed for predicates that are not needed for grounding variables in negative literals. In Lloyd and Topor [1986], it is shown that it is enough if all clauses in the definition of a predicate occurring in a positive literal in the query or in the body of a program clause are allowed; other program clauses need only be admissible in the sense that each variable that occurs in them occurs either in the head or in a positive literal of the body. As in Przymusinski [1988], the hierarchic condition can be replaced by a local hierarchical condition which partitions ground atoms, instead of predicates, into a hierarchy of levels. In Shepherdson [1985], Theorem 6.4, there is a generalization which allows for some non-hierarchical predicates, provided they have the finite tree property.

A natural weakening of the hierarchical condition gives the notion of a stratified program (Apt, Blair, and Walker [1988], Przymusinski [1988], Van Gelder [1988], Naqvi [1986]). This allows a program clause

$$p(t_1, \ldots, t_n) \leftarrow L_1 \wedge \ldots \wedge L_m$$

about an ith level predicate p to have positive literals of level i on the right, as long as the negative literals have level less than i. This corresponds to a natural view that a predicate ought to be fully defined before you negate it. Unfortunately the above completeness results do not extend to stratified programs. Example 12 of Apt, Blair, and Walker [1988] is the stratified program P:

$$p \leftarrow p, \quad q \leftarrow p, \quad q \leftarrow \neg p.$$

for which comp(P) $\models$ q but q is not derivable by SLDNF-resolution. However Barbuti and Martelli [1986], Theorem 5, have shown that the completeness results of Theorem 31 do apply to what they call structured programs. These are allowed, stratified programs with the additional property that the definite Horn program P, which results from the given program by deleting all negative literals in clause bodies, is determinate in the sense of the last section, i.e., ground categorical, i.e., for each ground atom A either A or $\neg$A is a consequence of comp(P).

One striking restriction of the completeness results of this section is that they give not only completeness but a sort of categoricity; each allowed query either succeeds or fails. In particular, comp(P) must be categorical for ground atoms, so all the programs they apply to not only have exactly one Herbrand model for comp(P) but are determinate on the Herbrand base. This is actually a necessary consequence of $\neg$-completeness for ground queries. For if A is a ground atom and Q is the query A $\wedge$ $\neg$A then $\neg$Q is a consequence of comp(P), and the only way Q can fail is by A succeeding or failing. It might be possible and worthwhile to modify SLDNF-resolution to fail such obviously false queries on sight, but I doubt if the general case of $\neg$-completeness for ground queries could be handled in this way. Requiring $\neg$-completeness for such queries is really an underhanded way of trying to extend the completeness for success from existentially quantified conjunctions to universally quantified disjunctions. And we have seen above that $\exists$-completeness must fail when there is no definite correct answer to the query. So, if one wants to get completeness results for non-ground categorical programs, one should probably aim only at θ-completeness for allowed queries. I do not know of any results of this kind apart from the ones for definite Horn programs in Theorem 28.

Semantics for Negation in Terms of Special Classes of Models

We saw in the section on the closed world assumption that cwa(P) was inconsistent for any program P implying indefinite information about ground atoms, and that it was consistent only if P had a least Herbrand model. In attempting to find a useful weaker assumption that would be consistent for all consistent programs P, Minker [1982] was led to suggest replacing least model by minimal model, i.e., model containing no proper submodel. He formulated the *generalized* (or extended) *closed world assumption* (see also Henschen and Park [1988], Gelfond et al. [1986], Lifschitz [1988]). He considered the case where there are no function symbols, but we allow these. However, we shall assume that P is a set of universal sentences (in most applications they will actually be universal quantifications of clauses). We may define gcwa(P), the theory obtained by applying the generalized closed world assumption to P, exactly the same as we defined cwa(P) except that instead of adding to P the set

$$\{\ \neg A:\ A\ \text{is false in some model of P}\}$$

which, since we are assuming P is a set of universal sentences, is equivalent to

$$\{\ \neg A:\ A\ \text{is false in some Herbrand model of P}\},$$

we add the set

$$\{\ \neg A:\ A\ \text{is false in all minimal Herbrand} \\ \text{models of P}\},$$

where, as usual, we identify a Herbrand model with the subset of the Herbrand base B_P which is true in it. Since we are talking mainly about Herbrand models in this section, we shall, from now on, sometimes drop the adjective Herbrand where it causes no confusion. The idea is that what we are really interested in are the minimal models of P, that we consider a sentence true if it is true in all minimal models, false if it is false in all minimal models, indefinite if it is true in one minimal model and false in another. An ideal sound and complete query evaluation procedure would be one that made a query succeed iff it were true in all minimal models, fail if it were false in all minimal models and gave no answer (e.g., an infinite computation) when the query was indefinite, i.e., true in some but not all minimal models.

We follow a slightly different development from Minker.

LEMMA 3

If P is a consistent set of universal sentences then P has a minimal Herbrand model.

Proof: Take an enumeration $A_1, A_2, \ldots$, of the ground atoms. Define M_i inductively, taking M_o as the empty set and forming M_i from M_{i-1} by adding to it:

$$A_i \text{ if } P \cup M_{i-1} \models A_i$$

$\neg A_i$ otherwise.

Take M to be the union of the M_i. Then M is a minimal Herbrand model for P. To see this note first that by induction on i, $P \cup M_i$ is consistent. So by compactness $P \cup M$ is consistent and since it is a set of universal sentences it has a Herbrand model, which can only be M. To show M is minimal, let M' be a submodel of M, i.e., such that all ground atoms which are false in M are false in M'. An easy induction shows that each A_i which is true in M is true in M', hence that $M' = M$. ∎

We now establish Minker's syntactic characterization of the GCWA:

LEMMA 4

A ground atom A is in a minimal Herbrand model of P iff there are ground atoms $A_i, \ldots, A_r$, $r \geq O$ such that

$$P \models (A \lor A_1 \lor \ldots \lor A_r) \text{ but } P \not\models (A_1 \lor \ldots \lor A_r).$$

Proof: If $P \not\models (A_1 \lor \ldots \lor A_r)$ then $P \cup \{\neg A_1, \ldots, \neg A_r\}$ is consistent so by Lemma 3 it has a minimal model.

If $P \models (A \lor A_1 \ldots \lor A_r)$ then $P \cup \{\neg A_1, \ldots, \neg A_r\} \models A$ so this model must contain A.

If A is in a minimal model M and $A_1, A_2, \ldots$ are all the ground atoms which are false in M, then

$$P \cup \{\neg A_1, \neg A_2, \ldots\} \cup \neg A\} \text{ is inconsistent,}$$

(otherwise there would be a proper submodel of M omitting A). By compactness some finite subset is inconsistent, i.e., for some r

$$P \cup \{\neg A_1, \ldots \neg A_r\} \cup \{\neg A\} \text{ is inconsistent,}$$

i.e., $P \models (A \lor A_1 \lor \dots \lor A_r)$.
But $P \not\models (A_1 \lor \dots \lor A_r)$ because $A_1 \lor \dots \lor A_r$ is false in M. ■

By choosing a minimal set $A_1, \dots, A_r$ such that

$$P \models (A \lor A_1 \lor \dots \lor A_r)$$

we can express the condition of the theorem by:
A belongs to a minimal positive ground clause which is a consequence of P.

THEOREM 32

1. A minimal model of P is a minimal model of gcwa(P), and conversely.

2. If P is consistent gcwa(P) is consistent.

3. If the existential quantification of a positive matrix is true in all minimal models of P it is a consequence of P.

4. If the existential quantification of a positive matrix is a consequence of gcwa(P) it is a consequence of P.

5. gcwa(P) is a consequence of cwa(P) and if cwa(P) is consistent it coincides with gcwa(P).

6. If Q is a consequence of gcwa(P) it is true in all minimal models of P.

In (3), (4) a positive matrix is a formula built up from atoms by the use of $\land, \lor$ only, i.e., without using $\lnot$.

Proof:

1. This follows immediately from the fact that the models of gcwa(P) are models of P that are contained in the union of all minimal models of P.

2. By Lemma 3, if P is consistent, it has a minimal model which we have just seen is also a model for gcwa(P).

3., 4.   If $\exists\phi$ is not a consequence of P then $P \cup A \ \lnot\phi$ is consistent, hence by Lemma 3 it has a minimal model. Since ϕ is positive, this is a minimal model for P since, if a proper submodel were a model for P, it would make more ground atoms negative, so would preserve the truth of $\forall \ \lnot\phi$ and would be a model for $P \cup \forall \ \lnot\phi$. By (1) it is also a model for gcwa(P).

5. If A is false in all minimal models of P, it is certainly false in some model, by Lemma 4, so gcwa(P) is a consequence of cwa(P). If cwa(P)

is consistent, then by Theorem 4 and Remark 2, P has a least model M which is obviously the only minimal model; so if A is false in some model it is false in M, hence, in all minimal models.

6.   Immediate consequence of (1). ∎

The result (3) means that in attempting to characterize the minimal models of P there is no point in adding to gcwa(P) the ground atoms that are true in all minimal models; they are already consequences of P. Sentence (4) says that gcwa(P) adds no new positive information. Although, by (1), all minimal models of P are models of gcwa(P), the converse is not true; there are models of gcwa(P) which are not minimal models of P; for example if P is p ∨ q then gcwa(P) contains no negative ground atoms and {p,q} is a model for it. The same example shows that the converse of (6) does not hold; (p ∧ ¬q) ∨ (q ∧ ¬p) is true in all minimal models of P but is not a consequence of gcwa(P). It does hold for existential quantifications of positive matrices, by (3), hence for the usual kind of positive query. It also holds for universal quantifications of positive matrices, because ∀xφ(x) is true in all minimal models of P iff φ(t) is true for all ground terms t in all minimal models of P, which is covered by the previous case. But in both these cases, gcwa(P) is not really involved, the query is true in all Herbrand models of P, i.e., is a consequence of P together with the domain-closure axiom DCA, so the negative ground atoms in gcwa(P) are not used. So quite apart from any incompleteness due to the computation procedure used to find consequences of it, gcwa(P) is an incomplete attempt to characterize the minimal models of P.

There is no simple relationship between comp(P) and gcwa(P), which is only to be expected since comp(P) depends on the way P is written, whereas gcwa(P), like cwa(P), has the merit of depending only on the logical content of P. Taking P as q ← ¬p shows that a model for gcwa(P) or a minimal model of P may not be a model for comp(P), and taking P as p ← p shows that a model for comp(P) may not be a model for gcwa(P) or a minimal model of P. The example q ← ¬p also shows that negation as failure is not sound with respect to the generalized closed world assumption (in contrast to the closed world assumption). For computation or proof procedures appropriate to it, see Henschen and Park [1988] and the references there.

Apt, Blair, and Walker [1988] propose a semantics for negation that combines this approach with that of the completed database, i.e., applies both kinds of default reasoning. They suggest that the models of P to study are those (Herbrand) models which are not only minimal but *supported*, i.e., a ground atom A is true only if there is a ground instance of a clause of P with head A and a body which is true. We saw in the section on fixpoint models that the supported models are precisely the fixpoints of T_P and Theorem 14 shows that these are the models of comp(P). Apt, Blair, and Walker say (after Lemma 3):

As explained in the introduction we are interested here in studying minimal and supported models. In view of Lemmas 2 and 3 this simply means we are looking for the minimal fixed points of the operator T_P.

It appears from this that they have in mind the second of the two distinct concepts below.

1.   minimal models of P which are fixpoints of T_P, or equivalently, models of comp(P)

2.   models of P which are minimal fixpoints of T_P or minimal models of comp(P).

The point is that a minimal model of P which is a model of comp(P) is clearly a minimal model of comp(P) but not vice-versa as the program $p \leftarrow q$, $q \leftarrow \neg p$, $q \leftarrow q$ shows. The only, and hence the minimal, model of comp(P) is $\{p,q\}$; the only minimal model of P is $\{p\}$. The model $\{p,q\}$ satisfies (2) but there is no model satisfying the stronger condition (1).

In their main result they establish the existence for *stratified* programs (defined below) of a model satisfying the stronger condition (1):

THEOREM 33

If P is a stratified program there is a minimal model of P which is also a model of comp(P). Hence comp(P) is consistent.

Proof: Apt, Blair, and Walker [1988]. ∎

There may be more than one model satisfying these conditions, e.g., if P is the stratified program $p \leftarrow p$, $q \leftarrow \neg p$ there are two such models $\{p\}$ and $\{q\}$. They show that there is one such model M_P which is defined in a natural way and propose that it be taken as defining the semantics for the program P, i.e., that an ideal query evaluation procedure should make a query Q succeed if Q is true in M_P and fail if Q is false in M_P. They give two equivalent ways of defining M_P. A *stratified* program P is one that can be partitioned

$$P = P_1 \ \dot{\cup} \ldots \dot{\cup} \ P_n,$$

so that if a predicate occurs positively in the body of a clause in P_i, all clauses where it occurs in the head are in P_j with $j \leq i$, and if a predicate occurs negatively in the body of a clause in P_i, then all clauses where it occurs in the head are in P_j with $j < i$. (So P_i consists of the clauses defining ith level predicates.) Their first definition of M_P is to start with the empty set, iterate T'_{P_1} ω times then T'_{P_2} ω times, ..., T'_{P_n} ω times. (The operator T'_P here is defined by

$T'_P(I) = T_P(I) \cup I$ and is more appropriate than T_P when that is nonmonotonic.) The other definition starts by defining $M(P_1)$ as the intersection of all Herbrand models of P_1, then $M(P)$ as the intersection of all Herbrand models of P_2 whose intersection with the Herbrand base of P_1 is $M(P_1)$, then ..., $M(P_n)$ as the intersection of all Herbrand models of P_n whose intersection with the Herbrand base of P_{n-1} is $M(P_{n-1})$. Finally define $M_P = M(P_n)$. For the program above, this model is $\{q\}$, which does seem to be better in accordance with default reasoning than the other minimal model of comp(P), namely $\{p\}$. There is no reason to suppose p is true, so p is taken to be false, hence q to be true. It seems natural to assign truth values to the predicates in the order in which they are defined, which is the essence of the above method. However, a strong point in favor of the model M_P is that they show it does not depend on the actual way a stratifiable program is stratified, i.e., divided into levels.

Notice that like comp(P), M_P depends not only on the logical content of P but on the way it is written, for $p \leftarrow \neg q$ and $q \leftarrow \neg p$ give different M_P. Apt, Blair, and Walker [1988] point out that one of the disadvantages of a semantics like this based on one model is that it can lead to non-computable syntax. We gave their example above for the similar case of the closed world assumption.

Since SLDNF-resolution is sound for comp(P) and M_P is a model of comp(P), it is certainly sound for M_P but, since more sentences will be true in M_P than in all models of comp(P), SLDNF-resolution will be even more incomplete for M_P than for comp(P). For example, with the program above where q is true in M_P but not in all models of comp(P), there is no chance of proving q by SLDNF-resolution. Apt, Blair, and Walker [1988] do give an interpreter for their semantics, which is sound and complete for stratified programs in the "Datalog" case where there are no function symbols but not complete when there are function symbols.

Przymusinski [1988] states very clearly the theme of this section:

> A model-theoretic approach to the theory of deductive databases is based on the idea of representing a database as a set DB of formulas of first order logic and by associating with DB a set M(DB) of one or more models of DB which describe the declarative meaning of the database or, in other words, its semantics. A sentence F is considered to be true in the database if and only if it is satisfied in all models M from M(DB).

He proposes an even more restricted class of models than the minimal, supported models of Apt, Blair, and Walker [1988], namely the class of perfect models. The argument for a semantics based on this class is that if one writes $p \vee q$, then one intends p,q to be treated equally; but, if one writes $p \leftarrow \neg q$ there is a presupposition, that in the absence of contrary evidence, q is false and hence p is true. He allows "disjunctive databases," i.e., clauses with more than one atom in the head, e.g.,

$$C_1 \vee \ldots \vee C_p \leftarrow A_1 \wedge \ldots \wedge A_m \wedge \neg B_1 \ldots \wedge \neg B_n,$$

and his basic notion of priority is that the C's here should have lower priority than the B's and no higher priority than the A's. To obtain greater generality, he defines this notion for ground atoms rather than predicates, i.e., if the above clause is a ground instance of a program clause he says that $C_i < B_j$, $C_i \leq A_k$. Taking the transitive closure of these relations establishes a relation on the ground atoms that is transitive (but may not be asymmetric and irreflexive if the program is not stratified).

His basic philosophy is

> ...if we have a model M of DB and if another model N is obtained by possibly adding some ground atoms to M and removing some other ground atoms from M, then we should consider the new model N to be preferable to M only if the addition of a lower priority atom A to N is justified by the simultaneous removal from M of a higher priority atom B (i.e., such that B > A). This reflects the general principle that we are willing to minimize higher priority predicates, even at the cost of enlarging predicates of lower priority, in an attempt to minimize high priority predicates as much as possible. A model M will be considered perfect if there are no models preferable to it. More formally:
>
> [Definition 2.] Suppose that M and N are two different models of a disjunctive database DB. We say that N is preferable to M (briefly, N < M) if for every ground atom A in N − M there is a ground atom B in M − N, such that B > A. We say that a model M of DB is perfect if there are no models preferable to M.

He extends the notion of stratifiability to disjunctive databases by requiring that in a clause

$$C_1 \vee \ldots \vee C_p \leftarrow A_1 \wedge \ldots \wedge A_m \wedge \neg B_1 \ldots \wedge \neg B_n$$

the predicates in $C_1,\ldots,C_p$ should all be of the same level i greater than that of the predicates in $B_1,\ldots,B_n$ and greater than or equal to those of the predicates in $A_1,\ldots,A_m$. He then weakens this to *local stratifiability* by applying it to ground atoms and instances of program clauses instead of to predicates and program clauses. (The number of levels is then allowed to be infinite.) It is equivalent to the nonexistence of increasing sequences in the above relation < between ground atoms.

He proves Theorem 4 and remark at the end of "Stratified and Locally Stratified Databases."

THEOREM 34
Every locally stratified disjunctive database has a perfect model. Moreover every stratified logic program P (i.e., where the head of each clause is a single

atom) has exactly one perfect model, and it coincides with the model M_p of Apt, Blair, and Walker [1988]. ∎

LEMMA 5

1. Every perfect model is minimal.

2. If the program is positive disjunctive, then a model is perfect iff it is minimal.

3. A model is perfect if there are no minimal models preferable to it.

(Positive disjunctive means the clauses are of the form

$$C_1 \vee \ldots \vee C_p \leftarrow A_1 \wedge \ldots \wedge A_m .)$$ ∎

He also establishes a relation between perfect models and the concept of prioritized circumscription introduced by McCarthy [1984] and further developed by Lifschitz [1985]:

> Let $S_1,\ldots,S_r$ be any decomposition of the set S of all predicates of a database DB into disjoint sets. A model M of DB is called a model of prioritized circumscription of DB with respect to priorities $S_1 > S_2 > \ldots > S_r$, or—briefly—a model of CIRC(DB, $S_1 > S_2 > \ldots > S_r$) if for every i = 1,...,r the extension in M of predicates from S_i is minimal among all models M′ of DB in which the extension of predicates from $S_1,S_2,\ldots,S_{i-1}$ coincides with the extension of these predicates in M.

He claims

THEOREM 35

Suppose that DB is a stratified disjunctive database and $\{S_1,S_2,\ldots,S_r\}$ is a stratification of DB. A model of DB is perfect if and only if it is a model of prioritized circumscription CIRC(DB,$S_1 > S_2 > \ldots > S_r$). ∎

Since for stratified programs the perfect models coincide with Apt, Blair, and Walker's [1988] model, these semantics based on perfect models suffer the same disadvantages as were pointed out for Apt, Blair, and Walker's [1988] model, in particular a stronger rule than negation is failure would be required for completeness.

Semantics for Negation as Failure in Terms of 3-Valued Logic

Three-valued logic seems particularly apt for dealing with programs, since they may either succeed or fail or go on forever giving no answer. And it seems particularly apt for database knowledge where we know some things are true, some things are false, and about other things we just do not know. Kleene [1952] introduced such a logic to deal with partial recursive functions and predicates. The three truth values are t, true, f, false, and u, undefined or un-known, and a connective has the value t (f) if it has that value in ordinary 2-valued logic for all possible replacements of u's by t or f, otherwise it has the value of u.

For example, $p \to q$ gets the truth value t if p is f or q is t but the value u if p,q are both u. (So $p \to p$ is not a tautology; if p has the value u it has the value u.) The universal quantifier is treated as an infinite conjunction so $\forall x \phi(x)$ is t if $\phi(a)$ is t for all a, f if $\phi(a)$ is f for some a, otherwise u (so it is the glb of truth values of the $\phi(a)$). Similarly, $\exists x \phi(x)$ is t if some $\phi(a)$ is t, f if all $\phi(a)$ are f, otherwise u.

This logic has been used in connection with logic programming by Mycroft [1983] and Lassez and Maher [1985]. Recent work of Fitting [1985] and Kunen [1987] provide an explanation of the incompleteness of negation as failure for 2-valued models. It turns out that it is also sound for comp(P) in 3-valued logic, so it can only derive those consequences that are true not only in all 2-valued models but also in all 3-valued models.

Use of the third truth value avoids the usual difficulty with non-Horn clauses that the operator T_P associated with a program P, which corresponds to one application of ground instances of the clauses regarded as rules, is no longer monotonic. To avoid asymmetric associations of T with true, let us call the corresponding operator for 3-valued logic Φ_P. This operates on pairs (T_o, F_o) of disjoint subsets of B_p, the Herbrand base of P, to produce a new pair

$$(T_1, F_1) = \Phi_P (T_o, F_o) ,$$

the idea being that if the elements of T_o are known to be true and the elements of F_o known to be false, then one application of the rules of P shows that the elements of T_1 are true and elements of F_1 are false.

Formally, for a ground atom A,

A $\in T_1$ iff some ground instance of a clause of P has head A and a body made true by (T_o, F_o),

A ∈ F$_1$ iff all ground instances of clauses of P with head A have body made false by (T$_o$,F$_o$).

So if A does not match the head of any clause of P it is, in accordance with the default reasoning behind negation as failure, put into F$_1$.

A little care is needed in defining the notion of a 3-valued model and the notion of comp(P). A 3-valued model of a set of sentences S is a set of objects together with interpretations of the various functions in a 2-valued manner. The equality relation "=" is interpreted as identity, the sentences in S must all evaluate to **t**, and so must what Kunen calls CET "Clark's Equational Theory," i.e., the equality and freeness axioms EA and FA. If we were to write comp(P) exactly as before as a set of completed definitions of predicates in the form

$$p(x_1, \ldots, x_n) \longleftrightarrow E_1 \vee \ldots \vee E_j$$

using the Kleene truth tables for ⟷, then we should be more or less committing ourselves to 2-valued models, for p⟷p is not **t** but **u** when p is **u**. Kunen therefore replaces this ⟷ with Kleene's weak equivalence ≅ which gives p ≅ q the value **t** if p,q have the same truth value, **f** otherwise. This saves comp(P) from the inconsistency that it can have under 2-valued logic. For example, if P is p ← ¬p then the 2-valued comp(P) is p ⟷ ¬p, which is inconsistent; what Kunen uses is p ≅ ¬p which has a model with p having the value **u**. (Note: Our use of ≅ agrees with Fitting but not with Kunen who uses ⟷ instead of our ≅ and ≡ instead of our ⟷.) Having done this, if we want comp(P) ⊨$_3$ P to hold, i.e., 3-valued models of comp(P) also to be models of P, we must replace the → in the clauses of P by ⊃ where p ⊃ q is the 2-valued "if p is **t** then q is **t**" with truth table

p\q	t	f	u
t	t	f	f
f	t	t	t
u	t	t	t.

(Actually, this result would still be true with the slightly stronger connective which also requires "if q is **f** then p is **f**" i.e., has truth table

p \ q	t	f	u
t	t	f	f
f	t	t	t
u	t	f	t.

It does not hold with $\rightarrow$ because the program $p \leftarrow p$ has completion $p \cong p$ that has a model where p is **u** which gives $p \leftarrow p$ the value **u** not **t**.)

We may identify a pair (T,F) of disjoint subsets of the Herbrand base with the 3-valued structure which gives all the elements of T the value **t**, all elements of F the value **f**, and all other elements of the Herbrand base the value **u**. We define $\Phi_p\!\uparrow\!\alpha$ like we defined $T_p\!\uparrow\!\alpha$, i.e., $\Phi_p\!\uparrow\!0 = (\emptyset,\emptyset)$, $\Phi_p\!\uparrow\!(\alpha + 1) = \Phi_p(\Phi_p\!\uparrow\!\alpha)$, $\Phi_p\!\uparrow\!\alpha = \bigcup_{\beta<\alpha} \Phi_p\!\uparrow\!\beta$ for α a limit ordinal.

We now have the analogue for Φ_p of the 2-valued properties of T_p:

THEOREM 36

1. Φ is monotonic.

2. Φ_p has a least fixpoint given by $\Phi_p \mid \alpha$ for some ordinal α.

3. If T,F are disjoint, then (T,F) is a 3-valued Herbrand model of comp(P) iff it is a fixpoint of Φ_p.

4. comp(P) is always consistent in 3-valued logic.

Proof: See Fitting [1985]. The monotonicity is obvious and (2) is a well known consequence of that. Part (3) also follows easily, as in the 2-valued case, and (4) follows from (2) and (3). ∎

However, the operator Φ_p is not in general continuous and so the closure ordinal α, i.e., the α such that $\Phi_p\!\uparrow\!\alpha$ is the least fixpoint, may be greater than ω as Example 2 shows. Fitting shows that α can be as high as Church-Kleene ω_1, the first nonrecursive ordinal. Both Fitting and Kunen show also that a semantics based on this least fixpoint as the sole model suffers from the same disadvantage as was pointed out for the closed world assumption, namely that the set of sentences, indeed even the set of ground atoms, that are true in this model may be non-recursively enumerable (as high as Π_1^1 complete in fact). The same is true of a semantics based on all 3-valued Herbrand models, for the programs used to construct the example just referred to can be taken to have only one Herbrand model.

Kunen proposes a very interesting and natural way of avoiding this non-computable syntax: Why should we consider only Herbrand models, why not consider all 3-valued models? In other words, ask whether Q is true in all 3-valued models of comp(P). He shows that an equivalent way of obtaining the same semantics is by using the operator Φ_P but chopping it off at ω:

THEOREM 37
A sentence ϕ has value **t** in all 3-valued models of comp(P) iff it has value **t** in $\Phi_P\!\uparrow\! n$ for some finite n.

Proof: See Kunen [1987]. ∎

There are three peculiar features of this result. First, in determining the truth value of ϕ in $\Phi_P \uparrow n$, quantifiers are interpreted as ranging over the Herbrand universe, yet we get equivalence to truth in *all* 3-valued models. This may be partly explained by the fact that *the truth of Theorem 37 depends on Φ_P being formed wrt the Herbrand base for the universal language KU which has, for each n, infinitely many n-ary function symbols.* For example, if P is simply p(a), then the Herbrand base for the language L_P is $\{p(a)\}$, and if Φ_P is evaluated wrt, this then $\forall x p(x)$ has value **t** in $\Phi_P\!\uparrow\!1$. But $\forall x p(x)$ is not true in all 3-valued (or even all 2-valued) models of comp(P), and it does not have value **t** in any $\Phi_P\!\uparrow\! n$ if Φ_P is evaluated wrt KU, because if b is a new constant p(b) has value **f** in $\Phi_P\!\uparrow\!1$. Second, truth in some $\Phi_P\!\uparrow\! n$ is not the same as truth in $\Phi_P\!\uparrow\!\omega$, which is not usually a model of comp(P). Third, the result only holds for sentences built up from the Kleene connectives $\wedge$, $\vee$, $\neg$, $\rightarrow$, $\leftrightarrow$, $\forall$, $\exists$, which have the property that if the function has the value of **t** or **f** and one argument changes from **u** to **t** or **f** the value of the function does not change. The weak equivalence $\cong$ used in the sentences defining the predicates in comp(P) does not have this property, so the sentences of comp(P)—which obviously have value **t** in all 3-valued models of comp(P)—may not evaluate to **t** in any $\Phi_P\,|\,n$. For example, if P is

$$p(0)$$
$$p(s(x)) \leftarrow p(x),$$

then comp(P) is

$$p(y) \cong [y = 0 \vee (\exists x)(y = s(x) \wedge p(x))].$$

This has value **f** in each $\Phi_P\!\uparrow\! n$ for finite n, because, for $y = s^n(0)$ the LHS is **u** but the RHS is **t**.

Kunen [1987] shows that whether ϕ has value **t** in $\Phi_P\!\uparrow\! n$ is decidable, given ϕ and n. This gives:

COROLLARY 5

The set of Q such that comp(P) $\models_3$ Q is recursively enumerable.

An alternative proof could be obtained by giving a complete and consistent deductive system for 3-valued logic, as Ebbinghaus [1969] has done for a very similar kind of 3-valued logic. ∎

For definite Horn clause programs 3-valued logic gives results which are in good agreement with those of 2-valued logic.

LEMMA 6

If P is a definite Horn clause program then

$$\Phi_P \!\uparrow\! \alpha \ = \ (T_P \!\uparrow\! \alpha, \ B_P - T_P \!\downarrow\! \alpha) \, .$$

Proof: Straightforward induction on α. ∎

Since the closure ordinal of $T_P\!\uparrow$ for a definite Horn clause program P is ω, this shows that the closure ordinal of $\Phi_P\!\uparrow$ is the same as that of $T_P\!\downarrow$, which as well known examples (e.g., Example 2) show can be greater than ω.

For those queries where the 2-valued semantics of negation as failure in terms of comp(P) is satisfactory (Theorem 27), the 3-valued semantics agrees with it:

THEOREM 38

If P is a definite Horn clause program and Q is an existential quantification of a conjunction of atoms, then the following are equivalent:

Q is true in all 2-valued models of comp(P)

Q is true in all 3-valued models of comp(P)

Q is true in all 2-valued Herbrand models of comp(P)

Q is true in all 3-valued Herbrand models of comp(P)

Q is true in all 2-valued models of P

Q is true in all 3-valued models of P

Q is true in all 2-valued Herbrand models of P

Q is true in all 3-valued Herbrand models of P.

Proof: Note that when we talk about 3-valued models of P here we mean P to be modified as above by replacing → by ⊃. When this is done, all 3-valued models of comp(P) are models of P, so all the classes of models described are contained in the class of 3-valued models of P. Since they all contain the class of 2-valued Herbrand models of comp(P), it is enough to show that if Q is true in all 2-valued Herbrand models of comp(P), it is true in all 3-valued models of P. The hypothesis implies that Q is true in $lfp(T_P)$. If

$$Q \text{ is } \exists x_1 \ldots \exists x_m (A_1(x_1, \ldots, x_r) \wedge \ldots \wedge A_s(x_1, \ldots, x_r))$$

then

$$A_1(t_1, \ldots, t_r) \wedge \ldots \wedge A_s(t_1, \ldots, t_r)$$

is true in $lfp(T_P)$ for some ground terms $t_1, \ldots, t_r$. Since $lfp(T_P) = T_P \uparrow \omega$ all the $A_i(t_1, \ldots, t_r)$ are in $T_P \uparrow n$ for some finite n. By induction on n this implies they are all true in all 3-valued models of P. ∎

The last step in the proof amounts to showing that the generic property of the least fixed point model of P given in Remark 1 extends to 3-valued models. If $\exists$ is replaced by $\forall$ here even the 2-valued parts of the result concerning Herbrand models fail if the language used is L_P, e.g., if P is $p(0), p(s(x)) \leftarrow p(x)$ and Q is $\forall x p(x)$. But Kunen [1987], Theorem 6.5, shows they are true if his Herbrand universe KU is used. In that case they can be further generalized to all positive sentences:

COROLLARY 6
The result of Theorem 38 holds for any positive sentence Q, i.e., one built up from atomic sentences using only $\wedge$, $\vee$, $\forall$, $\exists$, provided "Herbrand" is replaced by "Herbrand(KU)."

Proof: The proof is similar to that of Theorem 38 and is by structural induction on Q. The case where KU is needed is when Q is of the form $\forall x Q_1(x)$. Let c be a new constant, i.e., a constant in the language KU, different from all constants in P. If $\forall x Q_1(x)$ is true in $lfp(T_P)$ then Q (c) is true in $lfp(T_P)$, so by the induction hypothesis it is true in all 3-valued models of P. Since c does not occur in P, its assignment does not affect the truth of P, so Q (u) must be true for all individuals u in all 3-valued models of P, i.e., $\forall x Q_1(x)$ is true in all 3-valued models of P. ∎

The last step in this proof is a generalization of the genericity property (Remark 1) of $lfp(T_P)$ from existential sentences to positive sentences and from 2-valued to 3-valued logic, but only in the case when the Herbrand universe is KU (or sufficiently large to have enough new constants). The point is that new constants behave like variables.

Kunen states without proof that "any PROLOG-style interpreter will be sound under our semantics, provided that we remedy two features of standard PROLOG implementations which are commonly agreed to be in error. One is that we assume that unification is always done with an occur check. The other is in the treatment of a non-ground literal ..." Presumably he means to assert:

THEOREM 39
SLDNF-resolution is sound with respect to comp(P) in 3-valued logic, i.e., if a query

Q succeeds with answer θ then comp(P) $\models_3$ Qθ

Q fails then comp(P) $\models_3 \neg \exists$Q.

Proof: (Suggested) Check that the soundness proof in Lloyd [1984], pp. 74-80, holds for 3-valued logic. This needs a little care because all sorts of basic results, like $A \wedge B \rightarrow A$, are not valid in 3-valued logic, but one can use instead $P \models_3 A \wedge B$ implies $P \models_3 A$, which is true. Indeed I believe the result can be stated more strongly, and that, as in the 2-valued case (Corollary 4) we have some kind of "intuitionistic" soundness for 3-valued logic. By this I mean that $\models_3$ can be replaced by $\vdash_{3I}$, some "intuitionistic 3-valued derivability relation." Suitable rules for this (which appear adequate for the above proof) may be obtained either by taking a complete set of rules for 2-valued intuitionistic logic and discarding or modifying those that are not valid in 3-valued logic, or by taking a complete set of rules for 3-valued logic and discarding or modifying those that are not intuitionistically valid. ∎

Even those who find 3-valued logic unpalatable should take note of these results, for they help to explain the incompleteness of SLDNF-resolution. The reason you cannot derive all 2-valued consequences is because everything derivable must be true in all 3-valued models. It may be helpful to summarize here all the soundness results touched on in this paper and point out how they set upper bounds on the completeness of SLDNF-resolution.

Let us start from the extreme position that when you wrote a program P and asked a query Q, you were asking whether Q was true in all Herbrand(L_p) models of comp(P). In that case you would know there was no point in looking for a sound and complete proof procedure because, as Theorem 13 shows, the set of sentences true in all Herbrand(L_p) models of comp(P) may not be recursively enumerable. And if you used SLDNF-resolution you would know from the fact (Theorem 25) that it is sound wrt truth in all models of comp(P) that it must be incomplete for truth in all Herbrand(L_p) models of comp(P). If you take P to be $p(0)$, $p(s(x)) \leftarrow p(x)$, $s \leftarrow \neg p(x)$, $r \leftarrow \neg s$ and Q to be r, then Q is true in all Herbrand(L_p) models of P but a reason why the query Q does not succeed in SLDNF-resolution is that it is not true in *all* models of comp(P).

If what you really wanted to know was whether Q was true in *all* models of comp(P), then you would know that in theory a sound and complete proof procedure existed, but you would realize the incompleteness of SLDNF-resolution when you heard it was also sound wrt cwa(P). That would explain why taking P to be p ← ¬p did not make ¬p succeed, for although that is a consequence of comp(P) (since comp(P) is contradictory) it is not a consequence of cwa(P). This could also be explained by the soundness wrt 3-valued models, for ¬p is not true in all 3-valued models of comp(P) (written in 3-valued form as p ≅ ¬p). The soundness wrt intuitionistic derivability would explain why taking P as p ← q, p ← ¬q, q ← q does not make p succeed, for p is not intuitionistically derivable from comp(P) (which is equivalent to p ⟷ (q ∨ ¬q)). This could also by explained by the soundness wrt 3-valued derivability, for p is not true in all 3-valued models of comp(P) (e.g., the model with both p,q having truth value u). To sum up: For a query Q to succeed for a program P using SLDNF-resolution, Q must be true in all models of cwa(P), must be derivable in 2-valued intuitionistic logic from comp(P), and must be true in all 3-valued models of comp(P).

Although truth in all 3-valued models of comp(P) is one of the narrowest of these notions of consequences, it is not the end of the road. SLDNF-resolution is not in general complete wrt the 3-valued consequence relation even for allowed queries. Kunen gives the example of a program P:

```
p(x)  ←  isc(x)
p(x)  ←  nonc(x)
isc(c)
nonc(x)  ←  ¬isc(x)
```

whose 3-valued comp(P) implies

$$p(x) \cong (x = c \lor x \ne c).$$

Since Kunen uses a 2-valued equality relation, ∀xp(x) is true in all 3-valued models of comp(P), but the query p(x) does not succeed with answer the identity using SLDNF-resolution (though it does succeed with answer x = c). This can be explained using the 2-valued intuitionistic derivability relation, for ∀xp(x) is not intuitionistically derivable from 2-valued comp(P) since x = c ∨ x ≠ c is not intuitionistically provable. Although 3-valued logic already has a strong intuitionist flavor, I believe one can get a closer approximation to SLDNF-resolution by establishing soundness wrt some sort of "intuitionistic 3-valued" derivability relation as mentioned above. But I am not sure exactly how to formulate that.

Finally if one was really interested in whether Q was a consequence of P, rather than comp(P), then one should not be using SLDNF-resolution at all because it is not sound for this consequence relation.

Kunen does obtain a completeness proof in the propositional case:

THEOREM 40
If P is a set of sentences of propositional logic, then SLDNF-resolution is complete with respect to 3-valued models of comp(P). ∎

(Fitting and Kunen only consider programs built up using Kleene's 3-valued analogues of the 2-valued connectives. Schmitt [1986] considers a complete set of connectives for 3-valued logic. For example, as well as Kleene's negation which he calls $\neg$, he also has another negation $\sim$, where $\sim$p means "p is not true" (see truth table below). He also considers four kinds of literal: A, $\neg$A, $\sim$A, $\sim \neg$A. The last of these "A is not false" behaves like, and is called, a positive literal.

A	$\neg$A	$\sim$A	$\sim \neg$A
t	f	f	t
u	u	t	t
f	t	t	f

A clause is a disjunction of literals. Schmitt shows how to modify the resolution rule so that it is sound and complete; it is simply a matter of treating as complementary pairs each of A and $\neg$A, A and $\sim$A, $\sim \neg$A and $\neg$A. A Horn clause is defined in the usual way as one containing at most one positive literal. He shows that the results of Maltsev, Mahr and Makowsky, and Hodges on the relation of Horn theories to initial models, direct products, and substructures carry over to the 3-valued case. Definite Horn clauses can be written in the form

$$A \subset A_1 \land A_2 . . . \land A_n$$

where $A,A_1,...,A_n$ are positive literals and A $\supset$ B stands for $\sim$A $\lor$ B (this differs from our A $\subset$ B in being **u** if A is **t** and B is **u**, whereas ours is **f**; and it is not the same as our $\rightarrow$ either). He shows that the usual soundness and completeness results for SLD-resolution carry over provided you apply SLD-resolution to P augmented by all clauses $\sim \neg$A $\subset$ A for all atoms A. This work does not overlap with that of Fitting and Kunen because, although he considers a 3-valued logic with more connectives, Schmitt does not consider the relation of negation as failure to 3-valued models of comp(P).)

I think Kunen's semantics in terms of 3-valued models is the most satisfactory one for negation as failure because it comes closest to being complete and seems to provide a good intuition of the meaning attached to comp(P) by the procedure. However, the difficulties we have seen of finding a semantics wrt which SLDNF-resolution is sound and complete for general programs lends support to John Lloyd's view that a more profitable line of research is to try and extend the class of hierarchical programs and suitably allowed queries for which SLDNF-resolution is complete wrt the class of 2-valued consequences of comp(P). But in pursuing this aim a closer semantic approximation to SLDNF-resolution in the general case might be a useful tool as well as providing more insight into the logical meaning of a program when using SLDNF-resolution.

Acknowledgments

I would like to thank Jack Minker for inviting me to take part in the workshop and to contribute to these Proceedings and for submitting the paper to so many referees. I am grateful to them for giving their time and using their expertise to suggest improvements. I am grateful to John Crossley for stylistic improvements and particularly for inviting me to give a series of lectures on the content of this paper at Monash University. These meetings and lectures uncovered many errors, and the staff and graduate students of the computer science departments of both Monash and Melbourne universities pointed out more. I am also indebted to John Lloyd and Hervé Gallaire for corrections, and to Kenneth Kunen for patiently explaining his results. I would like to apologize in advance to readers for any mistakes that have survived all these critics and for the higher level errors that have been introduced in correcting earlier ones.

References

1. Apt, K. R., Blair, H., and Walker, A. [1988] Towards a Theory of Declarative Knowledge, in *Foundations of Deductive Database and Logic Programming* (J. Minker, Ed.), Morgan Kaufmann Publishers, Los Altos, CA, 89–148.

2. Apt, K. R. and Emden, M. H. van [1982] Contributions to the Theory of Logic Programming, *J.ACM* **29**, 841–863.

3. Barbuti, R. and Martelli, M. [1986] Completeness of SLDNF-resolution for Structured Programs, submitted to *Theoretical Computer Science* **21**.

4. Blair, H. A. [1982] The Recursion Theoretic Complexity of the Semantics of Predicate Logic as a Programming Language, *Information and Control* **54**, 25–47.

5. Blair, H. A. [1986] Decidability in the Herbrand Base, in *Proceedings Workshop on Foundations of Deductive Databases and Logic Programming* (J. Minker, Ed.), Washington, DC.

6. Borger, E. [1987] Unsolvable Decision Problems for PROLOG Programs, to appear in *Computer Theory and Logic* (E. Borger, Ed.), Lecture Notes in Computer Science, Springer-Verlag.

7. Carvalho, R. L. de, Maibaum, T. S. E., Pequeno, T. H. C., Pereda, A. A., and Veloso, P. A. S. [1980] A Model Theoretic Approach to the Theory of Abstract Data Types and Data Structures, *Research Report CS-80-22*, Waterloo, Ontario.

8. Clark, K. L. [1978] Negation as Failure, in *Logic and Data Base* (H. Gallaire and J. Minker, Eds.), Plenum, New York, 293–322.

9. Davis, M. [1983] The Prehistory and Early History of Automated Deduction, in *Automation of Reasoning* (J. Siekmann and G. Wrightson, Eds.), Springer, Berlin, vol. (1983), 1–28.

10. Ebbinghaus, H. D. [1969] Uber eine Pradikaten Logik mit Partiell Definierten Pradikaten and Funktionen, *Arch. math. Logik* **12**, 39–53.

11. Fitting, M. [1985] A Kripke-Kleene Semantics for General Logic Programs, *Logic Programming* **2**, 295–312.

12. Gabbay, D. M. [1985] N-Prolog: An Extension of Prolog with Hypothetical Implication. II. Logical Foundations, and Negation as Failure, ibid **2**(4):251–283.

13. Gabbay, D. M. [1986] Modal Provability Foundations for Negation by Failure, preprint.

14. Gabbay, D. M. and Sergot, M. J. [1986] Negation as Inconsistency, *J. Logic Programming* **3**(1):1–36.

15. Gallier, J. H. and Raatz, S. [1986a] HORNLOG: A Graph Based Interpreter for General Horn Clauses, Tech. Rep. MS-CIS-86-10, University of Pennsylvania; submitted to *J. Logic Programming*.

16. Gallier, J. H. and Raatz, S. [1986b] SLD-Resolution Methods for Horn Clauses with Equality Based on E-Unification, to appear, *J. Logic Programming*. Short version to appear, 1986 *IEEE Symposium on Logic Programming*, Salt Lake City, UT.

17. Gelfond, M., Przymusinska H., and Przymusinski, T. [1986] The Extended Closed World Assumption and Its Relationship to Parallel Circumscription, *Proceedings ACM SIGACT-SIGMOD Symposium on Principles of Database Systems*, Cambridge, MA, 133–139.

18. Goguen, J. A. and Burstall, R. M. [1984] Institutions: Abstract Model Theory for Computer Science, *Proc. of Logic Programming Workshop* (E. Clark and D. Kozen, Eds.), Lecture Notes in Computer Science **164**, Springer-Verlag, 221–256.

19. Haken, A. [1985] The Intractability of Resolution, *Theoretical Computer Science* **39**, 297–308.

20. Henschen, L. J. and Park, H-S. [1988] Compiling the GCWA in Indefinite Databases, in *Foundations of Deductive Databases and Logic Programming* (J. Minker, Ed.), Morgan Kaufmann Publishers, Los Altos, CA, 395–438.

21. Hodges, W. [1985] The Logical Basis of PROLOG, unpublished text of lecture, 1-10.

22. Jaffar, J., Lassez, J.- L., and Lloyd, J. W. [1983] Completeness of the Negation as Failure Rule, *IJCAI-83*, Karlsruhe, 500-506.

23. Jaffar, J., Lassez, J.- L., and Maher, M. J. [1984a] A Theory of Complete Logic Programs with Equality, *J. Logic Programming* **1**(3):211-223.

24. Jaffar, J., Lassez, J.- L., and Maher, M. J. [1984b] A Logic Programming Language Scheme, in *Logic Programming Relations, Functions and Equations* (D. DeGroot and G. Lindstrom, Eds.), Prentice Hall.   Also *Technical Report TR 84/15*, University of Melbourne.

25. Jaffar, J., Lassez, J.- L., and Maher, M. J. [1986a] Comments on "General Failure of Logic Programs," *J. Logic Programming* **3**(2):115-118.

26. Jaffar, J., Lassez, J.- L., and Maher, M. J. [1986b] Some Issues and Trends in the Semantics of Logic Programs, *Proceedings International Conference on Logic Programming*, 223-241.

27. Jaffar, J. and Stuckey, P. J. [1986] Canonical Logic Programs, *J. Logic Programming* **3**, 143-155.

28. Kleene, S. C. [1952] *Introduction to Metamathematics*, van Nostrand, New York.

29. Kowalski, R. [1979] *Logic for Problem Solving*, North Holland, New York.

30. Kunen, K. [1986] Negation in Logic Programming, to appear in *J. Logic Programming*, 15 pp.

31. Lassez, J.- L., and Maher, M. J. [1984] Closures and Fairness in the Semantics of Programming Logic, *Theoretical Computer Science* **29**, 167-184.

32. Lassez, J.- L. and Maher, M. J. [1985] Optimal Fixedpoints of Logic Programs, *Theoretical Computer Science* **39**, 15-25.

33. Lewis H. [1978] Renaming a Set of Clauses as a Horn Set, *JACM* **25**, 134-135.

34. Lifschitz, V. [1985] Computing Circumscription, *Proceedings IJCAI-85*, 121-127.

35. Lifschitz, V. [1988] On the Declarative Semantics of Logic Programs with Negation, *Foundations of Deductive Databases and Logic Programming* (J. Minker, Ed.), Morgan Kaufmann Publishers, Los Altos, CA, 177-192.

36. Lloyd, J. W. and Topor, R. W. [1984] Making PROLOG more Expressive, *J. Logic Programming* **1**, 225-240.

37. Lloyd, J. W. [1984] *Foundations of Logic Programming*, Springer, Berlin.

38. Lloyd, J. W. and Topor, R. W. [1985] A Basis for Deductive Data Base Systems, *J. Logic Programming* **2**, 93-110.

39. Lloyd, J. W. and Topor, R. W. [1986] A Basis for Deductive Data Base Systems, II, *J. Logic Programming* **3**, 55-68.

40. McCarthy, J. [1984] Applications of Circumscription to Formalizing Common Sense Knowledge, *AAAI Workshop on Non-Monotonic Reasoning*, 295–323.

41. Mahr, B. and Makowsky, J. A. [1983] Characterizing Specification Languages which Admit Initial Semantics, *Proc. 8th CAAP*, Lecture Notes in Computer Science **159**, Springer-Verlag, 300–316.

42. Makowsky, J. A. [1986] Why Horn Formulas Matter in Computer Science: Initial Structures and Generic Examples, *Techn. Report No. 329*, Technion Haifa, 1984 (extended abstract); in *Mathematical Foundations of Software Development, Proceedings of the International Joint Conference on Theory and Practice of Software Development (TAPSOFT)* (H. Ehrig et al., Eds.), Lecture Notes in Computer Science **185**, Springer (1985), 374–387, and (revised version) May 15, 1986, 1–28, preprint. The references in the text are to this most recent version.

43. Meltzer, B. [1983] Theorem-Proving for Computers: Some Results on Resolution and Renaming, in *Automation of Reasoning* **1** (J. Siekmann and G. Wrightson, Eds.), Springer, Berlin, 493–495.

44. Minker, J. [1982] On Indefinite Data Bases and the Closed World Assumption, *Proc. 6th Conf. Automated Deduction*, Lecture Notes in Computer Science **138**, Springer-Verlag, 292–308.

45. Minker, J. and Perlis, D. [1985] Computing Protected Circumscription, *J. Logic Programming* **2**, 1–24.

46. Mycroft, A. [1983] Logic Programs and Many-Valued Logic, *Proc. 1st STACS Conf.*

47. Naqvi, S. A. [1986] A Logic for Negation in Database Systems, in *Proceedings of Workshop on Foundations of Deductive Databases and Logic Programming* (J. Minker, Ed.), Washington, DC.

48. Plaisted, D. A. [1984] Complete Problems in the First-Order Predicate Calculus, *J. Comp. System Sciences* **29**, 8–35.

49. Przymusinski, T. C. [1988] On the Semantics of Stratified Deductive Databases, in *Foundations of Deductive Database and Logic Programming* (J. Minker, Ed.), Morgan Kaufmann Publishers, Los Altos, CA, 193–216.

50. Reiter, R. [1978] On Closed World Data Bases, in *Logic and Data Bases* (H. Gallaire and J. Minker, Eds.), Plenum, New York, 55–76.

51. Sakai, K. and Miyachi, T. [1983] Incorporating Naive Negation into PROLOG, *ICOT Technical Report:* TR-028.

52. Sato, T. [1982] Negation and Semantics of PROLOG Programs, *Proc. 1st International Conference on Logic Programming*, 169–174.

53. Schmitt, P. H. [1986] Computational Aspects of Three Valued Logic, *Proc. 8th Conf. Automated Deduction*, Lecture Notes in Computer Science **230**, Springer-Verlag, 190–198.

54. Shepherdson, J. C. [1984] Negation as Failure: A Comparison of Clark's Completed Data Base and Reiter's Closed World Assumption, *J. Logic Programming* **1**, 51-81.

55. Shepherdson, J. C. [1985] Negation as Failure II, *J. Logic Programming* **3**, 185-202.

56. Tärnlund, S. A. [1977] Horn Clause Compatibility, *BIT* **17**, 215-216.

57. Van Gelder, A. [1988] Negation as Failure Using Tight Derivations for General Logic Programs, *Foundations of Deductive Databases and Logic Programming* (J. Minker, Ed.), Morgan Kaufmann Publishers, Los Altos, CA, 149-176.

58. Voda, P. J. [1986] Choices in, and Limitations of, Logic Programming, *Proc. 3rd Int. Conf. Logic Programming*, Springer, 615-623.

Chapter

2

Towards a Theory of Declarative Knowledge

Krzysztof R. Apt[1]
C.W.I.,
Amsterdam, The Netherlands

Howard A. Blair[2]
CIS,
Syracuse University,
Syracuse, NY

Adrian Walker
IBM Thomas J. Watson Research Center,
Yorktown Heights, NY

Abstract

We identify a useful class of logic programs with negation, called *stratified programs*, that disallow certain combinations of recursion and negation. Programs in this class have a simple declarative and procedural meaning based, respectively, on model theory and a back-chaining interpreter. The standard model of a stratified program, which gives the program a declarative meaning

---

[1] Work performed during the author's visiting year at IBM Research Center, Yorktown Heights, NY 10598

[2] Work performed while the author was a consultant at IBM Research Center, Yorktown Heights, NY 10598

and is independent of the stratification, is characterized in two ways. One is based on a fixed point theory of nonmonotonic operators and the other on an abstract declarative characterization. The back-chaining interpreter also determines the standard model. Finally, we prove the consistency of Clark's completion for stratified programs and attempt to clarify the sources of some previously reported difficulties with negation in logic programming.

Introduction

The aim of this paper is to provide a formal basis for separating declarative and procedural matters in an extension of logic programming allowing negation in the presence of certain recursions. This should be viewed as part of a larger research program with the aim of extending logic programming so that it is more useful for expert systems, both as a formal basis and as a source of practical techniques.

Expert Systems

There is currently considerable interest in expert system shells that are based on logic programming. Logic programming certainly has several properties that should be seriously considered while searching for an appropriate formalism. Among other things, we expect that the knowledge in an expert system should be easy to examine and to change, and we expect the system to provide explanations of its results. At first sight, the knowledge in a logic program is easy to change, since it consists simply of facts and rules. From the *declarative* point of view, this is indeed the case. However, a common difficulty is that the addition of a rule with an intended declarative meaning has unintended *procedural* effects when the knowledge is interpreted by a particular inference engine. For example, the rule

(X is married to Y) if (Y is married to X)

has an obvious common sense declarative meaning, but it can cause control problems for several well-known inference mechanisms, including that of Prolog.

Similar issues arise in systems that are not based on logic, but logic as a formalism for expert systems has an important advantage: We can specify the *declarative meaning* of a collection of rules and facts using the techniques of model theory. This tells us what the consequences of the knowledge should be, independent of particular mechanisms for interpreting the knowledge. We can also specify various *procedural interpretations*, such as SLD resolution, and we can study the extent to which the interpretations live up to our model theoretic standard.

The extent to which an interpreter (or inference engine) behaves according to the declarative reading of knowledge can be crucial to its use by non-programmers, who wish to add knowledge to an expert system. Real world tasks about which knowledge is to be acquired can be complicated. It helps to manage this complexity if the declarative and procedural concerns can be separated. For example, order does not matter for declarative knowledge, but procedurally we might have to find just one of the possible orderings of a set of rules to make certain inference engines behave the way we wish.

At the higher, declarative level it should be sufficient to write down the knowledge correctly in the form of facts and rules. At the lower level, an inference engine should be available to handle the procedural and computational aspects, and to produce the intended declarative meaning.

Logic Programming

For any choice of formalism to succeed, it must be sufficiently expressive for the purposes at hand. Logic programming with definite clauses (see Kowalski [1978]) does not seem to be expressive enough for expert system shells. In particular, we need to express negation.

It is important to realize that use of negation indeed increases the expressive power of logic programming. This may sound paradoxical since, as is well known (see e.g., Tärnlund [1977]), logic programs without negation have the full power of recursion theory. But the point is that in many situations we compute over a finite domain, and this drastically changes the situation.

The realization of this fact led to extensive studies, started by Clark [1978], of the extensions of logic programming incorporating the use of negation. Unfortunately several difficulties have been revealed (see e.g., Shepherdson [1984, 1985, 1988]), and it seems fair to say that so far no satisfactory theory of negation has been proposed. In particular no positive result concerning the use of negation in the presence of recursion has been proved.

A certain amount is known about interpreters that behave according to model theory. For the case of logic programs without negation, both the declarative reading—through the least Herbrand model, and the procedural reading—through SLD resolution, are available and by the results of Apt and van Emden [1982], they naturally correspond through a completeness result. Brough and Walker [1984] showed that, even for function-free ("database like") programs without negation, a strong form of completeness cannot be achieved by any strictly top-down inference engine. Walker [1986b] described an implemented inference engine that uses a mixed top-down/bottom-up strategy that appears to overcome some of this difficulty, even with negation allowed.

Consider the treatment of negation in Prolog. Prolog is normally augmented with a definition of negation that says that $\neg P$ is true if we cannot prove P. This allows programs containing negation in the premises of rules to be executed. However, such programs must at present be written by programmers with an intimate knowledge of the Prolog interpreter's operation. We lack a declarative reading and have to rely on a highly intricate procedural interpretation instead.

One of the difficulties concerning the use of negation in logic programming is that this is an (almost classic) example of nonmonotonic reasoning. Indeed, suppose that by some means we infer from the logic program P a negative fact, say $\neg A$. Naturally we do not expect that $\neg A$ can then be inferred from P augmented by the fact A—otherwise a contradiction could be derived from P and A. Thus, the provability relation is no longer monotonic, and this makes it difficult to study.

Structure of the Paper

In this paper we achieve our goal by restricting the use of negation. We allow both recursion and negation, but we disallow recursion "through negation" as in

$$p \leftarrow \neg q,$$

$$q \leftarrow p$$

and we call the resulting programs *stratified*. They are formally defined in the section "Stratified Programs" below. These programs form a simple generalization of a class of programs introduced in the context of the deductive databases by Chandra and Harel [1985].

The declarative meaning of a stratified program is given in a semantic fashion—by certain of its minimal models. (A model is minimal if it has no proper subset that is also a model.) To see why we need minimality, consider the program $p \leftarrow p$. This has models $\{p\}$ and the empty set. $\{p\}$ is not minimal. We rule it out, since there is no way of proving p using the rule. The minimal models that we consider are those that are *supported*, in the sense that each item in such a model is either a fact in the program, or is the conclusion of a ground instance of a rule whose body is true in the model. To see why it is reasonable to require support, consider the program consisting of just the rule $p \leftarrow \neg q$. This program has minimal models $\{p\}$ and $\{q\}$, but only $\{p\}$ is supported. We rule $\{q\}$ out, on the grounds that there is no way of proving q using the rule as it stands.

To study models of logic programs we relate them in the section "From Models to Fixed Points" to fixed points of a natural operator originally introduced in van Emden and Kowalski [1976]. Unfortunately, in the presence of negation this operator is nonmonotonic and can have no fixed points. To resolve the difficulty we develop in the fifth section a fixed point theory of nonmonotonic operators, and in the section "Model Theory of Stratified Programs" apply it to the study of models of stratified programs. We believe that this theory can have other applications in the area of nonmonotonic reasoning.

The declarative meaning of a stratified program is given by exhibiting a particular supported minimal model that can be defined in a simple way by using the T operator of van Emden and Kowalski [1976]. This provides a logical interpretation of negation that also works procedurally.

The procedural reading of knowledge written in a form of a stratified program is provided by defining a top-down interpreter that makes rather simple use of bottom-up information. We define it in a recursive fashion and show in the two sections on the elementary interpreter and its existence that it admits a well-founded inductive definition when applied to stratified programs.

Then we show that the interpreter computes the chosen model of a stratified program, and that in the absence of function symbols the computation is effective and terminating. Finally, in the section "Other Views of Negation and Stratified Programs," we attempt to clarify the negation problem in logic programming and compare our treatment of negation with two other views proposed in the literature—those of Reiter [1978] and Clark [1978]. There we prove the consistency of Clark's completed database for stratified programs, again employing the fixed point techniques. We also explain why the unrestricted use of function symbols in general makes any interpreter nonterminating. The paper concludes by discussing other related work in the final section.

Preliminaries

In this section we recall the basic definitions concerning logic programs. Our only departure from customary treatment of the subject is that we study these programs in the presence of negation. Nothing will be said here on the computation process—only syntax and semantics will be discussed. We start by defining the syntax.

Syntax

We consider here a *first-order language* whose formulas are denoted by S. Its variables are denoted by x, y, and z terms by s, t, and atomic formulas (usually called *atoms*) in turn by the letters A, B, and C. An atom is called *ground* if no variable occurs in it. A *literal* is an atom A or its negation $\neg A$ and is denoted by the letter L. An *atom* is a *positive literal*, and the negation of an atom is a *negative literal*. A *clause* is a formula of the form

$$A \leftarrow L_1 \& ... \& L_m$$

where A is an atom, $L_1,...,L_m$ are literals and $m \geq 0$. A is the *head* (conclusion) of the clause and $L_1 \& ...\& L_m$ its *body* (hypothesis). Thus, negation is allowed in the body of a clause but not in its head. If m = 0 then, the clause is simply A and is called a *fact*. Otherwise it is called a *rule*. Finally a *program* is a finite set of clauses. A program whose clauses do not contain negation is called *positive*. In other words, in a positive program only positive literals occur in the bodies of the clauses. Such clauses are usually called *definite clauses*. We define *ground (P)* to be the set of all variable-free instances of clauses in P. Note that *ground (P)* depends on the underlying first-order language.

If a program P contains an atom $r(t_1,...,t_n)$, then r is a *relation* of P. We make the convention that no relation symbol occurs with different arities in P.

A *goal* is a formula of the form $\leftarrow L_1 \& ...\& L_m$ where $L_1,...,L_m$ are literals and $m \geq 0$.

A *substitution*

$$\theta \equiv (t_1/x_1)...(t_m/x_m)$$

is defined as usual: It replaces all free occurrences of the variables $x_1,...,x_m$ by the terms $t_1,...,t_m$, respectively. The replacement is performed simultaneously. $S\theta$ is the result of applying the substitution θ to the formula S. $S\theta$ is called an *instance* of S.

Semantics

The language of a program P is the first-order language determined by all and only the logical symbols occurring in P. The *Herbrand base* U_L of a first-order language L is defined as the set of all variable-free atoms of L. An *interpretation* for L is a subset of the Herbrand base of L. When L is the language of program P we may refer to U_P, the Herbrand base of P, and to interpretations for P. This definition for Herbrand interpretations will be convenient in later sections. Also we discuss the interaction between operators on interpretations of distinct but closely related programs.

The *truth* of a formula in an interpretation is defined as usual: Only those variable-free instances of atoms that are in I are considered to be true in I. A formula is *closed* if it contains no occurrence of a free variable. Formally, we proceed by induction.

DEFINITION 1
Let I be an interpretation.

1.   A formula S is, true in I iff each of its closed instances is true in I, that is, for each x occurring free in S, and each variable-free term $t,S(t/x)$ is true in I.

2.   A closed atom A is true in I iff $A \in I$.

3.   A closed formula $\neg S$ is true in I iff S is not true in I.

4.   A closed formula $\exists x.S$ is true in I iff for some variable free term t the formula $S(t/x)$ is true in I.

5.   A closed formula $\forall x.S$ is true in I iff (by (1)!) S is true in I.

6.   A closed formula $S_1 \leftarrow S_2$ is true in I iff S_2 is not true in I or S_1 is true in I.

7.   A closed formula $S_1 \& \ldots \& S_m$ is true in I iff each of the S_i is true in I.

8.   A closed formula $S_1 \vee \ldots \vee S_m$ is true in I iff one of the S_i is true in I.

9.   A closed formula $S_1 \leftrightarrow S_2$ is true in I iff (S_1 is true in I if and only if S_2 is true in I).   ∎

An interpretation M is a *model* for Γ if each formula in Γ is true in M (denoted $M \models \Gamma$). If Γ has a model, then Γ is *consistent*. The models here considered are usually called *Herbrand models*. It should be pointed out that they are not the most general models. Consequently, the notion of consistency we use here is a priori stronger than the usual one since it refers to the existence of a Herbrand model only. It is an important aspect of Herbrand's theorem that the two notions of consistency coincide for clauses.

If a model M of Γ is a subset of every other model of Γ, then we say that M is a *least* model of Γ. If M is a model of Γ such that no model of Γ is its proper subset, then we say that M is a *minimal* model of Γ. Thus, a least model is a minimal model, but not necessarily conversely.

Finally, we say that an interpretation I of a program P is *supported* if for each $A \in I$ there exists a clause $A_1 \leftarrow L_1 \& \ldots \& L_m$ in P and a substitution θ such that $I \models L_1\theta \& \ldots \& L_m\theta$, $A = A_1\theta$, and each $L_i\theta$ is ground. Thus, I is supported iff for each $A \in I$ there exists a clause in ground (P) with head A whose body is true in I.

Stratified Programs

We will now propose a treatment of negation in logic programming, which should be a solution to various difficulties exhibited in the literature. It is achieved through restricting its use and by proposing a new semantic interpretation. In the section on the existence of the interpreter we justify this semantic definition by proof theoretic means.

Our view of a safe use of negation is the following. When using negation we should refer to an *already known* relation. More specifically, first some relations should be defined (perhaps recursively) in terms of themselves *without* the use of negation. Next, some new relations can be defined in terms of themselves without the use of negation and in terms of the previous ones, possibly *with* the use of negation. This process can be iterated.

In such a way, from the semantic point of view we only negate relations whose meaning is fixed beforehand. It seems that most of the paradoxes concerning negation in logic programming violate this principle.

More precisely, we introduce the following definitions.

DEFINITION 2
Let P be a program.

1.   We say that the relation p *refers to* the relation r if there is a clause in P with p on its left-hand side and r on its right-hand side.

2.   By a *definition* of a relation symbol r we mean the subset of P consisting of all clauses with a formula on the left side whose relation symbol is r.

3.   A relation symbol r occurs *positively* in a positive literal and *negatively* in a negative literal.   ∎

These definitions formalize intuitive notions frequently used informally. We now provide the central definition of this section.

DEFINITION 3
A program P is called *stratified* if there is a partition

$$P = P_1 \dot{\cup} \dots \dot{\cup} P_n$$

such that the following two conditions hold for i = 1,...,n:

1.   if a relation symbol occurs positively in a clause in P_i, then its definition is contained within $\bigcup_{j \leq i} P_j$.

2.   if a relation symbol occurs negatively in a clause in P_i, then its definition is contained within

$$\bigcup_{j < i} P_j.$$

P_1 can be empty.

We say then that P is *stratified by* $P_1 \dot{\cup} \dots \dot{\cup} P_n$ and each P_i is called a *stratum* of P. Thus, each stratum defines new relations in terms of itself only positively and in terms of the relations from the previous strata, possibly negatively. We let $\bar{P}_i$ denote $P_1 \dot{\cup} \dots \dot{\cup} P_i$. Thus $\bar{P}_n = P$.   ∎

EXAMPLE 1

1. Let P be the following program:

$$p(x) \leftarrow \neg q,$$

$$r,$$

$$q \leftarrow q \& \neg r.$$

Then P is stratified by

$$P = \{r\} \cup \{q \leftarrow q \& \neg r\} \cup \{p(x) \leftarrow \neg q\}.$$

2. Let P be the following program:

$$p \leftarrow q,$$

$$q \leftarrow \neg p.$$

Then P is not stratified. Because of the second clause, the definition of p has to appear in a lower stratum than the definition of q. But p refers to q, so condition (1) cannot be satisfied.

The last example suggests the following simple test whether a program is stratified.

DEFINITION 4

By the *dependency graph* of a program P we mean the directed graph representing the relation *refers to* between the relation symbols of P. Formally, p *refers to* q in P iff there is a clause C in P in which p is the relation symbol in the head of C and q is the relation symbol of a literal in the body of C. Note that it may be that p refers to q via several clauses in P. In particular, for any pair of relation symbols p, q there is at most one edge (p,q) in the dependency graph of P. An edge (p,q) is *positive* [*negative*] iff there is a clause C in P in which p is the relation symbol in the head of C, and q is the relation symbol of a positive [negative] literal in the body of C. Note that an edge may be both positive and negative. ∎

LEMMA 1

A program P is stratified iff in its dependency graph there are no cycles containing a negative edge.

Proof: If the program is stratified, then the definition of each relation symbol is contained in some stratum. Assign to each relation the index of the stratum within which it is defined. If (p,q) is a positive edge in the dependency graph of P then the level assigned to q is smaller than or equal to that assigned to p, and if (p,q) is a negative edge, then the level assigned to q is strictly smaller than that assigned to p. Thus, there are no cycles in the dependency graph through a negative edge.

For the converse, decompose the dependency graph into *strongly connected* components, each of maximum cardinality (i.e., such that any two nodes in a component are connected in a cycle). Then the relation "there is an edge from component G to component H" is *well founded*, since it is finite, and contains no cycles. Thus, for some n the numbers 1,...,n can be assigned to the components so that if there is an edge from G to H, then the number assigned to H is smaller than that assigned to G. Now let P_i be the subset of the program P consisting of the definitions of all relations which lie within a component with the number i.

We claim that

$$P = P_1 \dot{\cup} \dots \dot{\cup} P_n$$

is a stratification of P. Indeed, if q is defined within some P_i and refers to r, then r lies in the same component or in a component with a smaller number. In other words, the definition of r is contained in P_j for some $j \leq i$. And if this reference is negative, then r lies in a component with a smaller number because by assumption there is no cycle through a negative edge. Thus, the definition of r is then contained in P_j for some $j < i$. ■

We will now study semantics of stratified programs. As explained in the introduction we are interested in models that are both minimal and supported. Our task is to prove that stratified programs indeed have such models.

From Models to Fixed Points

Van Emden and Kowalski [1976] proposed an elegant way of studying logic programs without negation. Their definitions still make perfect sense in the presence of negation. Their idea was to use a natural closure operator and equate the models of a program P with the pre-fixed points of the operator, which are simpler to analyze. This operator is usually called T_P. It maps interpretations of P into interpretations of P and is defined as follows:

$A \in T_P(I)$ iff for some clause $A_1 \leftarrow L_1 \& \dots \& L_m$ in P and substitution θ,

$I \models L_1 \theta \& \dots \& L_m \theta$ and $A = A_1 \theta$

We shall drop the subscript P if it is clear from the context to which program P the operator refers. Intuitively, $T_P(I)$ is the set of immediate conclusions of I, i.e., those which can be obtained by applying a rule from P only once. Note that $A \in T_P(I)$ iff there exists a clause in ground (P) with head A whose body is true in I.

Below, we shall study T as an operator, so it is perhaps useful to recall some terminology and well-known results. Since no greater generality is needed, we consider only the case of operators on complete lattices. We use $\subseteq$ to denote the order relation on the lattice.

We say that T is *monotonic* if $I_1 \subseteq I_2$ implies $T(I_1) \subseteq T(I_2)$. When $T(I) \subseteq I$ then we say that I is a *pre-fixed point* of T and when $T(I) = I$ then we say that I is a *fixed point* of T. The following classical result is at the heart of the van Emden and Kowalski [1976] approach.

THEOREM (KNASTER-TARSKI [1955])
A monotonic operator T has a least fixed point that is also the least pre-fixed point of T. ∎

Now suppose that T is one of the operators T_P on Herbrand interpretations. The Knaster-Tarski theorem's importance derives from the fact that for a positive program P the operator T_P is monotonic. Unfortunately, in the presence of negation, things change. In fact, in this paper we shall not make use of the Knaster-Tarski theorem. The following example explains the difficulties.

EXAMPLE 2
Let P be a program without negation. Then (see van Emden and Kowalski [1976]),

a. T_P is monotonic,

b. the intersection of two models of P is a model of P, and

c. P has a least model.

On the other hand, if P is a program with negation we have

d. T_P does not need to be monotonic,

e. Intersection of two models of P does not need to be a model of P, and

f. P may have no least model.

To see this, consider the program $P: A \leftarrow \neg B$

1. Take I_1 empty and $I_2 = \{B\}$. Then $T_P(I_1) = \{A\}$ whereas $T_P(I_2)$ is empty. Thus $I_1 \subseteq I_2$ but not $T_P(I_1) \subseteq T_P(I_2)$.

2. Take the above program P. Then $\{A\}$ and $\{B\}$ are models of P but their intersection is not.

3. P has two different minimal models: $\{A\}$ and $\{B\}$. ■

Several results concerning positive programs depend critically on the properties (a), (b), and (c). Fortunately, a very important property remains true.

LEMMA 2
Let P be a program. Then I is a model of P iff $T_P(I) \subseteq I$.

Proof: Essentially the same as the proof for programs without negation; see Lloyd [1984]. ■

This simple fact saves the whole approach based on the analysis of the operator T_P! Further, the notion of a supported model can also be naturally expressed in terms of the operator T_P. We have the following simple result.

LEMMA 3
Let P be a program. Then I is supported iff $T_P(I) \supseteq I$.

Proof: Direct from the definition. ■

As explained in the introduction, we are interested here in studying minimal and supported models. In view of Lemmas 2 and 3 this simply means that we are looking for minimal fixed points of the operator T_P. Thus, we are brought to study the fixed points of nonmonotonic operators. It is conceptually advantageous to carry out such an analysis in a completely general situation.

Fixed Point Theory of Nonmonotonic Operators

Powers

Here we study operators over an arbitrary, but fixed, complete lattice. To keep in mind the subsequent applications to logic programs and their interpretations, we denote the least element by ϕ and the elements of the lattice by I, J, M. The order relation on the lattice is denoted by $\subseteq$.

We start by defining *powers* of an operator T. We put

$$T{\uparrow}0(I) = I$$
$$T{\uparrow}(n + 1)\,(I) = T(T{\uparrow}n(I)) \cup T{\uparrow}n(I).$$
$$T{\uparrow}\omega(I) = \bigcup_{n=0}^{\infty} T{\uparrow}n(I)$$

$T{\uparrow}n(I)$ should not be confused with $T^n(I)$, which stands for the n fold application of T. If T is monotonic, then its ordinal powers can be (and usually are)
defined in a slightly simplified way by putting

$$T{\uparrow}(n + 1)\,(I) = T(T{\uparrow}n(I))$$

An obvious proof by induction shows that when T is monotonic both defini-
tions lead to the same value of $T{\uparrow}n(\phi)$ (but of $T{\uparrow}n(I)$ only when $I \subseteq T(I)$).

Clearly the process of computing powers of T can be extended beyond ω,
see Blair [1982], but we shall not need this.

Fixed Points

We now introduce the following definition.

DEFINITION 5

T is *finitary* if for every infinite sequence

$$I_0 \subseteq I_1 \subseteq \ldots$$

$$T(\bigcup_{n=0}^{\infty} I_n) \subseteq \bigcup_{n=0}^{\infty} T(I_n)$$

holds. Thus if $A \in T(\bigcup_{n=0}^{\infty} I_n)$ then for some n, $A \in T(I_n)$, which explains the
name. The following lemma shows the importance of this notion. ∎

LEMMA 4

If T is finitary then for all I

$$T(T{\uparrow}\omega(I)) \subseteq T{\uparrow}\omega(I).$$

Proof: We have

$T(T{\uparrow}\omega(I))$

$\subseteq \bigcup_{n=0}^{\infty} T(T{\uparrow}n(I))$ since T is finitary

$\subseteq T{\uparrow}\omega(I)$ since $T(T{\uparrow}n(I)) \subseteq T{\uparrow}(n + 1)(I)$. ∎

Thus, finitary operators have pre-fixed points which can be computed in a
natural way. In general finitary operators do not have fixed points, but under
some assumptions they do.

DEFINITION 6

T is *growing* if for all I, J, M

$$I \subseteq J \subseteq M \subseteq T{\uparrow}\omega(I)$$

implies

$$T(J) \subseteq T(M). \quad \blacksquare$$

The following lemma holds.

LEMMA 5

If T is growing then for all I

$$T{\uparrow}\omega(I) \subseteq I \cup T(T{\uparrow}\omega(I))$$

Proof: We have

$$A \in T{\uparrow}\omega(I) \Rightarrow A \in I \text{ or for some } n \geq 1,\, A \in T{\uparrow}n(I)$$
$$\Rightarrow A \in I \text{ or for some } n \geq 0,\, A \in T(T{\uparrow}n(I))$$

(by assumption) $\Rightarrow A \in I$ or $A \in T(T{\uparrow}\omega(I))$. $\quad \blacksquare$

COROLLARY 1

If T is finitary and growing then

$$T{\uparrow}\omega(\phi) = T(T{\uparrow}\omega(\phi)). \quad \blacksquare$$

Thus for finitary and growing T, $T{\uparrow}\omega(\phi)$ is a fixed point.

Iterations

Next, we study finite families of operators. Let $T_1, \dots, T_n$ be operators. We put

$$N_0 = I,$$
$$N_1 = T_1{\uparrow}\omega(N_0),$$
$$\dots$$
$$N_n = T_n{\uparrow}\omega(N_{n-1}).$$

Clearly $N_0 \subseteq N_1 \subseteq \dots \subseteq N_n$. Of course all N_i depend on I and it will be always clear from the context from which one. To concentrate attention on the fact that N_n is computed using T_i in an iterative fashion, we sometimes denote it by $iter(T_1, \dots, T_n, (I))$.

Our first task is to determine under which conditions $iter(T_1,\ldots,T_n,(I)$ is a fixed point of $\bigcup_{i=1}^{n} T_i$, where $(\bigcup_{i=1}^{n} T_i)(X) = \bigcup_{i=1}^{n} (T_i(X))$. For this purpose we introduce the following concept.

DEFINITION 7
A sequence of operators $T_1,\ldots,T_n$ is *local* if for all I,J and $i = 1,\ldots,n$

$$I \subseteq J \subseteq N_n$$

implies

$$T_i(J) = T_i(J \cap N_i).$$

Informally, locality means that each T_i is determined by its values on the subsets of N_i.

As an example of a non-local sequence of operators, consider T_{P_1}, T_{P_2} where $P_1 = \{q \leftarrow \neg p\}$ and $P_2 = \{p \leftarrow \neg p\}$. Then $I = \phi$, $N_1 = \{q\}$, and $N_2 = \{p,q\}$. Choose $J = \{p\}$. Then $T_{P_1}(J) = \phi$ but $T_{P_1}(J \cap N_1) = \{q\}$. ∎

We have the following two lemmas.

LEMMA 6
Suppose that the sequence $T_1,\ldots,T_n$ is local and that all T_i are finitary. Then

$$(\bigcup_{i=1}^{n} T_i)(iter(T_1,\ldots,T_n, I)) \subseteq iter(T_1,\ldots,T_n,I).$$

Proof: We have

$$\bigcup_{i=1}^{n} T_i(iter(T_1,\ldots,T_n, I))$$

$$\text{(by locality)} = \bigcup_{i=1}^{n} T_i(N_i)$$

$$\text{(by Lemma 4)} \subseteq \bigcup_{i=1}^{n} N_i$$

$$= iter(T_1,\ldots,T_n, I). \quad ∎$$

LEMMA 7
Suppose that the sequence $T_1,\ldots,T_n$ is local and each T_i is growing. Then

$$iter(T_1,\ldots,T_n,I) \subseteq I \cup (\bigcup_{i=1}^{n} T_i)(iter(T_1,\ldots,T_n,I)).$$

Proof: We prove it by induction on n. If $n = 1$, the lemma reduces to Lemma 5. For $n > 1$, assume the lemma holds for all $m < n$. Then

$$N_n$$

(by Lemma 5) $\qquad \subseteq N_{n-1} \cup T_n(N_n)$

(by ind. hypothesis) $\qquad \subseteq (I \cup (\bigcup_{i=1}^{n-1} T_i)(N_{n-1})) \cup T_n(N_n)$

(by locality) $\qquad = I \cup (\bigcup_{i=1}^{n} T_i)(N_n).$ ∎

COROLLARY 2

Suppose that sequence $T_1,\ldots,T_n$ is local and all T_i are finitary and growing. Then

$$iter(T_1,\ldots,T_n, I) = I \cup (\bigcup_{i=1}^{n} T_i)(iter(T_1,\ldots,T_n, I)). \quad ∎$$

Thus for a local sequence $T_1,\ldots,T_n$ of finitary and growing operators $iter(T_1,\ldots,T_n, \phi)$ is a fixed point of $\bigcup_{i=1}^{n} T_i$.

We now prove that under some assumptions $iter(T_1,\ldots,T_n, I)$ is a minimal pre-fixed point of $\bigcup_{i=1}^{n} T_i$ containing I. More precisely, we prove

THEOREM 1

Suppose that the sequence $T_1,\ldots,T_n$ is local and that all T_i are growing. If

$$I \subseteq J \subseteq iter(T_1,\ldots,T_n, I)$$

and

$$(\bigcup_{i=1}^{n} T_i)(J) \subseteq J$$

then

$$J = iter(T_1,\ldots,T_n, I).$$

Proof: We prove by induction on $j = 0,\ldots,n$ that

$$N_j \subseteq J. \tag{1}$$

For $j = 0$ it is part of the assumptions. Assume that the claim holds for some $j < n$. We now prove by induction on k that

$$T_{j+1}\!\uparrow\! k(N_j) \subseteq J. \tag{2}$$

For k = 0 this is just (1), So assume (2) holds for some $k \geq 0$. We have

$$T_{j+1} \uparrow (k+1)(N_j) \subseteq T_{j+1} (T_{j+1} \uparrow k(N_j)) \cup J$$

(by (2) and since T_{j+1} is growing) $\subseteq T_{j+1}(J \cap N_{j+1}) \cup J$

(by locality) $= T_{j+1}(J) \cup J$

(by the assumptions) $\subseteq J$.

Thus by induction for all k (2) holds, so $N_{j+1} \subseteq J$. This proves (1) for all $j = 0, \ldots, n$ and concludes the proof. ∎

Iteration Versus Simultaneity

Next, we relate $iter(T_1, \ldots, T_n, I)$ with $(\bigcup_{i=1}^{n} T_i) \uparrow \omega(I)$. We need the following notion.

DEFINITION 8
A sequence of operators $T_1, \ldots, T_n$ is *raising* if for all I, J, M and $i = 1, \ldots, n$

$$I \subseteq J \subseteq M \subseteq N_n$$

implies

$$T_i(J) \subseteq T_i(M). ∎$$

We have the following lemma.

LEMMA 8
Suppose that the sequence $T_1, \ldots, T_n$ is local and raising and that all T_i are finitary. Then

$$(\bigcup_{i=1}^{n} T_i) \uparrow \omega(I) \subseteq iter(T_1, \ldots, T_n, I).$$

Proof: We prove by induction on k that

$$(\bigcup_{i=1}^{n} T_i) \uparrow k(I) \subseteq iter(T_1, \ldots, T_n, I) \tag{3}$$

It clearly holds for $k = 0$. So assume (3) holds for some $k \geq 0$. To make the derivation more readable, denote $(\bigcup_{i=1}^{n} T_i) \uparrow k(I)$ by J. We have

$$(\bigcup_{i=1}^{n} T_i\!\uparrow\!(k+1))(I) = (\bigcup_{i=1}^{n} T_i)(J) \cup J$$

(by locality and (3) $= (\bigcup_{i=1}^{n} T_i)(J \cap N_i) \cup J$

(since $T_1,\ldots,T_n$ is raising) $\subseteq (\bigcup_{i=1}^{n} T_i)(N_i) \cup J$

(by Lemma 4) $\subseteq \bigcup_{i=1}^{n} N_i \cup J$

(by(3)) $\subseteq iter(T_1,\ldots,T_n, I).$

Thus, by induction (3) holds for all k, which completes the proof. ■

This leads us to the following theorem.

THEOREM 2
Suppose that the sequence $T_1,\ldots,T_n$ is local and raising. Suppose also that all T_i are finitary and growing. Then

$$iter(T_1,\ldots,T_n, I) = (\bigcup_{i=1}^{n} T_i)\!\uparrow\!\omega(I).$$

Proof: This time it suffices to combine previously proved results. First, observe that since all T_i are finitary, $\bigcup_{i=1}^{n} T_i$ is finitary, as well. Thus by Lemma 4

$$(\bigcup_{i=1}^{n} T_i)((\bigcup_{i=1}^{n} T_i)\!\uparrow\!\omega(I)) \subseteq (\bigcup_{i=1}^{n} T_i)\!\uparrow\!\omega(I).$$

Now, in view of Lemma 8 all assumptions of Theorem 1 are satisfied and the conclusion follows. ■

Independence

Finally, we study a condition under which the order of application of two operators is irrelevant. For this purpose we introduce the following notion.

DEFINITION 9
T_1 and T_2 are *independent* if for all I, J and M

1.   if $I \subseteq J \subseteq T_2\!\uparrow\!\omega(I)$ then $T_1(I \cup M) = T_1(J \cup M)$,

2.   if $I \subseteq J \subseteq T_1\!\uparrow\!\omega(I)$ then $T_2(I \cup M) = T_2(J \cup M)$. ■

Intuitively, in (1), T_1 makes no use of $J - I$. Consider $I \subseteq J \subseteq T_2\!\uparrow\!\omega(I)$ and $M = \phi$. Then $T_1(I) = T_1(J)$.

We have the following technical lemma.

LEMMA 9

Suppose that T_1 and T_2 are independent. Then for all $k \geq 1$

1. if $I \subseteq J \subseteq T_2 \uparrow \omega(I)$ then $T_1 \uparrow k(J) = T_1 \uparrow k(I) \cup J$,

2. if $I \subseteq J \subseteq T_1 \uparrow \omega(I)$ then $T_2 \uparrow k(J) = T_2 \uparrow k(I) \cup J$.

Proof: Suppose that $I \subseteq J \subseteq T_2 \uparrow \omega(I)$. Note that

$$T_1 \uparrow 1(J) = T_1 \uparrow 1(I) \cup J.$$

Suppose now the claim holds for some $k \geq 1$. We then have (1) by an obvious induction. By symmetry (2) holds as well, which proves the lemma. ∎

The lemma implies the following theorem.

THEOREM 3

Suppose that T_1 and T_2 are independent. Then for all I

$$T_1 \uparrow \omega(T_2 \uparrow \omega(I)) = T_2 \uparrow \omega(T_1 \uparrow \omega(I)).$$

Proof: We have

$$T_1 \uparrow \omega(T_2 \uparrow \omega(I)) = \bigcup_{k=1}^{\infty} T_1 \uparrow k(T_2 \uparrow \omega(I))$$

(by Lemma 9) $\qquad = \bigcup_{k=1}^{\infty} (T_1 \uparrow k(I) \cup T_2 \uparrow \omega(I))$

$\qquad\qquad\quad = T_1 \uparrow \omega(I) \cup T_2 \uparrow \omega(I)$

(by symmetry) $\qquad = T_2 \uparrow \omega(T_1 \uparrow \omega(I))$. ∎

It is time to relate the above results to logic programs.

Model Theory of Stratified Programs

Consider a program P stratified by

$$P = P_1 \dot\cup \ldots \dot\cup P_n.$$

We now define a standard interpretation of P by putting

$$M_1 = T_{P_1} \! \uparrow \! \omega(\phi),$$
$$M_2 = T_{P_2} \! \uparrow \! \omega(M_1),$$

...

$$M_n = T_{P_n} \! \uparrow \! \omega(M_{n-1}).$$

Let $M_P = M_n$.

In what sense is M_P standard? We prove in this and the next sections several results which support the claim that M_P is natural. Obviously our first task is to prove that M_P is a model of P.

This turns out to be an easy consequence of the results proved in the previous section.

Minimality and Supportedness of M_P

We first prove certain facts about the operators associated with logic programs.

THEOREM 4

For all programs P, T_P is finitary.

Proof: Straightforward and left to the reader. ∎

Next let us introduce the following useful notation.

$Neg_P = \{A : \neg A$ is a variable-free instance of a negative literal in a clause in $P\}$

$Def_P = \{A : A$ is a variable-free instance of a head of a clause in $P\}$

EXAMPLE 3

Let P be the following program:

$p(a),$

$r(x) \leftarrow \neg q(a),$

$p(x) \leftarrow \neg r(y).$

Then

$Neg_P = \{q(a), r(a)\}$

and

$Def_P = \{p(a), r(a)\}.$ ∎

We have the following simple lemma.

LEMMA 10

Let P be a subprogram of P'. Then

$$I \subseteq J \subseteq U_{P'} \text{ and } I \cap Neg_P = J \cap Neg_P$$

implies

$$T_P(I) \subseteq T_P(J).$$

Informally, the lemma says that each T_P is monotonic as long as its arguments do not differ on the elements of Neg_P. The reference to P' and $U_{P'}$ allows us to consider T_P on a larger space.

Proof: Suppose that $A \in T_P(I)$. Then there is a variable-free instance of a clause from P of the form

$$A \leftarrow L_1 \& \ldots \& L_m$$

where

$$I \models L_1, \ldots, I \models L_m.$$

If L_i is positive, then $L_i \in I$, so also $L_i \in J$ and consequently $J \models L_i$. If L_i is negative, then it is of the form $\neg B_i$ where $B_i \notin I$. Also $B_i \in Neg_P$. Thus $B_i \notin I \cap Neg_P$ and by the assumption $B_i \notin J \cap Neg_P$. Hence $B_i \notin J$ and consequently $J \models L_i$. Thus for all i, $J \models L_i$ which implies $A \in T_P(J)$. ∎

Next we introduce the following definition.

DEFINITION 10

A program is called *semi-positive* if none of its negated relation symbols occurs in a head of a clause. More formally, P is semi-positive if $Neg_P \cap Def_P = \phi$. ∎

The following is a consequence of the previous lemma.

THEOREM 5

If P is semi-positive, then T_P is growing.

Proof: First observe that if

$$I \subseteq J \subseteq M \subseteq T_P \uparrow \omega(I)$$

then, since $T_P \uparrow \omega(I) \subseteq I \cup Def_P$, we have

$$M \cap Neg_P \subseteq (I \cup Def_P) \cap Neg_P = I \cap Neg_P \subseteq J \cap Neg_P.$$

so

$$J \cap Neg_P = M \cap Neg_P.$$

Therefore by Lemma 10

$$T_P(J) \subseteq T_P(M). \quad \blacksquare$$

Informally, for semi-positive programs all arguments of T_P lying between I and $T_P \!\uparrow\! \omega(I)$ do not differ on the elements from Neg_P.

Now, consider a sequence of programs $P_1, \dots, P_n$.

DEFINITION 11

A sequence $P_1, \dots, P_n$ *defines new relations* if the following holds:
whenever a relation symbol occurs in a clause P_i, then its definition within $P_1 \cup \dots \cup P_n$ is contained in P_j for some $j \le i$. (Note that if the definition of a given relation symbol is empty, then that definition is contained within, in particular, P_1.)

More formally, a sequence $P_1, \dots, P_n$ defines new relations if for all $i = 1, \dots, n-1$

$$Def_{P_{i+1}} \cap U_{P_1 \cup \dots \cup P_i} = \phi. \quad \blacksquare$$

That is, none of the relation symbols defined in P_{i+1} is mentioned in $P_1, \dots, P_i$.

We have the following theorem.

THEOREM 6

If the sequence $P_1, \dots, P_n$ defines new relations, then the sequence of the operators $T_{P_1}, \dots, T_{P_n}$ considered on the space $U_{P_1 \cup \dots \cup P_n}$ is local.

Proof: As in the previous section we denote $iter(T_{P_1}, \dots, T_{P_i}. I)$ by N_i and let N_0 be I. We have for $i = 0, \dots n-1$

$$N_{i+1} - N_i \subseteq Def_{P_{i+1}}.$$

Thus for $i = 1, \dots, n$

$$N_n \cap U_{P_1 \cup \dots \cup P_i}$$
$$\subseteq (N_i \cup Def_{P_{i+1}} \cup \dots \cup Def_{P_n}) \cap U_{P_1 \cup \dots \cup P_i}$$
(since $P_1, \dots, P_n$ defines new relations) $\subseteq N_i \cap U_{P_1 \cup \dots \cup P_i}$
$$\subseteq N_n \cap U_{P_1 \cup \dots \cup P_i}.$$

Hence

$$N_i \cap U_{P_1 \cup \ldots \cup P_i} = N_n \cap U_{P_1 \cup \ldots \cup P_i}$$

Suppose now that

$$I \subseteq J \subseteq N_n.$$

Then for i = 1,...,n

$$J \cap U_{P_1 \cup \ldots \cup P_i} = J \cap N_n \cap U_{P_1 \cup \ldots \cup P_i}$$
$$= J \cap N_i \cap U_{P_1 \cup \ldots \cup P_i}.$$

But by the definition of T_P

$$T_{P_i}(J) = T_{P_i}(J \cap U_{P_1 \cup \ldots \cup P_i})$$
$$= T_{P_i}(J \cap N_i \cap U_{P_1 \cup \ldots \cup P_i})$$
$$= T_{P_i}(J \cap N_i)$$

as desired. ∎

Let us now relate the above theorems to stratfied programs. Suppose that P is stratified by

$$P = P_1 \dot{\cup} \ldots \dot{\cup} P_n.$$

Then by definition each P_i is semi-positive and the sequence $P_1,\ldots,P_n$ defines new relations. By Theorems 4 and 5 all operators T_{P_i} for $i = 1,\ldots n$ are finitary and growing. By Theorem 6 the sequence $T_{P_1} \ldots T_{P_n}$ is local. We are now in a position to apply Corollary 2. It implies

$$T_P(M_P) = M_P.$$

This in turn, in view of Lemmas 2 and 3, implies the following theorem.

THEOREM 7

1. M_P is a model of P.

2. M_P is supported. ∎

Also, by Theorem 1 and Lemma 2 we have

THEOREM 8
M_P is a minimal model of P. ■

Note that in view of Lemmas 6 and 2 and Theorems 4 and 6, M_P is a model of P whenever the sequence $P_1,\ldots,P_n$ defines new relations. But to prove that M_P is supported we also need Lemma 7, which requires that all T_{P_i} are growing. This condition is satisfied (see Theorem 5) if each P_i is semi-positive. Now it is easy to see that if the sequence $P_1,\ldots,P_n$ defines new relations and each P_i is semi-positive, then P is stratified by $P = P_1 \cup \ldots \cup P_n$. In other words, our general results on nonmonotonic operators do not allow us to conclude existence of supported models for other than stratified programs.

Independence of M_P from the Stratification

The definition of the model M_P for a stratified program P is somewhat unsatisfactory as it explicitly refers to the way P is stratified. We now prove that M_P does not depend on the stratification of P. This will support our claim that M_P is a natural model for P.

Again this easily follows from the results of the previous section. This time we use results of the second part of the section. We first introduce the following natural concept.

DEFINITION 12
Let P be a program.

1. *depends on* is the reflexive transitive closure of the relation *refers to* between the relation symbols of P.

2. By a *cluster* we mean a non-empty subset of P that is the union of a maximal collection of definitions that define relations that depend on one another. ■

The following example should clarify the definition.

EXAMPLE 4
Let P be

$p \leftarrow q,$

$r \leftarrow q \& q_1,$

$q \leftarrow r,$

$q_1.$

Then q and r depend on each other. Thus $\{p \leftarrow q\}$, $\{r \leftarrow q \& q_1, \quad q \leftarrow r\}$ and $\{q_1\}$ are the clusters of P. ∎

Note that P' is a cluster if it is non-empty and for each clause in P' with p on its left hand side and r on its right hand side. P' contains the definition of p and, if r depends on p, the definition of r.

We have the following simple lemma.

LEMMA 11
Let P be a program.

1. The clusters of P form a partition of P.

2. If P is stratified by $P_1 \overset{.}{\cup} \ldots \overset{.}{\cup} P_n$, then each stratum P_i is a union of clusters.

Proof: Consider the following relation between definitions from P:

$R_1 \geq R_2$ iff the relation defined by R_1 depends on the relation defined by R_2.

Let

$R_1 \approx R_2$ iff $R_1 \geq R_2$ and $R_2 \geq R_1$.

Then $\approx$ is an equivalence relation between the definitions from P.

To prove (1) it is now sufficient to observe that a cluster is just a union of definitions forming an equivalence class of $\approx$.

To prove (2) note that each definition from P is contained in a stratum. Let *index(R)* for a definition R be the index of the stratum it is contained in. (We shall also say that the index of a literal is the index of the definition of its relation symbol.) Then by the definition of stratification

$R_1 \geq R_1 \Rightarrow \text{index}(R_1) \geq \text{index}(R_2)$.

Thus

$R_1 \approx R_2 \Rightarrow \text{index}(R_1) = \text{index}(R_2)$.

so in view of the above characterization of clusters, each cluster is contained in a stratum. The claim now follows by (1). ∎

Consider now the relation $\geq$ defined in the last proof but now as a relation between clusters. In other words, given two clusters Q_1 and Q_2 we put

$Q_1 \geq Q_2$ iff for some definitions $R_1 \subseteq Q_1$

and $R_2 \subseteq Q_2$ we have $R_1 \geq R_2$.

Then, since $\approx$ is an equivalence relation, $\geq$ is a partial ordering between clusters.

Given now a program stratified by $P = P_1 \mathbin{\dot{\cup}} \ldots \mathbin{\dot{\cup}} P_n$, let $index(Q)$, for a cluster Q, be the index of a stratum it is contained in. Then for two clusters Q_1 and Q_2

$Q_1 \geq Q_2 \Rightarrow index(Q_1) \geq index(Q_2)$.

We now introduce the following definition.

DEFINITION 13
We say that two clusters Q_1, Q_2 are *unrelated* if neither $Q_1 \geq Q_2$ nor $Q_2 \geq Q_1$ holds.

Note that if Q_1 and Q_2 are unrelated, then $Def(Q_2) \cap U_{Q_1} = \phi$ and $Def(Q_1) \cap U_{Q_2} = \phi$. but not necessarily conversely. For example, if $P = \{p \leftarrow q, q \leftarrow r, r\}$ then the clusters $Q_1 = \{p \leftarrow q\}$ and $Q_2 = \{r\}$ are not unrelated but satisfy the above property. ■

The following is an immediate consequence of the above remarks.

LEMMA 12
Let P be a stratified program. Suppose that $P = P_1 \mathbin{\dot{\cup}} \ldots \mathbin{\dot{\cup}} P_k$ and $P = P'_1 \mathbin{\dot{\cup}} \ldots \mathbin{\dot{\cup}} P'_i$ are two different stratifications of P. If Q_1, Q_2 are two clusters such that for some i_1, i_2, j_1, j_2

$Q_1 \subseteq P_{i_1}, Q_2 \subseteq P_{i_2}, i_1 < i_2$

and

$Q_1 \subseteq P'_{j_1}, Q_2 \subseteq P'_{j_2}, j_1 > j_2$

then Q_1 and Q_2 are unrelated.

Proof: The conditions of the lemma simply state that the order of indexes of Q_1 and Q_2 in two stratifications of P is different. Thus neither $Q_1 \geq Q_2$ nor $Q_2 \geq Q_1$ holds. ■

We now link the notions of this and the previous sections.

THEOREM 9

Let Q_1, Q_2 be two clusters of a program P. Suppose that Q_1 and Q_2 are unrelated. Then T_{Q_1} and T_{Q_2} are independent.

Proof: Suppose that for some I, J

$$I \subseteq J \subseteq T_{Q_2} \uparrow \omega(I).$$

Then

$$J - I \subseteq Def_{Q_2},$$

so since Q_1 and Q_2 are unrelated.

$$(J - I) \cap U_{Q_1} = \phi.$$

Thus for any M

$$(I \cup M) \cap U_{Q_1} = (J \cup M) \cap U_{Q_1},$$

that is

$$T_{Q_1}(I \cup M) = T_{Q_1}(J \cup M).$$

By symmetry the other half of the independence definition holds as well. ∎

THEOREM 10

Let P be a program stratified by $P = P_1 \dot\cup \ldots \dot\cup P_k$ and suppose that $Q_1,\ldots,Q_n$ are the clusters of P_i for some i, $1 \leq i \leq n$. Then the sequence of operators $T_{Q_1},\ldots,T_{Q_n}$ considered on the space U_{P_i} is raising.

Proof: Since P_i is a stratum, it is a semi-positive program.
Suppose that

$$I \subseteq J \subseteq M \subseteq iter(T_{Q_1},\ldots,T_{Q_n}, I)$$

Then for any $j = 1,\ldots,n$

$$J \cap Neg_{Q_j} \subseteq (Def_{P_i} \cup I) \cap Neg_{Q_j}$$

(since P_i is semi-positive and $Neg_{Q_j} \subseteq Neg_{P_i}$) $= I \cap Neg_{Q_j}.$

Similarly

$$M \cap Neg_{Q_j} \subseteq I \cap Neg_{Q_j}.$$

It follows that

$$I \cap Neg_{Q_j} = J \cap Neg_{Q_j} = M \cap Neg_{Q_j}.$$

Now, by Lemma 10

$$T_{Q_j}(J) \subseteq T_{Q_j}(M). \quad \blacksquare$$

Finally we prove the following theorem.

THEOREM 11

Let P be a stratified program. Then M_P is independent of the stratification of P.

Proof: We use the previous two theorems.

Given two stratifications $P_1,\ldots,P_n$ and $P'_1,\ldots,P'_k$ of P, we say that they are *equivalent* if they yield the same model M_P, that is if

$$iter(T_{P_1},\ldots,T_{P_n}, \phi) = iter(T_{P'_1},\ldots,T_{P'_k}, \phi).$$

We now prove that any two stratifications of P are equivalent. So let $P_1,\ldots,P_n$ be a stratification of P. By Lemma 11 (2) each stratum is a union of clusters. Consider a stratum, say P_i, and a sequence of its clusters, say $Q_1,\ldots,Q_h$. This sequence can be rearranged so that for every j,m, $1 \leq j,m \leq h$

$$Q_j \geq Q_m \Rightarrow j \geq m.$$

Now $P_1,\ldots,P_{i-1}, Q_1,\ldots,Q_h, P_{i+1},\ldots,P_n$ is also a stratification of P. Moreover, by Theorems 6, 10, and 2 applied to $T_{Q_1}, \ldots,T_{Q_h}$ and T_{P_i}, it is a stratification equivalent to the previous one. Iterating this procedure for other strata we arrive at a stratification of P consisting of clusters which is equivalent to the original one. $\quad \blacksquare$

It now suffices to prove that any two stratifications of P consisting of clusters are equivalent. To this purpose we need the following simple lemma.

LEMMA 13

Let $a_1,\ldots,a_n$ and $b_1,\ldots,b_n$ be two permutations of n elements. Then $a_1,\ldots,a_n$ can be transformed into $b_1,\ldots,b_n$ by repeatedly exchanging two adjacent elements whose relative order in $b_1,\ldots,b_n$ is different.

Proof: Straightforward—use the bubble sort. ∎

We now complete the proof of Theorem 11. Let $Q_1,\ldots,Q_n$ and $Q'_1,\ldots,Q'_n$ be two stratifications of P consisting of clusters. If the relative order of two clusters Q_i and Q_j in these two sequences differs, then by Lemma 12 Q_i and Q_j are unrelated. Then by Theorem 4, T_{Q_i} and T_{Q_j} are independent. This together with the previous lemma concludes the proof. ∎

An Alternative Characterization of M_P

The definition of the model M_P is somewhat operational in the sense that it is defined in terms of the iterations of the operators T_{P_i}. We now offer another, equivalent definition, which while being less direct has the virtue of not referring to any computation mechanism.

Suppose that P is stratified by

$$P = P_1 \mathbin{\dot\cup} \ldots \mathbin{\dot\cup} P_n.$$

Recall that $\bar{P}_i$ denotes $P_1 \mathbin{\dot\cup} \ldots \mathbin{\dot\cup} P_i$. Put

$$M(\bar{P}_1) = \bigcap \{M : M \text{ is a supported model of } \bar{P}_1\}$$

$$M(\bar{P}_2) = \bigcap \{M : M \cap U_{\bar{P}_1} = M(\bar{P}_1) \text{ and M is a supported model of } \bar{P}_2\}$$

$$\ldots$$

$$M(\bar{P}_n) = \bigcap \{M : M \cap U_{\bar{P}_{n-1}} = M(\bar{P}_{n-1}) \text{ and M is a supported model of }$$
$$\bar{P}_n\}$$

We now prove the following theorem.

THEOREM 12
$$M_P = M(\bar{P}_n).$$

Proof: As expected we proceed by induction and prove that for all $i = 1,\ldots,n$ $M_i = M(\bar{P}_i)$.

For $i = 1$ it is the consequence of the fact that for a monotonic operator T, $T{\uparrow}k(\phi) = T^k(\phi)$ for all k, and a result of van Emden and Kowalski [1976] characterizing, for a positive program P,

$$\bigcup_{k=1}^{\infty} T_P^k(\emptyset) \text{ as } \bigcap \{M : T_P(M) = M\}.$$

Suppose now that the claim holds for some $i < n$. We then have by Theorem 7 applied to $\bar{P}_{i+1}$ that M_{i+1} is a supported model of $\bar{P}_{i+1}$ and, since the sequence $P_1, \ldots, P_{i+1}$ defines new relations,

$$M_{i+1} \cap U_{\bar{P}_i} = M_i \tag{1}$$

(by the induction hypothesis) $= M(\bar{P}_i)$.

Thus, from the definition of $M(\bar{P}_{i+1})$,

$$M(\bar{P}_{i+1}) \subseteq M_{i+1}.$$

To prove that equality actually holds, it is enough to show that $M(\bar{P}_{i+1})$ is a model of $\bar{P}_{i+1}$ and apply Theorem 8, which states that M_{i+1} is a minimal model of $\bar{P}_{i+1}$.
For this purpose we prove

$$T_{\bar{P}_{i+1}}(M(\bar{P}_{i+1})) \subseteq M(\bar{P}_{i+1}) \tag{2}$$

and use Lemma 2.
First note that by (1) and the definition of $M(\bar{P}_{i+1})$ we have

$$M(\bar{P}_{i+1}) \cap U_{\bar{P}_i} = M(\bar{P}_i). \tag{3}$$

Now take M such that $M \models \bar{P}_{i+1}$, M is a supported model of $\bar{P}_{i+1}$ and

$$M \cap U_{\bar{P}_i} = M(\bar{P}_i). \tag{4}$$

Then, by definition, $M(\bar{P}_{i+1}) \subseteq M$ and moreover by (4) $M \cap Neg_{\bar{P}_{i+1}} \subseteq U_{\bar{P}_i}^-$ as M is a supported model of $\bar{P}_{i+1}$. Thus

$$M(\bar{P}_{i+1}) \cap Neg_{\bar{P}_i+1} = M \cap U_{\bar{P}_i} \cap Neg_{\bar{P}_{i+1}}$$
$$= M \cap Neg_{\bar{P}_{i+1}}.$$

Now by Lemma 10

$$T_{\bar{P}_{i+1}}(M(\bar{P}_{i+1})) \subseteq T_{\bar{P}_{i+1}}(M)$$
$$= T_{\bar{P}_1}(M) \cup T_{\bar{P}_{i+1}}(M)$$
$$= T_{\bar{P}_1}(M \cap U_{\bar{P}_i}) \cup T_{\bar{P}_{i+1}}(M)$$

(by (4)) $= T_{\bar{P}_i}(M(\bar{P}_i)) \cup T_{\bar{P}_{i+1}}(M)$

(by ind. hyp., Lemma 2, Th. 7) $\subseteq M(\bar{P}_i) \cup T_{\bar{P}_{i+1}}(M)$

(by Lemma 2) $\subseteq M(\bar{P}_i) \cup M$

(by (4)). $= M.$

Since M was arbitrary, by the definition of $M(\bar{P}_{i+1})$ this proves (2), which concludes the proof. ∎

Note that the theorem does not hold when the assumption that M is supported in the definition of $M(\bar{P}_i)$ is dropped. Indeed, let P be $p \leftarrow \neg q$. Then P_1 is empty, so $U_{\bar{P}_1} = \emptyset$ and $M(\bar{P}_1) = M_1 = \emptyset$. On the other hand $M_2 = \{p\}$ whereas

$$\bigcap \{M : M \models \bar{P}_2 \text{ and } M \cap U_{\bar{P}_1} = \emptyset\} = \bigcap \{\{p\}, \{q\}\} = \emptyset.$$

An Elementary Interpreter

Our purpose in this and the next section is to study the foundations of a proof theory for logic programs with negation. The study begins with three deliberately naive intuitions about inference using the clauses of a program:

1. to prove a ground atom A find a ground instance $A \leftarrow L_1 \& \ldots \& L_n$ of a clause in the program and prove each of $L_1, \ldots, L_n$;

2. to prove $\neg A$ show there is no proof of A from the clauses of the program;

3. if there is a proof of A, then there is also a proof of A which does not, itself, depend (recursively) on a proof of A.

A little reflection should suggest that, while (3) is correct, for programs with negation (1) leads to incompleteness and (2) is unsound.

Apart from the problematic aspects of (1) and (2) regarding completeness and soundness there are other more serious and surprising difficulties. Below, we introduce an interpreter which formalizes (1), (2), and (3) in a straightforward way. For certain programs we will see that there are multiple interpretations of the formal definition of the interpreter; in this sense the interpreter is ambiguous. The same difficulties arise with other definitions of provability in the case of logic programs with negation. In particular we find that the definition of SLDNF-resolution given in Lloyd [1984, p. 76] suffers from the same kind of ambiguity. Moreover, it is not at all clear that (1), (2), and (3) are even consistent in the case of some programs.

In this section, we show that the ambiguity in the definition of the interpreter vanishes when we restrict to stratified programs, and in the next section we show that the definition is, formally, consistent under this restriction. Thus for a stratified program P the definition of the interpreter uniquely specifies which ground atoms are provable from P. We also show that this need not be the case when P is not stratified. Moreover, when P is stratified, the set of ground atoms provable from P is M_P. Since the interpreter uniquely determines the class of ground atoms provable from P independently of how P is stratified, this result gives yet another proof that M_P is independent of the stratification.

Typically, there are ground atoms that are true in M_P but are not logical consequences of P. Thus, from the point of view of first-order logic our proof procedure given by the interpreter is unsound. However, soundness and completeness notions depend on what concept of logical consequence is being considered. For example, there are true sentences in number theory that are not (first-order) logical consequences of Peano's axioms. An enriched proof procedure that, starting from Peano's axioms, would allow us to prove some of these sentences must necessarily be unsound from the point of view of ordinary first-order logic, but should certainly not be dismissed because of this. The point is that notions of logical consequence can be based on *intended* models rather than on *all* models.

This is the attitude we take here: A stratified program P has a unique intended model, namely M_P, and we reduce the notion of logical consequence from P to that of truth in M_P.

The interpreter uses ground instantiations of the clauses of the program. We do not claim such an interpreter is adequate for real programming, but it does have two important properties. First, it is an analytical tool for investigating the foundations of a proof theory for logic programs with negation. Second, it is easy to see how to implement it as an executable Prolog program that gives us an immediate extension from ground instances of clauses.

We give a (for the moment informal) example that illustrates what should be taken as a proof based on (1), (2), and (3).

EXAMPLE 5
Consider a program P:

$$p \leftarrow q \& \neg r,$$

$$q \leftarrow p,$$

$$q \leftarrow s,$$

$$r \leftarrow t,$$

$$s$$

and the tree T:

(Note that we are using T to stand for an operator, and T to stand for a tree. It will also be clear from context which is meant.) Our intention is to regard T as proving p from P in the following way: s is a fact in P, so P immediately proves s, hence q. Now, there is no proof tree for t, hence no proof tree for r. This establishes $\neg r$, and consequently p. The interpreter must also "trap" loops. In this example it would be useless to try to prove q by proving p. ■

We now formalize these notions. We first define the class of objects that will be used by the interpreter to construct proof trees.

DEFINITION 14
Let U be the Herbrand base of a language L. An *implication tree* over U is inductively defined by the following rules.

1.   For each $A \in U$, A and $\neg A$ are implication trees over U.

2.   If $T_1,...,T_n$ are (not necessarily distinct) implication trees, and $A \in U$, then

$$A(T_1,...,T_n)$$

is an implication tree over U. We may also denote this tree by

$$A \leftarrow T_1 \& \ldots \& T_n. \quad ■$$

When the context is clear we may sometimes omit the phrase "over U." An implication tree is identifiable with a (graphical) tree in the obvious way where we assume multiple copies of the same literal are distinguishable.

We will now introduce a sequence of restrictions on implication trees that will bring us to those trees that our interpreter can return as proof trees. Informally, it should be evident that along any path on a proof tree, the same ground literal need not occur more than once. Accordingly, we have the following definition.

DEFINITION 15
An implication tree T is *loop-free* iff T contains no path with two distinct occurrences of a node labelled A, for any $A \in U$. ■

Note that negative literals can only occur as leaves.

EXAMPLE 6
The implication tree given below is loop-free, and, we will see, proves q from

$q \leftarrow \neg q.$

$$q$$
$$|$$
$$\neg q$$

The class of implication trees over U of course ignores the structure of logic programs whose Herbrand bases are contained in U. Because we want to use implication trees to prove the consequences of logic programs, we must select those implication trees that can serve as proofs. We shall use the term "compatible" to link implication trees with programs in this way. Proposition 1 makes precise what it is that compatible implication trees do prove. ■

DEFINITION 16
Let T be an implication tree, and P a logic program.

1.   If T is $\neg A$, and A is ground, then T is *compatible* with P.

2.   If T is A, and A is ground, then T is *compatible* with P.

3.   If T is $A(T_1,...,T_n)$, T_i is *compatible* with P ($i = 1,...,n$), $B_1,...,B_n$ are the roots of $T_1,...,T_n$ respectively, and

$$A \leftarrow B_1 \& ... \& B_n$$

is in ground (P), then T is compatible with P. Here ground (P) stands for the set of all closed instances of clauses from P. ∎

The next definition allows the statement of Proposition 1 to be more succinct. Here and elsewhere, the symbol $\models$ is used to mean "first-order" logical provability.

DEFINITION 17
Let T be an implication tree compatible with P. A negative leaf $\neg A$ is *loop-trapped* if A occurs on the path from the root of T to $\neg A$. ∎

PROPOSITION 1
Let T be a loop-free implication tree compatible with P, and let A be the root of T. Suppose $\neg B_1, \ldots, \neg B_k$ are all and only the negative leaves of T that are *not* loop-trapped. Then

$$P \models A \vee B_1 \vee \ldots \vee B_k.$$

Proof: Straightforward by induction on the height of T. ∎

COROLLARY 3
Let T be a loop-free implication tree compatible with P in which every negative leaf is loop-trapped. Then

$$P \models \text{root(T)} ∎$$

In general, Proposition 1 and its corollary (fortunately!) do not have natural converses. That is, for a program that uses negation in a nontrivial way, a compatible implication tree may prove its root although not every negative leaf is loop-trapped. Consider the following example. (With the exception of Proposition 1, we are still being informal about "proof.")

EXAMPLE 7

P_1: $p \leftarrow q\&r,$

$q \leftarrow p,$

$q \leftarrow \neg s,$

$s \leftarrow p,$

$r.$

P_2: $p \leftarrow \neg q.$

First, in the case of program P_2

should indeed prove p since there is no proof of q. It is instructive to explicitly see the considerations in building an implication tree to prove p using P_1.

Step 1:

is an initial segment of an implication tree. r is a positive leaf that is also a fact in P_1. Thus, r is proved.

Step 2:   There are two possibilities for extending the initial segment of Step 1.

Alternative (a) is not an initial segment of any *loop-free* implication tree. Hence, there is no need to bother trying to prove p using alternative (a). Now, to use (b) we need to show that there is no proof of s. If there were, then we would have a proof of p and at the same time know that the alternative (b) fails to yield a proof. But (a) or (b) are, intuitively, the only ways of proving p. Thus, there is no proof of s, so (b) serves to prove p. We stress here that we are only giving evidence for what should be regarded as a proof, and are not trying to be rigorous. ■

We now define our interpreter. Let $\bar{U} = U \cup \neg U$, where $\neg U = \{\neg A \mid A \in U\}$.

DEFINITION 18

Let P be a logic program with Herbrand base U, and let IT be the set of implication trees over U. Then $I_p \subseteq \bar{U} \times \text{IT} \times 2^U$ is defined by

1. $I_P(A,A,S) \iff A$ is in ground (P), and $A \notin S$.

2. $I_P(A,A \leftarrow T_1 \& \ldots \& T_n, S) \iff A \notin S$, and for some $A \leftarrow B_1 \& \ldots \& B_n \notin$ ground (P) $I_P(B_1, T_1, \{A\} \cup S)$ and$\ldots$and $I_P(B_n, T_n, \{A\} \cup S)$

3. $I_P(\neg A, \neg A, S) \iff$ there does not exist a T such that $I_P(A, T, S)$.

4. Not $I_P(L,T,S)$ whenever $I_P(L,T,S)$ is not in any of the forms given in (1), (2), (3). ∎

The reader should verify that the interpreter constructs the proof tree for p using P_1 as outlined in the previous example. The third argument of I_P carries information for the loop trap.

DEFINITION 19
T is a *proof tree* (w.r.t.P) iff $\exists A[I_P(A, T, \phi)]$. If T is a proof tree with root A, we say that T proves A. ∎

The definition given for I_P is both ambiguous and computationally ineffective if P is left unconstrained. We shall see that the ambiguity vanishes if P is stratified. The noncomputability vanishes under additional constraints. In particular, if P is stratified, then any constraint on P that yields a decidable standard interpretation will result in I_P itself being a decidable relation.

The ambiguity in the definition of I_P lies in the fact that, in general, there is more than one relation on $\bar{U} \times \text{IT} \times 2^U$ that satisfies the definition. We shall demonstrate this difficulty with an example, then prove that the ambiguity essentially vanishes if P is stratified. In the following section we shall show that an unambiguous "bottom-up" inductive definition can be given that defines a unique relation on $\bar{U} \times \text{IT} \times 2^U$ that satisfies the definition of I_P.

EXAMPLE 8
Consider the following program P that is not stratified.

$q(0),$

$p(x) \leftarrow \neg p(s(x)).$

To simplify the notation, let n abbreviate

$\underbrace{s(s(\ldots s(0)\ldots))}_{n \text{ times}}$

Applying the interpreter to $p(0)$ we have

$$I_p(p(0), p(0), \phi) \text{ iff } I_p(\neg p(1), \neg p(1), \{p(0)\}).$$

$$\begin{array}{c} | \\ \neg p(1) \end{array}$$

$$\text{iff not } \exists T[I_p(p(1), T, \{p(0)\})]$$

We therefore have:

$$\begin{array}{ccc} p(0) & & p(1) \\ | & \text{proves } p(0) \text{ iff} & | & \text{is not a proof tree} \\ \neg p(1) & & \neg p(2) \end{array}$$

$$\begin{array}{ccc} & & p(2) \\ \text{iff} & & | & \text{proves } p(2) \\ & & \neg p(3) \end{array}$$

$$\begin{array}{ccc} & & p(3) \\ \text{iff} & & | & \text{is not a proof tree} \\ & & \neg p(4) \end{array}$$

$$\text{iff } \dots \text{ .}$$

Since this chain of equivalences is not terminating, we may suppose that every assertion in the chain is true, or that every assertion in the chain is false. In either case we satisfy the definition of I_p. ∎

EXAMPLE 9
The interpreter that we have given is, in general, meaningful as a terminating *procedure* only in very controlled circumstances; for instance, for function symbol free programs. To see nonterminating behavior on a program with function symbols, consider the stratified program P with the following clauses:

$$p(x) \leftarrow p(s(x)),$$

$$q \leftarrow \neg p(0).$$

In seeking to prove q, I_p costructs

$$\begin{array}{c} q \\ | \\ \neg p(0) \end{array}$$

In seeking to show that there is no proof tree for $p(0)$, I_P constructs the sequence of proof trees

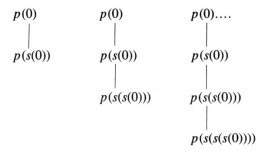

However, the unique relation on $\bar{U}_P \times \text{IT}_P \times 2^{U_P}$ that satisfies the definition of I_P is

$$\{<q, \begin{array}{c} q \\ | \\ \neg p(0) \end{array} ,S>| S \in 2^{U - \{q\}}\}. \quad \blacksquare$$

Next we show that the ambiguity in the definition of I_P essentially vanishes when P is stratified. By "essentially," we mean that when P is stratified, and if R is defined by

$$R(A,S) \iff \exists T [I_P(A,T,S)]$$

then R is uniquely determined. Now, as a matter of fact when P is stratified, the definition of I_P does uniquely determine I_P on $\bar{U} \times \text{IT} \times 2^U$, but it is convenient to defer the proof of this fact until after introducing a "bottom-up" definition for an interpretation of I_P in the next section.

Next we prove a technical lemma about loop-trapping in our interpreter. Note that the interpreter will not apply any rule to a goal A if A is in S. Normally, S is the set of proper ancestors of A. Now suppose that A is defined in stratum k of a program P. Intuitively, our lemma says that we can add to S all ground literals defined in the strata above k, without changing the behavior of the interpreter.

LEMMA 14

Let P be stratified by $P_1 \dot{\cup} ... \dot{\cup} P_n$. Let $V_j = Def_{Q_j}$ where $Q_j = P_j \cup ... \cup P_n$ ($j = 1,...,n$), and let $V_{n+1} = \phi$. For $j = 2,...,n+1$, $S \subseteq V_j$ and T compatible with $P_1 \cup ... \cup P_{j-1}$ the following holds:

$$I_P(\text{root(T)},\text{T},\phi) \iff I_P(\text{root(T)},\text{T},\ S) \tag{1}$$

Proof: Proceed by induction on j ($2 \leq j \leq n$).

$j = 2$: P_1 is a positive program. Since T is compatible with P_1 and $S \subseteq V_2$, no node in T occurs in S. The equivalence (1) follows immediately by a straightforward induction using clauses (1) and (2) in the definition of I_P.

$j \Rightarrow j + 1$: For each implication tree T and node N in T let S_{T_N} be the set of nodes occurring on the path in T from the root to the parent of N. (In particular, $S_{T.\text{root(T)}} = \phi$.) Recall Proposition 1. We proceed by strong induction.

Let T be compatible with $P_1 \dot{\cup} \dots \dot{\cup} P_j$. Then:

$\qquad I_P(\text{root(T)},\text{T},\phi)$

iff (by clauses (1) and (2) in the definition of I_P)

$\qquad I_P(\neg B, \neg B, S_{T,\neg a})$ $\qquad\qquad$ for every negative leaf
$\qquad\qquad\qquad\qquad\qquad\qquad\qquad\qquad$ $\neg B$ of T.

iff (by clause (3) in Definition 18)

$\qquad \text{not } I_P(B,\text{T}',S_{T,\neg B})$ $\qquad\qquad$ for every negative leaf
$\qquad\qquad\qquad\qquad\qquad\qquad\qquad\qquad$ $\neg B$ of T, and implication tree T$'$

iff (since not $I_P(\text{root(T}'), \text{T}',X)$ when T$'$ is not
$\qquad$ compatible with P)

$\qquad \text{not } I_P(B,\text{T}',S_{T,\neg B})$ $\qquad\qquad$ for every negative leaf
$\qquad\qquad\qquad\qquad\qquad\qquad\qquad\qquad$ $\neg B$ of T, and implication tree
$\qquad\qquad\qquad\qquad\qquad\qquad\qquad\qquad$ T$'$ compatible with $P_1 \cup \dots \cup P_k$
$\qquad\qquad\qquad\qquad\qquad\qquad\qquad\qquad$ where P_k is the stratum
$\qquad\qquad\qquad\qquad\qquad\qquad\qquad\qquad$ in which the relation symbol of
$\qquad\qquad\qquad\qquad\qquad\qquad\qquad\qquad$ B is defined.
$\qquad\qquad\qquad\qquad\qquad\qquad\qquad\qquad$ (Note that $k < j$.)

iff (by induction hypothesis, since $S_{T,\neg B} \subseteq V_{k+1}$)
$\qquad \text{not } I_P(B,\text{T}',\phi)$ $\qquad\qquad$ for every B and T$'$ as in
$\qquad\qquad\qquad\qquad\qquad\qquad\qquad\qquad$ the previous step

iff (again, by induction hypothesis)
$\qquad \text{not } I_P(B,\text{T}',S \cup S_{T,\neg B})$ $\qquad\qquad$ for every B, and T$'$ as in the

previous step

iff (by clause (3) of Definition 18)

$I_P(\neg B, \neg B, S \cup S_{T, \neg B})$ for every negative leaf
$\neg B$ of T

iff (by rules (1) and (2) of 18)

$I_P(\text{root}(T), T, S)$. (2) ∎

We now give the theorem that, in effect, says the interpreter unambiguously "computes" the standard model M_P of P, when P is stratified. The statement of the theorem may at first seem a bit arcane, but recall that the definition of I_P does not in general uniquely determine a relation on $\bar{U} \times \text{IT} \times 2^U$. We are about to show, under the assumption that P is stratified, that *if* the definition of I_P is satisfied on $\bar{U} \times \text{IT} \times 2^U$, then I_P does indeed prove precisely those A that are true in the standard model of P. Proving that I_P can be satisfied at all is somewhat harder. This is in part the point of the following section.

THEOREM 13
Let P be stratified. Suppose there is an interpretation of I_P on $\bar{U} \times \text{IT} \times 2^U$ that satisfies the definition of I_P. Under such an interpretation we have the following equivalences for all A in U_P:

1. $\exists T[I_P(A, T, \phi)]$ iff $A \in M_P$.
2. $I_P(\neg A, \neg A, \phi)$ iff $A \notin M_P$.

Proof: P is stratified by $P_1 \cup P_2 \cup \ldots \cup P_n$, for some $P_1, \ldots, P_n$. For each A in U, let r_A be the relation symbol occurring in A. If r_A is a relation symbol in the language in which P is a set of formulas (recall that the language with which P is associated may be larger than the language generated by symbols occurring in P), but r_A does not occur in P, then, by definiton, we shall say r_A is defined in P_1. Otherwise, r_A is defined in one of the P_i.
We proceed by induction on the index j of the stratum in which r_A is defined.

$j = 1$. $A \in M_P$ iff $A \in M_1$. The following equivalence holds:

$A \in T_{P1} \uparrow n(\phi)$ iff

there is a loop-free implication tree T compatible with P
such that height (T) $\leq n$ and $I_P(A, T, \phi)$.

This equivalence follows by an easy induction on n. $M_1 = \bigcup_{n=0}^{\infty} T_{P_1} \uparrow n(\phi)$.

Thus, (1) follows. (2) follows from (1), clause (3) of (18), and that all clauses about r_A are in P_1.

$j \Rightarrow j - 1$. The induction assumption we take is the following assertion. For every A such that r_A is defined in some stratum indexed by $j' \leq j$:

$$\exists T[I_P(A,T,\phi)] \text{ iff } A \in M_{j'},$$

$$\text{and } I_P(\neg A, \neg A, \phi) \text{ iff } A \notin M_{j'}. \tag{3}$$

To complete the proof it suffices to show that

For every A such that r_A is defined in P_{j+1}:

$$\exists T[I_P(A,T,\phi)] \text{ iff } A \in M_{j+1}$$

$$\text{and } I_P(\neg A, \neg A, \phi) \text{ iff } A \notin M_{j=1}. \tag{4}$$

Let $A \in U$ such that r_A is defined in P_{j+1}. If T is an implication tree that is not compatible with P_{j+1}, or $A \neq \text{root}(T)$, then not $I_P(A,T,X)$ for any $X \subseteq 2^U$, since it is easy to see that $I_P(A,T,X)$ is false if T is not compatible with P. Let T be compatible with P_{j+1}, and let $A = \text{root}(T)$. Then:

$I_P(A,T,\phi)$

iff (by clause (1) and (2) of Definition 18)
$\quad I_P(\neg B, \neg B, S_{T,\neg B})$ for every negative leaf $\neg B$ of T

iff (by clause (3) of Definition 18)
$\quad \text{not } I_P(B,T',S_{T,\neg B})$ for every negative leaf $\neg B$
                                      of T, and implication tree T'

iff (by Lemma 14)
$\quad \text{not } I_P(B,T',\phi)$ for every negative leaf
                                  B of T and implication tree T'

iff (by clause (3) of Definition 18)
$\quad I_P(\neg B, \neg B, \phi)$ for every negative leaf B of T

iff (by the induction hypothesis)
$\quad B \notin M_{j'}$ for every negative leaf B of T,
                                  where j' is the index
                                  of the relation symbol of B

So we have

$$I_P(A,T,\phi) \text{ iff} \tag{5}$$

$B \notin M_{j+1}$ for every negative leaf B of T

Now, suppose, $I_P(A,T,\phi)$. By Proposition 1,

$$P_{j+1} \models A \vee B_1 \vee \ldots \vee B_k \tag{6}$$

where $\neg B_i \ldots, \neg B_k$ are all and only the negative leaves of T.

$B_i \notin M_{j+1}$ $(i = 1,\ldots,k)$ by (5),

$M_{j+1} \models A \vee B_1 \vee \ldots \vee B_k$ by Theorem 7 and (6).

Therefore $A \in M_{j+1}$.

Conversely, suppose $A \in M_{j+1}$. Then $A \in T_{P_{j+1}} \uparrow m(M_1)$, for some finite m. A routine induction argument shows that there is an implication tree T (of height $\leq m$) that is compatible with P_{j+1}, has A as its root, and has the property that $B \notin M_j$ for every negative leaf B. Thus, $I_P(A,T,\phi)$. This completes the proof of the theorem. ■

Existence of the Interpreter

In this section we prove that an interpreter satisfying Definition 18 exists when P is a stratified program.

Theorem 13 shows that if the definition if I_P is satisfiable over $\bar{U}_P \times \text{IT} \times 2^{U_P}$, then the set of triples,

$$\{ < A, T, \emptyset > \}$$

in the satisfying relation is uniquely determined. It remains to show that the definition of I_P is, indeed, satisfiable over $\bar{U}_P \times \text{IT} \times 2^{U_P}$. The proof of Theorem 13 is almost sufficient for this purpose. What is lacking is a definition D of a relation R over $\bar{U}_P \times \text{IT} \times 2^{U_P}$ for which D is manifestly uniquely satisfiable and for which R satisfies the definition of I_P. For this purpose it suffices to give D as a "bottom-up" inductive definition.

Suppose that D has been given for R so that

$$\exists T[R(A,T,\emptyset)] \Rightarrow A \in M_P.$$

R itself then serves an an interpreter for stratified programs, and the difficulties concerning the ambiguity inherent in the definition of I_p vanish. Therefore, the objection may be raised that the definition of I_p may be bypassed in the development of our analysis of stratified programs. That is, why should we present two interpreters that are extensionally the same? The objection can be dispelled on two grounds. First, I_p is a "top-down," recursive, backward-chaining interpreter, and it will be seen that R is "bottom-up," inductive, and forward-chaining. Both points of view are independently interesting. Secondly, once we know that I_p presents no logical difficulties in the context of stratified programs, the definition of I_p is concise and simple. We now turn to the construction of R and prove that R satisfies the definition of I_p.

EXAMPLE 10
Let P be

$$q,$$

$$p \leftarrow \neg q.$$

Now,

$$I_p(p, p \leftarrow \neg q, \{q\})$$

follows from the definition of I_p, yet $p \notin M_P$. ∎

Example 10 illustrates that we can prove undesired consequences when starting from nonempty loop traps. The following construction circumvents this difficulty.

DEFINITION 20
If Q is obtained from P by the following construction, we say that Q *is the result of filtering* P *through* S.
Let L be a first-order language. U the Herbrand base of L, and let P be a stratified program in the language L with stratification given by

$$P = P_1 \dot\cup \ldots \dot\cup P_n$$

Let

$$P' = P'_1 \dot\cup \ldots \dot\cup P'_n$$

be the collection of ground instances of clauses in P.

Suppose $S \subseteq U$. Obtain

$$Q = Q_1 \dot{\cup} \ldots \dot{\cup} Q_n$$

from P' by removing all clauses with heads in S. ∎

DEFINITION 21
Let L be a first-order language with Herbrand base U. Let P be a stratified program in the language L with stratification given by

$$P = P_1 \dot{\cup} \ldots \dot{\cup} P_n$$

Let $S \subseteq U$, and let

$$Q^S = Q_1^S \dot{\cup} \ldots \dot{\cup} Q_n^S$$

be the result of filtering P through S.
   Let $A \in U$. Define

$$\text{index } (A) = \begin{cases} 1, \text{ if the relation symbol of } A \text{ is not defined in any stratum of } Q^S, \\ \\ k, \text{ if the relation symbol of } A \text{ is defined in stratum } Q_k^S \end{cases}$$

(Note that Q^S is in general a stratified program consisting of infinitely many ground clauses.) Let $M_1, \ldots, M_n$ be the models of $Q_1^S, \ldots, Q_n^S$ respectively where M_i is obtained from iter $(T_{Q_1^s}, \ldots, T_{Q_1^s}, \phi)$, (thus $M_{Q^S} = M_n$.) Let

   T be *proof tree with respect to S and P* iff

      T is a loop-free implication tree compatible with Q^S, has positive root,

      and for every negative leaf $\neg B$ of T, $B \notin M_{\text{index}(B)}$.

Finally, let R be the relation of $\bar{U} \times \text{IT} \times 2^U$ defined by

   $R(A,T,S) \iff \text{root } (T) = A$ and T is a proof tree with respect to S and
   P

and

   $R(\neg A, \neg A, S) \iff \text{not } R(A,T,S)$ for every implication tree T. ∎

COMMENT
It was claimed above that R would be given as a forward chaining interpreter. Note that R depends on Definition 20 which, in turn, depends on the $Q_1, \ldots, Q_n$.

In effect, we could use Definition 20 to construct proof trees in a "bottom-up" inductive way using $T_{Q_1},\ldots,T_{Q_n}$.

THEOREM 14
R satisfies the definition of I_P.

Proof: The proof is not deep, but for the sake of exposition of what is at stake we nonetheless give it.

Suppose that P, L, U, and S are as in Definition 21. Let $A \in U$, and let T be an implication tree with respect to U. To show that R satisfies the definition of I_P, we must show

$$R(A,T,S) \tag{1}$$

$$\Longleftrightarrow$$

$$T = A \text{ and } A \text{ is in ground}(P) \text{ and } A \notin S \tag{2}$$

or

$$T = A \leftarrow T_1 \&\ldots\&T_k \text{ and } A \notin S \text{ and for some} \tag{3}$$

$$(A \leftarrow B_1 \&\ldots\&B_k) \in \text{ground}(P):$$

$$R(B_1,T_1,\{A\} \cup S) \text{ and}\ldots\text{and } R(B_k,T_k,\{A\} \cup S)$$

and

$$R(\neg A, \neg A, S) \Longleftrightarrow \text{not } \exists T \in \text{IT such that } R(A,T,S). \tag{4}$$

Now, (4) is just a restatement of the second part of the definition of R.

From Definition 21, to show equivalence (1) it suffices to show

$$(2) \text{ or } (3) \text{ iff } T \text{ is a proof tree with respect to } S \text{ and } P, \text{ and root } (T) = A \tag{5}$$

Let Q be the result of filtering P through S. Suppose A is a head of a clause in Q. Let Q' be the result of filtering P through $\{A\} \cup S$. Q' does not differ from Q in strata below that stratum in which A occurs. Moreover, if A does not occur in T, then T is compatible with Q iff T is compatible with Q'.

Let T be an implication tree with positive root over U. There are two cases.

Case 1: $T = A$. Then T is a proof-tree with respect to S and P iff (2).

Case 2: $T = A \leftarrow T_1 \&\ldots\&T_k$. Without loss of generality we may suppose $A \in S$ and that $A \leftarrow \text{root}(T_1)\&\ldots\& \text{root}(T_k) \in \text{ground}(P)$, else both sides of (5) are false.

T is a proof tree w.r.t. S and P

   iff (by Definition 21)

      T is a loop-free implication tree compatible with Q and for every negative leaf $\neg B$ of T, $B \notin M_{index(B)}$, where $M_1,...M_n$ are the standard interpretations of $\bar{Q}_1,...,\bar{Q}_n$ respectively, where $\bar{Q}_i$ denotes $Q_1 \cup ... \cup Q_i$

   iff (since $B \in M_{index(B)}$, iff there is a proof tree w.r.t. S and Q with root B, see below)   (6)

      for each T_i, $i \in \{1,...,k\}$, if root(T_i) is positive, then T_i is a loop-free implication tree compatible with Q, and for every negative leaf $\neg B$ of $T_i, B \notin M_{index(B)}$,

      and

      if root(T_i)is negative, say $\neg C_i>$, then there is no proof tree with respect to S and Q with root C_1

   iff (since Q and Q' do not differ in strata below that in which A is defined)

      for each T_i, $i \in \{1,...,k\}$ if root (T_i) is positive, then T_i, is a loop-free implication tree compatible with Q', and for every negative leaf $\neg B$ of T_i, $B \notin M'_{index(B)}$, (where M'_j is the standard interpretation of Q'_j,$j = 1,...,k$)

      and

      if root (T_i) is negative, say $\neg C_i$, then there is no proof tree w.r.t. $\{A\} \cup S$ and Q' with root C_i, where Q' is the result of filtering P through $\{A\} \cup S$

 iff

      (3) where $B_i = \text{root}(T_i)$, $i \notin \{1,...,k\}$.

Equivalence (6) was justified by

   $B \in M_{index(B)}$ iff there is a proof tree w.r.t. S and Q with root B.

Proof trees with respect to S and Q are loop-free implication trees compatible with S and Q because Q contains no clause head in S. Thus the "if direction" of (6) follows from Proposition 1.

Suppose $B \in M_{index(B)}$. It is easy to show by an inductive construction that there is a loop free implication tree T compatible with Q for which every negative leaf $\neg C$ has the property that $C \notin M_{index(C)}$. Once again, since no clause head in Q occurs in S, T is a proof tree w.r.t. S and Q. ∎

COROLLARY 4

If P is a stratified program, then M_P, the standard model of P, is independent of the stratification of P.

Proof: The corollary follows directly from the statement of Theorem 13 since we have proved that the definition of I_P is satisfiable over $\bar{U} \times \text{IT} \times 2^U$. ∎

We conclude this section with a remark on the computational complexity of I_P. We showed in the previous section that in general I_P by itself does not yield a computation procedure capable of verifying that $A \in M_P$ even when M_P and all the lower stage standard interpretations are uniformly decidable. Nevertheless one of our principal areas of application is that of stratified programs without function symbols. For such programs I_P does indeed determine a useful computation procedure, since the Herbrand base of P is finite. From the point of view of worst case complexity, I_P is no worse than ordinary depth first, SLD-resolution-based interpreters for purely positive programs.

EXAMPLE 11

Let P_3 consist of

$$c_3(0,0,0),$$
$$c_3(X,Y,1) \leftarrow c_3(X,Y,0),$$
$$c_3(X,1,0) \leftarrow c_3(X,0,1),$$
$$c_3(1,0,0) \leftarrow c_3(0,1,1).$$

The goal $(\leftarrow c_3(1,1,1))$ produces a successful SLD path consisting of eight nodes. Similarly, I_{P_3} constructs a proof tree, with $c_3(1,1,1)$ as root of height eight. P_3 causes I_{P_3} as well as SLD-resolution to, in effect, run through a count-down of a 3-bit binary counter. It should be clear how to construct P_n from example P_3. ∎

Now, let P be a positive program in which no function symbols other than constants occur. Suppose P contains r relation symbols, each with arity $\leq a$, and c constants. Let U be the Herbrand base of P. Then

$$\text{size}(U) \leq rc^a,$$

Letting $\| T_P \| = $ least n such that $T_P{\uparrow}(n-1)(\phi) = T_P{\uparrow}n(\phi)$, we have

$$\| T_P \| \leq \text{size}(U).$$

For the programs P_n of example

$$|| \ T_{P_n} \ || = \text{size}(U) = 2^n$$

and both I_P as well as SLD-resolution are forced to, in effect, enumerate all of U when starting with ($\leftarrow c_n(1,...,1)$) as goal. Now, $\text{size}(P_n) = O(n)$. It follows that I_P as well as SLD-resolution require, in the worst case, $O(2^{size(P)})$ steps to succeed. Lastly, note that in our interpreter the loop check need only add a linear time complexity component, because we can represent S as an ordered tree; each path in the tree represents a literal A. Lookup and insertion time of A is $O(length(A))$.

Other Views of Negation and Stratified Programs

Our way of interpreting negation in the case of stratified programs is through choosing M_P as the set of true facts about P. It is helpful to relate this interpretation of negation with two other ones proposed in the literature.

Closed World Assumption (CWA)

Reiter [1978] proposed the *closed world assumption* (CWA) as a way of adding negative information to logic programs. According to this view any (atomic) fact which does not follow from a given program is assumed to be false. Thus by definition

$$CWA = P \cup \{ \neg A : A \text{ is a ground atom and not } P \models A \}.$$

where " $\models$ " stands for provability in first order logic. (Reiter disallowed function symbols but the problems discussed here do not depend on this assumption.)

This view is certainly a natural one when the program is just a collection of facts—if manager(Jones) is not in our database, then we usually conclude that Jones is not a manager. Moreover, Reiter [1978] proved that in the case of positive programs, CWA is consistent. But while trying to extend this view to arbitrary programs somehow our intuitions get lost and, we encounter difficulties (of which Reiter was perfectly aware). Restriction to stratified programs is no help. Consider, for example, the stratified program P: $p \leftarrow \neg q$. Then P is semantically equivalent to $p \lor q$, which implies neither p nor q. Thus, $CWA = P \cup \{ \neg p, \neg q \}$ and is inconsistent. The closed world assumption leads to difficulties here. Negation seems to be too strong when interpreted through CWA: Any uncertainty is resolved in a negative way.

Completions of Programs

Another way of adding negative information to the program is that proposed by Clark [1978] and called the *completion* of a program. His idea was to reinterpret the implications within the program as equivalences. In this way one adds to the program the "only if" part which allows us to infer negative consequences.

More formally the *completion* is defined as follows. (We slightly depart here from the original definition as we omit the equality axioms which are automatically satisified in Herbrand models when "=" is interpreted as identity.)

Let $x_1,\ldots,x_k$, be some variables not appearing in the program. First, transform each clause

$$p(t_1,\ldots,t_k) \leftarrow L_1 \& \ldots \& L_m$$

of P into

$$p(x_1,\ldots,x_k) \leftarrow \exists y_1,\ldots,y_i (x_1 = t_1) \& \ldots \& (x_k = t_k) \& L_1 \& \ldots \& L_m$$

where $y_1,\ldots,y_i$ are the variables of the original clause.

Next, change each set of the transformed clauses of the form

$$p(x_1,\ldots,x_k) \leftarrow S_1,$$

$$\vdots$$

$$p(x_1,\ldots,x_k) \leftarrow S_n,$$

where $n \geq 1$, into

$$\forall x_1,\ldots,x_k p(x_1,\ldots,x_k) \leftrightarrow S_1 \vee \ldots \vee S_n.$$

Then we denote by *comp(P)*, the *completion* of P, the formula consisting of the conjunction of these equivalences and of formulas

$$\forall x_1,\ldots,x_k \neg q(x_1,\ldots,x_k)$$

for each relation q which appears in the program but not in a head of a clause.

We wish to interpret "=" as identity. Therefore, we add the following clause to the definition of semantics: For two variable-free terms $s.t.$ $s = t$ is true in I iff s and t are identical. It is well known (see e.g., Shepherdson [1984]) that for positive programs comp(P) is consistent. We now prove that for stratified programs comp(P) is consistent as well.

In Apt and van Emden [1982] models of comp(P) for a positive program P were characterized as fixed points of T_P. Fortunately, this characterization remains true in the presence of negation. We have

THEOREM 15

Let P be a program. Then I is a model of comp(P) iff $T_P(I) = I$.

Proof: The definition of comp(P) we use is slightly different than those given in Apt and van Emden [1982] (called there the IFF definition) or Lloyd [1984]. Nevertheless, all steps of the (straightforward) proof remain the same. A doubting reader is encouraged to check the proof sketched in Lloyd [1984]. ■

This immediately implies the following theorem.

THEOREM 16

Let P be a stratified program. Then comp(P) is consistent.

Proof: We exhibited in the section on model theory a fixed point of T_P—which is the standard model M_P. Thus, M_P is a model of comp(P) which proves the consistency of *comp(P)*. ■

It is important to note that the views of negation represented by comp(P) and M_P do not coincide. Indeed, consider the stratified program P consisting of

$$p \leftarrow p, q \leftarrow \neg p.$$

Then comp(P) is

$$(p \leftrightarrow p) \ \& \ (q \leftrightarrow \neg p)$$

which is equivalent to $q \longleftrightarrow \neg p$. We thus have that it is not the case that $comp(P) \models \neg p$ whereas $M_P = \{q\}$. Hence $M_P \models \neg p$.

A Discussion

It is useful to have a closer look at the consequences of the fact that we interpret negation by model theoretic means. This implies that each atomic fact about a stratified program P is considered either true (when it belongs to the model M_P) or false (when it does not belong to the model M_P).

This duality does not need to take place when negation is interpreted through proof theoretic means. A common feature of the Clark [1978] and Reiter [1978] approaches to negation is to extend a given program P to a theory, say N_P, in which no new atomic facts can be proved and interpret negation by means of that theory. That is to say, for an atomic fact A

A is true iff $N_P \models A$

A is false iff $N_P \models \neg A$

Now, if N_P is not a complete theory, there is an atomic fact A which is neither true nor false. (We call here a theory T *complete* if for each atomic fact A either $T \models A$ or $T \models \neg A$ but not both.) When N_P is not complete, it is possible to establish a result of the form

A is true in all models of N_P iff A can be computed from P,

A is false in all models of N_P iff $\neg A$ can be computed from P.

In fact, when N_P is comp(P) this is the essence of the "completeness of the negation as failure" result proved in Jaffar, Lassez, and Lloyd [1983].

There, P is a positive program, N_P is *comp(P)*, and the computation mechanism is SLD resolution with negation as failure. More precisely, we have for all atoms A

comp(P) $\models A$ iff $\leftarrow A$ can be refuted from P,

comp(P) $\models \neg A$ iff $\leftarrow \neg A$ can be refuted from P.

(The first line in effect states the completeness of the SLD-resolution originally proved by Hill [1974].) The case when neither comp(P) $\models A$ nor comp(P) $\models \neg A$ is simply not handled: The refutation process then leads neither to success nor to a finite failure, hence it always diverges. Thus, for such A not truth value of A w.r.t. comp(P) is not defined. In such cases, of course, there will be models M_1, M_2 of comp(P) such that $M_1 \models A$, and $M_2 \models \neg A$.

The situation changes when N_P is a complete theory. Then without any restrictions on the syntax we cannot obtain a completeness result *even* in the case of positive programs. Indeed, suppose otherwise. Let W be a recursively enumerable, non-recursive set of natural numbers. By the result of Tärnlund [1977] there exists a positive program P such that for some relation p for all n

$P \models p(n)$ iff $n \in W$.

Since N_P is complete, we have for all n

$N_P \models p(n)$ iff $n \in W$,

$N_P \models \neg p(n)$ iff $n \notin W$.

Indeed, if $n \notin W$, then $P \models p(n)$ so $N_P \models p(n)$ since N_P extends P. And if $n \notin W$, then not $P \models p(n)$ so not $N_P \models p(n)$, since in N_P no new positive facts can be proved. This proves the first line and the second follows by the completeness of N_P.

This has two consequences. First is that the provability in N_P is not recursively enumerable (by the second equivalence) so N_P cannot be recursively axiomatized (see Rogers [1967]). Second, no completeness result for effective computation mechanisms is possible. Indeed, in case of completeness we have for all n

$$n \notin W \text{ iff } N_P \models \neg p(n)$$

$$\text{iff } p(n) \text{ is false}$$

$$\text{iff } \neg p(n) \text{ can be computed from } P$$

so the relation "A can be computed from P" is not recursively enumerable, that is, the computation mechanism is not effective.

An example of an interpretation of negation through a complete theory N_P is Reiter's closed world assumption for positive programs. Indeed, as mentioned in the subsection on the CWA, it is consistent for positive programs, and if not $(P + CWA) \models A$, then not $P \models A$ and consequently $(P + CWA) \models \neg A$. By the above remarks CWA cannot be recursively axiomatized and no completeness result for an effective computation mechanism is possible.

The same negative results hold for our interpretation of negation through the model M_P which acts as a complete theory. Thus, we define

$$A \text{ is true iff } M_P \models A$$

$$A \text{ is false iff not } M_P \models A$$

In general, while it is beyond the scope of this paper to prove it, it can be seen that for a stratified program P containing function symbols and having n strata, M_P can be non-recursively enumerable (in fact Σ_n^0-complete). The proof of this result is based on recursion-theoretic considerations similar to that of Blair [1982]. Thus, no effective procedure for computing M_P in general is possible.

The above discussion does not exclude a completeness result for stratified programs and the negation interpreted through Clark's completed database. We established the first, necessary, step by showing that for a stratified program P, comp(P) is consistent but we did not explore the issue any further. A warning should be issued to those wishing to investigate this problem. The following examples show that no completeness result w.r.t. comp(P) for SLD-resolution with negation as failure (called the SLDNF-resolution) or for our interpreter is possible.

EXAMPLE 12

Let P be the following program:

$p \leftarrow p,$

$q \leftarrow p,$

$q \leftarrow \neg p.$

Then P is stratified and comp(P) is equivalent to $(q \leftrightarrow p \lor \neg p)$, so *comp*($P$) $\models q$. On the other hand, there is no refutation of $\leftarrow q$ using SLDNF-resolution.

EXAMPLE 13

Let P be the following stratified program:

$p \leftarrow p,$

$q \leftarrow \neg p.$

Then comp(P) is equivalent to $q \leftrightarrow \neg p$ so not *comp*(P) $\models q$. However, our interpreter computes q. ∎

Thus, some other computation mechanisms have to be considered. On the other hand, we have the following conjecture.

DEFINITION 22

Let P be a program and p, q two relation symbols of P.

1. We say that p *depends positively* on q if p depends on q and in the dependency graph of P there is at least one path from p to q which contains exactly an even number (possibly 0) of negative edges.

2. We say the p *depends negatively* on q if p depends on q and in the dependency graph of P there is at least one path from p to q which contains exactly an odd number of negative edges.

3. We say that P is *strict* if for no relation symbols p and q of P, p depends both positively and negatively on q. ∎

DEFINITION 23

Let P be a program. Given a clause of P let

X stand for the set of the variables occurring on its left hand side.

Y for the set of the variables occurring in a positive literal of the body and

Z for the set of the variables occurring in a negative literal of the body.

We say that P satisfies the *strong covering axiom* if for each of its clauses

$$X \subseteq Y$$

and

$$Z \subseteq Y$$

holds. ∎

The first implication is called in Shepherdson [1984] the *covering axiom*. The strong covering axiom ensures that in the SLDNF-resolution only *ground* negative literals need be evaluated. We can now formulate our conjecture.

CONJECTURE 1
Let P be a strict stratified program which satisfies the strong covering axiom. Then for every ground literal L.

comp(P) $\models$ L iff $\dashv L$ can be refuted from P by SLDNF-resolution. ∎

(*Note*: Conjecture 1 was recently proved by Cavedon and Lloyd. Subsequently Kunen showed that the result holds even for non-stratified programs.)

Related Work

Syntax

As already mentioned in the introduction, stratified programs form a simple generalization of the class of formulas C given in section 5 of Chandra and Harel [1985], in which negation is handled in a similar, stratified way. The difference lies in the way the strata are related—for technical reasons, in their paper this is accomplished by additional relations which take care of the calls involving negative literals. Also, our class of semi-positive programs coincides with their class H'_j but they are concerned with different issues than we are and concentrate on the subject of definability of database queries. In particular, they do not allow function symbols.

Stratified programs were also introduced and studied independently in a recent paper of Van Gelder [1988] and, in the context of databases, in Naqvi [1986]. A form of stratification for logic programming without negation was first introduced by Sebelik and Stepanek [1982]. Our definition of stratified programs is a generalization of the concept of the *hierarchical constraint* of Clark [1978] according to which program relations can be assigned to levels so that each relation is defined only in terms of relations from the lower levels. The hierarchical constraint, in contrast to the stratificiation condition, rules out recursive definitions. In fact if we remove negation from the language, then programs reduce to positive programs. If we remove recursion from the language, then they reduce to programs with the hierarchical constraint. The notion of stratified programs has been further generalized to *locally stratified programs* in Przymusinski [1988].

Lloyd and Topor [1985] give a theoretical basis for deductive databases using PROLOG as the query evaluator. They show in particular that SLDNF-resolution does not *flounder* (does not reach a goal that contains only non-ground negative literals) with general programs and goals provided the program and goal is *allowed*. The concept of being *allowed* as applied to clauses is equivalent to our *strong covering axiom*.

Semantics

The semantics of logic programs with negation based on fixed points is a generalization of the approach originating with van Emden and Kowalski [1976] and further explored in Apt and van Emden [1982]. Chandra and Harel [1985] provide in an informal way a semantics for their class C of programs which corresponds to our model M_P where the partition of P is into appropriately ordered clusters.

An early approach to provide meaning to logic programs with negation was given by Minker [1982] in the context of deductive databases. For this purpose, he introduced the concept of a generalized closed world assumption (GCWA). Its semantic characterization employs minimal models.

The notion of minimality arises in many other studies of nonmonotonic reasoning as well—see e.g., the notion of *circumscription* due to McCarthy [1980]. In fact, recent work of Lifschitz [1988] provides an alternative definition of the model M_P in terms of a circumscription. His approach leads to a simpler proof of Theorem 11.

The notion of a supported model has also been introduced independently in Bidoit and Hull [1986] and called there a *causal model*. Przymusinski [1988] introduced the concept of a *perfect model* of a database and related it to circumscription and semantics of stratified databases. Stratified databases were recently studied in Apt and Pugin [1987], Lloyd, Sonenberg, and Topor [1986], and Topor and Sonenberg [1988].

Completeness Results in the Presence of Negation

In Clark [1978], a completeness result for programs with the hierarchical constraint is sketched. It relates completed programs with SLD-resolution with negation as failure. A rigorous proof is given in Shepherdson [1984]. Another completeness result is that of Jaffar, Lassez and Lloyd [1983] mentioned in the previous section but only for positive programs. See also Aquilano et al. [1986] for a completeness result in the presence of negation and absence of divergence ensured by syntactic criteria. A recent paper of Shepherdson [1988] provides an extensive overview of the use of negation in logic programming.

Nonmonotonic Reasoning

An entire issue of the journal *Artificial Intelligence* [1980] has been published on the subject and a conference organized (Proceedings [1984]). Gabbay [1985] provides a useful discussion of the problem of when a reasoning method can be viewed as a nonmonotonic logic. Our approach based on search for fixed points of nonmonotonic operators is very similar in nature to the one recently proposed by Sandewall [1985].

Interpreters and Other Computation Mechanisms

Our treatment of a computation mechanism in the form of an interpreter relates to the approach taken by Brough and Walker [1984], who studied interpreters with various stopping criteria for positive database-like programs.

Barbuti and Martelli [1986] prove the completeness of SLDNF-resolution for a sizeable class of naturally occurring logic programs called *structured* programs. Structured programs form a set of stratified programs.

Recently, Fitting [1985] and Gallier and Raatz [1987] proposed alternative computation mechanisms for logic programming based on, respectively, a tableau method and an interpreter using graph reduction.

Use of Logic Programming for Expert Systems

Walker [1986a] described an implemented expert system shell in Walker [1986a], called Syllog, which is based on logic programming. Syllog contains an inference engine that computes with database-like programs with negation allowed.

One of the important aspects of expert systems is the ability to reason in terms of uncertainty. Recently van Emden [1986] extended the results of Apt and van Emden [1982] to the case when the facts and rules have some certainty factor associated with them. His work can be viewed as orthogonal to ours.

Acknowledgment

We thank Ashok Chandra for helpful comments on the subject of this paper.

References

1. Aquilano, C., Barbuti, R., Bocchetti, P., and Martelli, M. [1986] Negation as Failure: Completeness of the Query Evaluation Process for Horn Clause Programs with Recursive Definitions, *Journal of Automated Reasoning* **2**, 155–170.

2. *Artificial Intelligence* [1980] **13**(1).

3. Apt, K. R. and Emden, M. H. van [1982] Contributions to the Theory of Logic Programming, *JACM* **29**(3):841–862.

4. Apt, K. R. and Pugin, J. M. [1987] Maintenance of Stratified Databases Viewed as a Belief Revision System, in *Proc. of the 6th ACM Symposium on Principles of Database Systems*, San Diego, CA, 136–145.

5. Blair, H. A. [1982] Recursion Theoretic Complexity of the Semantics of Predicate Logic as a Programming Language, *Information and Control* **54**, 25–46.

6. Bidoit, N. and Hull, R. [1986] Positivism Versus Minimalism in Deductive Databases, *Proc. of the 5th ACM SIGACT-SIGMOD Symposium on Principles of Database Systems*, Cambridge, MA, 123–132.

7. Barbuti, R. and Martelli, M. [1986] Completeness of the SLDNF-Resolution for a Class of Logic Programs, *Proc. of the 3rd International Conference on Logic Programming*, Lecture Notes in Computer Science, No. 227, Springer-Verlag, Berlin, 600–613.

8. Brough, D. and Walker, A. [1984] Some Practical Properties of Logic Programming Interpreters, *Proc. of the Japan FGCS84 Conference*, 149–156.

9. Cavedon, L. and Lloyd, J. W. [1987] Completeness Results for SLDNF-Resolution, Tech. Rep. 87/9, Dept. of Computer Science, Melbourne University.

10. Clark, K. L. [1978] Negation as Failure, in *Logic and Databases* (H. Gallaire and J. Minker, Eds.), Plenum Press, New York, 293–322.

11. Chandra, A. and Harel, D. [1985] Horn Clause Queries and Generalizations, *The Journal of Logic Programming* **2**(1):1–5.

12. Emden, M. H. van [1986] Quantitative Deduction and Its Fixpoint Theory, *Journal of Logic Programming* **3**(1):37–54.

13. Emden, M. H. van and Kowalski, R. A. [1976] The Semantics of Predicate Logic as a Programming Language, *JACM* **23**(4):733–742.

14. Fitting, M. [1985] Logic Programming Based on Logic, manuscript, Dept. of Math. and Computer Science, Lehman College, Bronx, NY.

15. Gabbay, D. [1985] Theoretical Foundations for Non-monotonic Reasoning in Expert Systems, in *Logics and Models of Concurrent Systems* (K. R. Apt, Ed.), Springer-Verlag, 439–458.

16. Gallier, J. and Raatz, S. [1988] A Graph-based Interpreter for General Horn Clauses, *Journal of Logic Programming*.

17. Hill, R. [1974] LUSH-Resolution and Its Completeness, *DCl Memo 78*, Department of Artificial Intelligence, University of Edinburgh.

18. Jaffar, J., Lassez, J.-L., and Lloyd, J. W. [1983] Completeness of the Negation as a Failure Rule, *IJCAI-83*, 500–506.

19. Kowalski, R. A. [1974] Predicate Logic as a Programming Language, *IFIP 74*, 569–574.

20. Kunen, K. [1987] Signed Data Dependencies in Logic Programs, Computer Sciences Technical Report 719, University of Wisconsin.

21. Lifschitz, V. [1988] On the Declarative Semantics of Logic Programs with Negation, in *Foundations of Deductive Databases and Logic Programming* (J. Minker, Ed.), Morgan Kaufmann, Publishers, Los Altos, CA, 177–192.

22. Lloyd, J. W. [1984] *Foundations of Logic Programming*, Springer-Verlag.

23. Lloyd, J. W., Sonenberg, E. A., and Topor, R. W. [1986] Integrity Constraint Checking in Stratified Databases, *Technical Report 86/5*, Dept. of Computer Science, University of Melbourne.

24. Lloyd, J. W. and Topor, R. W. [1985] A Basis for Deductive Database Systems II, *Journal of Logic Programming*, 3(1):55–67.

25. McCarthy, J. [1980] Circumscription—A Form of Nonmonotonic Reasoning, *Artificial Intelligence* 13(1):295–323.

26. Minker, J. [1982] On Indefinite Databases and the Closed World Assumption, *Proc. of the 6th Conference on Automated Deduction* (D. W. Loveland, Ed.), Lecture Notes in Computer Science 138, Springer-Verlag, Berlin, 292–308.

27. Naqvi, S. A. [1986] A Logic for Negation in Database Systems, in *Proc. of the Workshop on Foundations of Deductive Databases and Logic Programming*, Washington, DC, 378–387

28. *Proc. of the AAAI Workshop on Non-monotonic Reasoning* [1984].

29. Przymusinski, T. [1988] On the Semantics of Stratified Deductive Databases, in *Foundations of Deductive Databases and Logic Programming* (J. Minker, Ed.), Morgan Kaufmann Publishers, Los Altos, CA, 193–216.

30. Reiter, R. [1978] On Closed World Data Bases, in *Logic and Databases* (H. Gallaire and J. Minker, Eds.), Plenum Press, New York, 55–76.

31. Rogers, H. Jr. [1967] *Theory of Recursive Functions and Effective Computability*, McGraw-Hill.

32. Sandewall, E. [1985] A Functional Approach to Non-monotonic Logic, *IJCAI-85*, 100–106.

33. Sebelik, J. and Stepanek, P. [1982] Horn Clause Programs for Recursive Functions, in *Logic Programming* (K. Clark and S.-A. Tärnlund, Eds.), Academic Press, 325–340.

34. Shepherdson, J. C. [1984] Negation as Failure: A Comparison of Clark's Completed Data Base and Reiter's Closed World Assumption, *Journal of Logic Programming* **1**(1):51–81.

35. Shepherdson, J. C. [1985] Negation as Failure II, *Journal of Logic Programming* **2**(2):185–202.

36. Shepherdson, J. C. [1988] Negation in Logic Programming, in *Foundations of Deductive Databases and Logic Programming* (J. Minker, Ed.), Morgan Kaufmann Publishers, Los Altos, CA, 19–88.

37. Tärnlund, S. A. [1977] Horn Clause Compatibility, *BIT* **17**, 215–226.

38. Tarski, A. [1955] A Lattice-theoretical Fixpoint Theorem and Its Applications, *Pacific J. Math.* **5**, 285–309.

39. Topor, R. and Sonenberg, E. A. [1988] On Domain Independent Databases, in *Foundations of Deductive Databases and Logic Programming* (J. Minker, Ed.), Morgan Kaufmann Publishers, Los Altos, CA, 217–240.

40. Van Gelder, A. [1988] Negation as Failure Using Tight Derivations for General Logic Programs, in *Foundations of Deductive Databases and Logic Programming* (J. Minker, Ed.), Morgan Kaufmann Publishers, Los Altos, CA, 149–176.

41. Walker, A. [1986a] Syllog: An Approach to Prolog for Non-programmers, in *Logic Programming and Its Applications* (M. VanCaneghem and D.H.D. Warren, Eds.), Ablex, 32–49.

42. Walker, A. [1986b] A Knowledge Systems: Principles and Practice, *IBM Journal Res. Develop* **30**(1):2–13.

Chapter

3

Negation as Failure Using Tight Derivations for General Logic Programs

Allen Van Gelder

Stanford University
Stanford, CA

Abstract

A general logic program is a set of rules that have both positive and negative subgoals. We define negation in general logic programs as finite failure, but we limit proof attempts to *tight* derivations, that is, derivations expressed by trees in which no node has an identical ancestor. Consequently, many goals that do not fail finitely in other formulations do fail finitely in ours. Thus the negation-as-failure rule is strengthened, but at the cost of more careful (and expensive) program execution. We define the *tight tree semantics* as a pair of interpretations, *SS*, interpreted as the success set, and *FS*, interpreted as the failure set. We show that general logic programs with both the *bounded term size* property and *freedom from recursive negation* are "categorical" under the tight tree semantics; that is, every atom in the Herbrand base of the program is either in *SS* or *FS*. Then we show that programs with these properties have an equivalent *iterated fixed point semantics*, which has been studied by other researchers.

Introduction

Negation as failure has been studied extensively as a means of extending the power of logic programming without taking on the burden of full-fledged non-

Horn resolution. The negation-as-failure rule was introduced by Clark [1978] and is closely related to the *closed world assumption* of Reiter [1978]. A rigorous treatment of the Horn clause case, in which rules have only positive subgoals but the query may contain negative subgoals, may be found in Apt and van Emden [1982]. General logic programs, in which rules may also have negative subgoals, have been studied in Lloyd [1984], Le [1985a, 1985b], Shepherdson [1985, 1988], Naish [1985], Jaffar et al. [1986] and elsewhere (see Le [1985a] and Shepherdson [1985, 1988] for further bibliography).

We develop a semantics for general logic programs that is based upon the use of *tight* derivations. We say a derivation tree is *tight* if no node is identical to one of its own ancestors. Requiring tightness is a technique for avoiding redundant proofs (and nonterminating searches) while maintaining completeness that has been exploited in the theorem-proving community (Loveland [1978]).

Many of the infinite recursions for which Prolog is infamous can be avoided by requiring derivations to be tight. The necessary checking is generally not done because of the overhead and because it is unnecessary in many programs. The usability of Prolog would be considerably increased by the development of algorithms both to detect the danger of infinite recursion at "compile time" and to execute the program in a way that enforces tightness, yet is reasonably efficient. This is one of the research objectives of the Nail! project at Stanford University (Morris et al. [1986]). (Nail! stands for "Not *another* implementation of logic!") This paper takes a first step in that direction by defining an appropriate semantics for negation as failure using tight derivations.

Another problem with negation as failure is that some goals "slip through the cracks," in the sense that they neither succeed nor fail finitely. We define two properties of logic programs that "close up" these cracks. The *bounded term size* property ensures that no tight derivation tree has an infinite path, and *freedom from recursive negation* ensures that no two goals can "deadlock," each waiting for the other to fail. One of our main results is that programs with both these properties are "completely evaluated" by our semantics, in the sense that every goal is in either the success set or the failure set. Furthermore, when the bounded term size property is supplemented by a known bounding function, $f(n)$, it is decidable whether any goal in the Herbrand base succeeds or fails.

For programs with the two key properties, the bounded term size property and freedom from recursive negation, our second main result is that these programs have an equivalent *iterated fixed point semantics*. The iterated fixed point semantics can be formulated as truth in a certain circumscription theory (Lifschitz [1988]), and is thought by several researchers to be the "natural" interpretation for a general logic program (Apt et al. [1988], Lifschitz [1988], Morris et al. [1986], Topor and Sonenberg [1988]); we shall give some examples to support this view.

General Logic Programs and Safe Negation

In this section we introduce our notation and basic definitions and describe the class of general logic programs that we shall be considering in this paper. We define safe negation and exclude programs with unsafe negation from further consideration.

DEFINITION 1

A *general logic program* is a set of *general rules* that may have both positive and negative subgoals. A goal consists of a predicate symbol with terms as arguments, and may also be thought of as an atomic formula, or *atom*. A general rule is written with its *head*, or conclusion on the left, and its subgoals, if any, to the right of the symbol " $\leftarrow$," which may be read "if." For example,

$$p(X) \leftarrow a(X), \; \neg b(X).$$

in which $p(X)$ is the head, $a(X)$ is a positive subgoal, and $b(X)$ is a negative subgoal. The above rule also represents the *disjunctive clause*

$$p(X) \lor \neg a(X) \lor b(X)$$

A rule with no subgoals corresponds to a *positive unit clause*. (*Negative unit clauses* cannot occur in the program but can be derived and then used for further derivations.) A *Horn rule* is one with no negative subgoals, and a *Horn logic program* is one with only Horn rules. ∎

We shall be considering atoms in the Herbrand base and ground rules (clauses) whose variables have been instantiated to elements of the Herbrand universe. Whenever the term "ground" is used, it is intended to mean that every term is in the Herbrand universe.

DEFINITION 2

The *Herbrand instantiation* of a general logic program is the set of rules obtained by substituting terms in the Herbrand universe for variables in every possible way. An *instantiated logic program* is any subset of a Herbrand instantiation. Whereas "uninstantiated" logic programs are assumed to be a finite set of rules, instantiated logic programs may well be infinite. ∎

For simplicity in our discussion, we exclude equality ($=$) from the language. The extension to include equality is straightforward, following the methods presented in van Emden and Lloyd [1984] and Le [1985b]. However, to pave the way for such an extension we shall say two terms or atoms *match* if they are unifiable. Also, we say a ground atom *appears in* a set if it matches an atom in the set. In our discussion, *match* is a synonym for *unifiable*; ground terms or atoms match if and only if they are identical. In an extension that includes equality, ground terms or atoms *match* if they are equal in the appropriate equality theory.

Safe and Unsafe Negation

Unsafe negation is essentially complementation with respect to an ill-defined domain. Informally, unsafe negation occurs when we try to solve a negative subgoal containing free variables; we discuss some examples before giving a formal definition. Safe negation is similar to various other concepts, including "sound negation" (Naish [1985]), "safe formulas" in relational calculus (Ullman [1980]), and "domain independent databases" (Topor and Sonenberg [1988]).

One trivial source of unsafe negation can be eliminated syntactically. To avoid ambiguity in the quantification of a variable, we shall require that any variable that appears in a negative subgoal must also appear in the head of the rule or in a positive subgoal, thereby confirming that the variable is universally quantified at the scope of the entire rule. This involves no loss of generality, as rules may always be rewritten using the technique of *projection* to ensure that no variable appears only in negative subgoals.

EXAMPLE 1
Consider a program P_1 consisting of the following rather natural-appearing rule:

$$bachelor(X) \leftarrow male(X), \neg married(X,Y).$$

If Y is considered universally quantified at the scope of the rule, and this quantifier is pushed down, it becomes a universal quantifier immediately above the atom $married(X,Y)$. However, in Prolog, Y is necessarily free when the goal $? - married(X, Y)$ is undertaken, and so is existentially quantified, in effect. To avoid this source of confusion we shall insist that the rule be rewritten, e.g., as the pair of rules P'_1:

$$married1(X) \leftarrow married(X,Y).$$

$$bachelor(X) \leftarrow male(X), \neg married1(X). \quad \blacksquare$$

A more troublesome problem with unsafe negation arises when some subgoals can succeed without binding their arguments to ground terms.

EXAMPLE 2

Let $\mathbf{P}_2$ be the program

$p(X) \leftarrow a(X), d(X,Y).$

$d(X,Y) \leftarrow s(X,X), s(Y,Y), \neg s(X,Y).$

$s(U,U).$

$a(1).$

The subgoals $s(X,X)$ and $s(Y,Y)$ in the rule for d are not necessary but are included to emphasize the point that a program may be unsafe for negation even if every variable in a negative subgoal also appears in a positive subgoal. In the rule-based semantics, *SS* contains only $a(1)$ and $s(1,1)$, while $d(1,1)$ and $p(1)$ are in *FS*. However, adding the apparently unrelated fact $b(2)$ to the program means that now $d(1,2)$ is in *SS*, and so $p(1)$ switches from *FS* to *SS*. Such bizarre behavior is clearly undesirable in a practical system. ■

A detailed treatment of this problem is beyond the scope of this paper. The main idea is that in the example above, the Herband universe is not a sufficiently large domain of interpretation. (See Maher [1988] for related discussion.) Operationally, we want the negative subgoal $\neg d(1,Y)$ in the above example to succeed unless $d(1,Y)$ can ''succeed without binding Y.'' In general the problem is harder, and complex representations of goals are needed along the lines introduced in Lassez and Marriot [1986]. However, to avoid these issues, we shall deal only with logic programs that are safe for negation in the remainder of this paper. In order to define this term, we first need to define top-down-positive derivations.

DEFINITION 3

For our purposes, a *top-down-positive derivation* is a sequence $C_0,\ldots,C_n$ of conjunctive clauses made up of positive and negative subgoals. (Each conjunctive clause is the logical negative of a disjunctive clause in which positive subgoals become negative literals, and *vice versa*. The operation we describe is clearly equivalent to resolution on the corresponding disjunctive clauses.) C_0 is the top-level goal or goals. Each new clause C_{k+1} is formed from C_k by selecting a positive subgoal p in C_k and matching it with the head of some rule R to which θ_{k+1} has been applied. The substitution θ_{k+1} must leave C_k unchanged and must be a most general substitution that permits the remainder of the derivation to be performed. (See example below.) Then C_{k+1} consists of C_k with p removed and the subgoals of $R\theta_{k+1}$ added. A *positive-complete derivation* is a top-down-positive derivation in which the last clause has no positive subgoals. ■

DEFINITION 4

A general logic program is *safe for negation* if every top-down-positive derivation has the property that any variable in a negative subgoal is also in some positive subgoal of the same derived clause or in the top-level clause. ∎

The essential property of programs that are safe for negation is that whenever the top-level clause of a positive-complete derivation is variable free (ground), then so is the last clause, which contains only negative subgoals (or is empty). We see that this is not the case in $\mathbf{P}_2$ above because there is a positive-complete derivation that begins with $p(1)$ and ends with $\neg s(1,Y)$. However, experience with practical logic programs suggests that they usually are safe for negation.

One approach is to require that every variable in a rule appears in a positive subgoal (Apt et al. [1988], Topor and Sonenberg [1988]). It is clear that this ensures that the program is safe for negation, but it eliminates many "workhorse" routines of logic programming, such as

member(X, X.R).

member(X, Y.R) ← *member(X, R).*

A less restrictive syntactic condition that ensures safety for negation would be useful, but it is not easy to find. An algorithm that identifies a large class of safe-for-negation programs will appear in a future report and will be incorporated into the Nail! system.

Rule-based Negation-as-Failure Semantics

In this section we describe informally the semantics of general logic programs with negation as failure interpreted as the "traditional" finite failure (Clark [1978], Apt and van Emden [1982], Jaffar et al. [1983], Lloyd [1984]). The corresponding proof mechanism is frequently called *SLDNF resolution*. After defining the rule-based semantics, we discuss its connection with SLDNF resolution.

Informally, the rule-based semantics can be thought of as the theory (set of derivable ground clauses) corresponding to a proof system with these derivation rules:

1.   Resolve a (positive or negative) unit clause with a *subgoal* of a non-unit clause, deriving a smaller clause.

2. Remove subsumed clauses. (Recall that a clause is *subsumed* if another derived clause consists of a subset of its literals.)

3. If no rule head matches atom p, conclude $\neg p$.

where the proof system is applied to the Herbrand instantiation of a general logic program. As unit clauses are derived, they are collected in *SS* (if positive) and *FS* (if negative). See Figure 2 for an example.

For a given general logic program **P**, we shall be concerned with three kinds of sets: *success sets* (SS_k), *failure sets* (FS_k), and *remaining rules sets* (RR_k). To begin, we define $SS_0 = FS_0 = \emptyset$, and define RR_0 to be the Herbrand instantiation of **P**. For any ordinal k,[1] suppose we have three sets: SS_k, FS_k, and RR_k.

- SS_k is a set of atoms that are considered **true**.
- FS_k is a set of atoms that are considered **false**.
- RR_k is an instantiated logic program.

We define the triple $(SS_{k+1}, FS_{k+1}, RR_{k+1})$ in terms of (SS_k, FS_k, RR_k) by means of a transformation Φ, which we now describe. First create SS_{k+1} and FS_{k+1} by adding atoms to SS_k and FS_k, if possible, as follows:

- Initialize SS_{k+1} to SS_k. For each rule in RR_k with no subgoals, add the head of that rule to S_{k+1} (unless it already appears there).

- Initialize FS_{k+1} to FS_k. For each atom in the Herbrand base that matches the head of no rule in RR_k, add that atom to FS_{k+1} (unless it already appears there). When k is a successor ordinal, it is sufficient to consider only atoms that matched the head of some rule in RR_{k-1} (instead of the whole Herbrand base).

Now create RR_{k+1} by modifying RR_k as follows:

- Initialize RR_{k+1} to RR_k.

- Delete each rule in RR_{k+1} that has a positive subgoal in FS_{k+1} or has a negative subgoal in SS_{k+1}; these rules can never succeed.

---

[1] The semantics of general logic programs requires transfinite ordinals, $0,1,2,3,...,\omega, \omega + 1,$ $\omega + 2, \omega + 3,...,2\omega, 2\omega + 1,....$ A *successor* ordinal is one that has a greatest ordinal less than half itself, such as $1,2,\omega + 1$, etc. *Limit* ordinals lack this property, such as $\omega,2\omega$, etc.

- In each remaining rule in RR_{k+1}, delete all positive subgoals that appear in SS_{k+1} and delete all negative subgoals that appear in FS_{k+1}; these subgoals are considered proved and the rules "shrink" accordingly.

This completes the description of the transformation $\Phi(SS_k, FS_k, RR_k)$. Figure 2 illustrates the operation of Φ.

For each limit ordinal α, we define

$$SS_\alpha = \bigcup_{\beta < \alpha} SS_\beta \qquad FS_\alpha = \bigcup_{\beta < \alpha} FS_\beta \qquad RR_\alpha = \bigcap_{\beta < \alpha} RR_\beta.$$

Let Ω be the least nonconstructive ordinal, and define

$$SS = \bigcup_{\beta < \Omega} SS_\beta \qquad FS = \bigcup_{\beta < \Omega} FS_\beta.$$

Also, we say an atom in the Herbrand universe is *unclassified* if it is in neither SS nor FS.

DEFINITION 5

The *rule-based negation-as-failure semantics* (*rule-based semantics* for short) for a general logic program is the pair of sets (SS, FS) that is derived from SS_0, FS_0, RR_0, and the transformation Φ, as described above. Also, the "meaning of the logic program" with respect to the rule-based semantics is that atoms in SS are true, atoms in FS are false, and atoms in neither SS nor FS are unclassified. ∎

For integer k it is easy to see that each atom in SS_k has an SLDNF derivation of depth at most k and each atom in FS_k has failed finitely at that depth, in the sense of Apt and van Emden [1982] and Lloyd [1984]. Examples where transfinite ordinals play a role are given in Apt and van Emden [1982] and Jaffar et al. [1983].

The rule-based semantics is appealing for its uniformity and simplicity. Nevertheless, it can lead to some counter-intuitive results, as shown in the next section.

Counter-Intuitive Meanings of Rule-based Semantics

Rule-based semantics may give counter-intuitive meanings in several ways. We identify two categories of problems as *failure to fail* and *indefinite case*.

Failure to fail leads into the principal work of this paper. The *indefinite case* is related to *failure to fail*.

Failure to Fail

There are certain programs where it is obvious to a person that certain facts are unprovable, but the rule-based semantics does not put them into *FS*. In many cases they are related to Prolog's well known "left recursion loops."

EXAMPLE 3

Suppose we have a directed graph with two kinds of arcs, "bad" arcs (represented by *b*) and "good" arcs (represented by *g*). We want to define the following relations on the graph:

p(X,Y) A "poor" path is a sequence of "bad" arcs from X to Y.

e(X,Y) An "excellent" arc from X to Y is a "good" arc from X to Y such that there is no "poor" path from X to Y.

a(X,Y) Finally, we define Y to be "accessible" from X if there is a sequence of "excellent" arcs from X to Y.

The foregoing definitions are apparently expressed by the program $\mathbf{P}_3$ containing the following rules:

$p(X,Y) \leftarrow b(X,Y).$

$p(X,Y) \leftarrow b(X,U),\ p(U,Y).$

$e(X,Y) \leftarrow g(X,Y),\ \neg p(X,Y).$

$a(X,Y) \leftarrow e(X,Y).$

$a(X,Y) \leftarrow e(X,U),\ a(U,Y).$

Now suppose that the facts about b and g arcs are:

$b(1,2)\ \ g(2,3)$

$b(2,1)\ \ g(3,2)$

$b(3,4)$

$b(4,3)$

as suggested by Figure 1. The rule-based semantics with this program will duly compute *SS* that includes

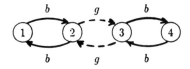

Figure 1: Directed Graph Discussed in Example 3

$$\{p(1,1), \ p(1,2), \ p(2,1), \ p(2,2),$$
$$p(3,3), \ p(3,4), \ p(4,3), \ p(4,4)\}$$

but it will leave e and a completely unclassified. The problem is that atoms like $p(1,3)$ and $p(2,3)$ cannot be put into FS_α for any ordinal α. This is because of the loop expressed by

$$p(1,3) \leftarrow b(1,2), \ p(2,3).$$
$$p(2,3) \leftarrow b(2,1), \ p(1,3).$$

Consequently, $e(2,3)$, among others, is never put into either SS or FS. ∎

Indefinite Case

In Example 3, the SS produced by the rule-based semantics was not a model, but it did represent the intersection of all models.[2] Here we show that SS very well may not be even that large; that is, there may be facts that are in all models, but are not put into SS by the rule-based semantics.

EXAMPLE 4
Let $\mathbf{P}_4$ be a program with the rules

$$p(X) \leftarrow a(X), \ c(X).$$
$$p(X) \leftarrow \neg a(X), \ d(X).$$
$$a(X) \leftarrow b(X).$$
$$b(X) \leftarrow a(X).$$

together with the facts:

$$c(1). \quad c(2). \quad d(2). \quad d(3).$$

---

[2] By *model* we shall always mean *Herbrand model*.

We observe that $p(2)$ is in all models. However, the rule-based semantics leaves a, and hence p, completely unclassified. The problem is that one of the cases $set\{a(2), \neg a(2)\}$ must hold but the semantics is not powerful enough to use this information. ∎

Tree-oriented Semantics for Negation as Failure

In this section we consider semantics in which remaining rules sets (RR_k) are replaced by sets of "remaining proof trees." First we define a *simple tree semantics* that is equivalent to the rule semantics of Definition 5 in the sense that it produces the same SS_k and FS_k. Then we propose a modification called the *tight tree semantics* that provides a strengthened form of finite failure.

Simple Tree Semantics

The simple tree negation-as-failure semantics is defined analogously to rule-based semantics with sets of remaining NF-trees (RT_k) replacing the sets of remaining rules.

DEFINITION 6
Given an instantiated general logic program RR_0, a *negation-as-failure derivation tree based on RR_0* (NF-tree for short) is a (possibly infinite) tree whose nodes are one of:

- a positive atom in the Herbrand base, which may have children;
- a negated atom in the Herbrand base, which must be a leaf;
- the constant *failed*, which is considered to be neither an atom nor a negated atom for our purposes, and must be a leaf.

For each internal node, either it has a *failed* child or there is some instantiated rule in RR_0 such that:

- The internal node matches the head of the instantiated rule.
- The children of the internal node can be placed in a one-to-one correspondence with matching subgoals of the rule (including the positive or negative polarity).

A *complete* NF-tree is one with no *failed* nodes. ∎

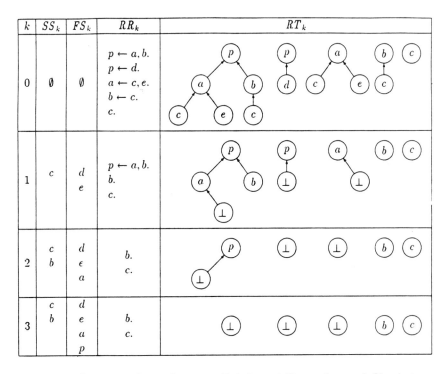

Figure 2: Correspondence between Rule-based Semantics and Simple-tree Semantics

DEFINITION 7

An atom p is said to be *NF-derivable* with respect to sets SS_k and FS_k and instantiated logic program RR_k if there is an NF-tree based on RR_k with p as root, such that each leaf of the tree is either a positive atom in SS_k or the negation of an atom in FS_k. In this case we say that the tree *NF-derives* p with respect to SS_k, FS_k, and RR_k. An atom is *finitely NF-derivable* if it is NF-derivable by a finite tree. ∎

As we did for the rule-based semantics, we define $SS_0 = FS_0 = \emptyset$ and define RR_0 to be the Herbrand instantiation of $\mathbf{P}$, a general logic program. Then RT_0 is defined to be the set of all complete NF-trees based on RR_0, as described in Definition 6.

For any ordinal k, suppose we have the triple (SS_k, FS_k, RT_k). We define the triple $(SS_{k+1}, FS_{k+1}, RR_{k+1})$ in terms of (SS_k, FS_k, RT_k) by means of a transformation Ψ, which we now describe. The close correspondence between this transformation and the Φ defined for rule-based semantics is illustrated in Figure 2. First, create SS_{k+1} and FS_{k+1} by adding atoms to SS_k and FS_k as follows:

- Initialize SS_{k+1} to SS_k. For each tree in RT_k consisting of a single node, add that atom to SS_{k+1} (unless it already appears there).

- Initialize FS_{k+1} to FS_k. For each atom in the Herbrand base that matches the root of no tree in RT_k, add that atom to FS_{k+1} (unless it already appears there). When k is a successor ordinal, it is sufficient to consider only atoms that matched the root of some tree in RT_{k-1} (instead of the whole Herbrand base).

Now create RT_{k+1} by modifying RT_k as follows:

- Initialize RT_{k+1} to RT_k.

- In each tree in RT_{k+1}, for each internal node, if it has a child containing *failed*, then replace that node and its subtree by the constant *failed*. (Do this just once; do not further propagate a *failed* that was created during this update step.) Trees that reduce to the single *failed* node have failed finitely.

- In each tree in RT_{k+1}, for each leaf, if it contains either a positive atom that appears in FS_{k+1} or a negated atom that appears in SS_{k+1}, then replace that leaf by the constant *failed*.

- In each tree in RT_{k+1}, delete all leaves (other than the root itself) that contain positive atoms that appear in SS_{k+1}, and delete all negated atoms (necessarily leaves) that appear in FS_{k+1}; these nodes are considered proved and the trees "shrink" accordingly.

This completes the description of the transformation $\Psi(SS_k, FS_k, RT_k)$. For each limit ordinal α, we define

$$SS_\alpha = \bigcup_{\beta < \alpha} SS_\beta \qquad FS_\alpha = \bigcup_{\beta < \alpha} FS_\beta \qquad RT_\alpha = \bigcap_{\beta < \alpha} RT_\beta.$$

Let Ω be the least nonconstructive ordinal, and define

$$SS = \bigcup_{\beta < \Omega} SS_\beta \qquad FS = \bigcup_{\beta < \Omega} FS_\beta \ .$$

DEFINITION 8
The *simple tree negation-as-failure semantics* (*simple tree semantics* for short) for a general logic program is the pair of sets (SS, FS) derived from SS_0, FS_0, RT_0, and the transformation Ψ, as described above. Also, the "meaning of the

logic program'' with respect to the simple tree semantics is that atoms in *SS* are true, atoms in *FS* are false, and atoms in neither *SS* nor *FS* are unclassified. ■

Note that the treatment of the constant *failed* is designed to maintain correspondence with rule-based semantics (see Figure 2.) The same values of *SS* and *FS* would be obtained if trees were completely failed as soon as one leaf failed, but the intermediate values of SS_α and FS_α would differ, in general.

LEMMA 1
Given a general logic program, for all ordinals $\alpha < \Omega$:

- The sets SS_α and FS_α in the rule-based semantics are the same as SS_α and FS_α in the simple tree semantics.

- Every subtree of a tree in RT_α is also a tree in RT_α.

- Every tree in RT_α is an NF-tree based on RR_α.

- For every rule in RR_α, there is a tree in RT_α such that its root matches the head, the root has no *failed* child, and the children of the root match the subgoals of the rule. (Possibly *failed* nodes occur at lower levels.)

Proof: Use induction on α and apply the definitions of Φ and Ψ. ■

THEOREM 1
Given a general logic program, the sets *SS* and *FS* in the rule-based semantics are the same as *SS* and *FS* in the simple tree semantics.

Proof: Immediate from Lemma 1. ■

Tight Tree Semantics

In this section we show that the tight tree semantics avoids the counter-intuitive ''failure-to-fail'' and ''indefinite-case'' results mentioned ''Counter-Intuitive Meanings of Rule-based Semantics'' for a large class of logic programs.

DEFINITION 9
A *tight negation-as-failure derivation tree* (*tight NF-tree* for short) is an NF-tree such that no node has an identical ancestor. Since ancestors are necessarily internal nodes, this condition only needs to be checked for nodes that are positive atoms. ■

Our strengthened form of finite failure is based on the use of tight NF-trees. Suppose we are trying to prove p. Recall that Herbrand's theorem essentially guarantees that if a set of clauses (including $\neg p$) is inconsistent, then some finite subset is inconsistent; this finite subset can be used to produce a finite derivation of p. Restricting attention to *tight* NF-trees is motivated by the following lemma.

LEMMA 2
For a given instantiated logic program, an atom is finitely NF-derived with respect to sets SS_k and FS_k if and only if it is finitely NF-derived by a *tight* NF-tree with respect to those sets.

Proof: Let t be a minimum (in node count) NF-tree that NF-derives atom p. Suppose node v contains positive atom a and has an ancestor v' that also contains a. Create a smaller NF-tree t' by replacing the subtree of t rooted at v' by the subtree rooted at v. Clearly t' NF-derives p, contradicting the minimality of t. Therefore, t must be tight. ∎

DEFINITION 10
The *tight tree negation-as-failure semantics* (*tight tree semantics* for short) has Ψ defined as for simple tree semantics (Definition 8). However, instead of starting at $(\emptyset, \emptyset, RT_0)$, the tight tree semantics starts at $(\emptyset, \emptyset, TT_0))$, where TT_0 is defined to be the subset of RT_0 consisting of *tight* NF-trees. Thereafter,

$$(SS_{k+1}, FS_{k+1}, TT_{k+1}) = \Psi(SS_k, FS_k, TT_k).$$

Definitions for limit ordinals and SS and FS are as before. ∎

EXAMPLE 5
Recall the program $\mathbf{P_3}$ from Example 3, that contained the rules:

$p(X,Y) \leftarrow b(X,Y).$

$p(X,Y) \leftarrow b(X,U),\ p(U,Y).$

$e(X,Y) \leftarrow g(X,Y),\ \neg p(X,Y).$

$a(X,Y) \leftarrow e(X,Y).$

$a(X,Y) \leftarrow e(X,U),\ a(U,Y).$

and the facts about *b* and *g*:

$b(1,2)$ $g(2,3)$

$b(2,1)$ $g(3,2)$

$b(3,4)$

$b(4,3)$

By considering only tight NF-trees, the looping problem disappears, and atoms like $p(1,3)$ and $p(2,3)$ can be put into FS_4. For example, $p(1,3)$ can reduce to $b(1,2)$ and $p(2,3)$, but then $p(2,3)$ cannot reduce to $b(2,1)$ and $p(1,3)$ because tightness is violated. The tight tree semantics with this program will therefore compute the more expected result that *SS* also includes

   $\{ e(2,3),\ e(3,2),\ a(2,2),\ a(2,3),\ a(3,2),\ a(3,3) \}$.
■

EXAMPLE 6
Recall that $\mathbf{P}_4$ in Example 4 is the program with rules

$p(X) \leftarrow a(X),\ c(X)$.

$p(X) \leftarrow \neg a(X),\ d(X)$.

$a(X) \leftarrow b(X)$.

$b(X) \leftarrow a(X)$.

together with the facts:

   $c(1)$. $c(2)$. $d(2)$. $d(3)$.

The rule-based semantics did not put $p(2)$ into *SS*, although it is in all models because it could not classify $a(2)$. The tight tree semantics prohibits the infinite nontight tree $a(2) \leftarrow b(2) \leftarrow a(2) \cdots$, puts $a(2)$ into FS_1, and then puts $p(2)$ into SS_2. But observe that, by the same token, the tight tree semantics puts $p(3)$ into SS_2, although it is *not* in all models. ■

The Bounded Term Size Property

Practical programs nearly always have the bounded term size property, defined below (unless they are buggy!). The natural tendency in problem solving is to reduce larger objects to smaller ones.

DEFINITION 11

We say a general logic program has the *bounded term size* property if it is safe for negation and there is a function $f(n)$ such that whenever the top level goal has no argument whose term size exceeds n, then no subgoal in any top-down-positive derivation (using most general unifiers, and expanding only positive subgoals) has an argument whose term size exceeds $f(n)$, whether the derivation is successful or not. (The size of a term is the count of its functors, constants, and variables.) ■

EXAMPLE 7

Consider the three argument reverse program P_5, in which it is intended that the first argument contain the unreversed part of a list, the second argument contain the already reversed part, and the third argument contain the complete reversed list. We assume lists are built with the binary functor " . " and that it is defined as an infix operator.

$rev(nil, R, R)$.

$rev(A . U, P, R) \leftarrow rev(U, A . P, R)$.

We see that this program has the bounded term size property with $f(n) = 2n$. Even though the goal

$? - rev(4.5.6.nil, 3.2.1.nil, nil)$

eventually fails, we have to consider how large the terms can grow in the meantime. In this case the largest term size starts at 7 and grows to 13. ■

It should be pointed out that it is undecidable in general whether a given program has the bounded term size property, for otherwise it would be possible to decide the halting problem. There is a clear correspondence between term size in derivations and term size in NF-trees.

LEMMA 3

If a general logic program has the bounded term size property, then every tight NF-tree for that program is finite.

Proof: An infinite tree of bounded degree must have an infinite path. But no term occurring on this path can have size greater than $f(n)$, where n is a bound on the size of terms in the root of the NF-tree. Since the alphabet of functors and constants is finite (we assume the program is finite), some atom on the infinite path must eventually repeat, violating tightness. ■

Freedom from Recursive Negation

The concept of freedom from recursive negation, defined below, is an important one for logic programs, and leads to our first main result. The same concept was developed independently in Apt, Blair, and Walker [1988] and Naqvi [1986], where it was called "stratified" and "layered," respectively. Other researchers adopted the term "stratified" (Lifschitz [1988], Przymusinski [1988]) but we prefer our own more descriptive terminology. In this section we show that programs that are free from recursive negation and have the bounded term size property are "categorical" under the tight tree semantics, whereas programs with recursive negation are not, in general. By "categorical," we mean that every atom in the Herbrand universe is in either *SS* or *FS*, and *SS* is a minimal model.

The definition of recursive negation is based on the concept of a *dependence graph* of the program. The nodes of this graph are the predicate symbols that appear in the goals and subgoals of the logic program. Where no confusion can arise we say "predicate" when we really mean "predicate symbol." Whenever predicate p is in the head of a rule and predicate q appears as a (positive or negative) subgoal, we put an arc $p \rightarrow q$ into the graph. This done, we identify the strongly connected components (SCCs) of the graph, which are the maximal sets of nodes that can all reach each other. The *reduced graph* of the dependence graph is obtained by combining all nodes in an SCC into a single node and eliminating arcs among them. Hence, the reduced graph is acyclic. SCC nodes with no out-arcs are considered leaves. Finally we define the *rank* of an SCC as its height in the reduced graph, with leaves having height 0. The rank of each predicate equals the rank of its SCC.

EXAMPLE 8

The dependence graph of $\mathbf{P}_3$ from Example 3 is shown in Figure 3. Eliminating the self-arcs gives the reduced graph in this case, from which we see that the ranks of b and g are 0, the rank of p is 1, the rank of e is 2, and the rank of a is 3. ∎

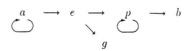

Figure 3: Dependence Graph of $\mathbf{P}_3$, Discussed in Example 8

In a loose sense, the ranks of SCCs correspond to levels of abstraction. In keeping with this view, we do not expect users to define less abstract items in terms of more abstract ones. Thus we do not view a rule like $p \leftarrow \neg q$ as a proper mechanism for deducing q when p is false; this is the essential difference between logic programs with negative subgoals and "pure" non-Horn clauses. However, if p and q are in the same SCC, then they are both at the same level of abstraction, and we believe that the user's intentions are then unclear. This motivates the following definition.

DEFINITION 12
We say a general logic program contains *recursive negation* if some rule has a negative subgoal in the same SCC as its head. A program in which this does not occur is said to be *free of recursive negation*. ∎

THEOREM 2
Let **P** be a general logic program with the bounded term size property that is free of recursive negation. Then the tight tree semantics for **P** partitions its Herbrand base into SS and FS; that is, every atom in the Herband base is classified. In addition, SS is a minimal (not necessarily minimum) model for **P**.

Proof: We partition the Herbrand base H according to the SCCs of the dependence graph into $H_1, \ldots, H_m$, where the SCCs are labeled $1, \ldots, m$ arbitrarily. That is, each atom in H whose predicate symbol is in SCC i goes into H_i. Denote the rank of SCC i by $rank(i)$ and define

$$H^{(k)} = \bigcup_{rank(i) \leq k} H_i.$$

Let $\mathbf{P}^{(k)}$ denote the program consisting of the rules of **P** whose heads have rank no greater than k, and let

$$SS_\alpha{}^{(k)} = SS_\alpha \cap H^{(k)} \qquad SS^{(k)} = SS \cap H^{(k)}$$

with corresponding definitions for $FS_\alpha^{(k)}$ and $FS^{(k)}$.

The critical observation is that the contents of $SS^{(j)}$ and $FS^{(j)}$, where $j < k$ are not influenced by atoms in $SS \cap H_i$ or $FS \cap H_i$, where $rank(i) = k$. We show by induction on k, the rank, that

1. For all SCCs i with $rank(i) = k$, $SS \cap H_i$ and $FS \cap H_i$ partition H_i;

2. $SS^{(k)} = SS_{(k+1)\omega}^{(k)}$ and $FS^{(k)} = FS_{(k+1)\omega}^{(k)}$.

3. $SS^{(k)}$ is a minimal model of $\mathbf{P}^{(k)}$.

For the base case, $k = 0$, (1) follows from Lemma 3 and the fact that $\mathbf{P}^{(0)}$ is a Horn clause program, so that "NF-derivable" coincides with "has a resolution proof." In this case $SS^{(0)}_\omega$ is known to be the minimum model of $\mathbf{P}^{(0)}$ (van Emden and Kowalski [1976]), establishing (2) and (3).

For the inductive step, let $k > 0$ and assume the inductive hypothesis for ranks less than k. Let α be an ordinal of the form $k\omega + h$, where h is a natural number. Let SCC i be any SCC with $rank(i) = k$. By freedom from recursive negation we know that if some rule whose head is in SCC i has a negative subgoal $\neg q$, then q is in an SCC whose rank is $j < k$. But $SS^{(j)}_\alpha = SS^{(j)}$ and $FS^{(j)}_\alpha = FS^{(j)}$ for the α under consideration. Therefore, all such negative subgoals are classified in "step" $k\omega + 1$; i.e., they are either removed from the trees or replaced by *failed*. For the remaining α in the range $k\omega < \alpha < k\omega + \omega$ the tight tree semantics behaves exactly as if the rules for SCCs at rank k were all Horn clauses. Therefore, (1), (2), and (3) follow by the same arguments used for rank 0. The only difference is that the model $SS^{(k)}$ is minimal, but not necessarily minimum. That is, removing an atom of rank $j > 0$ causes it to cease being a model, but then adding additional atoms of rank lower than j might restore the set to being a model that is not a superset of $SS^{(k)}$. ∎

EXAMPLE 9

To see that freedom from recursive negation (or some other condition in addition to bounded term sizes) is needed to prove the previous theorem, consider the program $\mathbf{P}_6$

$$p \leftarrow \neg q.$$

$$q \leftarrow \neg p.$$

We see that p and q are "deadlocked," each waiting for the other to either succeed or fail. Thus neither p nor q is classified in the tight tree semantics. ∎

COROLLARY 1

Let $\mathbf{P}$ be a general logic program that is free of recursive negation and has the bounded term size property, and in addition, let the bounding function $f(n)$ be known. Let SS and FS be based on the tight tree semantics operating on $\mathbf{P}$. Then for any ground atom p, it is decidable whether $p \in SS$.

Proof: Use induction on the rank of p. Perform a *tight* top-down proof search from top-level goal p, using resolution in the manner of Prolog on positive subgoals. Whenever variables are introduced, systematically try all substitutions of terms up to the allowable size $f(n)$, where n is the size of the largest term in p. (We did not say this was *efficient*.) By safety for negation, any variable in a negative subgoal also appears in a positive subgoal of the same clause (since the top-level clause was ground, see Definition 4), so $f(n)$ is always sufficient. Because of the bound on term size and because we prohibit any subgoal that has an identical ancestor, the depth of this part of the proof search (i.e., expanding positive subgoals) is finite. If the rank of p is 0, we are done; otherwise, when a negative subgoal, say $\neg q$, is encountered, by freedom from recursive negation, q has lower rank. By Theorem 2, q is in either SS or FS, and by the inductive hypothesis, it is decidable which. Thus the proof search for p either succeeds or fails finitely. ∎

It is hard to imagine a realistic situation in which we know that a bounding function $f(n)$ exists, but we cannot exhibit any such function. One obvious case when $f(n)$ is known is the function-free case. A less obvious, but at least partially analyzable, case is when function symbols are present, but the rules are such that arbitrarily large recursive term structures cannot be created. This is discussed further in the following section on practical methods.

When recursive terms can develop in the program, then analysis of $f(n)$ is much more difficult and only sketchy results are available (Naish [1983], Ullman [1985], Ullman and Van Gelder [1985]). These papers identify a few cases in which it can be proved that some arguments' term size definitely decreases around the recursive loop. Example 7 illustrated one such tractable case.

Iterated Least Fixed Point Semantics

An alternate semantics for general logic programs that are free from recursive negation, and one that is closer to certain implementations, is based on iterated least fixed points. For example, when the Herbrand base is finite, as it is in the function-free case, then the fixed points are also finite and can be computed by bottom-up methods. Our second main result is that the iterated least fixed point semantics, which we describe in this section, and the tight tree semantics are equivalent on general logic programs that have the bounded term size property and are free from recursive negation.

As is well-known (van Emden and Kowalski [1986], Aho and Ullman [1979], Apt and van Emden [1982]), a Horn clause program **P** has a natural semantics expressed as the least fixed point of a *modus ponens* operator T_P. Essentially, we define $SS_0 = \emptyset$, and whenever SS_k contains all the subgoals of an instantiated rule, then the operator T_P puts the head of the rule into SS_{k+1}. Then the success set SS of **P** is defined to be SS_ω, which is the least fixed point of T_P. The rule-based semantics in Definition 5 is in fact a generalization of this approach, in which the pair (SS,FS) is defined to be the least fixed point of a transformation that operates on both SS_k and FS_k simultaneously. We shall consider a different generalization.

DEFINITION 13

The operator $U_P(I)$, where I is a set of atoms, is defined as follows:

- $U_P(I)$ contains I.

- For any instantiated rule in **P**, if I contains all of the rule's *positive* sub-goals and none of the rule's *negative* subgoals, then $U_P(I)$ contains the head of the rule.

- $U_P(I)$ contains no other atoms.

Integer powers (i.e., iterated applications) of U_P are denoted by U_P^k, and we define

$$U_P^\omega(I) = \bigcup_{k < \omega} (U_P^k(I)).$$

■

For a given general logic program **P**, we find its strongly connected components and their ranks as described in the section "Freedom from Recursive Negation." Assume the program is found to be free of recursive negation. As before, let $\mathbf{P}^{(j)}$ consist of the rules of **P** whose heads have rank j. Then the *iterated fixed point semantics* of **P** is defined using the operators $U_{P^{(j)}}$.

For rank 0,

$$SS^{(0)} = U_{P^{(0)}}^\omega(\emptyset).$$

Recall that $\mathbf{P}^{(0)}$ consists of Horn clauses. Therefore, $SS^{(0)}$ is just the least fixed point of $T_{P^{(0)}}$.

For ranks $j > 0$,

$$SS^{(j)} = U_{P^{(j)}}^\omega(SS^{(j-1)}).$$

To justify the least fixed point nomenclature for ranks $j > 0$, we may define a modified program $P^{(j)+}$ consisting of the atoms of $SS^{(j-1)}$, regarded as facts, together with the rules of $\mathbf{P}^{(j)}$. Let D_j be the domain consisting of the atoms of the Herbrand universe that have rank j together with the atoms in $SS^{(j-1)}$. Then

$$SS^{(j)} = U_{P^{(j)+}}^\omega(\emptyset).$$

All of the atoms added to $SS^{(j)}$ are in D_j and, because **P** is free from recursive negation, none of these atoms can ever match a negative subgoal of a rule in $\mathbf{P}^{(j)+}$. This establishes the monotonicity of $U_{P^{(j)+}}$ in the domain D_j, and thus $SS^{(j)}$ is the least fixed point of $U_{P^{(j)+}}$ restricted to that domain.

The reader will notice that although $FS^{(j)}$ is not defined, for all practical purposes the iterated fixed point semantics treats $D_j - SS^{(j)}$ as the failure set of $\mathbf{P}^{(j)+}$.

THEOREM 3
Let **P** be a general logic program that has the bounded term size property and is free from recursive negation. Then the iterated fixed point semantics of **P** and the tight tree semantics of **P** are equivalent.

Proof: Use induction on rank. At rank 0 we have only Horn clauses. It is well known that the least fixed point of $T_{P^{(0)}}$, which is the same as the least fixed point of $U_{P^{(0)}}$, is the minimum model of **P**, and that every atom in the minimum model has a finite derivation tree (van Emden and Kowalski [1976], Apt and van Emden [1982]). By Lemma 2, every such atom also has a tight NF-tree. Thus $SS^{(0)}$ coincides in both semantics.

For rank $j > 0$ assume that $SS^{(i)}$ coincides in both semantics for ranks $i < j$. By Theorem 2, every atom of rank $i < j$ that is not in $SS^{(i)}$ is in $FS^{(i)}$ in the tight tree semantics. Now an easy induction on $k > 0$ shows that atom p is first added to $SS_k^{(j)}$ in the iterated fixed point semantics if and only if there is a complete tight NF-tree of height k (and no such tree of lesser height) that derives p in the tight tree semantics. It follows that $SS^{(j)}$ coincides in both semantics, completing the induction on j. ■

Practical Algorithms

The decidability proof in Corollary 1 called for the algorithm to "try all possible terms up to size $f(n)$" at certain points. Practical algorithms cannot afford to "try all possible terms," of course.[3] In many cases of practical interest, there is an order of goal reductions that allows all variables to be bound through unification, without invoking blind guessing. This is a research area in its own right.

---

[3] Actually, the interpreter described in Apt, Blair, and Walker [1988] does so in the function-free case!

The function-free case is an important special case that has received considerable study. In this case, the finiteness of the Herbrand universe can be exploited. This case is doubly important because it includes many of the well-known examples where top-down derivations do not terminate. (Transitive closures, as in Example 3 are typical.) It has been argued (Brough and Walker [1984]) that top-down methods cannot be "patched up" to fix these problems, that essentially different algorithms are needed. Various proposals to handle the function-free case efficiently have appeared (McKay and Shapiro [1981], Walker [1981], Henschen and Naqvi [1984], Porter [1985] Lozinskii [1985], Vieille [1986], Van Gelder [1986]). Their common themes are to introduce a bottom-up (forward reasoning) component into the evaluation procedure while attempting to evaluate only relevant portions of the Herbrand base. Although these studies do not consider negative subgoals, many of their results carry over without trouble when the program is free of recursive negation.

Programs with Nonrecursive Term Structure

As soon as a program contains any functor of positive arity, the Herbrand universe becomes infinite. However, it is still possible that all tight NF-trees are finite. Essentially, in order for a tight NF-tree to be infinite, it must be possible for the program to generate larger and larger terms during a top-down-positive derivation. For example, a rule like

$$lt(X,Y) \leftarrow lt(s(X),Y).$$

does just that. One way to rule out this possibility is to establish that the program cannot produce recursive terms at all, in either the top-down or the bottom-up direction. In this case there is a finite "reachable" subset of the Herbrand universe. The success set of the program under any reasonable semantics will lie within this finite subset, so the methods developed for the function-free case can normally be applied.

We shall sketch the description of a sufficient condition that resolution using most general unifiers cannot lead to arbitrarily large recursive term structures. Clearly it is sufficient to analyze each SCC separately for this purpose. In the discussion below, "functor" means a function symbol of positive arity; a constant is not regarded as a functor here. The idea is to look at the most general unifiers associated with each possible match of a positive subgoal to a rule head, look at the compound terms that occur in the program as predicate arguments, and build a directed *functor precedence graph* whose nodes are functors and variables (rules have disjoint sets of variables). For each substitution in some most general unifier, put an arc from the variable to each functor of the substitution term; put arcs both ways if two variables unify. For each term in the program, put an arc from each functor to each variable within its term. If no functor is in a cycle now, recursive terms cannot be built, at least not through resolution with most general unifiers, and $f(n)$ can be computed.

EXAMPLE 10
Suppose the only nontrivial rules are

$$p(f(X),g(X)) \leftarrow q(X,X).$$

$$q(U,V) \leftarrow p(U,V).$$

Then the functor precedence graph is

Since no functors are in cycles, recursive terms will not occur. ∎

However, if some functor *is* in a cycle, this is not conclusive evidence of recursive structure, because the sequence of unifications around the cycle may not actually compose.

EXAMPLE 11
Suppose the only nontrivial rules are

$$p(f(X),g(X)) \leftarrow q(X,X).$$

$$q(U,V) \leftarrow p(U,V).$$

Then the functor precedence graph is

$$
\begin{array}{ccc}
f & & g \\
\nearrow \searrow & & \nearrow \searrow \\
U \longleftrightarrow & X & \longleftrightarrow V
\end{array}
$$

Now both f and g are in cycles, yet recursive terms will not occur. To see why, make a "ghost" copy of the first rule

$$p(f(W),g(W)) \leftarrow q(W,W).$$

The substitution to resolve the first two rules on q is $\theta_1 = \{U := X; V := X\}$, which is read "replace U by X; replace V by X." The substitution to resolve the second rule with the "ghost" on p is $\theta_2 = \{U := f(W); V := g(W)\}$. Since these substitutions cannot be composed into a single substitution, the apparent loop will never be realized. ■

Conclusion

We have presented a new semantics, the *tight tree semantics*, for general logic programs that has advantages over the rule-based semantics in that a larger portion of the Herbrand base tends to be classified as belonging to either the success set or the failure set. We have defined a reasonable class of programs, namely those that have the bounded term size property and are free from recursive negation. We have shown that for this class the *entire* Herbrand base is classified as success or failure, and that an equivalent *iterated fixed point semantics* exists. Further work is needed to extend these results to programs with unsafe negation.

Acknowledgments

This work was supported by NSF grant IST-84-12791 and a grant of IBM Corporation.

References

1. Aho, A. V. and Ullman, J. D. [1979] Universality of Data Retrieval Languages, *6th ACM Symp. on Principles of Programming Languages*, 110–120.

2. Apt, K. R., Blair, H., and Walker A. [1988] Towards a Theory of Declarative Knowledge, *Foundations of Deductive Databases and Logic Programming* (J. Minker, Ed.), Morgan Kaufmann Publishers, Los Altos, CA, 89–148.

3. Apt, K. R. and Emden, M. H. van [1982] Contributions to the Theory of Logic Programming, *JACM* **29**(3):841–862.

4. Brough, D. R, and Walker, A. [1984] Some Practical Properties of Logic Programming Interpreters, *International Conference on Fifth Generation Computer Systems*, 149–156, Institute for New Generation Computing, Tokyo, Japan.

5. Clark, K. L. [1987] Negation as Failure, in *Logic and Databases*, (H. Gallaire and J. Minker, Eds.), Plenum Press, New York, 293–322.

6. Emden, M. H. van and Kowalski, R. A. [1976] The Semantics of Predicate Logic as a Programming Language, *JACM* **23**(4):733−742.

7. Emden, M. H. van and Lloyd, J. W. [1984] A Logical Reconstruction of Prolog II, *Journal of Logic Programming* **1**(4):143−149.

8. Henschen, L. J. and Naqvi, S. A. [1984] On Compiling Queries in First-Order Databases, *JACM* **31**(1):47−85.

9. Jaffar, J., Lassez, J.-L., and Lloyd, J. [1983] Completeness of the Negation-as-Failure Rule, *Int'l Joint Conf. on Artificial Intelligence*, 500−506.

10. Jaffar, J., Lassez, J.-L., and Maher, M. J. [1986] Comments on "General Failure of Logic Programs," *Journal of Logic Programming* **3**(2):115−118.

11. Le, V. T. [1985a] General Failure of Logic Programs, *Journal of Logic Programming* **2**(2):157−165.

12. Le, V. T. [1985b] Negation-as-Failure Rule for General Logic Programs with Equality, *Journal of Logic Programming* **2**(4):285−294.

13. Lifschitz, V. [1988] On the Declarative Semantics of Logic Programs with Negation, in *Foundations of Deductive Databases and Logic Programming* (J. Minker, Ed.), Morgan Kaufmann Publishers, Los Altos, CA, 177−192.

14. Lloyd, J. W. [1984] *Foundations of Logic Programming*, Springer-Verlag, New York.

15. Lassez, J. L. and Marriot, K. [1986] Explicit Representation of Terms Defined by Counter Examples, *Proc. Workshop on Foundations of Deductive Databases and Logic Programming* (J. Minker, Ed.), 659−677.

16. Loveland, D. W. [1978] *Automated Theorem Proving: A Logical Basis*, North Holland, Amsterdam.

17. Lozinskii, E. L. [1985] Evaluating Queries in Deductive Databases by Generating, *Proc. 9th Int. Joint Conf. on Artificial Intelligence*, 173−177.

18. Maher, M. J. [1988] Equivalences of Logic Programs, in *Foundations of Deductive Databases and Logic Programming* (J. Minker, Ed.), Morgan Kaufmann Publishers, Los Altos, CA, 627−658.

19. McKay D. and Shapiro, S. [1981] Using Active Connection Graphs for Reasoning with Recursive Rules, *Proc. 7th Int. Joint Conf. on Artificial Intelligence*, 368−374.

20. Morris, K., Ullman, J. D., and Van Gelder, A. [1986] Design Overview of the Nail! System, *Third Int'l Conf. on Logic Programming*, 554−568.

21. Naish, L. [1983] *Automatic Generation of Control for Logic Programs*, Technical Report 83/6, Dept. of Computer Science, University of Melbourne, Melbourne, Australia.

22. Naish, L. [1985] *Negation and Control in Prolog*. PhD thesis, University of Melbourne.

23. Naqvi, S. A., [1986] A Logic for Negation in Database Systems, in *Proc. Workshop on Foundations of Deductive Databases and Logic Programming* (J. Minker, Ed.), 378–387.

24. Porter III, Harry H. [1985] *Earley Deduction*, Technical Report CS/E 86-002, Oregon Graduate Center, Beaverton, OR.

25. Przymusinski, T. [1988] On the Semantics of Stratified Deductive Databases, in *Foundations of Deductive Databases and Logic Programming* (J. Minker, Ed.), Morgan Kaufmann Publishers, Los Altos, CA, 193–216.

26. Reiter, R. [1978] On Closed World Databases, in *Logic and Databases* (H. Gallaire and J. Minker, Eds.), Plenum Press, New York, 55–76.

27. Shepherdson, J. C. [1985] Negation as Failure, II, *Journal of Logic Programming* **2**(3):185–202.

28. Shepherdson, J. C. [1988] Negation in Logic Programming, in *Foundations of Deductive Databases and Logic Programming* (J. Minker, Ed.), Morgan Kaufmann Publishers, Los Altos, CA, 19–88.

29. Topor, R. and Sonenberg, E. A. [1988] On Domain Independent Databases, in *Foundations of Deductive Databases and Logic Programming* (J. Minker, Ed.), Morgan Kaufmann Publishers, Los Altos, CA, 217–240.

30. Ullman, J. D. [1980] *Principles of Database Systems*, Computer Science Press, Rockville, MD.

31. Ullman, J. D. [1985] Implementation of Logical Query Languages for Databases, *ACM Trans. on Database Systems* **10**(3):289–321.

32. Ullman, J. D. and Van Gelder, A. [1985] *Testing Applicability of Top-Down Capture Rules*, Technical Report STAN–CS–85–1046, Dept. of Computer Science, Stanford University, Stanford, CA.

33. Van Gelder, A. [1986] A Message Passing Framework for Logical Query Evaluation, *1986 ACM-SIGMOD Conf. on Management of Data*, 155–165.

34. Vieille, L. [1986] *Recursive Axioms in Deductive Databases: The Query Subquery Approach, Proceedings First International Conference on Expert Databases*, Charleston, SC, 179–194.

35. Walker, A. [1981] *Syllog: A Knowledge Based Data Management System*, Technical Report 034, Dept. of Computer Science, New York University.

4

On the Declarative Semantics of Logic Programs with Negation

Vladimir Lifschitz

Computer Science Department
Stanford University, Stanford, CA

Abstract

A logic program can be viewed as a set of predicate formulas, and its declarative meaning can be defined by specifying a certain Herbrand model of that set. For programs without negation, this model is defined either as the Herbrand model with the minimal set of positive ground atoms, or, equivalently, as the minimal fixed point of a certain operator associated with the program (van Emden and Kowalski). These solutions do not apply to general logic programs, because a program with negation may have many minimal Herbrand models, and the corresponding operator may have many minimal fixed points. Apt, Blair, and Walker and, independently, Van Gelder, introduced a class of *stratified* programs which disallows certain combinations of recursion and negation and showed how to use the fixed point approach to define a declarative semantics for such programs. Using the concept of circumscription, we extend the minimal model approach to stratified programs and show that it leads to the same semantics.

Introduction

Logic programming is based on the idea that substantial subsets of predicate calculus can be used as programming languages. A logic program is essentially a collection of predicate formulas, so that we can talk about the *models* of a logic program, about formulas that can be *derived* from it in predicate logic, and so forth. This is the *declarative* aspect of logic programming. On the other hand, we can accept the *procedural* view and, by specifying a logic programming interpreter, define *the process of computation* associated with a given program.

The investigation of the semantics of logic programs includes defining their declarative semantics and their procedural semantics and studying the relation between the two. In this paper we are interested primarily in the declarative interpretation of logic programs. But it should be remembered that a declarative semantics is useful only as long as it allows us to justify the correctness of the computational procedures employed in logic programming interpreters.

Given a logic program P and a query F without variables, what do we consider to be the right answer to the query? According to one possible definition, the answer is *yes* if F is a *logical consequence* of P, and *no* otherwise. This simple characterization provides a satisfactory declarative semantics for logic programming with Horn clauses (i.e., for programs without negation, as in pure Prolog). Consider, for instance, the program

$$p(1),$$

$$q(2), \tag{1}$$

$$r(x) \leftarrow q(x).$$

The answer to each of the queries $p(1)$, $q(2)$, and $r(2)$ is *yes* because they follow from (1) in predicate calculus; the answer to each of the queries $p(2)$, $q(1)$, and $r(1)$ is *no* because they do not follow from (1).

In view of Gödel's completeness theorem, this semantics can be equivalently expressed in terms of models: The answer to a query is *yes* iff the query is true in every model of the program. For a query with variables we can say that the answer is the set of tuples of values for the variables that make the query true in every model of the program.

On the other hand, we can take a somewhat different path and, instead of referring to *arbitrary* models of the program P, consider just *one* of them, the *canonical* model M_P. The answer to a query is the set of tuples of values for the variables that make the query true in that particular model. For program (1), for example, the canonical model has the universe $\{1,2\}$, with $p(x)$ true for $x = 1$, and $q(x)$ and $r(x)$ true for $x = 2$.

A general description of how the canonical model is constructed for logic programs without negation was given by van Emden and Kowalski [1976]. M_P is selected among the *Herbrand* models of P, i.e., among the models whose universe is the set of ground terms in the language of P, and whose object and function constants are interpreted in such a way that every ground term denotes itself. A Herbrand model is completely characterized by the set of ground atoms which are true in the model, and it is sometimes identified with this set. For instance, the model that defines the meaning of program (1) is represented by the set

$$\{p(1),q(2),r(2)\}. \qquad (2)$$

Another Herbrand model of (1) can be written as

$$\{p(1),p(2),q(1),q(2),r(1),r(2)\}. \qquad (3)$$

How do we select M_P among the Herbrand models of P? Herbrand models, viewed as sets of ground atoms, can be compared using set inclusion. For example, we can say that (2) is less than (3). A program P without negation has exactly one *minimal* Herbrand model, which is the intersection of all Herbrand models of P; in other words, a ground atom is true in that model iff it is true in every Herbrand model of P. According to van Emden and Kowalski, the meaning of P is represented by this minimal model. This description of the canonical model provides another declarative semantics for logic programming with Horn clauses, equivalent to the logical consequence semantics.

An equivalent description of the canonical model M_P is given by van Emden and Kowalski in the same paper, again for programs without negation, in terms of an operator T_P associated with P. When applied to a set M of ground atoms in the language of P, T_P produces the set $T_P(M)$ of ground atoms that follows from the facts in M by "one application" of one of the rules in P. The operator corresponding to program (1), for instance, transforms $\{q(1)\}$ into

$$\{p(1),q(2),r(1)\}.$$

The canonical model M_P can be characterized as the minimal fixed point of T_P:

$$M_P = T_P(\emptyset) \cup T_P(T_P(\emptyset)) \cup \dots$$

In case of program (1),

$$T_P(\emptyset) = \{p(1), q(2)\},$$
$$T_P(T_P(\emptyset)) = \{p(1),q(2),r(2)\},$$

and further applications of T_P do not add new elements. (In this example, the infinite union defining M_P can be replaced by its finite segment. But this is not necessarily so for programs with function symbols, when the Herbrand universe is infinite, and M_P may be infinite also.) Apt and van Emden [1982] prove other important properties of the fixed points of T_P.

We are interested in extending these ideas to logic programs with negation. Consider the program

$$p(1),$$

$$q(2), \tag{4}$$

$$r(x) \leftarrow \neg q(x).$$

The procedural interpretation of this program based on the familiar "negation as failure" principle suggests that the query $q(1)$ should be answered *no*, and then the query $r(1)$ should be answered *yes*. Let us see whether any of the declarative approaches outlined above can provide a justification for this.

1. *The Logical Consequence Semantics.* The formula $r(1)$ is *not* a logical consequence of (4). It is true in some models of (1) but certainly not in all of them. For instance, it is true in the Herbrand model

    $$\{p(1),q(2),r(1)\}, \tag{5}$$

    but false in

    $$\{p(1),q(1),q(2)\}. \tag{6}$$

    It appears then that the answer to the query $r(1)$ should have been negative.

2. *The Minimal Model Semantics.* Program (4) has *two* different minimal Herbrand models, (5) and (6). The "negation as failure" interpretation suggests that the meaning of (4) is correctly represented by the former. But how can we define in general terms why (5) is the "right" model? What complicates the matter is that the choice of M_p is apparently not invariant relative to logically equivalent transformations of P. The program

    $$p(1),$$

    $$q(2), \tag{7}$$

    $$q(x) \leftarrow \neg r(x),$$

    viewed as a set of formulas, is equivalent to (4), so that it has the same minimal models (5) and (6); but now (6) seems to correctly represent the meaning of the program.

3.   *The Fixed Point Semantics.* The operator T_P corresponding to program (4) has *two* different minimal fixed points, (5) and (6). How can we define in general terms why (5) is the "right" fixed point?

We have to conclude that the approaches that worked so well for logic programming with Horn clauses do not immediately provide a satisfactory declarative semantics for programs with negation.

An extension of the fixed point semantics applicable to some programs with negation was proposed recently by Apt, Blair, and Walker [1988] and independently by Van Gelder [1988]. (The extension is based on an idea discussed informally by Chandra and Harel [1985].) These authors introduced a class of general logic programs, called "stratified" or "free from recursive negation," and assign a unique Herbrand model M_P to every such program P using "iterated" fixed points. (The definitions will be reproduced below.) Programs (4) and (7) are stratified, and the iterated fixed point semantics assigns model (5) to (4) and model (6) to (7), as suggested by the procedural interpretation.

Here is an example of a program that is *not* stratified:

$p(1,2),$

$p(2,1),$ (8)

$q(x) \leftarrow p(x,y), \neg q(y).$

Its minimal Herbrand models are

$\{p(1,2),p(2,1),q(1)\}$

and

$\{p(1,2),p(2,1),q(2)\}.$

There seems to be no reasonable way to select one of them as canonical. Perhaps, one should not try to define a declarative meaning for (8) and other programs of this kind (at least as long as the meaning is to be conveyed by selecting a single model). When writing a stratified program, the programmer indicates what the declarative meaning of the program is by deciding whether a given atom should be placed in the head of a rule or, negated, in its body. Programs like (8) do not contain such "signals"; this is why it is not clear how to define a declarative semantics for arbitrary logic programs with negation. It is interesting to notice that the NAIL! system, currently under development at Stanford University (Morris, Ullman, and Van Gelder [1986]), explicitly prohibits non-stratified programs.

The iterated fixed point construction allows us to single out the canonical model M_P from among the minimal models of P; by itself, the minimality condition is not sufficient for defining the canonical model.

The purpose of this paper is to show that the situation becomes quite different if we take into account some recent work in the theory of circumscription (McCarthy [1986], Lifschitz [1986]). Applications of the idea of logical minimization to formalizing nonmonotonic aspects of commonsense reasoning have led to introducing some forms of minimization more general than the simple minimality condition used above. We will employ these more general forms of minimization to give a simple description of M_P in terms of minimality. This result can be viewed as an additional argument in favor of the declarative semantics of stratified programs proposed by Apt, Blair, Walker, and Van Gelder. It suggests, on the other hand, that the ideas of logic programming can be useful for implementing some special forms of circumscription.

Logic Programs and Circumscription

Consider a finite set of object, function, and predicate symbols that contains at least one object symbol and at least one predicate symbol. An *atom* is any atomic formula formed from these symbols and object variables. A *literal* is an atom A or its negation $\neg A$. A *clause* is a formula of the form

$$A \leftarrow L_1 \wedge \ldots \wedge L_m, \tag{9}$$

where A is an atom and $L_1,\ldots,L_m$ are literals, $m \geq 0$. A *program* is a finite set of clauses. We consider only programs that contain occurrences of all object, function, and predicate symbols. We identify a program P with the conjunction of the universal closures of its clauses.

In this paper we use the pointwise version of circumscription (Lifschitz [1986]) and define only a special case of this concept sufficient for our present purposes. Let $p_1,\ldots,p_l$ be distinct predicate symbols. The *(pointwise) circumscription of* one of these predicates, p_i, *relative to* $P(p_1,\ldots,p_l)$ with $p_1,\ldots,p_l$ *allowed to vary* is the second-order formula

$$P(p_1,\ldots,p_l) \wedge \forall x p'_1\ldots p'_l \neg [p_i(x) \wedge \neg p'_i(x) \wedge P(p'_1,\ldots,p'_l)], \tag{10}$$

where x is a tuple of distinct object variables, and $p'_1,\ldots,p'_l$ are distinct predicate variables of the same arities as $p_1,\ldots,p_l$. This formula expresses that it is impossible to change the value of p_i at any point x from *true* to *false* without losing the property P, even if we are allowed to make arbitrary additional changes in the values of $p_1,...,p_l$. In this sense, all values of p_i are "minimal". We denote (10) by $C_{pi}(P; p_1,...,p_l)$.

The definition of circumscription applies, of course, to arbitrary sentences; but here we are interested only in the case when P is a program.

EXAMPLE 1

Let P be program (1). The result of circumscribing p with all three predicates p, q, and r allowed to vary

$$C_p(P; p,q,r) \tag{11}$$

is equivalent to the conjunction of P and $\forall x(p(x) \equiv x = 1)$. To prove this fact, consider a model M of P. If the value of p at any point in the universe of M other than (the point representing) 1 is *true*, then it can be changed to *false* without losing properties (1). On the other hand, the first of formulas (1) shows that the value of p at 1 cannot be changed to *false*. In a similar way we check that circumscribing q,

$$C_q(P;p,q,r), \tag{12}$$

gives the conjunction of P and $\forall x(q(x) \equiv x = 2)$. The circumscription

$$C_r(P; p,q,r), \tag{13}$$

is equivalent to the conjunction of P and $\forall x(r(x) \equiv x = 2)$. (If the value of r at a point other than 2 is *true*, then we change the values of *both* r and q at that point to *false*, and it is clear that the new model will satisfy P.) It follows that the conjunction of all three circumscriptions (11), (12), and (13) is equivalent to

$$\forall x(p(x) \equiv x = 1) \land \forall x(q(x) \equiv x = 2) \land \forall x(r(x) \equiv x = 2).$$

This formula has exactly one Herbrand model, and that model is (2). Thus we have a characterization of M_P as *the only Herbrand model* of a certain *set of circumscriptions*, one for each predicate symbol in the language of P. ∎

By changing the set of predicates allowed to vary we can sometimes affect the result of circumscription. Removing predicates from this set generally makes the circumscription weaker because circumscription becomes the expression of minimality among a smaller number of alternatives. We will see that the possibility of deciding, for each predicate p, which other predicates are allowed to vary when p is minimized gives the additional flexibility needed for describing the semantics of programs with negation in terms of minimality.

EXAMPLE 2
Let us compare circumscriptions (11), (12), and (13) with

$$C_p(P;p), \tag{14}$$

$$C_q(P;q), \tag{15}$$

$$C_r(P;r). \tag{16}$$

It is easy to verify that (14) is equivalent to (11) and (15) to (12); but (16) gives the conjunction of P and $\forall\, x(r(x) \equiv q(x))$ and, thus, is weaker than (13). The Herbrand model

$$\{p(1),q(1),q(2),r(1),r(2)\}$$

satisfies (16), but not (13): It can be transformed into a model with a stronger r (namely, (2)), but only at the price of changing the interpretation of q as well. In spite of this difference, circumscriptions (14), (15), and (16) can be used instead of (11), (12), (13) to characterize model (2). ■

The characterization of M_P as the only Herbrand model of a set of circumscriptions in Example 1 can be extended to arbitrary programs without negation. Generally (in the presence of mutually recursive predicates), it may be essential that the list $p_1,...,p_l$ of predicates allowed to vary in the circumscriptions contain not only the minimized predicate, as in Example 2, but also other predicates used in the program.

Let us turn now to the case when P may contain negation. Then the set of circumscription formulas constructed as in Example 1 may have no Herbrand models.

EXAMPLE 3
Let P be program (4). Then circumscriptions (11) and (12) give again $\forall\, x(p(x) \equiv x = 1)$ and $\forall\, x(q(x) \equiv x = 2)$. The result of (13) is $\forall\, x\, \neg r(x)$. (Any value of r can be changed to *false* if the value of q at the same point is simultaneously changed to *true*.) Hence the only possible Herbrand model of (11), (12), and (13) is in this case

$$\{p(1),q(2)\}.$$

But the third clause of (4) is false in this model. It follows that no Herbrand model satisfies all three circumscriptions. (In fact, in the only model of (11), (12), and (13) for this program P we have $1 = 2$.) ■

It is easy to understand the source of this difficulty. The universal closure of the last clause of (4) is logically equivalent to $\forall\, x(q(x) \lor r(x))$. This sentence tells us that q and r cover the whole universe of the model. There is a conflict between the tasks of minimizing q and r.

In what sense then does model (5) minimize both q and r? The form of the last clause of (4) suggests that its intention is to use information about q for defining r. Among the possible interpretations of r, we want the one that is minimal, but minimal only under the assumption that q is given, i.e., minimal in the class of models *with the same q*. On the contrary, when q is minimized, we require that it be impossible to change any of its values to *false* even at the price of changing r arbitrarily.

In the language of circumscription, this kind of minimization can be expressed by formulas

$$C_p(P;p),\ C_q(P;q,r),\ C_r(P;r).\qquad\qquad (17)$$

If P is (4) then circumscriptions (17) hold in exactly one Herbrand model, and this model is (5).

This idea can be also expressed in terms of "priorities." When there is a conflict between the tasks of minimizing two predicates, like q and r in Example 3, we may wish to specify which minimization should be given a higher priority, i.e., whether we are ready to change values of q to *false* at the price of changing values of r to *true*, or the other way around. Model (5) corresponds to the first alternative, model (6) to the second. According to (17), predicate r is allowed to vary when q is minimized, but q must remain fixed when we minimize r. Thus we are willing to change r in order to make q stronger; in this sense, q is minimized at a higher priority than r.

For program (7), we would use the circumscriptions

$$C_p(P;p),\ C_q(P;q),\ C_r(P;q,r).$$

Model (6) is the only Herbrand model of P satisfying these three formulas.

In the general case, this idea can be expressed in terms of the *dependency graph* of P. Its nodes are the predicate symbols in the language of P, and it contains an edge (p,q) whenever there is a clause (9) in P that contains q in its head A and p in its body $L_1 \wedge \ldots \wedge L_m$. For instance, the dependency graph of program (4) has three nodes p, q, and r and one edge, (q,r).

We denote by S the set of predicate symbols in P, i.e., the set of nodes of its dependency graph. By $\leq$ we denote the pre-order on S defined by the dependency graph of P. In other words, we write $p \leq q$ if there is a path from p to q in the graph $(p,q \in S)$.

The model M_P will be defined by the circumscriptions that assign "higher priorities" to the predicates that are "smaller" with respect to this pre-order:

$$C_p(P;\{q : p \leq q\})\qquad (p \in S).\qquad\qquad (18)$$

In a model satisfying these circumscriptions, each predicate p is minimal at each point x in the sense that the value of $p(x)$ cannot be changed from *true* to *false*, even if we are allowed to simultaneously change any other values of p or any values of any predicates that follow p in the dependency graph of the program.

THEOREM 1
Any program P has at most one Herbrand model satisfying (18). ■

An edge (p,q) in the dependency graph of P is *negative* if, for some clause (9) in P, its head contains q and its body contains negated p. For instance, the edge (q, r) in the dependency graph of (4) is negative. P is *stratified* if in its dependency graph there are no cycles containing a negative edge (Apt, Blair, and Walker [1988]).

THEOREM 2
Any stratified program P has exactly one Herbrand model satisfying (18). ■

Theorem 1 is proved at the end of the paper. Theorem 2 follows from Theorem 1 and from Theorem 3 below.

Our minimal model semantics for stratified programs defines M_P to be the Herbrand model of (18). Theorem 2 expresses the correctness of this definition.

It is easy to see that the assertion of Theorem 2 does not hold for arbitrary programs. If P is (8) then (18) becomes the pair of formulas

$$C_p(P;p,q), \ C_q(P;q).$$

The second circumscription is false in all Herbrand models of (8).

Iterated Fixed Points

We will review now the iterated fixed point semantics of stratified programs according to Apt, Blair, and Walker [1988].

Let P be represented as the union of disjoint sets of clauses

$$P_1,\ldots,P_n, \tag{19}$$

with P_1 possibly empty. We say that (19) is a *stratification* of P if the following two conditions hold for $i = 1,\ldots,n$:

(i)   If a predicate p occurs in P_i then its definition is contained within $\bigcup_{j \leq i} P_j$;

(ii)   If a predicate p occurs in P_i under $\neg$ then its definition is contained within $\bigcup_{j < i} P_j$.

(The *definition* of p is the subset of P consisting of all clauses containing p on the left.) A program has a stratification iff it is stratified (Apt, Blair, and Walker [1988], Lemma 1).

Consider now a stratification (19) of a program P. For every $i = 1,...,n$, let T_i be the operator on Herbrand models (i.e., on sets of ground atoms) defined as follows: for every Herbrand model M and every ground atom A, $A \in T_i(M)$ iff $A \in M$ or, for some clause $A_1 \leftarrow L_1 \wedge ... \wedge L_m$ in P_i and some substitution θ of ground terms for variables, $L_1\theta,...,L_m\theta$ are true in M and $A = A_1\theta$.

The sets $M_0,...,M_n$ of ground atoms are defined by the equations:

$$M_0 = \emptyset,$$

$$M_i = \bigcup_{j \geq 0} T_i^j (M_{i-1}) \qquad (i = 1,...,n).$$

(T^j is T applied j times.) Apt, Blair, and Walker [1988] show that M_n is a model of P (Theorem 7), and that it does not depend on the choice of stratification (18) (Theorem 11). They propose to take this model M_n to be the denotation M_P of P.

The following theorem tells that this semantics is equivalent to the circumscriptive semantics defined above.

THEOREM 3
For any stratification (19) of a program P, M_n satisfies circumscriptions (18). ∎

By Theorem 1, M_n is the only Herbrand model of P satisfying (18). Thus the results of this paper give an alternative proof of the fact that M_n does not depend on the stratification.

Proof of Theorem 1

A Herbrand model of P is completely defined by the interpretations of all predicate constants in it. Consequently, we will prove Theorem 1 if we show that circumscriptions (18) allow us to derive an explicit definition of each predicate constant:

LEMMA

Let p be an n-ary predicate constant, x an n-tuple of distinct object variables. There exists a formula A(x) (possibly second-order) that has no parameters other than the members of x and contains no predicate constants other than equality, such that circumscriptions (18) imply $\forall x(p(x) \equiv A(x))$.

Proof: The lemma is proved by induction of the pre-order $\leq$ (which is well-founded, as is any pre-order on a finite set). Thus it is sufficient to find $A(x)$ which has all the required properties except that it may contain predicate constants that are $< p$ (i.e., constants q such that $q \leq p$ but not $p \leq q$); it will remain then to replace these constants in $A(x)$ by their explicit definitions.
Circumscription $C_p(P; \{q : p \leq q\})$ is

$$P(p_1, \ldots ,p_l) \wedge \forall xp'_1 \ldots p'_l \neg[p_1x \wedge \neg p'_1x \wedge P(p'_1, \ldots ,p'_l)],$$

where $p_1, \ldots ,p_l$ are all predicates q such that $p \leq q$; to simplify notation, we assume that p is p_1. This formula can be written as

$$P(p_1, \ldots ,p_l) \wedge \forall x[p_1(x) \supset \forall p'_1 \ldots p'_l(P(p'_1, \ldots ,p'_l) \supset p'_1(x))]. \quad (20)$$

The first term of (20) implies the converse of the conditional in the brackets, i.e.,

$$\forall x[\forall p'_1 \ldots p'_l(P(p'_1, \ldots , p'_l) \supset p'_1(x)) \supset p_1(x)]$$

(substitute $p_1, \ldots ,p_l$ for $p'_1, \ldots , p'_l$). Hence (20) can be rewritten in the form

$$P(p_1, \ldots , p_l) \wedge \forall x[p_1(x) \equiv \forall p'_1 \ldots p'_l(P(p'_1, \ldots , p'_l) \supset p'_1(x))]. \quad (21)$$

The second term of (21) has the required form, except that its right-hand side possibly contains predicate constants which are not $< p_1$. Let $p_1,\ldots,p_k$ ($k \leq l$) be the predicate constants from the same strongly connected component of the dependency graph as p_1, so that we have

$$p_1 \leq p_i, p_i \leq p_1 \quad (i = 1,\ldots,k),$$
$$p_1 < p_i \quad (i = k+1,\ldots,l).$$

Divide program P into three parts: P^1, consisting of the definitions of $p_1,\ldots,p_k$; P^2, consisting of the definitions of $p_{k+1},\ldots,p_l$; P^3, consisting of the definitions of all the other predicate symbols. It is clear that P^1 does not contain $p_{k+1},...,p_l$, and P^3 does not contain $p_1,...,p_l$; to emphasize this fact, we will write $P^1(p_1,...,p_k)$, $P^2(p_1,...,p_l)$ and P^3. Then the right-hand side of the equivalence in (21) can be written as

$$\forall\, p'_1 \cdots p'_l[(P^1(p'_1, \ldots, p'_k) \wedge P^2(p'_1, \ldots, p'_l) \wedge P^3) \supset p'_1(x)]. \qquad (22)$$

P^3 follows from the first term of (21) and thus can be dropped. Furthermore, P^2 is the only part of the formula containing $p'_{k+1},...,p'_l$, so that we can rewrite (22) as

$$\forall\, p'_1 \cdots p'_k[(P^1(p'_1, \ldots, p'_k) \wedge \exists\, p'_{k+1} \cdots p'_l P^2(p'_1, \ldots, p'_l)) \supset p'_1(x)]. \qquad (23)$$

To further simplify this formula, recall that P^2 consists of the definitions of $p_{k+1},...,p_l$. It follows that $\exists\, p'_{k+1}\cdots p'_l P^2(p'_1,...,p'_l)$ is identically true (by taking each of $p'_{k+1},...,p'_l$ identically true we can make the head of each clause in $P^2(p'_1,...,p'_l)$ true.) Hence (23) can be replaced by

$$\forall\, p'_1 \cdots p'_k[P^1(p'_1, \ldots, p'_k) \supset p'_1(x)],$$

so that the second term of (21) becomes

$$\forall\, x[p_1(x) \equiv \forall\, p'_1 \cdots p'_k(P^1(p'_1, \ldots, p'_k) \supset p'_1(x))].$$

It remains to notice that all predicate constants in $P^1(p_1,...,p_k)$ are $\leq p_1$, so that all predicate constants in $P^1(p'_1,...,p'_k)$ are $< p_1$. ∎

Proof of Theorem 3

Let $p_1,...,p_l$ be all elements of $\{q : p \leq q\}$. As in the previous proof, we will assume that p is p_1. We know that M_n is a model of $P(p_1,...,p_l)$; our goal is to show that this model satisfies the second term of the circumscription:

$$\forall\, xp'_1 \cdots p'_l \neg[p_1(x) \wedge \neg p'_1(x) \wedge P(p'_1, \ldots, p'_l)].$$

Assume that this is not the case. Then M_n satisfies

$$\exists\, xp'_1 \cdots p'_l[p_1(x) \wedge \neg p'_1(x) \wedge P(p'_1, \ldots, p'_l)]. \qquad (24)$$

This assumption can be stated in terms of models as follows. As usual in model theory, we write $M[\![q]\!]$ for the extension of a predicate q in a model M. Finding values of $p'_1,\ldots,p'_l$ that satisfy $P(p'_1,\ldots,p'_l)$ in M_n is equivalent to constructing a model of P that differs from M_n only by the interpretations of $p_1,\ldots,p_l$. Hence assumption (24) means that there exists a Herbrand model M' of P such that

(i) $M'[\![q]\!] = M_n[\![q]\!]$ for each $q \neq p_1, \ldots, p_l,$

(ii) $M_n[\![p_1]\!] \setminus M'[\![p_1]\!] \neq \emptyset$

The definition of each predicate constant is contained in some P_i. For each $i = 1,\ldots,n$, let D_i be the set of predicate constants whose definitions are contained in P_i. The description of the operators $T_1,T_2,\ldots$ shows then that, for any Herbrand model M and any predicate constant $q \in D_i, T_{i'}(M)[\![q]\!]$ may differ from $M[\![q]\!]$ only if $i' = i$. Hence

$$M_0[\![q]\!] = \ldots = M_{i-1}[\![q]\!] \quad (q \in D_i), \tag{25}$$

$$M_i[\![q]\!] = \ldots = M_n[\![q]\!] \quad (q \in D_i). \tag{26}$$

Since $M_0 = \emptyset$, (25) implies

$$M_{i-1}[\![q]\!] = \emptyset \quad (q \in D_i). \tag{27}$$

Let i_1 be such that $p_1 \in D_{i_1}$. If $q \in D_i$ for some $i < i_1$ then both property (i) of M' and formula (26) apply; it follows that

$$M_{i_1-1}[\![q]\!] = M'[\![q]\!] \quad (q \in \bigcup_{i < i_1} D_i). \tag{28}$$

Let us prove, by induction on j, that

$$T_{i_1}^j(M_{i_1-1})[\![q]\!] \subset M'[\![q]\!] \quad (q \in D_{i_1}). \tag{29}$$

For $j = 0$ this assertion follows from (27). Assume that (29) holds for some j and that, for some $q \in D_{i_1}$ and some tuple t of ground terms,

$$t \in T_{i_1}^{j+1}(M_{i_1-1})[\![q]\!], \text{ i.e.,}$$

$$q(t) \in T_{i_1}^{j+1}(M_{i_1-1}) = T_{i_1}(T_{i_1}^j(M_{i_1-1})).$$

Then, by the definition of T_{i_1}, either $q(t) \in T^j_{i_1}(M_{i_1-1})$ or, for some clause

$$A_1 \leftarrow L_1 \wedge \ldots \wedge L_m$$

from P_{i_1}, and some substitution θ, $A_1\theta$ is $q(t)$ and all literals $L_1\theta,\ldots,L_m\theta$ are true in $T^j_{i_1}(M_{i_1-1})$. In the first case, by the induction hypothesis, $t \in M'[\![q]\!]$. In the second case, let us show that all literals $L_1\theta,\ldots,L_m\theta$ are true in M'. Each of these literals has the form $q^*(t^*)$, possibly preceded by a negation, where q^* is a predicate constant and t^* is a tuple of ground terms. If

$$q^* \in \bigcup_{i < i_1} D_i$$

then, by (28), the literal is true in M'. If not then, by the definition of a stratification, the literal must be positive. Hence $q^*(t^*)$ is true in $T^j_{i_1}(M_{i_1-1})$, and it follows, by the induction hypothesis, that it is also true in M'. Thus all literals $L_1\theta,\ldots,L_m\theta$ are true in M'. Since M' is a model of P, it follows that $A_1\theta$, i.e., $q(t)$, is true in M' as well, so that again $t \in M'[\![q]\!]$. This completes the proof of (29). In particular,

$$T^j_{i_1}(M_{i_1-1})[\![p_1]\!] \subset M'[\![p_1]\!]. \tag{30}$$

Since

$$M_{i_1}[\![p_1]\!] = \bigcup_{j \geq 0} T^j_{i_1}(M_{i_1-1})[\![p_1]\!],$$

it follows from (30) that $M_{i_1}[\![p_1]\!] \subset M'[\![p_1]\!]$. Then, by (26), $M_n[\![p]\!] \subset M'[\![p]\!]$, in contradiction with property (ii) of M'.

Acknowledgments

I would like to thank Michael Gelfond and Allen Van Gelder for the discussions in which they called my attention to connections between circumscription and logic programming. In particular, Allen's observation that the dependency graph of a program contains an encoding of priorities has directly led me to the results presented in this paper. I am also grateful to Krzysztof Apt, John McCarthy, and Jack Minker for their comments on earlier drafts. This research was partially supported by DARPA under Contract N0039-82-C-0250.

References

1. Apt, K. R., Blair, H. and Walker, A. [1988], *Towards a Theory of Declarative Knowledge*, in *Foundations of Deductive Databases and Logic Programming* (J. Minker, Ed.), Morgan Kaufmann Publishers, Los Altos, CA, 89-148.

2. Apt, K. R. and van Emden, M. H. [1982], Contributions to the Theory of Logic Programming, *JACM* **29**(3):841-862.

3. Chandra, A. and Harel, D. [1985], Horn Clause Queries and Generalizations, *The Journal of Logic Programming* **1**, 1-15.

4. Emden, M. H. van and Kowalski, R. A. [1976], The Semantics of Predicate Logic as a Programming Language, *JACM* **23**(4):733-742.

5. Lifschitz, V. [1986], Pointwise Circumscription: Preliminary Report, *Proceedings AAAI-86* **1**, 406-410.

6. McCarthy, J. [1986], Applications of Circumscription to Formalizing Common-sense Knowledge, *Artificial Intelligence* **28**, 89-118.

7. Morris, K., Ullman, J. D. and Van Gelder, A. [1986], Design Overview of the NAIL! System, in Third International Conference on Logic Programming, *Lecture Notes in Computer Science* **225** (G. Goos and J. Hartmanis, Eds.), Springer-Verlag, 554-568.

8. Van Gelder, A. [1988], Negation as Failure Using Tight Derivations for General Logic Programs, in *Foundations of Deductive Databases and Logic Programming* (J. Minker, Ed.), Morgan Kaufmann Publishers, Los Altos, CA, 149-176.

5

On the Declarative Semantics of Deductive Databases and Logic Programs

Teodor C. Przymusinski

Department of Mathematical Science
University of Texas, El Paso, TX

Abstract

We investigate the declarative semantics of deductive databases and logic programs. We introduce the class of *perfect models* of a deductive database and argue that this class of models—enjoying many of the properties of the class of minimal models—provides a *correct intended semantics* for such databases, incorporating a natural form of the closed-world assumption.

We extend the notion of stratified logic programs onto the class of deductive databases, and we prove that every stratified database has perfect models and that every stratified logic program has exactly one such model. We show that perfect models are independent of the choice of a particular stratification and are, in fact, models of McCarthy's *prioritized circumscription*.

Finally, we introduce the class of *locally stratified* databases and logic programs (significantly extending the class of stratified databases) and show that all our results can be extended onto this broader class.

Introduction

A *model-theoretic approach* to the theory of deductive databases and logic programs is based on the idea of representing a database as a set DB of formulas of first-order logic and associating with DB a set M(DB) of one or more models of DB which describe the declarative meaning of the database or, in other words, its *semantics*. A sentence F is considered to be true in the database if and only if it is satisfied in all models M from M(DB) (see e.g., Gallaire, Minker, and Nicolas [1984], Reiter [1984]). In this paper, we follow the model-theoretic approach to investigate the declarative semantics of deductive databases and logic programs.

Although the minimal model semantics, i.e., the semantics based on the class of minimal models of DB (cf. Minker [1982], Gelfond et al. [1986a], Bossu and Siegel [1985], McCarthy [1984], Lifschitz [1985b], van Emden and Kowalski [1976]), seems suitable for the class of *positive* databases, i.e., those that do not permit negative premises in their clauses, it is not adequate for as it does in the case of positive programs (see e.g., Bossu and Siegel [1985], Lloyd [1984] and Section 3).

In this paper we introduce the class of *perfect models* of a deductive database and argue that this class of models provides a *correct intended semantics* for such databases, incorporating a natural form of the closed-world assumption. The class of perfect models is a subclass of the class of all minimal models, enjoying many of their natural properties. For positive databases, perfect models coincide with minimal models.

We extend the notion of stratified logic programs—introduced by Apt, Blair, and Walker [1988] and, independently, by Van Gelder [1988] (see also Naqvi [1986])—onto the class of deductive databases and we prove that *every stratified database has perfect models and that every stratified logic program has exactly one* such model. Moreover, this unique perfect model coincides with the models considered by Apt et al. We show that perfect models are independent of the choice of a particular stratification and are in fact models of McCarthy's *prioritized circumscription* (see McCarthy [1984] and Lifschitz [1985]).

Finally, we introduce the class of *locally stratified* databases and logic programs. This class significantly extends the class of stratified databases, by including many natural programs and databases, which fail to be stratified. We show that all our results can be extended onto this broader class.

In this paper we only discuss the *declarative* semantics of deductive databases and logic programs. *Procedural* issues are discussed in Przymusinski [1987] (see also Przymusinski [1986a], [1986b]). It is essential that a clear separation be achieved between declarative and procedural meaning of a database so that we know what *knowledge* it represents, regardless of particular *mechanisms* used to retrieve it (cf. Apt et al. [1988]).

Throughout this paper we allow function symbols and by a *model* of DB we always mean a *Herbrand model*, i.e., a subset of the Herbrand base of DB. The restriction to Herbrand models is only made to simplify the exposition. Analogous results are valid for arbitrary models. We expand on this subject in Przymusinski [1987].

Minimal Model Semantics

The model-theoretic approach is particularly well-understood in the case of the so called *(definite) Horn* databases, otherwise known as *positive logic programs*, i.e., databases consisting of clauses of the form:

$$A_1 \text{ \& } A_2 \text{ \& } \ldots \text{ \& } A_m \rightarrow C,$$

with m $\geq$ 0, and C and A_i denoting atomic formulas (atoms).

EXAMPLE 1

Suppose that our database DB consists of clauses

Physicist(x) $\rightarrow$ Good_mathematician(x)

Physicist(Einstein)

Businessman(Iacocca).

This database has several different models, the largest of which is the model M_{max} in which both men are at the same time businessmen, physicists, and good mathematicians. This model hardly seems to correctly describe the intended meaning of DB. In particular, there is nothing in this database to imply that Iacocca is a physicist or that Einstein is a businessman. In fact, we are inclined to believe that the lack of such information indicates that we can assume the contrary.

This database also has a smallest model M_{min} in which only Einstein is a physicist and good mathematician and only Iacocca is a businessman. This model seems to correctly reflect the semantics of DB, at the same time incorporating the classical case of the closed-world assumption, namely Reiter's CWA: if no reason exists for some positive statement to be true, we are allowed to infer that it is false (Reiter [1978]). ■

In view of the fact that every Horn database has exactly one minimal (i.e., smallest) model, the above example illustrates the following principle.

PRINCIPLE 1

The unique minimal model of a Horn database DB provides a natural semantics of DB, incorporating a suitable form of the closed-world assumption. ■

Horn databases constitute a fairly restricted class of deductive databases and do not allow the full expressive power of first order logic to be utilized. A natural extension of this class of databases is obtained by allowing disjunctions of atoms in the consequents of the clauses, thereby permitting general forms of disjunctive information. We will call such databases *positive disjunctive*. A positive disjunctive database therefore consists of a set of clauses of the form

$$A_1 \ \& \ A_2 \ \& \ \dots \ \& \ A_m \rightarrow C_1 \vee \dots \vee C_p,$$

where $m \geq 0$, $p \geq 1$, and A_i and C_k denote atoms.

EXAMPLE 2
Suppose that a database DB consists of clauses

Famous_man(x) → Successful_businessman(x) ∨ Renown_scientist(x)

Famous_man(Smith)

Good_mathematician(Jones)

Again, this database has several models, in the largest of which, M_{max}, both men, Smith and Jones, are successful businessmen, renowned scientists, good mathematicians, and famous men. This model obviously does not represent the intended meaning of DB.

It is however also easy to see that this database does not have a smallest model. How therefore are we supposed to define the semantics of DB? The problem fortunately has a natural solution: Even though DB does not have a smallest model, it has two models which are *minimal*, i.e., they do not contain any smaller models. In one of them, M_1, Smith is the only famous man, Jones is the only good mathematician, and Smith is the only successful businessman. The other model, M_2, differs from the first by making Smith the only renowned scientist instead of the only successful businessman. Both of these models seem to correctly capture *one aspect* of the intended meaning of DB, and together M_1 and M_2 define a proper semantics for DB: A sentence F is true in DB if and only if it is true in both models. In particular, it is true that Smith is either a famous businessman or a renowned scientist, but we do not know which. On the other hand, it is also true that Jones is neither a famous man, nor a successful businessman, nor a renowned scientist, since all of these are false in both minimal models. ■

It is well-known that for every model N of a positive disjunctive database DB there is a minimal model M of DB that is contained in N (Bossu and Siegel [1985]). In particular, every positive disjunctive database has at least one minimal model. The minimal model semantics corresponds to a natural form of the closed-world assumption, namely the so called Extended Closed-World Assumption (ECWA) (see Gelfond et al. [1986a]), which extends Minker's Generalized Closed World Assumption (Minker [1978]) (see also Yahya and Henschen [1985] and Gelfond et al. [1986b]). For Herbrand models, it is also equivalent to the semantics of parallel circumscription (with all predicates minimized) (McCarthy [1980], Lifschitz [1985a]). This leads to the following principle, generalizing Principle 1.

PRINCIPLE 2 (PRINCIPLE OF MINIMAL MODEL SEMANTICS)
The set MIN(DB) of all minimal models of a positive disjunctive database DB provides intended semantics of DB, incorporating a suitable form of the closed-world assumption. ■

Minimal Model Semantics Is Not Sufficient for General Databases

The expressive power of positive disjunctive databases is not sufficient for general databases. In practical applications, permitting negation in the premises of the rules greatly increases their expressiveness. We will call a database *disjunctive* if it consists of a set of clauses of the form:

$$A_1 \& \dots \& A_m \& \neg B_1 \& \dots \& \neg B_n \rightarrow C_1 \vee \dots \vee C_p,$$

where $m, n \geq 0$, $p \geq 1$, and A_i, B_j and C_k denote atoms.[1] If $p = 1$ for all clauses, then such a database is called a *(general) logic program* (see Lloyd [1984]).

With disjunctive databases the situation becomes more complex.

EXAMPLE 3
Suppose that we know that a typical businessman tends to avoid using advanced mathematics in his work, unless somehow he happens to be a good mathematician, and that Iacocca is a businessman, and that Einstein is a physicist. We can express these facts using negations as follows:

Businessman(x) & ¬Good_mathematician(x) → Avoids_math(x)   (1)

Businessman(Iacocca)

Physicist(Einstein)

This database DB has two minimal models M_1 and M_2. In both of them Iacocca is the only businessman and Einstein is the only physicist; but in M_1 Iacocca avoids advanced mathematics and in M_2 he is a good mathematician, instead. Do both of these models capture the intended meaning of DB?

---

[1] Such databases are called *positivistic* by Bidoit and Hull [1986].

Clearly not! By placing the negated predicate Good_mathematician(x) among the premises of the rule, we most likely intended to say that businessmen, in general, do not use advanced mathematics unless they happen to be good mathematicians. Since we have no reason to believe that Iacocca is a good mathematician, we are forced to infer that he does not use advanced mathematics. Therefore, only the first minimal model M_1 corresponds with the intended meaning of DB.

The reason for this asymmetry is easy to explain. The first clause (1) of DB is logically equivalent to the following clause (2) without negation:

$$\text{Businessman}(x) \rightarrow \text{Good\_mathematician}(x) \vee \text{Avoids\_math}(x) \qquad (2)$$

and models M_1 and M_2 are therefore also minimal models of the positive disjunctive database DB^*, obtained from DB by replacing (1) by (2). These models provide a correct semantics of DB^* because DB^* does not assign different priorities to the predicates Good_mathematician and Avoids_math treating them as equally plausible. The database DB, on the other hand, gives a *higher priority* to the predicate Good_mathematician than to the predicate Avoids_math. [2]

We can easily imagine the above priorities reversed. This is for instance the case in the following database:

Physicist(x) & $\neg$ Avoids_math(x) $\rightarrow$ Good_mathematician(x)

Businessman(Iacocca)

Physicist(Einstein),

which says that if x is a physicist and if we have no specific evidence showing that he avoids mathematics, then we are allowed to assume that he is a good mathematician. This shows that relative priorities among the predicates in the database are determined by the syntax of its clauses, with *consequents having lower priority than negated premises.* ∎

From the preceding example we can see that the set MIN(DB) of all minimal models of a disjunctive database *may contain models which do not properly interpret the declarative meaning of the database* and therefore we need to properly identify the class of those minimal models of DB which provides the correct, intended meaning of DB. The class of perfect models described in the next section fulfills those needs.

---

[2]According to the established convention (see e.g., Lifschitz [1985a]), higher priority means *higher priority for minimization*, i.e., predicate A has a higher priority than predicate B if A is supposed to be minimized before B is.

Perfect Model Semantics

In this section we introduce the class of *perfect models* of a disjunctive database. The class of perfect models is a subclass of the class of minimal models, enjoying many of its natural properties. We define the *perfect model semantics* of a disjunctive database DB to be the semantics based on the class PERF(DB) of perfect models of DB and we argue that this semantics correctly describes the intended meaning of disjunctive databases, at the same time generalizing the Principle of Minimal Model Semantics (Principle 2) for positive disjunctive databases.

Suppose that DB is any disjunctive database, i.e., DB consists of clauses K of the form:

$$A_1 \ \& \ \dots \ \& \ A_m \ \& \ \neg B_1 \ \& \ \dots \ \& \ \neg B_n \rightarrow C_1 \vee \dots \vee C_p,$$

where $m, n \geq 0$, $p \geq 1$, and A_i, B_j and C_k denote atoms. (In particular, suppose that DB is a general logic program.) We have observed before that the syntax of clauses determines relative *priorities* among the predicates in the database and that

I.   Negative premises should have *higher* priority than consequents.

 Moreover, we can assume that

II.   Positive premises should have priority *higher than or equal* to that of consequents.

 Indeed, if $A \rightarrow B$, then minimizing B immediately results in A being minimized, too. Consequently, A is always minimized before or at the same time that B is minimized. It is also natural to require that

III. Predicates appearing in the consequent of a given clause should have *the same* priority.

 Indeed, otherwise those predicates whose priority is higher should be converted into negative premises.

It will be convenient to generalize these observations slightly and talk about relative priorities between *ground atoms* instead of priorities between *predicate symbols*. More precisely, let L be any first order language which has an infinite supply of variables and contains all and only those constants,[3] function symbols, and predicate symbols that appear in DB. We consider L to be the underlying language of the first order theory DB and we denote by H the *Herbrand*

---

[3]But at least one.

base of L, i.e., the set of all ground atoms in L, i.e., atoms that do not contain variables. We call H the *Herbrand base of DB*. We denote by P the set of all predicate symbols of DB.

To formalize conditions I–III, we introduce a *priority relation* < between elements A and B of the Herbrand base H and an auxiliary relation ≤. If A < B, then we say the *B has priority higher than A* and if A ≤ B, then we say that the *priority of A is less than or equal to the priority of B*.

DEFINITION 1
Relations < and ≤ are defined by the following rules:

(PR1) (condition I) C < B, if B is a negative premise and C is one of the consequents in a ground instance of a clause from DB;

(PR2) (condition II) C ≤ A, if A is a positive premise and C is one of the consequents in a ground instance of a clause from DB;

(PR3) (condition III) C ≤ C′, if C and C′ are both consequents in a ground instance of a clause from DB;

augmented by obvious transitivity and closure rules:

(PR4) (transitivity of ≤) if A ≤ B and B ≤ C, then A ≤ C;

(PR5) (transitivity of <) if A ≤ B and B < C (resp. D < A) then A < C (resp. D < B);

(PR6) (< implies ≤) if A < B, then A ≤ B;

(PR7) (closure axiom) Nothing else satisfies < or ≤. ■

EXAMPLE 4
In the database given by

$$B(x) \ \& \ \neg G(x) \to A(x) \lor C(x)$$

$$P(x) \to G(x)$$

$$B(I)$$

we have A(I) < G(I), C(I) < G(I) (by PR1); A(I) ≤ B(I), C(I) ≤ B(I) G(I) ≤ P(I) (by PR2); and A(I) ≤ C(I), C(I) ≤ A(I) (by PR3). Consequently, A(I) < P(I), C(I) < P(I) (by PR5), but neither P(I) < C(I), nor A(I) < B(I) is true (by PR7). ■

Now that we have defined the priority relation < between ground atoms of DB, we are prepared to define the notion of a perfect model. It is our goal to *minimize high priority atoms as much as possible* and therefore we are willing to minimize the set of higher priority atoms in our models, even at the cost of enlarging the set of atoms of lower priority. It follows, that if M is a model of DB and if a new model N is obtained from M by possibly adding and/or removing some ground atoms from M, then we should consider the new model N to be *preferable* to M if and only if addition of a lower priority atom A to N is always *justified* by the simultaneous removal from M of a higher priority atom B, i.e., such that A < B. A model M will be considered *perfect*, if there are *no* models preferable to it. More formally:

DEFINITION 2[4]

Suppose that M and N are two *distinct* models of a disjunctive database DB. We say that N is *preferable* to M (or $N \ll M$), if for every ground atom A in $N - M$ there is a ground atom B in $M - N$, such that A < B. We say that a model M of DB is *perfect* if there are no models preferable to M.

We call the relation $\ll$ the *preference relation* between models. If M = N or $M \ll N$ then we write $M \leq N$. ∎

PROPOSITION 1

If $N \subset M$, then $N \ll M$. In particular, every perfect model is minimal.

Proof: The first assertion is obvious and the second immediately follows from the first. ∎

PROPOSITION 2

In a positive disjunctive database $M \ll N$ if and only if $M \subset N$. Consequently, a model is perfect if and only if it is minimal.

Proof: If DB is positive disjunctive, then the priority relation < is empty. Consequently, $M \ll N$ iff $M \subset N$. ∎

PROPOSITION 3

In order to show that a model M is perfect it suffices to show that there are no *minimal* models preferable to M.

Proof: Suppose that there are no minimal models preferable to M and suppose that N is a model such that $N \ll M$. Let K be a minimal model such that K is contained in N (see Bossu and Siegel [1985]). Then $K \ll M$, which is a contradiction. ∎

---

[4]D. Proudian pointed out that this ordering is similar to the multiset ordering considered in Dershowitz and Manna [1979].

EXAMPLE 5
Only model M_1 in Example 3 is perfect. Indeed:

$$M_1 = \{\text{Businessman(I)},\text{Physicist(E)},\text{Avoids\_math(I)}\},$$

$$M_2 = \{\text{Businessman(I)},\text{Physicist(E)},\text{Good\_mathematician(I)}\},$$

and we know that Good_mathematician(I) > Avoids_math(I) and therefore $M_1 \ll M_2$. Consequently, M_1 is perfect, but M_2 is not. ∎

Not every disjunctive database—nor even a logic program—has a perfect model:

EXAMPLE 6
The database:

$$\neg p(a) \to q(a) \text{ and } \neg q(a) \to p(a) \tag{5}$$

has only two minimal models $M_1 = \{p(a)\}$ and $M_2 = \{q(a)\}$ and since $p(a) < q(a)$ and $q(a) < p(a)$ we have $M_1 \ll M_2$ and $M_2 \ll M_1$, thus none of the models is perfect. The cause of this peculiarity is quite clear: our semantics is based on relative priorities between ground atoms and therefore we have to be consistent when assigning those priorities to avoid priority conflicts (cycles), which could render our semantics meaningless. ∎

EXAMPLE 7 (V. LIFSCHITZ)
For a more interesting example, consider the database DB defined by:

$$p(0)$$

$$\neg p(s(x)) \to p(x).$$

This database has infinitely many minimal models, but it is easy to verify that for any model N there is a model M such that $M \ll N$ and $N \ll M$, which implies that there are no perfect models of DB. It also shows that in this case the preference relation $\ll$ is not transitive. Notice that H contains an infinite sequence of atoms with increasing priorities, namely $p(0) < p(s(0)) < p(s(s(0)))$ ..., and therefore, intuitively, no matter how much we try to minimize high priority atoms we can never complete our task. ∎

DEFINITION 3
A relation $<$ is said to be *noetherian* if there is *no* infinite increasing sequence $A_0 < A_1 < A_2 < \cdots$. ∎

The non-existence of perfect models in the above examples and the fact that the preference relation $\ll$ was not transitive (and therefore not a partial order) turns out to be caused by the fact that the priority relation $<$ was not noetherian.

THEOREM 1

If the priority relation $<$ is noetherian, then both the priority relation $<$ and the preference relation $\ll$ are partial orders.[5]

Proof: If $<$ is noetherian then clearly there can be no atoms A such that $A < A$ and so $<$ must be a partial order. Since it is not true that $M \ll M$ for any model M, it suffices to show that the preference relation $\ll$ is transitive.

Suppose that $M \ll N$ and $N \ll R$, $A \in M - R$ and suppose that there is no $B > A$ such that $B \in R - M$. Since $<$ is noetherian, we can assume that A is a maximal atom with this property. Suppose first that $A \in N$. Then $A \in N - R$ and there is a $C > A$ such that $C \in R - N$. We can assume that C is a maximal atom with this property. Now, if C does not belong to M then $C \in R - M$, a contradiction. If $C \in M$, then $C \in M - N$ and there is a D such that $D > C$ and $D \in N - M$. If $D \in R$, then $D \in R - M$, a contradiction. Otherwise, $D \in N - R$ and there is an $E > D$ such that $E \in R - N$, but this contradicts the maximality of C.

Suppose now that A does not belong to N. Then $A \in M - N$ and there is a D such that $D > A$ and $D \in N - M$. We can assume that D is maximal. If $D \in R$ then we obtain a contradiction. Otherwise, $D \in N - R$ and there is a maximal E such that $E > D$ and $E \in R - N$. If E does not belong to M then we have a contradiction. Otherwise, $E \in M - N$ and there is an $F > E$ such that $F \in N - M$. This contradicts the maximality of D and completes the proof. ∎

As we will see in the next section (see Theorem 2 and Theorem 4), the fact that $<$ is noetherian also guarantees the existence of perfect models.

Finally, let us observe, that if in Definition 1 we introduced a relation between *predicate symbols* rather than between *ground atoms*, we would have an analogously defined transitive *predicate priority relation* $<_p$ between predicate symbols. This would be equivalent to stating that, for any two predicate symbols p and q:

$$p <_p q \text{ iff } p(\mathbf{a}) < p(\mathbf{b}), \text{ for some } \mathbf{a},\mathbf{b}. \quad \blacksquare$$

Due to the finiteness of the set of predicates, we can easily prove:

---

[5]By a *partial order* we mean an irreflexive and transitive relation.

PROPOSITION 4
The predicate priority relation $<_p$ is noetherian iff it is a partial order. Moreover, if $<_p$ is noetherian then so is $<$.

Proof: If there exists an infinite increasing (in the sense of $<_p$) sequence of elements of P, then two of its elements must have the same predicate symbol A, which implies that $A <_p A$ and shows that $<_p$ is not irreflexive. The converse is obvious.

If there exists an infinite increasing (in the sense of $<$) sequence of elements of H then two of its elements must have the same predicate symbol, which implies that $<_p$ is not noetherian. ∎

The property that the relation $<$ (resp. the relation $<_p$) is noetherian will lead us in the next section to the concepts of locally stratified (resp. stratified) databases.

Stratified and Locally Stratified Databases

Now we are ready to define the notions of a stratified and locally stratified database. For logic programs, the notion of a stratified database coincides with the notion of a stratified logic program as defined in Apt et al. [1988] and Van Gelder [1988] (see also Naqvi [1986]).

DEFINITION 4
A database DB is called *stratified* if it is possible to decompose the set P of all *predicates* of DB into disjoint sets $P_0, P_1, \cdots, P_r$, called *strata*, so that for every clause

$$A_1 \& \ldots \& A_m \& \neg B_1 \& \ldots \& \neg B_n \rightarrow C_1 \vee \ldots \vee C_p,$$

in DB we have that:

(i)   all the consequents C_i belong to the same stratum, say P_k;

(ii)   all the positive premises A_i belong to $\cup \{P_j: j \leq i\}$;

(ii)   all the negative premises B_i belong to $\cup \{P_j: j < i\}$.

Any particular decomposition $\{P_0, P_1, \cdots, P_r\}$ of P satisfying the above conditions is called a *stratification of DB*. ∎

DEFINITION 5
A database DB is called *locally stratified* if it is possible to decompose the *Herbrand base* H of DB into disjoint sets, called *strata*, $H_0, H_1, \cdots, H_\alpha, \cdots$, where $\alpha < \gamma$ and γ is a countable ordinal, so that for every *ground instance* of a clause

$$A_1 \& \ldots \& A_m \& \neg B_1 \& \ldots \& \neg B_n \rightarrow C_1 \vee \ldots \vee C_p,$$

in DB we have that:

(i)   all the consequents C_i belong to the same stratum, say P_k;

(ii) all the positive premises A_i belong to $\bigcup \{P_j: j \leq i\}$;

(iii) all the negative premises B_i belong to $\bigcup \{P_j: j < i\}$.

Any particular decomposition $\{H_0, H_1, \cdots, H_\alpha, \cdots\}$ of H satisfying the above conditions is called a *local stratification of DB*. ∎

In the above definitions, the decomposition of P or H determines priority levels (strata) of P or H, with lower level (stratum) denoting higher priority for minimization. The difference between the definitions of stratified and locally stratified databases is that in the latter case we decompose the Herbrand base H of DB instead of decomposing the set P of all predicate symbols of DB. Consequently, since in the presence of function symbols the Herbrand base is infinite, our decomposition may be infinite. We have however:

PROPOSITION 5
Every stratified database is locally stratified.

Proof: Any decomposition $D = P_0, P_1, \cdots, P_r$ of the set P of predicate symbols of DB immediately leads to the corresponding decomposition $E = H_0, H_1, \cdots, H_r$ of the Herbrand base H of DB defined by:

$$H_i = \{A \in H: \text{predicate symbol of A belongs to } P_i\}.$$

It is routine to verify that if D is a stratification of DB then E is a (finite) local stratification of DB. ∎

Before giving examples of stratified and locally stratified databases, we provide characterizations of stratified and locally stratified databases in terms of the priority relation $<$ and the predicate priority relation $<_P$:

THEOREM 2
A database DB is *locally stratified* if and only if the priority relation $<$ on H is noetherian. ∎

THEOREM 3
A database DB is *stratified* if and only if the predicate priority relation $<_p$ on P is noetherian (or, equivalently, if it is a partial order).[6]

Proof: Suppose that $\{H_0, \cdots, H_\alpha, \ldots\}$ is a local stratification of DB. Notice that if $A \in H_\alpha$ and if $B > A$, then $B \in H_\beta$, where $\beta < \alpha$. In view of the fact that the ordinals are well-ordered, this implies that the priority relation $<$ is noetherian.

Suppose now that $<$ is noetherian on H. Define H_0 to be the set of all maximal atoms in H, i.e., such atoms A for which there is no $B > A$. Since $<$ is noetherian, this set cannot be empty. Suppose that H_β was defined already for $\beta < \alpha$. Let $K = H - \cup \{H_\beta : \beta < \alpha\}$ and let H_α be the set of all maximal elements of K. Again, H_α cannot be empty. One easily shows that $\{H_0, \cdots, H_\alpha, \ldots\}$ is a local stratification of DB. An analogous proof works for stratified databases. ∎

It follows from the results of the previous section that in every locally stratified database—and thus also in every stratified database—the *preference relation* $\ll$ between models is a partial order. All the databases described so far in this paper, with the exception of Examples 6 and 7 are stratified. Databases in Examples 6 and 7 are not even locally stratified. We now present examples of locally stratified databases (in fact, logic programs) which are not stratified.

EXAMPLE 8
The following program gives a definition of even numbers:

even(0).

$\neg$even(X) $\rightarrow$ even(s(X)).

Here s(X) is meant to represent the successor function on the set of natural numbers. This program is not stratified because even $<_p$ even and so $<_p$ is not

---

[6]See Proposition 4.

a partial order, but it is locally stratified, because every increasing sequence of ground atoms is of the form:

$$\text{even}(s(s(s(...)))) < \text{even}(s(s(...))) < \text{even}(s(...)) < ... < s(0) < 0$$

and therefore it must be finite. ∎

EXAMPLE 9 (J. McCARTHY)
The following program DB describes the results of certain block-moving actions:

$$\neg ab(X,Y,S) \rightarrow on(X,Y,r(m(X,Y),S))$$

$$on(Z,X,S) \rightarrow ab(X,Y,S)$$

Here, "on(X,Y,S)" means that block X is on block Y in situation S; "r(E,S)" describes the result of event E in situation S; "m(X,Y)" is the action of moving X on Y and "ab(X,Y,S)" means that the action m(X,Y) in S is abnormal (i.e., does not lead to normal results). Consequently, the first clause says that unless something is abnormal, the result of moving X onto Y is that X is on Y. The second rule states that the situation is abnormal if some Z is already on X. The program is not stratified because ab $>_P$ on and on $\geq_P$ ab and consequently, ab $>_P$ ab. It is easy to check, however, that DB is locally stratified, because situation terms decrease in complexity and so every increasing sequence of atoms must be finite. ∎

Locally stratified programs of the above described type appear to be quite natural and useful in applications and seem to be essentially more expressive than stratified programs. Moreover, they have a well-defined declarative semantics (see Theorem 4) and it can be shown that for example SLDNF-resolution (see Lloyd [1984]) provides a sound query answering mechanism for this semantics (see Przymusinski [1987]). This seems to suggest that locally stratified programs should be included in the class of "permissible logic programs with negation." On the other hand, although it is quite easy to check whether a program or a database is stratified (the set P of predicates is finite), methods to verify local stratifiability of databases have yet to be developed. (This is an interesting open problem.)

Our basic result states that every model of a locally stratified database is "subsumed" by a perfect model, and therefore, in particular, every locally stratified database has at least one perfect model. This is analogous to the similar property of minimal models.

THEOREM 4 (BASIC)

For every model N of a locally stratified database DB there exists a perfect model M such that $M \leq N$. In particular, every locally stratified database has at least one perfect model.

Moreover, if DB is a logic program then DB has a unique perfect model M_{DB} and for every other model M we have $M_{DB} \leq M$. For stratified logic programs, M_{DB} coincides with the model constructed in Apt et al. [1988] and Van Gelder [1988].

Proof: Suppose that $\{H_0,...,H_\alpha,\cdots\}$, $\alpha < \beta$, is a local stratification of DB, and suppose that N is a model of DB, i.e., a subset of the Herbrand base H. Since we are only considering Herbrand models of DB, we can replace DB by the (possibly infinite) set DB$'$ of all ground instantiations of its clauses. For every $\alpha < \beta$ let DB_α be the set of all those clauses from DB$'$ whose consequents belong to H_α. For $0 < \alpha \leq \beta$ let H^α be $\cup \{H_\gamma : \gamma < \alpha\}$ and DB^α be $\cup \{DB_\gamma : \gamma < \alpha\}$. Obviously, DB$' = DB^\beta$ and $H = H^\beta$. If T is a subset of H, then by $T|\alpha$ we denote the restriction of T to H^α. ∎

Notice that from the definition of local stratifiability it follows that the set of all ground atoms of DB^α is contained in H^α, and therefore we can identify models of DB^α with subsets of H^α. The following lemma plays a crucial role in the proof of the theorem:

LEMMA 1

Suppose that S is a subset of H^α, which is a model of DB^α, for some $\alpha < \beta$. Suppose also that T is a subset of H^γ, where $\gamma = \alpha+1$, which is a model of DB^γ such that $S \leq T|\alpha$.

There exists a subset ME(S,T) of H^γ, called a *minimal extension of S modulo T*, with the following properties:

(i)   ME(S,T) is a model of DB^γ and ME(S,T)$|\alpha = S$;

(ii) ME(S,T) is a minimal model of $DB^\gamma \cup S$;

(iii) ME(S,T) $\leq$ T .

Moreover, properties (i)–(iii) imply:

(iv) ME(S,T) is perfect iff S is perfect;

(v)   if DB is a logic program, then ME(S,T) is unique.

Proof of Lemma 1: First modify the database DB_α as follows:

R1. Remove all clauses containing a negative premise $\neg B_i$ such that B_i is in S;

R2. Remove all clauses whose heads contain atoms belonging to T;

R3. From the remaining clauses remove all the negative premises (they are all satisfied in S);

and let D be the modified database.

Now consider a *positive disjunctive* database E defined as follows:

$$E = D \cup S \cup (T \cap H_\alpha),$$

and let a subset M of H^γ be a minimal model of E.

Notice that $M \upharpoonright \alpha = S$. Indeed, since consequents of clauses from D belong to H_α, the only elements from H^α "forced" to be in M are those from S. We will first decompose M into an increasing sequence M_n of subsets defined as follows. Let $M_0 = S \cup (T \cap H_\alpha)$. For $n \geq 0$, let $M_{n+1} = M_n \cup \{C \in M:$ there is a clause $A_1 \& \ldots \& A_m \rightarrow C_1 \vee \ldots \vee C_p$ in D such that $C = C_i$, for some i, and all A_j's belong to $M_n\}$.

Clearly, by definition, $M^* = \cup \{M_n\}$ is contained in M. Notice, however, that M^* is also a model of $E = D \cup S \cup (T \cap H_\alpha)$. Indeed, $S \cup (T \cap H_\alpha)$ is contained in M_0. If $A_1 \& \ldots \& A_m \rightarrow C_1 \vee \ldots \vee C_p$ is a clause in D such that all A_i's belong to M^*, then there is an r such that all A_i's belong to M_r, and since one of the C_i's must belong to M, it must also belong to M_{r+1}. This shows that the clause is satisfied by M^*. Since M was a minimal model of E, this implies that $M = M^*$ and thus $M = \cup \{M_n\}$.

We will now show that $M \leq T$. Take any $A \in M - T$. We are supposed to show that there is a $B > A$ such that $B \in T - M$. We can assume that A belongs to M_n, for some n. The proof is by induction on n. If $n = 0$, then $A \in$ S and thus $A \in S - T$ and since $S \leq T \upharpoonright \alpha$ there is a $B > A$ such that $B \in T - S$. Since $B \in M^\alpha$, this implies that $B \in T - M$.

Assume now that $n = r + 1$ and therefore $A \in M_{r+1}$. By definition of M_{r+1}, there must exist a clause:

$$A_1 \& \ldots \& A_m \rightarrow C_1 \vee \ldots \vee C_p$$

in D derived from a clause:

$$A_1 \& \ldots \& A_m \& \neg B_1 \& \ldots \& \neg B_n \rightarrow C_1 \vee \ldots \vee C_p,$$

in DB_α so that the following conditions are satisfied:

(a) there is an i such that C_i is equal to A;

(b) all A_i's belong to M_r;

(c) no B_j belongs to S;

(d) no C_j belongs to T.

If there is an A_i that does not belong to T, then $A_i \in M_r - T$ and in view of the inductive assumption, there is a $B > A_i$ such that $B \in T - M$ and clearly $B > A$. Suppose then that all the A_i's belong to T and ᴖone of the B_j's belongs to T. Since T is a model of DB_α, one of the atoms in $C_1 \vee \ldots \vee C_p$ must belong to T, but that contradicts (d). It follows that one of the B_j's must be in $T - S$ and clearly $B_j > A$. This shows that $M \leq T$.

Observe that M is a model of $S \cup DB^\gamma$. Indeed, since $M |\alpha = S$, S is contained in M. Every clause from DB^γ is satisfied in M, because either (a) it belongs to DB^α and is therefore satisfied by S, or (b) it contains a negative premise $\neg B$, such that $B \in S$ or (c) its head contains an atom from $T \cap H_\alpha$ and $T \cap H_\alpha$ is contained in M, or (d) its subset is in D and is therefore satisfied by M.

We can therefore find a minimal model $M' \subseteq M$ of $S \cup DB^\gamma$. We define $ME(S,T) = M'$. Conditions (i) and (ii) easily follow from the definition of $ME(S,T)$. Condition (iii) follows from the fact that $M \leq T$ and $M' \subseteq M$.

We now show that conditions (iv) and (v) follow from conditions (i)–(iii). To prove (iv), assume that S is perfect and that $ME(S,T)$ is not. There exists a model K of DB^γ such that $K \ll ME(S,T)$. Then obviously, $K' = K |\alpha \leq S$ and since S is perfect, $K' = S$. This implies that $K \subseteq ME(S,T)$ and since K is a model of $DB^\gamma \cup S$ and $ME(S,T)$ is a minimal such model, we must have $ME(S,T) = K$, which is impossible. Assume now that $ME(S,T)$ is perfect and S is not. Then there exists a model Z of DB^γ such that $Z \ll S$. Then, $ME(Z,ME(S,T)) \leq ME(S,T)$ and since $Z \neq S$ we have $ME(Z,ME(S,T)) \ll ME(S,T)$, which is again impossible.

Finally in order to prove (v), assume that DB is a logic program and observe that the model $ME(S,T)$ must be a minimal model of the positive logic program $H = S \cup G$, where G is the program obtained from DB_α after reductions R1 and R3 described above are performed. Indeed, $ME(S,T)$ is a model of H, because it is a model of DB^γ and $ME(S,T) |\alpha = S$. Moreover, if there existed a proper subset N of $ME(S,T)$, which is a model of H, then N would also satisfy (i), thus showing that $ME(S,T)$ violates (ii), which is impossible. Since every positive logic program has exactly one minimal model, $ME(S,T)$ must be unique. ∎

Proof of the theorem (continued): Using the above lemma, we will construct by induction on $0 < \gamma \le \beta$ subsets M^γ of H^γ satisfying the following conditions:

(a) M^γ is a perfect model of DB^γ;

(b) $M^\gamma \le N \upharpoonright \gamma$;

(c) $M^\gamma \upharpoonright \alpha = M^\alpha$, for $\alpha < \gamma$.

For $\gamma = 1$, DB^1 is positive disjunctive and so we let M^1 be any minimal model of DB^1 contained in $N \mid 1$. By Proposition 2, M^1 is perfect and $M^1 \le N \mid 1$.

Suppose that the construction has been performed for $\alpha < \gamma$. If γ is a limit ordinal then it suffices to set

$$M^\gamma = \bigcup M^\alpha, \alpha < \gamma.$$

It is clear that (c) holds. To prove (a), suppose that M^γ is not perfect. Then there is a model K of DB^γ such that $K \ll M^\gamma$. But then for every $\alpha < \gamma$ either $K \upharpoonright \alpha \ll M^\alpha$ or $K \upharpoonright \alpha = M^\alpha$. Since all of the M^α's are perfect only the latter can take place and consequently $M^\gamma = K$, which is impossible. To prove (b), take an $A \in M^\gamma - N \upharpoonright \gamma$. There exists an $\alpha < \gamma$ such that $A \in M^\alpha$. Consequently, A $\in M^\alpha$-$N \upharpoonright \alpha$ and therefore there is a $B > A$ such that $B \in N \upharpoonright \alpha$-$M^\alpha$ and thus $B \in N \upharpoonright \gamma$-$M^\gamma$.

Suppose now that $\gamma = \alpha + 1$. Then we define M^γ as $\text{ME}(M^\alpha, N \upharpoonright \gamma)$. It follows immediately from the lemma that all conditions (a)–(c) are satisfied.

The model $M = M^\beta$ is a perfect model of DB such that $M \le N$.

Observe that *the above constructed models M are the only perfect models of DB*. Indeed, for every model N there exists such a perfect model M, produced by the above construction, with the property that $M \le N$. Consequently, if N is perfect then it must be equal to M. Suppose now that DB is a logic program. By the lemma, the above construction produces a unique model M and therefore M is the unique perfect model of DB.

We have shown above that if DB is a logic program, then ME(S,T) is the unique minimal model of the positive logic program H = S U G, where G is the program obtained from DB_α after reductions R1 and R3 described above are performed. ME(S,T) is therefore independent of T. If DB is stratified by a decomposition $\{P_0, P_1, \cdots, P_r\}$ of P, then its unique perfect model M of DB is obtained by a finite iteration: let M^1 be the unique minimal model of DB^1 and for $n \le r$, let M^{n+1} be $\text{ME}(M^n)$. Since, in this case, the construction of M coincides with the construction used in Apt et al. [1988] and Van Gelder [1988], the resulting models are the same. This completes the proof of Theorem 4. ∎

The above theorem shows that the perfect model semantics is well-defined for any locally stratified disjunctive database DB and, in the special case when DB is a stratified logic program, the unique perfect model M_{DB} of DB coincides with the model introduced in Apt, et al. [1988] and Van Gelder [1988] (see also Naqvi [1986]). In this respect, it not only generalizes the results obtained in those papers (in two directions) onto the class of locally stratified disjunctive databases, but also provides a powerful justification of the selection of the model M_{DB}, by showing that it is not only "natural" (cf. Apt et al. [1988]), but is actually *uniquely determined by the perfect model semantics.*

In general, a locally stratified database may have many stratifications. However, since the notion of a perfect model clearly does not depend on a particular stratification, the set PERF(DB) of perfect models of DB is independent of the choice of a stratification. This gives a different (and easier) proof of the result from Apt et al. [1988] stating that their model does not depend on the choice of stratification.

Theorem 4, in conjunction with Propositions 1–3 also shows that *the class of perfect models of disjunctive databases is a natural extension of the class of minimal models of positive disjunctive databases.* This leads to the following extension of the previously stated Principle 2.

PRINCIPLE 3 (PRINCIPLE OF PERFECT MODEL SEMANTICS)
The set PERF(DB) of all perfect models of a database DB provides a natural intended declarative semantics of DB, incorporating a suitable form of the closed-world assumption.[7] Under this semantics, a sentence is considered true in DB if and only if it is true in all perfect models of DB. ∎

The fact that the Final Principle indeed generalizes previous Principle 2 follows immediately from Proposition 2.

EXAMPLE 10
Program DB from Example 8 has infinitely many minimal models. More precisely, any subset M of the set of natural numbers which contains 0, does not contain more than two consecutive numbers and whose complement does not contain any two consecutive numbers is a minimal model of DB. But it is easy to observe that the set E of even numbers is *the only perfect model of DB*, as expected. Indeed, if M ≠ E and if M is a minimal model of DB then there exists a k such that $k \in M$, but k ∉ E and the sets M and E coincide when restricted to the set of numbers less than k. Then, for every $m \in E - M$ we have that even(m) < even(k) and $k \in M - E$, which shows that E ≪ M.

On the other hand the program from Example 7 does not have any perfect models and it does not seem to have any reasonable intended semantics. ∎

---

[7]Next section explains the closed-world assumption used.

Relation to Prioritized Circumscription

It turns out that the perfect model semantics is equivalent to the appropriate form of prioritized circumscription. This again extends the well-known fact that standard (parallel) circumscription is equivalent to the minimal model semantics (cf. Principle 2).[8] This is also not surprising in view of the obvious similarities between the definitions of perfect models and models of prioritized circumscription. The author, however, believes that the notion of a perfect model is conceptually simpler and, in this particular context, more natural.

For simplicity, we state our results for stratified databases only. However, completely analogous results are valid for locally stratified databases. Prioritized circumscription was introduced by McCarthy [1980] and further developed by Lifschitz [1985a]. Below, we recall its model-theoretic characterization.

PROPOSITION 6 ([McCARTHY [1980], LIFSCHITZ [1985])

Suppose that $P_0, \cdots, P_n$, is *any* decomposition of the set P of all predicates of a database DB into disjoint sets. A model M of DB is a model of *prioritized circumscription of DB with respect to priorities* $P_0 > \ldots > P_n$ or, briefly, a model of $CIRC(DB, P_0 > \ldots > P_n)$, if for every $i \leq n$ the extension of predicates from P_i in M is minimal among all models N of DB for which the extension of predicates from $\cup \{P_j : j < i\}$ is equal to this extension in M. ∎

The following theorem establishes the equivalence of perfect models and models of prioritized circumscription for stratified databases.

THEOREM 5

Suppose that DB is a stratified database and $\{P_0, \cdots, P_n\}$ is a stratification of DB. A model of DB is perfect if and only if it is a model of prioritized circumscription $CIRC(DB, P_0 > \ldots > P_n)$.

Sketch of proof: Let $H_0, \cdots, H_n$ be the corresponding local stratification of DB as described in the proof of Proposition 5. We showed that the models constructed in the proof of Theorem 4 are the only perfect models of DB. Using this fact and conditions (i) and (ii) in Lemma 1 it is easy to verify by induction on n that every perfect model satisfies the condition in the definition of a model prioritized circumscription. Consequently, every perfect model is a model of prioritized circumscription.

To prove that every model of prioritized circumscription is perfect, again we use induction on n. For n = 0 this is obvious. For n > 0 we use the min-

---

[8]We recall that we only consider Herbrand models.

imality condition in the definition of a model of prioritized circumscription to show that models of prioritized circumscription must satisfy the conditions (i) and (ii) in Lemma 1 and must therefore be constructed exactly in the same way as the models constructed in the proof of Theorem 4. This shows that every such model must be perfect. ∎

COROLLARY 1

Suppose that $\{P_0,...,P_n\}$ and $\{T_0,...,T_m\}$ are two stratifications of the same database DB. Then M is a model of CIRC(DB,$P_0 > ... > P_n$) if and only if it is a model of CIRC(DB,$T_0 > ... > T_m$).

Proof: We know that the definition of a perfect model does not depend on the choice of the local stratification and that a model is perfect if and only if it is a model of prioritized circumscription with respect to some particular set of priorities. Consequently, models of prioritized circumscription for any two such sets of priorities must be identical. ∎

The above theorem provides further justification of the perfect model semantics, explains the form of closed-world assumption used in Principle 3 and further underscores the fact that the notion of a perfect model is a proper extension of the notion of a minimal model for the class of disjunctive databases. It also shows the independence of prioritized circumscription from the choice of stratification.

Related results for pointwise circumscription were obtained by Lifschitz [1988]. In Gelfond et al. [1986b] a syntactic characterization of the perfect model semantics—in the form of the so called Iterated Closed-World Assumption—is obtained.

Acknowledgments

The idea of local stratification arose in discussions with Michael Gelfond. The author is also grateful to Howard Blair, Vladimir Lifschitz, John McCarthy, Jack Minker, Halina Przymusinska, Allen Van Gelder, and two anonymous referees for suggesting examples, helpful discussions, and comments.

References

1. Apt, K., Blair, H. and Walker, A.[1988] Towards a Theory of Declarative Knowledge, in Foundations of Deductive Databases and Logic Programming (J. Minker, Ed.), Morgan Kaufmann Publishers, Los Altos, CA, 89–148.

2. Bidoit, N. and Hull, R. [1986] Positivism vs. Minimalism in Deductive Databases, *Proceedings ACM SIGACT-SIGMOD Symposium on Principles of Database Systems*, Cambridge, MA, 123–132.

3. Bossu, G. and Siegel, P. [1985] Saturation, Nonmonotonic Reasoning and the Closed World Assumption, *Artificial Intelligence* **25**, 13–63.

4. Dershowitz, N. and Manna, Z. [1979] Proving Termination with Multiset Orderings, *Communications ACM* **22**, 465–476.

5. Emden, M. H. van and Kowalski, R. A. [1976] The Semantics of Predicate Logic as a Programming Language, *JACM* **3**(4):733–742.

6. Gallaire, H., Minker, J., and Nicolas, J.-M. [1984] Logic and Databases: A Deductive Approach, *Computing Surveys* **16**, 153–185.

7. Gelfond, M., Przymusinska, H., and Przymusinski, T. [1986a] The Extended Closed World Assumption and Its Relationship to Parallel Circumscription, *Proceedings ACM SIGACT-SIGMOD Symposium on Principles of Database Systems*, Cambridge, MA, 133–139.

8. Gelfond, M., Przymusinska, H., and Przymusinski, T. [1986b] On the Relationship Between the Closed-world Assumption and Predicate Circumscription, submitted.

9. Lifschitz, V. [1985] Computing Circumscription, *Proceedings IJCAI–85*, 121–127.

10. Lifschitz, V. [1988] On the Declarative Semantics of Logic Programs with Negation, in *Foundations of Deductive Databases and Logic Programming* (J. Minker, Ed.), Morgan Kaufmann Publishers, Los Altos, CA, 177–192.

11. Lifschitz, V. [1985b] Closed World Data Bases and Circumscription, *Artificial Intelligence* **27**, 229–235.

12. Lloyd, J. W. [1984] Foundations of Logic Programming, Springer-Verlag, New York.

13. McCarthy, J. [1984] Applications of Circumscription to Formalizing Common Sense Knowledge, AAAI Workshop on Non-Monotonic Reasoning, 295–323.

14. Minker, J. [1982] On Indefinite Data Bases and the Closed World Assumption, *Proc. 6th Conference on Automated Deduction*, 292–308.

15. Naqvi, S. A. [1986] A Logic for Negation in Database Systems, *Proceedings of the Workshop on Foundations of Deductive Databases and Logic Programming* (J. Minker, Ed.), Washington, DC, 378–387.

16. Przymusinski, T. [1987] On the Declarative and Procedural Semantics of Stratified Deductive Databases and Logic Programs, *Journal of Logic Programming*, to appear.

17. Przymusinski, T. [1986a] Query Answering in Circumscriptive and Closed-World Theories, *Proceedings AAAI–86*, Philadelphia, PA, 186–190.

18. Przymusinski, T. [1986b] A Query Answering Algorithm for Circumscriptive Theories, *Proceedings of the ACM SIGART International Symposium on Methodologies for Intelligent Systems*, Knoxville, TN, 85–93.

19. Reiter, R. [1978] On Closed-World Data Bases, in *Logic and Data Bases* (H. Gallaire and J. Minker, Eds.), Plenum Press, New York, 55–76.

20. Reiter, R. [1984] Towards a Logical Reconstruction of Relational Database Theory, in *On Conceptual Modeling* (M. Brodie et al., Eds.), Springer-Verlag, 191–233.

21. Van Gelder, A. [1988] Negation as Failure Using Tight Derivations for General Logic Programs, in *Foundations of Deductive and Logic Programming* (J. Minker, Ed.), Morgan Kaufmann Publishers, Los Altos, CA, 149–176.

22. Yahya, A. and Henschen, L. [1985] Deduction in Non-Horn Databases, *Journal of Automated Reasoning* **1**(2):141–160.

6

On Domain Independent Databases

R. W. Topor
E. A. Sonenberg
Department of Computer Science
University of Melbourne
Parkville, Victoria
Australia

Abstract

We introduce and study the concept of domain independence to characterize the class of reasonable databases. A domain independent database is one for which the set of correct answers to an atomic query is independent of the domains of variables in the database statements. In particular, we prove that every "allowed" stratified database is domain independent and that every domain independent stratified database has an equivalent allowed database. We contrast these results with those of an earlier paper in which a different definition of a correct answer was used.

Introduction

The standard logical description of a relational database is that of a particular *interpretation* for a first order language. Within this framework, query evaluation is the process of finding the tuples for which a query (a first order formula) is true with respect to the given interpretation. It has long been recognized, however, that only certain formulas make reasonable queries in this setting (Di Paola [1969], Kuhns [1967]) in the sense that they yield the same answer whatever the domain of the interpretation. Such queries have been called "domain independent" and have been extensively studied (for example, see Nicolas and Demolombe [1983]). Simple examples of unreasonable queries are $\forall x p(x)$, whose truth depends on the domain of x, and $\neg p(x,a)$, whose set of correct answers depends on the domain of x.

In Topor [1986] it was observed that, for similar reasons, only certain deductive databases could be regarded as reasonable, and the concept of domain independent formulas was extended to that of domain independent databases. A class of "allowed" databases was introduced, and the relationship between allowed and domain independent databases was studied. A simple example of an unreasonable database is $\{ p(a) \leftarrow , q(a) \leftarrow \neg p(x) \}$, for which the query $q(a)$ is true if and only if a is the only constant in the domain of x.

Here, we restrict attention to stratified databases, give a modified definition of the class of domain independent databases, and investigate their properties with respect to the new definition. The definition of a domain independent database used here defines a correct answer for a query with respect to a database D in terms of truth with respect to a *particular model M_D* for D (Apt, Blair, and Walker [1988]). This contrasts with the definition in Topor [1986] that defined a correct answer in terms of *logical consequence* of comp(D) (Clark [1978]). Another definition of domain independent formulas and databases is given in Decker [1986b].

We prove that every allowed stratified database is domain independent and that every domain independent stratified database has an equivalent allowed database. We then describe how our results depend on which of two different definitions of a correct answer for a query with respect to a stratified database is used, and briefly compare the two definitions.

The next section contains basic definitions and properties of stratified databases and correct answers. After that, we describe domain independent and allowed formulas and their properties. We then introduce and define domain independent and allowed databases and study their relationship; this section contains our main results. The following section describes how our results depend on which definition of a correct answer is used. Finally, we present our conclusions.

We assume familiarity with the basic theory of logic programming, which can be found in Lloyd [1984]. The notation and terminology of this paper is consistent with Lloyd [1984] and Lloyd and Topor [1985, 1986].

Basic Concepts

In this section, we introduce the concepts of a deductive database and query. We define the class of stratified databases and give the definition of a correct answer.

Each database and query is assumed to be expressed in some first order function-free language with equality. In practice, typed languages should be used, but, for simplicity, we also restrict our attention to type-free languages throughout. $\forall(W)$ (resp., $\exists(W)$) denotes the universal (resp., existential) closure of the formula W. We assume that each such language contains only finitely many constants and predicates and at least one constant. For languages L_1 and L_2, we write $L_1 \leq L_2$ if L_2 extends L_1, that is, if L_2 contains at least all the constants and predicates in L_1.

The concepts of interpretation, model, Herbrand model, logical consequence, and so on, are defined in the usual way for first order theories. In the presence of the usual equality axioms, by Mendelson [1979, p. 83], we can assume throughout that every interpretation considered is *normal*, that is, equality is always assigned the identity relation.

One of our main aims is to study the way in which the set of correct answers to a query depends on the particular language used.

DEFINITION 1

A *database statement* is a first order formula of the form $\forall(A \leftarrow W)$, where A is an atom $p(t_1,\ldots,t_n)$, p is not =, and W is a first order formula. A is called the *head* and W the *body* of the statement. The formula W may be absent. In general, we adopt the standard convention of writing $\forall(A \leftarrow W)$ as $A \leftarrow W$. ■

DEFINITION 2

A *database D* is a finite set of database statements. The *language of D* is the language whose constants and predicates are those that occur in D. ■

DEFINITION 3

A *query* is a first order formula. ■

We assume without loss of generality that every query for a database is in the language of the database.

DEFINITION 4

Let Q be a query with free variables $x_1,\ldots,x_n$. An *answer* for Q is a substitution for some or all of the variables $x_1,\ldots,x_n$. ■

We shall be particularly concerned with the class of "stratified" databases and with the class of correct answers for a query with respect to a given database. To define stratified databases, we need to define the concept of an atom occurring positively or negatively in a formula, and the concept of a level mapping.

DEFINITION 5

An atom A *occurs positively* in A. If atom A occurs positively (resp., negatively) in a formula W, then A *occurs positively* (resp., *negatively*) in $\exists x W$ or $\forall x W$ or $W \wedge V$ or $W \vee V$ or $W \leftarrow V$. If atom A occurs positively (resp., negatively) in a formula W, then A *occurs negatively* (resp., *positively*) in $\sim W$ or $V \leftarrow W$. ∎

DEFINITION 6

A *level mapping* of a database is a mapping from its set of predicates to the natural numbers. We refer to the value of a predicate under the mapping as the *level* of the predicate. ∎

DEFINITION 7

A database is *definite* (Lloyd and Topor [1985]) if the body of every database statement is a conjunction of atoms.

A database is *hierarchical* (Clark [1978], Lloyd and Topor [1985]) if it has a level mapping such that, in every database statement $p(t_1, \ldots t_n) \leftarrow W$, the level of every predicate in W is less than the level of p.

A database is *stratified* (Lloyd, Sonenberg and Topor [1986]) if it has a level mapping such that, in every database statement $p(t_1, \ldots, t_n) \leftarrow W$, the level of the predicate of every atom occurring positively in W is less than or equal to the level of p and the level of the predicate of every atom occurring negatively in W is less than the level of p. ∎

Note that every definite database is stratified and that every hierarchical database is stratified. In the remainder of this paper, we will be primarily concerned with stratified databases. Also, without loss of generality, we will assume that the predicate levels in a stratified database are $0, 1, \ldots, k$, for some k.

The concept of a correct answer can be introduced by defining a particular model for a stratified database. First, we define a mapping T_D associated with a database D from the lattice of Herbrand interpretations for L into itself.

DEFINITION 8

Let D be a database, L a language extending that of D, and I a Herbrand interpretation for L. Then $T_D(I) = \{A\theta : A \leftarrow W$ is a statement in D, θ is a ground substitution for the variables in A and the free variables in W, and $W\theta$ is true wrt $I\}$. ∎

The following result is a special case of Proposition 2 in Lloyd et al. [1986].

LEMMA 1

Let D be a stratified database and L a language extending that of D.

1. Suppose D has maximum predicate level 0. Then T_D is monotonic.

2. Suppose D has maximum predicate level $k + 1$. Let D_k be the set of database statements $p(t_1,...,t_n) \leftarrow W$ in D such that p has level at most k. Suppose that M_k is a Herbrand interpretation for D_k and that M_k is a fixpoint of the mapping associated with D_k. Consider the complete lattice $C = \{M_k \cup S : S \subseteq \{p(c_1,...,c_n) : p \text{ has level } k + 1 \text{ and each } c_i \text{ is a constant of } L\}\}$, under set inclusion. Then C is a sublattice of the lattice of Herbrand interpretations for L and T_D, restricted to C, is well-defined and monotonic.

Proof: Straightforward. ∎

DEFINITION 9
Let D be a stratified database of maximum predicate level k and L a language extending that of D. Let M_{-1} be $\emptyset$. For $0 \leq j \leq k$ do the following. Let C_j be the complete lattice $\{M_{j-1} \cup S : S \subseteq \{p(c_1,...,c_n) : p \text{ has level } j \text{ and each } c_i \text{ is a constant of } L\}\}$, under set inclusion; let T_j be the restriction of T_D to C_j; and let M_j be $T_j \uparrow \omega$. Then, M_k is called the *standard model* for D wrt L and is denoted by $M(D,L)$. ∎

By Lemma 1, each T_j in this definition is monotonic and each $T_j \uparrow \omega$ is thus well-defined. Moreover, as the Herbrand base for L is finite, each $T_j \uparrow \omega$ is a fixpoint of T_j. We use this observation repeatedly below.

THEOREM 1
$M(D,L)$ is well-defined and is a minimal Herbrand model for D.

Proof: As noted above, each $T_j \uparrow \omega$ is a fixpoint of T_j and thus $T_j (T_j \uparrow \omega) \subseteq T_j \uparrow \omega$. By a proof similar to that of Proposition 6.4 of Lloyd [1984], each M_j is thus a (Herbrand) model for D_j. Moreover, each $T_j \uparrow \omega$ is the least fixpoint of T_j and thus, by Proposition 5.1 of Lloyd [1984], the least element I in C_j such that $T_j(I) \subseteq I$. Each M_j is thus well-defined and the least model for D_j whose restriction to D_{j-1} is M_{j-1}. It follows that $M(D,L)$ is well-defined and minimal. ∎

Note that $M(D,L)$ can depend on the language L.

EXAMPLE 1
Let D be the stratified database

$p(a) \leftarrow$

$q(x) \leftarrow \neg\, p(x)$

in language L. Then $M(D,L)$ is $\{p(a)\}$ if a is the only constant in L but $M(D,L)$ is $\{p(a), q(b)\}$ if a and b are the constants in L. ■

The model $M(D,L)$ was defined implicitly for stratified general databases by Chandra and Harel [1985] and explicitly for stratified general programs by Apt, Blair, and Walker [1988] where it was denoted by M_D. In each case, they used for L the language of D. The use of the word "standard" is motivated by a result in Apt et al. [1988] that states $M(D,L)$ is independent of the level mapping used to show D is stratified, by Lifschitz's demonstration that $M(D,L)$ arises naturally in an attempt to formalize default reasoning using circumscription (Lifschitz [1988]), and by Przymusinski's alternative, declarative, characterization of $M(D,L)$ in terms of perfect models (Przymusinski [1988]).

We can now define a correct answer for a query with respect to a database and a language.

DEFINITION 10
Let D be a stratified database, L a language extending that of D, and Q a query in L. A *correct answer* for Q wrt D and L is an answer θ for Q such that $\forall(Q\theta)$ is true in the standard model, $M(D,L)$, for D wrt L. ■

The concept of a correct answer gives a declarative description of the desired output from a query to a database with respect to a language. Note that the set of correct answers for a query with respect to a database and language can depend on the language.

EXAMPLE 1 (CONTINUED)
The set of correct answers for the query $q(x)$ is empty if a is the only constant in L but contains the substitution $\{x/b\}$ for each constant $b \neq a$ in L. ■

It is convenient to introduce the following definition at this point.

DEFINITION 11
Let D be a stratified database, L a language extending that of D, and Q a query in L. Then $ans(Q,D,L)$ is the set of all correct answers for Q wrt D and L that are ground substitutions for all free variables in Q. ■

Domain Independent Formulas

In this section, we review the definition and properties of domain independent formulas, introduce the class of "allowed" formulas, and study their relationship.

DEFINITION 12
Let W be a formula with k free variables and I an interpretation for W with domain U. If $k > 0$, $val(W,I)$ is the set of elements of U^k for which W is true wrt I. If $k = 0$, $val(W,I)$ is *true* or *false* depending on whether or not W is true wrt I. ∎

DEFINITION 13
A formula W is *domain independent* if, for all finite interpretations I_1 and I_2 for W that assign the same domain elements to the constants in W and the same relations to the predicates in W, $val(W,I_1) = val(W,I_2)$. ∎

That is, W is domain independent if the set of tuples for which W is true with respect to a finite interpretation I depends only on the domain elements assigned by I to the constants in W and on the relations assigned by I to the predicates in W, but not on the domains of the variables in W.

Note that domain independence of a formula is a model theoretic property and the domain independence of a closed formula is thus preserved under transformations that preserve logical equivalence.

EXAMPLE 2
Clearly, every valid closed formula is domain independent. The following formulas are also domain independent.

$p(x)$

$\exists x \exists y \, (p(x) \lor q(y))$

$\exists x \exists y (p(y) \rightarrow q(x,y))$

The following formulas are not domain independent.

$\neg \, p(x)$

$p(x) \lor q(y)$

$\forall y \, (p(y) \rightarrow q(x,y))$

$\exists x p(x) \land \exists x \neg p(x)$

We briefly explain the four counter-examples. Let U_I be the domain of an interpretation I, $P_I = val(p,I)$, and $Q_I = val(q,I)$. Then we can make the following observations.

$$val(\neg p(x),I) = U_I \backslash P_I.$$

$$val(p(x) \vee q(y),I) = P_I \times U_I \cup U_I \times Q_I.$$

$$val(\forall y(p(y) \rightarrow q(x,y)),I) = U_I \text{ if } val(p(y),I) = \emptyset.$$

$$val(\exists x p(x) \wedge \exists x \neg p(x),I) \text{ is true if and only if } \emptyset \subset P_I \subset U_I.$$

That is, for each formula W, there exist relations P_I and Q_I such that, for every interpretation I involving those relations, $val(W,I)$ depends on U_I. Each W should thus be considered an unreasonable query. ∎

Unfortunately, the class of domain independent formulas has the following property.

THEOREM 2 (DI PAOLA [1969], VARDI [1981])
The decision problem for the class of domain independent formulas is recursively unsolvable. ∎

As a result of Theorem 2, various subclasses of the domain independent formulas have been proposed. One important subclass of the domain independent formulas is the class of "safe" formulas, proposed by Ullman [1982] to ensure that $val(W,I)$ is finite even for those interpretations I with an infinite domain.

DEFINITION 14
Let W be a formula in language L and I an interpretation for L. Then $dom(W,I)$ is the set of domain elements that are assigned by I to constants in W or are components of tuples in relations that are assigned by I to predicates in W. ∎

DEFINITION 15
A formula $W(x_1,...,x_n)$ in language L is *safe* if, for all interpretations I for L, the following conditions hold.

1. If $W(d_1,...,d_n)$ is true wrt I then each d_i is in $dom(W,I)$.

2. If $\exists u F(u)$ is a subformula of W, then $F(d)$ true wrt I for some values of the free variables of F (besides u) implies that d is in $dom(W,I)$.

3. If $\forall u F(u)$ is a subformula of W, then $F(d)$ false wrt I for some values of the free variables of F (besides u) implies that d is in $dom(W,I)$.

As every safe formula, W has an equivalent relational algebra expression (Ullman [1982]), whose value in an interpretation I depends only on $dom(W,I)$. We have the following important observation. ∎

LEMMA 2 (NICOLAS AND DEMOLOMBE [1983])
Every safe formula is domain independent. ∎

The converse of Lemma 2 is false.

EXAMPLE 3
The following formulas are domain independent but not safe.

$\exists x(p(x) \vee q(a))$

$\exists x \neg p(x) \vee \forall y p(y)$

A recursive subclass of the domain independent formulas with a relatively simple definition is the class of "allowed" formulas, introduced in Topor [1986]. ∎

DEFINITION 16
A variable x is *pos* (positive) in a formula W if and only if one of the following cases holds.

x is pos in $p(t_1,\ldots,t_n)$ if x occurs in $p(t_1,\ldots,t_n)$ and p is not $=$.

x is pos in $x = t$ or $t = x$ if t is a constant.

x is pos in $\neg F$ if x is neg in F.

x is pos in $F \wedge G$ if x is pos in F or x is pos in G.

x is pos in $F \vee G$ if x is pos in F and x is pos in G.

x is pos in $F \rightarrow G$ if x is neg in F and x is pos in G.

x is pos in $\exists y F$ or $\forall y F$ if x is pos in F.

Similarly, x is *neg* (negative) in W if and only if one of the following cases holds.

x is neg in $\neg F$ if x is pos in F.

x is neg in $F \wedge G$ if x is neg in F and x is neg in G.

x is neg in $F \vee G$ if x is neg in F or x is neg in G.

x is neg in $F \rightarrow G$ if x is pos in F or x is neg in G.

x is neg in $\exists y F$ or $\forall y F$ if x is neg in F.

Note that a variable that occurs in a formula may be neither pos nor neg in the formula. For example, x is neither pos nor neg in $p(x) \lor q(y)$. If variable x is pos (resp., neg) in formula W, then x occurs in an atom that occurs positively (resp., negatively) in W (as in the definition of a stratified database). The converse, however, is false: If atom A occurs positively (resp., negatively) in formula W and variable x occurs in A, then x is not necessarily pos (resp., neg) in W. For example, $p(x)$ occurs positively in the above formula, but x is not pos in the formula. ■

DEFINITION 17
A formula W is *allowed* if the following conditions hold.

1. Every free variable in W is pos in W.
2. For every subformula $\exists xF$ of W, x is pos in F.
3. For every subformula $\forall xF$ of W, x is neg in F.

A query Q is *allowed* if Q is an allowed formula. ■

EXAMPLE 4
The following formulas are allowed.

$p(x)$

$p(x,y) \land \neg q(x)$

$p(x) \land \forall y(q(y) \to r(x,y))$

$\exists x \exists y(p(x) \land \neg(q(y) \to \forall z \neg r(x,y,z)))$

The following formulas are not allowed.

$\neg p(x)$	(*x not pos*)
$p(x) \lor q(y)$	(*x not pos*)
$\forall y p(x,y)$	(*y not neg*)
$\exists x \forall y(p(y) \to q(x,y))$	(*x not pos*)

Note that a formula that is allowed (resp., safe) may be logically equivalent to a formula that is not allowed (resp., safe), for example, $\exists xp(x) \lor q(a)$ and $\exists x(p(x) \lor q(a))$. ■

Allowed formulas have several important properties. First, there is the following key result.

THEOREM 3 (TOPOR [1986])
Every allowed formula is safe and hence domain independent. ∎

The proof that every allowed formula is safe is, by structural induction, using the similarity of the defining conditions. Second, allowed formulas can be transformed into particularly simple equivalent relational algebra expressions (Van Gelder and Topor [1987]). Finally, the evaluation of an allowed query, with respect to a database using SLDNF-resolution as described in Lloyd and Topor [1986], never terminates with a control error (i.e., it never "flounders").

Other recursive subclasses of the domain independent formulas are the range separable formulas (Codd [1972]), the evaluable formulas (Demolombe [1982]), and the range restricted formulas (Nicolas [1982]). Every allowed formula is evaluable, and every formula in prenex conjunctive normal form is evaluable if and only if it is range restricted. The class of range restricted formulas was generalized in Decker [1986a].

No expressive power is lost by restricting attention to allowed formulas because we can prove that every domain independent formula is equivalent to an allowed formula in the following sense.

THEOREM 4 (TOPOR [1986])
For every domain independent formula W in language L, there exists an allowed formula W' in L such that, for every finite interpretation I for L with $dom(W,I) \neq 0$, $val(W,I) = val(W',I)$. ∎

Examples in Nicolas and Demolombe [1983] and Topor [1986] show that the condition $dom(W,I) \neq \emptyset$ is essential in this result. The construction used in the proof of Theorem 4 to transform a formula W into an allowed formula W' is not useful in practice, as W' is only equivalent to W when W is domain independent—an undecidable condition.

Domain Independent Databases

Just as not all queries are reasonable, so not all deductive databases are reasonable. As the standard model, $M(D,L)$, for a stratified database D can depend on the language L, the set of correct answers for a perfectly reasonable (e.g., allowed) query can also depend on L. As the language L used to define $M(D,L)$ is often not given explicitly, this situation should be regarded as unacceptable.

When the language L is not given explicitly, it is often identified with the language of the database. In this case, the set of correct answers for a query can change, after a database update that is irrelevant to the query, but which changes the language of the database. Again, this situation should be regarded as unacceptable.

We now give three examples illustrating how the set of correct answers for a query can depend on L. In each example, the set of correct answers for a query changes when an otherwise irrelevant fact, such as $s(b) \leftarrow$, is added to the database. Example 1 above also illustrates the phenomenon.

EXAMPLE 5
Let D be the stratified database

$$p(a) \leftarrow$$

$$q(a) \leftarrow \forall x p(x))$$

in language L. Then $q(a)$ is true wrt $M(D,L)$ if and only if a is the only constant in L. That is, the identity substitution is a correct answer for the query $q(a)$ if a is the only constant in L; but there are no correct answers if L contains any other constants. Thus, D should not be considered a reasonable database. ∎

EXAMPLE 6
Let D be the stratified database

$$p(a) \leftarrow$$

$$q(x) \leftarrow$$

$$r(x) \leftarrow q(x) \wedge \neg p(x)$$

in language L and Q the query $r(x)$. If a is the only constant in L, there are no correct answers for Q wrt D and L. But, for every constant $b \neq a$ in L, $\{x/b\}$ is a correct (ground) answer for Q wrt D and L. Thus, D also should not be considered a reasonable database. ∎

EXAMPLE 7
Let D be the stratified database

$$p(a) \leftarrow$$

$$r(x,y) \leftarrow p(x) \vee q(y)$$

in language L and Q the query $r(x,y)$. Then, for every constant c in L, $\{x/a, y/c\}$ is a correct (ground) answer for Q wrt D and L. That is, the set of correct ground answers depends on L, so D also should not be considered a reasonable database. ∎

The following definition attempts to capture the concept of a reasonable database.

DEFINITION 18

A stratified database D is *domain independent* if, for all languages L_1 and L_2 extending that of D, and for all atoms A in L_1 and L_2, $ans(A,D,L_1) = ans(A,D,L_2)$. ∎

The use of ground answers in this definition is based on the assumption that a typical user of a database system is primarily interested in ground answers to a query.

Note that domain independence of a database D is a model theoretic property and is thus preserved under transformations that preserve $M(D,L)$. The following result gives two simpler ways of characterizing domain independence, which are often more useful in proofs.

LEMMA 3

Let D be a stratified database. Then the following conditions are equivalent.

1. D is domain independent.

2.   For all languages $L \leq L'$ extending that of D, and for all atoms A in L, $ans(A,D,L) = ans(A,D,L')$.

3.   For all languages $L \leq L'$ extending that of D, $M(D,L) = M(D,L')$.

Proof: Straightforward. ∎

Note that Lemma 3 holds even when L is restricted to be the language of D.

In fact, every domain independent database satisfies the stronger condition that, for every reasonable (e.g., allowed) query Q, and for every language L extending that of D and Q, the set of ground answers in $ans(Q,D,L)$ is independent of L.

THEOREM 5

Let D be a domain independent stratified database and $L \leq L'$ languages extending that of D. Then, for every domain independent query Q in L, $ans(Q,D,L) = ans(Q,D,L')$.

Proof: Straightforward, by Lemma 3. ∎

We now consider the decision problem for the class of domain independent databases. First we require another definition.

DEFINITION 19
A database is *general* (Lloyd [1984]) if the body of every database statement is a conjunction of literals. ∎

It is interesting to compare the following result with Theorem 2 above.

THEOREM 6
There is an algorithm to decide whether a stratified general database is domain independent.

Proof: Let D be a stratified general database, L the language of D, and $M = M(D,L)$ the standard model for D wrt L. As L is finite and function-free, M can be effectively computed. Then, it is straightforward to show that there exists a language $L' > L$ with $M(D,L') \neq M$ if and only if there exists an instance

$$(A \leftarrow B_1 \wedge \ldots \wedge B_m \wedge \neg C_1 \wedge \ldots \wedge \neg C_n)\theta$$

of a statement in D such that

1. θ is a ground substitution in L for the variables in $B_1 \wedge \ldots \wedge B_m$,

2. every ground literal $B_i\theta$ or $\neg C_j\theta$ is true wrt M, and

3. *either* (i) $A\theta$ is not ground, *or* (ii) $A\theta$ is ground, $A\theta$ is false wrt M, and there exists a nonground negative literal $\neg C_k\theta$ such that $\exists (\neg C_k\theta)$ is false wrt M.

This condition can be effectively tested, and the result follows by Lemma 3. ∎

It follows that there exist algorithms to decide whether a definite database is domain independent and whether a hierarchical database is domain independent. We have not yet determined, however, whether there is an algorithm to decide whether an arbitrary stratified database is domain independent.

Even if such an algorithm does exist, it will apparently require (in the worst case) the expensive construction of the standard model. It is thus desirable to search for recursive subclasses of the domain independent databases with simpler decision procedures. To this end, we introduce the class of "allowed" databases, as in Topor [1986].

DEFINITION 20
A database D is *allowed* if each statement in D is an allowed formula. ∎

That is, a database D is allowed if and only if, for every statement $\forall (A \leftarrow W)$ in D, every variable in A is free in W and W is an allowed formula. In particular, every unit clause $A \leftarrow$ in an allowed database is ground, and every relational database is allowed.

EXAMPLE 8
The following database is allowed.

$$p(a) \leftarrow$$

$$q(b,x) \leftarrow p(x) \lor q(x,c)$$

$$r(x,z) \leftarrow q(x,y) \land r(y,z) \land \neg p(x)$$

$$s(x,y) \leftarrow \exists z(p(x,y,z) \land \forall w(q(d,w) \rightarrow r(w,y)))$$

Similar classes of databases have been proposed by Bancilhon and Ramakrishnan [1986] for definite databases, by Clark [1978] and Shepherdson [1984] for databases in general form, and by Lloyd and Topor [1986]. These classes are related as follows. For definite databases, every "strongly safe" rule (Bancilhon and Ramakrishnan [1986]) is allowed, and every allowed rule is "bottom-up evaluable" (Bancilhon and Ramakrishnan [1986]). Every general clause $p(t_1,\ldots,t_n) \leftarrow L_1 \land \ldots \land L_n$ that satisfies the "covering axiom" (Shepherdson [1984]) and whose body $L_1 \land \ldots \land L_n$ is an allowed formula in the sense of Clark [1978] is allowed. If D is an allowed database and Q is an allowed query, then $D \cup \{ \leftarrow Q \}$ is allowed in the sense of Lloyd and Topor [1986]. It is interesting to note that although the various restrictions mentioned above were introduced to obtain completeness results for query evaluation processes, they also serve to ensure domain independence.

We now prove our main result that all allowed stratified databases are domain independent. This requires the following lemma of independent interest.

LEMMA 4
Let D be an allowed database, $L \leq L'$ languages extending that of D, I a Herbrand interpretation for L, and I' the Herbrand interpretation for L' containing the same set of ground atoms as I.

1. Let W be an allowed formula in L with free variables $x_1,\ldots,x_m$. If $W(c_1,\ldots,c_m)$ is true wrt I' for some tuple $c_1,\ldots,c_m$ of constants in L', then each c_i is in L.

2. Let T_D (resp., T'_D) be the mapping associated with D from the lattice of Herbrand interpretations for L (resp., L') into itself. Then $T_D(I) = T'_D(I')$.

Proof:

1. By Theorem 3, W is safe. Thus, each c_i is in $dom(W,I') = dom(W,I)$ and is hence in L.

2. Let $A \leftarrow V$ be a statement in D and $\theta = \{x_1/c_1,...,x_m/c_m\}$ a ground substitution for the variables in A and free variables in V. Then $A\theta$ is in $T_D(I)$ (resp., $T'_D(I')$) if and only if $V\theta$ is true wrt I (resp., I'). By part (a), we may assume that each c_i is in L. By Theorem 3, V is domain independent, so $V\theta$ is true wrt I if and only if $V\theta$ is true wrt I'. The result follows immediately. ■

THEOREM 7
Every allowed stratified database is domain independent.

Proof: Let D be an allowed stratified database and $L \leq L'$ languages that extend that of D. We show $M(D,L) = M(D,L')$ and the result then follows by Lemma 3. The proof is by induction on the maximum level, k, of the predicates in D.

Basis: $k = 0$. Using Lemma 4, it is easy to prove by induction on i that $T_D \uparrow i = T'_D \uparrow i$ for all $i \geq 0$. Then $M(D,L) = T_D \uparrow \omega = T'_D \uparrow \omega = M(D,L')$.

Induction step. Suppose the result holds for allowed stratified databases of maximum level $k \geq 0$ and D has maximum level $k + 1$. Let D_k be the set of database statements $p(t_1,...,t_n) \leftarrow W$ in D such that p has level at most k. By the induction hypothesis, $M(D_k,L) = M(D_k,L')$. Then, again using Lemma 4, the result follows. ■

In fact, this result holds for every stratified database D such that, for every statement $A \leftarrow W$ in D, every variable in A is free in W and W is a safe formula.

Theorem 7 has the following immediate corollaries.

COROLLARY 1
Every allowed definite database is domain independent. ■

COROLLARY 2
Every allowed hierarchical database is domain independent. ■

Note that a non-allowed definite database can be domain independent. An example is the database $\{p(x) \leftarrow q(y)\}$. Corollary 1 thus gives a syntactic description of a subclass of the domain independent definite databases.

COROLLARY 3

Let D be an allowed stratified database and $L \leq L'$ languages extending that of D. Then, for every allowed query Q in L, $ans(Q,D,L) = ans(Q,D,L')$.

Proof: Immediate, by Theorems 3, 5, and 7. ∎

The final theorem in this section shows that no expressive power is lost by restricting attention to allowed databases because we can prove that every domain independent stratified database is equivalent to an allowed database in the following sense.

THEOREM 8

Let D be a domain independent stratified database and L a language extending that of D. Then there exists an allowed stratified database D' in L such that, for every allowed query Q in L, $ans(Q,D,L) = ans(Q,D',L)$.

Proof: (Mark Wallace). Let D' be the set of ground unit clauses $A \leftarrow$ such that atom A is in $M(D,L)$. Then D' is clearly an allowed stratified database, and the result follows immediately. ∎

The construction of D' in the proof of Theorem 8 produces databases with an impractically large number of clauses. Moreover, it cannot be generalized to databases with functions. The following construction maintains the number of statements in the database.

Let $c_1,...,c_m$ be (all!) the constants in D. Let $DOM_D(x)$ denote the formula $x = c_1 \vee ... \vee x = c_m$. Then D' is constructed from D by modifying each statement $A \leftarrow W$ in D as follows.

1. For each free variable x_i in W that is not pos in W, add the conjunct $DOM_D(x_i)$ to the body of the statement.

2. Replace each subformula $\exists uF$ of W in which u is not pos in F by $\exists u(DOM_D(u) \wedge F)$.

3. Replace each subformula $\forall uF$ of W in which u is not neg in F by $\forall u(DOM_D(u) \rightarrow F)$.

Clearly, the resulting database D' is allowed and stratified, and it can be proved that, for any allowed query Q in L, $ans(Q,D,L) = ans(Q,D',L)$.

Unfortunately, this construction can produce databases with impractically large statements. Thus, it is desirable to find other constructions that produce simpler databases. A construction that avoids introducing the equalities in $DOM_D(x)$ for many domain independent databases has been suggested by Decker [1986a, 1986b].

The above theorems show that allowed stratified databases have the desirable declarative properties of being domain independent and of being as expressive as arbitrary domain independent databases. Results in Lloyd and Topor [1986] show that SLDNF-resolution never terminates with a control error (i.e., it never "flounders") when applied to allowed databases and queries. Results in Bancilhon and Ramakrishnan [1986] indicate that a similar property holds with respect to "bottom-up" query evaluation procedures. It is the combination of these desirable declarative and operational properties that makes allowed databases of such importance.

On Correct Answers

Two main definitions of a correct answer for a query with respect to a stratified database have been used in the literature. One is the definition used here, based on a particular Herbrand model designated the standard model $M(D,L)$. This definition has also been used for logic programs by Apt et al. [1988] and for databases by Chandra and Harel [1985]. We shall call this the *standard model* definition.

The other definition uses the completion, $comp_L(D)$, of a database D with respect to a language L. $comp_L(D)$ is a theory for which $M(D,L)$ is a model. It contains the completed definition for each predicate in L and an equality theory including the domain closure axioms for L. The equality theory, in the absence of functions, is used to restrict attention to Herbrand interpretations for L. Details may be found in Lloyd and Topor [1985] or Topor [1986].

DEFINITION 21
Let D be a database, L a language extending that of D, and Q a query in L. A *correct answer* for Q wrt $comp_L(D)$ is an answer θ for Q such that $\forall(Q\theta)$ is a logical consequence of $comp_L(D)$. ∎

This definition has been used for logic programs by Clark [1978] and Lloyd [1984] and for databases by Lloyd and Topor [1985, 1986] and Topor [1986]. We shall call this the *logical consequence* definition.

There seems to have been little explicit justification given by users of either definition for their choice. In this section, we show that the properties of domain independent databases depend on which definition of a correct answer is used.

First we state some simple consequences of the definitions.

THEOREM 9
Let D be a database, L a language extending that of D, Q a query in L, and θ a ground substitution for all free variables in Q.

1. If D is stratified and θ is a correct answer for Q wrt $comp_L(D)$ using the logical consequence definition, then θ is a correct answer for Q wrt D and L using the standard model definition.

2. If D is definite and Q is definite, or D is hierarchical, then θ is a correct answer for Q wrt $comp_L(D)$ using the logical consequence definition if and only if θ is a correct answer for Q wrt D and L using the standard model definition.

Proof: Straightforward. ∎

Part (2) cannot be extended to stratified databases.

EXAMPLE 9
Let D be the stratified database

$t(a) \leftarrow \forall x(p(x) \rightarrow q(x)).$

$p(a) \leftarrow$

$p(x) \leftarrow p(x)$

$q(a) \leftarrow$

in language L. Then $t(a)$ is true wrt $M(D,L)$ but $t(a)$ is not a logical consequence of $comp_L(D)$ for any L. ∎

Note that, for both definitions, if D and D' are distinct but logically equivalent databases, then the set of answers for a query can be different for D and D'.

Note also that the logical consequence definition is more general in that it can be used with a database that is not stratified provided its completion is consistent.

Now we compare the definitions with respect to the results presented here and in Topor [1986]. The definitions of a domain independent database are syntactically the same in each case but use different definitions of a correct answer. None of the examples given at the start of the previous section is domain independent under either definition. Consider the following example, however.

EXAMPLE 10
Let D be the allowed stratified database

$$t(a) \leftarrow \neg p(a)$$

$$p(a) \leftarrow \neg q(x) \wedge r(x)$$

$$q(a) \leftarrow$$

$$r(x) \leftarrow r(x)$$

in language L. By Theorem 7 above, D is domain independent using the standard model definition. However, $t(a)$ is a logical consequence of $comp_L(D)$ if and only if a is the only constant in L. Thus, D is not domain independent using the logical consequence definition. ■

The strongest statement about the relationship between allowed databases and domain independent databases using the logical consequence definition of a correct answer is the following.

THEOREM 10 (TOPOR [1986])
Let D be an allowed database. If D is either (a) definite, or (b) hierarchical, then D is domain independent. ■

Example 10 above shows that this result cannot be extended to stratified databases.

Similarly, the strongest statement we can make about the relationship between domain independent databases and domain independent queries using the logical consequence definition of a correct answer is the following.

THEOREM 11 (TOPOR [1986])
Let D be an allowed database, $L \leq L'$ languages extending that of D, and Q a query in L.

1. If D is definite and Q is definite, then $ans(Q,D,L) = ans(Q,D,L')$.

2. If D is hierarchical and Q is domain independent, then $ans(Q,D,L) = ans(Q,D,L')$ ■

Clearly this is a much weaker result than Theorem 5 above. The following example shows that part (1) cannot even be extended to allowed queries.

EXAMPLE 11
Let D be the allowed definite database

$p(a) \leftarrow$

$p(x) \leftarrow p(x)$

$q(a) \leftarrow$

in language L and Q the allowed query $\forall x(p(x) \rightarrow q(x))$. Then Q is a logical consequence of $\text{comp}_L(D)$ if and only if a is the only constant in L. ■

Note that each of the above counterexamples involves a database statement of the form $p(x) \leftarrow p(x)$. Although such a statement is a tautology, its presence changes the completed definition for p, and thus affects the set of correct answers when the logical consequence definition is used. By contrast, it has no effect on the standard model definition. The same phenomenon can occur with more complex statements, but it is not clear how to identify and exclude them.

Detailed comparisons of several definitions of correct answer, with respect to other declarative properties and to the existence of equivalent procedural semantics, are given by Shepherdson [1988] and Przymusinski [1988].

Conclusions

The examples at the start of "Domain Independent Databases" suggest that only domain independent databases should be used if answers obtained are to be independent of the (implicit) language containing the database and, hence, predictable. Even if the language is taken to contain only constants occurring in the database, only domain independent databases should be used if answers obtained are to be invariant (or stable) under updates that add new constants to other predicates in the database. This is the most important conclusion from this work.

Our work is based on the use of stratified databases—a large class of databases that allow both negation and recursion, that have a tractable model theory, and whose completions are always consistent—and the standard model semantics of stratified databases.

Although there may be an algorithm to decide whether a (stratified) database is domain independent, the corresponding decision procedure appears to be expensive, and it is thus desirable to use only databases in some simpler recursive subclass of the domain independent databases. We suggest the class of allowed stratified databases for this purpose.

This restriction will require the development of efficient transformations from the largest possible class of domain independent databases (and queries) into acceptably small allowed stratified databases (and allowed queries). Methods described by Decker [1986a, 1986b], Demolombe [1981], Topor

[1986], and Van Gelder and Topor [1987] may provide starting points for this work.

It would be desirable to extend the results in this paper to languages that include functions. This will require new definitions of allowed and domain independent formulas and a new proof that every allowed formula is domain independent. The proof that every allowed stratified database is domain independent should then hold without change. Possible definitions are proposed in Topor [1987].

The question of the relative merits of the two definitions of a correct answer for a query with respect to a stratified database also deserves further investigation. This question will probably be greatly influenced by the development of efficient query evaluation procedures with desirable properties with respect to one or the other of the definitions.

Acknowledgments

We thank John Lloyd, Allen Van Gelder, and Mark Wallace for useful discussions on the material in this paper, and a referee for detecting an incorrect proof of a now omitted "theorem."

References

1. Apt, K. R., Blair, H. A., and Walker A. [1988] Towards a Theory of Declarative Knowledge, in *Foundations of Deductive Databases and Logic Programming* (J. Minker, Ed.), Morgan Kaufmann, Publishers, Los Altos, CA, 89–148.

2. Bancilhon, F. and Ramakrishnan, R. [1986] An Amateur's Introduction to Recursive Query Processing Strategies, *Proc. ACM Int. Conf. on Management of Data*, Washington, DC, 16–52.

3. Chandra, A. K. and Harel, D. [1985] Horn Clause Queries and Generalizations, *J. Logic Programming* 2(1):1–15.

4. Clark, K. L. [1978] Negation as Failure, in *Logic and Data Bases* (H. Gallaire and J. Minker, Eds.), Plenum Press, New York, 293–322.

5. Codd, E. F. [1972] Relational Completeness of Data Base Sublanguages, in *Data Base Systems* (R. Rustin, Ed.), Prentice-Hall, Englewood Cliffs, NJ, 65–98.

6. Decker, H. [1986a] Integrity Enforcement in Deductive Databases, *Proc. 1st Int. Conf. on Expert Database Systems*, Charleston, SC, 271–285.

7. Decker, H. [1986b] Extending and Restricting Deductive Databases, Internal Report KB-21, ECRC, Munich.

8. Demolombe, R. [1981] Assigning Meaning to Ill-Defined Queries Expressed in Predicate Calculus Language, in *Advances in Data Base Theory, Vol. 1* (H. Gallaire, J. Minker, and J.-M. Nicolas, Eds.), Plenum Press, New York, 367-395.

9. Demolombe, R. [1982] Syntactical Characterization of a Subset of Domain Independent Formulas, Technical Report, ONERA-CERT, Toulouse.

10. Di Paola, R. A. [1969] The Recursive Unsolvability of the Decision Problem for the Class of Definite Formulas, *J. ACM* **16**(2):324-327.

11. Kuhns, J. L. [1967] Answering Questions by Computer: A Logical Study, RM-5428-PR, Rand Corp., Santa Monica, CA.

12. Lifschitz, V. [1988] On the Declarative Semantics of Logic Programs with Negation, in *Foundations of Deductive Databases and Logic Programming* (J. Minker, Ed.), Morgan Kaufmann Publishers, Los Altos, CA, 177-192.

13. Lloyd, J. W. [1984] *Foundations of Logic Programming*, Symbolic Computation Series, Springer-Verlag, Berlin.

14. Lloyd, J. W., Sonenberg, E. A., and Topor, R. W. [1986] Integrity Constraint Checking in Stratified Databases, Technical Report 86/5, Department of Computer Science, University of Melbourne. To appear in *J. Logic Programming*.

15. Lloyd, J. W. and Topor, R. W. [1985] A Basis for Deductive Database Systems, *J. Logic Programming* **2**(2):93-109.

16. Lloyd, J. W. and Topor, R. W. [1986] A Basis for Deductive Database Systems II, *J. Logic Programming* **3**(1):55-67.

17. Mendelson, E. [1979] *Introduction to Mathematical Logic*, 2nd Edition, Van Nostrand, Princeton, NJ.

18. Nicolas, J.-M. [1982] Logic for Improving Integrity Checking in Relational Data Bases, *Acta Informatica* **18**(3):227-253.

19. Nicolas, J.-M. and Demolombe, R. [1983] On the Stability of Relational Queries, Research Report, ONERA-CERT, Toulouse.

20. Przymusinski, T. C. [1988] Declarative Semantics of Deductive Databases and Logic Programs, in *Foundations of Deductive Databases and Logic Programming*, (J. Minker, Ed.), Morgan Kaufmann Publishers, Los Altos, CA, 193-216.

21. Shepherdson, J. C. [1984] Negation as Failure: A Comparison of Clark's Completed Data Base and Reiter's Closed World Assumption, *J. Logic Programming* **1**(1):51-79.

22. Shepherdson, J. C. [1988] Negation in Logic Programming, in *Foundations of Deductive Databases and Logic Programming* (J. Minker, Ed.), Morgan Kaufmann Publishers, Los Altos, CA, 19-88.

23. Topor, R. W. [1986] Domain Independent Formulas and Databases, Technical Report 86/11, Department of Computer Science, University of Melbourne. To appear in *Theoretical Computer Science*.

24. Ullman, J. D. [1982] *Principles of Database Systems*, 2nd Edition, Pitman, London.

25. Van Gelder, A. and Topor, R. W. [1987] Safety and Correct Translation of Relational Calculus Formulas, *Proc. 6th ACM Symp. on Principles of Database Systems*, San Diego, CA, 313–327.

26. Vardi, M. Y. [1981] The Decision Problem for Database Dependencies, *Inf. Proc. Letters* **12**(5):251–254.

II

FUNDAMENTAL ISSUES IN DEDUCTIVE DATABASES AND IMPLEMENTATION

7

Foundations of Semantic Query Optimization for Deductive Databases

U. S. Chakravarthy
CCA, Four Cambridge Center
Cambridge, MA

John Grant
Department of Computer and Information Sciences
Towson State University, Towson, MD

Jack Minker
Department of Computer Science and
University of Maryland Institute for Advanced Computer Studies
University of Maryland, College Park, MD

Abstract

Traditional query optimization concentrates on the properties of database operations and the efficient use of storage structures for relational databases. Semantic query optimization involves the use of integrity constraints in the optimization process. In several previous papers we described a method based on subsumption, which can be used both for standard relational databases and for deductive databases. This paper contains the formal definitions and proof of correctness of our semantic query optimization technique.

Introduction

Query optimization can be regarded as the process of transforming a query Q into a query Q' which can be evaluated more efficiently. Q' should be equivalent to Q in the sense that Q and Q' have the same answer for every database instance. Conventional query optimization involves many strategies including the optimization of access paths and storage structures. However, it does not take into account semantic knowledge about the database, that is, the integrity constraints that the database must satisfy.

Integrity constraints can be used to aid the search process or to transform a query into a semantically equivalent query; one that has the same answer for every database instance that satisfies the integrity constraints. Several researchers have previously used integrity constraints this way: for details see Hammer and McLeod [1975], McSkimin and Minker [1977], Aho, Sagiv, and Ullman [1979], Hammer and Zdonik [1980], King [1981], Kohli and Minker [1983], Xu [1983], Futo [1984], Jarke, Clifford and Vassiliou [1984].

Two papers presented at the workshop are relevant to the use and enforcement of integrity constraints as well as optimization in general. The paper by Sagiv [1988] indicates how Datalog programs can be optimized under the notion of uniform equivalence. The optimization proposed removes redundant (or useless) literals from a logic program, thereby reducing the number of joins required to compute answers to a query on the program. Optimization under uniform equivalence takes into account constraints that the database must satisfy.

The paper by Sadri and Kowalski [1988] deals with the enforcement of integrity constraints in a deductive database. It uses integrity constraints selectively whenever an update is made to make sure that no integrity constraint is violated. An extended version of SLDNF-resolution is applied for checking integrity constraints.

In this paper we formalize semantic query optimization within the framework of deductive databases. We use the compiled approach of Reiter [1978a] which decouples the deductive and data access processes. We extend the compiled axioms using the integrity constraints and use the extended axioms for answering queries. The extended axioms are obtained using subsumption in advance of query processing. This phase is called *semantic compilation*. The idea is that given a specific query we use the extended (semantically compiled) axioms, which take advantage of the restrictions on the database imposed by the integrity constraints, and so may yield the answer faster than the compiled axioms. Our algorithms are applicable to range-restricted, function-free, non-recursive axioms.

The organization of this paper is as follows. The section, "Overview of Semantic Query Optimization," provides a general overview of our method.

"Assumptions" contains our assumptions about the types of integrity constraints and structured deductive databases that we handle. The "Semantic Compilation" section contains both the semantic compilation process and its proof of correctness. In "Semantic Query Transformation" we formalize the transformation of a query using the semantically compiled axioms and establish the correctness of this transformation. "Extensions" concludes the paper with possible extensions to more general queries and databases.

Overview of Semantic Query Optimization

In this section we present a general overview of semantic query optimization. We describe the process of semantic query optimization as a two-phase approach; the compilation phase and the query transformation phase. These two phases will be discussed formally in "Semantic Compilation" and "Semantic Query Transformation" respectively. We compare our approach with the conventional query processing method for deductive databases using the compiled approach.

The standard approach to processing queries in deductive databases is represented in Figure 1 and discussed in more detail in the subsection "Query Transformation." The intensional axioms are compiled once using a theorem prover, prior to the submission of any query. The intensional axioms are not needed for query processing after compilation. The original query, which is given in terms of intensional as well as extensional predicates, is transformed into one or more queries using the compiled intensional axioms. These transformed queries contain only extensional and evaluable predicates. Then a plan is generated for each transformed query using a conventional query optimizer for relational databases. These plans are executed over the physical (extensional) database to obtain the answer for the original query. This method does not use any semantic knowledge about the database. The reader is referred to Ullman [1982], Chapter 8, for an exposition of various conventional query optimization techniques for relational databases.

The query optimization method formalized in this paper differs from the standard method in its ability to utilize semantic information about the database. Figure 2 represents query processing using the approach presented in this paper. A theorem prover is used during the semantic compilation phase. This phase involves the generation of semantically constrained axioms that contain portions of integrity constraints that may be useful during query processing. The intensional axioms and integrity constraints are not needed after semantic compilation. During the semantic query / optimization / transformation phase, semantically equivalent queries are generated using the semantically constrained axioms. The conventional query processor then chooses a minimum cost plan for evaluating these queries. Finally, this plan is executed to obtain the answer. Figure 3 contains a more detailed picture of the steps involved in semantic query optimization. The numbers inside the boxes cross-reference the algorithms and theorems of the paper.

Before going into details about semantic query optimization, it is useful to obtain the basic idea about the meaning of a key concept, the notion of residues. A compiled intensional axiom of the form

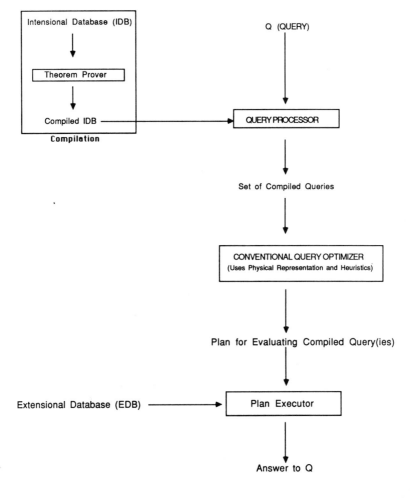

Figure 1: Conventional Query Processing for Non-Recursive Deductive Databases

$H \leftarrow P1^*,...,Pm^*$ (terms omitted)

is transformed to its semantically constrained form

$H \leftarrow P1^*,...,Pm^* \{R1,...,Rn\}$

where the Ri are residues. Let Ri have the form

$G \leftarrow F1,...,Fk$

and define Ri$'$ as not (F1,...,FK, not (G)). In the case of a unit residue, Ri$'$ is G; for the empty residue, Ri$'$ is fail.

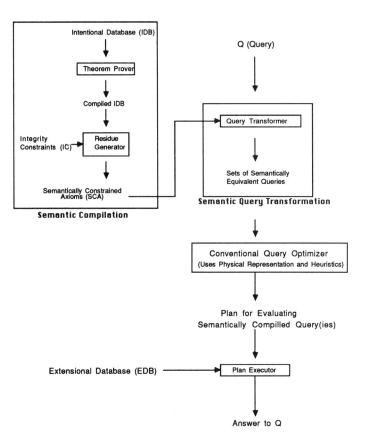

Figure 2: Query Processing Using Semantic Query Optimization

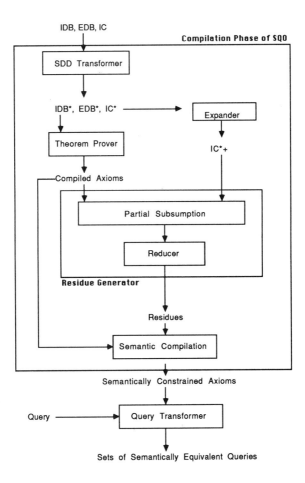

IDB, EDB, IC

Compilation Phase of SQO

SDD Transformer

IDB*, EDB*, IC*

Expander

Theorem Prover

IC*+

Compiled Axioms

Partial Subsumption

Reducer

Residue Generator

Residues

Semantic Compilation

Semantically Constrained Axioms

Query

Query Transformer

Sets of Semantically Equivalent Queries

Figure 3: Road Map of Semantic Query Processing (SQO)

Then the use of the residue Ri entails the addition of Ri' to the definition of H. In particular, if all n residues are used, then we obtain

$$H \leftarrow P1^*,\dots,Pm^*,R1',\dots,Rn'$$

as the meaning (declaratively and procedurally) of the semantically constrained axiom.

Two previous papers, Chakravarthy, Fishman, and Minker [1986] and Chakravarthy, Minker, and Grant [1986], have already dealt with our method of semantic query optimization. Those papers contain various realistic and practical examples as well as implementation trade-offs, primarily control strategies, that may be used in conjunction with semantic query optimization. The purpose of this paper is to provide the foundations for this method, formal definitions, and proofs of correctness.

Assumptions

In this section we start by presenting our assumptions concerning deductive databases. We also define the notion of a structured deductive database and show how to transform an arbitrary non-recursive database to one that is structured. We then prove that this transformation leads to an equivalent database in the absence of updates to the database.

We will use Prolog notation for clauses. We will have to switch sometimes between the standard older notation (as in Chang and Lee [1973]) and our own. It is easy to switch between the two. For example,

$H(x,y) \leftarrow R(x,z),S(z,y,b)$ is the Prolog clausal notation, which is

$\neg R(x,z) \lor \neg S(z,y,b) \lor H(x,y)$ in the standard clausal version.

The negative literals form the *body* of the clause and the positive literals form the *head*. For a *Horn clause* the head consists of at most a single atom. A *unit clause* is a Horn clause with a null body whose head has an atom. A *goal clause* has a null head. The *null clause*, which we write as *NC* has both a null body and a null head; it represents a contradiction. A *definite Horn clause* has exactly one positive literal and zero or more negative literals. A *definite implicational clause* has at least one atom in the body and exactly one atom in the head. For a *range-restricted clause* every variable in the head also appears in the body as arguments of nonevaluable predicates.

We assume for this paper that a database DB has the following components:

- EDB = a set of ground function-free unit clauses that represent tuples in relations: This is the *extensional database*,

- IDB = a set of non-recursive range-restricted function-free definite implicational clauses that represent definitions for relations: This is the *intensional database*,

- IC = a set of non-recursive range-restricted Horn clauses that represent the *integrity constraints*. (Skolem functions are allowed for extensional relations in the head.)

For convenience we assume that IDB clauses do not contain a constant or a repeated variable in the head. If such a clause does contain a constant or a repeated variable in the head, it is always possible to rewrite it, preserving logical equivalence by placing equalities in the body; in the subsection "Expanded (Variable Substituted) and Reduced Forms," the notion of expanded form is discussed where the body is expanded this way. Thus

$P(c,x1,...,xn) \leftarrow R1(\ ),...,Rk(\ )$ is rewritten as

$P(z,x1,...,xn) \leftarrow (z = c),R1(\ ),...,Rk(\ )$

where z is a new variable not present in the original clause. (In the background is a first-order language with the usual logical as well as the appropriate constant, function, and predicate symbols.) We assume a theory as described in Section 2.2.2 of Gallaire, Minker, and Nicolas [1984], one that includes the Closed World Assumption (CWA) as a metarule, i.e., $\vdash \neg P$ if not $\vdash P$. We will assume that all the *queries* are function-free goal clauses and mark the output variables by using a "*." These queries correspond to what are called existential conjunctive queries; the unmarked variables are assumed to be existentially quantified.

Integrity constraints are a set of clauses which the theory must obey, so that EDB ∪ IDB ∪ IC is consistent. Syntactically, both an axiom and an integrity constraint may be in the form of a definite implicational clause. The difference is the interpretation we have of the clauses. Also, there are, at best, only guidelines to classify a clause as an integrity constraint or as an axiom.

It is important to recognize that in some instances, an integrity constraint may be a definite implicational clause, and hence capable of generating new tuples (referred to as a generative integrity constraint) for the intensional or the hybrid relation of the consequent. We would like to assume that the integrity constraints are not generative, but are used only to verify the consistency of the database. This assumption is extremely useful from the viewpoint of enforcing integrity constraints efficiently, and it leads to the definition of a structured deductive database. A deductive database is *structured* if every relation is purely extensional or purely intensional and if all the integrity constraints are expressed using only extensional relations. The restrictions imposed by the notion of structured deductive database help in the enforcement of integrity constraints, since only the physically stored relations need to be checked. The notion of structured deductive database is discussed in Reiter [1978b] and Minker and Nicolas [1982] for recursive databases.

In the presence of generative integrity constraints, there are at least three ways of transforming a database to avoid the generation of tuples of an intensional relation: a) generative integrity constraints can be elevated to the status of intensional axioms; b) generative integrity constraints can be used to actually generate tuples into the extensional part of the hybrid relation corresponding to the integrity constraint whenever the corresponding base relations are updated; and c) a snapshot (an instance) of a deductive database can be transformed into a structured deductive database. As long as there are no updates affecting the generative integrity constraints, the transformation produces an equivalent database. This alternative permits a simple and efficient implementation for enforcing integrity constraints.

The algorithm sketched below transforms an instance of a deductive database into a structured deductive database according to c). This algorithm can be easily modified to obtain the effect of a) or b) described earlier.

ALGORITHM 1

The structured database $DB^* = \{EDB^*, IDB^*, IC^*\}$ is obtained from the database $DB = \{EDB, IDB, IC\}$ by the following steps:

1. Split each hybrid relation H into its intensional (H) and extensional (H^*) component, and add $H \leftarrow H^*$ to the IDB.

2. Delete the intensional relations from the body of every integrity constraint by substituting, after the appropriate unification, the body of each definition of the intensional relation in the integrity constraint.

3. Delete the intensional relations from the head of every integrity constraint by generating the tuples of the intensional relation, using EDB and IC, into an extensional relation. ■

EXAMPLE 1

EDB: $R1^*, R2^*, R3^*, R4^*, H2$

IDB:

$H1(x,y,z) \leftarrow R1^*(x,y), H3(y,z)$

$H2(x,z) \leftarrow R1^*(x,z), R2^*(z,c)$

$H3(x,y) \leftarrow R3^*(x,z), R2^*(z,y)$

IC:

$H1(x, y, a) \leftarrow R3^*(x, y), R4^*(y, a)$

$H2(x,z) \leftarrow R3^*(x,z)$

$\leftarrow H2(a,b)$

Step 1: Change the EDB by changing H2 to $H2^*$ and add $H2(x,y) \leftarrow H2^*(x,y)$ to the IDB.

Step 2: Remove $\leftarrow$H2(a,b) from IC and add the following to IC:

$\leftarrow$ R1*(a,b),R2*(b,c)

$\leftarrow$ H2*(a,b)

$\leftarrow$ R3*(a,b)

Final result after Step 3:

EDB*: R1*,R2*,R3*,R4*,H1* (added by using rule 1 in the previous IC),

H2* (enlarged by using rule 2 in the previous IC)

IDB*:

H1(x,y,z)$\leftarrow$ R1*(x,y),H3(y,z)

H3(x,y) $\leftarrow$ R3*(x,z),R2*(z,y)

H2(x,z) $\leftarrow$ R1*(x,z),R2*(z,c)

H2(x,y) $\leftarrow$ H2*(x,y)

H1(x,y,z) $\leftarrow$ H1*(x,y,z)

IC*:

$\leftarrow$ R1*(a,b),R2*(b,c)

$\leftarrow$ H2*(a,b)

$\leftarrow$ R3*(a,b) ∎

We wish to show that Algorithm 1 correctly transforms a database to a structured database (assuming no updates) according to c). By this we mean that (i) the extension of each relation in DB is the same in DB as in DB* and, (ii) that IC for DB is equivalent to IC* for DB*. If condition (i) is satisfied, that is, DB $\vdash$ R(a_1,...,a_n) iff DB* $\vdash$ R(a_1,...,a_n) for all relations in DB, then the answer to a query Q on DB must be identical to the answer to Q on DB*. Condition (ii) strengthens the notion of correctness.

THEOREM 1
Algorithm 1 correctly transforms a database DB to a structured database DB*.

Proof: It is clear that this algorithm does not change the extension of a relation in DB. To show the equivalence of IC and IC* we must consider an arbitrary instance of EDB* and show that DB satisfies IC iff DB* satisfies IC*. So suppose that IC contains G $\leftarrow$ F where F contains the intensional relation R. If DB satisfies G $\leftarrow$ F, then whenever F, including R, holds in DB, G must hold also. Let F′ be a replacement of F as performed in Step 2. If F′ holds in DB* then F must hold and so G must hold in DB*. If DB does not satisfy G ← F, then there must be a counterexample, which must also occur for one of the replacements of F. The case where G is empty is similar. Finally, Step 3 involves the generation of relations by generative integrity constraints; hence equivalence is maintained. ∎

For the rest of this paper we will assume that we are dealing with structured databases. We will also assume that the axioms (of IDB) are compiled. This means that all the intensional predicates are removed from the body of every clause in IDB by substituting for them their definitions (with the appropriate substitutions) (possibly several times). For example, in Example 1 the compiled axioms would be

$H1(x,y,z) \leftarrow R1^*(x,y),R3^*(y,u),R2^*(u,z)$

$H3(x,y) \leftarrow R3^*(x,z),R2^*(z,y)$

$H2(x,y) \leftarrow R1^*(x,z),R2^*(z,c)$

$H2(x,y) \leftarrow H2^*(x,y)$

$H1(x,y,z) \leftarrow H1^*(x,y,z)$

Only the first clause had to be changed, by applying the definition for $H3(x,y)$ from the second formula with the substitution $\{y/x,z/y,u/z\}$.

Semantic Compilation

In this section we formally describe and prove the correctness of semantic compilation. The basic notion is the subsumption of the body of an axiom in IDB by a part of an integrity constraint. The result of this partial subsumption is an instance of a part of the integrity constraint which we call a *residue*. In effect, a residue represents the interaction of an integrity constraint with an intensional axiom. We will show in "Semantic Query Transformation" how residues can be used to speed up query processing.

This section comprises several subsections. "Subsumption" contains preliminary material on subsumption. In "Expanded (Variable Substituted) and Reduced Forms," we show how to transform integrity constraints to expanded and reduced forms. We also prove the correctness of these transformations. "Partial Subsumption and Residue Generation" includes the partial subsumption algorithm that shows how residues are generated.

"Correctness of Residue Generation" has the proof of correctness for the partial subsumption algorithm. Finally, "Semantic Compilation" is an elaboration of the semantic compilation process.

Subsumption

We start this subsection by reviewing the notion of subsumption. We make two changes to the version in Chang and Lee [1973]: First, we use the Prolog notation; second, we modify the presentation of the algorithm in terms of refutation trees. A formula C *subsumes* a formula D if there is a substitution σ such that $C\sigma$ is a subclause of D. For example, if C = R(x,b) ← P(x,y),Q(y,z,b) and D = R(a,b) ← P(a,z),Q(z,z,b),S(a), then C subsumes D by the substitution $\{a/x, z/y\}$. In the subsumption algorithm, D is first instantiated to a ground clause by using new constants, not present in C or D. We will use k1,...,kn for these constants and call the substitution θ. In the example above, $\theta = \{k1/z\}$, so that $D\theta$ = R(a,b) ← P(a,k1), Q(k1,k1, b),S(a). Then $D\theta$ is negated leading to a set of literals, in this case $\neg D\theta$ = { ← R(a,b), P(a,k1) ← , Q(k1,k1,b) ← , S(a) ← }. The algorithm constructs linear refutation trees with C as the root, where each resolution must use an element of $D\theta$. For each tree, at each instance an element of $\neg D\theta$ is resolved with the present clause, starting with C. C subsumes D iff NC is obtained for at least one refutation tree. One refutation tree for the above example is

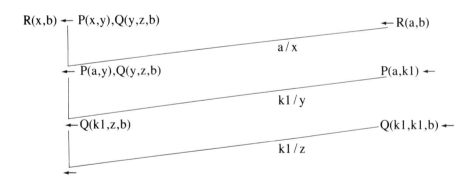

Suppose that an integrity constraint subsumes the body of an intensional axiom. This is a very unlikely situation, for it means that the intensional axiom contributes nothing to the definition of the intensional predicate. However, it may be the case that a subclause of an integrity constraint subsumes the body of an intensional axiom. Our method involves saving the rest of the integrity constraint, with the appropriate substitutions for subsumption, which we call a *residue*. It turns out that such residues may be useful during query processing.

To accomplish our objective, it is necessary to modify the integrity constraints initially and to modify the subsumption algorithm also. The following example illustrates the reason for this.

EXAMPLE 2

A: $H(x,z) \leftarrow R1^*(x,y),R2^*(y,z)$ is the compiled axiom

IC: $\leftarrow R2^*(u,a)$ is the integrity constraint.

The subsumption algorithm does not work here, because the axiom is first instantiated, and we simply obtain the result that IC does not subsume the body of A. However, if the query $\leftarrow H(x,a)$ were given, IC would subsume the body of the axiom for the instantiation in the query. Since this query has no answers, the computation of the join of $R1^*$ and $R2^*$ is a waste of time. Our objective is to anticipate this possibility in advance by including $\leftarrow (z = a)$ in the body of the compiled axiom. In fact, as we will see, $\leftarrow (z = a)$ will be the residue of IC for A after A is transformed to *expanded* form. ■

Expanded (Variable Substituted) and Reduced Forms

Constants and multiple occurrences of variables in integrity constraints cause the subsumption algorithm to fail to produce a nontrivial refutation tree. We solve this problem by showing how to transform an integrity constraint to one that is in expanded form. (We indicate the expanded form of a clause by writing a "+" after it. In the other papers on semantic query optimization we called the "expanded form" the "variable substituted form.") We start by presenting several examples to demonstrate the need for this form. Consider again Example 2. This example illustrates the replacement of a constant by a variable.

IC+: $\leftarrow R2^*(u,x1),(x1 = a).$

Now, the first literal in IC+ subsumes A; what remains of IC+ after substitution,

$\leftarrow (z = a),$ is the residue.

EXAMPLE 3

This example illustrates the replacement of multiple occurrences of a variable by distinct variables.

A: $H(x,z) \leftarrow R1^*(x,y),R2^*(y,z)$

IC: $\leftarrow R1^*(u,u).$

IC does not subsume A.

    IC+: $\leftarrow R1^*(u,x1),(x1 = u)$.

The first literal in IC+ subsumes A and the residue is $\leftarrow (x = y)$. ∎

EXAMPLE 4
This example illustrates variable substitution for evaluable predicates.

    A: $H(x,y) \leftarrow R1^*(x,y),GT(y,500)$

    IC: $\leftarrow R1^*(u,v),GT(v,400)$.

IC does not subsume A because of the presence of the different constants 400 and 500. We transform IC to IC+ by replacing $GT(r,t)$ with $GT(r,s),GE(s,t)$, where GT and GE are the evaluable predicates greater than and greater than or equal to, respectively.

    IC+: $\leftarrow R1^*(u,v),GT(v,x1),GE(x1,400)$.

Now the first two literals in IC+ subsume A leaving the residue

    $\leftarrow GE(500,400)$.

Since this residue is false, A does not contribute any tuples to the definition of H. ∎

Next we present the algorithm for transforming a clause to expanded form. We will use this algorithm to expand integrity constraints.

ALGORITHM 2
The expanded clause C+ is obtained from the clause C by modifying the body of C as follows:

1. An evaluable predicate that contains a constant and a variable is modified to two predicates with the original evaluable predicate containing two variables. For example, $GT(u,c)$ is replaced by $GT(u,x),GE(x,c)$.

2. An extensional predicate that contains a constant or a previously occurring variable is modified by changing the constant or the previously occurring variable to a new variable and adding the appropriate equality. ∎

Next we wish to show that Algorithm 2 works correctly. This means that C+ should be logically equivalent to C.

THEOREM 2

C+ is logically equivalent to C.

Proof: At each step in the construction of C+, the new formula is logically equivalent to C. ∎

In some cases we will wish to reduce a clause by eliminating predicates from it. This is essentially the reverse of expansion. (We indicate the reduced form of a clause C by writing ''−'' after it. We note that in some cases the reduction of a clause is the null clause.) In the following algorithm an atom is called true if it has the form t = t or if it represents a true evaluable predicate, such as GT(500,400). In the same way, an atom is called false if it has the form c = d where c and d are distinct constants or if it represents a false evaluable predicate such as GT(400,500).

ALGORITHM 3

The reduced clause C− is obtained from the clause C by modifying it as follows:

1.   Delete the head if it is a false atom.

2.   In the body of C

    a.   delete every duplicate occurrence of an atom,

    b.   delete every true atom,

    c.   perform the reverse of step 1) in Algorithm 2,

    d.   perform the reverse of step 2) in Algorithm 2. ∎

THEOREM 3

C− is logically equivalent to C.

Proof: At each step in the construction of C−, the new clause is logically equivalent to C. ∎

It should be clear from the construction that for every clause C, C−+− = C−. In general, we will assume that the clauses we start with, the integrity constraints and axioms are in reduced form. In that case, reduction is the inverse of expansion, that is, C+− = C.

Partial Subsumption and Residue Generation

In this section we formally define the notions of partial subsumption and the residue of an integrity constraint with respect to an intensional axiom. We present an algorithm to compute the residues that can be associated with an axiom for a given integrity constraint. We also define the notion of merge compatibility between an axiom and an integrity constraint.

DEFINITION 1

An integrity constraint IC *partially subsumes* an axiom A if IC does not subsume the body of A but a subclause of IC+ subsumes the body of A. ■

To define the notion of a residue we need first the notion of back substitution. We mentioned earlier, that when the subsumption algorithm is applied to check if C subsumes D, a substitution θ is applied first to transform D to a ground clause. Since this transformation assigns a new constant to each variable, it is possible to define the *back substitution* θ^{-1} which is the inverse of θ, that is, if $\theta = \{k1/x, k2/y\}$ then $\theta^{-1} = \{x/k1, y/k2\}$. We need an additional definition.

DEFINITION 2

A subclause D of a clause C is *nep-maximal* with respect to property P if D has property P, and for every clause D', $D \subseteq D' \subseteq C$, if D' has property P then D contains all the non-evaluable predicates in D'. ■

DEFINITION 3

A *residue* of an integrity constraint IC and an axiom A is $(((IC+ - IC + m)\sigma) -)\theta^{-1}$. IC+m is a nep-maximal subclause of IC+ which subsumes the body of A, θ is the substitution which reduces A to a ground instance, σ is the substitution which makes (IC+m)σ an instance of A, and the first "$-$" represents set subtraction. ■

According to this definition, there may be several residues of an integrity constraint for an axiom. This happens if a predicate occurs more than once in the body of an axiom or in the body of an integrity constraint. If the residue is NC we call it the *null residue*. This occurs if IC subsumes the body of A. We mentioned earlier that in this case the axiom adds no tuples to the intensional predicate. If the residue is IC+ itself, we refer to it as the *maximal residue*. Finally, a residue is called a *redundant residue* if it evaluates to true. For example, a residue whose head is (a = a), or which contains (b = c) in the body, is a redundant residue. Maximal and redundant residues are not useful for query optimization, because they do not indicate the interaction of the integrity constraint with the axiom in a useful manner. We use this criterion to determine whether or not an integrity constraint should be applied to an axiom and define the notion of merge compatibility.

DEFINITION 4

An integrity constraint is *merge compatible* with an axiom if at least one of the residues is non-redundant and non-maximal. ■

The partial subsumption algorithm is based on the subsumption algorithm to see if IC+ subsumes the body of A. The difference is that in the subsumption algorithm, as discussed earlier, we look for NC at the bottom of a refutation tree. In this case, however, we collect all the clauses at the bottom of the refutation trees as well as some clauses further up in the tree in case a non-evaluable predicate appears several times in an axiom. Then we reduce these clauses and apply back substitutions to obtain the residues. If the residues are all maximal or redundant, then IC is not merge compatible with A.

ALGORITHM 4

Input: An integrity constraint IC and an axiom A
Output: The residues of IC and A if IC is merge compatible with A, NOT_MERGE_COMPATIBLE is set to true if IC is not merge compatible with A, FULLY_SUBSUMES is set to true if IC subsumes A.
Method:

Obtain IC+ by Algorithm 2
Set $\theta = \{k1/v1,...,kn/vn\}$ where the vi, i = 1,...,n are the variables in A
and the ki are constants not occurring in either IC+ or A
/ * Let A have the form P ← L1,...,Ln */
Set UNIT_LITERALS = $\{L1\theta \leftarrow ,...,Ln\theta \leftarrow \}$
Set FULLY_SUBSUMES = FALSE
Set NOT_MERGE_COMPATIBLE = FALSE
Set RESIDUES = $\emptyset$
Set k = 0
Set RESOLVENTS^k = {IC+}
While RESOLVENTS^k ≠ $\emptyset$ and not(NC ∈ RESOLVENTS^k) Do
   For each C ∈ RESOLVENTS^k which either does not resolve with
      any element in UNIT_LITERALS or resolves only with an atom in
      UNIT_LITERALS whose
   non-evaluable predicate has been used in a previous resolution to obtain C
   Do   Set RESIDUES = RESIDUES ∪ {C}
   End For
   Set RESOLVENTS^{k+1} = {resolvents of C1 and C2 |
   C1 ∈ RESOLVENTS^k and C2 ∈ UNIT_LITERALS}
   Set k = k + 1
End While
If NC ∈ RESOLVENTS^k
   Then Set FULLY_SUBSUMES = TRUE
   Else If RESIDUES = {IC+}
       Then Set NOT_MERGE_COMPATIBLE = TRUE
       Else For each S ∈ RESIDUES Do
            Apply Algorithm 3 to reduce S / * This may
               generate NC */
            If a false atom occurs in the body or a true atom

                          in the head

                    Then   Delete S from RESIDUES / *redundant
                        residue / *
              End If
            End For
        End If
    End If
If NC $\in$ RESIDUES
  Then   Set FULLY_SUBSUMES = TRUE
  Else   If RESIDUES = $\emptyset$
            Then Set NOT_MERGE_COMPATIBLE = TRUE
            Else For each S $\in$ RESIDUES Do
                  Set S = Sθ^{-1}
              End For
        End If
End If ∎

We illustrate Algorithm 4 on two examples.

EXAMPLE 5

  A: H(u,v,w) $\leftarrow$ Q*(u),P*(v,w),R*(u,d)

  IC: $\leftarrow$ P*(x,y),Q*(y),R*(y,d)

Expanding IC we obtain

  IC+: $\leftarrow$ P*(x,y),Q*(x1),R*(x2,x3),(x1 = y),(x2 = y),(x3 = d)

  θ = {k1 / u,k2 / v,k3 / w}

  UNIT_LITERALS = {Q*(k1) $\leftarrow$, P*(k2,k3) $\leftarrow$, R*(k1,d) $\leftarrow$ }

  RESOLVENTS^3 = { $\leftarrow$ (k1 = k3),(k1 = k3),(d = d)}

  RESOLVENTS^4 = $\emptyset$

At this point RESIDUES = { $\leftarrow$ (k1 = k3),(k1 = k3),(d = d)}. By reduction we delete the extra atom (k1 = k3) first, and then, since the true atom (d = d) occurs in the body, we delete it. Now,

  RESIDUES = { $\leftarrow$ (k1 = k3)}.

Finally, by back substitution, we obtain the residue

  { $\leftarrow$ (u = w)}

In this example we obtain exactly one residue. The significance of this residue is that it represents the interaction of the axiom with the integrity constraint. So, for example, the query $\leftarrow$ H(y,x,y) can have no answers; it is unnecessary to join the Q^*, P^*, and R^* tables. We will return to this later. ■

EXAMPLE 6

A: H(u,v,w) $\leftarrow$ P*(u,d),S*(u,v),R*(v,w)

IC: $\leftarrow$ P*(a,b),Q*(x,a),R*(x,b)

Expanding IC we obtain

IC+: $\leftarrow$ P*(x1,x2),Q*(x,x3),R*(x4,x5),(x1 = a),(x2 = b),(x3 = a),(x4 = x),(x5 = b)

$\theta = \{k1/u,k2/v,k3/w\}$

UNIT_LITERALS = $\{P^*(k1,d) \leftarrow , S^*(k1,k2) \leftarrow , R^*(k2,k3) \leftarrow \}$

RESOLVENTS^2 =
$$\{ \leftarrow Q^*(x,x3),(k1 = a),(d = b),(x3 = a),(k2 = x),(k3 = b)\}$$

RESOLVENTS$^3 = \emptyset$

At this point

RESIDUES =
$$\{ \leftarrow Q^*(x,k3),(k1 = a),(d = b),(x3 = a),(k2 = x),(k3 = b)\}$$

The single residue has a false atom, (d = b), in the body, so it is deleted. Hence at the end

RESIDUES = $\emptyset$

and so IC is not merge compatible with A. ■

The Correctness of Residue Generation

In this section we show that Algorithm 4 works correctly, i.e., that it generates all nonredundant residues and that it indicates if the integrity constraint fully subsumes the body of the axiom or if the integrity constraint is not merge compatible with the axiom.

THEOREM 4
Algorithm 4 is correct.

Proof: There are several cases to consider.

Case 1: IC subsumes the body of A
  We must show that FULLY_SUBSUMES is set to TRUE. If IC+ subsumes the body of A then after the While loop NC $\in$ RESOLVENTS^k by the correctness of the Subsumption Algorithm, and so FULLY_SUBSUMES is set to TRUE. Now suppose that IC+ does not subsume the body of A. In this case the atoms of IC still resolve with the elements of UNIT_LITERALS, except that some of the substitutions are done on variables introduced during the expansion. So a residue at the end of the While loop consists of substitutions for the evaluable predicates in the body added during the expansion of IC to IC+. We need to show that the reduction of this residue is NC. This will be the case if all of these evaluable predicates evaluate to true.
  We consider the three types of additions of evaluable predicates. Suppose that IC contains the atom $P^*(y1,...,ym,c,c1,...,cn)$ in the body which is changed to $P^*(y1,...,ym,xi,c1,...,cn)$, $(xi = c)$ (where c is a constant). Since IC subsumes the body of A, there must be an atom in UNIT_LITERALS which resolves with A. When IC is resolved with the UNIT_LITERALS in the same way, we obtain the true atom $(c = c)$. Suppose next that IC contains the atom $P^*(y1,...,ym,z,c1,...,cn)$ in the body. The reason that z would be changed to xi is that z appears more than once in the atom or in another previous atom. We consider the second possibility; the first one is handled similarly. So suppose that

$$Q^*(z,z1,...,zg,d1,...,dk),P^*(y1,...,ym,z,c1,...,cn)$$

is changed to

$$Q^*(z,z1,...,zg,d1,...,dk),P^*(y1,...,ym,xi,c1,...,cn),(xi = z).$$

Again, since IC subsumes the body of A, the resolution must assign the same constant kj to z in P^* and Q^*, so, by the same resolution, the equality $(xi = z)$ is transformed to the true atom $(kj = kj)$. Finally, suppose that IC contains the atom GT(u,c), which is replaced by GT(u,v),GE(v,c). Since IC subsumes the body of A, there must be an element in UNIT_LITERALS, GT(k,c) $\leftarrow$, which resolves with GT(u,c). This resolution for IC+ leaves GE(c,c), which is true. The other evaluable predicates are handled in the same way. It is clear that NOT_MERGE_COMPATIBLE is set to FALSE.

Case 2: IC does not subsume the body of A.
  First we show that FULLY_SUBSUMES is set to FALSE. It is clear that if IC does not subsume the body of A, IC+ cannot subsume the body of A ei-

ther. So the only way that FULLY_SUBSUMES could be set to TRUE would be if one resolvent were a goal clause with only true atoms in the body. But then, going through the cases (c = c), (ki = ki), as well as GE(c,c) and LE(c,c), essentially going in the opposite direction to what we did in Case 1, we find that IC must have subsumed the body of A. But this contradicts the hypothesis. So FULLY_SUBSUMES is set to FALSE.

Case 2a: IC and A are not merge compatible.

This means that all the residues are either maximal or redundant. There can be only one maximal residue, IC+. In this case NOT_MERGE_COM-PATIBLE is set to TRUE after the While loop. Otherwise there may be several redundant residues. A redundant residue evaluates to true and is eliminated from RESIDUES in the If statement. Assuming that the residue computation is correct, which will be proved later, RESIDUES = $\emptyset$ and so NOT_MERGE_COMPATIBLE is set to TRUE.

Case 2b: IC and A are merge compatible.

This means that there is at least one residue that is not maximal and not redundant. Hence, assuming that the residue computation is correct, NOT_MERGE_COMPATIBLE is set to FALSE.

Now we must show that Algorithm 4 correctly computes all the residues. We do the general case where IC and A are merge compatible; the case where all the residues are redundant is similar.

($\rightarrow$) Suppose that R is a residue of IC and A according to the definition. We must show that R $\in$ RESIDUES at the end of Algorithm 4. Let IC+m be a nep-maximal subclause of IC+ which subsumes the body of A. We already showed that if we had started with IC+m, we would obtain NC after the While loop for some refutation tree using a substitution σ and the substitution θ which reduces the body of A to a ground instance. But we started with IC+. The same refutation tree can be constructed (with the left clause suitably modified) with the substitution σ since IC+m $\subseteq$ IC+, and instead of NC, we obtain (IC+ $-$ IC+m) $\in$ RESOLVENTS^k for some k. We must show that any more resolutions possible with UNIT_LITERALS must be with an atom whose non-evaluable predicate has been used previously. But this is clear; for another resolution in this refutation tree with a non-evaluable predicate not previously applied would contradict the nep-maximality of IC+m. The result follows, since the rest of the algorithm merely does the reduction ($-$) and the back substitution θ^{-1}.

($\leftarrow$) Suppose that R $\in$ RESIDUES at the end of Algorithm 4. We must show that R is a residue according to the definition of residues. Let R be derived from S, where S is a clause obtained at the end of the While loop. Then R = (S$-$)θ^{-1}; hence it suffices to show that S = (IC+ $-$ IC+$'$)σ where IC+$'$ is a nep-maximal subclause of IC+, which subsumes the body of A, and σ is the substitution which makes (IC+$'$)σ an instance of Aθ. It is clear from the construction that S has the form $(IC+ - IC+')\sigma$ for some $IC+'$. We must show that $IC+'$ subsumes the body of A. As in part ($\rightarrow$), using the same refutation tree and σ, if we start with $IC+\sigma$, we would obtain NC. The nep-maximality of $IC+'$ follows, since otherwise we would stay in the While loop because S could be resolved with a non-evaluable predicate in UNIT_LITERALS that was not used previously to obtain S. ∎

Semantic Compilation

We start this subsection by proving an important result about residues, one that will be helpful in showing that the application of residues preserves the semantic equivalence of queries. We also define the notions of a semantically constrained axiom and a semantically constrained (extensional) predicate. Finally, we describe the operations that constitute the process of semantic compilation.

THEOREM 5

Let IC be an integrity constraint and A an axiom defining the predicate H (H $\leftarrow$ $P1^*,...,Pn^*$, with terms omitted). Every residue of IC and A is a logical consequence of $IC \cup \{P1^*,...,Pn^*\}$.

Proof: By Theorem 2, IC is logically equivalent to IC+. It is known that the resolvent of two clauses is a logical consequence of the union of those clauses. In Algorithm 4 the resolution is done on IC+ and $Pi^*\theta$ at each step for some i, i = 1,...,n. However, the residue is obtained by applying θ^{-1} at the end, so that a residue could have been obtained by resolving IC+ and Pi^* at each step. Before a clause becomes a residue, it is reduced. But by Theorem 3, reduction preserves logical equivalence. ∎

The result of Theorem 5 means that whenever the axiom

A: H $\leftarrow$ $P1^*,...,Pn^*$

is applied to obtain the extension of H, for every integrity constraint IC, every residue represents a true formula for the database. So, for instance, in Example 5, the residue is $\leftarrow(u = w)$. This means that the axiom cannot generate any tuples for H with identical first and third values.

Now, for the purpose of defining the notion of semantic compilation, we extend the notion of (compiled) axiom by adding residues to obtain semantically constrained axioms.

DEFINITION 5

A *semantically constrained axiom (SCA)* is defined to have the form

$H \leftarrow P1^*,\ldots,Pm^* \; \{R1;\ldots;Rn\}$ (terms omitted).

Here,

$H \leftarrow P1^*,\ldots,Pm^*$

is a (compiled) axiom A, and R1,...,Rn are the residues of A with the integrity constraints that are merge compatible with A. ∎

The process of residue generation can be applied to extensional predicates also by applying the "axiom" $P^* \leftarrow P^*$ for the predicate P^*. This way we obtain semantically constrained extensional predicates which may be useful for processing queries for a non-deductive (or the extensional portion of a deductive) database.

Procedurally, a semantically constrained axiom, as given in the definition above, can be interpreted as follows. To solve H, solve the conjunction of literals $P1^*,\ldots,Pm^*$, without evaluating any Ri, i = 1,...,n, to false in the process of solving $P1^*,\ldots,Pm^*$.

Thus, a semantically constrained axiom incorporates semantic information (integrity constraints) into the axiom. We call the process of obtaining a semantically constrained axiom by obtaining all the residues of an axiom with all the integrity constraints *semantic integration*. Finally, *semantic compilation* is the process of semantic integration done for each axiom.

Semantic Query Transformation

In this section we show how residues are used in query processing. Semantic query optimization transforms a query into an equivalent query whose evaluation is easier. In the first subsection, "Query Transformation," we show how residues are used in the transformation of queries. The correctness of these transformations is proved in "The Correctness of Query Transformation." Several examples of semantic query optimization for specific databases appear in Chakravarthy, Fishman, and Minker [1986] and Chakravarthy, Minker, and Grant [1986].

Query Transformation

A query in a deductive database (using the compiled approach) is transformed into a set of queries on the extensional predicates first before processing. We show how residues are introduced into this process and how different types of residues may be incorporated into a query.

A query Q has the form

$$\leftarrow Q1(t11,\ldots,t1k_1),\ldots,Qn(tn1,\ldots,tnk_n)$$

where each Qi is a predicate. (Each term tij is a variable or constant.) The compilation of the query involves using the compiled axioms to make substitutions for all Qi which are intensional predicates. We will obtain a compiled query for each sequence of compiled axioms $\langle A1,\ldots,An\rangle$ where Ai is a compiled axiom for Qi. Now suppose that a compiled axiom Ai for Qi has the form:

$$Ai: Qi(t1,\ldots,tk_i) \leftarrow Pi1^*(\ ),\ldots,Pim_i^*(\ ),$$

where, for convenience we omit the terms in Pij^*. Let τi be a substitution which contains tij/tj for each variable tj, $j = 1,\ldots,k_i$, and which substitutes a distinct new variable, not previously used, for any additional variable present in $Pi1^*,\ldots,Pim_i^*$. For uniformity we can include extensional predicates in this scheme by writing

$$Qi^*(t1,\ldots,tk_i) \leftarrow Qi^*(t1,\ldots,tk_i).$$

Then, using a compiled axiom for each predicate Qi, we obtain the compiled query

$$CQ: \leftarrow P11^*(\ )\tau1,\ldots,P1m_1^*(\ )\tau1,P21^*(\ )\tau2,\ldots,Pnm_n^*(\ )\tau n.$$

The answers for the query are obtained by evaluating all the compiled queries and taking the union of the answers. We note that a compiled query which contains a false atom can have no answers, and can therefore be omitted.

In our case we want to use the semantically constrained axioms,

$$SCA: Qi(t1,\ldots,tk_i) \leftarrow Pi1^*(\ ),\ldots,Pim_i^*(\ )\ \{Ri1,\ldots,Rir_i\}$$

where each Rij is a residue. Let $\tau i'$ be a substitution which includes τi and which substitutes a distinct new variable, not previously used, for any additional variable present in $Ri1,\ldots,Rir_i$.

DEFINITION 6

A *semantically constrained query* SCQ for the query

$$Q: \leftarrow Q1(t11,\ldots,tik_1),\ldots,Qn(tn1,\ldots,tnk_n)$$

using the semantically constrained axioms

$$Qi(t1,...,tk_i) \leftarrow Pi1^*(\ ),...,Pim_i^*(\ ) \qquad \{Ri1,...,Rir_i\}\ i = 1,...,n$$

is

$$SCQ: \leftarrow P11^*(\ )\tau1',...,P1m_1^*(\ )\tau1',P21^*(\ )\tau2',...,Pnm_n^*(\ )\tau n'$$
$$\{R11\tau1'-,...,R1r_1\tau1'-,R21\tau2'-,...,Rnr_n\tau n'-\}.$$

(In SCQ the "−" stands for the reduction operator, because the residues may be simplified.) ∎

The next question is what to do with the residues in SCQ. A semantically constrained query may have many residues, and we can apply any subset of the set of residues in an attempt to optimize the query. We will discuss criteria for applying residues later. Now we show how residues may be applied by considering a single residue, which we write as R, at a time. We note that any residue that evaluates to true can be eliminated, and if any residue evaluates to false, then the query has no answers.

It is convenient to divide residues into four types: 1) the null clause (NC), 2) a goal clause, 3) a unit clause, and 4) a definite implicational clause. If the residue is NC then the query has no answers. We can think of the transformation as one that takes a query into NC. We consider two cases for a goal clause. First, if the residue subsumes the query, then the query has no answers. Again, the transformation takes the query into NC. For example, if Q: $\leftarrow Q1^*(x^*,a,b)$ and R: $\leftarrow Q1^*(u,a,v)$, then Q has no answers. A second possibility occurs where the residue restricts the solutions in some way. Suppose that for the same query, a residue is R': $\leftarrow GE(x^*,c)$. In this case the search for solutions can be restricted to values which are less than c. This may be helpful if there is an index for $Q1^*$ on the first attribute or if the elements of $Q1^*$ are ordered on the first attribute. Here the transformation adds $LT(x^*,c)$ to the query; in general, the opposite predicate (except for equality) replaces the one in the residue.

Now suppose that the residue is a unit clause. In this case there are several possibilities. In our setup we have a query Q: $\leftarrow Q1^*(\ ),...,Qn^*(\ )$ and residue R: $U(\ ) \leftarrow$, where U is an atom. The application of the residue consists of rewriting the query as

$$\leftarrow Q1^*(\ ),...,Qn^*(\ ),U(\ ).$$

If U is an evaluable predicate that instantiates or restricts a variable of the query, then it adds a selection condition. If U is a nonevaluable predicate that does not already exist in the query, then it introduces a join. The introduction of a join, however, is often not justified because a join is a time-consuming operation to perform. If U is a nonevaluable predicate that appears in the query, say $U = Qi^*$, then, in some cases both Qi^* and U may be removed from the query. This eliminates a join computation from the original query. This join elimination can be done if the resolution of SCQ and $U(\ ) \leftarrow$ can be performed and a resolvent obtained, which contains all the original output variables, and where the terms for all Qj^*, $j \neq i$ are not changed from the original query. The resolvent is then substituted for the query. In effect, the residue says that $Qi^*(\ )$ is in the database, and therefore no lookup is necessary. For example, if

$$Q: \leftarrow Q1^*(a,x^*,y), Q2^*(x^*,z), \qquad \text{and}$$
$$R: Q1^*(u,v,b) \leftarrow ,$$

then the resolvent is

$$\leftarrow Q2^*(x^*,z),$$

which is the new query.

The last case is the one where the residue is a definite implicational clause. Such a clause may be used to limit the search if the body of the residue must be true for the query. For example, let

$$Q: \leftarrow Q1^*(x^*,u,b), Q2^*(u,v) \qquad \text{and}$$
$$R: LT(u,500) \leftarrow Q1^*(x,u,b).$$

Such a residue may be derived from the integrity constraint

$$LT(u,500) \leftarrow Q2^*(u,v), Q1^*(x,u,z).$$

By using this residue, the query can be modified (restricted) to

$$\leftarrow Q1^*(x^*,u,b), Q2^*(u,v), LT(u,500).$$

The Correctness of Query Transformation

In this subsection we define the notion of semantic equivalence of queries. Then we show the correctness of the query transformations presented in the previous section by proving that the new query is semantically equivalent to the old query in every case.

We start by distinguishing among three different notions of equivalence for queries: logical, deductive, and semantic, in order of strength. Again we assume that the discussion takes place in a fixed language, but the definitions are general, independent of the language. Before presenting the formal definitions, we explain these notions in an intuitive manner. For relational databases, two queries are logically equivalent if they have the same answers in all databases. Here IC = $\emptyset$ and IDB = $\emptyset$. For deductive databases we introduce the notion of deductive equivalence with respect to a fixed IDB; this means that the queries must have the same answers for all databases with that IDB as the deductive definitions. Here IC = $\emptyset$ and IDB $\neq$ $\emptyset$. Finally, for semantic equivalence we include the integrity constraints in addition to the intensional axioms. Here IC $\neq$ $\emptyset$.

A *query* is a goal clause with explicitly specified variables, which we write as

$$\leftarrow Q(y1^*,\ldots,yn^*,z1,\ldots,zm,c1,\ldots,ck)$$

where the yi^* $i = 1,\ldots,n$ are the output variables, the zi $i = 1,\ldots,m$ are the existentially quantified variables, and the ci $i = 1,\ldots,k$ are constants. We say that

$$\leftarrow Q(y1^*,\ldots,yn^*,z1,\ldots,zm,c1,\ldots,ck)$$

is *logically equivalent* to

$$\leftarrow Q'(y1^*,\ldots,yn^*,z1,\ldots,zm,c1,\ldots,ck)$$

if for every EDB,

$$\text{EDB} \vdash \forall y1^*\ldots\forall yn^*(\exists z1\ldots\exists zm Q(y1^*,\ldots,yn^*,z1,\ldots,zm,c1,\ldots,ck) \longleftrightarrow$$

$$\exists z1\ldots\exists zm Q'(y1^*,\ldots,yn^*,z1,\ldots,zm,c1,\ldots,ck)).$$

Next, we say that

$$\leftarrow Q(y1^*,\ldots,yn^*,z1,\ldots,zm,c1,\ldots,ck)$$

is *deductively equivalent (with respect to IDB)* to

$$\leftarrow Q'(y1^*,\ldots,yn^*,z1,\ldots,zm,c1,\ldots,ck)$$

if for every DB with IDB,

$$\text{DB} \vdash \forall y1^*\ldots\forall yn^*(\exists z1\ldots\exists zm Q(y1^*,\ldots,yn^*,z1,\ldots,zm,c1,\ldots,ck) \longleftrightarrow$$

$$\exists z1\ldots\exists zm Q'(y1^*,\ldots,yn^*,z1,\ldots,zm,c1,\ldots,ck)).$$

DEFINITION 7

We say that

$$\leftarrow Q(y1^*,\ldots,yn^*,z1,\ldots,zm,c1,\ldots,ck)$$

is *semantically equivalent (with respect to IDB and IC)* to

$$\leftarrow Q'(y1^*,\ldots,yn^*,z1,\ldots,zm,c1,\ldots,ck)$$

if for every DB with IDB which satisfies IC,

$$DB \vdash \forall y1^*\ldots\forall yn^*(\exists z1\ldots\exists zmQ(y1^*,\ldots,yn^*,z1,\ldots,zm,c1,\ldots,ck) \longleftrightarrow$$

$$\exists z1\ldots\exists zmQ'(y1^*,\ldots,yn^*,z1,\ldots,zm,c1,\ldots,ck)). \blacksquare$$

This definition means that two queries are semantically equivalent if they have the same answers for any two databases that contain the same intensionally defined predicates and integrity constraints. Therefore we can safely substitute a query for another query if the two are semantically equivalent. We note that traditional query optimization deals with logical equivalence for relational databases and deductive equivalence for deductive databases. The notion of semantic equivalence applies both to relational databases where IDB = $\emptyset$ and to deductive databases where IDB $\neq \emptyset$. In the previous section we indicated various query transformations. The next theorem gives the correctness of those transformations.

THEOREM 6

The semantic query transformations presented in "Query Transformation" lead to semantically equivalent queries.

Proof: Consider a semantically constrained query

$$Q(y1^*,\ldots,yn^*,z1,\ldots,zm,c1,\ldots,ck) \qquad \{R1(\ ),\ldots,Rr(\ )\}.$$

Suppose that for a given database DB, $\langle a1,\ldots,an\rangle$ is an answer to the query with $\langle b1,\ldots,bm\rangle$ substituted for the existentially quantified variables. It follows from Theorem 5 that if

$$\tau = \{a1/y1^*,\ldots,an/yn^*,b1/z1,\ldots,bm/zm\}, \text{ then } R1(\ )\tau,\ldots,Rr(\ )\tau \text{ are}$$
all provable from DB.

Now we deal with the query transformations using the residues one at a time. We write R for a residue. Since NC represents a contradiction, if R is

NC, the query cannot have any answers. So it is semantically equivalent to NC. Next suppose that the residue is a goal clause. If the residue subsumes the query, and $\langle a1,...,an \rangle$ is an answer, the residue implies that $\langle a1,...,an \rangle$ is not an answer, which is a contradiction. Hence again, the query is semantically equivalent to NC. Suppose now that the residue has the form $\leftarrow$ GE(x^*,c). This means that for any solution, if a solves for x^*, then it is not the case that a $\geq$ c. Therefore, adding LT(x^*,c) does not change the set of solutions. The situation is similar for the other evaluable predicates.

Next we consider unit residues. Again, by using Theorem 5 we can add U ( ) to the query and retain semantic equivalence. We want to show that the join removal is justified. Starting with the query

$$\leftarrow Q1^*(\ ),...,Qn^*(\ ) \{U(\ ) \leftarrow \},$$

suppose that the resolution of the query and U( ) $\leftarrow$ can be performed as indicated earlier. We wish to show that the resolvent is semantically equivalent to the old query. So suppose that $\langle a1,...,an \rangle$ is an answer to the original query as at the beginning of the proof. Since the new query is just the old query with a literal removed and the output variables retained, $\langle a1,...,an \rangle$ is an answer for the resolvent, which is the new query. Conversely, suppose that $\langle a1,...,an \rangle$ is an answer for the new query (without the Qi^* term) and let v1,...vg be the variables in Qi^* which do not occur in the new query. We must show that DB $\vdash \exists v1...\exists vgQi^*(\ )\tau$ where τ is the substitution used for the new query. The residue $U^*(\ ) \leftarrow$ must have been obtained using some Qj^*, j $\neq$ i, because the integrity constraints are not recursive. Hence DB $\vdash U^*(\ )\tau$. But the way that the resolvent was obtained, there must be a substitution τ' which includes τ and which contains substitutions for each vi, such that DB $\vdash Qi^*(\ )\tau'$. This means that $\langle a1,...,an \rangle$ is an answer to the original query.

The last change is the one where the residue, a general Horn clause, is used to limit the search. The correctness of this search limitation policy follows immediately from the first paragraph of the proof. ∎

Extensions

In this paper we formally defined the notion of semantic query optimization and proved its correctness. We dealt with a restricted class of deductive databases where the intensional database contains non-recursive, function-free, range-restricted Horn clauses, while the integrity constraints are non-recursive range-restricted Horn clauses. All of our queries are existential conjunctive queries. It is possible to extend our results in certain restricted ways to more general databases and queries. In particular, Chakravarthy [1985] describes some aspects of semantic query optimization for non-Horn and recursive databases as well as for queries with universal quantification and negation.

Acknowledgments

We appreciate the excellent comments of the referees that led to considerable improvement in the presentation of this paper. Work on this paper was supported by the National Science Foundation under grant numbers DCR 8305992 and DCR 8412662, and by the Army Research Office under grant number DAAG-29-85-K-0177.

References

1. Aho, A. V., Sagiv, Y., and Ullman, J. D. [1979] Equivalences Among Relational Expressions, *Siam Journal of Computing* **8** , 218–246.

2. Chakravarthy, U. S. [1985] *Semantic Query Optimization in Deductive Databases,* Ph.D. Thesis, Department of Computer Science, University of Maryland, College Park, MD.

3. Chakravarthy, U. S., Fishman, D. H., and Minker, J. [1986] Semantic Query Optimization in Expert Systems and Database Systems, in *Expert Database Systems* (L. Kerschberg, Ed.), Benjamin/Cummings Publishing Co., Menlo Park, CA, 659–675.

4. Chakravarthy, U.S., Minker, J., and Grant, J. [1986] Semantic Query Optimization: Additional Constraints and Control Strategies, in *Expert Database Systems* (L. Kerschberg, Ed.), Benjamin/Cummings Publishing Co., Menlo Park, CA, 345–379.

5. Chang, C. L. and Lee, R.C.T. [1973] *Symbolic Logic and Mechanical Theorem Proving,* Academic Press, New York.

6. Futo, I. [1984] A Constraint Machine to Control Parallel Search of PRISM, Technical Note, Department of Computer Science, University of Maryland, College Park, MD.

7. Gallaire, H., Minker, J., and Nicolas, J.–M.[1984] Logic and Databases: A Deductive Approach, *ACM Computing Surveys* **16**, 153–185.

8. Hammer, M. M. and McLeod, D. J. [1975] Semantic Integrity in Relational Database Systems, *Proc. of the First VLDB Conference*, 25–47.

9. Hammer, M. M. and Zdonik, S. B. [1980] Knowledge Based Query Processing, *Proc. of the Sixth VLDB Conference*, 137–147.

10. Jarke, M., Clifford, J., and Vassiliou, Y. [1984] An Optimizing Prolog Front-End to a Relational Query System, *Proc. of the ACM-SIGMOD Conference,* 296–306.

11. King, J. J. [1981] *Query Optimization by Semantic Reasoning*, Ph.D. Thesis, Department of Computer Science, Stanford University, CA.

12. Kohli, M. and Minker, J. [1983] Intelligent Control Using Integrity Constraints, *Proc. of AAAI-83*, 202–205.

13. McSkimin, J. R. and Minker, J. [1977] The Use of a Semantic Network in a Deductive Query Answering System, *Proc of the Fifth IJCAI*, 50–58.

14. Minker, J. and Nicolas, J.-M. [1982] On Recursive Axioms in Deductive Databases, *Information Systems* **8**, 1–13.

15. Reiter, R. [1978a] Deductive Question-Answering on Relational Databases, in *Logic and Databases* (H. Gallaire and J. Minker, Eds.), Plenum Press, New York, 149–178.

16. Reiter, R. [1978b] On Structuring a First-Order Database, *Proc. of the Second CSCS National Conference*.

17. Sadri, F. and Kowalski, R. [1988] An Application of General Purpose Theorem-Proving to Database Integrity, in *Foundations of Deductive Databases and Logic Programming* (J. Minker, Ed.), Morgan Kaufmann Publishers, Los Altos, CA, 313–362.

18. Sagiv, Y. [1988] Optimizing Datalog Programs, in *Foundations of Deductive Databases and Logic Programming* (J. Minker, Ed.), Morgan Kaufmann Publishers, Los Altos, CA, 659–698.

19. Ullman, J. D. [1982] *Principles of Database Systems*, Second Edition, Computer Science Press.

20. Xu, G. D. [1983] Search Control in Semantic Query Optimization, Technical Report 83–9, University of Massachusetts, Department of Computer Science, Amherst, MA.

8

Intelligent Query Answering in Rule Based Systems[1]

Tomasz Imielinski
Department of Computer Science
Rutgers University, New Brunswick, NJ

Abstract

We propose that in large knowledge bases that are collections of atomic facts and general rules (Horn Clauses), the rules should be allowed to occur in the answer for a query. We introduce a new concept of an answer for a query which includes both atomic facts and general rules. We provide a method of transforming rules by relational algebra expressions built from projection, join, and selection and demonstrate how the answers consisting of both facts and general rules can be generated. This new concept of an answer could be used also when function symbols are allowed to occur in a database and the tuple oriented answer is infinite.

Introduction

In a large knowledge base system, data is represented both in the form of general laws (given as Horn clauses) and assertions representing specific facts (e.g., tuples of relations). We argue here that it is frequently beneficial to

---

[1]This is a modified version of the paper with the same title, which is to appear in the Journal of Logic Programming.

structure the answer for a query in a similar way, i.e., both in terms of tuples, as is traditionally the case, and in terms of general rules. This is simply a consequence of the general philosophy of logic programming which imposes a uniform view on programs (in this case queries and rules) and data (Kowalski [1979]). This is beneficial both from a conceptual and a computational point of view.

Conceptually, rules are often more informative and easier to comprehend than corresponding sets of derived tuples. For example, the fact that all students who specialize in a given area have to take all courses offered in this area can be represented better by a rule than by a corresponding derived set of tuples. This is the case regardless of whether this information is part of the database or part of an answer to a query. Computationally, we can benefit even more. It is much less expensive to evaluate rules over the answer to the query than over the database state itself, since the result of the query is much smaller than the database. Besides, rule transformation extends the algebraic spirit of query processing from purely relational databases to databases with rules and is also another example of "lazy evaluation" known in the area of programming languages.

Finally, this new concept of an answer to a query can be helpful in *resource limited computation* when we do not have enough resources to compute the full answer to a query. Indeed, we may interpret the answer with rules as a type of "abstracted" answer to a query. Such an answer can be specified further depending on the user's request. For example, if in the answer we include the rule saying "all prerequisites of courses," a user may want to know what these prerequisites are (see the next example) and in such a case our rule has to be evaluated. The query formulation process is, in this case, not only a process of choosing a proper formula to express a query but also choosing a *language* in which the answer to a query is acceptable to the user. Such a language could, for example, include predicates that can occur in the rules of the answer to a query. Needless to say, computing rules in answers is an option for the user and is applied only if he explicitly requests it. We would prefer also that, in case such a request is made, the necessary additional computation be cheaper than starting everything from the beginning. If rules in the answer to a query are evaluated yielding a set of tuples as the final answer for the query, the rules become *derived integrity constraints* in the view of the database (Hull [1984]).

A database formally consists of a *database extension* represented in the form of relations and a *database intension* which includes a set of rules R. The rules mentioned above are really *inference* rules, that is, rules that will derive missing, implicitly represented information from data stored explicitly as tuples in the database extension. Therefore, to query such a database, the database rules have to be used in the process of query evaluation. Formally, the answer to a query in such circumstances could be computed by closing the database under the underlying set of rules and then evaluating the query. We will say that rules from the database can be transformed by the query if some of the rules can be evaluated *after* the evaluation of the query without affecting the final result:

EXAMPLE 1

Assume that the set of all professors of a university is partitioned into research groups. Let the binary predicate Group(x,y) be true for x and y iff x and y belong to the same research group. In this case, it is natural to assume (or require) that professors from the same research group be able to teach the same courses. This can be represented formally by the following formula:

$$r_1 = \text{Teach}(x,y) \wedge \text{Group}(x,z) \rightarrow \text{Teach}(z,y)$$

In addition, we may have rules that express standard equivalence properties of the relation Group (reflexivity, symmetry, transitivity). We may require also that professors should be able to teach prerequisites of all the courses they are able to teach, which can be expressed by the following formula:

$$r_2 = \text{Teach}(x,y) \wedge \text{Prerequisite}(z,y) \rightarrow \text{Teach}(x,z)$$

where, additionally, the predicate Prerequisite satisfies the transitive closure rule.

Consider the query: "Give me all courses that Imielinski may teach." This query can be expressed by the following relational algebra expression:

$$\pi_{\text{Course}}\sigma_{\text{name = Imielinski}}(\text{Teach})$$

It is easy to see that the following rule, related to r_2, can be included in the answer to the query:

$$Q(y) \wedge \text{Prerequisite}(z,y) \rightarrow Q(z)$$

where Q denotes the query predicate. We say that this rule is *transformed* from r_2 modulo the query Q. This rule has also a very natural interpretation—together with the set of courses which will be returned, it simply says, "include prerequisites of the courses which were just printed out." If the user wants to know what these prerequisites are, he may request the evaluation of this rule. Notice that even in this case we will benefit computationally, since the new transformed rule will be evaluated over the result of the query which is much smaller than the database.

It is also clear that the rule r_1 is not transformable modulo this query and would have to be evaluated prior to the query itself.

The situation changes when we consider a different query

"Who can teach the Database course."

It is easy to see that the situation is totally reversed. Now the rule r_2 has to be evaluated prior to the query evaluation, while the rule r_1 can be transformed into the rule:

$$Q(x) \wedge Group(x,z) \rightarrow Q(z)$$

In other words the answer to the query can be described in natural language as "the groups of Imielinski, Smith,... et al. can teach databases."

Again, if the user wants to know who the members of a particular group are, he should request the evaluation of this rule. ∎

Formally, the rules in the answer to a query should be either expressed totally in terms of the *query predicate*, i.e., the predicate defined by the query, or by the query predicate and some other additional predicates that occur in the database. The choice of these additional predicates may be left to the user. The query predicate must appear both in the consequent and in the body of the rule (otherwise the query definition could trivially form such a rule). We will always denote the query predicate by Q.

In this paper we analyze conditions under which rule transformation is possible. First we describe conditions under which single rules can be transformed by single relational operations, then we generalize our discussion to relational expressions, and finally to sets of rules. The transformation of the sets of rules is particularly difficult—we always attempt to decompose the problem of transformation of sets of rules into the transformation of individual rules. We also demonstrate that even when a particular set of rules cannot be transformed, we can frequently construct an equivalent set of rules which can be transformed.

The paper is organized as follows. In the section, "Basic Notions," the basic concepts are introduced. General conditions for the transformation of rules are discussed in "Rules in Answers–Rule Transformation." The case of *single* rules is described in the subsection, "Transforming Single Rules." Transformation of *sets* of rules, which is much more difficult, is discussed in the subsection, "Transforming Sets of Rules." Some special cases of rule transformation are discussed also in the "Appendix" (in particular, the cases of bounded sets of rules and CONST rules). In the last section, "Infinite Answers, Functions, and Predicates," we talk briefly about the further generalization of the answer to a query to include predicates and function symbols. We also briefly discuss how the technique of including rules in answers to queries could be used in case of infinite answers occurring in databases with function symbols.

Basic Notions

We assume that the reader is familiar with the relational model of data (Ullman [1982]) and standard terminology of logic programming (Kowalski [1979], Gallaire, Minker, and Nicolas [1984]). By a literal P(t) we mean an atomic formula where P is the predicate name and t is a tuple of variables and / or constants, or the negation of such a formula. Rules have the form of function free Horn Clauses, where the P_i (t_i), i = 1, ..., n + 1 are atomic formulas:

$$P_1(t_1) \wedge P_2(t_2), \ldots \wedge P_n(t_n) \rightarrow P_{n+1}(t_{n+1}).$$

A rule with k atoms in its body will be called a *k-rule*. We say that a rule r *defines* a predicate p iff p occurs as a consequent of r. By *assertions* we mean atomic formulas of the form P(t) where t is a constant tuple. With a set of assertions we usually identify the relations built from the sets of tuples t such that P(t) is an atomic assertion. These relations will have columns identified either by *attributes* (Ullman [1982]) or by letters referring to attribute names. For example, in the predicate $P(x_1...x_n)$ the first position will be referred to by the number 1 or by A, the second by the number 2 or by B, etc. With sets of predicates, we associate *multirelations*, i.e., sets of relations each corresponding to an individual predicate. Further in the text, we identify sets of assertions with the corresponding multirelations.

A rule is *active* iff it serves as an inference rule; it is *passive* iff it is satisfied by the set of assertions. In the latter case, the rule does not yield new answers and is referred to as an *integrity constraint*. We assume further in the text that the database intension is built from the inference rules, R, and integrity constraints, IC. The division of the rules into passive and active is usually done at compile time for a database and holds for all possible database extensions.

A database state consists of two parts: a database *extension* and a database *intension*. The database extension is a set of assertions, S, stored in the form of a relational database. The database intension consists of Horn rules without functions. The database intension rules are used to generate additional, derived assertions from the database extension. Let r be a single rule. By r(S) we denote the result of one application of r to S; r(S) will contain S and some additional tuples generated by one application of r to S. By R(S), where R is a set of rules we mean $\cup$ {r(S): r $\in$ R}. $R^k(S)$ denotes the result of k applications of R to S. Finally $R^*(S)$ denotes the least fixpoint of R containing S.

We say that a rule is *typed* with respect to a certain predicate if each variable can occur only in a fixed position in any occurrence of this predicate. A predicate that occurs in the consequent of a rule is called a *consequent* predicate. We deal only with typed rules here. Further in the text we define two special families of rules—strongly typed rules and CONST rules.

We now describe the notion of a query more formally. Traditionally, queries in databases are expressed using two different formalisms: the relational algebra or the relational calculus (Ullman [1982]). The relational calculus is a variant of the predicate calculus with queries being open formulas of the language. Formally, by the *answer* to a query Q(x) in the database DB (which is viewed as a first order theory, a combination of database extension and intension), we mean the set of *all* substitutions of domain constants for the variable x such that the resulting formula is a semantic consequence of the database DB. If the database is relational (i.e., if the database state is a collection of relations) then for any query Q(x) we can compute the answer for this query by a *relational algebra expression* built from the well known (Ullman [1982]) relational algebra operations of projection, join, selection, union, and difference:

1. Selection: Denoted by $\sigma_E(R)$, where E is a selection condition generated by descriptors of the form (A = a) or (A = B) (where A,B are attribute names) and conjunction, disjunction, and negation. For example, $E = (A = a) \wedge (B = b) \vee \neg(A \neq B)$ is a selection condition. It is easy to see that selection conditions correspond to formulas expressed in the predicate calculus of equality without quantifiers.

2. Projection: Denoted $\pi_X(R)$, where X is a subset of the set of attributes of R, is defined as $\{t \mid \exists s \in R \text{ such that } t = s[X]\}$ where s[X] denotes the restriction of tuple s to the set of attributes X.

3. Natural Join: Denoted by $R \bowtie S$, is defined as the set of all tuples t defined over the union of the set of attributes of R and the set of attributes of S, such that the projection of tuple t over the set of attributes of R belongs to R and the projection of t over the set of attributes of S belongs to S.

4. Union and Difference: These are standard set theoretical operations on relations.

We refer to P-queries as queries built only from projections, PS-queries as queries built from projections and selections, and PSJ-queries as queries built from the projection, join, and selection.

The answer for a query is defined traditionally as a set of tuples. In the next section we modify this concept.

Rules in Answers–Rule Transformation

We now describe conditions under which we can include rules as part of the *answer* to a *query*. Generally speaking, in this section, we are interested in determining the formal limits of the degree to which we can algebraically manipulate "intensional" answers[2] without producing their equivalent "extensions" (sets of all tuples derived by the rule). Ideally, we would prefer to perform manipulations on rules without ever producing their extensions, or doing it only on explicit demand of the user. We show that, in general, this is not possible. This will be demonstrated by introducing proper correctness criteria for rule transformation and showing conditions under which a *correct* rule transformation can be accomplished.

We refer to a query usually by a relational algebra expression. This is more convenient in our approach, which is essentially bottom up.

Formally, we are interested in the following three situations:

1. *Total Transformation of Rules in Terms of the Query Predicate, Q.*

   In this case rules in the answer to a query are defined entirely in terms of the query predicate and can be "postponed" after the evaluation of the query. Formally, this corresponds to the following formula:

   For every set of assertions S, $Q(R^*(S)) = R_Q^*(Q(S))$

   where R_Q is the new "postponed" or transformed set of rules. In other words, the query and the set of rules should "commute" in the algebraic sense.

   Consider the predicate Teach(x,y,z) that denotes that a teacher x teaches a course y to a student z and the rule,

   r: Teach(x, Databases,z) $\rightarrow$ Teach(x, File Systems,z)

   If the query Q is a simple projection $\pi_{Teacher,Course}$ we can obtain the following rule as the answer for this query:

   $r_Q = Q(x,Databases) \rightarrow Q(x,File Systems)$

   It is easy to see that this rule r_Q satisfies the formula above, i.e., the original rule can be totally transformed. ∎

2. *Partial Transformation of Rules in Terms of the Query Predicate,Q.*

   Rules in the answer to a query are defined totally in terms of the query predicate but may be only partially postponed and some of them will

---

[2]Answers containing rules.

have to be performed prior to the evaluation of the query. In this case we have:

For every set of assertions S, $Q(R^*(S)) = R_0^*Q(R_0^*(S))$ where R_0 is the set of rules which have to be evaluated prior to the query itself (i.e., which cannot be postponed).

For example, take the rule r, defined above, and the query

$$Q = \sigma_{(Course \neq Database) \vee (Teacher \neq John)}(Teaches)$$

It is easy to see that the rule

$$r_0 = Teach(John, Databases, z) \rightarrow Teach(John, Compilers, z)$$

will have to be evaluated prior to the query, while

$$r_Q = (x \neq John) \wedge Q(x, Databases, z) \rightarrow Q(x, File Systems, z)$$

can be postponed until after the query evaluation. (Notice that we could really skip the condition $(x \neq John)$ in this rule.) ∎

3.   *Partial Transformation of Rules in Terms of Query Predicate and Concept Predicates*

The rules in the answer for a query are defined not only in terms of the query predicate but also in terms of other database predicates. In this case again we may have both the case of total rule transformation as in (1) and the case of partial query transformation as in (2). Formally this situation could be described by the same formula as in the second (above) case. The only difference is that the user has first to define the set of *concept* predicates (i.e., predicates in terms of which he is going to accept the answer to the query). The query Q is now no longer just a single relational expression (or formula of the predicate calculus). Rather, it is a pair (Q,C) consisting of the query Q and the set C of concept predicates.

The term ''concept'' is used here to reflect the fact that these predicates will be treated as ''atomic'' concepts that can then occur in rules in an answer to a query. We assume that concept predicates do not occur in the query itself (otherwise we could allow, trivially, the query definition as the possible answer for a query). By *concept rules* we mean rules in which all foreign predicates (i.e., those that do not occur in the consequent of the rule) are concept predicates. ∎

In all of these situations we assume that all rules in an answer to a query are recursive (i.e., they contain the query predicate *both* in the consequent and in the body of the rule). This assumption prevents us from considering trivial rule transformations as, for example, including a query definition (in the form of a Horn formula with a query predicate as a consequent) in an answer to a query. Besides, since recursive rules are the hardest to evaluate, their transformation could lead to significant computational gains.

Notice that in all the above cases the rule transformation is obtained *independently* of the set of assertions.

We must also point out here that we are interested in obtaining *active* rules in an answer to a query, that is, we want our rules to still play the role of inference rules as in the database itself. Certainly, we may talk also about transforming rules into *passive* rules in an answer to a query—this is, however, though, more in the spirit of *derived* integrity constraints considered, e.g., in Hull [1984] and Klug and Price [1982], and is not considered here.

Transforming Single Rules

We start by describing the method for a single rule transformation by a single relational expression.

We give precise conditions under which a single application of a given rule r can be transformed by a single relational operation. Later we consider the cases of arbitrary number of applications of a single rule as well as of a set of rules.

PROJECTION

Let π_X be a projection operation over an instance of a predicate occurring in the consequent of a rule and let l be any atom in which the consequent predicate occurs. By l[X] we denote the atom resulting from l by dropping all positions which correspond to the columns outside of X.

We have the following lemma:

LEMMA 1

A rule r is π_X-transformable[3] iff π_X does not project out either constants or variables, which occur in more than one atom in the body of the rule r. In this case, the result of the projection is the rule in which each occurrence of the atom l generated by the consequent predicate is replaced by its projection l[X].

Proof: If the condition of the lemma is not satisfied, we can construct two different database instances which have the same projection before the derivation

---

[3]That is, there exists a rule r' such that $\pi_X(r(S)) = r'(\pi_X(S))$.

of additional tuples by the rule r and different projections after the closure is computed. This demonstrates that the construction of the derived rule is impossible. If the conditions of the theorem are met, then it is easy to verify that the transformed rule satisfies the conditions of π_X-transformability. ■

EXAMPLE 2

Let $r = p(x,y,z',w) \wedge p(x',y,z,w) \rightarrow p(x,y,z,w)$.

Let $X = \{A,C\}$, then r is not π_X-transformable because the variable w is bound (it has two different occurrences). It is easy to see that for

	A	B	C	D			A	B	C	D
S1	a	b	c	d	and	S2	a	b	c	d
	a'	b	c'	d			a'	b	c'	d'

where a,b,...d' are domain constants, we have $\pi_{AC}(S_1) = \pi_{AC}(S_2)$ but not $\pi_{AC}(r(S_1)) = \pi_{AC}(r(S_2))$.

On the other hand if we take any X, such that $B \in X$ and $D \in X$, then the rule r is π_X-transformable. If $X = \{B,C,D\}$ then the rule:

$$\pi_X(r) = Q(y,z',w) \wedge Q(y,z,w') \rightarrow Q(y,z,w)$$

is part of the result of the query $Q = \pi_{BCD}(r)$.

In this case the rule r does not have to be evaluated but could remain active and be transformed independently into an *active* rule in the answer to the query. It is not necessary to evaluate the rule r over R in this case. Notice also that rule transformation does not require any accesses to the assertional part of the database and may even be done at compile time in many cases. In a similar way, the rule $r = P(x,y,z) \wedge W(y,y') \wedge U(z,w) \rightarrow P(x,y',w)$ is not π_{AB}-transformable because the variable z that is projected out is bound (by the predicate U). However, if we apply projection over the attributes B and C, then the rule can be transformed to the form

$$Q(y,z) \wedge W(y,y') \wedge U(z,w) \rightarrow Q(y,w)$$

where Q is a query predicate. ■

We now describe the join operation and the transformability of the rules by the join operation.

JOIN

Let r_1 and r_2 be two rules defined for relations R and S.

In order to determine the transformability of these rules we have to determine when the following holds:

$$r_1(R) \bowtie r_2(S) = r_Q(R \bowtie S)$$

Let $X = Y \cap Z$ be the common set of attributes for R and S. In order for the above equality to hold, the following necessary and sufficient conditions must be satisfied:

$$\pi_X(r_1(R)) = \pi_X(R) \text{ and}$$

$$\pi_X(r_2(S)) = \pi_X(S) \text{ for every R and S} \tag{1}$$

Condition 1 means that rules r_1 and r_2 leave the projection on X of R and S invariant. Indeed, otherwise rules r_1 and r_2 could produce some tuples which would contribute to the join if evaluated prior to the join itself. In consequence it would be incorrect to postpone their evaluation until after the join. This above condition is easy to test and can be done using standard methods of testing for the equivalence of relational expressions.

The rules r_1 and r_2 in this case transform to a set of rules rather than to just a single rule. The resulting set contains three rules denoted by r_1', r_2', and $r_\bowtie$ constructed in the following way:

Let r_1 define the predicate p. By a p-atom we mean an atom of the form $p(t_1, \ldots t_n)$. The rule r_1' is formed from the rule r_1 by replacing all p-atoms both in the body of the rule as well as in its consequent by Q-atoms where Q is a new predicate with arity corresponding to the arity of the join. Each p-atom l is replaced by the new Q-atom and has the same variables as l on the attributes corresponding to the attributes of p. The other positions of the new Q-atom are formed by a vector of new variables $z_{i_1}, \ldots, z_{i_n}$. These variables are the same for any new Q-atom replacing any p-atoms either in the body or in the consequent of the rule. All other atoms in r_1 remain unchanged. The rule r_2' is formed in an identical way.

There is also a third rule $r_\bowtie$ in the join, which is a unirelational recursive rule generated by the predicate Q. This rule is a proper join dependency corresponding to the join. It is formed in the following way:

There are two Q-atoms in the body each corresponding to one of the arguments of the join operation. The consequent atom has the form $Q(x_1, \ldots x_n)$ and the body Q-atom corresponding to the argument R has the same variables as the consequent atom on all attributes in Q corresponding to the attributes in R. The second atom is formed in an identical manner with respect to the second argument of the join. All other variables in the rule are pairwise different and different from the variables occurring in the consequent predicate.

The third rule always holds in the join of the two relations (with the sets of attributes Y and Z respectively). In other words, every join of the two relations R and S over the sets of attributes Y and Z satisfies this rule. It is, therefore, a derived integrity constraint or a passive rule in our previous terminology. This rule can be made active if we perform a "simplified" join, described below, over the tables R and S and add the rule $r_{\bowtie}$ as an additional rule that computes the remaining tuples if necessary. This simplified join has the following form:

For each tuple in R, find a tuple in S that can be joined with it, perform the join, and include the tuple in the result. Do the same thing for each tuple in S. Space is saved since we do not have to represent all combinations of tuples of R and tuples in S which match on X. These could always be generated by the rule $r_{\bowtie}$ "on demand." In such a case, the size of the result is, in the worst case, $\#R + \#S$ instead of $\#R \cdot \#S$. In this case the rule $r_{\bowtie}$ becomes the "active" part of the result. This method consists, therefore, of a good alternative way of evaluating a join.

EXAMPLE 3

Let R[A,B] and S[B,C] be two relational schemes. Let $r_1 = R(a,b_1) \to R(a,b_2)$ and $r_2 = S(b,c_1) \to S(b,c_2)$

This set of rules is not transformable because for $X = \{A,B\} \cap \{B,C\} = \{B\}$ the rule r_1 is not X-invariant, i.e., it does not satisfy condition (1). However, the rule r always holds in the result of this query.

The situation changes, when instead of the rule r_1, we consider the rule $r'_1 = R(a_1,b) \to R(a_2,b)$. The resulting set of rules is transformable. Indeed, condition (1) is now satisfied and the transformed set of rules has the following form:

$$r_1' = Q(a_1,b,y) \to Q(a_2,b,y)$$

$$r_2' = Q(z,b,c_1) \to Q(z,b,c_2)$$

$$r_\infty = Q(x,y,z') \wedge Q(x',y,z) \to Q(x,y,z)$$

We can make all three rules active in this case by evaluating a "simplified" join as described above. ∎

SELECTION

This is the most important operation, both because it is used frequently and also because it is the most "restrictive" as it produces small sets of answers even from large databases. It is definitely useful to evaluate rules over the result of a selection instead of evaluating them over the original database. This leads to a rule transformation which intuitively speaking "instantiates" the rule and makes it "more specific."

Let E be a selection condition. If t is a tuple (possibly with variables) by E(t) we denote a formula such that

$v(E(t))$ = true iff $E(v(t))$ is true, where v is the substitution of the domain constants for variables.

Let σ_E be the selection operation. There are two conditions under which the rule r can be transformed into either an active or a passive rule.

Let the rule r have the form $P(t_1),...P(t_n) \wedge W \rightarrow P(t_{n+1})$ where W is a conjunction of all the other literals in which the consequent predicate does not occur. We assume here again (as in the case of projection) that our rule is built only from concept predicates and the consequent predicate. We consider the following three cases:

1. The rule r is σ_E-transformable into an *active rule* iff $E(t_{n+1}) \leftrightarrow E(t_1) \wedge ... \wedge E(t_n)$. In this case we have $\sigma_E(r) = r$.

2. The rule $r = P(t_1) \wedge ... P(t_n) \wedge W \rightarrow P(t_{n+1})$ is σ_E-transformable into a *passive rule* iff $E(t_1) \wedge ... \wedge E(t_n) \rightarrow E(t_{n+1})$ holds.

3. The rule r is independent of the selection condition E iff $E(t_{n+1})$ is false. In this case the rule r does not have to be evaluated at all as far as the selection query is concerned.

Indeed, in Case 1 we have that $\sigma_E(r(R)) = r(\sigma_E(R))$. It is easy to see that the first condition is the necessary and sufficient condition for this equation to hold. In Case 2 this does not hold but the rule is still implied as the integrity constraint in the result.

In the situation when a rule cannot be transformed, we can decompose the rule into two parts, one of which is transformable while the other is not.

DEFINITION 1
Let $P(t_1)...P(t_n) \wedge W \rightarrow P(t_{n+1})$ be the rule. Let $E^* = E(t_1) \wedge ...E(t_n)$ and let

$E' = E^* \wedge E(t_{n+1})$ and
$-E' = \neg (E^*) \wedge E(t_{n+1})$

By r^E we denote the rule $E' \wedge P(t_1) \wedge ...P(t_n) \wedge W \rightarrow P(t_{n+1})$ and by r^{-E} we denote the rule $-E' \wedge P(t_1) \wedge ...P(t_n) \wedge W \rightarrow P(t_{n+1})$. If any of the preconditions E' or $-E'$ is false then the corresponding rule r^E or r^{-E} will be empty (the empty precondition is denoted by δ). ■

It is easy to see why the rule r^{-E} has to be evaluated prior to selection. It takes into account the tuples which themselves do not satisfy the selection condition but *contribute* to the selection condition through the original rule. Therefore this modified rule has to be evaluated prior to the query. On the other hand the rule r^E can be evaluated after the selection condition; indeed, all P-atoms in the body of the rule satisfy the selection condition so no information is lost by postponing evaluation of this rule.

EXAMPLE 4
Let our rule r have the form

$$P(x,y,z) \wedge W(z,u) \wedge U(y,v) \rightarrow P(x,u,v)$$

and let the selection condition $E = (A \neq a) \wedge ((B = b) \vee (C \neq c)))$.

This rule can be decomposed into two rules, r^E and r^{-E}. The rule r^E is given by:

$$r^E = P(x,y,z) \wedge W(z,u) \wedge U(y,v) \wedge E(x,y,z) \wedge (u = b) \vee (v \neq c) \rightarrow P(x,u,v)$$

The descriptor $(x \neq a)$ which seems to be missing above is implied by $E(x,y,z)$. The rule r^{-E} is given by:

$$r^{-E} = P(x,y,z) \wedge ((x = a) \vee ((y \neq b)) \wedge (z = c)) \wedge W(z,u) \wedge U(y,v) \wedge (x \neq a) \wedge ((u = b) \vee (v \neq c)) \rightarrow P(x,u,v)$$

Since the first rule belongs to the answer to the query, we can replace it by:

$$Q(x,y,z) \wedge W(z,u) \wedge U(y,v) \wedge (u = b) \vee (v \neq c)) \rightarrow Q(x,u,v)$$

where Q is the query predicate. ■

QUERIES
Now, we have to discuss transformations of individual rules by relational algebra expressions. The ideal situation would be if we could apply our transformation rules for the individual relational operators in a recursive way. Unfortunately it is not that simple and we have to restrict the syntax of the queries (expressions) to effectively use the rules introduced above. The most problematic operation is the natural join, since it generates a nonlinear recursive rule as the result of the rule transformation (i.e., a join dependency r). If, additionally, the argument predicates of the join were defined by some other recursive rules then, after applying the join, we produce (in case all rules are transformable) a *set* of not necessarily linear recursive rules as a set of trans-

formed rules. If there is another operation after the join operation in our expression it will not have a single rule as an argument but a set of complex rules. As we will see in the next section, the transformation of the set of recursive rules is considerably harder than the transformation of individual rules and is not always possible. Therefore, if we want to transform the rules effectively we should avoid expressions in which the join operation does not occur as the top (final) operation but is an argument of another operation. Notice that neither selection nor projection suffers from the above problem; they always transform single rules into single rules.

IDEMPOTENT RULES

So far we have described conditions for transforming single applications of a single rule by individual relational operations. These conditions can be applied directly in the case of an arbitrary number of applications of a single rule ($r^*(S)$) in the case of projection, selection, and join. Unfortunately, the decomposition of the rules modulo the selection condition cannot be generalized directly to the case of an arbitrary number of applications of a single rule. Such a decomposition is only possible when our rule r is *idempotent* (i.e., no more than one application of the rule is necessary in order to reach a fixpoint; the limit of the rule is equal to one). We will come back to this point when discussing the transformation of sets of rules.

Transforming Sets of Rules

Rules may be related to each other in a complicated way. In most cases we cannot simply apply the procedures described above to a set of rules on a rule by rule basis. Hull [1984] demonstrated a simple family of rules (template dependencies) such that a projection of it is not finitely specifiable by Horn Clauses. In other words he demonstrated that the set of rules holding in a simple projection may not be finite. We provide here his example.

EXAMPLE 5 (HULL [1984])
Let rules have the following form:

$$r_1 = P(a,b',c',d',e), P(a,b,c,d,e') \rightarrow P(a,b,c,d,e)$$

$$r_2 = P(a',b,c',d',e), P(a,b,c,d,e') \rightarrow P(a,b,c,d,e)$$

$$r_3 = P(a',b',c,d,e), P(a,b,c,d',e) \rightarrow P(a,b,c,d,e)$$

where a,b,c,d,e,a',b',c',d',e' are variables. Let us consider the projection π_{ABCD}. Hull demonstrated that the set of all relations which are the projections on ABCD of the relations satisfying this set of rules is not finitely specifiable by a set of Horn clauses. In our terms it means that the set of rules holding in the above projection is not even finitely specifiable. ∎

Frequently it also turns out that although a given set of rules is not transformable by the query, some other equivalent set of rules is. The following example illustrates the point:

EXAMPLE 6

Given two rules $p(a) \rightarrow p(b)$ and $p(b) \rightarrow p(c)$ and selection $\sigma_{(A = a)\lor(A = c)}$, we can get the implied rule $p(a) \rightarrow p(c)$ by application of modus ponens to the above two rules. In this case only the rule $p(b) \rightarrow p(c)$ should be evaluated before the query; the implied rule could be part of the answer. Therefore, the "closure" of this set of rules allows us to postpone one of the rules until after the query evaluation, which was not the case for the original set of rules. ∎

In this section we describe conditions under which sets of rules are transformable. In general we look for cases in which the transformation of a set of rules can be reduced to the transformation of a single rule or can be done on a rule by rule basis. In case the given set of rules is not transformable, we are interested in the construction of sets of rules that are equivalent to the given set but are "easier" to transform.

We select here some properties of sets of rules which make them easy to transform. We concentrate on the following two cases:

1. The "interaction" between rules is under control, so they can be transformed on a rule by rule basis.

2. The set of rules can be replaced by a single rule.

Limited "interaction" is assured by two properties called *modular decomposability* and *independence*. The transformation of a set of rules into a single rule is achieved by what we call the *saturating transformation*. These concepts are discussed below. First we define the notions of modular decomposability and independence. This is followed by a discussion of saturating transformation. Finally, in the appendix, we discuss how, for a given set of rules, under certain conditions, we can obtain an equivalent independent set of rules, which is easy to transform.

DEFINITION 2 (MODULAR DECOMPOSIBILITY)

We say that a set of rules R is *modularly decomposable* into $\langle R_0, R_1 \rangle$ (where the union of R_0 and R_1 is equal to R) iff

$$R^*(S) = R_0^*(R_1^*(S))$$

for any set of assertions S. ∎

Notice that the set R of rules may be modularly decomposable into $\langle R_0, R_1 \rangle$ but not into $\langle R_1, R_0 \rangle$.

DEFINITION 3 (STRONG INDEPENDENCE)

A set of rules R is *strongly independent* iff for any set of assertions S

$$R^*(S) = \bigcup_{r \in R} r(S). \quad \blacksquare$$

This notion is essentially equivalent to the notion of modular decomposition introduced in Lassez and Maher [1984].

DEFINITION 4 (INDEPENDENCE)

Independence is defined to be the same as strong independence but with respect to the closures of individual rules, i.e, with respect to r_i^*, instead of r_i for $i = 1, \ldots n$. $\blacksquare$

These definitions correspond to some kind of modularity since they express the fixpoint of a set of rules in terms of the fixpoints of subsets of this set of rules.

We say that a set of rules R is *totally* transformable by a query Q iff all individual rules in R are totally transformable.

We start our description of transformations of sets of rules from the situation when the set of rules is modularly decomposable. Later we analyze the transformation of independent sets of rules and show how, given a set of rules, to construct an independent set of rules which is equivalent to it.

In the next subsection we show two principal ways to transform rules in a database. The first method is applied to the situation when the set of rules is modularly decomposable. In the second method, the set of rules is transformed to a *single* rule. Finally, in the appendix we discuss general methods of constructing an independent set of rules which is equivalent to the given one.

Transforming Modularly Decomposable Sets of Rules

By a *totally transformable* set of rules we mean a set of rules such that each individual rule is directly transformable (i.e., it satisfies the condition that $Q(r^*(S)) = r_Q^*(Q(S))$).

We start with a transformation of a totally transformable set of rules. We assume that all these rules are concept rules, otherwise we have to first eliminate non-concept rules. A totally transformable set of rules can be transformed on a rule by rule basis in the case of queries that involve projections and selections. Indeed, such queries can be distributed over the union operator and our property follows directly. The join operator can be distributed too—in this case the "total transformability" of a set of rules is more restrictive. It requires that no rule violates the join requirement (specified in the join transformation rule). The transformation rules in this case require us to take each possible pair of rules, one "from each argument of the join," and perform a transformation according to the previously described join transformation rule.

The case of total transformability of a set of rules enables us, therefore, to reduce the problem of the transformation of a set of rules to the problem of the transformation of single rules. If the set of rules under consideration is not totally transformable, we have to do the following:

(i)   Identify a modular decomposition $\langle R_0, R_1 \rangle$ of the set R such that R_0 is totally transformable (clearly therefore we require that all rules in R_0 be concept rules).

(ii)   Evaluate all non-concept rules, and all rules which are in R_1 or are used by R_1[4] prior to the query Q and transform the rules from R_0 on a rule by rule basis.

Indeed, since the rules R_1 have to be evaluated prior to the query Q, all rules used by the rules from R_1 must also be evaluated regardless of whether they are concept or non-concept rules. Notice that in general we are interested in maximizing the subset R_0 such that $R = \langle R_0, R_1 \rangle$.

It is clear that modular decomposability of a set of rules allows the components of such decompositions to be treated as independent modules. As such, they can be transformed individually. It is also easy to see that even if a subset of rules is totally transformable but is not an independent submodule of the total set of rules, then the rule transformation is not possible.

Unfortunately, we do not have necessary and sufficient conditions for modular decomposability; we can only provide certain sufficient conditions. One such useful sufficient condition is presented here:

DEFINITION 5
Rule r_2 is *invariant* with respect to rule r_1 iff for any S

$$r_2(r_1(S)) = r_2(S) \quad \blacksquare$$

In other words rule r_2 is not "affected" by rule r_1. The condition given in Definition 5 can be checked easily using, for example, standard methods of testing the equivalence of relational expressions.

---

[4]A rule r is used by a rule s if either it defines some predicate, which occurs in the body of s, or it is used by some other rule, which defines some predicate occurring in the body of s.

We now have the following two sufficient conditions for modular decomposability:

Condition 1: Let $R = R_0 \cup R_1$. If all rules in R_1 are invariant with respect to all rules in R_0 then:

$$R^* = R_0^*(R_1^*)$$

The proof is a straightforward consequence of Definition 5. ∎

The other condition is related to a special class, called *strongly linear rules*:

A rule is called *strongly linear* if a consequent predicate occurs exactly once in the body of the rule and the rule is typed with respect to its consequent predicate. The body of a linear rule can be viewed as a conjunction of the atom generated by the consequent predicate and some formula which is a conjunction of atoms generated by foreign predicates. The latter formula is called the *writing formula* of the strongly linear rule. By an R-occurrence of a consequent predicate in a rule r, we mean the consequent atom. By an L-occurrence, we mean its occurrence (exactly one, since the rule is linear) in the body of r.

By Arg(r) we denote the set of positions of the L-occurrence of the consequent predicate that share variables with the writing formula. By Res(r) we denote the set of positions of the R-occurrence of the consequent predicate that share variables with the writing formula. Intuitively, Res(r) is the set of positions of the consequent predicate which are changed (written) by the rule r, while Arg(r) is the set of positions in the consequent predicate on which the changed positions depend.

Condition 2: Let R_1 and R_2 be two disjoint sets of strongly linear rules defining the same predicate. If for rule $r \in R_1$ and any rule $s \in R_2$ we have Arg(r) ∩ Arg(s) = ∅
then

$$R^*(S) = R_1^*(R_2^*(S)) = R_2^*(R_1^*(S))$$

for any S.
The proof is again trivial. ∎

Two sets of such linear rules are called *orthogonal*. Obviously, when we can establish the total transformability of a subset S of R, which is orthogonal to its complement in R, then we can simply transform S and evaluate all other rules (i.e., from $R \setminus S$) prior to the query. This is the case because orthogonality implies modular decomposability. We present now two examples illustrating the transformation of sets of rules.

Examples of Transformation of Sets of Rules

EXAMPLE 7
Let database predicates have the form:

Supply(x,y,z), meaning that supplier x supplies parts y to a project z

Subpart(u,v), meaning that part u is a subpart of v

Related(x,y), meaning that projects x and y are related (similar area)

Location(x,y), meaning that supplier x has location at y (he may have a number of locations)

Let our set of rules have a form:

$$r_1 = \text{Supply}(x,y,z) \wedge \text{Subpart}(u,y) \rightarrow \text{Supply}(x,u,z)$$

with the interpretation that if a supplier supplies a project with a part, he must supply this project with all subparts of this part.

$$r_2 = \text{Supply}(x,y,z) \wedge \text{Related}(w,z) \rightarrow \text{Supply}(x,y,w)$$

with the interpretation that a given supplier supplies all related projects.

Additionally we have the transitive closure rule for the Subpart relation, but do not assume that the predicate Related is transitive.

Let us assume that the predicates "Related" and "Subpart" are concept predicates. Notice first that again, as in the previous example, the rules r_1 and r_2 are orthogonal and may, therefore, be transformed independently.

Let $Q = \pi_{\text{Supplier,Part}}(\text{Supply}) \bowtie \text{Location}$

be our query. We may also consider Q to be a view,[5] that is, a mapping defining a new "derived" database. Such a definition mapping is frequently expressed by a relational algebra expression. Intensionally this query defines a view which is a table ("report") listing all suppliers, parts, and locations of these suppliers.

First, we have to compute the result of the transformation of our set of rules by a subquery $Q' = \pi_{\text{Supplier,Part}}(\text{Supply})$. We can consider rules r_1 and r_2 separately because they are orthogonal. Clearly r_2 is transformable into a trivial tautology and r_1 is transformed into:

$$Q'(x,y) \wedge \text{Subpart}(z,y) \rightarrow Q'(x,z)$$

---

[5] A view in the database literature is defined in Ullman [1982].

This rule is transformable by the join in our query Q since "it does not change" the projection over the attribute "Supplier." We now have to apply the join transformation and finally obtain the transformed set of rules:

$$r_3 = Q(x,y,z) \wedge \text{Subpart}(v,y) \rightarrow Q(x,v,z);$$

$$r_4 = Q(x,y,z) \wedge Q(u,y,w) \rightarrow Q(x,y,w)$$

Rule r_4 is our r rule for a join transformation (it is, in fact, a so-called join dependency). Notice the computational benefit stemming from the rule transformation here. The resulting query (or "view") could be stored economically by evaluating only the simplified join as described before and leaving the above two rules unevaluated. The rule r_3 could generate a huge number of tuples (because of the transitivity of the subpart predicate)—in this way these tuples do not have to be stored since they can always be generated by the corresponding rules. It is also clear that the answer to the query (view) is of the same type as exists in the database (i.e., information is stored both in terms of tuples and in terms of rules).

EXAMPLE 8
To illustrate modular decomposability we can consider Example 1 with two rules: the first with the "Group" predicate and the second with the "Prerequisite" predicate. Both rules are strongly linear and orthogonal. Therefore, for this set of rules $R = \{r_1, r_2\}$ we have that:

$$R^* = r_1{}^* r_2{}^*(S) = r_2{}^* r_1{}^*(S)$$

Clearly, as far as the first query is concerned, the rule r_2 is totally transformable, while r_1 is not. This is why the first rule has to be evaluated prior to the query, while the second one could be transformed. For the second query, from Example 1, the situation is exactly the opposite. In both cases we can transform the rules separately because of the possibility of modular decomposition. ■

An interesting situation occurs when a query is simply a selection operator (or is built from selection operators). When a rule r is not selection transformable we still may have a possibility, as the previous section indicates, to decompose the rule into two parts: r^E, which is transformable, and r^{-E}, which is not. This is the case, however, only when the rule r is *idempotent*. We would like to establish conditions under which a rule r can be decomposed in such a way when it is a member of a set of rules. A necessary condition is the idempotence of the rule. It is not, however, as was the case for transformation of a single rule, a sufficient condition. Let R' be the result of the replacement of r in the set R by $\{r^E, r^{-E}\}$. To achieve sufficiency we need the existence of a modular decomposition of R' into modular components R'_0 and R'_1 such that

r^E belongs to R'_0 and r^{-E} is in R'_1. Indeed, otherwise rules from R'_1 would have to be evaluated at least one more time after R'_0 contradicting the correctness of the transformation of R'_0.

In the next subsection we demonstrate a situation when a set of linear rules can be replaced by a *single linear rule*.

Saturating Transformation

In this section we prove a theorem stating that there exists a transformation of a set of strongly linear rules into a *single* idempotent rule. Consequently, the problem of the transformation of a set of rules can be reduced here to the problem of the transformation of a single rule. Before presenting this theorem let us define the notion of saturating transformation:

DEFINITION 6

Let $\Sigma = \{r_1,...r_k\}$ Let $\{w_1,...w_k\}$ be a set of writing formulas for $r_1,...r_k$ respectively.

By a *saturating* transformation T_Σ of Σ we mean the following one:

Add one additional predicate symbol T to the language. The rank of this symbol (the number of columns) should be equal to the cardinality of ACTIVE $= \cup \{\text{Arg}(r_j) \cup \text{Res}(r_j): r_j \in \Sigma\}$ times two. Intuitively, the predicate T will describe how the positions from ACTIVE will be changed by the rules, by showing their "new" values. That is why we need the predicate T with arity twice the cardinality of ACTIVE.

Replace Σ by

(i)   A single linear rule

$$r_T = p(x_1,...x_n) \wedge T(x_{i_1},...x_{i_p},z_{i_1},... z_{i_p}) \rightarrow p(u_1,...u_n)$$

where T is the predicate added to the language, ACTIVE $= \{i_1,...i_p\}$

and:

$$u_i = \begin{cases} z_{i_k} & \text{if } i = i_k \in \text{ACTIVE} \\ \\ x_i & \text{otherwise} \end{cases}$$

Some of the variables z_{i_k} may be equal to x_{i_k} (variables from the occurrence of the consequent predicate in the body of the rule), in case the position i_k is not changed by any rule.

(ii)   Add two sets of rules defining this additional predicate symbol T:

Initialization rules: For each writing formula w_i introduce the following rule:

$$w_i(x_{i_1}, \ldots x_{i_n}, u_{j_1}, \ldots u_{j_m}, y_{k_1}, \ldots y_{k_l}) \rightarrow T(x_1, \ldots x_k, z_1, \ldots z_k)$$

where x-variables on the left hand side denote the variables which occur both in the L-occurrence of the consequent predicate and in the writing formula, u-variables denote the variables which occur *only* in the writing formula (i.e., neither in L nor in an R-occurrence of the consequent predicate), and finally y-variables occur in the writing formula and in the R-occurrence of the consequent predicate. Moreover:

$$z_i = \begin{cases} x_i \text{ if i is not in Res}(w_i) \\ \\ y_i \text{ if } i \in \text{Res}(w_i) \end{cases}$$

where $\text{Res}(w_i)$ is the set of all positions of the consequent predicate p "changed" by the writing formula w_i. As it is easy to see, the effect of this added rule is that the predicate T leaves all positions unchanged with the exception of the ones written by w_i.

Continuation Rule:

This is the transitive closure of T, i.e

$$T(x_1, \ldots x_n, y_1, \ldots y_n) \wedge T(y_1, \ldots y_n, z_1, \ldots z_n) \rightarrow T(x_1, \ldots x_n, z_1, \ldots z_n)$$

■

Now we are ready to present our theorem.

THEOREM 1

Let Σ be a set of strongly linear p-rules (i.e., rules defining a predicate p). There exists a set of rules Σ' which is equivalent to Σ modulo p (i.e., both sets imply the same formulas about p) and such that p occurs only in one rule, which is strongly linear and idempotent.

Proof: Let Σ' be the result of the saturating transformation applied to Σ. It is easy to see that Σ' is equivalent to the original set of rules with respect to p. Indeed, any sequence of applications of the original linear rules $r_1, \ldots r_k$ can be "simulated" by the evaluation of a new single rule with the predicate T. In the same way any sequence of applications of a single new rule can be simulated by some sequence of applications of the original rules $r_1, \ldots r_k$. ■

Notice also another interesting interpretation of the above theorem: In order to compute the least fixpoint of strongly linear rules, it is sufficient to extend the relational algebra only by a transitive closure operator (to compute one of the transformed set of rules). The full power of least fixpoint queries is, therefore, much too large for strongly linear rules.

To benefit from such a transformation, a user must include T in the set of his concept predicates since otherwise a single new rule could not be transformed (rules with non-concept predicates are not transformed).

EXAMPLE 9

Assume that we have the following set of rules:

$$\text{MayTeach}(x,y) \wedge \text{Prefer}(x,y,z) \rightarrow \text{MayTeach}(x,z)$$

$$\text{MayTeach}(x,y) \wedge \text{Better}(x,y,v) \rightarrow \text{MayTeach}(v,y)$$

where the predicate Prefer(x,y,z) means that teacher x prefers course z to course y, and the predicate Better(x,y,v), where x and v are teachers and y is a course (subject), means that v knows y better than x does. The intuitive meaning of these two rules is that if a teacher is able to teach a given course he also has to be able to teach all courses that he prefers. The meaning of the second rule is that if a teacher x is able to teach a course y so must any teacher v who is a better teacher of y than x.

Suppose we have the query: Give me all teachers and the undergraduate courses[6] in which they may teach. It is easy to see that neither of these two rules is transformable with respect to this query. Indeed, this query is analogous to a pure selection query with respect to which neither of the two rules is transformable. If we apply a saturation transformation with respect to this set of rules we can transform the resulting rule.

Indeed, let us introduce the additional predicate

Betterknow(x,y,u,v) with the meaning u knows v better than x knows y.

and the rule,

$$r_T = \text{MayTeach}(x,y) \wedge \text{Betterknow}(x,y,u,v) \rightarrow \text{MayTeach}(u,v),$$

together with the rules defining the Betterknow predicate:

---

[6] Assuming we have an additional unary predicate Undergraduate(x) at our disposal.

$\text{Prefer}(x,y,z) \rightarrow \text{Betterknow}(x,y,x,z)^7$

$\text{Better}(y,z,u) \rightarrow \text{Betterknow}(y,u,z,u)$

$\text{Betterknow}(x,y,u,v) \wedge \text{Betterknow}(u,v,x',y') \rightarrow \text{Betterknow}(x,y,x',y')$

According to the above theorem, the second set of rules is equivalent to the original set of rules with respect to the predicate MayTeach. If the user u accepts the Betterknow predicate as the concept predicate, then the answer for the query would include the following rule:

$Q(x,y) \wedge \text{Betterknow}(x,y,u,v) \wedge \text{Undergraduate}(v) \rightarrow Q(u,v)$ ∎

Infinite Answers, Functions, and Predicates in the Answers for Queries

The concept of the answer to a query could be further revised to allow function symbols and even whole predicates to occur in it. For example, the term Brother(Mary) may occur in the answer to the query "Who lives with Mary?" even if we do not know the name of Mary's brother. Technically such an answer would result from aborting the unification (or semantic unification) in the query answering process. This way of representing answers could help in technically handling an *infinite* set of answers resulting from the presence of arithmetic functions (like successor) in database formulas. For example, we could represent the answer to some query by listing the set of objects and adding the rule "all successors" to the answer to a query. In this way "unsafe" queries could be given by a natural finite representation. This is the topic of ongoing research and will be reported elsewhere.

In a similar way, one can include predicates in the answer to a query. For instance, as the answer to the query "Who teaches undergraduate courses?" one may obtain the predicate "Assistant Professors." These answers may be further specified if such a request is made by the user. This "abstracted answer" is easier to obtain than in the full one. Besides, it may fully satisfy the user's needs at the moment. Techniques described in Chakravarthy et al. [1987] could be used here.

The abstracted answer may also be given to the user if the system itself finds the query too time consuming to process. Indeed, computing the answers to queries (remember we require *all* tuples which satisfy the query predicate to be included) may frequently be too hard. One way to cut the computational

---

[7]This name convention is based on a philosophical assumption that if x prefers to teach y than to teach z then x knows y better than he knows z.

cost is to approximate the answers to queries (i.e., not return all tuples satisfying the answers). However, this seems to be arbitrary. Another option is the one provided above—to give the complete answer to the query but in more "abstracted terms" possibly provided by the user as an option. In this case we may talk about complexity tailored computation which tailors the level of the details of the answer of the query to the computational resources. This is the topic of further research.

Related Work

The idea of including rules in answers first appeared in Kowalski [1979] but was not studied further. Related research includes work by Porto [1986], and by Chakravarthy et al. [1988]. In Porto [1986], the importance of different concepts of answers is stressed also. In Chakravarthy et al. [1988], integrity constraints are used to optimize the process of query answering. The methodology described there can also be viewed as a step in the direction of intelligent query processing, using intensional as well as extensional information.

Conclusions

We have proposed rule transformations as a technique for query processing that is beneficial both from the conceptual and the computational point of view. We have established the method of transformation of single rules by the relational operations of projection, join, and selection. We demonstrated that the situation becomes much more complex when we want to transform sets of rules, but in some cases we were still able to provide an algorithm to transform rules. We have defined classes of queries and rules for which rule transformation is advantageous. This includes queries built from projections and selection and limited occurrences of join.

An interesting extension of this work is to study the concepts of answers including unevaluated predicates and function symbols. An important future direction of this research is to develop the concept of a "complexity tailored" information system in which a user has a hierarchy of answers to a query at his or her disposal. The more abstracted answers would cost less than evaluating the answers, and the final choice of the type of answer can depend both on the computational resources of the system and the desires of a user.

Appendix

In the appendix, we demonstrate two interesting subcases when sets of rules can be transformed. The first subcase is based on the notion of *bounded* rules. The second subcase deals with the special case of CONST rules.

Transforming Sets of Bounded and Relatively Bounded Rules

Since the situation in which a set of rules is independent is rare, we seek different conditions to transform a set of rules. We are interested in a situation in which one can transform a set of rules into an independent set of rules.

We say that a set of rules R is *bounded* iff there exists a k such that for any database state S (i.e., the set of database assertions), $R^*(S) = R^k(S)$. We say that a set of rules R is p-bounded, where p is a predicate iff there exists a k such that for any $S = \langle S_1, \dots S_n \rangle$, $R^*(S)[p] = R^k(S)[p]$ where S[p] denotes the relation corresponding to the predicate p in the multirelation S. Such a predicate is called a *bounded predicate* and the smallest "k" with the above property is called the *limit* of the set of rules. Obviously the set of rules may, in general, be unbounded and at the same time p-bounded for some particular predicate p. The notion of boundness was first studied in Minker and Nicolas [1982].

A relation S_i is *closed* with respect to a set of rules R iff the smallest fixpoint of R containing $S = \langle S_1, \dots S_i, \dots S_n \rangle$ has the same i-th component as S (the fixpoint is a multirelation as well as a database extension). The rule r is *closed* in a database state S iff r(S) = S.

It turns out that when the set of rules is bounded (we discuss problems related to testing boundness at the end of this subsection) then it can be transformed to an equivalent independent set. More precisely, if a set of concept rules is p-bounded, where p is the predicate under consideration, we can always generate a finite set of rules which is equivalent to the original one and independent. This is so because, if the set of rules is bounded, only a finite bounded part of the Breadth First Resolution Tree (BFT) is relevant. An independent set R′ which is equivalent to R can be obtained by generating the p-closure for any predicate p. This p-closure can be generated by building a BFT with $:-p(x_1, \dots x_n)$ as the goal node. With each node of the BFT, we can associate the (answer) substitution θ generated down to this node. Let the node of the BFT have the form

$$:-P_1(t_1), \dots P_m(t_m)$$

With this node we can associate the following rule

$$P_1(t_1) \dots P_m(t_m) :-p(\theta(x_1) \dots \theta(x_n))$$

where p is the "goal" predicate.

Obviously, this rule follows by the resolution inference rule from the original set of rules. Notice that in case the node is empty (we do not expect this to happen in our case unless we allow pure assertions to occur in R), we obtain a "pure" answer substitution as the rule associated with the node.

The set of all rules associated with any node of the BFT for a goal :-p($x_1,...x_n$) is called the *p-closure* of the set of rules R. The closure of the set of rules can therefore be computed at compile time of the database by the "symbolic execution" of the set of rules (i.e., the execution of the set of rules of the database as a logic program). The closure (which simply corresponds to the logical closure of the set of rules by resolution) is of course logically equivalent to R. Moreover it is independent, as the following corollary shows:

COROLLARY 3
Let R be a p-bounded set of rules. The p-closure of R is independent. ∎

The symbolic execution of a set of rules has to be done only once at compile time of the database. The size of the resulting set of rules may still, in the worst case be exponential (with respect to the size of the set of rules). We do not see any better alternative: After all, if we do not evaluate the rules symbolically at compile time, we would have to do possibly exponential computations at run time, which is much more expensive. The additional advantage of the closure computation at compile time is the possibility of the *optimization* of the resulting, independent set of rules, in such a way that redundancy is avoided (for example, no two rules imply each other).

The above method will be useful only when the closure of a set of rules can be computed. It will be the case, for example, for sets of nonrecursive rules. Indeed, their BFT is finite, therefore, the process of closure generation always terminates in this case. The trouble is that the problem of deciding boundness is undecidable Gaifman [1986]. The hope is again in finding the special families of rules for which the boundness problem is decidable. Most of the work in this direction, summarized in Kanellakis [1988], is restricted to single recursive rules.The class of functional rules defined in Imielinski [1986] has the property that we can detect boundness of any *set* of functional rules. The transformation of such rules is considered in that paper too, and we will not elaborate on the transformation of the bounded set of rules any further.

EXAMPLE 10
Example 6 clearly illustrates the case when the original set of rules cannot be transformed, while the closure (in this case obviously finite) is independent and can be transformed on a rule by rule basis. ∎

Transforming Sets of CONST Rules

First we define the notion of a CONST rule.

CONST Rules. Let CONST be a family of unirelational rules (only one predicate occurs in the rule) that are typed with respect to their consequent predicates and such that the set of variables which occur in the body of the rule is a subset of the set of variables which occur in the consequent of the rule. We named these rules in this way because of the important role of constants. In fact, these rules can be viewed as describing properties and relationships between different constants in the database (see Example 11 below). We believe, that although in logic programming rules of this type are not very interesting, in the context of databases or expert systems they have important applications.

Any finite set of rules from CONST has, of course, finite breadth first resolution trees (BFT) which result from resolving the rules of the database against negations of each individual predicate.[8]

We deal here with sets of unrelational CONST rules. It is easy to see these sets of rules always have a finite BFT, therefore the closure computation is straightforward here.

The unrelational CONST rules have one more important feature: It turns out that if we deal only with rules from CONST, we do not have to compute the whole closure, but most frequently much less.

PROPOSITION 4

If rules are CONST, then the only rules which are π_X-transformable for any proper subset of the set of all attributes are 1-rules.

Proof: If a rule is a k-rule for $k > 1$ (i.e., a rule with k atoms in its body) then each position at each literal in the body of the rule consists of either a constant or the same variable (different variables may occur in different arguments of the predicate). Therefore, at each argument we have either a variable which is bound or a constant. According to our previous criterion such a rule is not projection transformable.

This fact has an important influence on the overall process of rule transformation in the case of the CONST rules. If any projection occurs in the query (which is most frequently the case) we may not even bother considering k-rules for $k > 1$. We may only restrict ourselves to 1-rules and their closure since according to our result no k-rule for $k > 1$ is transformed into a rule in the answer to the query. In other words we have only to symbolically evaluate the subset of 1-rules from R. This is a considerable simplification since in the case of the closure of 1-rules each rule in the closure is also a 1-rule, while in the case of an arbitrary closure the size of the rule (number of atoms) grows exponentially with respect to the number of times resolution is applied. Hence in this case much needed savings of space is achieved. Only in cases when we are dealing with the selection operation separately do we really have to compute the closure (although only in compile time).

---

[8] If we exclude trivial tautologies of the form $p(x_1, \ldots x_n) \rightarrow p(x_1, \ldots x_n)$.

As before, the general pattern of the transformation algorithm for a set of independent rules is that we apply the above projection, selection, and join on a rule by rule basis. Additionally, if the rule is not selection transformable, we can always decompose it into two parts, one of which is decomposable, and the other one which is not.

If a set of rules R is independent then the selection operation σ_E is simply performed by decomposing each rule. In this case for any rule $r \in R$ the rule r^E is an element of the answer. Moreover the resulting set of rules is independent too. In fact for a set of CONST rules we can simplify the rule transformation by describing it "at once" for the expressions built from projection (on a proper subset of the set of attributes) and selection:

$$\text{(PS-rule)} \quad \pi_X \sigma_E(r) = \begin{cases} \delta \text{ iff r is a k-rule for } k > 1 \text{ or} \\ \quad \pi_X(r) = \delta \text{ or} \\ \quad\quad\quad r^E = \delta \\ \\ \pi_X(r^E) \text{ otherwise} \end{cases}$$

We can easily generalize this transformation rule to the case when the rule is of the form:

$$E_r \wedge P(t_1) \wedge P(t_2) \ldots P(t_n) \wedge W \rightarrow P(t)$$

where E_r is the additional condition imposed on variables in the rule. For example such a rule may have the form:

$$(x \neq c_1) \wedge (y \neq b_2) \wedge P(x,y,d) \rightarrow P(x,y,e)$$

In this case $E_r = (x \neq c_1) \wedge (y \neq b_2)$. It is straightforward to generalize our projection, join and selection rules to capture this important modification.

This simplified transformation rule illustrates the point which we made before about the decisive influence of projection (only 1-closure has to be considered).

In general, there are classes of queries and classes of rules for which rule transformation will be very beneficial and classes of queries and rules for which it is better to apply traditional methods, since we are not going to gain much by rule transformation. Here is the classification together with a proper modification of the general "rule by rule" application of selection, projection and join transformation rules.

1. The class of PS-queries built only from projection (on the proper subset of the set of attributes) and selection.

This is a particularly good class of queries for which we can apply rule transformation. Indeed, in this case we only have to compute the closure of 1-rules (at compile time) by symbolic execution of the set of rules. It is a good idea to label each rule with its derivation tree (i.e., from which rules and how it was derived). In such a case we may also be able to eliminate some redundancies after rule transformation has been completed and possibly further decrease the number of rules which have to be evaluated prior to query evaluation. In general, rules that cannot be transformed will have to be evaluated prior to the evaluation of the query. In this way, elimination of redundancy could improve the overall computational benefit. In the case of CONST rules, this is relatively inexpensive since effectively we are going to deal only with 1-rules. Basically, if the given rule which is not transformable can be derived from some transformed rule, then it does not have to be evaluated at all, hence saving expensive computation.

The main procedure of rule transformation has the following form:

I.   Eliminate rules that are independent of the query, that is rules for which either $\pi_X(r) = \delta$ or $E(t_r)$ is false.

II. Apply the PS-rule to the set of rules on a rule by rule basis to compute the set of transformed rules.

III. Select the rules which have to be evaluated prior to the query (the set R_0 from the formula (**)). These are the k-rules for $k > 1$ and the r^{-E} rules. In the top down interpretation the rules computed in step (III) have to be included as part of the program computing the answer to the query. The rules computed in step (II) are included in the answer for the query.

Notice that from a practical point of view this is a very important class of queries. It corresponds for example to the query language "SQUARE" mappings (Ullman [1982]).

2.   The class of PSJ expressions built from the joins of PS-expressions.

This is a similar case when the closure of 1-rules is sufficient. We apply the same procedure as in (1) followed by the application of the join transformation rules (see the following example).

3.   The class of S-queries built purely from selection conditions. These queries require, in principle, computation of the full closure of the set of rules at compile time of the database. Then rule decomposition could be

applied on a rule by rule basis. The same applies to combinations of S queries with join.

This is effective only if the closure of a set of rules is not very large, which happens when the limit of a set (i.e., k such that $R^*(S) = R^k(S)$)is small. The limit of a set of rules measures, in fact, "how close" the set of rules R is to the independent set.

The queries of the first two groups are more frequent, however, since selection is usually followed by projection. ∎

In general, rule transformation can be applied when the set of rules is "loosely" connected, that is when the closure of the set of rules is not too large or in cases when we do not have to compute the full closure as for PS-queries. We claim that rule transformation should be applied every time it is possible to do so because of the obvious benefits. Furthermore, we note that we have only discussed conditions needed to obtain the complete set of rules in the answer to the query. If we relax the requirement of completeness, we can always apply our transformation (projection, selection, and join) rules directly to the set of rules to obtain only some rules in the answer. This may still be beneficial and does not require dealing with the closure.

EXAMPLE 11

Let our database scheme consist of two relation schemes:

TAKEN [Student,Program,Major,Minor,Course#]

and

DESCRIPTION [Course#,Credits,Field]

The relation TAKEN describes the courses taken by a given student during his stay at a university. Only those students who graduated from the university are stored in this relation, which provides a record of the curriculum of the student. The relation, DESCRIPTION, describes the number of credits for a given course. Notice that the relation TAKEN is not normalized—it may be interpreted as a view defined over two relations: one describing students (and their attributes) and the other describing the relationship between students and courses.

The domain of the attribute "Program" has two elements: "honors" and "regular," depending on whether the student was in the honor program or in the regular program. The attributes "Minor" and "Major" describe the corresponding minor and major fields (one each) for a given student. The relation DESCRIPTION is defined over three attributes, the last one, "Field," describes the field of a given course and has the same domain as the attributes "Major" and "Minor."

The following rules define instances of the database:

1. r_1 = "All students who major in economics and take the course #211 must take also course #241."

2. r_2 = "All students who minor in computer science and take the course #111 must take also course #211."

3. r_3 = "All honor students majoring in a given field must take all 400 level courses in that field."

The first two rules represent the prerequisite information. They can be represented by the following formulas:

4. $\forall_{s,y,z}$ TAKEN(s,y,Economics,z,211) $\rightarrow$ TAKEN(s,y,Economics,z, 241)

5. $\forall_{s,m,p}$ TAKEN(s,p,m,Computer Science,111) $\rightarrow$ TAKEN(s,p,m, computer science,211)

Consider another set of rules about the predicate "Description."

6. "All 400 level courses have 4 credits."

7. "All 300 level courses have 3 credits."

Consider the following query:

Q_1 = "Give me all the students, s, and courses, c, such that s is taking either #211 or #241" and that a student "s" is taking this course.

We could simply return the rule r_1 as part of the answer for the query. This is an illustration of the first case of our definition, when the rule can be *totally* transformed.

Consider a similar query which, however, requires additional work.

Q_2 = "Give me the set of all students who took either courses #111 or #241."

The answer for this query also contains a rule. However, this rule is no longer one of the rules r_1 or r_2. It is the consequence of these two rules by means of modus ponens. Namely, the rule which is part of the answer has the following form:

r_{12} = "All the minors in computer science who are majors in economics and who took #111 had taken also #241."

Again, instead of evaluating both r_1 and r_2 before the selection condition, we may only evaluate r_2 and "postpone" the evaluation of rule r_{12} or just include it in the answer without evaluating it. In the former case, rule r_{12} becomes a passive integrity constraint similar to those "derived constraints" holding in the view, in the latter case when the rule r_{12} remains unevaluated, it remains as an active, or an inference, rule.

Another query for which we could include rules as part of the answer is the following:

Q_3 = "Give me the set of all tuples of the relation TAKEN describing the students who took 400 level courses."

In this case a modified form of r_3 is part of the answer. That is,

"Honor students took all the courses"

since we are referring only to 400 level courses.

It is even more natural to keep the rules of the second scheme active. Indeed it definitely does not pay to physically store all the courses and the credits associated with them separately since we can always use the rules to derive the necessary data. It benefits also for the queries to manipulate over the unevaluated rules. For example, if we ask about the courses that have 3 credits, we could immediately include in the answer the statement "All 300 level courses" which can be evaluated later to the list of courses if the user wants to (Kowalski [1979] for similar argument). It could also be left as a meaningful part of the answer. ∎

EXAMPLE 12
Consider the following set R_S of rules defined over the relation p(ABC):

$$r_1 = p(x_A,b_1,x_C) \rightarrow p(x_A,b_2,x_C)$$
$$r_2 = p(x_A,x_B,c_1) \rightarrow p(x_A,x_B,c_2)$$
$$r_3 = (x_C \neq c_2) \wedge p(a_1,x_B,x_C) \wedge p(a_2, x_B,x_C) \rightarrow p(a_3,x_B,x_C)$$

where $b_1,b_2,c_1,c_2,a_1.a_2,a_3$ are constants and x_A,x_B and x_C are variables.

By symbolic execution of this set of rules (not demonstrated here) we can obtain the following closure of 1-rules and full closure of this set of rules:

The closure of 1-rules of R_S has the form:
$R_S \cup \{r_4\}$ where

$$r_4 = p(x_A,b_1,c_1) \rightarrow p(x_A,b_2,c_2)$$

the full closure of R_S additionally contains the following three rules:

$$(x_C \ne c_2) \wedge p(a_1,b_1,x_C) \wedge p(a_2,b_1,x_C) \rightarrow p(a_3,b_2,x_C)$$
$$(x_C \ne c_2) \wedge p(a_1,b_2,x_C) \wedge p(a_2,b_1,x_C) \rightarrow p(a_3,b_2,x_C)$$
$$(x_C \ne c_2) \wedge p(a_1,b_1,x_C) \wedge p(a_2,b_2,x_C) \rightarrow p(a_3,b_2,x_C)$$

Let us start from the S-queries. Given a selection query σ_E we can decompose each rule of the closure according to E-decomposition. Two extremal situations occur when $r^{-E} = \delta$ for all rules r and $r^E = \delta$ respectively. In the first case, all the rules can be transformed directly by selection and no rule has to be evaluated prior to selection. In the second case, no rule can be transformed. The first situation is equivalent to the total transformability of all the rules, i.e., it occurs when, for any rule r, we have $E(t_r) \leftrightarrow \wedge_{t \in T_r} E(t)$. This is the case, for example, for any selection condition that is implied by $E' = (A$ IN $X_A) \wedge ($ B IN $X_B) \wedge (C$ in $X_C)$ where X_A, X_B and X_C are subsets of the proper domains, $b_1, b_2 \in X_B$, $a_1, a_2, a_3 \in X_A$ and $c_1, c_2 \in X_C$. Indeed, as it is easy to verify, for each rule r, $r^{-E} = \delta$. Therefore in this case all rules are part of the answer for the selection query, which can be evaluated directly on the extension of the database (no rules have to be evaluated).

This situation is certainly optimal. Let us now consider a less optimal situation, for example when:

$$E = (B = b_1) \wedge (C = c_1) \vee (B = b_2) \wedge (C \ne c_1)$$

Here we have:

$$r_1^E = \delta$$

—since it is not possible to have both $E(t_1)$ and $E(t_r)$ true for this particular rule and this particular selection condition (t is the antecedent of the rule and t_r is the consequent of the rule)

$$r_1^{-E} = (x_C \ne c_1) \wedge p(x_A,b_1,x_C) \rightarrow p(a_A,b_2,x_C)$$

For r_2 we have in a similar way:

$$r_2^E = \delta \text{ for the same reasons as before}$$

and

$$r_2^{-E} = (x_B = b_2) \wedge p(x_A,x_B,c_1) \rightarrow p(x_A,x_B,c_2)$$

Finally for r_4 we have that

$$r_4{}^E = r_4 \text{ and } r_4{}^{-E} = \delta$$

Therefore, the rule r_4 may become the element of the answer for the query while the rules $r_1{}^{-E}$ and $r_2{}^{-E}$ will have to be evaluated prior to the query itself. The other rules of the closure of R_S can be transformed in a similar way. Notice the importance of the computation of the closure (the rule r_4 is not in the original set of rules)

PS-queries (queries built from selection and projection):

If we are dealing with a query involving projection we may restrict ourselves only to 1-rules from the closure. For example, $\pi_{BC}(\sigma_E(R))$ can be computed by totally disregarding 2-rules and applying the global transformation rules for PS-expressions and CONST rules for the above set of rules. Thus, if E is the selection condition considered above, which allows the total transformability of the rules then the projected rules have the form:

(1) $p(b_1,x_C) \rightarrow p(b_2,x_C)$

(2) $p(x_B,c_1) \rightarrow p(x_B,c_2)$

and

(3) $p(b_1,c_1) \rightarrow p(b_2,c_2)$

which is the modus ponens consequence of the first two rules. On the other hand for the selection condition E, considered above, only (3) will be transformed:

$$p(b,c_1) \rightarrow p(b_2,c_2)$$

Finally, consider queries built from join. Assume now that the relation R has 4 attributes ABCD. All rules are changed by adding one more position "D" to the predicate p and putting the variable x_D into this position. Suppose then that we have a second relation scheme T[DEF] with the following rules:

$$R_T = \{ \ T(x_D,e_1,x_F) \rightarrow T(x_D,e_2,x_F)$$
$$T(d_1,x_E,x_F) \rightarrow T(d_2,x_E,x_F)\}$$

Let the query have the form

$$\pi_{BCD}(\sigma_{A \neq a_3}(R) \bowtie \pi_{DE}(T))$$

From the join rules we immediately obtain that the second rule in R_T is not π_{DE}-transformable (it changes the projection on D). If we apply the CONST transformation rules we obtain that the only transformable rules are r_1, r_2, and r_3. Moreover the rule r_3 does not have to be evaluated, since $E(t_{r_3})$ is false.

Finally then, the rules which appear in the result of the left subexpression $Q' = \pi_{BCD}(\sigma_{1 \neq a_3}(R)))$ are:

$$Q'(b_1,x_C,x_D) \rightarrow Q'(b,x_C,x_D)$$
$$Q'(x_B,c_1,x_D) \rightarrow Q'(x_B,c_2,x_D)$$

The only rule which is join-transformable in the right argument of the join is the first rule in R_T. The second rule has to be evaluated prior to the join. Both rules about Q' are, however, join-transformable.

According to the join transformation rules we finally obtain the set of the following rules in the answer to this query:

$$Q(b_1,x_C,x_D,x_E) \rightarrow Q(b_2,x_C,x_D,x_E)$$
$$Q(x_B,c_1,x_D,x_E) \rightarrow Q(x_B,c_2,x_D,x_E)$$
$$Q(x_B,x_C,x_D,e_1) \rightarrow Q(x_B,x_C,x_D,e_2)$$

and the rule corresponding to the join operation:

$$Q(x_B,x_C,x_D,u) \wedge Q(y,z,x_D,x_E) \rightarrow Q(x_B,x_C,x_D,x_E).$$

In the top down interpretation this would mean that the program computing the answer for this query would only have to consist of the second rule in the set R_T; all other rules could just be included in the answer to the query. They could eventually be evaluated together with the set of answers obtained from the program computing the query. They could also be left in an unevaluated form as a part of data. ∎

Acknowledgment

The comments of anonymous referees are gratefully acknowledged.[9]

---

[9]Research for this paper was supported by NSF grant DCR 85-04140, on leave from Polish Academy of Science.

References

1. Chakravarthy, U. S., Grant, J., and Minker, J. [1988] Foundations of Semantic Query Optimization for Deductive Databases, in *Foundations of Deductive Database and Logic Programming* (J. Minker, Ed.), Morgan Kaufmann Publishers, Los Altos, CA, 243–273.

2. Gaifman, H. [1986] Abstract of Lecture Presented at Stanford University.

3. Gallaire, H., Minker, J., and Nicholas, J.-M. [1984] Logic and Databases—A Deductive Approach, *ACM Computing Surveys* **16**(2):153–198.

4. Hull, R. [1984] Finitely Specifiable Implicational Dependency Families, *JACM* **31**(2):210–227.

5. Imielinski, T. [1986] Functional Rules, University of Rutgers Report.

6. Kanellakis, P. [1988] Logic Programming and Parallel Complexity, in *Foundations of Deductive Databases and Logic Programming* (J. Minker, Ed.), Morgan Kaufmann Publishers, Los Altos, CA, 547–585.

7. Klug, A. and Price, R. [1982] Determining View Dependencies Using Tableaux, *ACM Transactions on Database Systems* **7**(3):361–381.

8. Kowalski, R. [1979] *Logic for Problem Solving*, Elsevier, North-Holland, New York.

9. Lassez, J. and Maher, M. [1984] Closure and Fairness in the Semantics of Programming Logic, *Theoretical Computer Science* **29**, 167–184.

10. Minker, J. and Nicolas, J.-M. [1982] On Recursive Axioms in Relational Databases, *Information Systems* **8**, 1–13.

11. Porto, A. [1986] Semantic Unification for KnowledgeBase Deduction, in *Proceedings of the Workshop on Deductive Databases and Logic Programming* (J. Minker, Ed.), Washington, DC, 102–118.

12. Ullman, J. D. [1982] *Principles of Database Systems*, Computer Science Press, Rockville, MD.

A Theorem-Proving Approach to
Database Integrity

Fariba Sadri
Robert Kowalski
Department of Computing
Imperial College of Science and Technology
London, England

Abstract

We propose an extension of the SLDNF proof procedure for checking integrity constraints in deductive databases. To achieve the effect of the simplification methods investigated by Nicolas [1982], Lloyd, Sonenberg, and Topor [1986], and Decker [1986], we use clauses corresponding to the updates as top clauses for the search space. This builds in the assumption that the database satisfied its integrity constraints prior to the transaction, and that, therefore, any violation of the constraints in the updated database must involve at least one of the updates in the transaction. Different simplification methods can be simulated by different strategies for literal selection and search.

The SLDNF proof procedure needs to be extended

to use as top clause any arbitrary deductive rule, denial, or negated fact,

to incorporate inference rules for reasoning about implicit deletions resulting from other deletions and additions, and

to allow an extended resolution step for reasoning forward from negated facts.

The choice of SLDNF facilitates the comparison of our Consistency Method for integrity checking with other simplification methods. However, SLDNF contains a number of inefficiencies. These can be avoided by incorporating the required features, such as negation as failure, and the ability to reason about implicit deletions in other, more efficient proof procedures.

Introduction

Informally speaking, integrity constraints are conditions that a database is required to satisfy as it changes through time. If an update violates these constraints, then typically the update is rejected or modified. Alternatively, in theory, the database itself, or even the constraints, could also be modified to restore integrity.

The following are some examples of integrity constraints:

(Throughout the paper, variables and function symbols are represented by letters in the lower case; predicate symbols, except for "$=$" and "$\leq$", and constant symbols start in the upper case.)

EXAMPLE 1
One of the most common kinds of constraint expresses a functional dependency. For example, "An employee can have only one salary," i.e.,

$\forall x \ \forall y \ \forall z \ [y = z \leftarrow$ Employee(x) and

Salary(x y) and

Salary(x z)] ∎

EXAMPLE 2
"No student can receive both an SERC grant and a British Council award."

$\forall x \ [\leftarrow$ Student(x) and

Receives(x SERC-grant) and

Receives(x Brit-Council-award)] ∎

EXAMPLE 3
"All students must have a lecturer as tutor."

$\forall x \ \exists y \ [($Lecturer(y) and Tutor(y x)$) - $Student(x)] ∎

EXAMPLE 4
"Lecturers without Ph.D.'s do not qualify for tenure."

$\forall$ x [$\leftarrow$ Lecturer(x) and

NOT Has-degree(x Ph.D.) and

Qualify-for-tenure(x)] ∎

This paper addresses the problem of determining if a deductive database (which may contain both facts and general rules) satisfies its integrity constraints, or more precisely, if a deductive database that satisfies its integrity constraints prior to a transaction continues to satisfy them afterwards.

We propose a way of exploiting the assumption that the database satisfies the constraints prior to the transaction, to avoid redundantly rechecking instances of the constraints that are satisfied in the database before and which are not affected by the transaction. This is the basis of all simplification methods for integrity checking in databases, including Nicolas's method for relational databases (Nicolas [1982]), Decker's (Decker [1986]), and Lloyd, Topor et al.'s (Topor, Keddis, and Wright [1985] and Lloyd, Sonenberg, and Topor [1986]) for deductive ones.

Lloyd and Topor [1985] first described a simplification algorithm for checking integrity constraints in databases consisting of *definite clauses*, that is clauses of the form

$A \leftarrow B_1$ and ... and B_n, $n \geq 0$,

where A and the B_i are atoms. They and their collaborators (Topor, Keddis, and Wright [1985], and Lloyd, Sonenberg, and Topor [1986]) then extended the algorithm to deal with deductive databases where database rules may have negative conditions as well as positive ones. For simplicity, from now on in this paper we call this more general algorithm the LT algorithm.

The main difference between our approach and the others is that we have tried to remain as much as possible within a general theorem-proving framework. In our method, we use an extension of SLDNF (Lloyd [1984]) and reason forward from the updates as top clauses. This allows us to take advantage of the assumption that the database satisfies the constraints prior to the transaction. We need to extend the SLDNF proof procedure to use as top clause any clause that might contribute to a proof of inconsistency, and to derive implicit deletions caused by other deletions and additions. This extended proof procedure has been implemented in Prolog by Soper [1986].

In the next section we explain more precisely what we mean by deductive databases, integrity constraints, and constraint satisfaction. The section, "The Proof Procedure," describes a simplified version of the proof procedure. The application of the proof procedure to integrity checking is exemplified in "The Consistency Method for Checking Integrity Constraints in Deductive Databases." The sections "Formalizing the Inference Rules for Implicit Deletions: The First Approach" and "Formalizing the Inference Rules for Implicit

Deletions: The Second Approach'' describe two different ways of formalizing the inference rules needed for reasoning about implicit deletions. In the section ''Comparison with Simplification Methods for Integrity Checking'' we compare our method with the Decker and LT algorithms for checking integrity of deductive databases. Finally, in the last section, we discuss the correctness and completeness of our method.

Definitions

Deductive Databases

A deductive database is a finite set of deductive rules, which are closed formulae of the form

$$A \leftarrow L_1 \text{ and} \dots \text{and } L_n, \quad n \geq 0,$$

where A is an atom, the L_i are literals (i.e.,atoms or negated atoms), and all the variables are assumed to be universally quantified in front of the formula in which they occur. A is called the *conclusion* of the rule and the L_i the *conditions*. If a condition is an atom, then it is a *positive condition* of the deductive rule. If a condition is a negated atom, then it is a *negative condition*. When $n = 0$, the deductive rule is also called a *fact*.

It is possible to transform more general formulae of the form $A \leftarrow W$ into a set of deductive rules. Here, A is an atom, W is an arbitrary first order formula, and all the variables in A and all the free variables in W are assumed to be universally quantified in front of the formula. Such transformations are described by Lloyd and Topor [1984].

For our integrity checking method, we assume that the database before and after any updates is *range-restricted*, that is, any variable that occurs in a deductive rule has an occurrence in a positive condition of the rule. This restriction corresponds exactly to Decker's ''range-restriction'' (Decker [1987]), and to the ''allowed'' condition of Lloyd and Topor [1986] and Topor and Sonenberg [1988]. This ensures that all negative conditions can be fully instantiated before they are evaluated by the negation as failure rule.

Integrity Constraints

Our integrity checking method deals directly with constraints of the form

$$\leftarrow L_1 \text{ and} \dots \text{and } L_n, \quad n > 0,$$

where the L_i are literals and all variables are assumed to be universally quantified in front of the constraint in which they occur. We call formulae of this kind *denials*, or sometimes *goals*. If a literal in a denial is an atom, then it is a *positive condition* of the denial; if a literal is a negated atom then, it is a *negative condition*.

Denials must also be range-restricted, that is, any variable that occurs in a negative condition of a constraint must also have an occurrence in a positive condition of the constraint.

It is also possible to deal with constraints that are in a more general form than denials. Given an arbitrary closed first-order formula W as a constraint, we can replace it by a new constraint "$\leftarrow A$" and add a rule

$$A \leftarrow NOT\ W$$

to the database, where A is a nullary predicate symbol that does not occur elsewhere in the database or the constraints. The rule "$A \leftarrow NOT\ W$" can then be transformed to a set of deductive rules as described by Lloyd and Topor [1984]. Because the resulting deductive rules must be range restricted, a corresponding range-restriction on the form of the integrity constraint W is imposed.

If W is in clausal form, that is in the form

$$B_1\ or \ldots or\ B_m \leftarrow A_1\ and \ldots and\ A_n, \quad n \geq 0, \quad m \geq 0,$$

where the A_i and the B_i are atoms, then W can simply be rewritten directly as the denial

$$\leftarrow A_1\ and \ldots and\ A_n\ and\ NOT\ B_1\ and \ldots and\ NOT\ B_m.$$

Throughout this paper we restrict our attention to sets of integrity constraints that are mutually consistent. Thus we do not allow, for example, both

$$A \leftarrow \quad and \quad \leftarrow A$$

to belong to the same set of integrity constraints.

Constraint Satisfaction

The most common definition of constraint satisfaction is that a database D satisfies its constraints I, where I is a set of closed formulae, if and only if every formula in I is a logical consequence of the completion of D. We call this the *theoremhood* view of constraint satisfaction.

The *completion* of a database D, denoted Comp(D), consists essentially of D together with the only-if version of the rules in D and an appropriate equality theory. For a more precise definition of completion, see Clark [1978] or Lloyd [1984]. We assume that the completion of a database contains a denial of the form $\leftarrow P(x_1 \ldots x_n)$ for every n-ary predicate P in the underlying language which is not defined in the database (i.e., does not occur in the conclusion of a deductive rule). In practice, for convenience, only the database is represented explicitly and reasoning with its completion is implemented through the negation as finite failure rule (Clark [1978]).

Our method appeals to an alternative definition of constraint satisfaction. According to this definition, a database D satisfies integrity constraints I if and only if the completion of D is consistent with I. We call this the *consistency* view of constraint satisfaction. Our method also uses negation as failure to implement reasoning with the completion of the database. In the sequel, the connective "NOT" denotes negation by failure.

The two definitions of constraint satisfaction are equivalent if for any closed formula W in the language of the database and the constraints, either W or its negation is a logical consequence of the completion of the database. The completion of such a database is said to be *complete*. The two definitions can give different results when the database includes recursive definitions.

Notice that if the completion of the database is consistent, then any theorem of the completion is consistent with the completion. Thus, if such a database satisfies its constraints according to the theoremhood view, then it also satisfies them according to the consistency view. We discuss the relationship between the two definitions further in "The Consistency Method for Checking Integrity Constraints in Deductive Databases," Theorem 2.

The Proof Procedure

The proof procedure that we propose is a linear resolution procedure which is an extension of SLDNF. Our method uses this proof procedure for reasoning forward from updates. In this section, we first describe the SLDNF proof procedure and then define our proof procedure for a restricted case which does not require reasoning about implicit deletions. Later, in the sections " Formalizing the Inference Rules for Implicit Deletions: The First Approach" and "Formalizing the Inference Rules for Implicit Deletions: The Second Approach," we extend the proof procedure to deal with implicit deletions as well.

The reader may wish to skip the more formal parts of this section on a first reading, and look first at Examples 5 through 10.

The SLDNF Proof Procedure

A *computation rule* is a rule that selects a literal from any denial. A computation rule is *safe* if and only if it does not select negative conditions unless they are ground, i.e., contain no variables.

Let S be a set of deductive rules, G a denial, and R a safe computation rule. An *SLDNF-derivation* of $S \cup \{G\}$, where "$\cup$" denotes the set union operation, via R is a sequence (possibly infinite), G_0, G_1, G_2,... such that $G_0 = G$, and for all i, $i \geq 0$, G_{i+1} is obtained from G_i by one of (1) or (2) as follows:

1. Let G_i be "$\leftarrow L_1$ and...and L_n," and suppose R selects a positive condition L_k from G_i. Then G_{i+1} is the resolvent on L_k of G_i and some input clause in S.

    Here, by "resolvent" we mean the obvious generalization of the standard notion of resolvent: Let C be a deductive rule

    $$A \leftarrow L'_1 \text{ and...and } L'_m$$

    in input set S such that A and L_k unify with most general unifier (mgu) θ.

    Then by "resolvent" of G_i and C on L_k we mean the formula

    $$\leftarrow (L_1 \text{ and...and } L_{k-1} \text{ and } L_{k+1} \text{ and...and } L_n$$
    $$\text{and } L'_1 \text{ and...and } L'_m)\theta.$$

2. Let G_i be "$\leftarrow L_1$ and...and L_n," and suppose R selects from G_i a literal L_k, which is a negated atom "NOT A." Then G_{i+1} is G_i with L_k removed if the goal "$\leftarrow$ NOT A" succeeds. "$\leftarrow$ NOT A" *succeeds* if the goal "$\leftarrow$A" fails finitely, i.e., if for some safe computation rule R' the SLDNF-search space for $S \cup \{\leftarrow A\}$ fails finitely.

An *SLDNF-refutation* of $S \cup \{G\}$ via R is an SLDNF-derivation of $S \cup \{G\}$ via R which ends at the empty clause.

A goal G *succeeds* from input set S if and only if there is an SLDNF-refutation of $S \cup \{G\}$. If a goal "$\leftarrow$W" succeeds from input set S, then "$\exists x_1,...,\exists x_n W$" is a logical consequence of Comp(S), where $x_1,...x_n$ are all the free variables occurring in W.

A *finitely failed SLDNF-derivation* is an SLDNF-derivation G_0, G_1,...,G_n, $n \geq 0$, such that the selected literal of G_n is either a negative condition "NOT A" and "$\leftarrow$A" succeeds, or the selected literal is a positive condition and G_n has no resolvent on this literal with any of the deductive rules in the input set.

An *SLDNF-search space* for $S \cup \{G_0\}$ via R is the set of all SLDNF-derivations for $S \cup \{G_0\}$ via R such that

1. any finite derivation in the set is either a refutation or a finitely failed derivation, and

2.   for any two derivations of the form

$$G_0, G_1, ..., G_k, G_{k+1}, ...$$
$$G_0, G_1, ..., G_k, G'_{k+1}, ...$$

the same literal is selected from G_k.

Here, the second condition means that we only consider computation rules that are functions from derivations to literals, such that for a derivation G_0, $G_1, ..., G_n$ the computation rule selects a literal from G_n. Note that computation rules are not functions from a set of goals to a set of literals. Such a rule is more restrictive because it forces the selection of the same literal from two identical goals occurring on different derivations in the search space.

A *finitely failed SLDNF-search space* is a search space that consists entirely of finitely failed derivations.

The SLDNF proof procedure has been proved correct (sound) for any set of deductive rules and goals (Clark [1978]) and complete for certain restricted cases (Clark [1978], Jaffar, Lassez, and Lloyd [1983]).

Our Proof Procedure

As mentioned earlier, to exploit the assumption that the database satisfies its integrity constraints prior to the transaction, our integrity checking method reasons forward from the updates. We introduce the integrity checking method through a series of examples later in "The Consistency Method for Checking Integrity Constraints in Deductive Databases". Here, however, to motivate the proof procedure that we have developed for the integrity checking, we describe the type of formulae that we need to consider as top clauses.

If an update is an addition of a deductive rule R, then we select R as top clause as it stands. If an update is a deletion of a fact A, which is not implicit (i.e., derivable) in the updated database, then we use the negated fact "NOT A" as top clause, and thus in effect reason forward from the fact that A is not provable in the updated database. The processing of updates that are deletions of facts will be described in more detail in the sections "The Consistency Method for Checking Integrity Constraints in Deductive Databases" and "Formalizing the Inference Rules for Implicit Deletions: The First Approach". Note that "NOT A" is a metalevel notion, which is not logically equivalent to the object level denial "←A." "NOT A" holds if and only if SLDNF (or equivalently our proof procedure) fails finitely to prove A. By Clark's correctness result for SLDNF (Clark [1978]), "NOT A" implies that "←A" follows from Comp(D), but not vice versa.

If an update is a deletion of a deductive rule which is not a fact, then we determine what instances of the conclusion of this rule are deleted as a result of the deletion of the rule and select as top clauses the negation of these deleted instances.

In addition to deductive rules and negated atoms, we also allow denials as top clauses in our proof procedure. This allows us to deal with insertions of new integrity constraints and also to evaluate queries. As will become clear, our proof procedure is equivalent to SLDNF when a denial is used as top clause.

In the sequel, we use the term ''clause'' loosely to refer to any deductive rule, denial, or negated fact.

A computation rule (also called a literal selection rule) in our proof procedure is a rule that selects a literal from any clause. Safe computation rules are as defined for SLDNF.

Let input set S be a set of deductive rules and denials. Let C_0 be a clause in S or a negated fact. If C_0 is a negated fact ''NOT A'' then ''$\leftarrow$A '' must fail finitely from S using SLDNF. Let R be a safe computation rule. A *derivation* via R with top clause C_0 is a sequence (possibly infinite) $C_0, C_1, \ldots$ such that the C_i, for $i > 0$, are deductive rules or denials, and for all i, $i \geq 0$, C_{i+1} is obtained from C_i as follows:

1. Suppose R selects from C_i a literal L which is not a negative condition of C_i. Then C_{i+1} is the resolvent on L of C_i and some input clause in S. We allow the ''extended'' resolution of clauses ''NOT A'' and ''B $\leftarrow$ NOT A' and C,'' on the underlined literals if the atoms A and A' unify. θ is the mgu of ''NOT A'' and ''NOT A''' if and only if it is the mgu of A and A'. The resolvent is then $(B \leftarrow C)\theta$. We need this extended resolution step to reason forward from deletions, as will become clear shortly.

2. Suppose R selects from C_i a negative condition ''NOT A.'' Then C_{i+1} is C_i with the selected literal ''NOT A'' removed if the goal ''$\leftarrow$NOT A'' succeeds. ''$\leftarrow$NOT A'' *succeeds* if the goal ''$\leftarrow$A'' fails finitely, i.e., if for some safe computation rule R' the search space with top clause ''$\leftarrow$A'' fails finitely. Either SLDNF or our proof procedure can be used for this subsidiary computation. The two are identical whenever the top clause is a denial. (In such a case, all clauses C_i in the derivation are also denials.)

NOTES

1. Steps (1) and (2) above are extensions of steps (1) and (2) respectively in the description of SLDNF-derivation.

2. A selected condition ''NOT A'' can only be eliminated through the negation as failure rule. A selected conclusion ''NOT A,'' however, can only be eliminated through (extended) resolution with an input clause. In this simplified version of the proof procedure, only the top clause can have such a conclusion. Therefore, an extended resolution step can only be applied to obtain the second clause in a derivation from the top clause.

Similarly to the definition of SLDNF, a *refutation* in our proof procedure is a derivation that ends at the empty clause, and a goal G *succeeds* if and only if there is a refutation with G as top clause.

A *finitely failed derivation* is a derivation C_0, C_1,... ,C_n, $n \geq 0$, such that C_n is not the empty clause, and it is not possible to construct a derivation C_0, C_1,..., C_n, C_{n+1}.

A *search space* for S via R with top clause C_0 is the set of all derivations via R with C_0 as top clause satisfying the same conditions (1) and (2) as in the definition of SLDNF-search space. Note that a search space via R with top clause C_0 contains all refutations via R with C_0 as top clause.

A *finitely failed search space* is a search space that consists entirely of finitely failed derivations.

THEOREM 1

(Correctness of the proof procedure as described above.)

Let input set S be the union of a set D of deductive rules, and a set I of denials.

If there is a refutation with input set S and top clause C_0, then Comp(D) $\cup$ I is logically inconsistent.

Proof: The theorem follows from the more general fact that if $C_0,C_1,..., C_n$ is a derivation, then C_n is a logical consequence of Comp(D) $\cup$ I. (Note that strictly speaking, whenever we refer to logical consequences of Comp(D) $\cup$ I we need to reinterpret all negations as classical negations.) This can be shown by induction on n:

1. C_0 is a logical consequence of Comp(D) $\cup$ I by definition of top clause.

2. Suppose C_{n-1} is a logical consequence of Comp(D) $\cup$ I. Then so is C_n, because each of the possible steps for deriving C_n from C_{n-1} is logically correct: Standard resolution is correct; extended resolution is an obviously correct extension of resolution; and negation by failure in SLDNF is correct. ∎

COROLLARY 1

If a goal "←W" succeeds by means of our proof procedure with input set S, then "$\exists x_1 ... \exists x_n$ W" is a logical consequence of Comp(D), where $x_1,...,x_n$ are all the free variables occurring in W.

Proof: Since "←W" is in I, by Theorem 1 Comp(D) $\cup$ I is inconsistent. Moreover, only one occurrence of a denial can participate in any refutation. Therefore, "←W" is inconsistent with Comp(D) and the corollary follows. ∎

EXAMPLE 5

Suppose the input set consists of the following:

D:

    1.   R(x y) ← Q(y) and P(x)

    2.   Q(x) ← M(x) and NOT N(x)

    3.   T(x) ← Q(x)

    4.   M(x) ← K(x)

    5.   M(B)

    6.   M(C)

    7.   P(A)

    8.   S(A B)

I:

    9.   ← S(A B) and R(A B)

    10.   ← T(x) and NOT P(x) ∎

The first diagram is a representation of a refutation with the atom "M(B)" as top clause. "[ ]" denotes the empty clause. When more than one literal is candidate for selection, the selected literal is underlined.

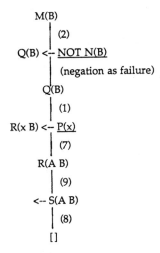

Figure 1: A Refutation for Example 5 with a Fact as Top Clause

Figure 2 represents an alternative search space for the same input set with the negated fact "NOT P(C)" as top clause:

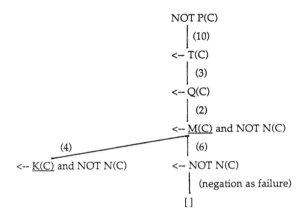

Figure 2: A Search Space for Example 5 with a Negated Fact as Top Clause

Both diagrams show that Comp(D) ∪ I is inconsistent. The second one shows that the finite failure of fact P(C) contributes to an inconsistency.

In the next section, we introduce our integrity checking method through a series of examples. The description of the method in the general case is presented in "Formalizing the Inference Rules for Implicit Deletions: The Second Approach."

The Consistency Method for Checking Integrity Constraints in Deductive Databases

In general every update in a transaction needs to be considered as a candidate top clause for the attempted refutation. The input set consists of the integrity constraints and the updated database.

In this paper, we concentrate on updates that modify only the database and not the integrity constraints. In the section "Updates that Are Additions or Deletions of Integrity Constraints", however, we discuss briefly how our method can also be used to deal with additions and deletions of integrity constraints.

In the sequel we use D_0 and D to name the database before and after the transaction, respectively, T to name the transaction and I to name the set of integrity constraints on D_0 and D.

Updates that Are Additions

EXAMPLE 6

In this example the transaction consists of a single insertion and the database is relational, that is, it consists only of facts that contain no variables. "Rank(x y)" expresses that x has rank y, and "Proj(x y)" expresses that x works on project y.

D_0:

1. Rank(John Lect)

2. Rank(Tom Prof)

3. Rank(Peter RA)

4. Proj(John LAW)

5. Proj(Tom LOGICALC)

6. Proj(Peter PARLOG)

7. Proj(Jo LOGICALC)

8. Proj(Mary LOGICALC)

I:

(IC)   ←Rank(x RA) and Proj(x LOGICALC)

The constraint states that no RA (research assistant) works on project LOGICALC.

T:

Insert Rank(Jo RA). ∎

Let us assume (correctly) that D_0 satisfies its constraint. To determine whether the updated database, i.e., $D = D_0 \cup \{Rank(Jo\ RA)\}$, still satisfies the constraint we apply the proof procedure with the update as top clause and $D \cup I$ as input set. We obtain the following search space shown in Figure 3.

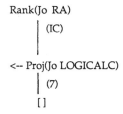

Figure 3: A Search for Example 6, with the Update as Top Clause, Showing a Violation of Integrity

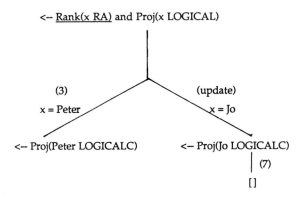

Figure 4: A Search Space for Example 6 with the Constraint as Top Clause

The search space consists of a single refutation illustrating that the update violates the integrity constraint.

The advantage of selecting the update as top clause is that it limits attention to the relevant instantiations of the deductive rules and the integrity constraints.

If the completion of the database is consistent, then any inconsistency must involve an integrity constraint. The completion of a relational database is always consistent. Thus, in this example, instead of the update, we can choose the constraint as top clause while still using the updated database as input set. This results in the search space shown in Figure 4, given the literal selection rule indicated by underlining. Because the top clause is a denial, the same search space is obtained by both our proof procedure and by SLDNF.

This search space also demonstrates that the updated database violates the integrity constraint. However, it is somewhat larger than the previous search space because it does not take advantage of the assumption that the constraint was satisfied before the update.

It is instructive to compare the search space in Figure 4 with an SLDNF-search space for proving that (IC) is a theorem of the completion of D. To prove the theoremhood of (IC) we have to negate it and use it as top clause for an attempted SLDNF-refutation. The negation of (IC), however, is

$$\exists x(\text{Rank}(x\ \text{RA}) \text{ and } \text{Proj}(x\ \text{LOGICALC}))$$

which is not in an appropriate form for SLDNF. We can overcome this problem by defining a new relation "Constraint-Violated" as follows:

$$\text{Constraint-Violated} \leftarrow \text{Rank}(x\ \text{RA}) \text{ and } \text{Proj}(x\ \text{LOGICALC}),$$

and then using the goal

$$\leftarrow \text{NOT Constraint-Violated}$$

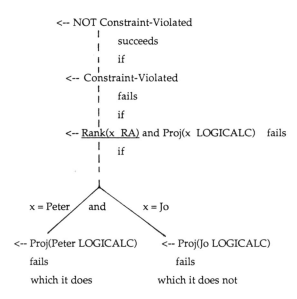

Figure 5: An SLDNF-Search Space for Example 6

as top clause. With this top clause we obtain the SLDNF-search space shown in Figure 5, where broken vertical lines represent subsidiary computations involved in applying the negation as failure rule.

Because SLDNF is complete for relational databases, the finitely failed search space in Figure 5 shows that (IC) is not a theorem of the completion of D. Notice that except for the first two steps and the success/failure labels Figure 5 is identical to Figure 4. Thus, although the two views of integrity are conceptually very different, operationally, the work involved in checking consistency, with the constraint as top clause, is virtually the same as the work involved in proving theoremhood of the constraint. In general we can prove the following.

THEOREM 2

Let S be a deductive database, and let "←C" be an integrity constraint on S, where C is a conjunction of literals. Then there exists a refutation with "←C" as top clause and S as input set by our proof procedure (and equivalently by SLDNF), which shows that the constraint is inconsistent with Comp(S), if and only if the attempt to show by SLDNF that the constraint is a theorem fails finitely. Moreover, there exists an SLDNF proof of the integrity constraint as a theorem if and only if the attempt to show that the constraint is inconsistent fails finitely, by our proof procedure with the constraint as top clause (and equivalently by SLDNF).

Proof: The proof is a direct generalization of the preceding example. ∎

COROLLARY 2
If Comp(S) is consistent and there is a finitely failed search space obtained from our proof procedure with S as input set and ''←C'' as top clause, then Comp(S) ∪ {←C} is consistent, and therefore the constraint ''←C'' is satisfied in S according to the consistency view.

Proof: The proof follows trivially from the second part of Theorem 2 and from the fact that any theorem of a consistent theory is itself consistent with the theory. ∎

A sufficient condition for the consistency of Comp(S) is that S be *stratified* (Apt, Blair, and Walker [1988]). A deductive database is stratified if there is a mapping M from its set of predicate symbols to natural numbers (the non-negated integers) such that for every database rule R = [P(t$_1$ ... t$_n$) ← Conditions]

$M(Q) \leq M(P)$ if Q is a predicate of a positive condition of R, and

$M(S) < M(P)$ if S is a predicate of a negative condition of R.

Thus the stratification condition allows recursion but in a limited form. It excludes rules such as ''P ← NOT P.''

Notice that unlike Theorem 1, Theorem 2 only deals with the case where we take the integrity constraints and not the updates as top clauses. This latter case will be treated in the section ''Correctness and Completeness of the Consistency Method.''

Our method for integrity checking lends itself more readily to the consistency view of constraint satisfaction. We believe, however, that the method can be modified to cater for the theoremhood view, as well, while still using the updates as top clauses. But we will not pursue this possibility further in this paper.

The next example concerns a database that contains a deductive rule which is not a fact. This example illustrates why in our method integrity constraints have to be rewritten as denials.

EXAMPLE 7
In this example ''Acc(x y)'' expresses that x has access to machine y.

D_0:

1. Rank(John Lect)

2. Rank(Mary Prof)

3. Proj(John P1)

4. Proj(Mary P2)

5. Acc(x VAX) ← Proj(x P1)

I:

(IC) Rank(x Lect) ← Proj(x P1)

T:

Insert Proj(Tom P1). ∎

Assume (correctly) that D_0 satisfies the constraint. The integrity constraint is not in the form required for our integrity checking method. If we use the constraint as it stands and select the update as top clause, we obtain the search space shown in Figure 6.

This search space fails to demonstrate any inconsistency. The completion of the updated database, however, is inconsistent with the integrity constraint because together they logically imply both

"Rank(Tom Lect)" and "NOT Rank(Tom Lect)."

To simulate reasoning with the completion of the database we rewrite the constraint in the form

← Proj(x P1) and NOT Rank(x Lect),

where "NOT" is negation by failure, while reasoning with the database rather than with its completion.

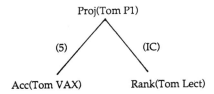

Figure 6: A Search for Example 7 with the Update as Top Clause

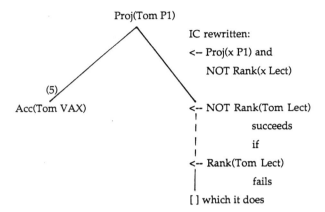

Proj(Tom P1)

IC rewritten:
<-- Proj(x P1) and
    NOT Rank(x Lect)

(5)
Acc(Tom VAX)

<-- NOT Rank(Tom Lect)
            succeeds
            if
<-- Rank(Tom Lect)
            fails
[ ] which it does

Figure 7: A Search Space for Example 7 with the Update as Top Clause, Using the Rewritten Form of the Integrity Constraint

The search space shown in Figure 7, still with the update as top clause, but using the rewritten form of (IC), demonstrates that the updated database violates the integrity constraint.

The search space consists of two derivations. The one on the left, where the update is resolved with the deductive rule in the database, is a finitely failed derivation. The one on the right, where the update is resolved with (IC), is a refutation and shows that the constraint is violated.

The insertion into the database of deductive rules that are not facts is treated exactly as the addition of facts, as shown in the following example.

EXAMPLE 8

D_0:

1.   Eligible(x SERC-grant) ← Student(x) and

Citizen(x UK)

2.   Eligible(x Brit-Council-award) ← Student(x) and

Citizen(x y) and

Dependent-territory(y)

3.   Dependent-territory(Falkland-Islands)

4.   Student(Mary)

5.   Citizen(Mary Falkland-Islands)

6.   Student(Tom)

7.   Citizen(Tom UK)

I:

(IC)   ← Eligible(x SERC-grant) and

Eligible(x Brit-Council-award)

The constraint states that no one is eligible for both an SERC grant and a British Council award.

T:

Insert Citizen(x UK) ← Citizen(x Falkland-Islands). ■

As before we use the update as top clause and the updated database and the constraint as input set. The refutation, shown in Figure 8, shows that the update violates the constraint.

The complete search space contains two other derivations that fail finitely.

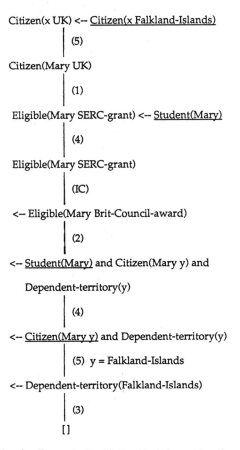

Citizen(x UK) <-- Citizen(x Falkland-Islands)

| (5)

Citizen(Mary UK)

| (1)

Eligible(Mary SERC-grant) <-- Student(Mary)

| (4)

Eligible(Mary SERC-grant)

| (IC)

<-- Eligible(Mary Brit-Council-award)

| (2)

<-- Student(Mary) and Citizen(Mary y) and

Dependent-territory(y)

| (4)

<-- Citizen(Mary y) and Dependent-territory(y)

| (5) y = Falkland-Islands

<-- Dependent-territory(Falkland-Islands)

| (3)

[]

Figure 8: A Refutation for Example 8 with the Update as Top Clause

Updates that Are Deletions

Suppose that a user asks for a fact A to be deleted from a deductive database. A may be explicit or implicit or both. If it is implicit, then to "delete" A it is necessary to modify some of the clauses in the database. In general, several modifications will achieve the desired effect. The choice of modification can be made autonomously by the database management system or by interaction with the user. In this paper, however, we do not address this problem.

Here, we assume that the transaction is in the form suitable for our method; that is, it consists of a set, al, and a set, dl, of deductive rules such that the rules in al are to be explicitly added to the database, and such that all rules occurring explicitly in the database that are variants of a rule in dl are to be explicitly deleted from the database. (A clause C is a *variant* of a clause C′ if C is identical to C′ up to a renaming of variables.) This allows an update that is the explicit deletion of a fact which is both explicit and implicit in the database. Such an update would delete the explicit occurrence only.

We assume further that al does not contain any variants of rules in dl. Thus, for example, a transaction cannot include the addition of a rule "P(x) ← Q(x y)" and the deletion of a rule "P(z) ← Q(z x)." If the original transaction is not in the required form then it must be suitably preprocessed.

We consider first a simple example of deleting a fact from a relational database.

EXAMPLE 9

D_0:
1. Rank(John Lect)
2. Rank(Mary Lect)
3. Rank(Tom Prof)
4. Proj(John P1)
5. Proj(Mary P1)
6. Proj(Tom P2)

I:

(IC) Rank(x Lect) ← Proj(x P1)

which is rewritten as

← Proj(x P1) and NOT Rank(x Lect).

T:

Delete Rank(John Lect). ■

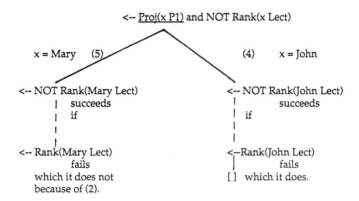

Figure 9: A Search Space for Example 9 with the Constraint as Top Clause

Before applying our method to this example, we show, below, the search space with the integrity constraint as top clause and the updated database, that is, $D_0 - \{\text{Rank(John Lect)}\}$, as input set, where "$-$" denotes set difference. This search space (Figure 9) shows clearly that the integrity constraint is violated in the updated database because the proof of "Rank(John Lect)" fails.

In our approach to achieve the same effect by reasoning forward from the update, we use as top clause the negated fact "NOT Rank(John Lect)," which represents the update. The search space shown in Figure 10, with this negated fact as top clause, shows that the update violates the integrity constraint. Note that the updated database, and therefore the input set, do not explicitly contain the negated fact "NOT Rank(John Lect)."

The first step in the search space is an extended resolution step between the negated fact

NOT Rank(John Lect)

and the integrity constraint

← Proj(x P1) and NOT Rank(x Lect)

on the underlined literals.

Note that in this example the database is relational and, therefore, the fact that is to be deleted by the transaction can only be explicit in the database. In general, however, in a deductive database, facts can be implicit as well as explicit. In such a database, given a transaction including an update of deleting a fact A we need to ensure that A is not provable in the updated database before

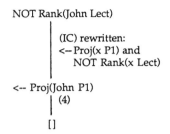

Figure 10: A Search for Example 9 with the Update as Top Clause

reasoning forward from "NOT A." If A is still provable in the updated database, then the update, which only deletes the explicit occurrence of A, does not alter the logical content of the database, and there is, therefore, no need to consider the update as a top clause for integrity checking.

Because of the possible presence of negation by failure in the deductive rules, deletion of facts can implicitly add new facts to the database. Using the extended resolution rule to reason forward from negation as failure is also crucial to cater for such cases as illustrated in the following example.

EXAMPLE 10

In this example "Teaches(x y)" means x teaches on course y.

D_0:
1. Teaches(John Databases)

2. Rank(John Lect)

3. Rank(Mary Lect)

4. Proj(John P1)

5. Proj(Mary P1)

6. Academic-visitor(x) ← Teaches(x Databases) and

   NOT Rank(x Lect)

I:

(IC) ← Proj(x P1) and Academic-Visitor(x)

T:

Delete Rank(John Lect) ■

Here the update leads to an inconsistency because the deletion of a fact results in the addition of a fact, which violates the integrity constraint, as shown in Figure 11.

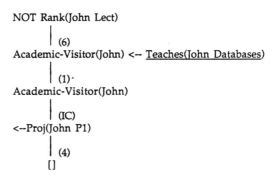

NOT Rank(John Lect)

   | (6)

Academic-Visitor(John) <-- <u>Teaches(John Databases)</u>

   | (1)·

Academic-Visitor(John)

   | (IC)

<--Proj(John P1)

   | (4)

[]

Figure 11: A Search Space for Example 10 with the Update as Top Clause

Updates that Require Additional Inference Rules

In deductive databases the deletion of explicitly present facts can cause the deletion of other implicit facts. Consider the following very simple propositional database, for example:

D_0: A

    B ← A

Fact B is provable in this database. However, if fact A were deleted, B would no longer be provable. The deletion of A would *implicitly delete* B. To check integrity of deductive databases it is necessary to detect such implicit deletions. This requires the addition of a new inference rule, as illustrated in the following example.

EXAMPLE 11

In this example

    ''Sup(x y)'' expresses that x supports project y, and

    ''Alloc(x y)'' expresses that project x is allocated machine y.

    D_0:

      Sup(SERC P1)

      Sup(BP P2)

      Sup(MOD P3)

      Alloc(x VAX) ← Sup(SERC x)

      Alloc(x IBM) ← Sup(BP x)

      Alloc(x SUN) ← Sup(MOD x)

I:
    (IC) Alloc(P1 VAX) or Alloc(P1 SUN)

which states that project P1 is allocated either the VAX or the SUN. (IC) is rewritten as

    ← NOT Alloc(P1 VAX) and NOT Alloc(P1 SUN).

T:
    Delete   Sup(SERC P1). ∎

The fact "Sup(SERC P1)" is only explicit in D_0 and, thus, it is not provable in the updated database.

Intuitively speaking, the deletion of the fact "Sup(SERC P1)" also "deletes" the previously derivable fact "Alloc(P1 VAX)." More formally, "←Alloc(P1 VAX)" is a new logical consequence of the completion of the updated database $D_0 - \{ Sup(SERC \ P1) \}$. Since "←Alloc(P1 SUN)" is also a logical consequence of this completion, the update violates the integrity constraint.

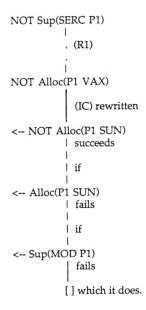

Figure 12: A Refutation for Example 11 with the Update as Top Clause

One way to deduce that ''Alloc(P1 VAX)'' is deleted from the updated database is to reason as follows:

(R1)

because NOT Sup(SERC P1)

and Alloc(x VAX) ← Sup(SERC x)

and we have no other way of showing Alloc(P1 VAX)

therefore NOT Alloc(P1 VAX).

Such a rule allows us to reason with the completed database without having to represent the completion of the database explicitly. It can also be thought of as a rule that allows us to reason forward from negation as failure. We will formalize and generalize the reasoning in (R1) later. Assuming for now that we have such a formalization, the incomplete refutation, shown in Figure 12, shows that the updated database violates the integrity constraint. The refutation is incomplete because we have ignored the details of (R1).

Because of the presence of negation as failure in the deductive rules, an addition can also cause implicit deletions. We need another inference rule to cater for such a case, as illustrated in the following example.

EXAMPLE 12

D_0:

    1.   Overseas-student(x) ← Student(x) and NOT Resident(x UK)

    2.   Student(Jim)

    3.   Eligible(Jim Brit-Council-award)

I:

    (IC)   Overseas-student(x) ← Eligible(x Brit-Council-award)

which is rewritten in the form

       ← Eligible(x Brit-Council-award) and NOT Overseas-student(x)

T:

    Insert Resident(Jim UK). ∎

Intuitively speaking, the insertion of the fact ''Resident(Jim UK)'' ''deletes'' the previously derivable fact ''Overseas-student(Jim),'' and thus violates the integrity constraint. To deduce this implicit deletion we need to reason that

(R2)

because Resident(Jim UK)

and Overseas-student(x) ← Student(x) and NOT Resident(x UK)

and we have no other way of showing Overseas-student(Jim)

therefore NOT Overseas-student(Jim).

Later we will show how this reasoning can be formalized in general. Assuming that we have the required formalization, the incomplete refutation (Figure 13) shows that the update violates the integrity constraint. The refutation is incomplete because the details of (R2) are ignored.

Finally, we require another inference rule for dealing with deletion of deductive rules that are not facts. Following Decker [1986], the approach that we have taken is to determine what instances of the conclusion of a deleted rule are also deleted as a result. The negations of these deleted facts are then taken as candidate top clauses for the attempted refutation. We show a formalization of the required inference rule, later.

Transactions with Multiple Updates

In general, when a single transaction consists of several updates, each update is a candidate top clause. The input set, as usual, consists of the constraints and the updated database. If an update leads to a refutation then the transaction violates the integrity constraints. (The proof of inconsistency can then be analyzed to determine which of the updates contribute to the inconsistency and to identify candidate clauses for revision to restore consistency.) If all the updates

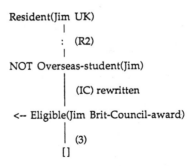

Figure 13: A Refutation for Example 12 with the Update as Top Clause

lead to finitely failed search spaces, and our method is complete for the given case, then the transaction satisfies the constraints.

We believe that our method is as complete as SLDNF. We will discuss this point later in "Correctness and Completeness of the Consistency Method." SLDNF has been proved complete for several restricted classes of databases (Clark [1978], Jaffar, Lassez, and Lloyd [1983]), which include hierarchical databases such as those before and after the update in the following example. (A database is *hierarchical* if it contains no recursion. See Clark [1978] for a more precise definition.)

EXAMPLE 13

D_0:

1. Employed(Tom)

2. Self-employed(Tom)

3. Lecturer(Dick)

4. Lecturer(Harry)

5. Lecturer(Bill)

6. Eligible-for-state-pension(Dick)

7. Eligible-for-state-pension(Harry)

8. Eligible-for-state-pension(Bill)

I:

(IC)   Eligible-for-state-pension(x) $\leftarrow$ Lecturer(x)

which is rewritten as

$\leftarrow$ Lecturer(x) and NOT Eligible-for-state-pension(x)

T:

{ Insert 9. Lecturer(Tom)

10. Eligible-for-state-pension(x) $\leftarrow$

Employed(x) and

NOT Self-employed(x)

Delete Self-employed(Tom)} ∎

Assume (correctly) that D_0 satisfies the constraint. The transaction consists of three updates. To check if D satisfies the constraint, each of the three updates must be considered as top clause. In each case the input set consists of the constraint and the updated database, that is,

$$(D_0 \cup \{(9), (10)\}) - \{(2)\}.$$

It is not difficult to see, intuitively, that the updated database satisfies the constraint. The transaction could violate the constraint only if it added a new lecturer who was not eligible for state pension, or if it deleted the eligibility of some continuing lecturer. The second case does not arise because the transaction adds more ways of concluding eligibility rather than deleting the existing ways. The first case does not arise because, although the transaction adds Tom as a lecturer, it also implicitly adds Tom's eligibility for state pension.

In Figure 14, we show the three search spaces that result from taking each of the updates in the transaction as top clause. All three search spaces fail

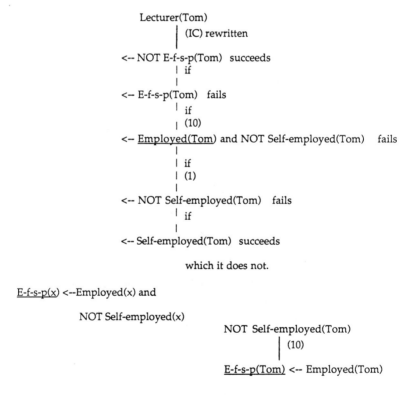

Figure 14: Three Finitely Failed Search Spaces for Example 13 with the Three Updates in the Transaction as Top Clauses

finitely. Thus, assuming that our method is as complete as SLDNF, we can conclude that the transaction satisfies the constraint.

In the search spaces, we have abbreviated the predicate symbol "Eligible-for-state-pension" to "E-f-s-p." Each of the three search spaces consists of a single derivation. The second search space consists only of the top clause, and the third consists of two clauses.

Updates that Are Additions or Deletions of Integrity Constraints

It is easy to deal with additions and deletions of integrity constraints. Additions of constraints are handled exactly as additions of deductive rules. Thus, if a constraint IC is to be added, then IC is selected as top clause for the proof procedure. Of course, if IC is not in the form of a denial, then first it has to be transformed to the required form as described in the subsection "Integrity Constraints." The deletion of a constraint cannot possibly cause an inconsistency, and therefore, there is no need to check integrity for an update that deletes a constraint.

In the sequel, we assume that updates only modify the database and not the constraints. This assumption is relaxed in Kowalski, Sadri, and Soper [1987]. Also, without loss of generality, we assume that constraints are in the form of denials.

Formalizing the Inference Rules for Implicit Deletions: The First Approach

There are at least two different ways of formalizing the inference rules that we need for reasoning about implicit deletions. The first way, discussed in this section, is to formalize the inference rules as metalevel rules which are included in the input set. The second way, discussed in the next section, is to formalize the inference rules as part of the proof procedure. The first approach is probably easier to understand, but the second approach is better for reasons we will explain later.

Let "Deleted(D D_0 f)" express that fact f is deleted in D in the sense that f is a logical consequence of $\text{Comp}(D_0)$, but not of $\text{Comp}(D)$. This can be formalized by a metarule:

(MR)

Deleted(D D_0 f) $\leftarrow$ Demo(D_0 f) and NOT Demo(D f),

where Demo is the standard SLDNF provability relation. Demo(d g) means that the conjunction of literals g is provable from d using SLDNF, or equivalently using our proof procedure with "$\leftarrow g$" as top clause.

We could write this rule more generally using variables for the first two arguments of "Deleted," and adding a condition Result(d d_0 t) to express that d is the database that results from d_0 by means of a transaction t. This would be necessary if we were to embed our integrity checking method into a more general knowledge assimilation system which processes a stream of transactions. In the context of this paper, however, such generality makes the notation more cumbersome without providing any benefits.

The use of (MR) as it stands would give rise to a blind and very inefficient search to find out what facts are deleted from the database as a result of the transaction. We can improve efficiency by adding to (MR) extra conditions to reduce the search. (MR1) and (MR2), below, both result from adding extra conditions to (MR). (MR1) is a general rule corresponding to (R1) in Example 11. (MR2) corresponds to (R2) in Example 12.

(MR1)

> Deleted(D D_0 f) ← NOT p and
> In(f–b D) and
> On(p b) and
> Demo(D_0 f) and
> NOT Demo(D f)

In(c d) means clause c is in database d, and On(p b) means literal p occurs in b which is a conjunction of literals. The symbol " – " is a metalevel infix function symbol naming the object level implication "←." Similarly, below we use "not" as a prefix function symbol naming the negation symbol "NOT."

(MR2)

> Deleted(D D_0 f) ← p and
> In(f–b D) and
> On(not(p) b) and
> Demo(D_0 f) and
> NOT Demo(D f)

As mentioned in the last section, we need another inference rule to deal with deletion of rules that are not facts. Suppose "Transact(D D_0 al dl)" expresses that database D results from updating database D_0 by a transaction consisting of a set of additions al and a set of deletions dl. Then we use rule (MR3) to determine what instances of the conclusion of a deleted rule are deleted as a result.

(MR3)

$$\text{Deleted}(D \, D_0 \, f) \leftarrow \text{Transact}(D \, D_0 \, al \, dl) \text{ and}$$
$$\text{In}(f\!\leftarrow\!b \, dl) \text{ and}$$
$$\text{Demo}(D_0 \, f) \text{ and}$$
$$\text{NOT Demo}(D \, f)$$

This same rule also deals correctly with the special case where "$f \leftarrow b$" names a deductive rule which is a fact, i.e., when b is empty.

The relationship between "Deleted" and negation as failure can be described by the rule:

(MR4)

$$\text{NOT } f \leftarrow \text{Deleted}(D \, D_0 \, f)$$

Note that D, the updated database, is explicit in the condition of (MR4) but implicit in the conclusion. This is to conform with the simplified syntax of negation as failure. Essentially, (MR1)–(MR4) together formalize a correct but partial definition of negation by failure as unprovability. Their purpose is to allow us to determine what facts are deleted (i.e., have become unprovable) as a result of the update.

NOTES

1. These metarules do not treat unification explicitly. The required unification steps would automatically be performed if the rules were executed by a Prolog-like system. Although this is common Prolog practice its logical status is problematic. These problems can be avoided by defining unification explicitly and by adding extra conditions to the metarules to compute the required mgu's and the resulting instantiated formulae, as is the case in the standard definition of provability (see Kowalski [1979], for example).

2. The "Demo" and "NOT Demo" conditions in the metarules can be solved either by running metalevel definitions of "Demo" and "NOT Demo" or by using reflection as in FOL (Weyhrauch [1980]) or in amalgamation logic (Bowen and Kowalski [1982]). To solve "Demo($D_0 \, f$)" by reflection, we show that the goal named f can be solved by SLDNF in the database named D_0. To solve "NOT Demo(D f)" by reflection we show that the goal named f fails finitely by SLDNF in the database named D.

3. The variables p in (MR1) and (MR2) and f in (MR4) are supposed to range over object level facts. These variables, however, do not always

occur as arguments of metalevel predicates or functions in these rules. Thus, our metarules (MR1), (MR2), and (MR4) are not strictly well-formed (although, in practice, they work when using a Prolog-like execution mechanism).

This problem can be avoided by replacing the occurrences of p in the first conditions of (MR1) and (MR2) and the occurrence of f in the conclusion of (MR4) by well-formed atoms Demo(D p) and Demo(D f). This, however, introduces other complications because it requires additional reflection rules and modifications to the extended resolution step.

4. Note that (MR1)–(MR4), together with the standard and the extended resolution rules, cater for the propagation of the effects of initial additions and deletions through chains of database rules.

In this scheme metarules (MR1)–(MR4) are part of the input set. Candidate top clauses correspond to the updates as follows. If R is a deductive rule that is to be added to the database, then R is a candidate top clause. On the other hand, to deal with deletions we select as top clause and thus reason forward from the metalevel fact "Transact(D D_0 al dl)." This is for the sake of convenience, because the top clause then immediately resolves with metarule (MR3), thus automatically dealing with all the deletions of dl.

As mentioned earlier, the metarules give us a partial definition of negation as failure. Therefore, for the sake of efficiency, they should only be used forward. Otherwise, if used backward, they would only duplicate the effect of the normal negation as failure rule. This restriction and the above scheme for selecting top clauses ensure that rules (MR1)–(MR3) are entered only through their first condition.

Notice that we need to extend the proof procedure described in the subsection, "Our Proof Procedure," to allow in derivations, formulae of the form

$$\text{NOT } A \leftarrow L_1 \text{ and} \dots \text{and } L_n, \quad n \geq 1,$$

where A is an atom and the L_i are literals. This extension is trivial, as we already allow negated facts in derivations. We extend the term "clause" to include formulae of the above form. A formal definition of the proof procedure incorporating this extension is given in the next section.

The inclusion of the metarules in the input set is not entirely satisfactory from a methodological point of view. The metarules would have to be distinguished from the other input clauses. As well as requiring special control restrictions, the metarules must be protected against modification by user updates. These problems and the naming problem, described in note (3) above, can be avoided by formalizing (MR1)–(MR4) as inference rules in the definition of the proof procedure.

The next section describes this alternative approach and formalizes the general case of our proof procedure which is an extension of the simplified version described in the subsection "Our Proof Procedure."

Formalizing the Inference Rules for Implicit Deletions: The Second Approach

In this section we first formalize the top-most levels of the resolution (standard and extended) and the negation as failure rules. Then we formalize the inference rules for implicit deletions. To describe the proof procedure we use logic as metalanguage. Although our definitions are intended as an abstract and general description, they are actually runnable in Prolog. As before, the definitions do not make explicit the unification steps involved.

The proof procedure is formalized by the definition of a relation "Inconsistent." Inconsistent(s c) holds if and only if there is a refutation with top clause c and input set s, using our proof procedure. The following relationship holds between the relations "Demo" and "Inconsistent." For all deductive databases d and conjunctions of literals g, where the variables in g are assumed to be existentially quantified in front of g

$$\text{Demo}(d\ g) \longleftrightarrow \text{Inconsistent}(d\text{-}g).$$

The base case for "Inconsistent" is defined by:

(I1)

Inconsistent(s [])

Rule (I2) formalizes the standard and extended resolution rules, and (I3) formalizes the negation as failure rule.

(I2)

Inconsistent(s c) ←
    Select-literal(l c a) and
    In(d s) and
    Resolvent(d c l a r) and
    Inconsistent(s r)

Here Select-literal(l c a) expresses that literal l is selected from the a-side (Conclusion or Condition) of clause c. This relation must describe a safe computation rule. To conform to our earlier assumption that computation rules are functions from derivations to literals, we would have to change the second parameter of the relation ''Inconsistent'' to denote the entire derivation ending at clause c. Other minor modifications would also need to be made. We ignore these changes for the sake of simplicity.

Resolvent(d c l a r) expresses that r is the resolvent of clauses d and c on the literal l occurring on the a-side of c. We assume that ''Resolvent'' is defined in such a way that it deals appropriately with clauses c that have negated conclusions and zero or more conditions. The a-side parameter is necessary to ensure that the negation as failure rule is only applied to negative conditions and not to negated conclusions.

(I3)

> Inconsistent(s c) ←
>> Select-literal(not(p) c Condition) and
>> NOT Inconsistent(s ←p) and
>> Remove-literal(c not(p) Condition c') and
>> Inconsistent(s c')

Remove-literal(c l a c') expresses that c' is clause c with literal l removed from its a-side.

(I1), (I2), and (I3), together with the subsidiary definitions needed for them, extend the proof procedure as described in ''Our Proof Procedure'' to include in derivations clauses with negated conclusions and any number of conditions. We now formalize the inference rules for reasoning about implicit deletions. Inference rules (I4) and (I5) correspond to metarules (MR1) and (MR2) respectively, and incorporate (MR4) as well.

(I4)

> Inconsistent(D ∪ I not(p)←c) ←
>> Select-literal(not(p) not(p)←c Conclusion) and
>> In(f←b D) and
>> On(p b) and
>> Demo(D_0 f) and
>> NOT Demo(D f) and
>> Inconsistent(D ∪ I not(f)←c)

(I5)

> Inconsistent(D ∪ I p←c) ←
>> Select-literal(p p←c Conclusion) and
>> In(f←b D) and

On(not(p) b) and
Demo(D_0 f) and
NOT Demo(D f) and
Inconsistent(D $\cup$ I not(f)–c)

(We can equivalently replace the "Demo" and "NOT Demo" conditions of (I4) and (I5) by "Inconsistent(D_0–f)" and "NOT Inconsistent(D–f)", respectively.) Finally, we use rules (I6) and (I7) to consider automatically all top clauses associated with the updates in the transaction. (I6) corresponds to metarule (MR3), and (I7) allows us to consider as top clause each of the deductive rules that are to be added by the transaction.

In (I6) and (I7), the term "transact(D D_0 al dl)" represents the transaction and names the relation "Transact(D D_0 al dl)" used earlier in the metarules.

(I6)

IC-Violated(D $\cup$ I transact(D D_0 al dl)) ←
    In(f–b dl) and
    Demo(D_0 f) and
    NOT Demo(D f) and
    Inconsistent(D $\cup$ I not(f))

(I7)

IC-Violated(D $\cup$ I transact(D D_0 al dl)) ←
    In(c al) and
    Inconsistent(D $\cup$ I c)

To check the satisfaction of integrity constraints I in database D obtained by a transaction consisting of a set of additions, al, and a set of deletions, dl, we evaluate the query

    ← IC-Violated(D $\cup$ I transact(D D_0 al dl)).

The inference rule approach has a number of advantages over the metarule approach described in the previous section. The inference rules are part of the proof procedure and not the input set. They, therefore, cannot be modified by user updates. For the sake of efficiency the metarules should be used forward only, unlike the other deductive rules in the input set that can be used backward as well as forward. This is an undesirable and ad hoc restriction, which is avoided in the inference rule approach. Furthermore, the inference rules are well-formed, whereas the metarules are not.

The metarule and the inference rule approaches have been implemented in Prolog by Paul Soper. For a description of the implementation see Soper [1986] or Kowalski, Sadri, and Soper [1987].

Comparison with Simplification Methods for Integrity Checking

The features required for our method, such as rules for deriving implicit deletions, can be incorporated in proof procedures other than SLDNF. The choice of SLDNF, however, facilitates the comparison of our method with other algorithms for integrity checking. It is possible to obtain different algorithms from our method by adopting different strategies for literal selection and for searching the resulting search space. Two such strategies allow us to approximate the simplification algorithms of Decker [1986], and Lloyd, Topor, et al. (Lloyd, Sonenberg, and Topor [1986], and Topor, Keddis, and Wright [1985]).

Both these algorithms are extensions of Nicolas's simplification algorithm for relational databases (Nicolas [1982]) and are based on the theoremhood view of constraint satisfaction. To avoid floundering, they impose restrictions identical to ours on variable occurrences in database rules and integrity constraints. (Floundering occurs when a clause in a derivation consists entirely of non-ground negative conditions. In such a case no literal can be selected from the clause by any safe computation rule.) Lloyd, Sonenberg, and Topor [1986] have proved the LT algorithm correct for stratified deductive databases.

Decker reasons forward from the update to compute the facts that are added to or deleted from the database, simplifies the integrity constraints using syntactic criteria similar to Nicolas's, and evaluates the simplified constraints in the updated database. For efficiency's sake, he interleaves the derivation of added and deleted facts with the evaluation of the simplified constraints. He uses special purpose procedures to implement reasoning forward from the update and to simplify the integrity constraints. To evaluate the constraints he uses a proof procedure similar to SLDNF.

The LT algorithm is similar to Decker's. The main difference is that to find appropriate instantiations for the integrity constraints, they only process the rules in the database which are not facts.

The strategy that allows our method to approximate Decker's is that of always selecting a condition of a clause in preference to the conclusion, if there is one. A form of depth first search for traversing the resulting search space then corresponds to Decker's interleaving of the three parts of his algorithm.

The opposite strategy of selecting the conclusion in preference to conditions approximates the LT algorithm.

The following example illustrates how the two algorithms compare with one another and with our method.

EXAMPLE 14

D_0:

  1. $R(x\ y) \leftarrow P(x)$ and $Q(y)$

  2. $S(x\ y) \leftarrow R(x\ y)$

  3. $Q(B)$

  4. $M(y) \leftarrow$ NOT $P(x)$ and $N(x\ y)$

  5. $N(A\ A)$

  6. $K(x) \leftarrow P(x)$ and $L(x)$

  7. $H(x) \leftarrow K(x)$

  8. $J(A)$

I:
   (IC1) $W(x\ y) \leftarrow S(x\ y)$
   (IC2) $M(x) \leftarrow T(x)$
   (IC3) $\leftarrow H(x)$ and $J(x)$

T:
   Insert $P(A)$.

Suppose (correctly) that D_0 satisfies the constraints. ∎

DECKER'S ALGORITHM
(For a complete description of Decker's algorithm see Decker [1986].)
   The facts added to D_0 as a result of the update are

   $ADD = \{P(A),\ R(A\ B),\ S(A\ B)\}.$

There is only one fact that is deleted from D_0; $DEL = \{M(A)\}$.
Decker computes the sets ADD and DEL in stages:

$$Add^0 = \{P(A)\}$$
$$Del^0 = \{\}$$
$$Add^1 = \{R(A\ B)\}$$
$$Del^1 = \{M(A)\}$$
$$Add^2 = \{S(A\ B)\}$$
$$Del^2 = \{\}.$$

After computing each set Add^n or Del^n, the constraints are tested to determine if they are affected by a fact in Add^n or Del^n. The fact ''M(A)'' in Del^1 matches the conclusion of (IC2). Therefore the simplified constraint ''$\leftarrow$T(A)'' has to be evaluated in the updated database. This is then proved to be a theorem of the completion of the updated database, using a proof procedure similar to SLDNF. Next the fact ''S(A B)'' in Add^2 matches the condition of (IC1). The simplified constraint ''W(A B) $\leftarrow$'' is then evaluated by attempting to prove that it is a theorem. The attempt fails finitely, showing that the update violates the constraint. (The fact that ''W(A B)'' is not a theorem of Comp(D) follows from the correctness of SLDNF and the consistency of Comp(D).)

It is possible to add a stopping criterion for computing the sets Add^n and Del^n. For example, if for some n every fact in Add^n and Del^n occurs in an earlier Add or Del set, respectively, then there is no need to compute Add^p or Del^p, for $p > n$. In general, however, in the presence of recursion and function symbols an update may result in an infinite number of implicit additions or deletions. In such a case it is crucial to interleave the three parts of the algorithm to increase the likelihood of finding an integrity violation if one exists.

To simulate Decker's algorithm, we use our proof procedure with the update as top clause and with the first literal selection strategy described earlier. This results in the search space shown in Figure 15.

The strategy that searches this tree in the order indicated by the numbers at the clauses simulates Decker's algorithm almost exactly. The computations involved in the middle derivation of the search space need to be performed in Decker's evaluation of set Add^1, even though they do not lead to the derivation of any facts in that set. The rightmost derivation corresponds to Decker's evaluation of set Del^1 and his simplification and evaluation of constraint (IC2). The leftmost derivation corresponds to his evaluation of sets Add^1 and Add^2 and the simplification and evaluation of (IC1).

The main difference between Decker's algorithm and our approximation of it is that he checks if a fact derivable as a consequence of an update is provable in the database prior to the transaction, and reasons forward from the fact only if it is not. We reason forward from all facts that are consequences of the updates. We could simulate Decker's algorithm exactly by adding extra conditions to inference rules (I2), (I3), and (I7) so that we reason forward from facts derivable from the updated database only if they were not derivable from the previous database.

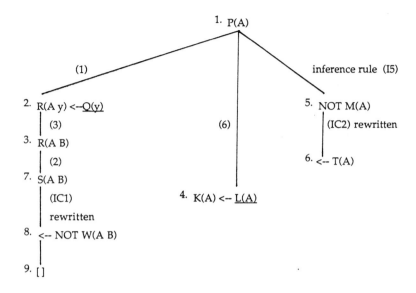

Figure 15: A Search Space for Example 14 Illustrating Our Approximation of Decker's Algorithm

THE LT ALGORITHM

(For a complete description of this algorithm see Lloyd, Sonenberg, and Topor [1986] or Topor, Keddis, and Wright [1985].)

To apply the LT algorithm to Example 14:

- First two sets of atoms, POS and NEG, are computed using only the update and the deductive rules that are not facts.

$$POS = \{P(A),R(A \ y),K(A),S(A \ y),H(A)\}$$
$$NEG = \{M(y)\}.$$

Like Decker's algorithm, the LT algorithm computes these sets in stages.

Every ground atom added to the database as a result of the update is an instance of an atom in POS. However, POS could contain additional atoms no instances of which are added to the database. The same is true of the set NEG for ground atoms that are deleted.

- Then, using sets POS and NEG, the constraints are appropriately instantiated. The instances of the integrity constraints that have to be evaluated in this example are the formulae

1. $W(A \ y) \leftarrow S(A \ y)$

2. $M(x) \leftarrow T(x)$

3. $\leftarrow H(A)$ and $J(A)$

- These are evaluated using the SLDNF proof procedure. This evaluation shows that constraints (2) and (3) are satisfied but (1) is violated. The violation of (1) is shown by the following finitely failed search space.

As before we introduce a new relation, "Constraint-Violated," with the definition

Constraint-Violated $\leftarrow S(A \ y)$ and NOT $W(A \ y)$,

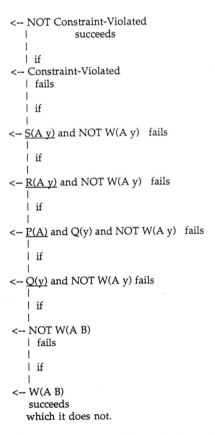

```
<-- NOT Constraint-Violated
    |           succeeds
    |
    | if
<-- Constraint-Violated
    | fails
    |
    | if
    |
<-- S(A y) and NOT W(A y)   fails
    |
    | if
    |
<-- R(A y) and NOT W(A y)   fails
    |
    | if
    |
<-- P(A) and Q(y) and NOT W(A y)   fails
    |
    | if
    |
<-- Q(y) and NOT W(A y) fails
    |
    | if
    |
<-- NOT W(A B)
    | fails
    |
    | if
    |
<-- W(A B)
    succeeds
    which it does not.
```

Figure 16: A Finitely Failed SLDNF-Search Space for Example 14 Showing that the First Constraint Is Not a Theorem of Comp(D)

and choose the goal

    ← NOT Constraint-Violated

as the top clause of the SLDNF-search space.

Like the Decker algorithm, the LT algorithm needs stopping conditions and interleaving to increase the likelihood of detecting a violation of integrity.

One of the inefficiencies of the LT method is that some of the information obtained during the computation of the sets POS and NEG may be thrown away and have to be recomputed when evaluating the instantiated constraints. This redundancy is avoided in our simulation of their algorithm. The search space shown in Figure 17 is obtained with our method when using the second literal selection strategy, described earlier.

The search strategy indicated by the numbers at the clauses allows us to approximate the LT algorithm. Where two clauses have the same number the order in which they are investigated does not matter.

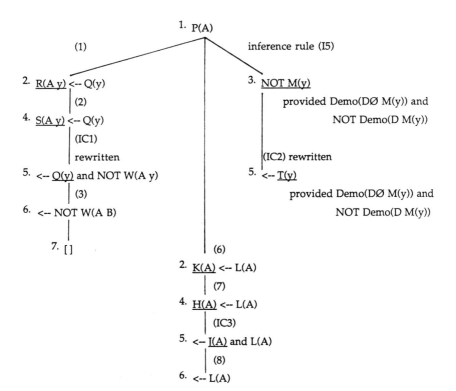

Figure 17: A Search Space for Example 14 Illustrating Our Approximation of the LT Algorithm

The unifications computed on the leftmost and the middle derivations of this search space down to the clauses numbered (4) correspond exactly to those needed for constructing the set POS. The computation on the rightmost derivation down to the clause numbered (3) corresponds exactly to that needed for constructing the set NEG. The computations involved in the other clauses of the derivations correspond to the instantiation and evaluation of the integrity constraints in the LT algorithm. Notice that the work involved from clause (5) down to clause (7) on the leftmost derivation corresponds to the second half of the SLDNF-search space in Figure 16. The first half of this SLDNF-search space duplicates some of the work done in the construction of POS in the LT algorithm. This inefficiency is avoided in our approach.

Notice that the "Demo" and "Not Demo" conditions in the rightmost derivation are not strictly part of the object level derivation. They are metalevel conditions coming from an application of (I5). To simulate the LT algorithm the selection of these two conditions has been deferred. As an alternative, these metalevel conditions can be amalgamated into the object level and can be activated by the object level selection rule. This effect can be obtained by replacing (I5) by

Inconsistent(D $\cup$ I p$\leftarrow$c) $\leftarrow$
    Select-literal(p p$\leftarrow$c Conclusion) and
    In(f$\leftarrow$b D) and
    On(not(p) b) and
    Inconsistent(D $\cup$ I not(f)$\leftarrow$(c *and* demo(D_0 f) *and*
        not(demo(Df)))).

Here "demo" is a prefix function symbol naming the relation "Demo," and "*and*" is an infix function symbol naming the connective "and." An extra level of reflection rules is needed to execute the "demo" and "not demo" conditions when they are selected. Similar modifications could be made to the other inference rules.

The two search spaces in Figures 15 and 17, simulating the Decker and LT algorithms, show that neither algorithm is more efficient than the other in all cases. The two spaces have a similar structure. The work involved in the leftmost refutation is about the same in both search spaces. However, the middle derivation involves less work in the simulation of Decker's algorithm than in the simulation of LT's; whereas the work involved in the rightmost derivation is greater in the simulation of Decker's algorithm, because Decker, in effect, evaluates the "Demo" and "NOT Demo" conditions but the LT algorithm does not. We believe that it is an advantage of our method that we can dynamically employ suitable selection and search strategies to obtain the best performance.

We have chosen to embed our method for checking integrity within a linear proof procedure in order to facilitate comparison with the other integrity check-

ing algorithms. As a consequence, our proof procedure inherits the inefficiencies of linear proof procedures, which are documented in Kowalski
[1975], for example. One such inefficiency is illustrated by the following example.

EXAMPLE 15

D_0:

1. $N(x) \leftarrow P(x)$

2. $R(x\ y) \leftarrow P(x)$ and $Q(y)$

3. $Q(B)$

4. $M(A)$

I:
(IC) $\leftarrow N(x)$ and $R(x\ y)$ and $M(y)$

T:

Insert $P(A)$. ∎

Using our method, with the latter of the two literal selection strategies
described earlier, we can obtain the search space, shown in Figure 18, showing
that the updated database satisfies the constraint. (Our method is complete for
this example, as will be argued in the next section. Therefore, the finite failure
of the search space with the update as top clause implies the satisfaction of the
constraint in the updated database.)

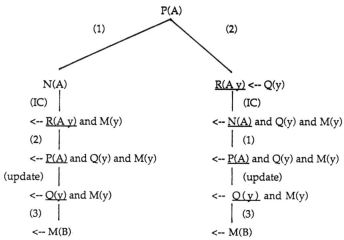

Figure 18: A Search Space for Example 15 Showing an Inefficiency of Our
Proof Procedure

Notice the duplication of work on the last three clauses of the two derivations. This inefficiency is avoided in the LT algorithm. We can also avoid this and other inefficiencies by employing better theorem proving techniques, such as the connection graph proof procedure (Kowalski [1975]), in our method.

Correctness and Completeness of the Consistency Method

Recall that, according to our definition of constraint satisfaction, database D satisfies constraints I if and only if Comp(D) $\cup$ I is consistent. In this section we discuss the correctness and completeness of our integrity checking method (as formalized by the inference rules in "Formalizing the Inference Rules for Implicit Deletions: The Second Approach") relative to this specification.

Recall also that our proof procedure is identical to SLDNF whenever the top clause is a denial. Therefore, it is as correct and as complete as SLDNF when the integrity constraints are chosen as top clauses. SLDNF has been proved correct in general by Clark [1978], complete for hierarchical databases by Clark [1978], and complete for databases consisting of definite clauses by Jaffar, Lassez, and Lloyd [1983]. It has also been conjectured complete for certain classes of stratified databases by Apt, Blair, and Walker [1988]. By Corollary 2 to Theorem 2, if Comp(D) is consistent and for all constraints IC in I there is a finitely failed search space with IC as top clause, then

$$\text{Comp(D)} \cup I$$

is consistent and therefore database D satisfies I. The case where the updates are chosen as top clauses is more complicated.

Correctness When Updates Are Top Clauses

Theorem 1 shows the correctness of our proof procedure without inference rules for implicit deletion. In general we have the following.

THEOREM 3
Let S be an input set consisting of a set D of deductive rules and a set I of denials. Let C_0 be a top clause, which is either a clause in S or the negation of a fact that fails finitely from D. If there is a refutation by means of our proof procedure with top clause C_0 then Comp(D) $\cup$ I is inconsistent.

Proof: We prove more generally, by induction on n, that if $C_0, C_1,...,C_n$ is a derivation then C_n is a logical consequence of Comp(D) $\cup$ I. (Recall that, when referring to logical consequences of Comp(D) $\cup$ I, we interpret all negations as classical negations.)

Base case $n = 0$: C_0 is an obvious consequence of Comp(D) $\cup$ I if C_0 is a clause in S. By the correctness of SLDNF, C_0 is also a consequence of Comp(D) if it is the negation of a fact that fails finitely from D.

Induction step: Suppose C_i is a logical consequence of Comp(D) $\cup$ I, and C_{i+1} is obtained from C_i by one of the following rules:

1.   standard resolution, (I2),

2.   extended resolution, (I2),

3.   negation by failure, (I3),

4.   inference rules for implicit deletion, (I4) and (I5).

We have already shown, in the proof of Theorem 1, that C_{i+1} is a logical consequence of Comp(D) U I in cases (1), (2), and (3).

It remains to show that this also holds when C_{i+1} is obtained from C_i by (I4) or (I5). In both cases C_{i+1} has the form

NOT f ← c

for some fact f such that the condition

NOT Demo(D f)

holds. But this condition holds if and only if f fails finitely from D. But then, by the correctness of negation as failure, "NOT f" is a logical consequence of Comp(D) $\cup$ I and therefore so is "NOT f ← c." ∎

In this argument we have assumed that the condition "NOT Demo(D f)" is evaluated before the clause "NOT f ← c" is derived, as it would be if the conditions in (I4) and (I5) were executed in Prolog order. But the logical content of these inference rules is independent of the choice of safe computation rules for evaluating their conditions. The above proof therefore implies the correctness of the method for any safe computation rule, such as that employed in our simulation of the LT algorithm in Example 14.

Completeness When Updates Are Top Clauses

We define the set of top clauses associated with transaction T, TC(T), as follows:

TC(T) = {r : r is a rule inserted by T} $\cup$
            {NOT f : NOT Demo(D f) and Demo(D_0 f) and
                      (f is a fact deleted explicitly by T or
                       f is a ground instance of the conclusion
                       of a rule deleted explicitly by T)}.

When we talk of using one of the updates in T as top clause, strictly speaking we mean using a member of TC(T) as top clause.

Recall that our method of integrity checking is based on the assumption that D_0 satisfies the constraints prior to the transaction. With this assumption, we believe that our method is as complete as SLDNF. That is, if there is an SLDNF-refutation with an integrity constraint as top clause then there is a refutation by means of our proof procedure with an update as top clause.

We shall prove the completeness of our method for the special, but non-trivial case, where the database consists of definite clauses, the integrity constraints are denials without negative conditions, and the transaction consists only of additions. The proof procedure in this case is non-trivial because it is neither a special case of SL (Kowalski and Kuehner [1971]) (because SL has a more restricted last-in-first-out computation rule), nor a special case of SLD (Lloyd [1984]) (because the top clause for SLD must be a denial, although SLD allows an equally liberal computation rule as our proof procedure). SLD is a linear proof procedure that takes definite clauses as input set and denials without negative conditions as top clauses. It is identical to SLDNF except that it does not employ the negation as failure rule. SLD has been proved complete by Hill [1974]. Thus if D is inconsistent with a constraint IC, then for any computation rule R there exists an SLD-refutation of $D \cup \{IC\}$ via R. We prove the completeness of our method for this special case by proving that the method is as complete as SLD.

Since Comp(D_0) is consistent with the constraints, any inconsistency after the transaction must involve at least one of the updates. Therefore, in any SLD-refutation with a constraint as top clause, showing the violation of the constraint in the updated database, one of the input clauses contributing to the refutation must be an update. Thus to prove the completeness of our method relative to SLD, it is sufficient to prove the following.

THEOREM 4

Suppose there is an SLD-refutation R with input set S and with a denial IC as top clause. Then, for every computation rule CR and for every input clause C contributing to the refutation, there is a refutation via CR with input set $S \cup \{IC\}$ by means of our proof procedure with C as top clause. (An input clause C contributes to a derivation $C_0, C_1,\ldots,C_n$ if and only if for some i,

$$0 \le i < n, C_{i+1}$$

is obtained by the resolution of C and C_i.)

Proof: The proof reduces to the case where S and IC are variable-free. The general case follows from the variable-free case by the standard techniques of (1) first applying Herbrand's Theorem (Chang and Lee [1973]) to obtain a variable-free unsatisfiable set of instances $S' \cup \{IC'\}$ of $S \cup \{IC\}$, and transforming R to a variable-free SLD-refutation R' of $S' \cup \{IC'\}$ to which a ground instance C' of C contributes, (2) transforming R' to a ground refutation R'' by means of our proof procedure with C' as top clause, and finally (3) applying the "lifting lemma" (Chang and Lee [1973]) to obtain the desired refutation R* (isomorphic to R'') of S ∪ {IC} with top clause C. Because this general technique is so standard for resolution proofs of (relative) completeness, we shall deal here only with part (2) which is specific to this theorem.

First, transform R' into the form of an and-tree TR: The top node of TR is the denial IC' with subtrees for every condition A_i in IC'. These subtrees are joined to the top node by arcs connecting the conditions A_i with the conclusions of the rules in S' with which they resolve in R'. The top of TR then has the form

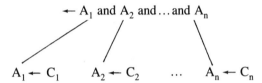

$$\leftarrow A_1 \text{ and } A_2 \text{ and} \ldots \text{and } A_n$$

$$A_1 \leftarrow C_1 \qquad A_2 \leftarrow C_2 \qquad \ldots \qquad A_n \leftarrow C_n$$

where the C_i denote (possibly empty) conjunctions of literals. By an induction argument the subtrees with top node $\leftarrow C_i$ can be constructed similarly. Notice that the and-tree is actually a special form of connection graph linking occurrences of clauses in S' ∪ {IC'}. The same clause can occur in different subtrees. Every occurrence of an atom in TR is linked to only one other occurrence of an atom. Thus every link represents a possible resolution between the clauses.

The original SLD-refutation R' is one particular linear traversal of TR, starting with the top node IC'. The desired refutation R'' is just an alternative linear traversal of TR starting with an occurrence of C' instead.

R'' can be constructed by course of values induction on the number of arcs in TR: Suppose C' occurs at a node N in TR of the form

$$(A) \leftarrow B_1 \text{ and } B_2 \text{ and} \ldots B_m.$$

Each atom in N is linked to exactly one other atom in a node in TR. N may have zero or more conditions and may or may not have any conclusion. Suppose that computation rule CR selects an occurrence of an atom (conclusion or condition) in C and that B is the ground instance of this atom occurrence in C'. Let C'' be the resolvent on B of C' with the clause to which B is linked in TR. Replace the two nodes in TR by the one node which is the resolvent, letting the resolvent inherit all the unselected links from the parent clauses (exactly as in the connection graph proof procedure). The resulting tree TR' has exactly one less link than TR. By induction hypothesis for every computation rule CR' there exists a refutation R''' of S' ∪ {IC'} with top clause C''. Choose CR' to be the computation rule that selects from a clause C'_n ending a derivation $C'_0, \ldots C'_n$ of $S' \cup \{IC'\}$ the ground instance of the same atom occurrence that CR selects from the clause C_n ending a derivation C, $C_0, \ldots, C_n$ of $S \cup \{IC\}$, where $C'_0, \ldots, C'_n$ is the ground derivation isomorphic to $C_0, \ldots, C_n$. The desired refutation R'' is then just C' followed by R'''. ∎

It is possible to extend the proof of Theorem 4 to prove completeness for a more general case where the database still consists of definite clauses and all the updates are additions but where integrity constraints may have negative conditions. SLDNF is complete for such a case in the following sense. If a constraint IC is inconsistent with Comp(D) then for every safe computation rule CR there is an SLDNF-refutation of $D \cup \{IC\}$ via CR. This follows fairly easily from the completeness results of SLD (Hill [1974]) and SLDNF (Jaffar, Lassez, and Lloyd [1983]). We prove the completeness of our method for this case by proving it as complete as SLDNF.

Since D_0 satisfies the constraint, one of the updates in the transaction must contribute to any SLDNF-refutation of $D \cup \{IC\}$ (that is, an update must be an input clause used in the solution of a positive condition of IC). If this were not the case then there would be some ground instance "NOT A," say, of a negative condition of IC such that "NOT A" is provable by SLDNF in D, but not in D_0. Therefore there is a finitely failed SLD-search space for $D \cup \{\leftarrow A\}$. But the search space for $D \cup \{\leftarrow A\}$ includes the search space for $D_0 \cup \{\leftarrow A\}$ because D includes D_0 and both consist of definite clauses. Therefore there must be a finitely failed SLD-search space for $D_0 \cup \{\leftarrow A\}$, which implies that D_0 violates IC contrary to assumption. Thus to prove our method as complete as SLDNF in this case it is sufficient to prove the following.

THEOREM 5
Suppose there is an SLDNF-refutation R with input set S consisting of definite clauses, and denial IC as top clause. Then for every safe computation rule CR and every input clause C contributing to the refutation there is a refutation via CR by means of our proof procedure with C as top clause and $S \cup \{IC\}$ as input set.

Proof: The SLDNF-refutation R without its auxiliary negation as failure subproofs has the same structure as an SLD-refutation, except for the solution of negative conditions. If for every auxiliary subproof of a ground negative condition "NOT A" in R we add a negative fact "NOT A" to the database, and then rename such negated atoms systematically by means of new and distinct positive ground atoms, we transform R into a form to which Theorem 4 applies. Thus we can construct a refutation via CR by means of our proof procedure with C as top clause. If we now undo the renaming and restore the auxiliary negation as failure subproofs, we obtain the desired refutation. ∎

As well as ensuring the completeness of the method, the special cases covered in Theorems 4 and 5 have another major advantage. The proof procedure in these cases can be implemented with efficiencies comparable to that of Prolog implementations, as described in Kowalski, Sadri, and Soper [1987].

We have not yet proved the analogue of Theorem 5 for the general case. The main difficulty comes from the need to generalize the and-tree in the proof of Theorem 4 to a tree including auxiliary proofs of negation as failure. These auxiliary proofs are not simple and-trees but include entire finitely failed search spaces. This suggests that we may be able to deal with this case by converting finitely failed search spaces into direct proofs of negative conditions using Comp(D) as in Clark's proof of the correctness of SLDNF (Clark [1978]).

The correctness of our proof procedure justifies concluding that if we obtain a refutation with our proof procedure then the updated database violates the constraints. Completeness justifies concluding that if our proof procedure fails finitely with all the updates as top clauses then integrity is maintained in the updated database.

Conclusion

In this paper we have presented a method for checking integrity constraints in deductive databases. The method extends the backward reasoning control strategy of logic programming in order to reason forward from updates. In particular, the method incorporates additional rules for negation as failure to reason forward from deletions. We have argued that our method can be used to approximate other integrity checking algorithms for deductive databases.

Acknowledgments

We are grateful to Hendrik Decker, Kave Eshghi, Jean-Marie Nicolas, Paul Soper, and Rodney Topor for helpful discussions. We are also indebted to the referees for their constructive comments. This work was supported by the Science and Engineering Research Council.

References

1. Apt, K. B., Blair, H., and Walker, A. [1988] Towards a Theory of Declarative Knowledge, in *Foundations of Deductive Databases and Logic Programming* (J. Minker, Ed.), Morgan Kaufmann Publishers, Los Altos, CA, 89–148.

2. Bowen, K. A. and Kowalski, R. A. [1982] Amalgamating Language and Metalanguage in Logic Programming, in *Logic Programming* (K. L. Clark and S.-A. Tärnlund, Eds.), Academic Press, 153–172.

3. Chang, C. L. and Lee, R. C. T. [1973] Symbolic Logic and Mechanical Theorem Proving, Academic Press.

4. Clark, K. L. [1978] Negation as Failure, in *Logic and Data Bases* (H. Gallaire and J. Minker, Eds.), Plenum, New York, 293–322.

5. Decker, H. [1986] Integrity Enforcement on Deductive Databases, *Proc. EDS 86*, Charleston, SC, 271–285.

6. Decker, H. [1987] The Range Form or How to Avoid Floundering, Internal Report KB-26, ECRC, Munich.

7. Hill, R. [1974] LUSH-Resolution and Its Completeness, DCL Memo 78, Department of Artificial Intelligence, University of Edinburgh.

8. Jaffar, J., Lassez, J-L., and Lloyd, J. W. [1983] Completeness of the Negation as Failure Rule, *IJCAI-83*, Karlsruhe, 500–506.

9. Kowalski, R. A. [1975] A Proof Procedure Using Connection Graphs, *JACM* **22** (4): 572–595.

10. Kowalski, R. A. [1979] Logic for Problem Solving, Elsevier North Holland.

11. Kowalski, R. A. and Kuehner, D. [1971] Linear Resolution with Selection Function, *Artificial Intelligence* **2**, 227–260.

12. Kowalski, R., Sadri, F., and Soper P. [1987] Integrity Checking in Deductive Databases, in *Proc. 13th VLDB*, Brighton, England, 61–69.

13. Lloyd, J. W. [1984] Foundations of Logic Programming, Springer-Verlag, Symbolic Computation Series.

14. Lloyd, J. W., Sonenberg, E. A., and Topor, R. W. [1986] Integrity Constraint Checking in Stratified Databases, Technical Report 86/5, Department of Computing Science, University of Melbourne.

15. Lloyd, J. W. and Topor, R. W. [1984] Making Prolog More Expressive, *J. Logic Programming* **1**(3):225–240.

16. Lloyd, J. W. and Topor, R. W. [1985] A Basis for Deductive Database Systems, *J. Logic Programming* **2**(2):93–109.

17. Lloyd, J. W. and Topor, R. W. [1986] A Basis for Deductive Database Systems II, *J. Logic Programming* **3**(1):55–67.

18. Nicolas, J. M. [1982] Logic for Improving Integrity Checking in Relational Data Bases, Acta Informatica **18**(3):227–253.

19. Soper, P. J. R. [1986] Integrity Checking in Deductive Databases, M.Sc. thesis, Department of Computing, Imperial College, University of London.

20. Topor, R. W., Keddis, T., and Wright, D. W. [1985] Deductive Database Tools, Technical Report 84/7 (Revised August 23, 1985), Department of Computer Science, University of Melbourne, Parkville, Vic. 3052. Shorter version in *Australian Computer Journal* **17**(4):163–173.

21. Topor, R. W. and Sonenberg, E. A. [1988] On Domain Independent Databases, in *Foundations of Deductive Databases and Logic Programming* (J. Minker, Ed.), Morgan Kaufmann Publishers, Los Altos, CA, 217–240.

22. Weyhrauch, R. [1980] Prolegomena to a Theory of Mechanized Formal Reasoning, *Artificial Intelligence* **13**, 133–170.

10

A Logic-based Language for Database Updates

Sanjay Manchanda
David Scott Warren
Department of Computer Science
State University of New York at Stony Brook
Stony Brook, NY

Abstract

We propose a logic programming language for writing database update programs. The language is called DLP, for Dynamic Logic Programming. Update programs in the language are logic programs augmented with simple update operations; they have a declarative semantics in a dynamic logic of updates. This semantics provides a logical theory of database updates. DLP supports data-definition, view definition, querying, updating, and general computing; therefore, it can serve as a uniform interface to a logic database. We present an application of DLP and its semantics to the view update problem. A view update translator is an update program in DLP and must satisfy certain conditions for correctly translating update requests on a particular view. It is shown that very simple syntactic transformations on a view definition can be used to obtain correct view update translators for the view.

Introduction

The field of logic databases uses the language of mathematical logic for describing the database and its operations. Typically, first-order predicate logic is used as the representation language and query language for the database, while its inferential mechanisms are used to deduce new information from the database. However, little work has been done on a logic programming language that supports updates. In general, database updates are not very well understood, as is apparent in the primitive update facilities offered by current database systems. For example, users who interact with a database through views are not allowed to update through the same mechanism—or are disallowed any update privileges. One problem with trying to incorporate updates in the logic database paradigm is that if the database is represented as a first-order theory, then an update operation is a modification of this underlying theory. This implies that an update operation cannot be expressed within the first-order predicate logic—a different logic is required.

A logic program that queries and updates a database is analogous to the usual Pascal program that tests and manipulates its environment. The major difference is that the environment of a procedural program is a mapping from variables to values, while the environment of a logic program is a mapping from predicate symbols to relations. Dynamic logics (see Harel [1979]) are logics for reasoning about programs that test and change an environment. Therefore, it should be possible to construct a dynamic logic of update programs. We develop such a logic. This logic is the basis of a logic programming language called DLP. The language is based on Horn Clause logic programs with negation. The guiding principles behind the design of DLP are that it should have an intuitive declarative semantics, and it should be practical and efficiently implementable.

A database relation can be defined in two ways: by listing its tuples explicitly, that is, specifying its *extension*, or by means of rules, that is, specifying its *intension*. We call a relation defined directly by listing its tuples, a *base relation*, and a relation defined (wholly or partially) by means of rules, a *rule-defined relation*. Usually, a database user does not have access to the rule definitions and he cannot modify them. He is allowed to see only the relations they define, although as we shall see later, it may be possible to support updating of some rule-defined relations by updating the base relations that are used in their definition. Therefore, the basic update operations in DLP are the addition and deletion of a tuple from a base relation.[1] Assume that a user wants to add the tuple (sam,machines) to the employee-department base relation, ed. In DLP he will indicate this update request by the *update query* ←
⟨+ed(sam,machines)⟩. The query may be interpreted as a request to move to a database in which ed(sam,machines) is true. Similarly, a delete request will be indicated by ← ⟨−ed(sam,machines)⟩, which is interpreted as a request to move to a database in which ed(sam,machines) is false. To continue the analogy with procedural programs, these two statements correspond to the assignment statement of a procedural program—the basic statement that

---

[1]Replacements are not handled as atomic actions in our framework.

changes state. Note however, that the procedural component of DLP has a simple declarative basis: The only command is to "make something true (or false)."

The user also may want to query a database besides updating it. Assume that the user first wants to add the tuple (sam,machines) to ed, and then to find sam's manager. If em is the employee-manager relation, then the DLP update query

$$Q: \leftarrow \langle +ed(sam,machines) \rangle (em(sam,Mgr))$$

accomplishes the task. Here, in the usual Prolog convention, Mgr is an existentially quantified variable. The parentheses around em(sam,Mgr) emphasize that this query is evaluated in the updated database.

This statement should be compared with the dynamic logic formula, $\langle P \rangle \alpha$, where P is a formula of a language of programs and α is an assertion. For example, $\langle X := a \rangle X = a$ is a formula of Harel's Regular Dynamic Logic (RDL), which uses a regular language of programs. In a dynamic logic, programs are viewed as operators on states, where a state can be thought of as a mapping from all the variables in the program to some value domain. The programs can be non-deterministic, that is, they can transform a current state to several possible final states. Correspondingly, a dynamic logic assigns a binary relation on states as the denotation of a program. Declaratively, the wff $\langle P \rangle \alpha$ is true in a current state, if there exists a state accessible from the current state in the denotation of P such that α is true in the new state. In the RDL, the statement $X := a$ returns a state in which X has value a, irrespective of what its value was earlier; hence the formula $\langle X := a \rangle X = a$ is true in every state.

In the dynamic logic of updates, the state consists of the extension of the relations in the database. The declarative semantics of the update query Q given above is that Q is true in a current database, if there exists a database accessible from the current database in the denotation of +ed(sam,machines), and em(sam,Mgr) is true in that new database. The denotation of the literal +ed(sam,machines) is a binary relation on databases such that the new database is identical to the old database except that ed(sam,machines) is true in the new database. Observe that the literal +ed(sam,machines) is not an ordinary first-order literal since it does not denote a relation on terms; we call it a *dynamic literal*.

For reasons of security, brevity, and so on, it may be useful to hide portions of the actual database from the user. This is usually done through the view mechanism. A view is associated with a *view relation* and a *view definition*. A view relation is a rule-defined relation that is made to appear like a base relation to the user. The rules that define the view relation constitute the view definition. If a user wants to update a view, then the user's update request must be translated down to a set of updates on the base relations. The essential correctness condition of a view update is that this update on the base relations must in turn imply the intended update on the view. The problem of view updates is that this translation process is ambiguous (see for example, Furtado and Sevcik [1979]). Let the em view be defined as:

$$em(Ename,Mgr) \leftarrow ed(Ename,Dept) \ \& \ dm(Dept,Mgr)$$

Consider the update request $\leftarrow \langle+em(sam,john)\rangle$ where john is currently the manager of the machines department and sam works in the foundry department. There are many possible ways of satisfying this update request. To name a couple of possibilities, either sam can be made an employee in machines or john can be made the manager of foundry.

Some of these ambiguities can be resolved by using a view update *translator*. A translator specifies a particular policy for updating a view. We may have an *add translator* for translating add requests on the view, and a *delete translator* for translating delete requests on the view. In this paper, the translator is actually an update program. The following translator implements the policy of adding tuples to the ed relation only. It assumes that an employee can work in two departments, and adds the employee to the manager's department. Of course, more complex policies can also be programmed. It is specified as the following *update rule* of DLP:

$$\langle+em(Ename,Mgr)\rangle \leftarrow \langle+ed(Ename,Dept)\rangle(dm(Dept,Mgr))$$

Not every update rule is a viable translator for a particular view. A translator must satisfy certain conditions for correctly translating update requests on a particular view. For example, a minimal correctness condition is that for some value of Ename and Mgr, em(Ename,Mgr) should be true after the procedure +em(Ename,Mgr) succeeds. We explore reasonable translators for views and examine their relationship to view definitions. We demonstrate a set of syntactic transformations, which transform view definitions into correct translators. These transformations are valid for a reasonable class of views.

The paper is divided into two parts. In the first part, we introduce the language DLP and give its formal syntax and semantics. In the second part, we apply to the problem of defining correct view update translators the machinery that is developed in the first part.

Related Work

This paper extends the ideas developed in Warren [1984]. The semantics of DLP is related to the theory of updates developed by Farinas and Herzig [1986], who also build upon Warren's work. However they do not support deletion or update procedures. Abiteboul and Grahne [1985] discuss update specification and implementation for incomplete-information databases, using the notion of tables proposed by Imielinski and Lipski [1984]. We do not discuss updates on incomplete-information databases in any detail in this paper. However, their semantics for updates is related to the semantics of DLP, and some of their ideas are applicable to its implementation. Wilkins [1986] also has a theory of updates based on a possible world semantics. Her assumptions and development are considerably different from ours—for example, she supports the insertion of arbitrary formulas in the database. Abiteboul and Vianu [1987] have proposed a procedural language for writing database transactions. Except for Warren [1984], none of the proposals mentioned above supports update procedures.

We follow a model-theoretic approach to the semantics of updates; that is, an update is understood to be a mapping from a set of models to another set of models. A syntactic approach to the theory of updates can be found in Fagin, Kuper, Ullman, and Vardi [1986]. They represent the database as a first-order theory and specify an update as a condition that is to be satisfied by the resulting database. This approach is non-constructive and turns out to be intractable. Casanova and Furtado [1984] have a motivation similar to ours in proposing the use of an extended temporal logic for specifying database integrity constraints. However, they do not address the actual database update problem.

Most of the work on view updates has focused on developing criteria and algorithms for view update translation (see Furtado and Sevcik [1979], Bancilhon and Spyratos [1981], Dayal and Bernstein [1982], Keller [1985]). We concentrate on developing a language for expressing view update translators. Carlson and Arora [1983] have proposed the UPM language for expressing updates. Unlike DLP, UPM is a purely operational language in which no attempt is made to automatically verify the correctness of view update programs.

Syntax of DLP

The framework used for describing the database in logic is similar to the one used by Kowalski [1978]. A database is described by a first-order language L. L has a finite number of constant symbols and predicate symbols. It has an infinite number of variable symbols and no function symbols. Quantifiers are not explicitly specified but the conventions of Prolog are used to determine the quantification of variables. The predicate symbols of L can be divided into three disjoint sets: *base* predicate symbols, *rule* predicate symbols and *dynamic* predicate symbols. Additionally, for every base predicate symbol p_b in the language, there is a dynamic predicate symbol of the form $+p_b$ and $-p_b$. These symbols are called *dynamic base predicate* symbols. A base predicate symbol denotes a base relation and a rule predicate symbol denotes a rule-defined relation. A dynamic predicate symbol denotes a binary relation on databases, and it is used to express updates.

A *term* is a constant symbol or a variable symbol. The syntax of DLP is an extension of Prolog syntax. Accordingly, we will use words starting with lower case letters for constant symbols, and words starting with upper case letters for variables. An atom formed from a base predicate symbol is called a *base atom*; an atom formed from a rule predicate symbol is called a *rule atom*; and an atom formed from a dynamic predicate symbol is called a *dynamic atom*. If A is a base or rule atom, then A and $\neg A$ are *literals*. For uniformity, a dynamic atom will also be called a dynamic literal. However, note that negative dynamic literals are not allowed. The reserved word *true* is considered to be a literal. The well-formed formulas (wffs) of DLP are defined as follows.

1. A *conjunction C*, defined as $C ::= L \mid C1\&C2$, where L is a rule literal or a base literal, and $C1$ and $C2$ are conjunctions.

2. A *rule* defined as $H \leftarrow C$, where H is a rule atom also called the *head* of the rule. C is a conjunction, called the *body* of the rule.

3. A *dynamic conjunction D*, defined as $D ::= L \mid L\&D \mid \langle E \rangle (D)$, where E is a dynamic literal.

4. An *update rule*, defined as $\langle E \rangle \leftarrow D$, where $\langle E \rangle$ is the head of the update rule, and D, a dynamic conjunction, is its body.

Views are a restricted version of rules, and view update translators are a restricted version of update rules. They are discussed in the second half of the paper. Note that a dynamic literal can only occur within angular brackets, and it is always followed by a dynamic conjunction in parentheses. We will find it convenient to use the following abbreviation.

$$\langle E \rangle (true) \equiv \langle E \rangle$$

A *database description* Δ is a triple (F,R,U) where

> F is the extensional portion of the database description.
>
> R is the intensional portion of the database description.
>
> U is the update portion of the database description.

F is a set of positive ground base literals also called the base facts. R is a set of rules and U is a set of update rules. Only the base predicate symbols are allowed to occur in the base facts; only the rule predicate symbols are allowed to occur in the heads of rules; only the dynamic predicate symbols are allowed to occur in the heads of update rules. Note that no negated predicate symbols can occur in the extensional portion of the database description. Also note that the usage of the word facts is more restricted than standard Prolog usage, since

Prolog facts can contain variables. In DLP, a Prolog fact such as p(X,a). will be represented explicitly as the rule $p(X,a) \leftarrow true$.

A *query* is a formula of the form $\leftarrow C$, where C is a conjunction. An *update query* is a formula of the form $\leftarrow D$, where D is a dynamic conjunction. The variables of a query and an update query are assumed to be existentially quantified over the entire conjunction.

Informal Introduction to DLP

The semantics and the proof theory of DLP is a proper extension of the semantics and proof theory of Pure Prolog. We will find it convenient to explain the informal execution of DLP program's in a Prolog-like fashion, assuming its left-to-right, top-to-bottom control strategy. Of course, the semantics of DLP, as well as its proof theory, is independent of any control strategy. In this section, we will discuss queries and procedures that add and delete tuples from base relations only. No updates will be allowed on rule-defined relations.

The user interacts with the DLP system by posing an update query. Let ed be the employee-department base relation, es, the employee-salary base relation, and edp, the employee-department-project rule-defined relation. The following query, Q1, checks that joe's salary is 20k, adds him as an employee in the weapons department, and finds the project to which he has been assigned.

```
Q1: ← es(joe,20K)&
         (+ed(joe,weapons))(edp(joe,weapons,Proj))
```

Operationally, Q1 checks to see if es(joe,20K) is true in the current database, adds the tuple (joe,weapons) to ed, and then finds the value of Proj for which edp(joe,weapons,Proj) is true in the updated database. The tuple is added to the ed relation only if it was not already present, that is, no duplicates are allowed in the database. Just as Prolog returns the variable bindings as the answer to a query, DLP returns not only the variable bindings but also the updated database as the answer. Of course, DLP does not have to print the whole new database as the answer. It will print out all the base facts that were added or deleted during the execution of the update query. Therefore, for Q1, DLP will return an instantiation for Proj and indicate that the base fact ed(joe,weapons) was added—if it was not already present in the original database. If joe's salary is not 20K or if he has not been assigned any project, then Q1 will evaluate to false; it will fail and the database will remain unchanged.

The declarative semantics of the query Q1 is obtained by viewing it as a dynamic logic formula. At this point, the reader may wish to review the portion of the "Introduction" that explains the basic concepts of dynamic logic. The atom +ed(joe,weapons) is a dynamic atom whose meaning is a binary relation on databases. We will call this meaning its *dynamic meaning*. If p_b is a base predicate, then the dynamic meaning of dynamic atoms of the form $+p_b(\bar{c})$ and $-p_b(\bar{c})$ is fixed. Informally, $+p_b(\bar{c})$ can be viewed as an operator on databases that returns a new database by adding $p_b(\bar{c})$ to the old database. Similarly, $-p_b(\bar{c})$ returns a new database by deleting $p_b(\bar{c})$ from the old database. Just like the addition operation, the deletion operation returns the old database if $p_b(\bar{c})$ is already absent from the old database. Thus DLP has predefined operators for adding and deleting tuples from any base relation.

Now the declarative semantics of Q1 can be given. Q1 is true in a current database I, if es(joe,20K) is true in I; and if there exists a new database J accessible from I through +ed(joe,weapons) (that is, (I,J) belongs to the dynamic meaning of +ed(joe,weapons)); and there exists a value for Proj, such that edp(joe,weapons,Proj) is true in the new database. The parentheses around edp(joe,weapons,Proj) emphasize the fact that it is evaluated in the new database.

The denotation of a dynamic atom is a binary relation on the set of all possible databases. A possible database is also called a *database state*. We want to view $+p_b(\bar{c})$ as returning a database state in which $p_b(\bar{c})$ is true, and $-p_b(\bar{c})$ as returning a database state in which $\neg p_b(\bar{c})$ is true. This gives a simple declarative basis to the add and delete operations. We formalize this idea by defining the database state to be a minimal Herbrand model and by interpreting negation with respect to this minimal model. Let us tentatively define a database state to be a minimal Herbrand model of the set of formulas obtained by the union of the set of rules specified in the database description, and a possible set of base facts. The set of base facts given in the database description determines the initial database state. During execution, the current database state keeps changing. Syntactically, base facts are added and deleted. Semantically, the computation proceeds from one minimal model to another minimal model.

We say that the literal $p(\bar{c})$ is true in a database state if $p(\bar{c})$ belongs to the database state, and the literal $\neg p(\bar{c})$ is true in a database state if $p(\bar{c})$ does not belong to the database state. It should be noted that the body of a rule is an arbitrary conjunction that can contain negative literals. Therefore, a rule in R is equivalent to a first-order clause with at least one positive literal. It follows that the set of clauses $F \cup R$ can have more than one minimal model, that is, there is no unique least model as in the case of Horn Clauses, (see van Emden and Kowalski [1976]). Hence, it may be argued that the tentative definition of a database state is not precise.

This problem can be solved by selecting a particular minimal model of the facts and rules in preference to the other minimal models. This selected model is declared then to be the database state. The concept of negation with respect to minimal models, and the selection of a particular minimal model, is discussed elsewhere in this book by Przymusinski [1988], Lifschitz [1988], Van

Gelder [1988], and Apt, Blair, and Walker [1988]. A set of base facts and rules can be viewed as a logic program with negated literals allowed in the body of rules. By assigning priorities to the predicate symbols in the program according to the structure of the rules, it is possible to select a specific minimal model of the program via a fixpoint construction (Apt, Blair, and Walker [1988]) or via a set of circumscriptions (Lifschitz [1988]). A sufficient syntactic condition that allows this minimal model to be chosen is called *stratification*, which essentially disallows recursion through negation (for a definition, see Apt, Blair, and Walker [1988]). It can be argued that this chosen model is the model intended by the programmer. Przymusinski [1988] defines the notion of a *perfect* model and shows that a stratified program always has exactly one perfect model. This model is identical to the minimal model chosen by Apt et al. and by Lifschitz. If a set of rules is stratifiable, then the program consisting of the rules and some possible set of base facts is stratifiable. Accordingly, we restrict our attention to stratifiable sets of rules for the rest of the paper and assume that each state is actually a perfect model.

DEFINITION 1

A database state is the perfect model of the set of formulas obtained by the union of the set of rules specified in the database description and some set of base facts. ∎

This gives us the machinery for defining the basic update operations. Let I be a database state. Since I is a Herbrand model, it is merely a set of rule and base atoms. Let $I|_b$ be the restriction of I to the base atoms in I. The dynamic meaning of a dynamic atom E will be written as $M_d(E)$.

DEFINITION 2

$$M_d(+p_b(\bar{c})) = \{(I,J) : J|_b = I|_b \cup \{p_b(\bar{c})\} \text{ and } J \text{ is the perfect model}$$
$$\text{of } J|_b \cup R\},$$

$$M_d(-p_b(\bar{c})) = \{(I,J) : J|_b = I|_b \setminus \{p_b(\bar{c})\} \text{ and } J \text{ is the perfect model}$$
$$\text{of } J|_b \cup R\}. \quad \blacksquare$$

Update queries are not restricted to a single update literal. Nested updates are allowed. For example,

```
Q2: ← ⟨+ep(joe,peace)⟩
            (edp(henry,Dept,peace) & ⟨+ed(joe,Dept)⟩)
```

Assume that henry is the project leader of the peace project. The update query Q2 adds joe to the peace project, finds henry's department in the updated database, and adds joe to the same department. Note that ⟨+ep(joe,Dept)⟩ is an abbreviation of ⟨+ep(joe,Dept)⟩(true). Q2 is true in a current database state *I*, if there exists a database state *J* such that (*I,J*) belongs to M_d(+ep(joe,peace)); and there exists a constant *c*, such that edp(henry,*c*,peace) is true in *J*; and there exists a database state *K*, such that (*J,K*) belongs to M_d(+ed(joe,*c*)).

Observe that dynamic conjunctions are restricted to be nested to the right. For example, the following query Q3 is not a well-formed formula of DLP. The reason for this restriction is that in order to use the language for database updates, we want every dynamic conjunction to determine a binary relation on database states.

> Q3: ← ⟨+ed(joe,weapons)⟩ & ⟨+ep(joe,peace)⟩

Q3 has a well-defined declarative semantics in the dynamic logic. Q3 is true in a current database state if there exists a database state accessible from the current database state obtained by adding ed(joe,weapons) to the current database state, and if there exists a (possibly some other) database state obtained by adding ep(joe,peace) to the current state. However, Q3 is not acceptable as a dynamic conjunction because it cannot be given a dynamic meaning as a binary relation on database states. The problem is that the new database state in which to continue execution could be one in which either literal has been added, or one in which both have been added—it is not clear which one should be selected.

It is possible to write update procedures in DLP. An update procedure is a set of update rules that have the same dynamic predicate in the head. An update procedure defines a new operator on database states. Assume that a company wants to hire an employee in a particular department only if the average salary in the department stays below a certain limit after the hire. Then, the hire update procedure can be expressed as follows.

> ⟨hire(Ename,Sal,Dept)⟩ ←
>   ⟨+es(Ename,Sal)⟩
>   (⟨+ed(Ename,Dept)⟩
>   (avg_sal(Dept,Avg) & Avg < 50k))

Here hire is a dynamic predicate. The update query ← ⟨hire(joe, 60k,weapons)⟩, will add information about joe in the database, compute the average salary of the weapons department, and return the updated database if this average is less than 50k. If this average is greater than or equal to 50k, the procedure will fail and no updates will be performed.

The body of the update rule defines the dynamic meaning of hire. The body is a dynamic conjunction, denoting a binary relation on database states. A tuple of database states (I,K) belongs to this relation, if—given the values of Ename, Sal, and Dept—there exists J accessible from I through +es(Ename,Sal) and there exists K accessible from J through +ed(Ename, Dept) such that in K, the average salary of the department Dept, is less than 50k. The update rule states that a state K is accessible from I through hire(Ename,Sal,Dept), if K is accessible through the body of the update rule for hire. That is, if an update rule is of the form ⟨*Head*⟩ ◄─ *Body*, then its semantics is: $M_d(Body) \subseteq M_d(Head)$. Note that the dynamic meaning of dynamic base predicate symbols is a *function* on states, that is, base relation updates always succeed. Meanwhile, the dynamic meaning of other dynamic predicate symbols is really a binary relation. That is, an update procedure may fail indicating that there is no state accessible from the current state. Since the semantics of an update rule is different from that of a Prolog type of rule, the two rules use a different syntax. The " ← " sign is used for defining rules, and the " ◄─ " sign is used for defining update rules.

Updates can be non-deterministic. For example, if a company wants to enroll its employees in a refresher course which has several sections, it may want to use the following update procedure.

```
⟨enroll(Ename)⟩  ◄─ ⟨sec1(Ename)⟩
                      (size(sec1,N) & N < 30)

⟨enroll(Ename)⟩  ◄─ ⟨sec2(Ename)⟩
                      (size(sec2,N) & N < 20)
```

When called with an employee name, the enroll procedure will non-deterministically try to enroll an employee in a section. If neither section is full, then the procedure will either return a database state with the employee enrolled in Section 1 or will return a database state with the employee enrolled in Section 2. Clearly, a Prolog type of backtracking strategy can be used to execute an enroll update query. The top rule for enroll will be executed first. It will add the employee to Section 1 and then check the size of the section. If the size is less than 30, the update query will succeed; otherwise, this database will be backtracked over, that is, the tuple that was added to the sec1 relation will be removed—then, the second rule will be tried in the same manner.

Update procedures can call other update procedures. Also, update procedures can be recursive. For example, consider the definition of the update procedure inc_sal(Inc), which increments the salary of each employee by the amount Inc.

```
exists_emp ← es(Ename,Sal)

⟨inc_sal(Inc)⟩ ← ¬exists_emp
⟨inc_sal(Inc)⟩ ←
        ⟨-es(Ename,Sal)⟩
        (NewSal is Sal + Inc &
        ⟨inc_sal(Inc)⟩(⟨+es(Ename,NewSal)⟩)))
```

The first rule in the definition of inc_sal says that if there are no employees in a current database state I, then the same database state should be returned as the updated database state, that is, $(I,I) \in M_d(\texttt{inc\_sal(Inc)})$. The second rule says that a database state L is accessible from a current database state I through inc_sal(Inc) (that is, $(I,L) \in M_d(\texttt{inc\_sal}$ $\texttt{(Inc)})$), if I and L satisfy the conjunction of the following statements: The state J is accessible from I by non-deterministically deleting an employee-salary tuple for an employee of name Ename; NewSal is his new salary in J; K is accessible from J by incrementing the salaries of all the employees in J; L is accessible from K by adding the employee-salary tuple for the employee of name Ename.

It is instructive to see how inc_sal can be executed using Prolog's control strategy. When inc_sal is called, it will first check to see if all the employees have been deleted. If all the employees have been deleted, it will succeed. Otherwise, it will delete a tuple from the es relation, instantiating the variables Ename and Sal in the process. Then, it will compute the new salary for this employee and call itself recursively. The recursive call will return after incrementing all the other employees' salaries. Following its return, the new es tuple for the employee of name Ename will be added to the database.

Formal Semantics of DLP

A dynamic logic has a Kripke semantics (Kripke [1963], Pratt [1976]) based on the concept of a *state* or a *possible world*. Let $\Delta = (F,R,U)$ be a database description and L its associated first-order language. Let H_c be the Herbrand Universe of L, and H_b its Herbrand Base. Then a structure for L is $N = (G,S,M_d)$, where:

S is a *set of states*, such that $S \subseteq 2^{H_b}$.

$G \in S$, is the current state.

M_d is a *dynamic meaning* function. For a dynamic predicate symbol p_d of arity n, and a tuple of constants $\bar{c}$ from H_c^n, M_d defines a binary relation on the set of states S, that is: $M_d(p_d)$: $H_c^n \rightharpoonup S \times S$, or alternatively, $M_d(p_d(\bar{c})) \subseteq S \times S$.

Additionally, all structures must satisfy the following constraints.

1. There is a bijection between the set of all possible sets of base facts and the set of states. Let H_B be the restriction of the Herbrand Base to the set of all possible positive base literals. Then 2^{H_B} is the set of all possible sets of base facts. A state is a set of ground rules and base atoms. Let $I\,|_b$ be the restriction of state I to the base atoms in I. Then the bijection $2^{H_B} \rightarrow S$ is defined as:

    For each $f \in 2^{H_B}$, there exists precisely one $I \in S$, such that $I\,|_b = f$.

    In other words, any possible set of base facts maps to a unique state which contains this set of base facts as a subset.

2. Dynamic base predicate symbols have a *fixed* dynamic meaning as follows:

    For $I, J \in S$, $\bar{c} \in H_c^n$,

    $$M_d(+p_b(\bar{c})) = \{(I,J) : J\,|_b = I\,|_b \cup \{p_b(\bar{c})\}\}$$

    $$M_d(-p_b(\bar{c})) = \{(I,J) : J\,|_b = I\,|_b \setminus \{p_b(\bar{c})\}\}$$

We give here the definition of the truth value of a well-formed formula, given a state I and a variable assignment s. Given a tuple of terms $\bar{t}$, $\bar{t}[s]$ denotes a tuple of constants from H_c. Given a well-formed formula $p(\bar{t})$, $p(\bar{t})[s]$ denotes the ground well-formed formula obtained after applying the variable assignment to it as a substitution. It follows from the definition of M_d, that $M_d(p_d(\bar{t})[s])$ denotes a binary relation on states. In the following definitions, the truth of a well-formed formula is defined with respect to an understood structure N.

1. If p is a base or rule predicate symbol then

    $$I \vDash p(\bar{t})[s] \text{ iff } p(\bar{t})[s] \in I.$$

2. If p is a base or rule predicate symbol then

    $$I \vDash \neg p(\bar{t})[s] \text{ iff } p(\bar{t})[s] \notin I.$$

3. If $H \leftarrow C$ is a rule then

    $$I \vDash (H \leftarrow C)[s] \text{ iff when } I \vDash C[s] \text{ then } I \vDash H[s].$$

4. If p_d is a dynamic predicate symbol then

$$I \models ((p_d(\bar{t}))(D))[s] \text{ iff there exists a state J such that}$$
$$(I,J) \in M_d(p_d(\bar{t})[s]) \text{ and } J \models D[s] \ .$$

5. If $L\&D$ is a dynamic conjunction then

$$I \models (L\&D)[s] \text{ iff } I \models L[s] \text{ and } I \models D[s].$$

The dynamic meaning function on predicate symbols can be extended to dynamic conjunctions. That is, besides a truth value, a dynamic conjunction has a dynamic meaning which is a relation on states. The extension of the dynamic meaning function to dynamic conjunctions is denoted as $\bar{M}_d$. It is defined as follows.

1. If p is a base or rule predicate symbol,

$$\bar{M}_d(p(\bar{t})[s]) = \{(I,I) : I \models p(\bar{t})[s]\} \ .$$

2. If p_d is a dynamic predicate symbol,

$$\bar{M}_d((p_d(\bar{t}))(D)[s]) = \{(I,J) : \text{for some } K, (I,K) \in M_d(p_d(\bar{t})[s]) \text{ and}$$
$$(K, J) \in \bar{M}_d(D[s])\}$$

3. $\bar{M}_d((L\&D)[s]) = \{(I,J) : I \models L[s] \text{ and } (I,J) \in \bar{M}_d(D[s])\}$

An update rule $\langle E \rangle \ - \ D$, is true if for all variable assignments s, $\bar{M}_d(D[s]) \subseteq M_d(E[s])$. In this case we say that U *satisfies* $\langle E \rangle \leftarrow D$.

N satisfies a set of rules if it satisfies every rule in the set. Given a database description $\Delta = (F,R,U)$, and a structure $N = (G,S,M_d)$, N is a model of Δ if:

(a)   for all $I \in S$, $I \models R$.

(b) N satisfies U.

(c) $G|_b = F$.

G is needed in the model to ensure that database descriptions having the same set of rules but different extensional portions have different models.

N is a *minimal* model of Δ if:

(a) N is a model of Δ.

(b)   Every state $I \in S$ is a minimal model of $(I|_b \cup R)$.

(c)   There is no structure $N' = (G,S,M'_d)$ different from N such that[2]

(i) N' is a model of Δ.

(ii)   For every dynamic predicate p_d and $\bar{c} \in H^n_c$, $M'_d(p_d(\bar{c})) \subseteq M_d(p_d(\bar{c}))$.

We call a minimal model an *M-model* if each state $I \in S$ is a perfect model of $I|_b \cup R$. We are interested only in M-models of database descriptions. The proof of uniqueness of the M-model requires the following lemma.

LEMMA 1
Let X be a set of structures whose elements are of the form $N^i = (G,S,M^i_d)$, that is, they differ only in the dynamic meaning function. Let $N^l = (G,S,M^l_d)$ be a structure such that $M^l_d(p_d(\bar{c})) = \cap_i M^i_d(p_d(\bar{c}))$ for all p_d and $\bar{c}$. Then for any ground dynamic conjunction D, $\bar{M}^l_d(D) \subseteq \cap_i \bar{M}^i_d(D)$.

Proof: By induction on the structure of ground dynamic conjunctions.

Base Case: $D = p(\bar{c})$.
Here $\bar{M}^i_d(D) = \cap_i \bar{M}^i_d(D) = \bar{M}^l_d(D) = (I,I) : I| = p(\bar{c})$. Therefore, the result follows for this case.
Induction Step: Two cases arise.

Case 1: $D = \langle p_d(\bar{c})\rangle(D1)$.
By the definition of $\bar{M}_d$, $\cap_i\bar{M}^i_d(D) = \cap_i\{(I,J) : (I,K) \in M^i_d(p_d(\bar{c}))$ and $(K,J) \in \bar{M}^i_d(D1)\}$. It follows that $\{(I,J) : (I,K) \in \cap_i M^i_d(p_d(\bar{c}))$ and $(K,J) \in \cap_i\bar{M}^i_d(D1)\} \subseteq \cap_i \bar{M}^i_d(D)$. To see this, consider a representative tuple (I,J) belonging to the left-hand side; it is easy to show that it belongs to the right-hand side. By the induction hypothesis, $\bar{M}^l_d(D1) \subseteq \cap_i \bar{M}^i_d(D1)$, and by definition $M^l_d(p_d(\bar{c})) = \cap_iM^i_d(p_d(\bar{c}))$. Therefore, $\bar{M}^l_d(D) \subseteq \cap_i\bar{M}^i_d(D)$.

Case 2: $D = L\&D1$. Similar to Case 1. ■

THEOREM 1
A database description has a unique M-model.

Proof: Let $N = (G,S,M_d)$ be a model of a database description $\Delta = (F,R,U)$. If N is an M-model, then there exists a state I in S for each $f \in 2^{H_B}$, such that $I|_b = f$, and I is a perfect model of $I|_b \cup R$. As discussed in the last section,

---

[2]Note that N' has the same set of states as N.

we are assuming that R is stratifiable. From the definition of stratification (see Apt, Blair, and Walker [1988]), it follows that the logic program $I|_b \cup R$ is stratifiable. Przymusinski [1988] shows that a stratifiable logic program has exactly one perfect model. Therefore, each state in S always exists and is unique. Any two sets of states must contain the same number of states, since there is a bijection between the set of states and the set of all possible sets of facts. This proves that if N is an M-model, then S always exists and is unique.

The current state G is the perfect model of $F \cup R$. Once the database description is fixed, F is fixed, and G too, always exists and is unique.

We have proved that all M-models of a database description must have the same set of states and the same current state. Consider the following relation on models of Δ, all having the same set of states S, and the same current state G: $N^1 \leq N^2$ iff $M_d^1(p_d)(\bar{c}) \subseteq M_d^2(p_d)(\bar{c})$, for all p_d and $\bar{c}$. This relation induces a partial order on the set of models, since set inclusion induces a partial order on the set of dynamic meanings. We will prove now that any set X of such models has a greatest lower bound. Let $N^i = (G,S,M_d^i)$ be a typical element of X. Consider the structure $N^l = (G,S,M_d^l)$, where $M_d^l(p_d(\bar{c})) = \cap_i M_d^i(p_d(\bar{c}))$, for all p_d and $\bar{c}$. Clearly $N^l \leq N^i$ for any $N^i \in X$. We have to prove that N^l is a model of Δ. Since N^l has the set of states S, every state in N^l satisfies every rule in R. Consider a ground update rule of the form $\langle E \rangle \leftarrow D$. Since the update rule is true in any N^i, we have $\bar{M}_d^i(D) \subseteq M_d^i(E)$. Therefore, $\cap_i \bar{M}_d^i(D) \subseteq \cap_i M_d^i(E)$. By Lemma 1, we have $\bar{M}_d^l(D) \subseteq M_d^l(E)$. Therefore, N^l satisfies any ground update rule, and N^l is a model of Δ. Since any set of such models of Δ has a greatest lower bound, the set of all such models has a unique least element. From the definition of the M-model, it follows that this unique least model is the M-model of Δ. To complete the argument, it is necessary to prove that Δ always has at least one model. We do this by constructing the top element of the partial order. Consider the structure, $N^T = (S,G,M_d^T)$, where $M_d^T(p_d(\bar{c}) = S \times S$ for all p_d and $\bar{c}$. The definition of M_d^T ensures that any update rule in U will be true in N^T, thereby making it a model of Δ. Therefore, the M-model of Δ exists and is unique. ∎

Implementation Issues of DLP

The proof theory of DLP is an extension of the proof theory of Prolog. A complete description of the proof theory and implementation of DLP is beyond the scope of this paper, however, we give a simple and incomplete interpreter for DLP. It is a proper extension of Prolog's standard interpreter. The interpreter operates on positive programs, that is, no negation is permitted. Also, Prolog's left-to-right literal selection rule is assumed; the interpreter always selects the leftmost conjunct for execution. An additional restriction is placed on update rules: It is assumed that any dynamic base literal is ground when it is executed. The interpreter is based on a sound and complete proof theory for DLP without negation, given in Manchanda [1987a].

The interpreter accepts a database description (F,R,U) and a query Q. It has to provide a method of adding facts to and deleting facts from the database. This is done by maintaining two sets of facts: the add set (AS) and the delete set (DS). AS and DS are initially empty. The interpreter reduces the given query to a new query while producing new add and delete sets. It succeeds when the query is reduced to empty. The interpreter is given as a non-deterministic procedure, all choices within it are assumed to be non-deterministic. A single cycle of the interpreter is outlined below.

INTERPRETER

Case 1: $Q = L\&D$ where L is a base literal. Choose a base fact in AS, or in F, which unifies with L, with unifying substitution s. The new query is $D[s]$.

Case 2: $Q = L\&D$ where L is a rule literal. Choose a rule in R, $H \leftarrow C$, such that H unifies with L, with unifying substitution s. The new query is $(C\&D)[s]$.

Case 3: $Q = \langle + p_b(\bar{t})\rangle(D)$. Choose a fact in DS that unifies with $p_b(\bar{t})$. Remove this fact from DS. If $p_b(\bar{t})$ is not in F then add it to set AS. The new query is D.

Case 4: $Q = \langle - p_b(\bar{t})\rangle(D)$. Choose (a) or (b); if neither (a) nor (b) can be chosen, then choose (c). (a): Choose a fact in AS that unifies with $p_b(\bar{t})$. Remove this fact from AS. The new query is D. (b): Choose a fact in F that unifies with $p_b(\bar{t})$. Add $p_b(\bar{t})$ to DS. The new query is D. (c): The new query is D.

Case 5: $Q = \langle p_d(\bar{t})\rangle (D)$. Choose an update rule, $\langle E \rangle \leftarrow F$, such that $p_d(\bar{t})$ unifies with E, with substitution s. The new query is $In(D,F)[s]$, where $In(D,F)$ is a formula obtained by adding D as the last and innermost conjunct of F. It is defined inductively as: $In(D,L) = L \& D$, $In(D,L\&D1) = L \& In(D,D1)$, $In(D,\langle E\rangle(D1)) = \langle E\rangle(In(D,D1))$. ∎

If at any step, no more choices can be made, the interpreter fails. On success, the updates in AS and DS can be applied to the current set of base facts to obtain the new set of base facts. It is easy to prove that the interpreter is sound for the declarative semantics described in the last section. The soundness of the interpreter also follows from the soundness of the proof system given in Manchanda [1987a]. The add and delete set together form an *intentions list* of deferred updates, which may be used for concurrency control and recovery purposes. Manchanda, Sengupta, and Warren [1986] describe how the intentions list may be used in conjunction with an *optimistic concurrency control* algorithm (see Agrawal et al. [1987]) for supporting concurrent updates on the database system.

In theory, the completeness of the interpreter is not affected by the fact that updates are required to be ground when they are executed. Since the variables of a query are existentially quantified, it is possible to construct a dovetailing proof procedure that accepts a query, constructs all ground instances of it, and uses the interpreter to try to prove each ground instance. Also, if this is done, the assumption of the left-to-right conjunct selection rule can be relaxed. The interpreter can be extended to handle negation by incorporating Apt, Blair, and Walker's [1988] interpreter for ground queries over logic programs with negation.

Now we motivate some issues that arise in a more practical treatment of non-ground updates. Consider the update queries Q4 and Q5.

Q4: ← Sal = 30k & ⟨+es(mark,Sal)⟩
Q5: ← ⟨+es(mark,Sal)⟩ (Sal = 30k)

Since Sal is existentially quantified, the declarative semantics decrees that the two queries should return the same updated database. However, consider what happens when Q5 is executed in the obvious way, that is, first the tuple (mark,Sal) is added to the database and then the equality is executed. When the tuple is added, Sal is an existentially quantified variable, and its value is unknown. It behaves temporarily as a *marked null* value until it is assigned its actual value. This was noted in Warren [1984]. A detailed treatment of logical null values can be found in Reiter [1986].

In this example, the null value was short lived. However, consider the update query ← ⟨+es(mark,Sal)⟩. It asserts the existence of a database in which mark has some unspecified salary. Every possible value of Sal determines a different database. It is not clear which database should be returned after executing the update query. One solution is to simply choose an arbitrary value for Sal. A better solution is to add the tuple to the database along with the null value. This complicates answers to queries, for example, the query ← es(mark,20k) should return an answer like "Yes, if Sal = 20k." Several people discuss question answering in incomplete information databases with null values, for example, see Reiter [1986], Grant and Minker [1986], Imielinski [1986], Yahya and Henschen [1985]. Deletion requires special treatment in the presence of null values. For example, consider the delete request ← ⟨-p(a,X)⟩ on the set of facts {p(a,Y), p(a,b)}. Since both X and Y are existentially quantified, several new databases are possible. For example, a possible new database is {p(a,b)}, where X = Y ≠ b; another possibility is {p(a,Y),p(a,b)}, where X ≠ Y and X ≠ b. A sound treatment of deletion requires the maintenance of inequality constraints in the interpreter. A similar remark applies if it is desired to implement negation as negation by failure. These issues are discussed in Manchanda [1987b].

View Updates

A database view is a rule-defined relation that is made to appear as a base relation to the user. The actual base relations used to define the view may be hidden from the user in the interest of brevity, security, and so on. A user's update request on the view has to be translated down to the base relations and then performed in such a way that the user sees the view relation as having been updated. In general, a view defines a many-to-many mapping from the base relation tuples to the view tuples. This makes the translation process ambiguous. These ambiguities are resolved by specifying a view update translator for the view. In this paper, the translator is an update program that not only does the translation, it also does the updates. In general, an add translator is required for translating add requests on the view, and a delete translator is required for translating delete requests on the view.

Not all rule predicates are used as views. We distinguish certain rule predicates by calling them view predicates and also refer to the corresponding rules as *view definitions*. Consider the definition of the edp view.

```
edp(Ename,Dept,Proj)  ←
          ed(Ename,Dept) &
          ep(Ename,Proj)
```

Here ep is the employee-project base relation. Assume that the user wants to delete the tuple (joe,weapons,peace) from the edp view. How should he specify this update request? Since the view relation is being treated as a base relation, we introduce dynamic predicate symbols of the form +edp and −edp—just like we introduced $+p_b$ and $-p_b$ earlier on for base predicate p_b. When we need to distinguish between the different types of dynamic predicate symbols, we qualify them as "dynamic base predicate" or "dynamic view predicate" symbols. Now the user can specify his delete request as ← ⟨−edp(joe,weapons,peace)⟩. The declarative understanding of this request is that the user wants edp(joe,weapons,peace) to be false in the updated state. Similarly, the dynamic meaning of +edp(joe, weapons, peace) should be defined such that edp(joe,weapons, peace) is true in the updated database state.

DEFINITION 3
An add(delete) translator for a view predicate p_v is a set of update rules such that each rule has a head of the form $+p_v(\bar{t})(-p_v(\bar{t}))$. ∎

Unlike the meaning of a dynamic base predicate, the meaning of a dynamic view predicate is not predefined, it is defined by the corresponding view update translator. Consider the translation of the delete request specified above. To delete the tuple (joe,weapons,peace) from the edp relation, either (joe,weapons) must be deleted from ed or (joe,peace) must be deleted from ep. Declaratively, edp(joe,weapons,peace) is false in a database state if either ed(joe,weapons) is false in the database or if ep(joe,peace) is false in the database. The database administrator (henceforth DBA) may decide that a user of the edp view has the authority to remove people from a project, but not from a department. He can indicate the desired translation for the update request by specifying the following delete translator δ for the view.

$$δ: \ ⟨-edp(Ename,Dept,Proj)⟩ \longleftarrow$$
$$ed(Ename,Dept) \ \& $$
$$⟨-ep(Ename,Proj)⟩$$

The declarative semantics of δ is that there exists a database reachable from the current state in which edp(Ename,Dept,Proj) is false, if ed(Ename,Dept) is true in the current database state, and there exists a database state reachable from the current database state in which ep(Ename,Proj) is false. Note that a state in which ep(Ename,Proj) is false is always reachable from the current state by simply deleting ep(Ename,Proj), since ep is a base predicate. The translator is intuitively correct because if the update succeeds, then ¬edp(Ename,Dept, Proj) is true in the updated database.

In the rest of the paper, we define two correctness conditions for translators and specify some syntactic transformations for converting view definitions to translators. We treat only a very restricted class of rules as view definitions. Some of these restrictions are more severe than is necessary. They are needed to simplify the presentation of the ideas. Our purpose here is to motivate the primary ideas underlying this application of the logical theory of database updates; it is not to provide a complete treatment of this topic. We place the following restrictions on view definitions and view update translators.

1.   There is at most one defining rule for each view definition and view update translator.

2.   No negative literals are allowed in the bodies of view definitions.

3.   Views and view update translators cannot be recursively defined.

Condition 1 means that union views are not allowed. The framework of this paper can be extended to handle union views. However, we exclude them for reasons of brevity. The same reasons apply for Condition 2. Condition 3 disallows recursive view definitions because the semantics of updating a recursive view is not well understood. We will modify our definition of the database description to be the 5-tuple (F,R,U,V,T), where V is a set of view definitions, and T is a set of translators.

For the purposes of view updating, it is useful to treat a view definition as an if and only-if rule. The idea of interpreting the if definitions of a logic program as iff definitions was first used by Clark [1978] to formalize the concept of negation in logic programs. Given a logic program, he defines a *completed database* (CDB) that contains the iff definitions. The restrictions placed on view definitions enable us to simplify his original definition. The simplified definition is:

Given a view definition of the form $L \leftarrow C$, its *completion* is given by $L \longleftrightarrow \exists X_1,...,X_n C$, where $X_1,...,X_n$ are variables that occur in C but not in L. A predicate q of arity n that does not have a defining rule is assigned the formula $\neg q(X_1,...,X_n)$ in the completion. A base fact remains unchanged in the completion of the program.

The idea of completing the view definitions is consistent with our semantics. This follows from the following (slightly rephrased) result which is proved in Apt, Blair, and Walker [1988]:

If a logic program P is stratified then the perfect model of P is also a model of comp(P).

Here comp(P) refers to the completion of P. This means that any conclusion that follows from the completion of the view definitions is true in each state (of course, the reverse is not necessarily true). The completion of a view is especially useful in reasoning about translations of delete requests.

The theorems that follow require the following lemma. It states that in the M-model, the dynamic meaning of the body of an update translator is not just a subset of the dynamic meaning of the head, it is actually equal to it.

LEMMA 2

Given a database description Δ and its M-model $N = (G,S,M_d)$, if $\langle p_d(\bar{t})\rangle \leftarrow D$ is a translator in Δ, then $M_d(p_d(\bar{t})[s]) = \bar{M}_d(D[s])$, for all variable assignments s.

Proof: Since N satisfies the update rule we must have that $\bar{M}_d(D[s]) \subseteq M_d(p_d(\bar{t})[s])$. If $\bar{M}_d(D[s]) \neq M_d(p_d(\bar{t})[s])$ then consider the structure N' that is identical to N except that the dynamic meaning of p_d in N' is given by: $M'_d(p_d(\bar{t})[s]) = \bar{M}'_d(D[s])$. We say that a dynamic predicate q *depends on* a dynamic predicate r, if r occurs in a defining update rule for q. Since recursive definitions are not allowed, no dynamic predicate occurring in D can depend

on p_d. Therefore, the dynamic meaning of D is unchanged in N' i.e. $\bar{M}_d(D) = \bar{M}'_d(D)$. Then clearly $M'_d(p_d)(\bar{c}) \subset M_d(p_d)(\bar{c})$ for all $\bar{c} \in H_c^n$.
Now we show that N' is a model of Δ. Since N' is identical to N except on the dynamic meaning of p_d, we only have to show that N' satisfies every update rule in Δ. Consider any update rule τ in Δ. Three cases arise.

Case (a): τ is the given update rule $\langle p_d(\bar{t}) \rangle \leftarrow D$. Then clearly, τ is true in N'. If τ is not the given update rule, then it is some other update rule $\langle q_d(\bar{t}) \rangle \leftarrow B$.

Case (b): B contains a dynamic predicate that depends on p_d. Since τ is true in N, we have $\bar{M}_d(B[s]) \subseteq M_d(q_d(\bar{t})[s])$. Since $M'_d(p_d)(\bar{c}) \subset M_d(p_d)(\bar{c})$, clearly $\bar{M}'_d(B[s]) \subseteq \bar{M}_d(B[s])$. This can be verified by a simple induction on the structure on dynamic conjunctions. Therefore, $\bar{M}'_d(B[s]) \subseteq M_d(q_d(\bar{t})[s])$. Since N and N' differ only on the the dynamic meaning of p_d, we have $M_d(q_d(\bar{t})[s]) = M'_d(q_d(\bar{t})[s])$. Therefore, $\bar{M}'_d(B[s]) \subseteq M'_d(q_d(\bar{t})[s])$ and τ is true in N'.

Case (c): B does not contain a dynamic predicate that depends on p_d. Then $\bar{M}_d(B) = \bar{M}'_d(B)$ and $M_d(q_d(\bar{t})[s]) = M'_d(q_d(\bar{t})[s])$ and τ is true in N' since it is true in N.

This proves that N' is a model of Δ. However, since $M'_d(p_d) \subseteq M_d(p_d)$, this implies that N is not an M-model, which leads to a contradiction. Therefore, the initial assumption was incorrect and $M_d(p_d(\bar{t})[s]) = \bar{M}_d(D[s])$. ∎

Correctness Conditions for Translators

In this section we define two weak correctness conditions for translators and show how to verify that the translators are correct.

Semantic Correctness

If a translator accepts an add request $\leftarrow \langle +p_v(c_1,\ldots,c_n) \rangle$, then the minimal constraint for the translator to perform the addition correctly is that $p_v(c_1,\ldots,c_n)$ should be true after the addition is done. A similar statement applies to delete requests. A translator whose updates satisfy this condition is termed *semantically correct*.

DEFINITION 4
Let Δ be a database description whose M-model is $N = (G,S,M_d)$.

1. The translator $\langle +p_v(\bar{t}) \rangle \longleftarrow D$ is semantically correct in Δ if
    for all variable assignments s, for all $I,J \in S$, if $(I,J) \in M_d(+p_v(\bar{t})[s])$
    then $J \models p_v(\bar{t})[s]$.

2. The translator $\langle -p_v(\bar{t}) \rangle \longleftarrow D$ is semantically correct in Δ if
    for all variable assignments s, for all $I,J \in S$, if $(I,J) \in M_d(-p_v(\bar{t})[s])$
    then $J \models \neg p_v(\bar{t})[s]$. ■

Note that there is an important difference between base relation updates and view updates. An update on a base relation *always* succeeds, while an update on a view may *fail*. Consider the add translator α given below. The translator is semantically correct. However, if joe does not work in the sales department then the update request $\longleftarrow \langle +\text{edp(joe,sales,peace)} \rangle$ will fail, since the literal ed(joe,sales) evaluates to false in the current database. No update will be performed, and the database will remain unchanged. In this case, we say that the translator has *rejected* the update. If the update query succeeds, we say that the translator *accepts* the update. In this case, the DLP formula $\langle +\text{edp(joe,sales,peace)} \rangle$ (edp(joe,sales,peace)) is not true in every state even though the translator is correct. In standard dynamic logic, semantic correctness can be expressed as the requirement that for all $\bar{c} \in H_b^n$, $[+p_v(\bar{c})](p_v(\bar{c}))$ and $[-p_v(\bar{c})](\neg p_v(\bar{c}))$ should be true in every state. Here, "[ ]" is a connective of standard dynamic logic that corresponds to the "for all" quantification on states. That is, $I \models [p_d(\bar{t})](D)[s]$ iff for all $(I,J) \in M_d(p_d(\bar{t})[s])$, $J \models D[s]$. Note that the dynamic meaning of a dynamic base predicate is a function on states, therefore: $[+p_b(\bar{c})](p_b(\bar{c})) \equiv \langle +p_b(\bar{c}) \rangle (p_b(\bar{c}))$, and $[-p_b(\bar{c})](\neg p_b(\bar{c})) \equiv \langle -p_b(\bar{c}) \rangle (\neg p_b(\bar{c}))$.

The above definition can be used to verify that the following translator α is semantically correct in Δ.

```
α: ⟨+edp(Ename,Dept,Proj)⟩ ⟵
        ed(Ename,Dept) &
        ⟨+ep(Ename,Proj)⟩
```

If α is true in the M-model $N = (G,S,M_d)$ of Δ, then for a variable assignment s: $M_d(+\text{edp(Ename,Dept,Proj)}[s]) = \bar{M}_d(\text{ed(Ename,Dept)} \And \langle +\text{ep(Ename,Proj)} \rangle [s])$. This implies that $M_d(+\text{edp(Ename,Dept, Proj)}[s]) = \{(I,J) : I,J \in S, I \models \text{ed(Ename,Dept)} [s], (I,J) \in M_d(+\text{ep(Ename,Proj)} [s])\}$. Since ep is a base predicate, $J \models \text{ed(Ename, Dept)}[s]$ and $J \models \text{ep(Ename,Proj)}[s]$. Since all states satisfy the view definition for edp, this implies that $J \models \text{edp(Ename,Dept,Proj)}[s]$. Therefore, $M_d(+\text{edp(Ename,Dept,Proj)}[s]) = \{(I,J) : I \models \text{ed(Ename,Dept)}[s], J \models \text{edp(Ename, Dept,Proj)}[s]\}$. Therefore, α is semantically correct.

Note that we could add more predicates as conditions in α and it would still be correct. For example, we may want to add an employee to a project only if he satisfies the prerequisites required for the project. Let satisfiespreq(Ename,Proj) be a predicate that is true, if an employee of name Ename satisfies the prerequisites for the project Proj. Then, the following translator rejects an update request for an employee if he does not satisfy the prerequisites.

⟨+edp(Ename,Dept,Proj)⟩ ◀—
        satisfiespreq(Ename,Proj) &
        ed(Ename,Dept) &
        ⟨+ep(Ename,Proj)⟩

It is easy to see that the translator is correct. This suggests a possible way of handling static and dynamic integrity constraints in the framework. As an example of a translator that may fail to be correct, consider the add translator β for the edp view.

β: ⟨+edp(Ename,Dept,Proj)⟩ ◀—
        ⟨+playsbaseball(Ename)⟩

Clearly, β is unrelated to the view definition for edp. For any M-model N of Δ, we must have M_d(+edp(Ename,Dept,Proj)[s]) = M_d(+playsbaseball (Ename)[s]). Let playsbaseball be a base predicate. Consider the database state K = {ed(joe,weapons)}, and another database state $K1$ = {ed(joe,weapons), playsbaseball(bob)}. If the database description contains only the edp view and β, then from β, it follows that $(K,K1) \in M_d(\langle$ +edp (bob,somedept,someproj)⟩). However $K1 \not\models$ edp(bob, somedept,someproj). Therefore, β is semantically incorrect.

Semantic Acceptability

If there is an update request to add a tuple already in the view, or to delete a tuple not in the view, then the update should not change the database. A translator whose updates satisfy this condition is termed *semantically acceptable* (see Bancilhon and Spyratos [1981]).

DEFINITION 5

Let Δ be a database description whose M-model is $N = (G,S,M_d)$.

1. The translator $\langle+p_v(\bar{t})\rangle$ ◀— D is semantically acceptable in Δ if for all variable assignments s, for all $I,J \in S$, if $(I,J) \in M_d(+p_v(\bar{t})[s])$ and $I \models p_v(\bar{t})[s]$ then $I = J$.

2.   The translator $\langle -p_v(\bar{t}) \rangle \leftarrow D$ is semantically acceptable in Δ if for all variable assignments s, for all $I,J \in S$, if $(I,J) \in M_d(-p_v(\bar{t})[s])$ and $I \models \neg p_v(\bar{t})[s]$ then $I = J$. ■

For example consider the following delete translator η for the edp view.

     η: $\langle$-edp(Ename,Dept,Proj)$\rangle$ $\leftarrow$
              $\langle$-ed(Ename,Dept)$\rangle$
              ($\langle$-ep(Ename,Proj)$\rangle$)

For all values of Ename, Dept, and Proj, η returns a state (say J) in which ¬ ep(Ename,Proj) is true. Recall that the completion of the view definition is true in every state in an M-model. If ¬ ep(Ename,Proj) is true in J, then the completion of the edp view implies that ¬ edp(Ename,Dept,Proj) is true in J. Therefore, η is semantically correct in a Δ that contains the edp view. However, η is not semantically acceptable. Let the current database state I be a state in which an employee mark works only in the weapons department, and on the peace project. For η to be semantically acceptable, the update query $\leftarrow \langle$-edp(mark,sales,peace)$\rangle$ should succeed without changing the database—since the specified tuple is already not in the view. However, the translator will return a new state J in which mark has been taken off the peace project. Therefore, η is not semantically acceptable. Note that one way of guaranteeing semantic acceptability is to include always the entire body of the view definition in the translator to check if the requested tuple is in the view before actually doing any updates. The following delete translator η′ is semantically acceptable. It satisfies case (b) of the definition vacuously, because there are no I, J and s such that: $(I,J) \in M_d(-$edp(Ename,Dept, Proj)$[s])$, and $I \models \neg$ edp(Ename,Dept,Proj)$[s]$.

     η′: $\langle$-edp(Ename,Dept,Proj)$\rangle$ $\leftarrow$
              ed(Ename,Dept) & ep(Ename,Proj) &
              $\langle$-ed(Ename,Dept)$\rangle$ ($\langle$-ep(Ename,Proj)$\rangle$)

Observe that correctness is a property that can be ascribed not just to the translator, but also to the dynamic meaning of the dynamic view predicate defined by the translator. In this sense, the dynamic meaning of a dynamic base predicate is always semantically correct and acceptable.

Defining View Update Translators

This section describes syntactic transformations on view definitions that generate semantically correct and acceptable view update translators.
A view definition can be represented as:

$$p_v(\bar{u}) \leftarrow Cond \ \& \ q_1(\bar{t}_1)\&...\&q_p(\bar{t}_p)$$

where each q_i is either a rule predicate, a base predicate, or a view predicate. The literal corresponding to the view predicate is called a *view literal*. *Cond* is a condition formula, that is, a conjunction over zero or more of the predicates: equality, inequality, arithmetic comparisons. The terms in the literals and the condition formula together specify the join and selection conditions on the predicates used to construct the view.

Add Translators

Assume that we have a database description Δ that does not contain a translator for p_v, but it contains a view definition for p_v. We give below a set of transformations that generate semantically correct and acceptable add translators for p_v. The main part of the transformation consists of converting base and view literals to dynamic literals; this can be considered as the process of annotating the literals with "$+$" and "$\langle \ \rangle$." For example, a view or base literal, $q_i(\bar{t})$, could be annotated to become $\langle +q_i(\bar{t})\rangle$. Of course, this really creates a new formula in the well-defined formal language, DLP. Note that we are considering only translators that translate add requests to add requests. If the view definition is allowed to contain negative literals in its body, it may make sense to translate add requests to delete requests. We do not handle that case here, although it is certainly a possible extension of this work.

Transformations   Convert the view definition of the form:
$p_v(\bar{u}) \leftarrow Cond\&C$, into update rules of the form: $\langle +p_v(\bar{u})\rangle \leftarrow Cond \ \& \ \lambda(C)$, where λ is a syntactic mapping that maps a conjunction to several possible dynamic conjunctions. $\lambda(C)$ represents any one dynamic conjunction obtained by applying λ to C. Each possible value of $\lambda(C)$ gives rise to a different transformation. Let q_b be a base predicate symbol, q_v a view predicate symbol, and q_r a rule predicate symbol. Then λ can be defined as follows:

$$\lambda(q_r(\bar{t})) = q_r(\bar{t})$$
$$\lambda(q_r(\bar{t})\&C1) = q_r(\bar{t})\&\lambda(C1)$$
$$\lambda(q_b(\bar{t})) = q_b(\bar{t}) \text{ or } \langle +q_b(\bar{t})\rangle(true)$$
$$\lambda(q_b(\bar{t})\&C1) = q_b(\bar{t})\&\lambda(C1) \text{ or } \langle +q_b(\bar{t})\rangle(\lambda(C1))$$
$$\lambda(q_v(\bar{t})) = q_v(\bar{t}) \text{ or } \langle +q_v(\bar{t})\rangle(true)$$
$$\lambda(q_v(\bar{t})\&C1) = q_v(\bar{t})\&\lambda(C1) \text{ or } \langle +q_v(\bar{t})\rangle(\lambda(C1))$$

Also, $\lambda(true) = true$. The "or" represents a choice in the annotation of a base or view literal. All correct earlier examples conform to such transformations. If every dynamic literal $\langle +q(\bar{t})\rangle$ in the body of α makes $q(\bar{t})$ true after the update, then the translator is semantically correct and acceptable.

THEOREM 2

An add translator α, obtained by the above transformation procedure, is semantically correct and acceptable in a database description Δ, if the translators corresponding to the dynamic view predicates in the body of α are semantically correct and acceptable in Δ.

Proof: Observe that $\lambda(C)$ determines C uniquely. We first prove that if $(I,J) \in \bar{M}_d(\lambda(C)[s])$ then: (a) $J \models C[s]$, (b) If $I \models C[s]$ then $I = J$. We use induction on the structure of dynamic conjunctions.

Base Case: $\lambda(C) = L$, where L is a rule, base or view literal.

The result is obvious since $\bar{M}_d(L[s]) = \{(I,I): I \models L[s]\}$, and $C = \lambda(C) = L$.
Induction Step: Two cases arise.

Case 1: $\lambda(C) = \langle +q(\bar{t}) \rangle\ (\lambda(C1))$.

$\bar{M}_d(\lambda(C)[s]) = \{(I,J) : (I,K) \in M_d(+q(\bar{t})[s])$ and $(K,J) \in \bar{M}_d(\lambda(C1)[s])\}$. If q is a view predicate, then by the semantic correctness of its translator, we have that $K \models q(\bar{t})[s]$. If q is a base predicate, then also we have $K \models q(\bar{t})[s]$. By the induction hypothesis, $J \models C1[s]$. Since no deletions are permitted, J must have been obtained from K by adding one or more tuples to K. Therefore if $K \models q(\bar{t})[s]$ then $J \models q(\bar{t})[s]$. Then since $q(\bar{t})\&C1 = C$, we must have that $J \models C$. This proves Part (a). If q is a view predicate, then by the semantic acceptability of its translator, we must have that if $I \models q(\bar{t})[s]$ then $I = K$. If q is a base predicate, then the same result holds. By the inductive hypothesis, if $K \models C1[s]$ then $K = J$. Therefore, if $I \models C[s]$ then $I = K = J$. This proves Part (b).

Case 2: $\lambda(C) = L\ \&\ \lambda(C1)$. The proof is similar to the proof of Case 1.

By the definition of M_d, it follows from (a) and (b) that if $(I,J) \in \bar{M}_d(Cond \& \lambda(C)[s])$ then (i) $J \models (Cond\&C)[s]$, and (ii) If $I \models (Cond\&C)[s]$ then $I = J$. By Lemma 2, we have $M_d(+p_v(\bar{u})[s]) = \bar{M}_d((Cond\&\lambda(C))[s])$. Since the completion of the view definition is true in every state, $J \models p_v(\bar{u})[s]$ iff $J \models (Cond\&C)[s]$. Then from (i), we have that: If $(I,J) \in M_d(+p_v)(\bar{u})[s]$ then $J \models p_v(\bar{u})[s]$. This proves semantic correctness. From (ii), we have that: If $I \models p_v(\bar{u})[s]$ then $I = J$. This proves semantic acceptability. ∎

Delete Translators

Transformations   Convert the view definition of the form $p_v(\bar{u}) \leftarrow Cond\&C$, into update rules of the form: $\langle -p_v(\bar{u}) \rangle \leftarrow Cond\&C\ \&\ \mu(C)$, where μ is a syntactic mapping that maps a conjunction into several possible dynamic conjunctions. $\mu(C)$ represents one of these possible dynamic conjunctions, which is restricted to contain *at least one* dynamic literal. μ is defined as follows.

$$\mu(q_r(\bar{t})) = \textit{true}$$
$$\mu(q_r(t) \ \& \ C1) = \mu(C1)$$
$$\mu(q_b(\bar{t})) = \textit{true} \text{ or } \langle -q_b(\bar{t})\rangle(\textit{true})$$
$$\mu(q_b(\bar{t}) \ \&C1) = \mu(C1) \text{ or } \langle -q_b(\bar{t})\rangle(\mu(C1))$$
$$\mu(q_v(\bar{t})) = \textit{true} \text{ or } \langle -q_v(\bar{t})\rangle(\textit{true})$$
$$\mu(q_v(\bar{t})\&C1) = \mu(C1) \text{ or } \langle -q_v(\bar{t})\rangle(\mu(C1))$$

Also, $\mu(\textit{true}) = \textit{true}$. Consider the employee-manager view transformed into the delete translator δ.

```
em(Ename,Mgr) ←
        ed(Ename,Dept)   &
        dm(Dept,Mgr)
```

```
δ: ⟨-em(Ename,Mgr)⟩ ←
        ed(Ename,Dept) &
        dm(Dept,Mgr) & ⟨-dm(Dept,Mgr)⟩
```

In this case, the literals `dm(Dept,Mgr)` and `ed(Ename,Dept)` do not contribute to the semantic correctness of δ. However, such literals are specified in the transformation because, in general, they are necessary for semantic acceptability. For example, if we had the chosen to annotate `ed(Ename,Dept)` as well, then both these literals would be required.

Unfortunately not all the translators that can be defined in this way are semantically correct. In fact δ is not semantically correct! Consider the query $\leftarrow\langle -\text{em}(\text{sam,john})\rangle$. Consider a state I, in which `sam` works in two departments: `foundry` and `machines`. Also, `john` is the manager of `foundry` and `machines` in I. Since `dm` is a base relation, there is a state J accessible from I, which is identical to I, except that `john` is not the manager of `foundry` in J. Clearly, $M_d(-\text{em}(\text{sam,john}))$ contains the pair (I,J). However, in state J, `john` is the manager of `machines` and `sam` works in `machines`; therefore `john` is `sam`'s manager. This implies that the translator is not semantically correct. The problem here is that there is more than one pair of database tuples that satisfy the view tuple, while the translator deletes only one pair. For doing the translation correctly, it is necessary to treat `Dept` as being universally quantified in the body of the rule (the reason for this is explained in the proof below). This would require an extension of the language to handle universally quantified variables in queries. Instead, we choose to restrict the view definition, such that it has no variables in the body that do not occur in the head. This solves the problem. In database terminology, this corresponds to the restriction that the view is not allowed to project out non-selecting attributes.

THEOREM 3

A delete translator δ obtained by the above transformation is semantically correct and acceptable in Δ if

1. The translators corresponding to the dynamic view predicates in the body of δ are semantically correct and acceptable in Δ.

2. All the variables that occur in the body of δ also occur in its head.

Proof: Consider the general form of the view definition specified earlier in the section:

$$p_v(\bar{u}) \leftarrow Cond\& \; q_1(\bar{t}_1)\&...\&q_p(\bar{t}_p).$$

Recall that its completion is:

$$p_v(\bar{u}) \longleftrightarrow \exists X_1...,X_n Cond\&q_1(\bar{t}_1)\&...\&q_p(\bar{t}_p),$$

where X_i is a variable that occurs in the body but not in the head. Since Condition 2 of the Theorem 3 forbids such variables, they can be removed from the completion. Removing the variables and negating both sides we have the formula: $\neg p_v(\bar{u}) \longleftrightarrow \neg Cond \vee \neg q_1(\bar{t}_1) \vee...\vee \neg q_p(\bar{t}_p))$.

Note that if X_i's were not removed, they would be universally quantified in the above formula. Since the completion of the view definition is true in all states of an M-model, so is the previous formula. Let s be a variable assignment for all the variables in the rule. Then, in order to make $\neg p_v(\bar{u})[s]$ true, it is necessary to make at least one $\neg q_i(\bar{t}_i)[s]$ true. The given transformation converts at least one $q_i(\bar{t}_i)$ to $\langle - q_i(\bar{t}_i)\rangle$. Since the delete translator for q_i is correct, if (I,J) $\in M_d(- q_i(\bar{t}_i)[s])$, then $J \models \neg q_i(\bar{t}_i)[s])$. Therefore, δ is semantically correct. For semantic acceptability, observe that if a state $I \models \neg p_v(\bar{u})[s]$ then it must falsify at least one q_i literal. However, in this case, since the entire body of the view definition is included in δ, the body of δ can never be true in I—that is, there cannot exist a J such that $(I,J) \in M_d(- p_v(\bar{u})[s])$. Therefore, Condition (b) of Definition 5 is vacuously satisfied for all such I. Therefore, δ is semantically acceptable. ∎

Conclusion

We have developed a language that incorporates database update operations within the logic programming framework. The semantics of the language provides a theory of database updates. Its usefulness has been demonstrated, in part, by applying it to the problem of view updates. An efficient implementation of the language, suitable for writing large update programs, is required before this approach to database updates becomes practically useful. Several extensions to DLP are possible. It is relatively simple to extend DLP to handle delete queries with universally quantified variables. An extension of DLP that allows hypothetical reasoning is described in Manchanda [1987a].

Acknowledgments

We wish to thank the referees for their useful comments. We have benefited from discussions with Michael Kifer and Michael Gelfond.

References

1. Abiteboul, S. and Grahne, G. [1985] Update Semantics for Incomplete Databases, *Proceedings of VLDB 85*, Stockholm, 1–12.

2. Abiteboul, S. and Vianu, V. [1987] A Transaction Language Complete for Database Update and Specification, *Proceedings of the 5th ACM PODS*, San Diego, 260–268.

3. Agrawal, D., Bernstein, A. J., Gupta, P., and Sengupta, S. [1987] Distributed Optimistic Concurrency Control with Reduced Rollback, *Distributed Computing* **2**(1):45–59.

4. Apt, K. R., Blair, H., and Walker, A. [1988] Towards a Theory of Declarative Knowledge, in *Foundations of Deductive Databases and Logic Programming* (J. Minker, Ed.), Morgan Kaufmann Publishers, Los Altos, CA, 89–148.

5. Bancilhon, F. and Spyratos, N. [1981] Update Semantics of Relational Views, *ACM Transactions on Database Systems* **6**(4):557–575.

6. Carlson, C. R. and Arora, A. K. [1983] UPM: A Formal Tool for Expressing Database Update Semantics, in *Entity-Relationship Approach to Software Engineering* (C. G. Davis et al., Eds.), Elsevier Science Publishers.

7. Casanova, M. A. and Furtado, A. L. [1984] A Family of Temporal Languages for the Description of Transition Constraints, in *Advances in Database Theory*, Volume 2 (H. Gallaire, J. Minker, and J. M. Nicolas, Eds.), Plenum Press, New York, 211–238.

8. Clark, K. L. [1978] Negation as Failure, in *Logic and Databases* (H. Gallaire and J. Minker, Eds.), Plenum Press, New York, 293–322.

9. Dayal, U. and Bernstein, P. A. [1982] On the Correct Translation of Update Operations on Relational Views, *ACM Transactions on Database Systems* **8**(3): 381–416.

10. Emden, M. H. van and Kowalski, R. A. [1976] The Semantics of Predicate Logic as a Programming Language, *JACM* **23**(4):733–742.

11. Fagin, R., Kuper, G. M., Ullman, J. D., and Vardi, M. Y. [1986] Updating Logical Databases, in *Advances in Computing Research*, Volume 3 (P. Kanellakis, Ed.), Jai Press, 1–18.

12. Farinas, L. and Herzig, A. [1986] Reasoning about Database Updates, in *Workshop on Foundations of Deductive Databases and Logic Programming* (J. Minker, Ed.), Washington, DC, 53–67.

13. Furtado, A. L. and Sevcik, K. C. [1979] Permitting Updates through Views of Data Bases, *Information Systems* **4**(4):269–283.

14. Grant, J. and Minker, J. [1986] Answering Queries in Indefinite Databases and the Null Value problem, in *Advances in Computing Research* (P. Kanellakis, Ed.), 247–267.

15. Harel, D. [1979] *First-Order Dynamic Logic, Lecture Notes in Computer Science*, Springer-Verlag.

16. Imielinski, T. [1986] Automated Deduction in Databases with Incomplete Information, in *Workshop on Foundations of Deductive Databases and Logic Programming* (J. Minker, Ed.), Washington, DC, 242–283.

17. Imielinski, T. and Lipski, W. [1984] Incomplete Information in Relational Databases, *JACM* **31**(4):761–791.

18. Keller, A. [1985] Algorithms for Translating View Updates to Database Updates for Views Involving Selections, Projections, and Joins, in *Proceedings of the 4th ACM PODS*, 154–163.

19. Kowalski, R. [1978] Logic for Data Description, in *Logic and Databases* (H. Gallaire and J. Minker, Eds.), Plenum Press, New York, 77–103.

20. Kripke, S. [1963] Semantical Considerations on Modal Logic, *Acta Philosophica Fennica* **16**, Helsinki, 83–94.

21. Lifschitz, V. [1988] On the Declarative Semantics of Logic Programs with Negation, in *Foundations of Deductive Databases and Logic Programming*, (J. Minker, Ed.), Morgan Kaufmann Publishers, Los Altos, CA, 177–192.

22. Manchanda, S. [1987a] *A Dynamic Logic Programming Language*, Technical Report 87/01, SUNY at Stony Brook, Stony Brook, NY 11794.

23. Manchanda, S. [1987b] *A Dynamic Logic Programming Language for Relational Updates*, SUNY at Stony Brook, Stony Brook, NY 11794. Ph.D thesis.

24. Manchanda, S., Sengupta, S., and Warren, D. S. [1986] *Concurrent Updates in a Prolog Database System*, Technical Report 86/28, SUNY at Stony Brook, Stony Brook, NY 11794.

25. Pratt, V. R. [1976] Semantical Considerations on Floyd-Hoare Logic, *Proceedings of the 17th IEEE FOCS*, 109–121.

26. Przymusinksi, T. C. [1988] On the Semantics of Stratified Databases, in *Foundations of Deductive Databases and Logic Programming* (J. Minker, Ed.), Morgan Kaufmann Publishers, Los Altos, CA, 193–216.

27. Reiter, R. [1986] A Sound and Sometimes Complete Query Evaluation Algorithm for Relational Databases with Null Values, *JACM* **33**(2):349–370.

28. Van Gelder, A. [1988] Negation as Failure Using Tight Derivations for General Logic Programs, in *Foundations of Deductive Databases and Logic Programming* (J. Minker, Ed.), Morgan Kaufmann Publishers, Los Altos, CA, 149–176.

29. Warren, D. S. [1984] Database Updates in Pure Prolog, *Proceedings of the International Conference on Fifth Generation Computer Systems*, ICOT, Tokyo, 244–253.

30. Wilkins, M. W. [1986] A Model-Theoretic Approach to Updating Logical Databases, *Proceedings of the 5th ACM PODS*, 224–234.

31. Yahya, A. and Henschen, L. J. [1985] Deduction in Non-Horn Databases, in *Journal of Automated Reasoning* **1**(1):141–160.

11

Compiling the GCWA in Indefinite Deductive Databases

Lawrence J. Henschen
Hyung-Sik Park
Electrical Engineering and Computer Science
Northwestern University, Evanston, IL

Abstract

This paper presents several fundamental results on compiling the GCWA (Generalized Closed World Assumption) in IDDB (Indefinite Deductive Databases). We do not allow function symbols, but we do allow non-Horn clauses. Further, although the GCWA is used to derive negative assumptions, we do allow also negative clauses to occur explicitly. We show a fundamental relationship between indefiniteness and GCWA inference. We consider three representation alternatives to separate the CDB (Clausal DB) from the RDB (Relational DB). We present the basic ideas and some effective ways for compiling GCWA inference on the CDB and evaluating it through the RDB in a non-recursive IDDB. We also present a basic idea on compiling the GCWA in a recursive IDDB by a pattern generation method. Finally, we introduce decomposition and evaluation theorems to evaluate disjunctive and conjunctive ground queries.

Introduction

The reader is assumed to be familiar with the logic approach to databases, especially with the concept of query compilation relative to an intensional database (IDB) (Henschen and Naqvi [1984], Reiter [1978a], Ullman [1985]).

395

This paper presents several fundamental results on compiling generalized closed world (GCWA) inference, i.e., generating queries that will correctly answer a question, such as "Can we assume a ground formula F to be false?", in an IDDB (Indefinite Deductive Database) under the GCWA (Generalized Closed World Assumption) (Minker [1982]). An IDDB is a deductive database that allows negative clauses and non-Horn clauses in addition to Horn clauses. (As in other deductive database research, we do not allow function symbols.) Since the volume of negative facts may be too huge to be explicitly represented, deductive databases have traditionally treated negative information implicitly. Although the negation of a ground atom can be assumed to be true straightforwardly by negation as (finite) failure (Clark [1978], Reiter [1978b]) in a Horn database, a generalized metarule (Bossu and Siegel [1985], Minker [1982]) must be used in a DB with non-Horn clauses. The GCWA is based on the concept of a minimal model. (All references to interpretations and models in this paper will mean Herbrand interpretations and models.) A minimal model is a model of a database such that no proper subset of the true atoms is also a model of that database. The semantic definition of GCWA says that a ground atom A is false with respect to IDDB under the GCWA iff it is false in every minimal model of IDDB. It is very difficult to evaluate this condition directly. We therefore introduce a compiling technique based on an equivalent syntactic condition to help overcome the computational problems and also to separate deduction from data retrieval.

Three methods for dealing with the GCWA have been reported recently. First, Grant and Minker [1986] (GM) developed an algebraic method for testing if a candidate tuple $a1 + \ldots + an$ is an answer to a query $Q(y)$; that is, if DB $\vdash Q(a1) \vee \ldots \vee Q(an)$. This is a much broader problem than the YES/NO type questions discussed in the present paper. Second, Yahya and Henschen (YH) (Yahya and Henschen [1985]) developed a deductive method that can determine whether or not a conjunction of ground atoms can be assumed false in a non-Horn database under an extended GCWA. Third, Bossu and Siegel (BS) (Bossu and Siegel [1985]) developed a deductive method that can answer a query by subimplication. Subimplication is a generalization of the GCWA that handles databases having no minimal model. It reduces to the GCWA if the database has no function symbols. Of the three methods, YH is most closely related to the present work. However, these three methods have the following weak points: GM requires the system to generate all database models; YH requires the query to be decomposed into several subqueries that must all be proved at query evaluation time; BS requires many subsumption tests in the computation of characteristic clauses and characteristic formulas. None of these methods seems practical enough for application to large databases.

Very closely related to the notion of the GCWA is that of negation-as-failure in logic programming. The recent results on stratified programs (for example, Apt et al., [1988], Lifschitz [1988], Van Gelder [1988], and

Przymusinski [1988]) have clarified the theory of negation-as-failure and show the clear distinction between these two approaches to non-Horn clauses. Consider the two forms

$$P \rightarrow Q \vee R$$

and

$$P \And \neg R \rightarrow Q.$$

For the second formula to be part of a stratified logic program, all the clauses that define R positively must occur in an earlier level of the program. That is, it must be possible to prove all positive instances of R that are desired without using the above rule. In essence, this imposes an implied ordering on the predicates Q and R; R is to be considered first, and only if R fails does the program infer Q. This may indeed be the desired meaning for many applications. For example, in the rule

$$DEPT(x,CS) \And -CHMN(x) \rightarrow LOAD(x,4)$$

the meaning is to check *first* that x is not the chairman before concluding that the teaching load is 4. The important theoretical result for stratified programs is that a *unique* minimal model can be constructed by iterated minimization—first minimize the predicates in level O, then in level 1, etc. Unfortunately, in many situations it is not possible to assign a priority between Q and R. For example, in the rule

$$FB(x,A) \And MB(x,O) \rightarrow BP(x,A) \vee BP(x,O),$$

x's possible blood type may be A or O without there being any priority or preference. In such cases there is no reasonable candidate for a unique minimal model, and there are four possible values for a ground atom, namely, true, provably false, assumably false, and indefinite. The question of when a ground atom can be assumed false requires algorithms to compute negative information under the GCWA.

A major difficulty in computing with the GCWA is that ordinary resolution applied to an IDDB cannot distinguish between ground atoms that are indefinite and those that can be assumed false under the GCWA. This difficulty will be illustrated by an example in the next section. In order to overcome this problem we will investigate the relationships between indefiniteness and GCWA inference in an IDDB. We will also discuss certain tradeoffs among three schemes for representing explicit negative data. We then will develop the GCWA inference engine by introducing a compilation technique for ID-

DBs similar in spirit to compilation for Horn databases (Chang [1981], Henschen and Naqvi [1984], Reiter [1978a]).

Indefinite Databases and GCWA Inference

In this paper, we use the following notations: P and R, ... for arbitrary predicate symbols; u, v, w, x, ... for vectors of variables; a, b, c, ... for vectors of constants; CL for a clause; K for a ground clause; "DB $\vdash Q$" for "Q is a logical consequence of DB"; "DB $\not\vdash Q$" for "Q is not a logical consequence of DB"; "DB $\vdash_{GCWA} \neg Q$" for "$\neg Q$ can be assumed by GCWA"; and "DB $\not\vdash_{GCWA} \neg Q$" for "$\neg Q$ cannot be assumed by GCWA." A clause may be written as a list of literals without commas, or it may be written with the symbol "v" for OR to emphasize the structure of the clause.

A deductive database is an extension of the proof theoretic relational DB (Reiter [1984]) in which new facts may be derived from the set of explicit facts, called the EDB(Extensional DB), by using the deductive general laws, called the IDB(Intensional DB). We assume throughout that any database under consideration is consistent. There are two kinds of deductive databases relevant to our study—DDDB (Definite Deductive Databases) and IDDB (Indefinite Deductive Databases)—and their properties are quite different. A DDDB allows only function-free Horn definite clauses, whereas an IDDB allows function-free non-Horn clauses as well as negative clauses. For an extensive survey of deductive databases, refer to Gallaire, Minker, and Nicolas [1984].

Since a typical database will have vast amounts of negative information, such information should be implicitly represented. Reiter [1978b] developed the *closed world assumption* (CWA) that says that a negative ground unit clause, $\neg P$, can be assumed to be true for a DDDB if P cannot be derived from DDDB. However, the CWA leads to inconsistencies when used with an IDDB. For example, let IDDB = $\{P\ Q\}$. IDDB $\not\vdash P$. Hence IDDB $\vdash_{CWA}$ $\neg P$. Similarly for Q. However, IDDB $\cup \{\neg P, \neg Q\}$ is inconsistent. Minker [1982] suggested *semantic* and *syntactic definitions* of the *GCWA* for handling negative information implicitly in an IDDB and showed that they are equivalent. The GCWA, like the CWA, is based on the concept of a minimal model. Recall that an (Herbrand) interpretation is specified by listing the ground atoms that are to be true. Then a *minimal model* of a database DB is a model of DB such that no proper subset of the set of true atoms is also a model of DB. It is easy to show that a ground atom A is *true* in every model of DB iff it is true in every minimal model of DB.

SEMANTIC DEFINITION OF GCWA
A ground atom A can be assumed to be false with respect to IDDB iff A is not in any minimal model of IDDB. ∎

SYNTACTIC DEFINITION OF GCWA
A ground atom A can be assumed to be false with respect to IDDB iff DB $\not\vdash$ A and for any positive ground clause K, IDDB $\vdash$ K if IDDB $\vdash$ A v K. ∎

In an indefinite database IDDB, then, there are three possibilities for a ground atom A:

1.   IDDB $\vdash$ A, in which case A is in all models (minimal or otherwise), and we say that A is true in IDDB.

2. A is in no minimal model of IDDB, and we say that A is false in IDDB.

3.   There are minimal models $M1$ and $M2$ such that A is in $M1$ and not in $M2$, and we say that A is indefinite in IDDB.

Note that in case 2 there are two possibilities, namely, A is no model at all so that A is provably false (DB $\vdash$ $\neg A$), and A is in no minimal model so that it can be assumed false by the GCWA.

EXAMPLE 1
Let DB $= \{P\ Q, R\ S, \neg S, R\ T\}$. Then, there are two minimal models of DB: $M_1 = \{P, R\}$ and $M_2 = \{Q, R\}$. Consider the following unit queries.

$\mathbf{Q_1}$ $= R$. This query is *true* in DB.
Semantic justification: R is in M_1 and M_2, and hence in all models of DB.
Syntactic justification: DB $\vdash$ R.

$\mathbf{Q_2}$ $= P$. This query is *indefinite* in DB.
Semantic justification: P is in M_1, but not in M_2.
Syntactic justification: DB $\not\vdash$ P. However, DB $\vdash$ P v Q, but DB $\not\vdash$ Q.

$\mathbf{Q_3}$ $= S$. This query is *provably false* in DB.
Semantic justification: S is not in any model of DB.
Syntactic justification: DB $\vdash$ $\neg S$.

$\mathbf{Q_4}$ $= T$. This query can be *assumed false* in DB by GCWA.
Semantic justification: T is not in M_1 or in M_2.
Syntactic justification: DB $\vdash$ $T R$ but DB $\not\vdash$ R.
Hence, there is no K such that DB $\vdash$ T K, and DB $\not\vdash$ K. Also, DB $\not\vdash$ T. ∎

As Q_2 and Q_4 show, there is no difference between the indefinite and assumed false cases when the ordinary approach (of trying to prove the query or its negation) is applied. Hence, we need to develop specialized inference engines to evaluate the GCWA. We introduce some basic notions for analyzing indefiniteness as follows:

DEFINITION 1
PIGC[DB] is the set of positive, non-Horn clauses C such that

1.   DB $\vdash C$ and

2.   no proper subclause of C is derivable from DB.

If A is a ground atom, then *PIGC*[A] consists of members of PIGC[DB] that contain A. A clause *pigc* denotes a member of PIGC[DB]. When DB is clear from context, we write PIGC. ■

We introduce three auxiliary functions.

DEFINITION 2

True[A] iff DB $\vdash A$.

Indef[A] iff A is indefinite in DB.

False[A] iff NOT True[A] and NOT Indef[A]. ■

Notice that the above makes no distinction between provably false and false by assumption. Our main purpose is to determine which of the three values Q has—true, false, or indefinite. If it was important for a user to distinguish between the two false cases, additional tests would have to be made.

LEMMA 1 (MINKER'S LEMMA (Minker [1982]*)*
Let CP be the set of all positive ground clauses derivable from DB. Then CP and DB have the same minimal models. ■

LEMMA 2
A ground atom A is indefinite iff there is a positive ground clause K such that A v K is in PIGC. ■

THEOREM 1 (INDEFINITENESS THEOREM)
Indef[A] iff PIGC[A] is not empty. ■

THEOREM 2 (GCWA THEOREM)

False[A] iff NOT True[A] and PIGC[A] is empty. ∎

Proofs: Proofs of all theorems are provided in the appendix.

Theorems 1 and 2 say that the PIGC characterizes the indefiniteness of an IDDB. That is, it seems unavoidable to consider PIGC in some form or other for answering Indef[A] and False[A]. However, since it is obviously infeasible to derive PIGC in general, we should develop an appropriate mechanism to handle only PIGC[A], that is, the portion of PIGC relevant to the atom being evaluated.

Compilation and Representation Alternatives

In this section, we introduce the two important sets NH and PSUB, which provide a basis for compilation, and consider three alternative representations to separate deduction from retrieval.

Basic Concept of Compilation

The goal of compiling is to separate the deductive process from the data retrieval process. For the problem at hand, namely determining PIGC[A], we need to find which resolvents of IDB clauses could lead to positive ground clauses containing A when data from the database is taken into consideration. Further, such a positive ground clause must not be subsumed by another positive clause. A simple example will illustrate the basic approach. Suppose the database contained the clauses

$$\neg P(x) \neg Q(y) \neg S(z) R(x,y,z) T(x,y,z),$$

$$\neg O(w) S(w) U(w), \quad \text{and}$$

$$\neg M(v) T(v,10,u) U(u),$$

where P, Q, M, and O are simple relations stored in the EDB. Suppose we had the query, "Is $R(JOHN,10,TOYS)$ indefinite or false?" The resolvent, $\neg P(x) \neg Q(y) \neg O(z) R(x,y,z) T(x,y,z) U(z)$, could produce a positive ground clause containing $R(JOHN,10,TOYS)$ if the appropriate data were in the relations P, Q, and O. On the other hand, if $JOHN$ were in M, the third clause would derive a positive ground clause subsuming the one containing $R(JOHN,10,TOYS)$; that is, $R(JOHN,10,TOYS)$ $T(JOHN,10,TOYS)$ $U(TOYS)$ would not be in PIGC after all. Thus, we may answer false or indefinite after retrieving the appropriate data from P, Q, O, and M and testing the resulting clauses for subsumption. Notice that if the third clause had contained $T(v,25,u)$ instead, there would be no possibility for subsumption, and $R(JOHN,10,TOYS)$ $T(JOHN,10,TOYS)$ $U(TOYS)$ would definitely be in PIGC. As with regular query compilation, the above kinds of analyses can be carried out without specific values for the attributes of R, and the deductive analysis separated from the data retrieval.

Basic Notions for Compilation

In order to carry out the deductive analysis for compiling queries with respect to PIGC, we identify certain sets of clauses. The IIDB(Indefinite IDB) consists of indefinite general clauses. The DIDB(Definite IDB) consists of definite general clauses. The IEDB(Indefinite EDB) consists of non-Horn ground clauses. The DEDB(Definite EDB) consists of ground atoms. As will be seen below, the precise details of compiling will depend on whether negative clauses and clauses in IEDB are used at compile time or are to be handled at evaluation time. Therefore, we call *CDB(Clausal Database)* the set of clauses that are to be used in the compile phase and *RDB(Relational Database)* the clauses to be used at evaluation time.

DEFINITION 3

For an arbitrary predicate P, $NH[P]$ is the set of non-Horn clauses, C, such that

1. $DB \vdash C$,

2. C contains a positive occurrence of P,

3. the negative literals of C all refer to EDB predicates   and

4. C is not subsumed by any clause derivable from CDB. ■

DEFINITION 4

Let a clause CL1 be written as CLR1 v CLC1 where CLR1 contains all the literals of CL1 which can be resolved against the RDB relations (i.e., negative literals for which there are positive RDB relations and positive literals for which there are negative RDB relations). Similarly, let CL2 = CLR2 v CLC2. Then CL1 *potentially subsumes* CL2 iff CLC1 subsumes CLC2. ■

The idea is that, while CL1 may not subsume CL2 in the ordinary way, a clause obtained by resolving CL1 against the RDB could subsume one obtained by resolving CL2 against the RDB. For example, $\neg M(v)$ $T(v,10,u)$ $U(u)$ from the previous section potentially subsumes $\neg P(x)$ $\neg Q(y)$ $\neg O(z)$ $R(x,y,z)$ $T(x,y,z)$ $U(z)$ because, depending on the data in relations P, Q, O, and M, the derived instance of $T(v,10,u)$ $U(u)$, could subsume the derived instance of $T(x,y,z)$ $R(x,y,z)$ $U(z)$ as discussed previously. Thus, P, Q, O, and M are not considered in testing for potential subsumption. If we had negative ground unit clauses in the RDB, the corresponding positive literals would also not be considered.

DEFINITION 5
PSUB[cl] denotes the set of clauses which potentially subsumes the clause cl and is derivable from the CDB. If S is a set of clauses, *PSUB[S]* denotes the union of PSUB[cl] for each cl in S. ■

The sets NH[P] and PSUB[NH[P]] can be used to generate PIGC[A] for a ground atom A whose predicate is P if the negative data is used properly.

Representation Theorem

To see why the negative data plays a crucial role, we consider three representation alternatives.

REPRESENTATION 1

(a)   CDB = IIDB $\cup$ DIDB $\cup$ negative nonunit clauses

(b)   RDB = IEDB $\cup$ DEDB $\cup$ negative unit ground facts

REPRESENTATION 2

(a)   CDB = IIDB $\cup$ DIDB $\cup$ IEDB $\cup$ negative nonunit clauses

(b)   RDB = DEDB $\cup$ negative unit ground facts

REPRESENTATION 3

(a)   CDB = IIDB $\cup$ DIDB $\cup$ IEDB $\cup$ negative clauses

(b)   RDB = DEDB

EXAMPLE 2
Let DB =

{1. $\dashv P(x)\ Q(x)$,

2. $\dashv U(x)\ S(x)\ V(x)$,

3. $\dashv T(x)\ P(x)\ R(x)\ S(x)$,

4. $\dashv Q(a)$,

5. $\dashv S(a)$,

6. $T(a)$,

7. $U(a)$,

8. $\dashv V(b)$}.

In *Representation 2*, CDB = {1,2,3} and RDB {4,5,6,7,8}. Then

$$\mathrm{NH}[P] = \{\dashv T(x)\ P(x)\ R(x)\ S(x)\}$$

and

$$\mathrm{PSUB[NH}[P]] = \{\dashv U(x)\ S(x)\ V(x),\ \dashv T(x)\ Q(x)\ R(x)\ S(x)\}.$$

$T(a)$ and $\dashv S(a)$ are in RDB, so $P(a)\ R(a)$ is derivable from NH[P]. But $T(a)$, $\dashv S(a)$, and $\dashv Q(a)$ are also in RDB, making $R(a)$ derivable as well (from the second psub clause). Therefore, $P(a)\ R(a)$ is not in PIGC. Hence PIGC[$P(a)$] is empty.

In *Representation 3*, CDB = {1,2,3,4,5,8} and RDB = {6,7}. Then, performing resolution on the CDB yields the following resolvents:

$\dashv T(x)\ R(x)\ S(x)\ Q(x)$,

$\dashv P(a)$,

$\dashv U(a)\ V(a)$,

$\dashv U(b)\ S(b)$, and

$\dashv T(a)\ R(a)$.

Hence, NH[P] = {$\dashv T(x)\ P(x)\ R(x)\ S(x)$}, as before, but PSUB[NH[P]] = {$\dashv T(a)\ R(a),\ \dashv U(b)\ S(b)$}. As before, ⌐IGC[$P(a)$] is empty. ∎

In Example 2, notice that the clause $\dashv U(x)S(x)V(x)$ should be in PSUB[NH[P]] for Representation 2, since the literal $V(x)$ may be resolved with the negative data in the RDB, and these resolutions are made at evaluation time, not at compile time. In Representation 3, any negative information about V would have to be in the CDB and would therefore be resolved at compile time. Notice also that clause 2 could lead to a Horn clause with positive literal over S because there is explicit negative information about V which can remove the second positive literal. Thus, in Representation 2, clause 2 would be included in the set of compiled clauses that could prove S atoms true. Of course, in Representation 3, any such negative information over V would be present in the CDB and used at compile time to actually generate the Horn clause.

THEOREM 3 (REPRESENTATION THEOREM)

Let A be a ground atom whose predicate is P.

1. In Representation 1, PIGC[A] of DB may not be equivalent to PIGC[A] of RDB $\cup$ NH[P] $\cup$ PSUB[NH[P]].

2. In Representation 2, PIGC[A] of DB is equivalent to PIGC[A] of RDB $\cup$ NH[P] $\cup$ PSUB[NH[P]].

3. In Representation 3, PIGC[A] of DB is equivalent to PIGC[A] of RDB $\cup$ NH[P] $\cup$ PSUB[NH[P]]. ■

The *Representation Theorem* indicates that Representations 2 and 3 enable us to compile the CDB with respect to NH[P] and PSUB[NH[P]] before evaluation time. In order to avoid extra overhead in the deduction at compile time, we may prefer *Representation 1*. However, the ordinary relational table is not adequate for storing indefinite clauses, and additional operations would be needed at evaluation time. Representation 2 needs an additional RDB operation for handling the negative unit ground clauses, while Representation 3 needs additional resolutions on the CDB. When the negative ground facts are updated, some modifications to the compiled programs are needed in Representation 3 but not in Representation 2. However, when the volume of explicit negative ground facts is not very large and updates to them are not frequent, Representation 3 may be preferred, since it reduces the size of NH[P] and PSUB[NH[P]], and it incorporates the traditional relational DB as the RDB.

Compiling the GCWA in a Non-Recursive IDDB

Based on the preceding remarks, one approach to compilation, then, is to generate all possible resolvents from clauses in the CDB and decide for each predicate P which clauses could verify True[A] for a ground atom over P and which ones belong to NH[*P*] and PSUB[NH[*P*]]. As indicated, this is determined by which representation is used. This may be impractical, or even impossible, in more complicated cases. For example, the two clauses

$$\neg P(x)\, Q(x,a1)\, Q(x,a2) \text{ and } \neg Q(u,v)\, \neg Q(v,w)\, R(u,w)$$

have a resolvent

$$\neg P(y)\, \neg Q(a2,x)\, R(y,x)\, Q(y,a1),$$

which is a recursive rule and produces infinitely many resolvents. Even in the absence of such situations, there may in general be many clauses derivable from the CDB during compilation. We show in the following sections that in many of these situations not all clauses derivable in the compile step are necessary to answer Indef[*A*]. We will develop *reduced NH* sets for certain cases and prove that if an excluded clause can verify the indefiniteness of *A*, then one of the retained clauses can also verify its indefiniteness. We write NHr[*P*] to denote a subset of NH[*P*] obtained by any of these reductions.

NH Reduction

In this section, we assume that DB is in Representation 3. If DB is in Representation 2, some modifications to the previous definition of PSUB are needed to apply the following NH-reduction theorems. This will be discussed later in "Explicit Negative Facts and NH Reduction."

Primitive Types of Clausal Branch

In the inference network of the CDB, we introduce five primitive types of clausal branch:

Type of branch	Natural logic form	Clausal logic form
Linear chain	$P \rightarrow Q$	$\neg P \vee Q$
Forward OR branch	$P \rightarrow Q$ or R	$\neg P \vee Q \vee R$
Backward OR branch	P or $Q \rightarrow R$	$\neg P \vee R, \neg Q \vee R$
Forward AND branch	$P \rightarrow Q$ and R	$\neg P \vee Q, \neg P \vee R$
Backward AND branch	P and $Q \rightarrow R$	$\neg P \vee \neg Q \vee R$

Linear Chain Reduction

THEOREM 4 (LINEAR CHAIN REDUCTION THEOREM)
Let CDB contain a set of clauses of the form

$$\{P1 \rightarrow P2, P2 \rightarrow P3, ..., Pn{-}1 \rightarrow Pn\},$$

where $P2$, $P3$, ..., and Pn do not appear in any other clauses. Then, $NH[Pn] = NH[P2]$ and $PSUB[NH[Pn]] = PSUB1 \cup PSUB^*$, where PSUB1 denotes the set of clauses obtained by replacing $P1$ in $PSUB[P1]$ by Pn and PSUB* is the set $\{P1 \rightarrow Pn, P2 \rightarrow Pn, ..., Pn{-}1 \rightarrow Pn\}$. ∎

Theorem 4 does not exclude clauses but it does show that linear chains do not increase the size of $NH[Pn]$.

Forward OR-branch Reduction

THEOREM 5 (FORWARD OR-BRANCH REDUCTION THEOREM I)
Let CDB contain

1. $P(x) \rightarrow Q(x,a_1) \vee Q(x,a_2) \vee ... \vee Q(x,a_n)$ and

2. $Q(x,y) \rightarrow R(x,y)$,

where predicate symbols P, Q, and R may have arbitrary arguments and only common variables are explicitly represented. Then for any constant a, $Indef[Q(a,a_i)]$ can be determined from

$$P(x) \rightarrow Q(x,a_1) \vee ... \vee Q(x,a_{i-1}) \vee R(x,a_i) \vee$$

$$Q(x,a_{i+1}) \vee ... \vee Q(x,a_n),$$

and clauses obtained by resolving 2 with 1 more than once can be excluded from $NH[Q]$. ∎

EXAMPLE 3
Let CDB =

$\{$1. FATHER(a,c) FATHER(b,c),

2. FATHER$(x,y) \rightarrow$ PARENT$(x,y)\}$,

where FATHER is a base relation in RDB (and the P-part of clause 1 is empty). Then,

$$\text{NHr[PARENT]} = \{\text{PARENT}(a,c)\ \text{FATHER}(b,c),$$
$$\text{FATHER}(a,c)\ \text{PARENT}(b,c)\},\quad \text{but}$$
$$\text{NH[PARENT]} = \text{NHr[PARENT]} \cup \{\text{PARENT}(a,c)\ \text{PARENT}(b,c)\}.\ \blacksquare$$

THEOREM 6 (FORWARD OR-BRANCH REDUCTION THEOREM II)
Let CDB contain

1. $P(x) \rightarrow Q1(x,a_1) \vee Q2(x,a_2) \vee \ldots \vee Qn(x,a_n)$
2. $Q1(x,y) \rightarrow R1(x,y)$

$\ldots \ldots$

$n + 1.\ Qn(x,y) \rightarrow Rn(x,y),$

where different predicate symbols P, $Q1$, ..., Qn, $R1$, ..., Rn may have arbitrary arguments. Then for any constant a, $\text{Indef}[Ri(a,a_i)]$ can be computed from

$$P(x) \rightarrow Q1(x,a_1) \vee .. \vee Qi-1(x,a_{i-1}) \vee Ri(x,a_i) \vee Qi + 1(x,a_{i+1}) \vee \ldots \vee Qn(x,a_n),$$

and clauses obtained by resolving 1 with more than one of 2 through $n + 1$ can be excluded from each NH[Ri]. $\blacksquare$

EXAMPLE 4
Let CDB =

$\{1.\ \text{PHANTOM}(a)\ \text{MIG}(a),$

$\quad 2.\ \text{PHANTOM}(x) \rightarrow \text{FRIEND}(x),$

$\quad 3.\ \text{MIG}(x) \rightarrow \text{ENEMY}(x),$

$\quad 4.\ \text{ENEMY}(x) \rightarrow \text{DOWN}(x)\},$

where PHANTOM and MIG are the base relations in the RDB (and the P-part is again empty). Then,

$$\text{NHr[FRIEND]} = \{\text{FRIEND}(a)\ \text{MIG}(a)\},$$

while

NH[FRIEND] = {FRIEND(a) MIG(a),

FRIEND(a) ENEMY(a),

FRIEND(a) DOWN(a)}.

PSUB[NHr[FRIEND]] = {PHANTOM(x) $\rightarrow$ FRIEND(x),
MIG(x) $\rightarrow$ ENEMY(x)}. ■

Backward OR-Branch Reduction

THEOREM 7 (BACKWARD OR-BRANCH REDUCTION THEOREM)
Let CDB contain

1. $P1(x) \rightarrow Q11(x,a_{11}) \vee Q12(x,a_{12}) \vee \dots \vee Q1s1(x,a_{1s1})$
2. $P2(x) \rightarrow Q21(x,a_{21}) \vee Q22(x,a_{22}) \vee \dots \vee Q2s2(x,a_{2s2})$

. . . .

m. $Pm(x) \rightarrow Qm1(x,a_{m1}) \vee Qm2(x,a_{m2}) \vee \dots \vee Qmsm(x,a_{msm})$

$m + 1$. $Q11(x,y) \rightarrow R(x,y)$

$m + 2$. $Q21(x,y) \rightarrow R(x,y)$

. . . . . .

$2m$. $Qm1(x,y) \rightarrow R(x,y)$,

where the Qij's may or may not be distinct. Then, a reduced set for NH[R] can be taken as NHr1 $\cup$ NHr2 $\cup \dots \cup$ NHrm, where NHri denotes a reduced Nhi for

CDBi = {$Pi(x) \rightarrow Qi1(x,a_{i1}) \vee Qi2(x,a_{i2}) \vee \dots \vee Qisi(x,a_{isi})$,
$Qi1(x,y) \rightarrow R(x,y)$}

and NHri can be computed by the Forward OR-Branch Theorem I or II depending on whether the Qij's are all alike or not. ■

Forward AND-Branch Reduction

THEOREM 8 (FORWARD AND-BRANCH REDUCTION THEOREM)
Let CDB contain

1. $P(x) \rightarrow Q1(x,a_1) \vee Q2(x,a_2) \vee \dots \vee Qn(x,a_n)$
2. $Q1(x,y) \rightarrow R1(x,y)$

3. $Q1(x,y) \rightarrow R2(x,y)$

$\cdots\cdots$

$m + 1.$ $Q1(x,y) \rightarrow Rm(x,y)$

Then clauses obtained by resolving clause 1 with a clause from 2 through $m + 1$ other than clause $i + 1$ can be excluded from NH[Ri]. ∎

This theorem says that a forward AND-branch can also be treated independently as a forward OR-branch.

Backward AND-Branch Reduction

LEMMA 3
Let CDB contain

1. $P(x) \rightarrow Q(x,a_1) \vee \ldots \vee Q(x,a_n)$
2. $Q(x_1,x_2) \,\&\, Q(x_2,x_3) \rightarrow R(x_1,x_3).$

Then clauses derived from 1 and 2 which contain more than one R are not needed to compute Indef[$R(c1,c2)$]. ∎

The significant effect of Lemma 3 is illustrated with the following example. Let CDB =

$\{1.$ $P(x) \rightarrow Q(x,a_1) \vee Q(x,a_2)$

$2.$ $Q(x_1,x_2) \,\&\, Q(x_2,x_3) \rightarrow R(x_1,x_3)\}.$

Then, NHr consists of only 8 clauses, while NH consists of infinitely many clauses since it has a recursive literal over Q.
NHr =

$\{3.$ $(2,1)\, \neg Q(a_2,x_1)\, \neg P(x_2)\, R(x_2,x_1)\, Q(x_2,a_1)$

$4.$ $(2,1)\, \neg Q(a_1,x_1)\, \neg P(x_2)\, R(x_2,x_1)\, Q(x_2,a_2)$

$5.$ $(2,1)\, \neg Q(x_1,x_2)\, \neg P(x_2)\, R(x_1,a_2)\, Q(x_2,a_1)$

$6.$ $(2,1)\, \neg Q(x_1,x_2)\, \neg P(x_2)\, R(x_1,a_1)\, Q(x_2,a_2)$

$7.$ $(3,1)\, \neg P(x_1)\, \neg P(a_2)\, R(x_1,a_2)\, Q(x_1,a_1)\, Q(a_2,a_1)$

$8.$ $(3,1)\, \neg P(x_1)\, \neg P(a_2)\, R(x_1,a_1)\, Q(x_1,a_1)\, Q(a_2,a_2)$

$9.$ $(4,1)\, \neg P(x_1)\, \neg P(a_1)\, R(x_1,a_2)\, Q(x_1,a_2)\, Q(a_1,a_1)$

$10.$ $(4,1)\, \neg P(x_1)\, \neg P(a_1)\, R(x_1,a_1)\, Q(x_1,a_2)\, Q(a_1,a_2)\}$

Notice that this type of DB cannot be treated simply since each clause in NHr has a recursive literal over Q. In a later section we present a basic idea on compiling the GCWA in a simple recursive IDDB.

EXAMPLE 5
Let CDB =

$$\{1.\ F(a,c)\ F(b,c) \qquad 2.\ \neg F(x,y)\ \neg F(y,z)\ GF(x,z)\}.$$

Then, NH[GF] =

$$\{3.\ \neg F(c,x_1)\ GF(b,x_1)\ F(a,c) \qquad 4.\ \neg F(c,x_1)\ GF(a,x_1)\ F(b,c)$$

$$5.\ \neg F(x_1,b)\ GF(x_1,c)\ F(a,c) \qquad 6.\ \neg F(x_1,a)\ GF(x_1,c)\ F(b,c)$$

$$7.\ \neg F(c,x_1)\ GF(b,x_1)\ \neg F(x_2,a)\ GF(x_2,c)$$

$$8.\ \neg F(c,x_1)\ GF(b,x_1)\ \neg F(c,x_2)\ GF(a,x_2)$$

$$9.\ \neg F(c,x_1)\ GF(a,x_1)\ \neg F(x_2,b)\ GF(x_2,c)$$

$$10.\ \neg F(x_1,b)\ GF(x_1,b)\ \neg F(x_2,a)\ GF(x_2,c)\},$$

NHr[GF] contains only clauses 3–6. Notice that in this case NH[GF] consists of a finite number of clauses because clause 1 is ground. ∎

LEMMA 4
Let CDB contain

$$1.\ P(x) \rightarrow Q(x,a_1) \vee \ldots \vee Q(x,a_n)$$

$$2.\ Q(x_1,x_2)\ \&\ Q(x_2,x_3)\ \&\ \ldots\ \&\ Q(x_{m-1},x_m) \rightarrow R(x_1,x_m).$$

Then resolvents of 1 and 2 containing more than one R can be excluded from NH[R]. ∎

THEOREM 9 (BACKWARD AND-BRANCH REDUCTION THEOREM I)
Let CDB contain

$$1.\ P1(x) \rightarrow Q(x,a_{1,1}) \vee \ldots \vee Q(x,a_{1,n1})$$

$$2.\ P2(x) \rightarrow Q(x,a_{2,1}) \vee \ldots \vee Q(x,a_{2,n2})$$

$$\cdots \cdots \cdots$$

$$m.\ Pm(x) \rightarrow Q(x,a_{m,1}) \vee \ldots \vee Q(x,a_{m,nm})$$

$$m+1.\ Q(x_1,x_2)\ \&\ Q(x_2,x_3)\ \&\ ..\ \&\ Q(x_{k-1},x_k) \rightarrow R(x_1,x_k).$$

Then resolvents of clause 1 with more than one of the remaining clauses can be excluded from NH[R]. ∎

EXAMPLE 6
Let CDB =

$\{$1. $F(a,c) \vee F(b,c)$ 2. $F(c,e) \vee F(d,e)$

3. $\neg F(x,y) \vee \neg F(y,z) \vee GF(x,z)\}$.

Then, NHr[GF] =

$\{$4. $\neg F(e,x) \vee GF(d,x) \vee F(c,e)$ 5. $\neg F(e,x) \vee GF(c,x) \vee F(d,e)$

6. $\neg F(c,x) \vee GF(b,x) \vee F(a,c)$ 7. $\neg F(c,x) \vee GF(a,x) \vee F(b,c)$

8. $\neg F(x,d) \vee GF(x,e) \vee F(c,e)$ 9. $\neg F(x,c) \vee GF(x,e) \vee F(d,e)$

10. $\neg F(x,b) \vee GF(x,c) \vee F(a,c)$ 11. $\neg F(x,a) \vee GF(x,c) \vee F(b,c)$

12. $GF(b,e) \vee F(a,c) \vee F(d,e)$ 13. $GF(a,e) \vee F(b,c) \vee F(d,e)\}$

NHr[GF] consists of 10 clauses, while NH[GF] consists of 37 clauses. ∎

THEOREM 10 (BACKWARD AND-BRANCH REDUCTION THEOREM II)
Let CDB =

$\{$1. $P1(x) \rightarrow Q(x,a_1) \vee \ldots \vee Q(x,a_n)$

2. $P2(x) \rightarrow R(x,b_1) \vee \ldots \vee R(x,b_m)$

3. $Q(x,z) \& R(z,y) \rightarrow S(x,y)\}$.

Then any resolvent of 1, 2, and 3 containing more than one S can be excluded from NH[S]. ∎

EXAMPLE 7
Let CDB =

$\{$1. $F(a,c) \ F(b,c)$ 2. $B(d,a) \ B(d,e)$

3. $\neg F(x,y) \ \neg B(z,x) \ U(z,y)\}$.

Then, NH[U] =

$\{$4. $(3,1) \ \neg B(x_1,b) \ U(x_1,c) \ F(a,c)$

5. $(3,1) \ \neg B(x_1,a) \ U(x_1,c) \ F(b,c)$

6. $(3,2) \neg F(e,x_1) \ U(d,x_1) \ B(d,a)$

7. $(3,2) \neg F(a,x_1) \ U(d,x_1) \ B(d,e)$

8. $(4,3) \neg B(x_1,b) \ U(x_1,c) \neg B(x_2,a) \ U(x_2,c)$

9. $(5,2) \ U(d,c) \ F(b,c) \ B(d,e)$

10. $(6,5) \neg F(e,x_1) \ U(d,x_1) \ U(d,c) \ F(b,c)$

11. $(6,3) \neg F(e,x_1) \ U(d,x_1) \neg F(a,x_2) \ U(d,x_2)$

12. $(7,4) \ U(d,c) \ B(d,e) \neg B(x_1,b) \ U(x_1,c)$

13. $(8,6) \neg B(x_1,b) \ U(x_1,c) \ U(d,c) \neg F(e,x_2) \ U(d,x_2)\}$

while NHr[U] = $\{4, 5, 6, 7, 9\}$. ∎

Explicit Negative Facts and NH-Reduction

In this section, we show the relationship between explicit negative facts and NH-reduction. In particular, if DB is in Representation 2, the explicit negative facts make it difficult to compute NH in a forward OR-branch as shown in the following example.

EXAMPLE 8
Let CDB =

{1. PHANTOM(a) MIG(a),

2. PHANTOM(x) → FRIEND(x),

3. MIG(x) → ENEMY(x)},

where PHANTOM and MIG are base relations, and FRIEND and ENEMY may have explicit negative facts stored in the RDB. NHr[FRIEND] = {FRIEND(a) MIG(a)}, while NH[FRIEND] also contains the clause FRIEND(a) ENEMY(a). PSUB[NHr[FRIEND]] = {PHANTOM(x) → FRIEND(x), MIG(x) → ENEMY(x)}.

Suppose we are using Representation 2 and we add ¬ENEMY(a). This fact will be placed in the RDB. Then ¬MIG(a) is derived by resolving MIG(x) → ENEMY(x) in PSUB[NHr[FRIEND]] and ¬ENEMY(a) in RDB, and this resolves with FRIEND(a) MIG(a) in NHr[FRIEND]. Hence, FRIEND(a) is true.

On the other hand, if we are using Representation 3, the above fact, ¬ENEMY(a), would be added to the CDB. Then CDB =

{1. PHANTOM(a) MIG(a),

2. PHANTOM(x) → FRIEND(x),

3. MIG(*x*) → ENEMY(*x*),

4. ¬ ENEMY(*a*) } .

Additional resolutions in the compile phase due to this update are

5. (3,4) ¬ MIG(*a*)

6. (1,5) PHANTOM(*a*)

7. (2,6) FRIEND(*a*)

Thus, FRIEND(*a*) is true, as before. Since FRIEND(*a*) subsumes FRIEND(*a*) MIG(*a*), NHr[FRIEND] and PSUB[NHr[FRIEND]] are empty. In addition, it is necessary to add PHANTOM(*a*) to the RDB. ∎

We observe, then, that in Representation 2 with a *reduced* NH set, the evaluator apparently must perform some of the deductions that were eliminated by the reduction, as in the resolution of ¬ ENEMY(*a*) with clause 3. The full NH set already contains a clause derived from clause 3, and this derived clause reacts directly with the RDB. This problem stems from the existence of explicit negative facts for a predicate which also has general definitions in the IDB; in the present case, ENEMY is defined partly by clause 3 and partly by the negative fact ¬ ENEMY(*a*). When this happens, the PSUB sets for the reduced NH sets must include clauses that can resolve with clauses in NH or with other clauses in PSUB itself, and the evaluator must perform all possible resolutions after data retrieval. In the example, NHr[FRIEND] = {*nh1*: FRIEND(*a*) MIG(*a*)}, and clause 3 resolves with *nh1*. Therefore, PSUB[NH[FRIEND]] must include clause 3. Then the evaluation of PSUB will produce ¬ MIG(*a*), and the evaluator must resolve this new clause with *nh1*. We note that if explicit negative facts are not allowed over defined relations, these complications do not occur.

NH-Inheritance

In this section, we introduce two kinds of NH-inheritance, namely linear and combinatorial NH-inheritances, to utilize previously compiled NH-information.

NH-Inheritance Network

In addition to eliminating clauses from the NH sets, it is also possible to reduce the compiling effort by generating these sets in a particular order. To this end we introduce a kind of AND/OR graph, called an NH-inheritance network.

Definition: NH-Inheritance Network   An NH-inheritance network consists of relation nodes, axiom nodes, AND-edges, and OR-edges. Relation nodes represent relation symbols. Axiom nodes represent clauses. If C is the clause $\neg L_1 \dots \neg L_n M_1 \dots M_m$, then the relation node for L_i is connected to the axiom node for C with an AND edge, and the relation node for M_i is connected to the axiom node for C with an OR edge. ∎

The NH sets can be computed in the order in which the predicates are used to define one another. We first compute NH for each base relation. Then NH is computed for each predicate that depends only on base relations, and so on.

EXAMPLE 9
Let CDB =

     {CL1. $P(x,y) \rightarrow Q(x,y)$,

       CL2. $R(a,c)\ R(b,c)$,

       CL3. $Q(x,y)\ \&\ R(y,z) \rightarrow S(x,z)$,

       CL4. $\neg R(a,d)$}.

Since we are concerned with only the hierarchical relationship among relation symbols in the CDB, we do not include arguments in the following graph. We compute NH[P] and NH[R] first, then NH[Q], and finally NH[S]. We show later that in many cases the successive NH sets can be computed directly from the earlier ones without the need for extensive deduction.

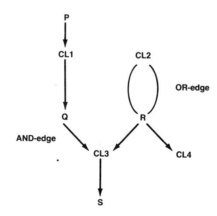

Linear NH-Inheritance

In this section, we introduce the linear NH-inheritance property in a forward/backward OR-branch or a forward AND-branch.

THEOREM 11 (LINEAR NH-INHERITANCE THEOREM)

Let DB be a non-recursive IDDB, CDB contain the clause

$P(x_1,x_2,y_1,y_2) \rightarrow Q(x_1,x_2,z)$, and let

$NH[P] =$

$\{nh \mid nh = P(t_1,t_2,t_3,t_4) \vee K$, where K may contain not only positive but also negative literals and zero or more positive literals over $P\}$

and $PSUB[NH[P]] = PS1 \cup PS2$
where $PS1 = \{psub1 \mid psub1 = P(u_1,u_2,u_3,u_4) \vee K1\}$
and $PS2 = \{psub2 \mid psub2 \text{ does not contain } P\}$.
Suppose Q does not appear positively in any other clause.
Then, $NH[Q] = \{nh \mid nh = Q(t_1,t_2,t_5) \vee K$
and $P(t_1,t_2,t_3,t_4) \vee K$ is in $NH[P]\}$
and $PSUB[NH[Q]] =$

$\{psub1 \mid psub1 = Q(u_1,u_2,u_5) \vee K1$

and $P(u_1,u_2,u_3,u_4) \vee K1$ is in $PS1\}$

$\cup PS2.$ ∎

COROLLARY 1

Let DB be a non-recursive IDDB, CDB contain a set of clauses of the form $\{P1 \rightarrow Q, ..., Pn \rightarrow Q\}$, and let

$NH[Pi] = \{nh \mid nh = Pi \vee Ki\}$

for each $i = 1,...,n$ and $PSUB[NH[Pi] = PS1i \cup PS2i$,
where $PS1i = \{psub1 \mid psub1 = Pi \vee K1i\}$
and $PS2i = \{psub2 \mid psub2 \text{ does not contain } Pi\}$
and where the arguments of each literal are not explicitly represented for convenience and positive literals over Q appear only in those clauses. Then,

$NH[Q] = NH1[Q] \cup ... \cup NHn[Q]$

and $PSUB[NH[Q]] = PSUB1[NH[Q]] \cup ... \cup PSUBn[NH[Q]]$,
where $NHi[Q] = \{nh \mid nh = Q \lor Ki$ and $Pi \lor Ki$ is in $NH[Pi]\}$
and $PSUBi[NH[Q]] = \{psub1 \mid psub1 = Qi \lor Ki$ and

$$Pi \lor Ki \text{ is in } PS1i\}$$

$\cup PS2i$. ∎

COROLLARY 2
Let DB be a non-recursive IDDB, CDB contain a clause of the form
$P(x_1,x_2,y_1,y_2) \twoheadrightarrow Q(x_1,x_2,b_1) \lor ... \lor Q(x_1,x_2,b_n)$, and let $NH[P] = \{nh \mid$
$nh = P(t_1,t_2,t_3,t_4) \lor K\}$, and $PSUB[NH[P]] = PS1 \cup PS2$ as in Theorem 11.
Suppose Q does not occur positively in any other clause. Then,

$$NH[Q] = \{nh \mid nh = Q(t_1,t_2,b_1) \lor ... \lor Q(t_1,t_2,b_n) \lor K$$

$$\text{and } P(x_1,x_2,y_1,y_2) \lor K \text{ is in } NH[P]\}$$

and $PSUB[NH[Q]] = PS2$. ∎

The linear NH-inheritance theorem and its corollaries say that NH and
PSUB for Q can be formed directly from those for P with linear time complexity. We can avoid the combinatorial explosion in NH-computation in the
forward / backward OR-branch and forward AND-branch if DB allows negative facts only in the base relation, as shown in Example 8.

EXAMPLE 10
Let a non-recursive DB contain the set of clauses

$$\{\neg P1(x) \ P2(x,a_1) \ P2(x,a_2),$$

$$\neg P2(x,y) \ P3(x,y),$$

$$\neg P3(x,y) \ P4(x,y),$$

$$\neg P4(x,y) \ P5(y,c_1) \ P5(y,c_2)\},$$

where $P4$ and $P5$ do not appear positively in any other clauses. Then

$$NH[P3] = \{\neg P1(x) \ \neg P1(y) \ P3(x,a_1) \ P3(y,a_2)\},$$

and $PSUB[NH[P3]] = \{\neg P2(x,y) \ P3(x,y)\}$.

By applying the Linear NH-Inheritance Theorem (or OR-branch Reduction
Theorem),

$\text{NH}[P4] = \{ P4(x,a_1) \neg P1(x)\, P3(y,a_2) \neg P1(y),$

$\qquad\qquad P4(y,a_2) \neg P1(y)\, P3(x,a_1) \neg P1(x) \}$

and $\text{PSUB}[\text{NH}[P4]] = \{ P4(x,y) \neg P2(x,y) \}.$

Also,

$\text{NH}[P5] = \{ P5(a_1,c_1)\, P5(a_1,c_2) \neg P1(x)\, P3(x,a_2) \neg P1(y),$

$\qquad\qquad P5(a_2,c_1)\, P5(a_2,c_2) \neg P1(x)\, P3(x,a_1) \neg P1(y) \}$

and $\text{PSUB}[\text{NH}[P5]]$ is empty. ∎

Example 10 illustrates why the OR-Branch Reduction Theorem is a special case of the Linear NH-Inheritance Theorem.

Combinatorial NH-Inheritance

In this section, we discuss NH-inheritance in a backward AND-branch.

THEOREM 12 (COMBINATORIAL NH-INHERITANCE THEOREM)
Let DB be a non-recursive IDDB, CDB contain a clause of the form
$\text{CL*} = P1(x_1,x_2)\ \&\ \ldots\ \&\ Pn(x_n,x_{n+1}) \rightarrow Q(x_1,x_n),$
and suppose

$\text{NH}[P1] = \{ nh1 \mid nh1 = P1(t_{1,1},t_{1,2}) \vee \text{K1} \},$

$\qquad \ldots,$

$\text{NH}[Pn] = \{ nhn \mid nhn = Pn(t_{n,1},t_{n,:}\ \vee \text{Kn} \},$

and $\text{PSUB}[\text{NH}[Pi]] = \{ hi \mid hi = \text{Pi}(x\quad \vee \text{KNi},$ where KNi denotes a negative subclause of $hi \}.$
Then, $\text{NH}[Q] = \{ nh \mid nh$ contains exactly one Q and is a resolvent obtained by resolving CL* with one clause from each NH[Pi]$\},$
and $\text{PSUB}[\text{NH}[[Q]] =$

$\{ hi \mid hi = Q(x_i,x_{i+1}) \vee \neg P1(x_1,x_2) \vee \ldots \vee$

$\neg Pi{-}1(x_{i-1},x_i) \vee \neg Pi+1(x_{i+1},x_{i+2}) \vee \ldots \vee \neg Pn(x_n,x_{n+1})$

$\vee \text{KNi where } Pi(x_i,y_i) \vee \text{KNi is in PSUB}[\text{NH}[Pi]] \}.$ ∎

The combinatorial NH-Inheritance Theorem states that NH and PSUB for Q can be formed directly from those for $P1$, $P2$, $\ldots$, and Pn with some combinatorial explosion. Such combinatorial explosion seems unavoidable in a backward AND-branch unless we restrict the number of such backward AND-branches and the number of partially derived relations in them.

Compiling Unit Queries in Recursive IDDB

Recently, several research reports (Bancilhon and Ramakrishnan [1987] Chang [1981], Henschen and Naqvi [1984], Han [1985]) showed that many practical recursive axioms can be compiled into specific patterns of negative clauses in recursive Horn databases. However, it seems very difficult to find some regular patterns for the positive parts of non-Horn clauses in a recursive IDDB, in addition to the patterns for their negative parts. We show that those patterns may be found in certain recursive IDDBs by utilizing the compiled patterns of recursive axioms in Horn databases. We call the patterns for positive parts and negative parts of non-Horn clauses in NH positive and negative patterns, respectively. NH is assumed to be reduced by the NH-reduction theorems given in the previous section.

We take a typical set of transitive recursive axioms,

$$\{\texttt{Father}(x,y) \;\rightarrow\; \texttt{Ancestor}(x,y),$$

$$\texttt{Father}(x,z) \;\&\; \texttt{Ancestor}(z,y) \;\rightarrow\; \texttt{Ancestor}(x,y)\}$$

to illustrate our basic idea for compiling recursive axioms in an IDDB. Let a query Q = Ancestor(*JOHN*,?), i.e., find all descendants of *John*. Then, we obtain negative clauses consisting of arbitrarily many instances of the relation Father of the form $\neg\,$Father($JOHN,x_2$) $\neg\,$Father(x_2,x_3) .... $\neg\,$Father(x_{n-1},x_n) by resolving the given axiom set and $\neg\,$Ancestor($JOHN$,?). In other words, Q can be compiled into the form of Father$^+$, where Father$^+$ denotes zero or more join operations over the relation Father in the RDB. Then, we obtain all descendants of *JOHN* by repeatedly joining the relation Father until no more descendants of *JOHN* can be newly generated. That is, we can compile the given recursive axiom in Horn databases and evaluate it over the RDB with a definite termination mechanism. Now, suppose we allow non-Horn ground clauses for the relation Father to make a simple recursive IDDB, e.g.,

$$\begin{aligned}
\text{CDB} = \{&1.\ \ F(a,c)\ \ F(b,c) \\
&2.\ \ \neg F(x,y)\ \ A(x,y) \\
&3.\ \ \neg F(x,z)\ \ \neg A(z,y)\ \ A(x,y)\}.
\end{aligned}$$

Then, we introduce the following theorem to show that the positive and negative patterns may be found in this recursive IDDB by utilizing the compiled patterns of recursive axioms in the Horn case.

LEMMA 5
Let CDB =

> {F(a,c) F(b,c),
> $\neg$F(x,y) A(x,y),
> $\neg$F(x,z) $\neg$A(z,y) A(x,y)},

and call the set *Se* =

> $\{\neg F(x_1,x_2) A(x_1,x_2), \neg F(x_1,x_2) \neg F(x_2,x_3) A(x_1,x_3),$
>
> ......,
>
> $\neg F(x_1,x_2) \neg F(x_2,x_3) ... \neg F(x_{n-1},x_n) A(x_1,x_n), ...\}$

the set of exit expressions. Then, NH[*A*] can be obtained by resolving F(a,c) F(b,c) with each clause of *Se*. ∎

THEOREM 13 (RECURSIVE AXIOM ORDERING THEOREM)
Let CDB = *Si* $\cup$ $\{\neg F(x,y) A(x,y), \neg F(x,z) \neg A(z,y) A(x,y)\}$, where *Si* denotes a set of positive non-Horn ground clauses over F, and let *Se* be as in Lemma 5. Then, NH[*A*] can be obtained by resolving *Si* with *Se* instead of with the recursive axiom. ∎

Theorem 13 implies that we could first perform resolution on only the given transitive recursive axiom set to obtain the patterns of negative clauses in the Horn part of the database, and then perform resolution on those patterns and non-Horn clauses to obtain the positive patterns and their associated negative patterns for the recursive part. This is illustrated in the following example.

EXAMPLE 11
Let CDB =

> {CL1. F(a,c) F(b,c),
> CL2. $\neg$F(x,y) A(x,y),
> CL3. $\neg$F(x,z) $\neg$A(z,y) A(x,y)}

and F consist of acyclic data in RDB. Then, find the positive and negative patterns for NH[*A*]. #*L* denotes the level of recursion.

```
---- #L = 0
 1. F(a,c) F(b,c)
 2. ¬F(x₁,x₂) A(x₁,x₂)
 3.(2,1) A(b,c) F(a,c)
 4.(2,1) A(a,c) F(b,c)
```

```
---- #L = 1
 1. F(a,c) F(b,c)
 2. ¬F(x₁,x₂) ¬F(x₂,x₃) A(x₁,x₃)
 3.(2,1) ¬F(c,x₁) A(b,x₁) F(a,c)
 4.(2,1) ¬F(c,x₁) A(a,x₁) F(b,c)
 5.(2,1) ¬F(x₁,b) A(x₁,c) F(a,c)
 6.(2,1) ¬F(x₁,a) A(x₁,c) F(b,c)
```

```
---- #L = 2
 1. F(a,c) F(b,c)
 2. ¬F(x₁,x₂) ¬F(x₂,x₃) ¬F(x₃,x₄) A(x₁,x₄)
 3.(2,1) ¬F(c,x₁) ¬F(x₁,x₂) A(b,x₂) F(a,c)
 4.(2,1) ¬F(c,x₁) ¬F(x₁,x₂) A(a,x₂) F(b,c)
 5.(2,1) ¬F(x₁,b) ¬F(c,x₂) A(x₁,x₂) F(a,c)
 6.(2,1) ¬F(x₁,a) ¬F(c,x₂) A(x₁,x₂) F(b,c)
 7.(2,1) ¬F(x₁,x₂) ¬F(x₂,b) A(x₁,c) F(a,c)
 8.(2,1) ¬F(x₁,x₂) ¬F(x₂,a) A(x₁,c) F(b,c)
```

```
---- #L = 3
 1. F(a,c) F(b,c)
 2. ¬F(x₁,x₂) ¬F(x₂,x₃) ¬F(x₃,x₄) ¬F(x₄,x₅) A(x₁,x₅)
 3.(2,1) ¬F(c,x₁) ¬F(x₁,x₂) ¬F(x₂,x₃) A(a,x₃) F(b,c)
 4.(2,1) ¬F(x₁,a) ¬F(c,x₂) ¬F(x₂,x₃) A(x₁,x₃) F(b,c)
 5.(2,1) ¬F(x₁,x₂) ¬F(x₂,a) ¬F(c,x₃) A(x₁,x₃) F(b,c)
 6.(2,1) ¬F(x₁,x₂) ¬F(x₂,x₃) ¬F(x₃,a) A(x₁,c) F(b,c)
 7.(2,1) ¬F(c,x₁) ¬F(x₁,x₂) ¬F(x₂,x₃) A(b,x₃) F(a,c)
 8.(2,1) ¬F(x₁,b) ¬F(c,x₂) ¬F(x₂,x₃) A(x₁,x₃) F(a,c)
 9.(2,1) ¬F(x₁,x₂) ¬F(x₂,b) ¬F(c,x₃) A(x₁,x₃) F(a,c)
10.(2,1) ¬F(x₁,x₂) ¬F(x₂,x₃) ¬F(x₃,b) A(x₁,c) F(a,c)
```

```
---- #L = 4
 1. F(a,c) F(b,c)
 2. ¬F(x₁,x₂) ¬F(x₂,x₃) ¬F(x₃,x₄)
    ¬F(x₄,x₅) ¬F(x₅,x₆) A(x₁,x₆)
 3.(2,1) ¬F(c,x₁) ¬F(x₁,x₂) ¬F(x₂,x₃) ¬F(x₃,x₄)
         A(a,x₄) F(b,c)
```

4.(2,1) $\neg F(x_1,a)$ $\neg F(c,x_2)$ $\neg F(x_2,x_3)$ $\neg F(x_3,x_4)$
$A(x_1,x_4)$ $F(b,c)$

5.(2,1) $\neg F(x_1,x_2)$ $\neg F(x_2,a)$ $\neg F(c,x_3)$ $\neg F(x_3,x_4)$
$A(x_1,x_4)$ $F(b,c)$

6.(2,1) $\neg F(x_1,x_2)$ $\neg F(x_2,x_3)$ $\neg F(x_3,a)$ $\neg F(c,x_4)$
$A(x_1,x_4)$ $F(b,c)$

7.(2,1) $\neg F(x_1,x_2)$ $\neg F(x_2,x_3)$ $\neg F(x_3,x_4)$ $\neg F(x_4,a)$
$A(x_1,c)$ $F(b,c)$

8.(2,1) $\neg F(c,x_1)$ $\neg F(x_1,x_2)$ $\neg F(x_2,x_3)$ $\neg F(x_3,x_4)$
$A(b,x_4)$ $F(a,c)$

9.(2,1) $\neg F(x_1,b)$ $\neg F(c,x_2)$ $\neg F(x_2,x_3)$ $\neg F(x_3,x_4)$
$A(x_1,x_4)$ $F(a,c)$

10.(2,1) $\neg F(x_1,x_2)$ $\neg F(x_2,b)$ $\neg F(c,x_3)$ $\neg F(x_3,x_4)$
$A(x_1,x_4)$ $F(a,c)$

11.(2,1) $\neg F(x_1,x_2)$ $\neg F(x_2,x_3)$ $\neg F(x_3,b)$ $\neg F(c,x_4)$
$A(x_1,x_4)$ $F(a,c)$

12.(2,1) $\neg F(x_1,x_2)$ $\neg F(x_2,x_3)$ $\neg F(x_3,x_4)$ $\neg F(x_4,b)$
$A(x_1,c)$ $F(a,c)$

Notice that we do not need to generate the following resolvents during the above resolution process.

1. Resolvents including more than one positive literal over A, e.g., $A(a,c)$ $A(b,c)$ in LOOP# = 0, due to the NH-reduction theorems.

2. Resolvents generated by resolving upon either $F(a,c)$ or $F(b,c)$ two or more times, e.g., (3,1) $\neg F(c,b)$ $A(b,c)$ $F(a,c)$ and (4,1) $\neg F(c,a)$ $A(a,c)$ $F(b,c)$ in LOOP# = 2, due to the acyclicity of data in F.

3. Any resolvent of the form $\neg F(\_,\_)$ ... $\neg F(\_,\_)$ $A(\_,\_)$ $F(a,c)$ $F(b,c)$ obtained by resolving with $F(a,c)$ v $F(b,c)$ twice, once on each ground literal, because it is subsumed by $F(a,c)$ $F(b,c)$.

In the above NH set, we can find the following 8 positive patterns:

PPAT1... $A(b,c)$ $F(a,c)$ PPAT2... $A(a,c)$ $F(b,c)$
PPAT3... $A(b,x)$ $F(a,c)$ PPAT4... $A(a,x)$ $F(b,c)$
PPAT5... $A(x,c)$ $F(a,c)$ PPAT6... $A(x,c)$ $F(b,c)$
PPAT7... $A(x,y)$ $F(a,c)$ PPAT8... $A(x,y)$ $F(b,c)$

Notice that those patterns can be found in level 0,1, and 2, and no positive pattern is newly generated in levels 3 and 4. Then, we can find the negative patterns associated with each positive pattern as follows:

```
For PPAT1...A(b,c) F(a,c),
L#0. A(b,c) F(a,c)
```

Hence, no negative pattern.

```
For PPAT3...A(b,x) F(a,c),
L#1. ¬F(c,x) A(b,x) F(a,c)
L#2. ¬F(c,x₁) ¬F(x₁,x₂) A(b,x₂) F(a,c)
L#3. ¬F(c,x₁) ¬F(x₁,x₂) ¬F(x₂,x₃) A(b,x₃) F(a,c)
L#4. ¬F(c,x₁) ¬F(x₁,x₂) ¬F(x₂,x₃)
     ¬F(x₃,x₄) A(b,x₄) F(a,c)
```

Hence, its associated negative pattern is $\neg F(c,x)\ \neg F^*$, where F^* denotes transitive closure over the relation F.

```
For PPAT8...A(x,y) F(b,c),
L#2. ¬F(x₁,a) ¬F(c,x₂) A(x₁,x₂) F(a,c)
L#3. ¬F(x₁,a) ¬F(c,x₂) ¬F(x₂,x₃) A(x₁,x₃) F(a,c)
     ¬F(x₁,x₂) ¬F(x₂,a) ¬F(c,x₃) A(x₁,x₃) F(a,c)
L#4. ¬F(x₁,a) ¬F(c,x₂) ¬F(x₂,x₃)
     ¬F(x₃,x₄) A(x₁,x₄) F(a,c)
     ¬F(x₁,x₂) ¬F(x₂,a) ¬F(c,x₃) ¬F(x₃,x₄)
     A(x₁,x₄) F(a,c)
     ¬F(x₁,x₂) ¬F(x₂,x₃) ¬F(x₃,a) ¬F(c,x₄)
     A(x₁,x₄) F(a,c)
```

Hence, its associated negative pattern is $\neg F^*\ \neg F(x,a)\ \neg F(c,y)\ \neg F^*$.
By the above analysis of NH-patterns, we can obtain NH[A] =

```
{A(b,c) F(a,c),
 A(a,c) F(b,c),
 ¬F(c,x₁) ¬F* A(b,xₙ) F(a,c),
       . . . . . .
 ¬F* ¬F(xᵢ,a) ¬F(c,xᵢ₊₁) ¬F* A(x₁,xₙ) F(b,c)}  and
PSUB[NH[A]] = {¬F(x₁,x₂) A(x₁,x₂)}.
```

This idea may be applied to other recursive axioms, but it is still very naive. In particular, it depends heavily on the number and pattern of indefinite data in CDB. Even when DB allows simple recursive axioms and small amounts of indefinite data, it seems very difficult to find some regular NH-patterns. Hence, we should find much more practical restrictions for recursive IDDBs than those like acyclicity of data in the above example. ∎

Complex Query Evaluation by Decomposition

In this section, we introduce the query decomposition and evaluation theorems to evaluate disjunctive and conjunctive queries by decomposing them into their unit subqueries and utilizing the compiled information of such subqueries.

Query Decomposition Theorem

THEOREM 14 (QUERY DECOMPOSITION THEOREM)
Let CL1 and CL2 be ground clauses. "*" denotes "don't care" and "t," "f," and "i" denote "true," "false," and "indefinite," respectively.

1. Disjunctive decomposition			2. Conjunctive decomposition		
CL1	CL2	CL1 v CL2	CL1	CL2	CL1 & CL2
t	*	t	f	*	f
f	*	CL2	t	*	CL2
i	i	i or t	i	i	i or f
.					
.					

Notice that the Decomposition Theorem shows a duality between disjunctive and conjunctive decomposition. ∎

Simple Disjunctive Query Evaluation

Disjunctive ground queries can be evaluated as follows. Let $DQ = L1 \lor L2 \lor \ldots \lor Ln$. Then, determine the value of each literal Li by utilizing the compiled program for Li. If all Li are indefinite, we need some additional operations to determine the value of DQ. We consider two ways to handle this case: the resolution-refutation method and the PIGC-generation method. Both methods are restricted to the case when each Li is positive. The case when some Li are negative seems much more complex.

In the resolution-refutation method, we may perform a straightforward refutation proof search for DB $\cup$ $-$DQ to infer the value of DQ. If a refutation is generated, DQ is true. Otherwise, DQ is indefinite. This can be compiled easily in Representation 3 as follows: Add $-$DQ to CDB, perform resolution on CDB, and gather negative clauses newly generated.

EXAMPLE 12

Let DB = $\{P \; Q\}$, $\Gamma Q1 = P \; Q$, and DQ2 = $\neg P \dashv Q$. The minimal models of DB are $M1 = \{P\}$ and $M2 = \{Q\}$. Hence, both P and Q are indefinite, and DQ1 and DQ2 are both true under the GCWA with respect to DB. However, DB $\cup$ $-$DQ1 has a refutation, while DB $\cup$ $-$DQ2 does not. ■

In the PIGC-generation method, DQ may be evaluated by utilizing the compiled program of unit queries and invoking the following theorem.

THEOREM 15 (DISJUNCTIVE QUERY EVALUATION THEOREM)

Let DQ = $P1$ $\vee$ ... $\vee$ Pm, where Pi's are ground atoms and are all indefinite with respect to DB. Then, if there exists a pigc in PIGC that subsumes DQ, DQ is true with respect to DB. Otherwise, DQ is indefinite with respect to DB. ■

EXAMPLE 13

Let DB = $\{ P \; R, Q \; S \}$ and DQ = $P \; Q \; R$. Then, $M1 = \{ P, Q \}$, $M2 = \{P, S\}$, $M3 = \{R, Q\}$, and $M4 = \{R, S\}$ are the minimal models of DB. P, Q, and R are all indefinite. Since we can generate $P \vee R$ subsuming DQ, DQ is true. Notice that DQ may be compiled. ■

Simple Conjunctive Query Evaluation

Queries consisting of a conjunction of ground atoms can be evaluated as follows. Let CQ = $L1$ & $L2$ & .... & Ln. If all Li are indefinite, we have a PIGC-generation method as follows.

LEMMA 6

Let $P1$, ..., Pm be a set of distinct ground atoms of DB, and let DB contain the clauses

```
P1 v K11,  P1 v K12,  ...
P2 v K21,  P2 v K22,  ...
        .
        .
        .
Pm v Km1,  Pm v Km2,  ...        .
```

where the i-th row consists of all clauses containing the literal Pi. (Note, this implies that a clause may be in more than one row.) Then the atoms $P1$, ..., Pm appear together in some minimal model if and only if the following two conditions hold:

C1.   For each $i = 1$, ..., m, there is a Kij that contains none of the other Pn's;

C2. There exists some set S^* of ground atoms formed by taking the union of atoms from one Kij from each row such that S^* contains none of the atoms $P1$, ..., Pm and every clause in PIGC which does not contain any of $P1$, ..., Pm (i.e., is not one of the clauses listed above) contains a literal not in S^*. ■

THEOREM 16 (CONJUNCTIVE EVALUATION THEOREM)
Let $CQ = P1$ & ... & Pm, where the Pi are ground atoms that are all indefinite with respect to DB. If the two conditions in Lemma 6 hold, CQ is also indefinite with respect to DB. Otherwise, CQ is false. ■

EXAMPLE 14
Let DB = $\{P\,Q, P\,R\,S, R\,T\}$.
Then, $M1 = \{P, R\}$, $M2 = \{P, T\}$, $M3 = \{Q, R\}$, AND $M4 = \{Q, S, T\}$ are the minimal models.
P, Q, R, S, and T are all indefinite ground atoms.

1. For $CQ1 = P$ & Q & R,

    Semantic justification: There is no minimal model containing all of P, Q, and R. Hence, CQ1 is false.

    Syntactic justification: Find P v K1s such that K1s contains none of Q and R by generating pigc's of P: $P\,Q$ contains Q, $P\,R\,S$ contains R, and there are no more pigc's containing P. Since there is no such P v K1s, DB fails C1. Hence, CQ1 is false.

2. For $CQ2 = Q$ & S & T,

    Semantic justification: Minimal model $M4$ contains all of Q, S, and T. Hence, CQ2 is indefinite.

    Syntactic justification: $Q\,P$, $S\,P\,R$, and $T\,R$ satisfy condition C1 in Lemma 6. Now let $S^* = \{P, R\}$. Since there is no Pj v Kjt such that Pj is in S^* and Kjt contains none of Q, S, and T, DB also satisfies condition C2 in Lemma 6. Hence, CQ is indefinite with respect to DB. ■

EXAMPLE 15
Let DB = $\{P\,Q\,R, S\,T, Q\,T\}$ and $CQ = P$ & S. $M1 = \{P, T\}$, $M2 = \{S, Q\}$, $M3 = \{Q, T\}$, and $M4 = \{R, T\}$ are the minimal models of DB.

Semantic justification: There is no minimal model containing P and S. Hence, CQ is false.

Syntactic justification: Let $P1 = P$, $P2 = S$, and $P3 = Q$. Then, $P1$ v $K11 = P\,Q\,R$ and $P2$ v $K21 = S\,T$ verify condition C1 in Lemma 6. The only candidate for S^* is $\{Q, R, T\}$ by taking the union of K11 and K21. However, $P3$ v K31 $= Q\ T$ consists of only atoms in $\{Q, R, T\}$. Since DB has no other candidate for S^*, condition C2 fails. Hence, CQ is false with respect to DB. ∎

More Complex Query Evaluation

THEOREM 17 (CNF QUERY EVALUATION THEOREM)
Let CNQ = CL1 & CL2 & ... & CLm, where all the ground clauses CLi are indefinite with respect to DB. Let DNQ = $X1$ v $X2$ v ... v Xn, where DNQ is a disjunctive normal form of CNQ and $Xi = Pi1$ & $Pi2$ & ... & Pik. Then, CNQ is indefinite iff there exists at least one Xi indefinite. Notice that CNQ and DNQ cannot be true due to the conjunctive decomposition theorem, and that all $Pi1$, ..., Pik are not necessarily indefinite. ∎

EXAMPLE 16
Let DB = $\{P\ Q\ S, Q\ R\ S\}$ and CNQ = $(P$ v $Q)$ & $(R$ v $S)$. Then, $M1 = \{P, R\}$, $M2 = \{Q\}$, and $M3 = \{S\}$ are the minimal models of DB. All P, Q, R, and S are indefinite. Let DNQ =

$$(P\ \&\ R)\ \text{v}\ (P\ \&\ S)\ \text{v}\ (Q\ \&\ R)\ \text{v}\ (Q\ \&\ S)$$

which we will write as K1 v K2 v K3 v K4. K1 is indefinite with respect to DB, since it is true with respect to $M1$ but false with respect to $M2$ and $M3$. Hence, DNQ and CNQ are indefinite with respect to DB. ∎

Note that if CNQ or DNQ contains negative literals, the techniques of the preceding two sections do not apply. This most general case still remains an open problem.

Summary and Further Work

Our goal is to develop effective inference engines for indefinite databases. We have shown that PIGC is the key to determining when a ground atom is indefinite or can be assumed false under the GCWA. Further, we have shown which sets of resolvents must be generated in a compile phase in order to separate deduction from data retrieval. We have shown that two of the three obvious representation schemes allow such clause sets to be generated in a separate compile phase. We have shown which sets of reduction rules can be used in a compile phase in order to eliminate many redundant resolvents, and what kind of compilation strategy is globally effective to inherit previously compiled information in a non-recursive IDDB. Further, we have indicated how simple recursive axioms might be handled in a recursive IDDB. Finally, we have shown how conjunction and disjunction can be handled.

Work beyond that described in this paper is needed to implement the actual compilation as follows:

1.   Develop the actual algorithms to generate just the right resolvents in an effective way incorporating NH-reduction and NH-inheritance rules.

2.   Develop a more general methodology to handle more complex recursive axioms in an IDDB.

3.   Develop the evaluation theorems to handle more complex queries containing negative literals.

Of course, the main goal of finding indefinite answers to *open* queries remains unsolved. It is our hope that results on answering ground atomic queries may provide some insight into the more general problem. It would also be interesting to determine which of the results in this paper carry over to the extended GCWA of Yahya and Henschen [1985]. Finally, Representation 1 seems to offer many advantages for the compilation aspects of this problem, and we are currently working on the necessary extensions to the evaluation phase in order to be able to use Representation 1.

Acknowledgment

We gratefully acknowledge support from the National Science Foundation under grant number DCR-8608311 that made this work possible.

Appendix

Proofs

Proof of Lemma 1   Refer to Minker's proof (Minker [1982]).   ■

Proof of Lemma 2   Let PGC denote the set of all positive (not necessarily minimal) ground clauses derivable from DB.

ONLY-IF PART
We prove this by contradiction. Suppose that CL = $A \vee K$ is in PIGC but A is not indefinite in DB. Then there are no minimal models M, M' of DB such

that A is in M and A is not in M'. By Lemma 1, there are no minimal models M, M' of PGC such that A is in M and A is not in M'. There are two cases.

Case 1: A appears in some, and hence all, minimal model(s) of PGC. Then, PGC $\vdash$ A. Hence, CL is not in PIGC, since A subsumes CL.

Case 2: A does not appear in any minimal model of PGC. Then, PGC $\vdash_{GCWA} \neg A$. Then the (non-empty) positive ground clause K is in PGC by the syntactic definition of GCWA. Hence, CL is not in PIGC, since K subsumes CL.

Therefore, CL $= A \lor K$ in PIGC implies that A is indefinite in DB.

IF-PART
This proof can be done, straightforwardly, by the semantic definition of indefiniteness. Suppose that A is indefinite in DB. By Lemma 1, A is indefinite in PGC. By the definition of indefiniteness, A is in some minimal model of PGC and not in some other minimal model of PGC. Then, DB $\not\vdash$ A. Clearly, A must occur in some minimal positive clause or it would never need to be true. Hence $A \lor K$ is in PIGC for some K. ∎

Proof of Theorem 1
Indef[A]

```
<--> C = A v C' in PIGC, by Lemma 2
<--> PIGC[A] is not empty, by definition of PIGC[A].  ∎
```

Proof of Theorem 2 Trivial.

Proof of Theorem 3

1. *Representation 1*:
    We show a counter example. Let DIDB $= \neg P(x) \lor Q(x)$ }, IEDB $= \{P(a) \lor P(b)$ }, and IIDB $=$ DEDB $=$ empty. Then, NH[P] is empty. Hence, PIGC of RDB $\cup$ NH[P] $= \{P(a) \lor P(b)\}$. However, PIGC of DB is $\{ P(a) \lor P(b), P(b) \lor Q(a), P(a) \lor Q(b), Q(a) \lor Q(b) \}$.

2. *Representation 2*:
    This can be shown easily by using the reordering of resolution steps deriving a pigc in PIGC[A], as follows: Suppose that a positive(negative) unit ground input clause, say $P(\neg P)$, is involved in the i-th binary resolution step for deriving an arbitrary pigc. We can move $P(\neg P)$ down to the bottom of the resolution sequence without generating more pigc's. Therefore, we can separate the resolution steps containing unit ground input clauses from the resolution steps not containing them. We also need

to move resolution on negative literals in non-Horn clauses up so that NH[P] clauses are in the middle. PSUB[NH[P]] can be separated in the same manner. Now, RDB can be separated from CDB.

3. *Representation 3*:
   This case follows immediately from the proof of case 2 by excluding the negative unit ground clauses in the reordering. ∎

Proof of Theorem 4 Trivial. ∎

Proof of Theorem 5 If Indef[$R(a,a_i)$] is false, the proof is easy: NH and PSUB cannot yield a pigc containing $R(a,a_i)$ and since NHr is a subset of NH, it also cannot yield such a pigc. We prove the indefinite case by induction on #R, where #R is the maximum number of R literals appearing in a non-Horn clause derivable from CDB.

INDUCTION BASIS: (#R = 2)
Then, CDB =

$$\{1. \quad P(x) \quad \rightarrow \quad Q(x,a_1) \; v \; Q(x,a_2)$$
$$2. \quad Q(x,y) \quad \rightarrow \quad R(x,y)\}.$$

We show that Indef[$R(a,a_i)$] can be computed from NHr[R] $\cup$ PSUB[NHr[R]] $\cup$ RDB instead of NH[R] $\cup$ PSUB[NH[R]] $\cup$ RDB. Without loss of generality, we prove it with respect to Indef[$R(a,a_1)$]. Then, we need to show that $R(a,a_1)$ v $Q(a,a_2)$ is in PIGC[$R(a,a_1)$] if $R(a,a_1)$ v $R(a,a_2)$ is in PIGC[$R(a,a_1)$] because of resolving 1 and 2. Suppose that $R(a,a_1)$ v $R(a,a_2)$ is in PIGC[$R(a,a_1)$] because of 1 and 2. This implies the following: $P(a)$ is true; that is, it is in RDB. Both $R(a,a_1)$ and $R(a,a_2)$ are indefinite. $Q(a,a_2)$ is not true, since $\neg Q(x,y)$ v $R(x,y)$ is in PSUB[NH[R]] and $R(a,a_2)$ is indefinite. That is, $Q(a,a_1)$ is not in RDB. $Q(a,a_2)$ is not false, since $P(a)$ is true, $\neg P(a)$ v $R(a,a_1)$ v $Q(a,a_2)$ is derivable from NH[R] and $R(a,a_1)$ is indefinite. (This can be justified easily: $\neg Q(a,a_2)$ is not in the RDB, since DB is in Representation 3.) Hence, $Q(a,a_2)$ must be indefinite. Hence, $R(a,a_1)$ v $Q(a,a_2)$ is in PIGC[$R(a,a_1)$].

INDUCTION STEP

INDUCTION HYPOTHESIS: (#R ≤ n)
Let #$R \leq n$, and $R(a,a_i)$ v K and $R(a,a_i)$ v K' be derivable from NH, where K consists of literals over R and Q, K' consists of only literals over Q. Then, if Indef[$R(a,a_i)$] can be computed from $R(a,a_i)$ v K $\cup$ PSUB[NH[R]] $\cup$ RDB, it can be computed from $R(a,a_i)$ v K' $\cup$ PSUB[NHr[R]] $\cup$ RDB.

INDUCTION: (#R ≤ n + 1)
We show that if Indef[$R(a,a_i)$] can be computed from $R(a,a_i)$ v K v $R(a,a_{n+1})$ ∪ PSUB[NH[R]] ∪ RDB, it can be computed from $R(a,a_i)$ v K v $Q(a,a_{n+1})$ ∪ PSUB[NH[R]] ∪ RDB. Then, by induction, it can be computed from $R(a,a_i)$ v K' v $Q(a,a_{n+1})$ ∪ PSUB[NHr[R]] ∪ RDB. First, suppose that $R(a,a_i)$ v K v ($R(a,a_{n+1})$) is in PIGC[$R(a,a_i)$]. Then, $P(a)$ is true; $R(a,a_i)$, K, and $R(a,a_{n+1})$ are indefinite. $Q(a,a_{n+1})$ is not true, since $\neg Q(x,y)$ v $R(x,y)$ is in PSUB[NH[R]] and $R(a,a_{n+1})$ is indefinite. $Q(a,a_{n+1})$ is not false, since $P(a)$ is true, $\neg P(a)$ v $R(a,a_i)$ v K v $Q(a,a_{n+1})$ is derivable from NH[R] and $R(a,a_i)$ v K v $R(a,a_{n+1})$ is derivable from PIGC[$R(a,a_i)$]. Hence, $Q(a,a_{n+1})$ is indefinite. Hence, $R(a,a_i)$ v K v $Q(a,a_{n+1})$ is in PIGC[$R(a,a_i)$]. Second, a proper subclause of $R(a,a_i)$ v K v $R(a,a_{n+1})$ cannot be in PIGC, since DB is in Representation 3. ∎

Proof of Theorem 6 We prove the indefinite case by induction on #R, where #R is the number of R literals appearing in non-Horn clauses derivable from CDB.

INDUCTION BASIS: (#R = 2)
Then, CDB =

```
{1.  P(x)    →   Q1(x,a₁) v Q2(x,a₂)
 2.  Q1(x,y) →   R1(x,y)
 3.  Q2(x,y) →   R2(x,y)}.
```

We need to show that $R1(a,a_1)$ v $Q2(a,a_2)$ is in PIGC[$R1(a,a_1)$] if $R1(a,a_1)$ v $R2(a,a_2)$ is. Suppose that $R1(a,a_1)$ v $R2(a,a_2)$ is in PIGC[$R1(a,a_1)$]. This implies the following: $P(a)$ is true; that is, it is in RDB. Both $R1(a,a_1)$ and $R2(a,a_2)$ are indefinite. $Q2(a,a_2)$ is not in the RDB, since $\neg Q2(x,y)$ v $R2(x,y)$ is in PSUB[NH[$R2$]] and $R2(a,a_2)$ is indefinite. $\neg Q2(a,a_2)$ is not in the RDB, since $P(a)$ is true, $\dashv P(a)$ v $R1(a,a_1)$ v $Q2(a,a_2)$ is derivable from NH[$R1$], and $R1(a,a_1)$ is indefinite. Hence, $Q2(a,a_2)$ must be indefinite, and $R1(a,a_1)$ v $Q2(a,a_2)$ is in PIGC[$R1(a,a_1)$].

INDUCTION STEP
This is similar to the proof of Theorem 5. ∎

Proof of Theorem 7 This proof is similar to the proof of Theorems 5 and 6. ∎

Proof of Theorem 8 This proof is similar to the proof of Theorems 5 and 6. ∎

Proof of Lemma 3 Let $h = \neg Q(x_1,x_2) \vee \neg Q(x_2,x_3) \vee R(x_1,x_3)$. Let $nhi = R(\$1,\$2) \vee KN1 \vee KP1$, where $\$1$ and $\$2$ denote either a variable or a constant, KN1 is a negative subclause not containing a literal over R, and KP1 is a positive subclause not containing a literal over R but containing the literal $Q(\$1,\$2)$. Then, nhi and h can resolve in two ways, depending on which Q literal in h is used, to yield a clause $[R(\$1,\$2) \vee KN2 \vee KP2]*s_0$, and KN2 is either KN1 $\vee \neg Q(x_2,x_3)$ or KN1 $\vee \neg Q(x_1,x_2)$, KP2 is either (KP1 $\neg Q(x_1,x_2))\vee R(x_1,x_3)$ or (KP1 $\neg Q(x_2,x_3)) \vee R(x_1,x_3)$, and s_0 denotes an m.g.u. (most general unifier) of $Q(\$1,\$2)$ and the Q literal resolved upon in h. Now suppose that nhj yields a clause, pigc2, in $PIGC[R(c_1,c_2)]$. We show that nhi will also yield a clause, pigc1, in $PIGC[R(c_1,c_2)]$.

Suppose that pigc2 $= R(c_1,c_2) \vee KP2*s_0*s_2$, where s_2 is an m.g.u of KN2 and RDB and $R(c_1,c_2) = R(\$1,\$2)*s_0*s_2$. We have the following cases depending on the form of KN2.

Case 1: KN2 is KN1 $\vee \neg Q(x_2,x_3)$. Since KN2 can be resolved away using the RDB, KN2$*s_0*s_2$ must be false. That is, KN1$*s_0*s_2$ and $\neg Q(x_2,x_3)*s_0*s_2$ are false. Obviously, $R(c1,c2)$ is indefinite, and KP2$*s_0*s_2$ is also indefinite. That is, (KP1 $\neg Q(x_1,x_2)) *s_0*s_2$ and $R(x_1,x_3)*s_0*s_2$ are indefinite. Since KN1$*s_0*s_2$ is false and nhi is in NHr, $[R(\$1,\$2) \vee KP1]*s_0*s_2$ is derivable from NHr $\cup$ RDB, where KP1 contains at least one $Q(\$3,\$4)$ unifiable with $Q(x,y)$. In order to prove that pigc1 $= [R(\$1,S2) \vee Q(\$3,\$4)]*s_0*s_2$ is in PIGC, we need to show that $Q(\$3,\$4)*s_0*s_2$ is indefinite, that is, $Q(x_1,x_2)*s_0*s_2$ indefinite.

1. Suppose that $Q(x_1,x_2)*s_0*s_2$ is true. Then, $R(x_1,x_3)*s_0*s_2$ is true, since $Q(x_1,x_2)*s_0*s_2$ and $Q(x_2,x_3)*s_0*s_2$ are true, and $[\neg Q(x_1,x_2) \vee \neg Q(x_2,x_3) \vee R(x_1,x_3)]*s_0*s_2$ is implied by h. This contradicts that $R(x_1,x_3)*s_0*s_2$ is indefinite. Hence, $Q(x_1,x_2)*s_0*s_2$ is not true.

2. $Q(x_1,x_2)*s_0*s_2$ is not false, since DB is in representation 3.

Case 2: KN2 is KN1 $\vee \neg Q(x_1,x_2)$. This proof is similar to the first case.

Note that pigc2 cannot be a proper subclause of the positive part of nhj, since DB is in Representation 3. ∎

Proof of Lemma 4 This proof is similar to the proof of Lemma 3 except for the number of Q's in CL2. We can prove this theorem by replacing $\neg Q(x_1,x_2)*s_0*s_2$ and $\neg Q(x_2,x_3)*s_0*s_2$ in KN2 of Lemma 3 with $(\neg Q(x_1,x_2) \vee \ldots \vee \neg Q(x_{i-1},x_i) \vee \neg Q(x_{i+1},x_{i+2}) \vee \ldots \vee \neg Q(x_{m-1},x_m))*s_0*s_2$. ∎

Proof of Theorem 9 This follows immediately from Lemmas 3 and 4. ∎

Proof of Theorem 10 The proof is similar to the proof of Lemma 4. We can prove it by letting $h = \neg Q(x,z) \vee \neg R(z,y) \vee S(x,y)$, $nhi = S(\$1,\$2) \vee$

KN1 v KP1, and $nhj = [R(\$1,\$2)$ v KN2 v KP2]$*s_0$, where KP1 contains $Q(\$3,\$4)$ and / or $R(\$5,\$6)$, KN2 = KN1 v $\neg Q(\$3,\$4)$ or KN1 v $\neg R(\$5,\$6)$, KP2 = (KP1 $\neg Q(\$3,\$4)$) v $S(x,y)$ or (KP1 $\neg R(\$5,\$6)$) v $S(x,y)$. ■

Proof of Theorem 11 Notice that K does not contain a negative literal over P, since DB is non-recursive.

Case 1: Suppose no clause contains a literal over P. Then CDB has no clauses containing more than one positive literal over P, but of course there will be some clause containing exactly one such literal. Let CL be such a clause. By resolving CL and $P(x_1,x_2,y_1y_2) \rightarrow Q(x_1,x_2,z)$, each literal over P in Cl can be replaced by a literal over Q. Then, we can obtain NH[Q] by inheriting the generation pattern of NH[P].

Case 2: Suppose some clauses contain one or more P's. Then CDB has some clauses containing more than one positive literal over P. Let CL be such a clause. By applying the OR-branch reduction theorem to {CL, $P(x_1,x_2,y_1,y_2) \rightarrow Q(x_1,x_2,z)$}, we need only generate their resolvents containing one Q.

Then, we can obtain NH[Q] by inheriting the generation pattern of NH[P]. ■

Proof of Theorem 12 Since DB is non-recursive, NH[Q] can be obtained by resolving CL* with clauses only in $nh1$, ..., and nhn, and PSUB[Q] by resolving CL* with clauses only in PSUB[$nh[Pi]$]. Then, NH[Q] and PSUB[Q] given in Theorem 11 can be constructed by applying the backward AND-branch reduction theorem. ■

Proof of Lemma 5

```
Let Si = {F(a,c) F(b,c)},
Sr = {¬F(x₁,x₂) ¬A(x₂,x₃) A(x₁,x₃),
      ¬F(x₁,x₂) ¬F(x₂,x₃) ¬A(x₃,x₄) A(x₁,x₄),
      . . . . . .
      ¬F(x₁,x₂) .... ¬F(xₙ₋₂,xₙ₋₁) ¬A(xₙ₋₁,xₙ) A(x₁,xₙ),
      . . . . . . . },
```

and *Se* as in the statement of the lemma.
Se and *Sr* are obtained by performing resolution on the set of recursive axioms, {$\neg F(x,y) A(x,y)$, $\neg F(x,z) \neg A(z,y) A(x,y)$}. Let CLi, CLr, and CLe denote clauses in *Si*, *Sr*, and *Se*, respectively. Let (CL1,CL2,CL3,...) denote a resolvent obtained by resolving (CL1,CL2), resolving its resolvent with CL3, and so on. Then, we have the following five possibilities for successive resolutions in the generation of NH[A]:

```
R1.  (CLi,CLe,CLr)
R2.  (CLi,CLr,CLe)
R3.  (CLr,CLe,CLi)
R4.  (CLi,CLe,CLi)
R5.  (CLi,CLr,CLi)
```

Notice that we may neglect the following two alternatives for the next resolution step, due to the NH-reduction theorem.

1. resolution including CLe two or more times, e.g., (CLi,CLe,CLe).

2. resolution including CLr two or more times, e.g., (CLi,CLr,CLr).

Also, resolutions (CLi,CLr,CLi,CLe,...) and (CLi,CLe,CLi,CLr,...) can be reformatted into (CLi,CLr,CLe,CLi,...) and (CLi,CLe,CLr,CLi,...), respectively. Hence, we need consider only *R1*, *R2*, and *R3* for the next resolution. It is a straightforward exercise in resolution theory to prove the following two facts:

F1. Clauses in NH derived by (CLi,CLr,CLe) and (CLi,CLe,CLr) are the same as those by (CLr,CLe,CLi).

F1. Clauses derived by (CLr,CLe) are in *Se*.

Hence, NH[*A*] can be generated by (CLe,CLi,CLi,...) without involving CLr. ■

Proof of Theorem 13   This follows immediately from Lemma 5, except the reformation of resolution resolving more than one non-Horn clause from *Si*. ■

Proof of Theorem 14   All cases of this theorem can be proved easily except the case of when both CL1 and CL2 are indefinite.

1. *Disjunctive case*: Clearly, if both CL1 and CL2 are indefinite, CL1 v CL2 cannot be false since CL1, and therefore CL1 v CL2, must be true in at least one minimal model. We show by example that CL1 v CL2 may be either indefinite or true. Let DB = $\{P\ R,\ Q\ S,\ \neg P\ \neg Q\}$. Then, $M1 = \{R, S\}$, $M2 = \{P, S\}$, and $M3 = \{Q, R\}$ are the minimal models of DB. Let DB$'$ = $\{P\ R,\ Q\ S\}$. Then, $M1' = \{P, Q\}$, $M2' = \{P, S\}$, $M3' = \{R, Q\}$, and $M4' = (R, S)$ are the minimal models of DB$'$. Let CL1 = $\neg P$ and CL2 = $\neg Q$. Then, both CL1 and CL2 are indefinite with respect to DB and DB$'$. However, CL1 v CL2 is true with respect to DB, but indefinite with respect to DB$'$.

2. *Conjunctive case*: First, if both CL1 and CL2 are indefinite, CL1 & CL2 cannot be true since there exists at least one minimal model falsifying it. Again, consider two example databases. Let DB = $\{P\ Q\}$. Then, $M1 = \{P\}$ and $M2 = \{Q\}$ are the minimal models of DB. Let DB$' = \{P\ R,\ Q\ S\}$. Then, $M1' = \{P,\ Q\}$, $M2' = \{P,\ S\}$, $M3' = \{R,\ Q\}$, and $M4' = \{R,\ S\}$ are the minimal models of DB$'$. Let CL1 = Q and CL2 = Q. Then, both CL1 and CL2 are indefinite with respect to DB and DB$'$, while CL1 & CL2 is false with respect to DB and indefinite with respect to DB$'$. ∎

Proof of Theorem 15

1. Suppose there is a pigc consisting of only atoms of DQ. Any minimal model contains at least one ground atom of such a pigc. Hence, DQ is true in all minimal models.

2. Now suppose there is no pigc consisting of only atoms of DQ. Since all the Pi's of DQ are indefinite, DQ is indefinite or true by the disjunctive theorem. Hence, if there is a minimal model, M^*, falsifying DQ, DQ is indefinite with respect to DB. Such an M^* can be constructed by selecting atoms from literals of pigc's which are different from literals of DQ. ∎

Proof of Lemma 6

IF PART

Suppose DB satisfies the two conditions. Then there are three kinds of clauses in PIGC: (1) Pi v Kis satisfying condition 1, i.e., Kis contains no other Pj literals; (2) the set of Pj v Kjt, one from each row, corresponding to the choice of S^*; (3) other clauses, say Cls, containing none of the Pi atoms and none of the atoms in S^*. Now each Cls contains an atom, say Us, not among the Pi, $i = 1,...,m$, or S^*. We form a minimal model of DB in the following way. First, include all atoms V such that the unit clause V is derivable from DB. (Of course, none of these atoms can occur in PIGC.) Next, include $P1$, ..., Pm. These will satisfy all type 1 and type 2 clauses. Further, by condition 1 and the definition of S^*, deleting any Pi will falsify some type 1 or 2 clause in the partial model being developed. We complete the minimal model by considering each type 3 clause in turn. If it has already been made true, it can be ignored. Otherwise, it contains none of the atoms $P1$, ..., Pm (or it would be true) and does contain an atom Us. Add Us to the partial model. Note that Us cannot make any of the $Kjt's$ from type 2 clauses true, so none of the Pj atoms may be deleted from the model being constructed. The end result is a minimal model of DB containing $P1$, ..., Pm. ∎

ONLY-IF PART
Suppose $P1$, ..., Pm appear together in some minimal model, say M^*. We prove that each condition must hold.

Condition 1: Suppose for some i, every Kis contains one of the other Pj atoms. Then clearly Pi could be deleted from M^*, contradicting the minimality of M^*.

Condition 2: Since M^* is minimal, deleting Pi from M^* must falsify some clause $Pi \vee Kis\langle i \rangle$. Then no literal of $Kis\langle i \rangle$ can appear in M^*. In particular, no atom of $Kis\langle i \rangle$ can be one of the other Pj atoms. Let S^* be the union of $K1s\langle 1 \rangle$, ..., $Kms\langle s \rangle$. Then S^* has no atom appearing in M^* and contains none of $P1$, ..., Pm. However, M^* makes every clause in DB true, and hence every clause in PIGC true. Let C be a clause not containing any of $P1$, ..., Pm. Since C is true in M^*, C must contain some atom of M^*, and that atom cannot be in S^*. ∎

Proof of Theorem 16 By the Conjunctive Decomposition Theorem, CQ is indefinite or false. If DB satisfies the two conditions, all Pi's commonly appear in at least one minimal model, by Lemma 6. Hence, CQ is true with respect to that model. Hence, CQ is indefinite with respect to DB. If DB doesn't satisfy the two conditions, there is no minimal model containing all $P1$, ..., Pm. Hence, CQ is false with respect to DB. ∎

Proof of Theorem 17

IF PART

(1) All CL1,..., and CLm are indefinite.

→(2) All ground atoms appearing in Q are "indefinite" or "false," and (3) CNQ is not true by (1) and the disjunctive decomposition theorem.

→(4) All $X1$,..., and Xn are "indefinite" or "false" by (2) and the conjunctive decomposition theorem.

→(5) DNQ is "indefinite" or "true," by (4), some Xi being indefinite, and the disjunctive decomposition theorem.

→(6) CNQ is indefinite, by (3) and CNQ having the same value as DNQ.

ONLY-IF PART
Trivial. ∎

References

1. Apt, K., Blair, H., and Walker, A. [1988] Towards a Theory of Declarative Knowledge, in *Foundations of Deductive Databases and Logic Programming* (J. Minker, Ed.), Morgan Kaufmann Publishers, Los Altos, CA, 89–148.

2. Bossu, G. and Siegel, P. [1985] Saturation, Nonmonotonic Reasoning and the Closed-World Assumption, *Artificial Intelligence* **25**, 13–63.

3. Bancilhon, F. and Ramakrishnan, P. [1987] An Amateur's Introduction to Recursive Query Processing Strategies, in *Proc. ACM-SIGMOD Conference on Management of Data*, Washington, DC, 16–52.

4. Chang, C. L. [1981] On Evaluation of Queries Containing Derived Relations, in *Advances in Data Base Theory, Vol. 1* (H. Gallaire, J. Minker, and J. M. Nicolas, Eds.), Plenum Press, New York, 235–260.

5. Clark, K. L. [1978] Negation as Failure, in *Logic and Databases* (H. Gallaire and J. Minker, Eds.), Plenum Press, New York, 293–324.

6. Gallaire, H., Minker, J., and Nicolas, J. [1984] Logic and Databases: A Deductive Approach, *ACM Computing Surveys* **10**, 153–185.

7. Grant, J. and Minker, J. [1986] Answering Queries in Indefinite Databases and the Null Value Problem, in *Advances in Computing Theory*, Vol. 3, *The Theory of Databases* (P. Kanellakis, Guest Ed.), JAI Press, Greenwich, CT, 247–267.

8. Han, J. [1985] Pattern-based and Knowledge-directed Query Compilation for Recursive Data Bases, Ph.D. thesis, University of Wisconsin—Madison.

9. Henschen, L. J. and Naqvi, S. [1984] On Compiling Queries in Recursive First-Order Databases, *JACM* **31**,47–85.

10. Henschen, L. J. and Park, H-S, [1986] Indefinite and GCWA Inference in Indefinite Deductive Databases, in *Proceedings of AAAI-86*, Philadelphia, PA, 193–241.

11. Lifschitz, V. [1988] On the Declarative Semantics of Logic Programs with Negation, in *Foundations of Deductive Databases and Logic Programming* (J. Minker, Ed.), Morgan Kaufmann Publishers, Los Altos, CA, 177–192.

12. Minker, J. [1982] On Indefinite Databases and the Closed World Assumption, in *Lecture Notes in Computer Science* **138**, Springer-Verlag, 292–308.

13. Przymusinski, T. [1988] On the Semantics of Stratified Deductive Databases, in *Foundations of Deductive Databases and Logic Programming* (J. Minker, Ed.) Morgan Kaufmann Publishers, Los Altos, CA, 193–216.

14. Reiter, R. [1978a] Deductive Question Answering on Relational Databases, in *Logic and Data Bases* (H. Gallaire and J. Minker, Eds.), Plenum Press, New York, 149–177.

15. Reiter, R. [1978b] On Closed World Databases, in *Logic and Databases* (H. Gallaire and J. Minker, Eds.), Plenum Press, New York, 55–76.

16. Reiter, R. [1984] Towards a Logical Reconstruction of Relational Database Theory, in *On Conceptual Modelling* (M. L. Brodie, J. Mylopoulos, and J. W. Schmit, Eds.), Springer-Verlag, New York, 163–189.

17. Ullman, J. D. [1985] Implementation of Logical Query Languages for Databases, *ACM Trans. on Database Systems* **10**, 289–321.

18. Van Gelder, A. [1988] Negation as Failure Using Tight Derivations for Logic Programs, in *Foundations of Deductive Databases and Logic Programming* (J. Minker, Ed.), Morgan Kaufmann Publishers, Los Altos, CA, 149–176.

19. Yahya, A. and Henschen, L. J. [1985], Deduction in Non-Horn Databases, *Journal of Automated Reasoning* **1**, 141–160.

12

Performance Evaluation of Data Intensive Logic Programs

Francois Bancilhon
MCC, Austin, TX

Raghu Ramakrishnan
MCC, Austin, TX, and
University of Texas, Austin, TX

Abstract

We present an analytical evaluation of the performance of several recursive query evaluation strategies on a set of four queries, over a range of data. We derive expressions for the cost of each strategy, using a simple model to characterize the data, plot these costs for specific configurations of the data, and discuss the results. We identify three important factors which influence the performance of these strategies.

Introduction

The database community has recently manifested a strong interest in the problem of computing "logic queries" against relational databases. Of course, database researchers already know how to evaluate logic queries: The view mechanism, as offered by most relational systems, is a form of support for a restricted set of logic queries which are non-recursive. The problem of efficiently supporting recursive queries, is however, still open.

Gallaire, Minker, and Nicolas [1984] present an overview of work in deductive databases. In the past five years, following the pioneering work by Chang [1981], McKay and Shapiro [1981], and Henschen and Naqvi [1984], numerous strategies have been proposed to deal with recursion in logic queries. The positive side of this work is that there are many algorithms offered to solve *the* problem. The negative side is that we do not know how to make a choice of an algorithm.

A strategy is defined by (i) an application domain (i.e., a class of rules for which it applies) and (ii) an algorithm for replying to queries given such a set of rules. We believe that strategies should be compared according to the following criteria: (i) size of the application domain (the larger the better), (ii) performance of the strategy (the faster the better), and (iii) ease of implementation (the simpler the better). In this paper, we address the second point in some detail.

In Bancilhon and Ramakrishnan [1986], we give a complete description of our understanding of several strategies and of their application domains, and we demonstrate each of them through examples. The strategies covered are: *Naive Evaluation* (Bancilhon [1986]), *Semi-Naive Evaluation* (Bancilhon [1986]), *Iterative Query-Subquery* (Vieille [1986]), *Recursive Query-Subquery* (Vieille [1986]), *Henschen-Naqvi* (Henschen and Naqvi [1984]), *Prolog* (Roussel [1975]), *APEX* (Lozinskii [1985]), *Aho-Ullman* (Aho and Ullman [1979]), *Static Filtering* (Kifer and Lozinskii [1986a]), *Magic Sets* (Bancilhon et al. [1986a]), and *Counting* (Sacca and Zaniolo [1986]). In this paper, we also consider a strategy that was not covered in our previous paper (Bancilhon and Ramakrishnan) [1986] and the {*Generalized Magic Sets*} strategy (Beeri and Ramakrishnan [1987]).

In the next section, we present descriptions of these methods. We then compare the performance of these strategies. We choose a simple set of typical queries, a simple characterization of the data, and a simple cost function, and give an analytical evaluation of the cost of each strategy. The results provide a first insight into the relative merits of all the proposed strategies.

The rest of the paper is organized as follows: In "The Methods," we present descriptions of the various methods, in "Framework for Performance Evaluation," we present the framework for our performance evaluation, and in "Notation and Preliminary Derivations," we introduce some notation and preliminary derivations. We present the performance analysis in "Analysis of the Query Evaluation Strategies." We summarize and interpret this analysis in "Graphical Comparison of the Costs." We discuss related work on performance evaluation in "Related Work" and present our conclusions in the section Conclusions and Caveats. We include graphs showing the relative performance of the various strategies over a range of queries and data in an appendix.

The Methods

We shall use the same example for most of the methods. The intensional database and query are:

R1 ancestor(X,Y) :- parent(X,Z),ancestor(Z,Y).

R2 ancestor(X,Y) :- parent(X,Y).

R3 query(X) :- ancestor(aa,X).

The extensional database is:

parent(a,aa).

parent(a,ab).

parent(aa,aaa).

parent(aa,aab).

parent(aaa,aaaa).

parent(c,ca).

The material in this section is taken from Bancilhon and Ramakrishnan [1986], and the reader should refer to it for detailed definitions (although we now present a few important definitions). A rule in the intensional database is *range restricted* if every variable in the head appears somewhere in the body. A rule is *bottom-up evaluable* if at each step in the bottom-up evaluation the set of values for each variable is finite. (This is a stronger restriction than range restriction if evaluable predicates, such as arithmetic operators, are present.)

Naive Evaluation

Naive Evaluation is a bottom-up, compiled, iterative strategy. Its application domain is the set of bottom-up evaluable rules. In a first phase, the rules that derive the query are compiled into an iterative program. The compilation process uses a reduced rule / goal graph. It first selects all the rules that derive the query. A temporary relation is assigned to each derived predicate in this set of rules. A statement that computes the value of the output predicate from the value of the input predicates is associated with each rule node in the graph. With each set of mutually recursive rules, there is associated a loop that applies the rules in that set until no new tuple is generated. Each temporary relation is initialized to the empty set. Then computation proceeds from the base predicates capturing the nodes of the graph.

In this example, the rules which derive the query are {R1, R2, R3}, and there are two temporary relations: ancestor and query. The method consists in applying R2 to parent, producing a new value for ancestor, then applying R1 to ancestor until no new tuple is generated, then applying R3.

The object program is:

> **begin**
>
> initialize ancestor to the empty set;
>
> evaluate (ancestor(X,Y) :- parent(X,Y));
>
> insert the result in ancestor;
>
> **while** "new tuples are generated" **do**
>
> **begin**
>
> evaluate (ancestor(X,Y) :- parent(X,Z), ancestor(Z,Y)) using the
>
> current value of ancestor;
>
> insert the result in ancestor
>
> **end**;
>
> evaluate (query(X) :- ancestor(aa,X));
>
> insert the result in query
>
> **end**.

The execution of the program against the data proceeds follows:

Step 1: Apply R2.
The resulting state is:

> ancestor = {(a,aa), (a,ab), (aa,aaa), (aa,aab), (aaa,aaaa), (c,ca)}
>
> query = { }

Step 2: Apply R1.
The following new tuples are generated:

> ancestor: {(a,aaa), (a,aab), (aa,aaaa)}

And the resulting state is:

> ancestor = {(a,aa), (a,ab), (aa,aaa), (aa,aab), (aaa,aaaa), (c,ca), (a,aaa),
>   (a,aab), (aa,aaaa)}
>
> query = { }

New tuples have been generated, so we continue:

Step 3: Apply R1.
The following tuples are generated:

> ancestor: {(a,aaa), (a,aab), (aa,aaaa), (a,aaaa)}

The new state is:

> ancestor = {(a,aa), (a,ab), (aa,aaa), (aa,aab), (aaa,aaaa), (c,ca), (a,aaa),
>   (a,aab), (aa,aaaa), (a,aaaa)}
>
> query = { }

Because (a,aaaa) is new, we continue:

Step 4: Apply R2.
The following tuples are generated:

> ancestor: {(a,aaa), (a,aab), (aa,aaaa), (a,aaaa)}

Because there are no new tuples, the state does not change and we move to R3.

Step 5: Apply R3.
The following tuples are produced:

> query: {(aa,aaa), (aa,aaaa)}

The new state is:

> ancestor = {(a,aa), (a,ab), (aa,aaa), (aa,aab), (aaa,aaaa), (c,ca), (a,aaa),
>   (a,aab), (aa,aaaa), (a,aaaa)}
>
> query = {(aa,aaa), (aa,aaaa)}.

The algorithm terminates.

In this example, we note the following problems: (i) The entire relation is evaluated, i.e., the set of potentially relevant facts is the set of facts of the base predicates which derive the query; (ii) Step 3 completely duplicates Step 2.

Naive Evaluation is the most widely described method in the literature. It has been presented in a number of papers under different forms. The inference engine of SNIP, presented in McKay and Shapiro [1981], is in fact an interpreted version of Naive Evaluation. The method described in Chang [1981], while based on a very interesting language paradigm and restricted to linear systems, is a compiled version of Naive Evaluation based on relational algebra. The method in Marque-Pucheu [1983] is a compiled version of Naive Evaluation using a different algebra of relations. The method in Bayer [1985] is another description of Naive Evaluation. The framework presented in Delobel [1986] also uses Naive Evaluation as its inference strategy. SNIP is, to our knowledge, the only existing implementation in the general case.

Semi-Naive Evaluation

Semi-Naive Evaluation is a bottom-up, compiled and iterative strategy. Its application range is the set of bottom-up evaluable rules. This method uses the same approach as Naive Evaluation, but it tries to cut down on the number of duplications. It behaves exactly as Naive Evaluation, except for the loop mechanism where it tries to be smarter.

Let us first try to give an idea of the method as an extension of Naive Evaluation. Let p be a recursive predicate: Consider a recursive rule having p as a head predicate and let us write this rule:

$$p :- \phi(p1,p2,\ldots,pn,q1,q2,\ldots,qm).$$

where ϕ is a first order formula, $p1,p2,\ldots,pn$ are mutually recursive to p, and $q1,q2,\ldots,qm$ are base or derived predicates, which are not mutually recursive to p.

In the Naive Evaluation strategy, all the qi's are fully evaluated when we start computing p and the pi's. On the other hand, p and the pi's are all evaluated inside the same loop (together with the rest of the predicates mutually recursive to p).

Let pj(i) be the value of the predicate pj at the i-th iteration of the loop. At this iteration, we compute

$$\phi(p1(i),p2(i),\ldots,pn(i),q1,q2,\ldots,qm).$$

During that same iteration, each pj receives a set of new tuples. Let us call this new set dpj(i). Thus the value of pj at the beginning of step $(i + 1)$ is $pj(i) + dpj(i)$ (where + denotes union).

At step (i + 1) we evaluate

$$\phi((p1(i) + dp1(i)),...,(pn(i) + dpn(i)),q1,...,qm),$$

which, of course, recomputes the previous expression (because ϕ is monotonic). The ideal, however, is to compute only the *new* tuples, i.e, the expression:

$$d\phi(p1(i),dp1(i),...,pn(i),dpn(i),q1,...,qm) =$$
$$\phi((p1(i) + dp1(i)),...,(pn(i) + dpn(i)),q1,...,qm) -$$
$$\phi(p1(i),...,pn(i),q1,...,qm)$$

The basic principle of the semi-naive method is the evaluation of the differential of ϕ instead of the entire ϕ at each step. The problem is to come up with a first order expression for $d\phi$ that does not contain any difference operator. Let us assume there is such an expression and describe the algorithm. With each recursive predicate p are associated four temporary relations—p.before, p.after, dp.before, and dp.after. The object program for a loop is as follows:

> **while** "the state changes" **do**
> **begin**
> **for** all mutually recursive predicates p **do**
> > **begin**
> > initialize dp.after to the empty set;
> > initialize p.after to p.before;
> > **end**
> **for** each mutually recursive rule **do**
> > **begin**
> > evaluate $d\phi(p1,dp1,...,pn,dpn,q1,...,qn)$ using the current values of
> > pi.before for pi and of dpi.before for dpi;
> > add the resulting tuples to dp.after;
> > add the resulting tuples to p.after
> > **end**
> **end**.

We now have to provide a way to generate dφ from φ. The problem is not solved in its entirety and only a number of transformations are known. In Bancilhon [1985], some transformations are given in terms of the relational algebra.

It should be noted, however, that for the method to work, the only property we have to guarantee is that:

$$\phi(p1 + dp1,...) - \phi(p1,...) \subseteq d\phi(p1,dp1,...) \subseteq \phi(p1 + dp1,...)$$

Clearly, the closer dφ(p1,dp1,...) is to (φ(p1 + dp1,...) − φ(p1,...)), the better the optimization. In the worst case, where we use φ for dφ, Semi-Naive Evaluation behaves as Naive Evaluation. Here are some simple examples of rewrite rules:

if φ(p,q) = p(X,Y),q(Y,Z), **then** dφ(p,dp,q) = dp(X,Y),q(Y,Z)

More generally, when φ is linear in p, the expression for dφ is obtained by replacing p by dp.

if φ(p1,p2) = p1(X,Y),p2(Y,Z),

then dφ(p,dp) = p1(X,Y),dp2(Y,Z) +
    dp1(X,Y),p2(Y,Z) + dp1(X,Y),dp2(Y,Z)

Note that this is not an exact differential but a reasonable approximation.

The idea of Semi-Naive Evaluation underlies many papers. A complete description of the method based on relational algebra is given in Bancilhon [1985]. The idea is also present in Bayer [1985].

It should also be pointed out that, in the particular case of linear rules, because the differential of φ(p) is simply φ(dp), it is sufficient to have an inference engine that only uses the new tuples. Therefore, many methods that are restricted to linear rules do indeed use Semi-Naive Evaluation. Note also that when the rules are not linear, applying Naive Evaluation only to the "new tuples" is an incorrect method (in the sense that it does not produce the whole answer to the query). This can be checked easily on the recursive rule:

ancestor(X,Y) :− ancestor(X,Z),ancestor(Z,Y).

In this case, if we only feed the new tuples at the next stage, the relation that we compute consists of the ancestors whose distance to one another is a power of two.

To our knowledge, outside of the special case of linear rules, the method as a whole has not been implemented.

Iterative Query / Subquery

Iterative Query / Subquery (QSQI) is an interpreted, top-down strategy. Its application domain is the set of range restricted rules without evaluable predicates. The method associates a temporary relation with every relation which derives the query, but the computation of the predicates deriving the query is done at run time. QSQI also stores a set of queries that are currently being evaluated. When several queries correspond to the same query form, QSQI stores and executes them as a single object. For instance, if we have the queries p(a,X) and p(b,X), we can view this as query p({a,b},X). We call such an object a *generalized query*. The state memorized by the algorithm is a pair ⟨Q,R⟩, where Q is a set of generalized queries, and R is a set of derived relations, together with their current values.

The iterative interpreter is as follows:

Initial state is ⟨{query(X)},{}⟩

while the state changes **do**

  for all generalized queries in Q **do**

    for all rules whose head matches the generalized query **do**

    begin

    unify rule with the generalized query;

    (i.e., propagate the constants. This generates new generalized queries for each derived predicate in the body by looking up the base relations.)

    generate new tuples;

    (by replacing each base predicate on the right by its value and every derived predicate by its current temporary value.)

    add these new tuples to R;

    add these new generalized queries to Q

    end

Let us now run this interpreter against our example logic database:
The initial state is: ⟨{query(X)},{}⟩

STEP 1

We try to solve query(X). Only rule R3 applies. Unification produces the generalized query ancestor({aa},X). This generates temporary relations for query and ancestor with empty set values. Attempts at generating tuples for this generalized query fail. The new state vector is:

$$\langle \{ \text{query}(X), \text{ancestor}(aa,X) \}, \{ \text{ancestor} = \{ \} , \text{query} = \{ \} \} \rangle$$

STEP 2

. A new generalized query has been generated, so the algorithm continues. We try to evaluate each of the generalized queries: Query(X) does not give anything new, so we try ancestor($\{aa\}$,X).

Using rule R2, and unifying, we obtain parent(aa,X). This is a base relation, so we can produce a set of tuples. Thus a value for ancestor is generated that contains all the tuples of parent(aa,X) and the new state vector is:

$$\langle \{ \text{query}(X), \text{ancestor}(aa,X) \},$$
$$\{ \text{ancestor} = \{ (aa,aaa),(aa,aab) \} , \text{query} = \{ \} \} \rangle$$

We now solve ancestor(aa,X) using R1. Unification produces the expression:

parent(aa,Z),ancestor(Z,Y).

We try to generate new tuples from this expansion and the current ancestor value but obtain no tuples. We also generate new generalized queries by looking up parent and instantiating Z. This produces the new expression:

parent(aa,$\{aaa,aab\}$),ancestor($\{aaa,aab\}$,Z).

This creates two new queries that are added to the generalized query, and the new state is:

$$\langle \{ \text{query}(X), \text{ancestor}(\{aa,aaa,aab\},X) \},$$
$$\{ \text{ancestor} = \{ (aa,aaa),(aa,aab) \} , \text{query} = \{ \} \} \rangle$$

STEP 3

New generalized queries and new tuples have been generated, so the algorithm continues. We first solve query(X) using R3 and obtain the value $\{$(aa,aaa), (aa,aab)$\}$ for query. The resulting new state is:

$$\langle \{ \text{query}(X), \text{ancestor}(\{aa,aaa,aab\},X) \},$$
$$\{ \text{ancestor} = \{ (aa,aaa),(aa,aab) \} , \text{query} = \{ (aa,aaa),(aa,aab) \} \} \rangle$$

We now try to solve ancestor({aa,aaa,aab},X). Using R2, we obtain parent({aa,aaa,aab),X), which is a base relation, and generate the following tuples in ancestor: {(aa,aaa),(aa,aab),(aaa,aaaa)}. This produces the new state:

⟨{query(X),ancestor({aa,aaa,aab},X)},

    {ancestor = {(aa,aaa),(aa,aab),(aaa,aaaa)},

        query = {(aa,aaa),(aa,aab)}}⟩

We now solve ancestor({aa,aaa,aab},X)} using R1 and obtain: p({aa,aaa,aab},Z),ancestor(Z,Y). We bind Z by going to the parent relation, and obtain: p({aa,aaa,aab},{aaa,aab,aaaa}), ancestor({aaa,aab,aaaa},Y). This generates the new generalized query ancestor({aaa,aab,aaaa},Y) and the new state:

⟨{query(X),ancestor({aa,aaa,aab,aaaa},X)},

    {ancestor = {(aa,aaa),(aa,aab),(aaa,aaaa)},

query = {(aa,aaa),(aa,aab)}}⟩

STEP 4
A new generalized query has been generated, so the algorithm continues. Solving the ancestor queries using R2 produces no new tuples, and solving it with R3 produces neither a new generalized query nor any tuples. The algorithm terminates.

Concerning the performance of the method, one can note that (i) the set of potentially relevant facts is better than for naive (in this example it is optimal), and (ii) QSQI has the same duplication problem as Naive Evaluation: each step entirely duplicates the previous strategy.

The concept of Iterative Query / Subquery is presented in Vieille [1986]. To our knowledge it has not been implemented.

Recursive Query / Subquery or Extension Tables

Recursive Query / Subquery (QSQR) is a top-down interpreted recursive strategy. The application domain is the set of range restricted rules without evaluable predicates. It is, of course, a recursive version of the previous strategy. As before, we maintain temporary values of derived relations and a set of generalized queries. The state memorized by the algorithm is still a pair ⟨Q,R⟩, where Q is a set of generalized queries and R is a set of derived relations together with their current values. The algorithm uses a selection function which, given a rule, can choose the first and the next derived predicate in the body to be "solved."

The recursive interpreter is as follows:

procedure evaluate(q)   (* q is a generalized query *)

begin

while "new tuples are generated" **do**

  for all rules whose head matches the generalized query **do**

    begin

    unify the rule with the generalized query; (i.e., propagate

      the constants)

    until there are no more derived predicates on the right **do**

      begin

      choose the first / next derived predicate according to the

        selection function;

      generate the corresponding generalized query;

      (This is done by replacing in the rule each base predicate
        by its value and each previously solved derived predicate by
        its current value.)

      eliminate from that generalized query the queries that are

        already in Q;

      this produces a new generalized query q′;

      add q′ to Q;

      evaluate(q′)

      end;

    replace each evaluated predicate by its value and evaluate

      the generalized query q;

    (This can be done in some order without waiting for all predicates

      to be evaluated.)

    add the results in R;

    return the results

    end

end.

The initial state is $\langle \{query(X)\}, \{\} \rangle$, evaluate(query(X)).

It is important to note that this version of QSQ is very similar to Prolog. It solves goals in a top-down fashion using recursion, and it considers the literals ordered in the rule (the order is defined by the selection function). The important differences with Prolog are: (i) The method is set-at-a-time instead of tuple-at-a-time, through the generalized query concept, and (ii) as pointed out in Dietrich and Warren [1985], the method uses a dynamic programming approach of storing the intermediate results and re-using them when needed. This dynamic programming feature also solves the problem of cycles in the facts—while Prolog will run in an infinite loop in the presence of such cycles, QSQR will detect them and stop the computation when no new tuple is generated. Thus, QSQR is complete over its application domain, whereas Prolog is not.

The ancestor example is now annotated using the algorithm:

evaluate(query(X))

use rule R3

query(X) :- ancestor(aa,X)

this generates the query ancestor($\{aa\}$,X)

new state is: $\langle \{ancestor(\{aa\},X), query(X)\}, \{\} \rangle$

evaluate(ancestor($\{aa\}$,X)

Step 1 of the iteration

use rule R1

ancestor($\{aa\}$,Y) :- parent($\{aa\}$,Z), ancestor(Z,Y).

by looking up parent we get the bindings $\{aaa,aab\}$ for Z.

this generates the query ancestor($\{aaa,aab\}$,X)

new state is: $\langle \{ancestor(\{aa,aaa,aab\},X), query(X)\}, \{\} \rangle$

evaluate (ancestor($\{aaa,aab\}$,X))

(this is a recursive call)

Step 1.1

use R1

ancestor($\{aaa,aab\}$,Y) :- parent($\{aaa,aab\}$,Z),ancestor(Z,Y).

by looking up parent to obtain the binding $\{aaaa\}$ for Z and the

new state is: $\langle \{ancestor(\{aa,aaa,aab,aaaa\},X), query(X)\}, \{\} \rangle$

evaluate(ancestor({aaaa},X))

(this is a recursive call)

   Step 1.1.1

   use R1

   ancestor({aaaa},Y) :– parent({aaaa},Z),ancestor(Z,Y).

   by looking up parent we obtain no binding for Z

   use R2

   ancestor({aaaa},Y) :– parent({aaaa},Y)

   which fails to return any tuple

   end of **evaluate**(ancestor({aaaa},X))

   Step 1.1.2

   nothing new is produced

   end of **evaluate**(ancestor({aaaa},Y))

use R2

ancestor({aaa,aab},Y) :– parent({aaa,aab},Y)

returns the tuple ancestor(aaa,aaaa) and the

new state is: ⟨{ancestor({aa,aaa,aab,aaaa},X),

query(X)}, {ancestor = {(aaa,aaaa)}}⟩

   Step 1.2

   same as Step 1, nothing new produced

   end of **evaluate** (ancestor({aaa,aab},X))

use rule R2

ancestor({aa},X) :– parent({aa},Y)

returns the tuples ancestor(aa,aaa) and ancestor(aa,aab) and the

new state is: ⟨{ancestor({aa,aaa,aab,aaaa},X), query(X)},

   {ancestor = {(aaa,aaaa), (aa,aaa),(aa,aab)}}⟩
      (aa,aaa),(aa,aab)}}⟩

Step 2

nothing new produced

end of **evaluate**({aa},X)

generate tuples from R3 and the

new state is: ⟨{ancestor({aa,aaa,aab,aaaa},X), query(X)},

{ancestor = {(aaa,aaaa),(aa,aaa),(aa,aab)},query = (aaa,aaaa),

(aa,aaa),(aa,aab)}}⟩

end of **evaluate**(query(X))

The Recursive Query / Subquery method is described in Vieille [1986]. A compiled version has been implemented on top of the INGRES relational system. In Dietrich and Warren [1985], along with a good survey of some of these strategies, a method called "extension tables" is presented. It is, up to a few details, the same method.

Henschen-Naqvi

Henschen-Naqvi is a top-down, compiled and iterative method. The application domain is that of linear range restricted rules. The method has a compilation phase which generates an iterative program. That iterative program is then run against the data base. The general strategy is fairly complex to understand, and we shall restrict ourselves to describing it in the "typical case," which is:

p(X,Y) :- up(X,XU),p(XU,YU),down(YU,Y).

p(X,Y) :- flat(X,Y).

query(X) :- p(a,X).

Note that the relation names *up* and *down* are not to be confused with the notions "top-down" or "bottom-up," which are characteristics of evaluation strategies. Let us introduce some simple notation that will make reading the algorithm much simpler. Since we are only dealing with binary relations, we can view these as set-to-set mappings. Thus, the relation r associates with each set A a set B, consisting of all elements related to A by r. We denote A.r the image of A by r, and we have:

$$A.r = \{ y \mid r(x,y) \text{ and } x \in A \}$$

If we view relations as mappings, we can compose them, and we denote r.s the composition of r and s. Therefore:

A.(r.s) = (A.r).s

This approach is similar to the formalism described in Gardarin and Maindreville [1986]. We denote the composition of relation r n times with itself r^n. Finally we denote set union by '+'. Once this notation is introduced, it is easy to see that the answer to the query is

{a}.flat + {a}.up.flat.down + {a}.up.up.flat.down.down + ... + {a}.up^n.flat.down^n + ...

The state memorized by the algorithm is a pair $\langle V,E \rangle$, where V is the value of a unary relation and E is an expression. At each step, using V and E, we compute some new tuples and compute the new values of V and E.

The iterative program is as follows:

V : = {a};

E : = λ;   / * the empty string */

while "new tuples are generated in V" **do**

  begin

  / * produce some answer tuples */

  answer : = answer + V.flat.E;

  / * compute the new value */

  V : = V.up;

  / * compute the new expression */

  E : = E | .down;

  end.

Note that E is an *expression* and is augmented each time around the loop by concatenating ".down" to it through the "cons" operator. As can be seen from this program, at step i, the value V represents {a}.up^i and the expression E represents down^i. Therefore the tuples produced are:

{a}.up^i.flat.down^i.

This is not meant to be a complete description of the method, but a description of its behavior in the typical case.

The Henschen-Naqvi method is described in Henschen and Naqvi [1984]. The method has been implemented in the case described here. This implementation can be found in Laskowski [1984]. An equivalent strategy is described using a different formalism in Gardarin and Maindreville [1986]. The performance of the strategy is compared to Semi-Naive Evaluation and another method (not described here) in Han and Lu [1986].

Prolog

Prolog (Roussel [1975]) is a top-down, interpreted and recursive method. The application domain of Prolog is difficult to state precisely: (i) It is data dependent in the sense that the facts have to be acyclic for the interpreter to terminate, and (ii) there is no simple syntactic characterization of a terminating Prolog program. The job of characterizing the "good" rules is left to the programmer.

We consider its execution model to be well known and will not describe it. In fact, Prolog is a programming language and not a general strategy to evaluate Horn clauses. We essentially mention Prolog for the sake of completeness and because it is interesting to compare its performance to the other strategies.

APEX

APEX is a strategy that is difficult to categorize. It is partly compiled in the sense that a graph similar to the predicate connection graph is produced from the rules, which takes care of some of the preprocessing needed for interpretation. It is not fully compiled in the sense that the program that runs against the database is still unique (but driven by the graph). It is, however, clearly recursive, because the interpreter program is recursive. Finally, it is partly top-down and partly bottom-up as will be seen in the interpreter.

The application domain of APEX is the set of range restricted rules which contain no constants and no evaluable predicates. The interpreter takes the form of a recursive procedure, which, given a query, produces a set of tuples for this query. It is as follows:

    procedure solve(query,answer)

    begin

    answer := { };

    if query q is on a base relation

then evaluate q against the date base

else

  begin

    select the relevant facts for q in the base predicates;

    put them in relevant;

    while new tuples are generated **do**

      begin

      for each rule **do** (this can be done in parallel)

        begin

          instantiate the right predicates with the relevant facts and produce

            tuples for the left predicate;

          add these tuples to the set of relevant facts;

          initialize the set of useful facts to the set of relevant facts;

          for each literal on the right **do** (this can be done in parallel)

            begin

            for each matching relevant fact **do**

              begin

                plug the fact in the rule and propagate the constants;

                this generates a new rule and a new set of queries;

                for all these new queries q' **do**

                  begin

                  solve(q',answer(q')) (this is the recursion step)

                  add answer(q') to the useful facts

                end

              end

          instantiate the right predicates with the useful facts;

          produce tuples for the left predicate;

          add these to the relevant facts;

extract the answer to q from the relevant facts

end

end

end

end.

end;

solve(query(X),answer).

Let us now run this program against the ancestor example. We cannot have a constant in the rules and we must modify our rule set and directly solve the query ancestor(aa,X):

solve (ancestor(aa,X), answer)

we first select the relevant base facts.

relevant = {parent(aa,aaa),parent(aa,aab)};

we now start the main iteration:

Step 1

rule R1

ancestor(X,Y) :– parent(X,Z), ancestor(Z,Y)

    we cannot produce any new tuple from this rule because ancestor

    does not yet have any relevant fact

    useful = {parent(aa,aaa),parent(aa,aab)};

    process parent(X,Z)

      use parent(aa,aaa)

        the new rule is

        parent(aa,aaa),ancestor(aaa,Y)

        solve(ancestor(aaa,Y),answer1)

        ...(this call is not described)

        this returns

        {ancestor(aaa,aaaa)}, which we add to useful

useful = { parent(aa,aaa),

parent(aa,aab),ancestor(aaa,aaaa) };

use parent(aa,aab)

the new rule is

parent(aa,aab),ancestor(aab,Y)

solve(ancestor(aab,Y),answer2)

...(this call is not described)

this returns nothing

process ancestor(Z,Y)

we instantiate parent and ancestor with the useful facts.

this produces ancestor(aa,aaaa)

we add it to the relevant facts:

relevant = { parent(aa,aaa),parent(aa,aab), ancestor(aa,aaaa) };

rule R2

ancestor(X,Y) :– parent(X,Y)

using the relevant facts we produce { ancestor(aa,aaa),ancestor(aa,aab) }

we add these to relevant:

relevant = { parent(aa,aaa),parent(aa,aab),ancestor(aa,aaa),

ancestor(aa,aab), ancestor(aa,aaaa) };

this rule does not produce any subquery

Step 2

will not produce anything new,

and so the algorithm stops.

The APEX method is desrcribed in Lozinskii [1985]. The method has been implemented.

Aho-Ullman

Aho and Ullman (Aho and Ullman [1979]) present an algorithm for optimizing recursive queries by commuting selections with the least fixpoint operator (LFP). The input is an expression

$$\sigma_F(LFP(r = f(r))$$

where f(r) is a monotonic relational algebra expression (under the ordering of set inclusion) and contains at most one occurrence of r. The output is an equivalent expression where the selection has been pushed through as far as possible.

We introduce their notation and ideas through an example. Consider:

a(X,Y) :- a(X,Z), p(Z,Y).

a(X,Y) :- p(X,Y).

q(X) :- a(john,X).

Aho-Ullman write this as:

$$\sigma_{a_1 = john}(LFP(a = a.p \cup p))$$

In this definition, *a* is a relation which is defined by a *fixpoint* equation in relational algebra, and *p* is a base relation. If we start with *a* empty and repeatedly compute *a* using the rule a = a.p $\cup$ p, at some iteration, there is no change (since the relation *p* is finite). Because the function used in the fixpoint equation is monotonic, this is the *least fixpoint* of the fixpoint equation (Tarski [1955]). It is the smallest relation *a* that satisfies the equation, i.e., contains every tuple that can be generated by using the fixpoint rule, and no tuple that cannot. The query is simply the selection $a_1 = john$ applied to this relation. Thus, the query is a selection applied to the transitive closure of p.

We now describe how the Aho-Ullman algorithm optimizes this query. We use '.' to denote composition, which is a join followed by projecting out the join attributes. We begin with the expression

$$\sigma_{a_1 = john}(a)$$

and by replacing a by f(a) we generate

$$\sigma_{a_1 = john}(a.p \cup p)).$$

By distributing the selection across the join, we obtain

$$\sigma_{a_1 = john}(a.p) \cup \sigma_{a_1 = john}(p).$$

Since the selection in the first subexpression only involves the first attribute of a, we can rewrite it as

$$\sigma_{a_1 = john}(a).p$$

We observe that this contains the subexpression

$$\sigma_{a_1 = john}(a)$$

which was the first expression in the series. If we denote this by E, the desired optimized expression is then

$$LFP(E = E.p \cup \sigma_{a_i = john} (p)).$$

This is equivalent to the Horn Clause query:

a(john,Y) :– a(john,Z), p(Z,Y).

a(john,Y) :– p(john,Y).

q(X) :– a(john,X).

The essence of the strategy is to construct a series of equivalent expressions starting with the expression $\sigma_F(r)$ and repeatedly replacing the single occurrence of r by the expression f(r). Note that each of these expressions contains just one occurrence of R. In each expression we push the selection as far inside as possible. Selection distributes across union, commutes with another selection, and can be pushed ahead of a projection. However, it distributes across a Cartesian product $Y \times Z$ only if the selection applies to components from just one of the two arguments Y and Z. The algorithm fails to commute the selection with the LFP operator if the (single) occurrence of r is in one of the arguments of a Cartesian product across which we cannot distribute the selection. We stop when this happens or when we find an expression of the form $h(g(\sigma_F(r)))$ and one of the previous expressions in the series is of the form $h(\sigma_F(r))$. In the latter case, the equivalent expression that we are looking for is $h(LFP(s = g(s)))$, and we have succeeded in pushing the selection ahead of the LFP operator.

We note in conclusion that the expression f(r) must contain no more than one occurrence of *r*. For instance, the algorithm does not apply in this case:

$$\sigma_{a_1 = john}(LFP(a = a.a \cup p))$$

Aho and Ullman also present a similar strategy for commuting projections with the LFP operator, but we do not discuss it here.

Static Filtering

The Static Filtering algorithm is an extension of the Aho-Ullman algorithm described above. However, rules are represented as rule / goal graphs rather than as relational algebra expressions, and the strategy is described in terms of *filters* that are applied to the arcs of the graph. It is convenient to think of the data as flowing through the graph along the arcs. A *filter* on an arc is a selection that can be applied to the tuples flowing through that arc, and is used to reduce the number of tuples that are generated. Transforming a given rule / goal graph into an equivalent graph with (additional) filters on some arcs is equivalent to rewriting the corresponding set of rules.

The execution of a query starts with the nodes corresponding to the base relations sending all their tuples through all arcs that leave them. Each axiom node that receives tuples, generates tuples for its head predicate and passes them on through all its outgoing arcs. A relation node saves all new tuples that it receives and passes them on through its outgoing arcs. Computation stops (with the answer being the set of tuples in the query node) when there is no more change in the tuples stored at the various nodes at some iteration. We note that this is simply Semi-Naive Evaluation.

Given filters on all the arcs leaving a node, we can "push" them through the node as follows. If the node is a relation node, we simply place the disjunction of the filters on each incoming arc. If the node is an axiom node, we place on each incoming arc the strongest consequence of the disjunction that can be expressed purely in terms of the variables of the literal corresponding to this arc.

The objective of the optimization algorithm is to place the "strongest" possible filters on each arc. Starting with the filter that represents the constant in the query, it repeatedly pushes filters through the nodes at which the corresponding arcs are incident. Since the number of possible filters is finite, this algorithm terminates. It stops when further pushing of filters does not change the graph, and the graph at this point is equivalent to the original graph (although the graph at intermediate steps may not). Note that since the disjunction of "true" with any predicate is "true," if any arc in a loop is assigned the filter "true," all arcs in the loop are subsequently assigned the filter "true."

Consider the transitive closure example that we optimized using the Aho-Ullman algorithm. We would represent it by the following axioms:

R1 a(X,Y) :- a(X,Z), p(Z,Y).

R2 a(X,Y) :- p(X,Y).

R3 q(X) :- a(john,X).

Given in Figure 1 is the corresponding system graph, before and after optimization (we have omitted the variables in the axioms for clarity).

We begin the optimization by pushing the selection through the relation node a. Thus, the arcs from R1 to *a* and from R2 to *a* both receive the filter '1 = john' (we have simplified the conventions for keeping track of variables—"1" refers to the first attribute of the corresponding head predicate). We then push these filters through the corresponding axiom nodes, R1 and R2. Pushing "1 = john" through node R2 puts the filter "p_1 = john" on the arc from p to R2. Pushing "1 = john" through node R1 puts the filter "a_1 = john" on the arc from a to R1. Note that it does not put anything on the arc from p to R1 (empty filters are equivalent to "true"). There are no arcs entering p, and the filter on the arc from a to R1 does not change the disjunction of the filters on arcs leaving a (which is still 'a_1 = john'). So the algorithm terminates here.

The analogy with the Aho-Ullman algorithm is easily seen when we recognize that a filter is a selection, pushing through a relation node is distribution across a ∪ and pushing through an axiom node is distribution across a Cartesian product. In general, the optimizations achieved by the two algorithms are identical. However, the Static Filtering algorithm is more general, successfully optimizing some expressions containing more than one occurrence of the defined predicate. An example is the expression

$$\sigma_{a_1 = \text{john}}(\text{LFP}(a = (a.p \cup a.q \cup p))).$$

The Aho-Ullman algorithm does not apply in this case because there are two occurrences of R in f(R). The Static Filtering algorithm optimizes this to

$$\text{LFP}((\sigma_{a_1 = \text{john}}(a).p) \cup (\sigma_{a_1 = \text{john}}(a).q) \cup (\sigma_{a_1 = \text{john}}(p))).$$

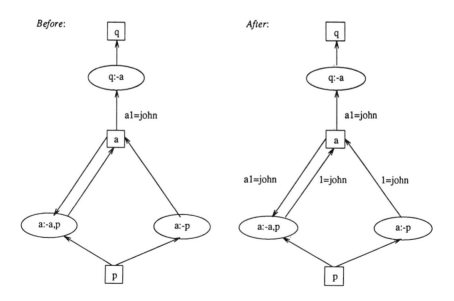

Figure 1.

Essentially, it improves upon the Aho-Ullman algorithm in that it is able to distribute selection across some unions where both arguments contain r.

Further, the algorithm can work directly upon certain mutually recursive rules, for example

R1 r(X,Y) :– b(X), s(X,Y).

R2 s(X,Y) :– c(X), r(X,Y).

R3 q(X) :– r(X,john).

Before applying the Aho-Ullman algorithm, these rules must be rewritten as follows

R1 r(X,Y) :– b(X), c(X), r(X,Y).

R2 q(X) :– r(X,john).

Note that the Static Filtering algorithm fails to optimize both

$\sigma_{a_1 \ = \ john}$ (LFP(a = a.a $\cup$ p)), and

$\sigma_{a_1 \ = \ john}$ (LFP(a = a.p $\cup$ p.a $\cup$ p)).

In this description, we have treated only the "static" filtering approach of Kifer and Lozinskii. Elsewhere, they have also proposed "dynamic" filters (Kifer and Lozinskii [1986b]), which are not determined at compile time but are computed at run time; this approach is similar to Generalized Magic Sets, discussed later in this section.

Magic Sets

The idea of the Magic Sets optimization is to simulate the sideways passing of bindings à la Prolog by the introduction of new rules. This cuts down on the number of potentially relevant facts. The application domain is the set of bottom-up evaluable rules. We shall describe the strategy in detail, using as an example a modified version of the same-generation rule set:

sg(X,Y) :– p(X,XP),p(Y,YP),sg(YP,XP).

sg(X,X).

query(X) :– sg(a,X).

Note that in this version the two variables, XP and YP, have been permuted. Note also that the second rule is not range restricted. The first step of the magic set transformation is the introduction of adornments and the generation of adorned rules.

Given a system of rules, the *adorned rule system* (Ullman [1985]) is obtained as follows:

For each rule r and for each adornment a of the predicate on the left, generate an adorned rule: Define recursively an argument of a predicate in the rule r to be *distinguished* (Henschen and Naqvi [1984]) if either it is bound in the adornment a, or it is a constant, or it appears in a base predicate occurrence that has a distinguished variable. Thus, the sources of bindings are (i) the constants and (ii) the bindings in the head of the rule. These bindings are propagated through the base predicates. If we consider each distinguished argument to be bound, this defines an adornment for each derived literal on the right. The adorned rule is obtained by replacing each derived literal by its adorned version.

If we consider the rule

sg(X,Y) :– p(X,XP),p(Y,YP),sg(YP,XP).

with adornment bf on the head predicate, then X is distinguished because it is bound in sg(X,Y). XP is distinguished because X is distinguished, and p(X,XP) is a base predicate. These are the only distinguished variables. Thus the new adorned rule is

sg^{bf}(X,Y) :– p(X,XP),p(Y,YP),sg^{fb}(YP,XP).

If we consider a set of rules, this process generates a set of adorned rules. The set of adorned rules has size K.R where R is the size of the original set of rules and K is a factor exponential in the number of attributes per derived predicate. So, for instance, if every predicate has three attributes, then the adorned system is eight times larger than the original system. However, we do not need the entire adorned system and we only keep the adorned rules that derive the query. In our example, the reachable adorned system is:

sg^{bf}(X,Y) :– p(X,XP),p(Y,YP),sg^{fb}(YP,XP).

sg^{fb}(X,Y) :– p(X,XP),p(Y,YP),sg^{bf}(YP,XP).

sg^{bf}(X,X).

sg^{fb}(X,X).

$query^{f}$(X) :– sg^{bf}(a,X).

Clearly, this new set of rules is equivalent to the original set in the sense that it will generate the same answer to the query.

The magic set optimization consists in generating, from the given set of rules, a new set of rules that are equivalent to the original set with respect to the query, and such that their bottom-up evaluation is more efficient. This transformation is done as follows: (i) For each occurrence of a derived predicate on the right of an adorned rule, we generate a magic rule. (ii) For each adorned rule we generate a modified rule. The magic rule is generated as follows: (i) choose an adorned literal predicate p on the right of the adorned rule r, (ii) erase all other derived literals on the right, (iii) in the derived predicate occurrence, replace the name of the predicate by *magic.p*^{a} where *a* is the literal adornment, and erase the non-distinguished variables, (iv) erase all the non-distinguished base predicates, (v) in the left hand side, erase all the non-distinguished variables and replace the name of the predicate by *magic.p*$1^{a'}$, where p1 is the predicate on the left, and a′ is the adornment of the predicate p1, and finally (vi) exchange the two magic predicates.

For instance the adorned rule:

$$sg^{bf}(X,Y) :- p(X,XP),p(Y,YP),sg^{fb}(YP,XP).$$

generates the magic rule:

$$magic^{fb}(XP) :- p(X,XP), magic^{bf}(X).$$

Note that the magic rules simulate the passing of bound arguments through backward chaining. (We have dropped the suffix ''sg'' in naming the magic predicates since it is clear from the context.)

The modified rule is generated as follows: For each rule whose head is p.a, add on the right hand side the predicate magic.p.a(X) where X is the list of distinguished variables in that occurrence of p. For instance the adorned rule:

$$sg^{bf}(X,Y) :- p(X,XP),p(Y,YP),sg^{fb}(YP,XP).$$

generates the modified rule:

$$sg^{bf}(X,Y) :- p(X,XP),p(Y,YP),magic^{bf}(X), sg^{fb}(YP,XP).$$

Finally the complete modified set of rules for our example is:

$$magic^{fb}(XP) :- p(X,XP), magic^{bf}(X).$$
$$magic^{bf}(YP) :- p(Y,YP),magic^{fb}(Y).$$
$$magic^{bf}(a).$$
$$sg^{bf}(X,Y) :- p(X,XP),p(Y,YP),magic^{bf}(X),sg^{fb}(YP,XP).$$

$sg^{fb}(X,Y) :- p(X,XP),p(Y,YP),magic^{fb}(Y),sg^{bf}(YP,XP).$

$sg^{bf}(X,X) :- magic^{bf}(X).$

$sg^{fb}(X,X) :- magic^{bf}(X).$

$query.f(X) :- sg^{bf}(a,X).$

The idea of the magic sets strategy was presented in Bancilhon et al. [1986b] and the precise algorithm is described in Bancilhon et al. [1986a]. To our knowledge, the strategy is not implemented.

Counting and Reverse Counting

Counting and Reverse Counting are derived from the magic sets optimization strategy. They apply under two conditions: (i) the data is acyclic, and (ii) there is at most one recursive rule for each predicate, and it is linear. We first describe counting using the "typical" single linear rule system:

$p(X,Y) :- flat(X,Y).$

$p(X,Y) :- up(X,XU),p(XU,YU),down(YU,Y).$

$query(Y) :- p(a,Y).$

The idea consists of introducing magic sets (called *counting* sets) in which elements are numbered by their distance to the element a. Remember that the magic set essentially marks all the *up* ancestors of a and then applies the rules in a bottom-up fashion to only the marked ancestors. In the counting strategy, at the same time we mark the ancestors of "john," we number them by their distance from a. Then we can "augment" the p predicate by numbering its tuples and generate them by levels as follows:

$counting(a,0).$

$counting(X,I) :- counting(Y,J),up(Y,X),I = J + 1.$

$p'(X,Y,I) :- counting(X,I),flat(X,Y).$

$p'(X,Y,I) :- counting(X,I),up(X,XU),$
$\quad p'(XU,YU,J),down(YU,Y),I = J - 1.$

$query(X) :- p'(a,X,0).$

Thus at each step, instead of using the entire magic set, we only use the tuples of the correct level, thus minimizing the set of relevant tuples. But in fact, it is useless to compute the first attribute of the p predicate. Thus the system can be further optimized into:

counting(a,0).

counting(X,I) :–counting(Y,J),up(Y,X),I = J + 1.

p''(Y,I) :– counting(X,I),flat(X,Y).

p''(Y,I) :– p''(YU,J),down(YU,Y),I = J − 1,J > 0.

query(X) :– p''(Y,0).

It is interesting to notice that this new set of rules, in fact, simulates a stack.

Reverse counting is another variation around the same idea. It works as follows: (i) first compute the magic set, then (ii) for each element b in the magic set number all its *down* descendants and its *up* descendants and add to the answer all the *down* descendants having the same number as a (because a is in the *up* descendants). This gives the following equivalent system:

magic(a).

magic(Y) :– magic(X),up(X,Y).

des.up(X,X,0) :– magic(X).

des.down(X',Y,0) :– magic(X'),flat(X',Y).

des.up(X',X,I) :– des.up(X',Y,J),up(X,Y),I = J + 1.

des.down(X',X,I) :– des.down(X',Y,J),down(Y,X),I = J + 1.

query(Y) :– des.up(X',a,Y),des.down(X',Y,I).

This can be slightly optimized by limiting ourselves to the b's which will join with *flat* and restricting the *down* des's to be in the magic set. This generates the following system:

magic(a).

magic(Y) :– magic(X),up(X,Y).

des.up(X,X,0) :– magic(X),flat(X,Y).

des.down(X',Y,0) :– magic(X'),flat(X',Y).

des.up(X',X,I) :– magic(X),des.up(X',Y,J),up(X,Y),I = J + 1.

des.down(X',X,I) :– des.down(X',Y,J),down(Y,X),I = J + 1.

sg(a,Y) :– des.up(X',a,Y),des.down(X',Y,I).

Note that we still have the problem of a "late termination" on *down* because we number *all* the descendants in *down*, even those of a lower generation than a.

The idea of Counting was presented in Bancilhon et al. [1986b] and a formal description of counting and of an extension called "Magic Counting" was presented in the single rule case in Sacca and Zaniolo [1986]. Reverse Counting is described in Bancilhon et al. [1986a]. They have not been implemented.

Generalized Magic Sets

A generalization of the Magic Sets method is described in Beeri and Ramakrishnan [1987]. The intuition is that the Magic Sets method works essentially by passing bindings obtained by solving body predicates "sideways" in the rule to restrict the computation of other body predicates. The notion of *sideways information passing* is formalized in terms of labeled graphs. A sideways information passing graph is associated with each rule, and these graphs are used to define the Magic Sets transformation. (In general, many such graphs exist for each rule, each reflecting one way of solving the predicates in the body of the rule; we may choose any one of these and associate it with the rule.)

There are examples, such as transitive closure defined using double recursion, in which the original Magic Sets transformation achieves no improvement over Semi-Naive Evaluation. Intuitively, this is because the only form of sideways information passing that it implements consists of using base predicates to bind variables. Thus, in the same generation example discussed earlier, the predicate *p* is used to bind the variable XP. The method, however, fails to pass information through derived predicates, and so it fails with transitive closure expressed using double recursion (since the recursive rule contains no base predicates in the body). Consider the rule:

a(X,Y) :– a(X,Z), a(Z,Y).

Given a query a(john,Y), the Magic Sets method recognizes that X is bound (since it is bound in the adornment *bf* corresponding to the head of the rule). However, Z is considered free. So it generates the following adorned rule:

$a^{bf}(X,Y) :\!- a^{bf}(X,Z),a^{ff}(Z,Y).$

Clearly, the method computes the entire ancestor relation. To succeed in binding Z, the first occurrence of *a* in the body must be used.

The generalized version of the method succeeds in passing information through derived predicates as well. As with the original Magic Sets strategy, a set of *adorned rules* is first obtained from the given rules, and these adorned rules are then used to produce the optimized set of rules. Both these steps are now directed, however, by the notion of *sideways information passing graphs* (sips). A sip corresponding to the above rule which binds Z is:

$$h \to_X a.1, \, h,a.1 \to_Z a.2$$

The predicate h denotes the bound part of the head. This graph indicates that the head binds X and this is used in solving the first occurrence of a. Further, this solution is used to bind Z in solving the second occurrence of a. This generates the adorned rule:

$$a^{bf}(X,Y) :- a^{bf}(X,Z), \, a^{bf}(Z,Y).$$

The magic rules corresponding to the two occurrences of a are:

magic(X) :- magic(X).

magic(Z) :- magic(X), $a^{bf}(X,Z)$.

The first rule is trivial and may be discarded. In addition, we obtain the rule "magic(john)" from the query. The modified rules are obtained exactly as in the Magic Sets method, by adding magic predicates to the body of the rule.

We do not present the details here. The reader is referred to Beeri and Ramakrishnan [1987], where Counting and variants of both Magic Sets and Counting are generalized as well. The "Alexandre" strategy described in Rohmer and Lescoeur [1985] is essentially a variant of the Generalized Magic Sets strategy. The dynamic filtering approach of Kifer and Lozinskii is similar to the Generalized Magic Sets strategy, although it cannot implement some sideways information passing graphs. The dynamic filters essentially perform as magic sets, but this is a run-time strategy, and the overhead of computing and applying the filters falls outside our framework. We do not discuss dynamic filtering further in this paper.

Framework for Performance Evaluation

We now turn to the problem of comparing the above strategies. To perform a comparison of the strategies we must:

1. Choose a set of rules and queries that will represent our benchmark.

2. Choose some test data that will represent our extensional database.

3.   Choose a cost function to measure the performance of each strategy.

4.   Evaluate the performance of each query against the extensional databases.

We first describe the four queries used as "typical" intensional databases. Then, we present our characterization of the data. Each relation is characterized by four parameters and it is argued that a number of familiar data structures, e.g., trees, can be described in this framework. We describe our cost metric, which is the size of the intermediate results before duplicate elimination. We present analytical cost functions for each query evaluation strategy on each query. The cost functions are plotted for three sets of data—tree, inverted tree, and cylinder. We discuss these results informally.

Workload: Sample Intensional Databases and Queries

Instead of generating a general mix, we have chosen four queries that have the properties of exercising various important features of the strategies. We are fully aware that this set is insufficient to provide a complete benchmark, but we view this work as a first step toward a better understanding of the performance behavior of the various strategies.

The queries used are three different versions of the ancestor query and a version of the same-generation query. The first one is just a classical ancestor rule and query with the first attribute bound.

QUERY 1

a(X,Y) :– p(X,Y).

a(X,Y) :– p(X,Z),a(Z,Y).

query(X) :– a(john,X).

Because most strategies are representation dependent, we have studied the same example with the second attribute bound instead of the first. This will allow us to determine which strategies can solve both cases.

QUERY 2

a(X,Y) :– p(X,Y).

a(X,Y) :– p(X,Z),a(Z,Y).

query(X) :– a(X,john).

The third version of the ancestor example specifies ancestor using double recursion. This enables us to see how the strategies react to the non-linear case. Since this example is fully symmetric, it is sufficient to test it with its first attribute bound.

QUERY 3

a(X,Y) :- p(X,Y).

a(X,Y) :- a(X,Z),a(Z,Y).

query(X) :- a(john,X).

Finally, to study something more complex than transitive closure, we have chosen a generalized version of the same generation example, bound on its first attribute.

QUERY 4

p(X,Y) :- flat(X,Y).

p(X,Y) :- up(X,XU),p(XU,YU), down(YU,Y).

query(X) :- p(john,X).

Characterizing Data: Sample Extensional Databases

Because we decided on an analytical approach, we had to obtain tractable formulae for the cost of each strategy against each query. Therefore, each relation must be characterized by a *small* set of parameters. Fortunately, because of the choice of our workload, we can restrict our attention to binary relations. We represent every binary relation by a directed graph and view tuples as edges and domain elements as nodes. Nodes are arranged in layers and each edge goes from a node in one layer to a node in the next. Note that in these graphs each node has at least one in-edge or one out-edge. Nodes in the first layer have no incoming edges and nodes in the last layer have no outgoing edges. We assume that edges are randomly distributed with a uniform distribution.

This formalism does not represent cycles. Nor does it represent shortcuts, where a shortcut is the existence of two paths of different length going from one point to another. Clearly, they would violate our assumption that nodes were arranged in layers with edges going from nodes in one layer to the next.

Let R be a binary relation and A be a set. Recall that we denote by A.R the set:

$$A.R = \{y \mid x \in A \text{ and } R(x,y) \}$$

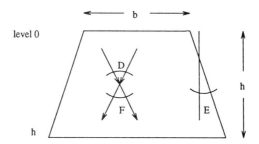

Figure 2: The Canonical Data Structure

We characterize a binary relation R by:

1. F_R the *fan-out* factor,

2. D_R the *duplication* factor,

3. h_R the *height*, and

4. b_R the *base*.

F_R and D_R are defined as follows: Given a "random" set A of n nodes from R, the size of A.R is n F_R before duplicate elimination. D_R is the duplication factor in A.R, i.e., the ratio of the size of A.R before and after duplicate elimination. Thus the size of A.R after duplicate elimination is n F_R / D_R.

We call $E_R = F_R / D_R$ the *expansion* factor of R.

The base b_R is the number of nodes that do not have any antecedents. The height h_R is the length of the longest chain in R.

When no confusion is possible, we shall simply use F, D, h, and b instead of F_R, D_R, h_R, and b_R.

The typical structure, shown in Figure 2, consists of a number of layers. There are $(h_R + 1)$ layers of nodes in the structure, numbered from top to bottom (as 0 to h). There are b_R nodes in level 0.

This "parametrized structure" is fairly general and can represent a number of typical configurations:

A binary balanced tree of height k is defined by:

F = 2; D = 1; h = k; b = 1

The same binary tree upside down is defined by:

$F = 1$; $D = 2$; $h = k$, $b = 2^k$

A list of length k is defined by:

$F = 1$; $D = 1$; $h = k$; $b = 1$

A set of n lists of length k is defined by:

$F = 1$; $D = 1$; $h = k$; $b = n$

A parent relation, where each person has two children and each child has two parents, is defined by:

$F = 2$; $D = 2$; $h =$ number of generations; $b =$ number of people of unknown parentage

We emphasize that we assume the data to be *random* with a uniform distribution. Thus, the values F and D are average values. Our characterization of a binary tree, for instance, describes a random (but layered) data structure in which the average values of F and D are 2 and 1 respectively. An actual binary tree has a regular pattern (*each* internal node has exactly one incoming and two outgoing edges incident on it), and this is not captured by our characterization. Our assumption that the duplication factor is independent of the size is a very crude approximation. For instance, it implies that if you start from one node you still generate some duplicate nodes. Obviously the duplication factor increases with the size of the start set. Therefore, our approximation overestimates the number of duplicate nodes. However, it becomes reasonable as the size of the start set becomes large. It is also dependent upon our assumption that the data is random and not regular.

Let us now turn to the problem of characterizing inter-relation relationships. Let A and B be two sets. The *transfer ratio* of A with respect to B, denoted $T_{A.B}$, is the number such that given a random set of n nodes in A, the size of A $\cap$ B after duplicate elimination is $n\, T_{A.B}$. In other words, given a set of nodes in A, the transfer ratio is the fraction of these nodes which also appear in set B. Note that $0 \leq T \leq 1$. This definition can be extended to binary relations by considering only the columns of the relations. We shall denote the i-th column of R by Ri. Thus, given two binary relations, R and S, the number of tuples in the (ternary) result of the join of R and S is $n\, T_{R2.S1}$, where n is the number of tuples in R.

The Cost Metrics

We have chosen for our cost measure the number of *successful inferences* performed by the system.
Consider a rule:

$$p :\!- q1, q2, \ldots, qn$$

A *successful inference* (or *firing*) associated with this rule is of the form (*id, t, t1, t2,…,tn*), where *t1* through *tn* are (ground) tuples in *q1* through *qn* and *t* is a tuple in *p*. It denotes that the truth of *t1* through *tn* is used to establish that *t* is true, by applying the given rule. There is (conceptually) an identifier *id* associated with an inference because it is possible that the inference is repeatedly made, and we wish to measure this.

The simplest way to obtain this cost function is to measure the size of the intermediate results *before* duplicate elimination. We note that this cost measure does not count *unsuccessful* inferences, i.e., uses of the rule in which the tuples *t1* through *tn* fail to establish *t* (for example, because they do not agree on the values they assign to common variables). Also, since the cost measure is independent of the number of *q*'s, in this model the measure of complexity of the join, the cartesian product, intersection, and selection is the size of the result; the measure of complexity of union is the sum of the sizes of the arguments (each tuple present in both argument is going to fire twice); and the measure of complexity of projection is the size of the argument. Readers familiar with performance evaluation of relational queries might be surprised by these measures.

Our concern, however, is primarily with recursive queries. In particular, all but one of our queries (ancestor using double recursion) are *linear*, i.e., the body of each recursive rule contains exactly one occurrence of the recursive predicate. We justify our measurement of only successful inferences by the observation that the number of successful inferences (for the recursive predicate) at one step constitutes the operand at the next step. We justify the approximation in estimating the cost of a join in terms of the size of just one of the operands as follows. The join represented by the predicates in the body of a rule may be thought of as a fixed "operator" which is repeatedly applied to the relation corresponding to the recursive predicate. It is reasonable to assume that the cost of each such application is proportional to the size of this relation (the operand). By measuring the size of this intermediate relation over all steps, we obtain a cost that is proportional to the actual cost.

In essence, our cost is a measure of one important factor in the performance of a query evaluation system, the number of successful inferences, rather than a measure of the actual run-time performance. This cost model is studied further in Bancilhon [1985].

Notation and Preliminary Derivations

In this section, we explain the notation and terminology used in analytically deriving the cost functions. We also derive some expressions that are used in the analysis of some of the strategies. The derivations of these expressions are of some interest in their own right since they are good examples of the techniques we use in subsequent analyses. We denote multiplication by simply juxtaposing the operands. Where there is ambiguity, parentheses are used to clarify the expression, or we use * to denote multiplication. We denote the number of nodes at level i in relation R by $n_R(i)$, the total number of nodes in R by N_R, and the total number of edges in R (which is the number of tuples in R) by A_R. Where no confusion is possible, we drop the subscripts.

We denote the sum of the (h + 1)st elements of the geometric series of ratio E by gsum(E,h), thus:

$$gsum(E,h) = (1 + E + E^2 + E^3 + ...+ E^h)$$

From the definition of the expansion factor E, we have $n(i + 1) = n(i)E$. So the total number of nodes is:

$$N = b(1 + E + E^2 + E^3 + ...+ E^h)$$
$$= (b)gsum(E,h)$$

Clearly, the number of edges entering level i is $n(i - 1)F$, and the number of edges leaving level i is $n(i)F$. Thus the total number of edges is:

$$A = bF + bEF + bE^2F + ... + bE^{(h-1)}F$$
$$= bF(1 + E + E^2 + ... + E^{(h-1)})$$
$$= (bF)gsum(E,h - 1)$$

We denote by h′ the *average* level:

$$h' = h - \left\lfloor \frac{\sum_{i=1}^{h} (i*n(i))}{N} \right\rfloor$$

It denotes the mean level at which we pick a node, assuming nodes are uniformly distributed. We have actually defined h′ as the distance of the mean level from the highest level h for notational convenience, since this is a quantity we use extensively.

We define the length of an arc (a,b) in the transitive closure of R (which is denoted by R*) to be the length of the path of R that generates it. (Note that this is well-defined because there are no shortcuts.) Since an arc is represented by its end points, the number of arcs of length k with a given first node can be computed as the number of distinct nodes reachable from the given node by a path of length k. So, starting from a given node, on the average we can reach E distinct nodes by a path of length 1, E^2 distinct nodes by a path of length 2, and so on. The number of arcs of length k going from level i to level (i + k) is thus:

$$n(i)E^k = n(i + k)$$

Of course, if D is not one, this is an approximation which depends on our assumption of random data. In particular, it breaks down for regular data, such as an actual inverted tree. The intuition is as follows. The parameters F and D are used to estimate the number of *arcs* of length k, as opposed to the number of *paths* of length k. Several paths may generate the same arc (i.e., they have the same end points). Thus, we use the parameters F and D to estimate this "duplication" of arcs. This approximation depends upon the randomness of data. In an inverted tree, for instance, the number of paths is exactly the number of arcs because there is a unique path between any two points. The inverted tree is one instance of a family of data structures with given values of F(= 1) and D(= 2), and in this particular instance, due to the regular pattern in the data, the above approximation breaks down. In general, however, for such a structure the number of paths is *not* equal to the number of arcs; and if the data is randomly (and uniformly) distributed, our approximation is accurate.

We denote by $a_{R*}(k)$ the number of arcs of length exactly k in R*. Where the context is clear, we write a(k). The value of a(k) is obtained by summing all the arcs of length k that enter level i for i = k to h. Thus:

$$a(k) = n(k) + n(k + 1) + \ldots + n(h)$$
$$= n(k)\ gsum(E, h - k)$$

Finally, given a relation R(A,B), its transpose $R^T(B,A)$ is defined to be such that $R^T(B,A)$ holds iff R(A,B) holds, for all pairs (A,B). We have the following relationships:

$$F_{R^T} = D_R,$$
$$D_{R^T} = F_R,$$

$$E_{R^T} = 1/E_R,$$

$$h_{R^T} = h_R,$$

$$h'_{R^T} = h_R - h'_R, \text{ and}$$

$$b_{R^T} = b_R E_R{}^{h_R}.$$

Analysis of the Query Evaluation Strategies

In this section, we analyze the performance of each strategy on the set of sample queries.

Query Form Ancestor.bf

R1   a(X,Y) :- p(X,Y).

R2   a(X,Y) :- p(X,Z),a(Z,Y).

R3   query(X) :- a(john,X).

Naive Evaluation   We begin the computation of the answer by firing R1 (Step 1). The number of successful firings is the number of arcs in p (which is the number of arcs of length 1 in the transitive closure of p). There are no successful firings of R2 at this step since the relation a is empty. At the next step, we fire R1 again, and in addition, there are successful firings of R2 since the previous step added some tuples to the relation a. The number of successful firings of R2 is a(2), where a(2) is the number of arcs of length 2 in the transitive closure of p. At the next step, the number of successful firings of R2 is (a(2) + a(3)), since the relation a now contains all arcs of length 1 or 2. We repeat this process until no new tuples are added to a at some step. This occurs after Step h.

We now generalize the above argument. At Step i we generate all the arcs of length $\leq$ i. Thus all arcs of length i are going to be generated at (h − i + 1) steps. Further, because of duplication, a given arc is computed more than once at each step. Thus, the number of successful firings is greater than the number of arcs generated. If we assume that we perform duplicate elimination at the end of each step, a given arc is computed D times at each step. To see this, consider an arc that is extended in a given step. The step essentially extends this arc by adding an edge to one end point. The number of new arcs generated is the number of new nodes reached, and there is a duplication factor D in this set of nodes.

Finally, we fire R3 once to produce the answer. The number of successful firings of R3 is the size of the answer set. This is equal to the number of nodes in the subtree rooted at "john," and is thus:

$$= E + E^2 + \dots + E^{h'}$$

$$= (E)\text{gsum}(E, h' - 1)$$

Thus the total number of successful firings is:

$$D \sum_{i=1}^{h} (h - i + 1)a(i) + (E)\text{gsum}(E, h' - 1).$$

Semi-Naive Evaluation   The performance of the Semi-Naive strategy is similar to Naive Evaluation, with the difference that we do not recompute arcs. At each step, we use for relation a only the tuples that were computed for it in the previous step. Thus, at Step i we generate all arcs of length exactly i, with a duplication rate of D.

The number of successful firings is therefore:

$$D \sum_{i=1}^{h} a(i) + (E)\text{gsum}(E, h' - 1).$$

QSQ, Iterative   At Step 1, we compute all arcs in p (i.e., arcs of length 1 in the transitive closure of p) leaving "john." At Step 2, we compute all arcs leaving nodes that are reachable from "john" by an arc of length 1, and also recompute all arcs of length 1 leaving "john." At Step 3, we compute all arcs leaving nodes that are reachable from "john" by an arc of length 2. We also compute all arcs in the transitive closure of the tree of height 2 rooted at "john" (and in doing so, duplicate all the work done in Step 1). At Step j, we compute all arcs leaving nodes that are reachable from "john" by an arc of length $(j - 1)$. There are DE^j such arcs. We also compute the transitive closure of the tree of height $(j - 1)$ rooted at "john." This involves computing $D \sum_{i=1}^{j-1} a(i,j)$ arcs, where $a(i,j)$ denotes the number of arcs of length i in the transitive closure of a subtree of height $(j - 1)$ in relation p. However, at the last step, Step $(h' + 1)$, we simply compute the transitive closure of the tree of height h' rooted at "john" (i.e., the entire subtree rooted at "john"). The cost is thus:

Step 1: DE

Step 2: $DE^2 + DE$

Step 3 : $$DE^3 + D \sum_{i=1}^{2} a(i,2)$$

...

Step j: $$DE^j + D \sum_{i=1}^{j-1} a(i,j)$$

...

Step h' + 1: $$D \sum_{i=1}^{h'} a(i,h')$$

The total cost is the sum of all these costs:

$$(D + E)gsum(E,h' - 1) + D \sum_{j=1}^{h'} \sum_{i=1}^{j} a(i,j)$$

QSQ, Recursive   The query asks for all nodes reachable from "john," and in answering it, we generate similar queries for each node that are reachable from "john" via a path of length 1. Each of these queries in turn generates similar queries for nodes reachable from them by a path of length 1, and so on. At each node, the answers to the subqueries generated at that node are arcs such that the first element is the given node. The answer to the query at a given node is computed by composing the arc from the node to its child with the answer arcs generated at that child, for every child.

Thus, we compute each arc in the transitive closure of the subtree rooted at "john," and each arc is computed exactly once. The number of arcs in the transitive closure is $\sum_{i=1}^{h'} a(i)$. Since the subtree has height h' and b = 1, we have $a(i) = E^i gsum(E,h' - i)$. As before, we also assume a duplication factor of D. Finally, rule R3 is fired to produce the answer, the cost being the size of the answer set. The total cost is therefore:

$$(E)gsum(E,h' - 1) + D \sum_{i=1}^{h'} E^i gsum(E,h' - i)$$

Henschen-Naqvi   The Henschen-Naqvi method evaluates the sequence of expressions:

p(john,X)

p(john,X1),p(X1,X2)

p(john,X1),p(X1,X2),p(X2,X3)

etc.

At each step, the previous expression is extended by one join. The cost of doing this (assuming duplicate elimination) is:

$$ED + E^2D + \ldots + E^{h'}D$$
$$= (DE)\text{gsum}(E,h' - 1)$$
$$= (F)\text{gsum}(E,h' - 1)$$

We also fire R3 to produce the answer. Thus the total cost is:

$$(F + E)\text{gsum}(E,h' - 1)$$

Prolog   In this case, Prolog performs very much like QSQR, setting up the same subqueries. But since Prolog does not perform duplicate elimination, the subquery at a given node is solved as often as there are paths to the node. This is equivalent to QSQR operating on a similar data structure with $E = F$ and $D = 1$. Thus, the cost is similar to that for QSQR, with F substituted for E:

$$(E)\text{gsum}(E,h' - 1) + \sum_{i=1}^{h'} (F^i)\text{gsum}(F,h' - i)$$

APEX   The relevant facts for the given query are all $p(\text{john},X)$. For each value x of X, we generate a new subquery $a(x,X1)$. So the behavior is identical to that of QSQR. The cost is, therefore:

$$(E)\text{gsum}(E,h' - 1) + D \sum_{i=1}^{h'} E^i\text{gsum}(E,h' - i)$$

Static Filtering   The optimization algorithm for the system graph fails to yield any improvement. The unoptimized system graph performs semi-naive computation (since we store all intermediate results and do not recompute them). The cost is, therefore:

$$D \sum_{i=1}^{h} a(i) + (E)\text{gsum}(E,h' - 1)$$

Magic Sets   The rule system is rewritten as follows:

R'1   magic(john).

R'2   magic(X) :− magic(Y),p(Y,X).

R'3   a(X,Y) :− magic(X),p(X,Y).

R'4   a(X,Y) :- magic(X),p(X,Z),a(Z,Y).

R'5   query(X) :- a(john,X).

We first compute the *magic set* by firing R'1 and R'2 repeatedly. We then evaluate a(X,Y) using the semi-naive algorithm on R'3 and R'4. Because of the magic predicate, this amounts to semi-naive computation of the subtree rooted at john. The cost of this step is thus $D \sum_{i=1}^{h'} a(i)$. Since the height of the subtree is h' and b = 1, this can be rewritten as $D \sum_{i=1}^{h'} E^i gsum(E,h' - i)$.

Finally, we answer the query by firing R'5. Thus the cost is:

Firings of R1 and R2: $(F)gsum(E,h' - 1)$

Firings of R3 and R4: $D \sum_{i=1}^{h'} E^i gsum(E,h' - i)$

Firings of R5: $(E)gsum(E,h' - 1)$

And the total cost is:

$$(F + E)gsum(E,h' - 1) + D \sum_{i=1}^{h'} E^i gsum(E,h' - i)$$

Counting   The system is rewritten as follows:

R'1   counting(john,0).

R'2   counting(X,I + 1) :- counting(Y,I),p(Y,X).

R'3   query(X) :- counting(X,I).

We first fire rules R'1 and R'2 repeatedly to compute the *counting* set, and then we fire R'3. In firing R'1 and R'2, we are essentially computing nodes rather than arcs. At Step i, we find nodes that are at a distance i from "john." The cost of this phase is thus:

$$ED + E^2D + ... + E^{h'}D$$

$$= (DE)gsum(E,h' - 1)$$

$$= (F)gsum(E,h' - 1)$$

The total cost is, therefore:

$$(F + E)gsum(E,h' - 1)$$

Generalized Magic Sets It performs exactly like the Magic Sets strategy.

Query Form Ancestor.fb

R1   a(X,Y) :- p(X,Y).

R2   a(X,Y) :- p(X,Z),a(Z,Y).

R3   query(X) :- a(X,john).

Naive Evaluation As before, the Naive strategy computes the transitive closure of the entire relation p. Therefore the cost of the first phase remains unchanged. However, the cost of firing R3 changes since the size of the answer set is different. By binding the second argument, we are effectively looking at the transpose of the data graph, and so, by the properties of the transpose, the size of the answer set is now:

$$(1/E)\text{gsum}(1/E, h' - 1)$$

The total cost is therefore:

$$D \sum_{i=1}^{h} (h - i + 1)\, a(i) + (1/E)\text{gsum}(1/E, h - h' - 1)$$

Semi-Naive Evaluation We compute the transitive closure of p, proceeding as before. We then fire R3 to find the answer, the cost being the size of the answer set. The cost is therefore:

$$D \sum_{i=1}^{h} a(i) + (1/E)\text{gsum}(1/E, h - h' - 1)$$

QSQ, Iterative We only generate subqueries of the form $a(X,\text{john})$. At Step 1, we compute all arcs in p (i.e., arcs of length 1 in the transitive closure of p) that enter the node "john." At Step 2 we compute all arcs of length 2 entering "john," and also recompute the arcs computed in Step 1. At Step i, we compute all arcs of length i in the transitive closure of p which enter node "john," and recompute all arcs computed in Steps 1 through i − 1. Also, we work with the transpose of p. Using the properties of a transpose, we substitute F for D, $1/E$ for E, and h − h' for h'. This yields the following expressions for the cost of each step:

Step 1: $F\,(1/E)$

Step 2: $F\,(1/E + (1/E)^2)$

Step 3: $F (1/E + (1/E)^2 + (1/E)^3)$

...

Step j: $F (\sum_{i=1}^{j} (1/E)^i)$

...

Step h − h': $F (\sum_{i=1}^{h-h'} (1/E)^{h-h'})$

Finally, we fire rule R3 to produce the answer. The total cost is therefore:

$$F \sum_{j=1}^{h-h'} \sum_{i=1}^{j} (1/E)^i + (1/E)\text{gsum}(1/E, h - h' - 1)$$

QSQ, Recursive   As in the iterative case, we only generate queries of the form $a(X,john)$. However, we do not recompute arcs, and therefore, at Step i, we only compute arcs of length i in the transitive closure of p which enter ''john.'' Proceeding as in the iterative case, the cost of Step i is:

Step i: $F ((1/E)^i)$

We also fire rule R3 to produce the answer. The total cost is thus:

$(D + 1/E)\text{gsum}(1/E, h - h' - 1)$

Henschen-Naqvi   The method evaluates the sequence of expressions:

$p(X,john)$;

$p(X2,X1), p(X1,john)$;

$p(X3,X2), p(X2,X1), p(X1,john)$ etc.

etc.

Thus, the computation   essentially   to the previous case, but again, we work with the transpose of p instead of p.
The total cost is:

$(D + 1/E)\text{gsum}(1/E, h - h' - 1)$

Prolog   We generate each path in the data structure p and check to see if it ends in ''john.''

The number of paths of length 1 starting from a given node at level i and reaching level (i + 1) is F^l. The number of paths of length 1 going from level i to level (i + 1) is thus:

$n(i)F^l$

The total number of paths of length 1 is obtained by summing all the arcs of length 1 that enter level j for j = 1 to h:

$$= F^l(n(1) + n(2) + \ldots + n(h - 1))$$
$$= F^l(b + bE + \ldots + b\,E^{h-1})$$
$$= (F^l b)gsum(E, h - 1)$$

The cost, which is the total number of paths, plus the cost of firing R3, is thus:

$$(1/E)gsum(1/E, h - h' - 1) + \sum_{l=1}^{h} bF^l gsum(E, h - 1)$$

APEX The relevant facts are all p(X,john). By substituting one of these facts in R2, we generate the subquery a(john,Y). Further, we generate the sequence of subqueries:

p(X,john); p(X,Z) where p(Z,john); p(X,Z1) where p(Z1,Z),
p(Z,john); ...

This computes the inverted tree rooted at "john" in *p*. The cost of this step (which is similar to the execution of QSQR) is:

$$(D)gsum(1/E, h - h' - 1)$$

The answers generated for each of these subqueries is added to the set of relevant facts. Thus for each fact p(x,y) that we generate, we also generate the subquery a(y,Y) by substitution in R2. So we eventually compute all the descendants of all the ancestors of "john." This is Semi-Naive computation over the data structure with $b = (1/E)^{(h-h')}$ and height h. The cost of this step:

$$D(1/E)^{(h-h')} \sum_{i=1}^{h} E^i gsum(E, h - i))$$

The cost of firing R3, however, is still the size of the answer set. The total cost, therefore:

$$(D + 1/E)\text{gsum}(1/E, h - h' - 1) + D(1/E)^{(h-h')} \sum_{i=1}^{h} E^i \text{gsum}(E, h - i))$$

Static Filtering   The optimizer recognizes that the second argument of *a* in the body of R2 is always "john" and so we only generate queries of the form *a*(X,john). Since we use Semi-Naive Evaluation, arcs are not recomputed, and so the cost is identical to QSQR. Including the cost of firing R3 to produce the answers, the cost is:

$$(D + 1/E)\text{gsum}(1/E, h - h' - 1)$$

Magic Sets   We rewrite the rules as follows:

R'1   magic(john).

R'2   a(X,Y) :– magic(Y),p(X,Y).

R'3   a(X,Y) :– magic(Y),p(X,Z),a(Z,Y).

R'4   query(X) :– a(X,john).

We first fire R'1 to compute the magic set. We then compute a(X,Y) by using Semi-Naive Evaluation on R'2 and R'3. This is equivalent to computing all arcs of the form a(X,john) in the transitive closure of the inverted tree rooted at "john" using Semi-Naive Evaluation. This is similar to the computation of the magic set in the previous query (with the first argument bound), and the cost of this step is $D\text{gsum}(1/E, h - h' - 1)$.

Finally, we fire R'4 to answer the query, the cost of this step being the size of the answer set. The total cost is:

$$1 + (D + 1/E)\text{gsum}(1/E, h - h' - 1)$$

Counting   We generate the following rule:

counting(I + 1, Y) :– counting(I, Y).

The computation of the counting sets, therefore, does not terminate, and the strategy does not work.

Generalized Magic Sets   It performs exactly like the Magic Sets strategy.

Query Form Ancestor.bf, Doubly Recursive Version

R1 $a(X,Y) :\!- p(X,Y).$

R2 $a(X,Y) :\!- a(X,Z),a(Z,Y).$

R3 $query(X) :\!- a(john,X).$

Naive Evaluation We first fire R1 and R2 until no new tuples are generated, and finally we fire R3 to produce the answer.

At Step i, we generate all arcs of length less or equal to 2^{i-1}. Each arc of length k (k > 1) is generated $k - 1$ times at each step (because there are $k - 1$ ways of generating an arc of length k from two sub-arcs of length less than k). Further, in each of these $k - 1$ ways of generating an arc, the arc is generated more than once because of duplication. In the case that an arc of length k is generated by appending a single edge to an arc of length $k - 1$, the duplication is represented by a factor D. In the symmetric case that it is generated by adding an edge to the front of an arc of length $k - 1$, the duplication is represented by a factor F! In the other $k - 3$ cases, our model does not provide an estimate of the duplication. We approximate by assuming a duplication factor D uniformly. Also, since it takes log(h) steps to compute the transitive closure, each arc of length k is going to be re-computed at $\log(h) - \log(k) + 1$ steps. (*Note:* This is a simplification. At Step i, only paths of length $\leq 2^{(i-2)}$ are available. So some of the $(k - 1)$ possible generations of a path of length k are generated in the next step.) Thus, the number of successful firings can be computed as follows:

Firings of R1 and R2: $D(\log(h) + 1) a(1)$

$$+ D \sum_{i=2}^{h} (\log(h/i) + 1)(i - 1)a(i)$$

Firings of R3: $(E)gsum(E,h' - 1)$

And the total cost is:

$$(E)gsum(E,h' - 1) + D(\log(h) + 1) a(1) + D \sum_{i=2}^{h} (\log(h/i) + 1)(i - 1) a(i)$$

Semi-Naive Evaluation We first fire R1, then fire R2 repeatedly until no new tuples are generated, and finally fire R3 to produce the answer. At Step 1, we fire R1 to produce all arcs of length 1. At Step i (i > 1), we generate all arcs of length l, $2^{(i-2)} < l \leq 2^{i-1}$. Each arc of length l is generated $l - 1$ times (because there are $l - 1$ ways of generating an arc of length l from two sub-arcs of length less than l), with a duplication factor D (approximating as before). However, each arc is generated at exactly one step. Hence, the number of successful firings can be computed as follows:

Firings of R1 and R2: $(D)a(1) + D \sum\limits_{i=2}^{h} (i - 1) a(i)$

Firings of R3: $(E)gsum(E,h' - 1)$

And the total cost is:

$$(E)gsum(E,h' - 1) + (D)a(1) + D \sum\limits_{i=2}^{h} (i - 1) a(i)$$

QSQ, Iterative   As in the previous two queries, QSQI improves on Naive Evaluation by restricting itself to the subtree rooted at john. At Step i, we generate all arcs of length less than or equal to 2^{i-1} in this subtree, generating each arc of length l, $l - 1$ times, with a duplication factor D. Using the cost expression for Naive Evaluation, we obtain the following expression for the cost of QSQI:

$$(E)gsum(E,h' - 1) + D(\log(h') + 1)(E)gsum(E,h' - 1)$$
$$+ D \sum\limits_{i=2}^{h'} (\log(h'/i) + 1)(i - 1)(E^i gsum(E, h' - i))$$

QSQ, Recursive   Proceeding as in the first query, it is easy to see that QSQR restricts itself to the subtree rooted at "john" while performing Semi-Naive Evaluation. Using the cost expression for Semi-Naive Evaluation, we obtain the following cost expression for QSQR:

$$(E)gsum(E,h' - 1) + (DE)gsum(E,h' - 1) + D \sum\limits_{i=2}^{h'} (i - 1)$$
$$(E^i gsum(E,h' - i))$$

Henschen-Naqvi   Henschen-Naqvi does not apply in this case.

Prolog   Prolog does not terminate.

APEX   The relevant facts initially are all p(john,X).

By substituting the relevant facts in R1, we generate facts a(john,X) for X such that p(john,X). By substituting them in R2 we generate the subqueries a(X,john) and a(john,Z). The answers to each of these subqueries are added to the set of relevant facts.

Eventually we compute all descendants of every ancestor of "john" and all ancestors of every descendant of "john." This amounts to the Semi-Naive Computation of the structure with $b' = (1/E)^{h-h'}$, $E' = E$, $D' = D$, and height h, and the inverted structure with $E^{h'}$ elements on level h. The latter is simply a structure with $b' = E^{h'}$, $E' = 1/E$, $D' = F$, and $h' = h$.

Finally, we fire R3 once to produce the answer, the cost being the size of the answer set. The total cost is thus:

$$(E)gsum(E,h'-1) + (D)(1/E)^{h-h'-1}gsum(E,h-1)$$
$$+ (1/E)^{h-h'}(D \sum_{i=2}^{h} (i-1)E^i gsum(E,h-i))$$
$$+ (F)E^{h'-1}gsum(1/E,h-1)$$
$$+ E^{h'}(F \sum_{i=2}^{h} (i-1)(1/E)^i gsum(1/E,h-i))$$

Static Filtering   The optimization strategy fails to make any improvements and so it reduces to Semi-Naive Evaluation. The cost is therefore:

$$(E)gsum(E,h'-1) + (D)a(1) + D \sum_{i=2}^{h} (i-1)a(i)$$

Magic Sets   The magic set fails to bring any improvement in the sense that it generates the predicate a.ff as a reachable adorned predicate. Thus the performance is the same as the Semi-Naive Algorithm (assuming that we use the Semi-Naive Algorithm in the bottom-up phase).

The cost:

$$(E)gsum(E,h'-1) + (D)a(1) + D \sum_{i=2}^{h} (i-1)a(i)$$

Counting   Counting does not apply.

Generalized Magic Sets   The rules are rewritten as follows:

R'1   magic(john).

R'2   magic(Z) :– magic(X), a(X,Z).

R'3   a(X,Y) :– magic(X), p(X,Y).

R'4   a(X,Y) :– magic(X), a(X,Z), a(Z,Y).

R'5   query(X) :– a(john,X).

Rules R'1 and R'2 compute the transitive closure of a rooted at "john," which is nothing but the transitive closure of p rooted at "john." The magic predicate now restricts the computation of R'3 and R'4 to the subtree rooted at "john." This computation is done using Semi-Naive Evaluation, and finally, the answer is computed using R'5. The costs for the firings of rules R'1 and R'2 and rule R'5 are the same as in the first query. The cost of rules R'3 and R'4 can be computed easily by using the cost expression for Semi-Naive Evaluation. Thus, the total cost is:

$$(F + E)\text{gsum}(E,h' - 1) + (DE)\text{gsum}(E,h' - 1)$$
$$+ D \sum_{i=2}^{h'} (i - 1)\,(E^i\text{gsum}(E,h' - i))$$

Query Form Same-Generation.bf

R1 $p(X,Y) :\!- flat(X,Y).$

R2 $p(X,Y) :\!- up(X,XU),p(XU,YU),down(YU,Y).$

R3 $query(X) :\!- p(john,X).$

In the following, $h'_{up.down} = \min(h'_{up}, h'_{down})$, and $h_{up.down} = \min(h_{iup}, h_{down})$.

Naive Evaluation   We fire R1 and R2 repeatedly until no new tuples are generated, and then we fire R3 to produce the answer. At step $(i + 1)$ (in the firings of R1 and R2), we generate all arcs with a segment of length $\leq i$ in up, and there are a total of $(h_{up.down} + 1)$ steps where $h_{up.down}$ is $\min(h'_{up}, h'_{down})$. So each arc with a segment of length i in up is generated at $(h_{up.down} - i + 1)$ steps. The cost may be computed as follows:

Firings of R1: $(h_{up.down} + 1)A_{flat}$ (Note: A_{flat} = total number of arcs in $flat$)

Firings of R2: $a_{up}(1)T_{up2.flat1}E_{flat}T_{flat2.down1}E_{down}D_{down}h_{up.down}$

     $+ \ a_{up}(2)T_{up2.flat1}E_{flat}T_{flat2.down1}E^2_{down}D_{down}(h_{up.down-1})$

     $+ \ ...$

     $+ \ a_{up}(i)T_{up2.flat1}E_{flat}T_{flat2.down1}E^i_{down}D_{down}(h_{up.down} - i + 1)$

     $+ \ ...$

     $+ \ a_{up}(h_{up.down})T_{up2.flat1}E_{flat}T_{flat2.down1}E^{h_{up.down}}_{down}D_{down}$

Thus the total number of firings due to R2 is:

$$T_{up2.flat1}E_{flat}T_{flat2.down1}D_{down} \sum_{i=1}^{h_{up.down}} (h_{up.down} - i + 1)a_{up}(i)E^i_{down}$$

Firings of R3:

The cost of firing R3 is equal to the size of the answer set. The derivation of the following expression for the size of the answer set is given in the analysis of the Henschen-Naqvi strategy:

$$= T_{up2.flat1} E_{flat} T_{flat2.down1} D_{down} \sum_{i=1}^{h'_{up.down}} (E_{up} E_{down})^i$$

The total cost is therefore:

$$(h_{up.down}+1)A_{flat}$$
$$+ T_{up2.flat1} E_{flat} T_{flat2.down1} D_{down} \sum_{i=1}^{h_{up.down}} (h_{up.down} - i + 1)a_{up}(i) E_{down}^i$$
$$+ T_{up2.flat1} E_{flat} T_{flat2.down1} D_{down} \sum_{i=1}^{h'_{up.down}} (E_{up}E_{down})^i$$

Note: We assume that the join *up.p.down* is generated as follows: (1) Obtain a tuple from the current relation for *p*. (2) Look for matching tuples in *up*. (3) Look for matching tuples in *down*. (4) Take the cartesian product of the first column of the tuples from *up* and the second column of the tuples from *down*.

Semi-Naive Evaluation   We first fire R1, and then fire R2 repeatedly until no new tuples are generated for *sg*, and finally fire R3 to produce the answer. We compute the cost as follows.

At step 1, we compute p(1) = flat

At step 2, we compute p(2) = up.flat.down = up.p(1).down

...

At step i, we compute p(i) = up.p(i − 1).down

...

Up to step $h_{up.down}$.

We now compute the number of successful firings. At the i-th step (in the firings of R2), we generate all arcs with a segment of length exactly i in *up*.

Firings of R1: A_{flat}

Firings of R2: $a_{up}(1)T_{up2.flat1}E_{flat}T_{flat2.down1}E_{down}D_{down}$

$\quad + \; a_{up}(2)T_{up2.flat1}E_{flat}T_{flat2.down1}E_{down}^2 \, D_{down}$

$\quad + \; ...$

$\quad + \; a_{up}(i)T_{up2.flat1}E_{flat}T_{flat2.down1}E_{down}^i \, D_{down}$

$\quad + \; ...$

$\quad + \; a_{up}(\, h_{up.down})T_{up2.flat1}E_{flat}T_{flat2.down1}E_{down}^{h_{up.down}}D_{down}$

Thus the total number of firings due to R2 is:

$$T_{up2.flat1}E_{flat}T_{flat2.down1}D_{down}(a_{up}(1)E_{down}$$
$$+ \; a_{up}(2)E_{down}^2 \; + \; ... \; + \; a_{up}(h_{up.down})E_{down}^{h_{up.down}}$$
$$= \; T_{up2.flat1}E_{flat}T_{flat2.down1}D_{down} \sum_{i=1}^{h_{up.down}} a_{up}(i)E_{down}^i$$

Firings of R3: $\; T_{up2.flat1}E_{flat}T_{flat2.down1}D_{down} \sum_{i=1}^{h'_{up.down}} (E_{up} \, E_{down})^i$

The total cost is therefore:

$$A_{flat} + T_{up2.flat1}E_{flat}T_{flat2.down1}D_{down} \sum_{i=1}^{h_{up.down}} a_{up}(i)E_{down}^i$$

$$+ \; T_{up2.flat1}E_{flat}T_{flat2.down1}D_{down} \sum_{i=1}^{h'_{up.down}} (E_{up}E_{down})^i$$

QSQ, Iterative In the following description, by "path" we refer to a path with equal segments in *up* and *down* linked through an edge in *flat*. In (partially) solving the known subqueries, at Step i, we find the following paths (with a firing corresponding to each):

all paths from "john" with a segment of length $\leq (i - 1)$ in *up* +

all paths from nodes at distance 1 (in *up*) from "john" with a segment of length $\leq (i - 2)$ in *up* +

...

all paths from nodes at distance $(i - 1)$ from "john" with a segment of length $= 0$ in *up*.

There are a total of ($h'_{up.down}$ + 1) steps. In addition, we set up $D E^i$ new subqueries at Step i. In fact, we may set up new subqueries even when the previous steps generate no new paths, since this is done for i = 1 to h'_{up}.

The paths with a segment of length i in *up* are computed by the following join:

up.sg.down

The join at Step i is computed in 3 stages. For a given start node (in *up*), we find all paths starting from one of its children and having a segment of length i − 1 in *up* (and in *down*). We do this by simply using the paths we found in Steps 1 through i − 1 (i.e., in the partial results for *sg* computed in these steps). The number of such paths, for a given child, is:

$$E_{up}^{(i-1)}T_{up2.flat1}E_{flat}T_{flat2.down1}E_{down}^{(i-1)}$$

The second step of the join appends these paths to the arcs linking the start node to its children. In the third stage of the join, the resulting paths (in each of which the segment in *down* is one arc shorter than the segment in *up*) are extended by appending each node in *down* to which there is an arc from the last node on the path.

The total cost of the join which computes a path of length i is thus:

(Stage 1) F_{up} +

(Stage 2) $E_{up}(E_{up}^{(i-1)} T_{up2.flat1}E_{flat}T_{flat2.down1}E_{down}^{(i-2)} F_{down})$ +

(Stage 3) $E_{up}E_{up}^{(i-1)} T_{up2.flat1}E_{flat}T_{flat2.down1}E_{down}^{(i-1)} F_{down}$

If we denote this by C(i), the cost of Steps 1 through ($h'_{up.down}$ + 1) is:

$$\sum_{i=1}^{h'_{up.down}+1} \sum_{j=0}^{i-1} C(j) + E_{up}\sum_{j=0}^{i-2} C(j) + \ldots E_{up}^{i-1} \sum_{j=0}^{0} C(j)$$

This can be rewritten as:

$$\sum_{i=0}^{h'_{up.down}} \sum_{j=0}^{i} C(j)gsum(E_{up},h'_{up.down} - i)$$

The cost of setting up the subqueries is:

$$D_{up}E_{up}gsum(E_{up},h'u - 1)\}$$

Finally, we fire R3 to produce the answer, the cost being the size of the answer set.

The total cost is the sum of these costs, and after replacing 'C(i)' by the corresponding expression, it is:

$$\sum_{i=1}^{h'_{up.down}+1} (i)\ F_{up} gsum(E_{up}, h'_{up.down} - i)$$

$$\sum_{i=1}^{h'_{up.down}+1} \left[T_{up2.flat1}\ E_{flat} T_{flat2.down1} D_{down} \sum_{j=0}^{i} E_{up}^{j} E_{down}^{j-1}\ gsum(E_{up},\ h'_{up.down} - i) \right]$$

$$+ \sum_{i=1}^{h'_{up.down}+1} \left[T_{up2.flat1}\ E_{flat} T_{flat2.down1} D_{down} \sum_{j=0}^{i} E_{up}^{j} E_{down}^{j}\ gsum(E_{up},\ h'_{up.down} - i) \right]$$

$$+\ D_{up} E_{up} gsum(E_{up}, h'_{up} - 1) + T_{up2.flat1} E_{flat} T_{flat2.down1}\ D_{down} \sum_{i=1}^{h'_{up.down}} E_{up} E_{down})^{i}$$

QSQ, Recursive   By a similar analysis, we arrive at the same cost expression C(i). However, in the recursive version, we do not recompute paths. At Step i, we find:

all paths from "john" with a segment of length $\leq (i - 1)$ in up +

all paths from nodes at distance 1 (in up) from "john" with a segment of length $\leq (i - 2)$ in up +

...

all paths from nodes at distance $(i - 1)$ from "john" with a segment of length ≤ 0 in up.

There are a total of $(h'_{up.down} + 1)$ steps.

In addition, as in QSQI, we set up D E^{i} new subqueries at Step i. This is done for i = 1 to h'_{up}, and so we may set up new subqueries even when the previous steps generate no new paths.

The cost of setting up the subqueries is the same as in QSQI, but the cost of Steps 1 to $(h'_{up.down}+1)$ is now:

$$\sum_{i=1}^{h'_{up.down}+1} C(i - 1) + E_{up}\ C(i - 2) +...+ E_{up}^{i-1} C(0)$$

This can be rewritten as:

$$\sum_{i=0}^{h'_{up.down}} C(i) gsum(E_{up}, h'_{up.down} - i)$$

As before, we fire R3 to produce the answer, the cost being the size of the answer set.

The total cost, after replacing 'C(i)' by the corresponding expression, is:

$$
\sum_{i=0}^{h'_{up.down}} \left[F_{up}gsum(E_{up},h'_{up.down} - i) \right.
$$

$$
\left. + T_{up2.flat1}E_{flat}T_{flat2.down1}D_{down}E_{up}^{i}E_{down}^{i-1}\, gsum(E_{up},h'_{up.down} - i)(1 + E_{down}) \right]
$$

$$
+ D_{up}E_{up}gsum(E_{up},h'_{up} - 1) + T_{up2.flat1}E_{flat}T_{flat2.down1}D_{down}\sum_{i=1}^{h'_{up.down}}(E_{up}E_{down})^{i}
$$

Henschen-Naqvi   In the Henschen-Naqvi algorithm, we start from the query node and at Step i find all nodes reachable from it by a path of length i in *up*. We do this by using the set of nodes at a distance i − 1 (found in the previous step and stored) and stepping one level through *up*. We then find the set of nodes reachable from these nodes by an arc in *flat*, and Step i levels through *down* starting from this set. Thus, at Step i of the Henschen-Naqvi algorithm:

we evaluate the value Vi = Vi − 1.up, and

we evaluate Output = Vi.flat down^i, and put it in the result.

Vi is initially "john," and we stop when Vi is empty, i.e., after h'u steps. Evaluation of V0, V1,...,Vh':

$$
E_{up}D_{up} + \{Eu\ sup\ 2\}D_{up} + ... + \{Eu\ sup\ \{h'u\}\}D_{up}
$$
$$
= F_{up}(1 + E_{up} + \{Eu\ sup\ 2\} + ... + \{Eu\ sup\ \{h'u - 1\}\}
$$
$$
= F_{up}gsum(E_{up},h'_{up}-1)
$$

To evaluate Vi.flat down^i, we have to evaluate successively:

Vi.flat	E_{up}^{i}	$T_{up2.flat1}\ F_{flat}$
Vi.flat.down	E_{up}^{i}	$T_{up2.flat1}E_{flat}T_{flat2.down1}F_{down}$
Vi.flat down^2	E_{up}^{i}	$T_{up2.flat1}E_{flat}T_{flat2.down1}E_{down}F_{down}$
...		
Vi.flat down^i	E_{up}^{i}	$T_{up2.flat1}E_{flat}T_{flat2.down1}E_{down}^{(i-1)}\ F_{down}$

Thus the total sum for Vi.flat down^i is:

$$E_{up}^i \, T_{up2.flat1}F_{flat} + E_{up}^i \, T_{up2.flat1}E_{flat}T_{flat2.down1}F_{down}(1 + E_{down} + E_{down}^2$$

$$+ \dots + E_{down}^{(i-1)}$$

$$= E_{up}^i \, T_{up2.flat1}F_{flat} + E_{up}^i \, T_{up2.flat1}E_{flat}T_{flat2.down1}F_{down}\text{gsum}(E_{down}, i-1)$$

This has to be computed at each step. Thus we have to sum this for $i = 1$ to $h'_{up.down}$, where $h'_{up.down}$ is min(h'_{up}, h'_{down}). This yields:

$$\sum_{i=1}^{h'_{up.down}} (E_{up}^i T_{up2.flat1}F_{flat}$$

$$+ \, T_{up2.flat1}E_{flat}T_{flat2.down1}F_{down}E_{up}^i \, \text{gsum}(E_{down}, i-1))$$

Finally, we fire R3 once to produce the answer. The cost of this step is the size of the answer set. We can compute this easily since the answer is the union of all the results Vi.flat down^i. It is equal to:

$$T_{up2.flat1}E_{flat}T_{flat2.down1}F_{down}(E_{up} + \dots$$

$$+ \, E_{up}^i \, E_{down}^{(i-1)} + \dots + E_{up}^{h'_{up.down}} E_{down}^{(h'_{up.down}-1)})$$

$$= T_{up2.flat1}E_{flat} \, T_{flat2.down1}D_{down} \sum_{i=1}^{h'_{up.down}} (E_{up}E_{down})^i$$

This expression is also used in analyzing some of the other strategies.

The total cost of the Henschen-Naqvi strategy is thus:

$$F_{up}\text{gsum}(E_{up}, h'_{up} - 1)$$

$$+ \sum_{i=1}^{h'_{up.down}} (E_{up}^i \, T_{up2.flat1}F_{flat}$$

$$+ \, T_{up2.flat1}E_{flat}T_{flat2.down1}F_{down}E_{up}^i \, \text{gsum}(E_{down}, i-1))$$

$$+ \, T_{up2.flat1}E_{flat}T_{flat2.down1}D_{down} \sum_{i=1}^{h'_{up.down}} (E_{up}E_{down})^i$$

Prolog   Prolog behaves like QSQR except that it does not perform duplicate elimination. So the expression for the cost of the iterative QSQ algorithm should be modified by replacing all E's by the corresponding F's. However, the cost of firing R3 is still the size of the answer set; hence that subcost is unchanged. The cost of Prolog is therefore:

$$\sum_{i=0}^{h'_{up.down}} \left[F_{up}gsum(F_{up}, h'_{up.down} - i)\} \right.$$

$$+ T_{up2.flat1}F_{flat}T_{flat2.down1}D_{down}F_{up}^i F_{down}^{i-1} gsum(F_{up},h'_{up.down} - i)(1 + F_{down})\right]$$

$$+ D_{up}F_{up}gsum(F_{up},h'_{up} - 1)$$

$$+ T_{up2.flat1}E_{flat} T_{flat2.down1} D_{down} \sum_{i=1}^{h'_{up.down}} (E_{up} E_{down})^i$$

APEX The relevant facts are initially flat(john,X) and up(john,X). By substituting the facts up(john,X) in R2, we generate the expression:

up(john,XU),p(XU,YU),down(YU,Y)

This contains the subquery p(XU,YU) where up(john,XU). Expanding this again in the same way, repeatedly, we generate the same set of queries as QSQR, and so the cost of this phase is identical to the cost of setting up and computing subqueries in QSQR:

$$D_{up}E_{up}gsum(E_{up},h'_{up} - 1)$$

$$+ \sum_{i=0}^{h'_{up.down}} \left[(F_{up} \, gsum(E_{up} , h'_{up.down} - i) \right.$$

$$+ T_{up2.flat1}E_{flat}T_{flat2.down1}D_{down}E_{up}^i E_{down}^{i-1} gsum(E_{up},h'_{up.down} - i)(1+E_{down})\right]$$

Further, the answers to each of these subqueries are added to the set of relevant facts, and new facts are generated by substituting them into R2. For example, an answer (john, peter) would generate all paths with a segment in *up* containing the node "john" and a segment in *down*, of equal length, containing the node "peter." If "jim" is a child of "john" in *up*, and we have an answer (jim, joe), this would similarly generate all such paths containing "jim," and these would include all of the paths generated due to (john, peter) if the answer (john, peter) was obtained through a path passing via "jim." However, since APEX performs duplicate elimination, this will be detected and these paths will be generated exactly once. Thus, to measure the extra paths generated, we begin with the answers (X, Y) (from the first phase) in which X was furthest (at a distance $h'_{up.down}$) from "john." The number of such answers is:

$$E_{up}^{h'_{up.down}} (T_{up2.flat1}E_{flat}T_{flat2.down1})$$

Note that all these answers are actually facts in *flat*. By substituting one of these answers into R2, we generate $E_{up} E_{down}$ paths with a segment of length 1 in *up* and *down*. By substituting these into R2, we generate paths with a segment of length 2 in *up*, and so on. In this way we generate all such paths with a segment of length i in *up* where $i = 1$ to $\min((h_{up} - (h'_{up} - h'_{up.down})), h'_{down})$. To see this, we note that we begin with answers that are at a distance $h'_{up.down}$ from "john," and "john" is h'_{up} levels from the the lowest level of *up*. Thus we can extend the answers by up to $h_{up} - (h'_{up} - h'_{up.down})$ arcs in *up*, and by up to h'_{down} levels in *down*. Since the segments in *up* and *down* must be equal in any valid extension, the lower of these two values denotes the length of the longest possible extension.

Each such extension represents a firing. So the cost of this phase is:

$$T_{up2.flat1} \, E_{flat} \, T_{flat2.down1} \, E_{up}^{h'_{up.down}}$$
$$\text{gsum}((1/E_{up})E_{down}, \min((h_{up} - (h'_{up} - h'_{up.down})), h'_{down}))$$

Finally, we fire R3 to produce the answers to the query. The cost of this step, as usual, is the size of the answer set.

The total cost, which is the sum of all these costs, is therefore:

$$D_{up}E_{up}\text{gsum}(E_{up}, h'_{up} - 1)$$

$$+ \sum_{i=0}^{h'_{up.down}} \Bigg[(\,F_{up}\text{gsum}(E_{up}, h'_{up.down} - i)$$

$$+ T_{up2.flat1}E_{flat}T_{flat2.down1}D_{down}E_{up}^{i}\,E_{down}^{i-1} \; \text{gsum}(E_{up}, h'_{up.down} - i)(1 + E_{down}) \Bigg]$$

$$+ T_{up2.flat1}E_{flat}T_{flat2.down1}E_{up}^{h'_{up.down}}$$
$$\text{gsum}((1/E_{up})E_{down}, \min((h_{up} - (h'_{up} - h'_{up.down})), h'_{down}))$$

$$+ T_{up2.flat1}E_{flat}T_{flat2.down1}D_{down} \sum_{i=1}^{h'_{up.down}} (E_{up}E_{down})^{i}$$

Static Filtering The Static Filtering algorithm reduces to the Semi-Naive strategy since the optimizer fails to make any improvements.

The cost is, therefore:

$$A_{flat} + T_{up2.flat1} \, E_{flat} \, T_{flat2.down1} \, D_{down} \, \Big(\sum_{i=1}^{h_{up.down}} (a_{up}(i)E_{down}^{i}) $$

$$+ T_{up2.flat1}E_{flat}T_{flat2.down1}F_{down} \sum_{i=1}^{h'_{up.down}} (E_{up}E_{down})^{i}$$

Magic Sets The modified system is:

R'1   magic(john).

R'2   magic(XU) :– magic(X),up(X,XU).

R'3   p(X,Y) :– magic(X),flat(X,Y).

R'4   p(X,Y) :– magic(X),up(X,XU),p(XU,YU),down(YU,Y).

R'5   query(X) :– p(john,X).

We first compute the magic set. Then we compute p(X,Y) using Semi-Naive Evaluation. The presence of the magic predicates means we only consider the part of *up* which is the subtree rooted at "john". So the cost is:

Firings of R'1 and R'2: $F_{up}\text{gsum}(E_{up},h'_{up} - 1)$

Firings of R'3: $T_{up2.flat1}F_{flat}E_{up}\text{gsum}(E_{up},h'_{up} - 1)$

Firings of R'4: $T_{up2.flat1}E_{flat}T_{flat2.down1}D_{down}$

$$(E^1_{up}\ \text{gsum}(E_{up},h'_{up} - 1)E_{down}$$

$$+ E^2_{up}\ \text{gsum}(E_{up},h'_{up} - 2)E^2_{down}$$

$$+ E^{h'_{up.down}}_{up}\ \text{gsum}(E_{up},h'_{up}-h'_{up.down})E^{h'_{up.down}}_{down})$$

$$= T_{up2.flat1}E_{flat}T_{flat2.down1}D_{down} \sum_{i=1}^{h'_{up.down}} E^i_{up}\ \text{gsum}(E_{up},h'_{up} - i)E^i_{down}$$

Firings of R'5: $T_{up2.flat1}E_{flat}T_{flat2.down1}D_{down} \sum_{i=1}^{h'_{up.down}} (E_{up}E_{down})^i$

The total cost is thus:

$$F_{up}\text{gsum}(E_{up},h'_{up} - 1) + T_{up2.flat1}F_{flat}E_{up}\text{gsum}(E_{up},h'_{up} - 1)$$

$$+ T_{up2.flat1}E_{flat}T_{flat2.down1}D_{down} \sum_{i=1}^{h'_{up.down}} E^i_{up}\ \text{gsum}(E_{up},h'_u - i)\ E^i_{down}$$

$$+ T_{up2.flat1}E_{flat}T_{flat2.down1}D_{down} \sum_{i=1}^{h'_{up.down}} (E_{up}E_{down})^i$$

Counting   We first rewrite the rule set as follows:

R'1   counting(john,0).

R'2   counting(XU,I + 1) :– counting(X,I),up(X,XU).

R'3   p(Y,I) :– counting(X,I),flat(X,Y).

R'4 $p(Y,I) :- p(YU,I + 1),down(YU,Y).$

R'5 $query(Y) :- p(Y,0).$

Next, we compute the counting set using R'1 and R'2. We then fire R'3 and obtain sets of nodes in *flat*, each set numbered with the distance from "john" (in *up*) of the nodes it contains. We then fire R'4 repeatedly, traversing down one level each time. The cost of this step can be computed as follows. For each set numbered i, we find the elements that are also present in *down*. Let us denote this set Si. Consider the set of elements in Si which are also in *down*. They generate $E_{down}D_{down}$ firings in stepping one level through *down* to produce nodes in *down* at level i − 1. In the best case, the set of nodes produced thus is always contained in the set of nodes at level i − 1 that is computed by firing rule R3 (i.e., Si − 1), and this is detected by duplicate elimination. In the worst case, these two sets are disjoint. Thus, in the best case, each set Si effectively generates just $E_{down}D_{down}$ arcs (firings of R'4) in stepping through *down*. In the worst case, each set Si generates $gsum(E_{down},i)D_{down}$ arcs in stepping through *down*.

Finally, we fire R'5 to produce the answer; the cost is the size of the answer set. We can now compute the cost:

The number of elements in counting(X,I) is:

$$E_{up}^I$$

Thus the number of elements in p(Y,I) is:

$$E_{up}^I T_{up2.flat1} E_{flat}$$

And the number that are also present in *down* is:

$$E_{up}^I T_{up2.flat1} E_{flat} T_{flat2.down1}$$

Firings of R'1 and R'2:	$F_{up} gsum(E_{up}, h'_{up} - 1)$
Firings of R'3:	$T_{up2.flat1} F_{flat} E_{up} gsum(E_{up}, h'_{up} - 1)$
Firings of R'4—Best Case:	$\displaystyle\sum_{i=1}^{h'_{up.down}} E_{up}^i\ T_{up2.flat1} E_{flat} T_{flat2.down1} E_{down} D_{down}$
Firings of R'4—Worst Case:	$\displaystyle\sum_{i=1}^{h'_{up.down}} E_{up}^i T_{up2.flat1} E_{flat} T_{flat2.down1}$ $gsum(E_{down},i)D_{down}$
Firings of R5:	$T_{up2.flat1} E_{flat} T_{flat2.down1} D_{down} \displaystyle\sum_{i=1}^{h'_{up.down}} (E_{up} E_{down})^i$

Total cost—Best Case:

$$F_{up}\text{gsum}(E_{up},h'_{up} - 1) + T_{up2.flat1}F_{flat}E_{up}\text{gsum}(E_{up},h'_{up} - 1)$$
$$+ \sum_{i=1}^{h'_{up.down}} T_{up2.flat1}E_{flat}T_{flat2.down1}D_{down}E^i_{up}\,E_{down}$$
$$+ T_{up2.flat}\,E_{flat}\,T_{flat2.down1}\,D_{down}\sum_{i=1}^{h'_{up.down}} (E_{up}\,E_{down})^i$$

Total cost—Worst Case:

$$F_{up}\text{gsum}(E_{up},h'_{up} - 1) + T_{up2.flat1}F_{flat}E_{up}\text{gsum}(E_{up},h'_{up}-1)$$
$$+ \sum_{i=1}^{h'_{up.down}} T_{up2.flat1}E_{flat}T_{flat2.down1}D_{down}E^i_{up}\text{gsum}(E_{down},i)$$
$$+ T_{up2.flat1}E_{flat}T_{flat2.down1}D_{down}\sum_{i=1}^{h'_{up.down}} (E_{up}E_{down})^i$$

Generalized Magic Sets   It performs exactly like the Magic Sets strategy.

Graphical Comparison of the Costs

The curves given in the appendix show the relative performance of the various strategies on each of the sample queries for three sets of data. They are relations in which the tuples are arranged in a tree structure, an inverted tree structure, and a "cylinder." A cylinder is a structure in which each layer has b nodes and each node has on the average two incoming and two outgoing arcs. We present below a sample relation of each type:

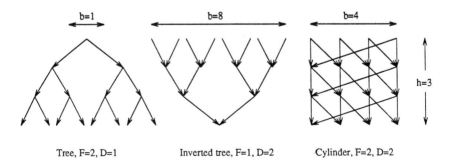

Tree, F=2, D=1   Inverted tree, F=1, D=2   Cylinder, F=2, D=2

Figure 3.

The choice of these structures was made in order to study the effects of uneven distribution of the data and the effects of duplication. We have fixed the sizes of all relations at 100,000 tuples. For the tree structure, we vary the shape by changing the fan-out F while keeping the number of arcs (which is the number of tuples) constant. Clearly, decreasing the fan-out increases the depth of the structure and vice-versa. Similarly, the shape of the inverted tree is varied by varying the duplication factor. The shape of the cylinder is varied by varying the ratio of breadth b to height h, again keeping the number of arcs constant.

For each query and data structure, we plot the cost of each strategy against the shape of the data (measured in terms of the parameter used to vary it). Thus, for each query, we plot cost vs. F for the tree, cost vs. D for the inverted tree, and cost vs. b/h for the cylinder. We do this for each strategy. The cost is computed using the cost functions listed in the appendix. We have sometimes displayed a subset of the curves (for the same query and data structure) over a different range to allow a better comparison.

For the ancestor queries, we plot the cost of each strategy for the cases when the parent relation has 100,000 tuples and the data in it has the shape of a tree, an inverted tree and a cylinder.

For the same generation example, we have assumed that the relations *up* and *down* are identical and that the fan-out and duplication for the relation *flat* are both equal to 1. We have also assumed that the transfer ratio from up to *flat* is equal to the transfer ratio from flat to down. We have assumed that all three relations (*up*, *flat*, and *down*) have 100,000 tuples. We plot the cost of each strategy as the shape of *up* and *down* varies for a total of six cases: the cases when the structure is a tree, an inverted tree, and a cylinder, with the transfer ratio equal to 1 and 0.01 (100% and 1% respectively).

Summary of the Curves

There are several important points to be seen in the curves. For a given query, there is a clear ordering of the various strategies that usually holds over the entire range of data. The difference in performance between strategies is by orders of magnitude, emphasizing the importance of choosing the right strategy. The cost of the optimal strategy is less than 10,000 in each of the queries we have considered over the entire range of data. The size of the data is 100,000 tuples. This indicates that recursive queries can be implemented efficiently.

We present a summary of the ordering of the strategies, as seen in the corresponding curves. We use $\ll$ to denote an order of magnitude or greater difference in performance, and for a given query, we list in parentheses those strategies that perform identically for all data. We refer to the various strategies using the following acronyms for brevity: HN (Henschen-Naqvi), C (Counting), MS (Magic Sets), QSQR, QSQI, APEX, P (Prolog), SN (Semi-Naive), N (Naive), and SF (Static Filtering).

QUERY 1 (ANCESTOR.BF)

Tree: (HN,C) $\ll$ (QSQR,APEX) = P $\approx$ (MS,GMS) $\ll$
   QSQI $\ll$ (SN,SF) $\ll$ N

Inverted tree: (HN,C) $\ll$ (QSQR,APEX) $\approx$ (MS,GMS) $\ll$ P $\ll$
   QSQI $\ll$ (SN,SF) $\ll$ N

Cylinder: (HN,C) $\ll$ (QSQR,APEX) $\approx$ (MS,GMS) $\ll$
   QSQI $\ll$ (SN,SF) $\ll$ N $\ll$ P

QUERY 2 (ANCESTOR.FB)

All data: (HN,MS,GMS,QSQR,SF) $\ll$ APEX $\approx$ QSQI $\ll$ SN $\ll$ N $\approx$ P

QUERY 3 (ANCESTOR.BF, NON-LINEAR)

All data: QSQR $\approx$ GMS $\ll$ QSQI $\ll$ APEX $\ll$ (SN,MS,SF) $\ll$ N

(HN, Counting, and Prolog do not apply)

QUERY 4 (SAME GENERATION.BF)

Tree: C $\ll$ HN $\approx$ (MS,GMS) $\ll$ QSQR = P $\ll$
   APEX $\ll$ QSQI $\ll$ (SN,SF) $\ll$ N

Inverted tree: C $\ll$ HN $\approx$ (MS,GMS) $\ll$ QSQR $\approx$
   APEX $\ll$ P $\approx$ QSQI $\ll$ (SN,SF) $\ll$ N

Cylinder: C $\ll$ HN $\approx$ (MS,GMS) $\ll$ QSQR $\ll$
   APEX $\ll$ QSQI $\ll$ (SN,SF) $\ll$ N $\ll$ P

To summarize the ancestor results, the following order is seen to hold for the ancestor queries:

(HN, C) $\ll$ QSQR $\approx$ (MS,GMS) $\ll$ APEX $\approx$ QSQI $\ll$ SN $\ll$ N

There are some exceptions and additions to the above ordering. In the non-linear case, Henschen-Naqvi and Counting do not apply, and Magic Sets reduces to Semi-Naive. Static Filtering performs like Semi-Naive, except in the case where the second argument is bound, and in this case it performs like QSQR. APEX performs like QSQR in the case where the first argument is bound. Prolog performs poorly when it cannot propagate the constant in the query (the case where the second argument is bound), as expected. When it can propagate the constant, its performance degrades sharply with duplication, especially as the depth of the data structure increases. This is readily seen from the curves for the cylinder.

To summarize the same generation results, we have:

$$C \ll HN \approx (MS, GMS) \ll QSQR \ll APEX \ll QSQI \ll$$
$$(SN, SF) \ll (P, N)$$

Prolog behaves like QSQR when there is no duplication (tree). With duplication, its performance degrades so sharply with an increase in the depth of the data structure that we have classified it with Naive, although it performs better than Semi-Naive over a wide range.

Interpreting the Results

These results indicate that the following three factors greatly influence the performance:

1. The amount of *duplication* of work,

2. The size of the set of *relevant facts*, and

3. The size (number and arity) of intermediate relations.

By duplication of work, we refer to the repeated firing of a rule on the same data. This can occur due to duplication in the data (e.g., Prolog), or due to an iterative control strategy that does not remember previous firings (e.g., QSQI and Naive). Consider the second factor. A fact p(a) is *relevant* to a given query q iff there exists a derivation p(a) $\rightarrow^*$ q(b) for some b in the answer set. If we know all the relevant facts in advance, instead of using the database to reply to the query, we can use the relevant part of the database only, thus cutting down on the set of facts to be processed. It is, in general, impossible to find all the relevant facts in advance without spending as much effort as in replying to the query. Thus, all methods have a way of finding a super-set of relevant facts. We call this set the *set of potentially relevant facts*. As this set becomes smaller, i.e., contains fewer and fewer facts that are *not* relevant, the work done in evaluating the query clearly decreases. The third factor is hard to define precisely. Strategies that only look at sets of nodes rather than sets of arcs perform better than those that look at sets of arcs, by an order of magnitude or more. They are less generally applicable since this often involves a loss of information. This usually leads to non-termination unless the database has certain properties, such as linearity of rules and acyclicity of the extensional database. And of course, strategies that create more intermediate relations pay for it in increased costs, since the addition of a tuple to a relation (intermediate or otherwise) represents a firing.

The following discussion is intended to clarify these issues, as well as to explain the performance of the various strategies in terms of the three factors.

The Ancestor Queries   We begin by looking at the ancestor queries. The effect of duplication is seen by considering Prolog and QSQI, both of which do duplicate work, for different reasons. When the first argument is bound, Prolog performs like QSQR on a tree data structure, where exactly one arc enters each node (equivalently, there is exactly one way of deriving a given answer). With duplication (i.e., on the average more than one arc enters a given node), performance degrades dramatically. Prolog's performance for the same query on a cylinder is comparable to Naive Evaluation, a difference of several orders of magnitude! We note that the set of relevant facts is comparable in the two cases, being the set of nodes reachable from the node denoting the constant in the query (which will henceforth be referred to as the query node). However, in the case of the cylinder, these nodes can be reached along several paths and Prolog infers them afresh along each path. QSQI performs duplicate computation for a different reason, which is that its iterative control strategy does not remember previous firings. Essentially, there are as many steps (executions of the control loop) as the longest path from the query node, and all nodes reached by a path of length less than or equal to i are recomputed at all steps after the i-th. This can be seen by comparing QSQR and QSQI and noting that QSQI is orders of magnitude worse in all cases. QSQR uses the same set of relevant facts (the reachable nodes) and differs only in that it has a recursive control strategy that precisely avoids this duplication. Naive Evaluation also does a lot of duplicate work, for the same reason as QSQI, i.e., it does not remember previous firings. Semi-Naive differs from Naive only in that it remembers all previous firings and does not repeat them. Thus, the effect of duplication can also be seen in the difference between Naive and Semi-Naive.

The effect of a smaller set of relevant facts can be seen in the vast difference between Magic Sets and Semi-Naive. Magic Sets is simply Semi-Naive applied to the set of relevant facts, which is determined to be the set of reachable nodes except in the doubly recursive case. In this case, the first phase of the Magic Sets strategy, which computes the set of relevant facts, fails and the Magic Sets strategy degenerates to Semi-Naive. This effect can also be seen in the behavior of Prolog on a tree data structure (which means we eliminate the effect of duplication) when the first argument is free. Prolog's depth first strategy is unable to propagate the constant in the second argument of the query. In other words, it must consider all facts in the database, and its performance degrades by several orders of magnitude. Similarly, the Static Filtering strategy degenerates to Semi-Naive when the optimization algorithm fails to push down the constant in the query. We note that pushing the constant (i.e., the selection that it represents) is equivalent to cutting down on the number of relevant facts.

QSQR succeeds in restricting the set of relevant facts to the set of nodes reachable from the query node even in the non-linear version of ancestor. It does this at the cost of implementing the recursive control, which is a cost that we do not understand at this stage. QSQI also succeeds in restricting the set of relevant facts but performs a great deal of duplicate computation. The Magic Sets algorithm uses the entire parent relation for the set of relevant facts and so degenerates to Semi-Naive. APEX, for reasons explained below, also uses a much larger set of relevant facts. So, although it improves upon Semi-Naive Computation in this case, it is much worse than QSQR. The Generalized Magic Sets strategy, however, succeeds in restricting the set of relevant facts to those reachable from the query node, thus illustrating its wider applicability. Henschen-Naqvi and Counting do not apply and Prolog does not terminate.

The behavior of APEX illustrates the interesting distinction between the set of relevant facts and the set of *useful* facts. The first step in the APEX strategy is to find what APEX calls the set of relevant facts (which is actually a subset of the set of relevant facts as we have defined it, since it does not include all facts that could derive an answer). In the ancestor examples, these are facts from the relation parent, and the firing of the first rule adds them to the ancestor relation. Subsequently, these facts are substituted (in turn) into both the parent and ancestor predicates in the body of the second rule. Except in the first case, this leads to subqueries whose answers are not relevant. For example, in the case where the second argument is bound to "john," the set of relevant (à la APEX) facts is the set of facts p(X,john). By substituting these into the parent predicate in the second rule, we generate the query a(john,?). This computes the ancestors of "john," whereas the given query a(?,john) asks for the descendants of john. This is because APEX does not make the distinction that facts of the form p(X,john) are relevant to the query a(?,john) only when substituted into the ancestor predicate in the second rule. This is a distinction that the Magic Sets strategy makes, and it thereby reduces the number of useless firings.

We now consider the third factor, the arity of the intermediate relations. The two strategies that use unary intermediate relations are the Henschen-Naqvi and Counting strategies. In essence, at Step i they compute the set of relevant facts which is at a distance i from the query node. Let us denote this set by Si. At the next step, they compute the set of those nodes in parent to which there is an arc from a node in Si. Thus, they compute all nodes reachable from "john," and further they compute each node at most D times where D is the duplication factor. However, the unary relations strategy fails to terminate if the query node is in a cycle. Also, neither the Henschen-Naqvi nor the Counting strategy applies when there are non-linear rules.

Magic Sets computes exactly the same set of relevant facts and does no duplicate work. However, in the second phase at Step i it computes all arcs in the transitive closure of parent (restricted to the set of relevant facts) of length

i. In particular, this includes all arcs of length i rooted at "john." This is the answer, and this is essentially all that the more specialized methods, Henschen-Naqvi and Counting, compute. Everything else that the Magic Sets strategy does is useless computation. Thus, the cost of the Magic Sets strategy is the number of arcs in the transitive closure of the subtree rooted at "john" (i.e., the subtree of nodes reachable from john).

The recursive control of QSQR generates subqueries using precisely the nodes in set Si at Step i, and the answer to each of these subqueries is the set of all nodes in the subtree rooted at that node. By induction, it is easy to see that the total cost involved in computing a query is the number of arcs in the transitive closure of the subgraph rooted at that query node. (The cost is thus similar to that of Magic Sets.) The intermediate relations here are the (binary) sets of answers to each subquery. This seems to indicate the power of a recursive control strategy since it succeeds in reducing both the set of relevant facts and the amount of duplicate work.

The Same Generation Query   We conclude this discussion by explaining the performance of the various strategies in the same generation query in terms of these three factors. Counting has the best performance since it uses the smallest set of relevant facts (the nodes of *up* which are reachable from the query node), does not do duplicate computation, and further, uses unary intermediate relations. It executes the query in two phases. In the first phase, at Step i, it computes the set of all nodes in *up* that are reachable from the query node via a path of length i. In the second phase, it first computes the nodes of *down* that are reachable from this set via an arc of *flat*, still retaining the distance of each set from the query node. In subsequent iterations, it steps through *down* once each time, such that each node in a set that is i steps away from the query node in *up* is the root of paths of length i in *down*.

Henschen-Naqvi uses the same set of relevant facts and is a unary strategy, but it does a large amount of duplicate work. It is a single phase algorithm, which does the same amount of work as the first phase of Counting in computing sets of *up* nodes along with their distances from the query node. However, it steps through *down* i times for each set at a distance i from the query node in *up*. Since it does not keep track of the work it does in Step i at Step i + 1, it repeats much of the work in stepping through *down*. (Unless, of course, the data is such that there is no duplication of work. This corresponds to the data configuration in the worst case for Counting— the additional book-keeping done by Counting is unnecessary since the data ensures that there is no duplication of work in stepping through *down*.)

The set of relevant facts for Magic Sets and QSQR is again the set of *up* nodes reachable from the query node. They do not perform duplicate computation. However, they work with binary relations, in effect computing all paths with equal lengths in *up* and *down* linked by a single arc in flat. Thus, their performance is inferior to that of Counting. Further, QSQR's left to right strategy forces us to create intermediate relations for up^* and $up^*.sg$, where up^* denotes the transitive closure of up. Since the Magic Sets strategy does not impose any order of evaluation, we can do with the single intermediate relation sg. The cost of the additional inferences required to create the intermediate relations causes a large difference in the costs of the two strategies.

Our graphs show the performance of Magic Sets to be identical to that of Henschen-Naqvi. It is to be expected that they perform similarly since the duplicate work done by Henschen-Naqvi is offset by the fact that they work with binary relations. However, their performance is not really identical. It appears to be so in our curves for two reasons. The first is our approximation of the number of arcs of length 1 to n(l)gsum(E,h − 1). The second is the fact that we plot the curves for cases where up and $down$ are identical. Under these conditions, the expressions for the performance of these methods become identical.

QSQI is similar to QSQR except that at each step it duplicates the work of the previous steps, and so it is inferior to Magic Sets and QSQR. Semi-Naive uses binary relations, and although it does not do duplicate work, this is outweighed by the fact that the set of relevant facts is all the nodes in up, therefore, it performs worse than QSQI. Static Filtering degenerates to Semi-Naive since the optimization strategy fails to make any improvements to the system graph. Prolog is similar to QSQR when there is no duplication in the data, but its cost increases exponentially with the depth of the data structure when there is duplication. Naive Evaluation uses the entire set of nodes in up as relevant facts, does duplicate work since it does not remember firings, and uses binary intermediate relations. With the exception of Prolog over a certain range, it is clearly the worst strategy.

Finally, we note that when the transfer ratio T is 0.01 (1%), the cost of computing the answer by Naive or Semi-Naive Evaluation is essentially that of computing all arcs in the relation *flat*, and so the two methods perform almost identically.

Related Work

The performance issue was addressed informally through the discussion of a set of examples in Bancilhon et al. [1986b]. Han and Lu [1986] contains a study of the performance of a set of four evaluation strategies (including Naive and Henschen-Naqvi and two others not considered here) on the same generation example using randomly generated data. Their model is based on the selectivity of the join and select operations and the sizes of the data relations. They consider both CPU and IO cost. We have chosen to concentrate on one aspect of the problem, which is the number of successful firings (measured using the sizes of the intermediate relations), and have studied a wider range of strategies, queries, and data.

Conclusions and Caveats

We have presented a performance comparison of ten methods. Even though the "benchmark" we have used is incomplete, the cost measure too elementary, and the approximations crude, we found the results to be valuable. The robustness of the results (at least on our workload), both in terms of the order of magnitude differences between the costs of the strategies and in terms of invariance of the results to the parameters which we varied, was a surprise. We have also been able to explain most of our results through three factors: duplication, relevant facts, and unary vs. binary. While the first two factors were well known, the third one came as a surprise, even though it was probably already understood in Sacca and Zaniolo [1986].

Our conclusions may be summarized as follows:

1. For a given query, there is a clear ordering of the strategies.

2. The more specialized strategies perform significantly better.

3. Recursion is a powerful control structure that reduces the number of relevant facts and eliminates duplicate work.

4. The choice of the right strategy is critical since the differences in performance are by orders of magnitude.

5. Three factors that greatly influence performance are: (i) duplication of work, (ii) the set of relevant facts, and (iii) the number and arity of the intermediate relations.

The results seem robust in that the performance of the various strategies usually differ by orders of magnitude, which allows a wide latitude for the approximations in the model and cost evaluation. Also, the curves rarely intersect, which means that the relative ordering of the strategies is maintained in most cases over the entire range of data.

However, it must be emphasized that our cost function makes some crude approximations. The cost of join is linear in the size of the result, a consequence of our using the size of intermediate relations as the cost measure. We also ignore the cost of disk accesses and the cost of implementing a recursive control strategy. Our model suffers from the approximation that duplication is independent of the size of the start set.

Finally, our sample data and queries are limited, and the results must be extrapolated to other data and queries with caution, especially since the results show some variance in the relative performance of the strategies for different sets of data and queries. In particular, our benchmark is limited to the type of data and query where there is a *large* amount of data and the size of the answer to the query is *small*. This clearly favors the "smart" strategies and obscures, for instance, the fact that Semi-Naive performs as well as any other strategy when computing the entire transitive closure of a relation (Bancilhon [1986]). Further, our data contains no cycles or shortcuts. This is an important limitation since it favors some of the specialized strategies. For instance, there are cases where Counting performs worse than Magic Sets (Bancilhon et al. [1986a]). This is not shown by our results since these cases involve shortcuts in the data.

Acknowledgments

We thank the anonymous referees for numerous comments which improved the technical content and presentation of this paper.

References

1. Aho, A. and Ullman, J. D. [1979] Universality of Data Retrieval Languages, *Proc. 6th ACM Symposium on Principles of Programming Languages*, 110–120.

2. Bancilhon, F. [1986] Naive Evaluation of Recursively Defined Relations, in *On Knowledge Base Management Systems—Integrating Database and AI Systems* (M. Brodie and J. Mylopoulos, Eds.), Springer-Verlag, 165–178.

3. Bancilhon, F. [1985] A Note on the Performance of Rule Based Systems, *MCC Technical Report DB-022-85*.

4. Bancilhon, F., Maier, D., Sagiv, Y., and Ullman, J. D. [1986a] Magic Sets and Other Strange Ways to Implement Logic Programs, *Proc. 5th ACM SIGMOD-SIGACT Symposium on Principles of Database Systems*, 1–15.

5. Bancilhon, F., Maier, D., Sagiv, Y., and Ullman J. D. [1986b] Magic Sets: Algorithms and Examples, unpublished manuscript.

6. Bancilhon, F. and Ramakrishnan, R. [1986] An Amateur's Introduction to Recursive Query Processing Strategies, *Proc. SIGMOD 86*, 16–52.

7. Bayer, R. [1985] Query Evaluation and Recursion in Deductive Database Systems, unpublished manuscript.

8. Beeri, C. and Ramakrishnan, R. [1987] On the Power of Magic, *Proc. 6th ACM SIGMOD-SIGACT-SIGART Symposium on Principles of Database Systems*, 269–283.

9. Chang, C. [1981] On the Evaluation of Queries Containing Derived Relations in Relational Databases, in *Advances in Data Base Theory, Vol.1* (H. Gallaire, J. Minker, and J. M. Nicolas, Eds.), Plenum Press, New York, 235–260.

10. Delobel, C. [1986] Bases de Donnees et Bases de Connaissances: Une Approche Systemique a l'Aide d'une Algebre Matricielle des Relations, *Journees Francophones*, Grenoble, January 1986, 101–134.

11. Dietrich, S. W. and Warren, D. S. [1985] Dynamic Programming Strategies for the Evaluation of Recursive Queries, unpublished report.

12. Gallaire, H., Minker, J., and Nicolas, J.-M. [1984] Logic and Data Bases: A Deductive Approach, *Computing Surveys* **16**(2):153–185.

13. Gardarin, G. and de Maindreville, Ch. [1986] Evaluation of Database Recursive Logic Programs as Recurrent Function Series, *Proc. SIGMOD 86*, Washington, DC, 177–186.

14. Han, J. and Lu, H. [1986] Some Performance Results on Recursive Query Processing in Relational Database Systems, *Proc. Data Engineering Conference*, Los Angeles, CA, 533–539.

15. Henschen, L. and Naqvi, S. [1984] On Compiling Queries in Recursive First-Order Data Bases, *JACM* **31**, 47–85.

16. Kifer, M. and Lozinskii, E. [1986a] Filtering Data Flow in Deductive Databases, *Proc. International Conference on Database Theory, Lecture Notes in Computer Science, No. 243*, Springer-Verlag, 186–202.

17. Kifer, M. and Lozinskii, E. [1986b] A Framework for an Efficient Implementation of Deductive Databases, *Proc. 6th Advanced Database Symposium*, 109–116.

18. Laskowski, K. [1984] Compiling Recursive Axioms in First Order Databases, Masters Thesis, Northwestern University.

19. Lozinskii, E. [1985] Evaluating Queries in Deductive Databases by Generating, *Proc. 11th International Joint Conference on Artificial Intelligence*, 173–177.

20. Marque-Pucheu, G. [1983] Algebraic Structure of Answers in a Recursive Logic Database, to appear in Acta Informatica.

21. McKay, D. and Shapiro, S. [1981] Using Active Connection Graphs for Reasoning with Recursive Rules, *Proc. 7th International Joint Conference on Artificial Intelligence*, 368–374.

22. Rohmer, J. and Lescoeur, R. [1985] La Methode Alexandre: Une Solution pour Traiter les Axiomes Recursifs dans les Bases de Donnees Deductives, *Colloque Reconnaissance de Formes et Intelligence Artificielle*, Grenoble, November 1985, 125–146.

23. Roussel, P. [1975] PROLOG, Manuel de Reference et de Utilisation, Groupe Intelligence Artificielle, Universite Aix-Marseille II.

24. Sacca, D. and Zaniolo, C. [1986] On the Implementation of a Simple Class of Logic Queries for Databases, *Proc. 5th ACM SIGMOD-SIGACT Symposium on Principles of Database Systems*, 16–23.

25. Tarski, A. [1955] A Lattice Theoretical Fixpoint Theorem and Its Applications, *Pacific Journal of Mathematics* **5**, 285–309.

26. Ullman, J. D. [1985] Implementation of Logical Query Languages for Databases, *Transactions on Database Systems* **10**(3):289–321.

27. Vieille, L. [1986] Recursive Axioms in Deductive Databases: The Query/Subquery Approach *Proc. First Intl. Conference on Expert Database Systems*, Charleston, 179–194.

Query 1, Tree data

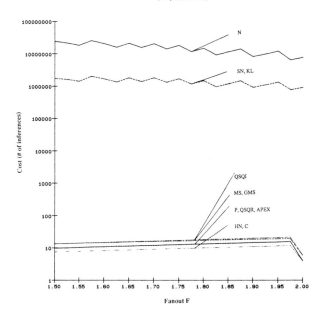

ABF_INV

Query 1, Inverted tree data

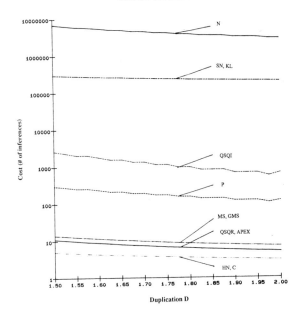

Query 1, Cylinder data

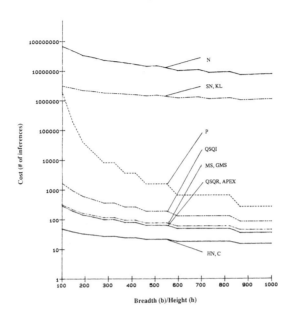

Query 2, Cylinder data

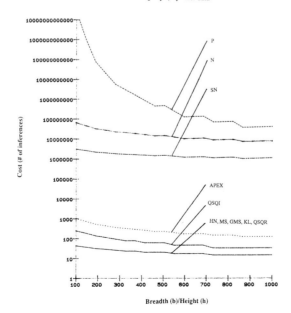

Query 2, Tree data

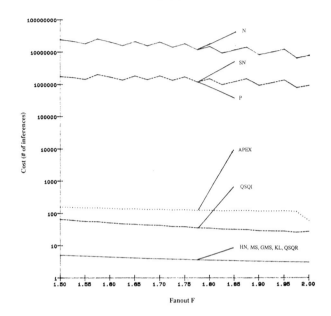

Query 3, Tree data

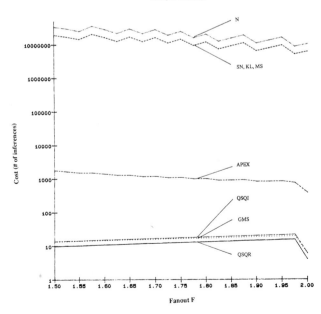

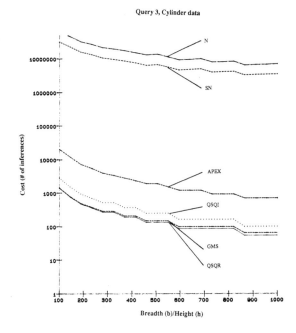

Query 3, Cylinder data

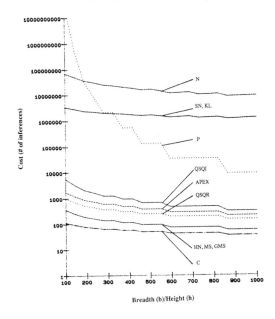

Query 4, Cylinder data with Join Selectivity = 100%

Query 4, Tree data with Join Selectivity = 100%

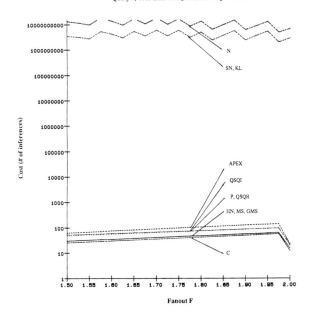

Query 4, Tree data with Join Selectivity = 100%

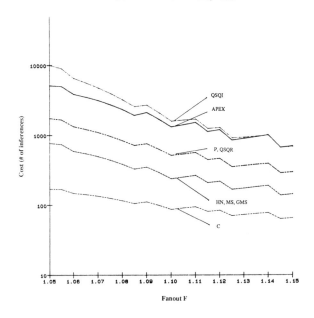

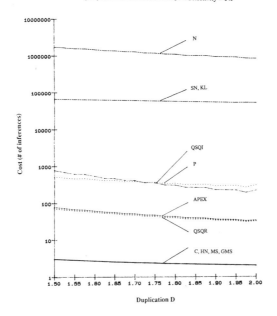

Query 4, Inverted tree data with Join Selectivity = 1%

SG_INV

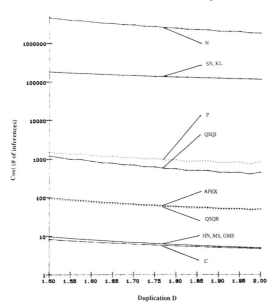

Query 4, Inverted tree data with Join Selectivity = 100%

13

A Superjoin Algorithm for Deductive Databases

James A. Thom
Department of Computer Science
Royal Melbourne Institute of Technology,
Australia

Kotagiri Ramamohanarao
Department of Computer Science
University of Melbourne,
Australia

Lee Naish
Department of Computer Science
University of Melbourne,
Australia

Abstract

This paper describes a join algorithm suitable for deductive as well as relational databases that are accessed by computers with large main memories. Using multi-key hashing and appropriate buffering, joins can be performed on very large relations more efficiently than with existing methods. This algorithm fits naturally into PROLOG top-down computations and can be made very flexible by incorporating additional PROLOG features. It can also be used with bottom-up query evaluation strategies.

519

Introduction

The join operator is both a frequently used relational operator and an expensive one in relational database systems. Several join algorithms have been discussed in the recent literature, including Bratbergsengen [1984], DeWitt et al. [1984], Jarke and Koch [1984], and Ullman [1985], for example, nested-loops, sort-merge, and hash-join.

We propose another join algorithm, the *superjoin* algorithm. This algorithm, based on multi-key hashing, partitions the join to enable efficient buffer management. The superjoin algorithm is suitable for large relational databases accessed from computers with large main memories. One of the properties of the superjoin algorithm is that it maintains excellent performance from very small relations to very large relations. The superjoin algorithm also supports queries containing arbitrary constraints, disjunctions, negations, and existential quantifiers. These additional properties are especially useful for deductive database systems.

This paper is organized as follows. In "Background" we introduce the notation used in this paper, multi-key hashing, and partial match joins.

We describe how, using multi-key hashing and appropriate partitioning, joins can be performed on very large relations in a very efficient way. If there is suitable buffering of pages, then each page of each relation need be read into main memory at most once. An algorithm is described that minimizes the number of buffers required. An implementation of this algorithm, in PROLOG, is given in Appendix 1 and some examples are listed in Appendix 2.

We describe how the superjoin fits naturally into PROLOG's top-down computation, including PROLOG features such as negation and existential quantifiers. A complete deductive database system would include a higher level that would handle rules and recursion. The system would transform a query into possibly several sub-queries to be processed efficiently by the superjoin. The superjoin would access a low-level interface to the external database.

We analyze the performance of the superjoin algorithm, and compare it with other well known join algorithms.

Our conclusion is that the superjoin provides a flexible and powerful database primitive, and at the same time provides superior efficiency to that of existing join algorithms.

Background

Notation

Throughout this paper we shall use a notation based on PROLOG's implementation of Horn Clause logic (Clocksin and Mellish [1981]). The term *predicate* is used as equivalent to the term *relation,* and *fact* is used as equivalent to *tuple.*

Predicate (relation) names are written in lower case, strings are written with double quotes, and variables are written in upper case. A fact (tuple) can be written

```
p("x1", "y1")
```

which is a fact about "x1" and "y1" from the predicate "p." A *query* can be written

```
?- p(X, "y1")
```

which would find all values for the first attribute (the variable X) for those facts in "p" where the second attribute is "y1." Conjunctions are constructed with ',' and disjunctions with ';'. Thus, the query

```
?- p(X,Y), q(Y,Z)    QUERY 1
```

would join "p" with "q," joining on the second attribute of "p" and the first attribute of "q" (the *join variable* Y).

Multi-key Hashing

There are various schemes for accessing predicates stored using multi-key hashing, including Rothnie and Lozano [1974], Rivest [1976], Aho and Ullman [1979], Ramamohanarao et al. [1983], and Ramamohanarao and Shepherd [1986]. Many schemes are variations and enhancements on a common scheme that we shall describe here.

Consider a partial match query on a single predicate. We assume a predicate is stored on disc in the pages of one file. Each tuple has a fixed number of attributes, denoted a_1, a_2,...,a_k. A *partial match query* is a specification of the value of zero or more of these k attributes. The answer to a query is the collection of all tuples in the file that have the specified values for the specified attributes.

Tuples are allocated to pages within the file by means of a hashing scheme that allocates zero or more bits to each attribute of the tuple. Consider a static file consisting of 2^d pages, where $d \geq 0$. The pages are numbered from 0 to $2^d - 1$. Each attribute a_i has a hashing function h_i that maps from the key space of a_i to a bit string. From this string d_i bits are selected, such that $d_1 + ... + d_k = d$. By computing the hash values of all the attribute values of a tuple, it is possible to compute the page number in which the tuple is stored. This requires the use of a *choice vector,* which defines a mapping between the strings of d_i bits and the page number. The choice vector was introduced for handling dynamic files in Lloyd and Ramamohanarao [1982] and in Ramamohanarao et al. [1983]. A choice vector specifies a permutation of the k d_i bits selected from the hash values of the attributes. Here we use a slightly simplified notation for choice vectors.

Suppose the hash functions h_i map "y0" to the string of bits "...000" and "y1" to "...001" and "y2" to "...010" and similarly for "z0 ," "z1 ," "z2," and so on. For each attribute, we choose the last d_i bits to construct the choice vector.

Consider a predicate q(Y,Z), the hash functions h_1 and h_2 would map the value Y to a string "...$Y_3Y_2Y_1$" and the value Z to a string "...$Z_3Z_2Z_1$" respectively, where Y_i and Z_i can take values 0 or 1. We loosely refer to these strings of subscripted variables as bit strings. If q(Y,Z) is stored in 2^3 pages, then we might set $d_1 = 2$ and $d_2 = 1$. Thus the bits Y_2Y_1 and Z_1 would be selected from the bit strings generated by the hash functions.

The choice vector could be any one permutation of these bit strings, such as $Y_1Z_1Y_2$. Thus tuples would be stored in the file as shown in the "q" predicate in Figure 1.

For a query containing variables, only some of the bits will be specified. Thus several pages will need to be searched. Consider the query:

```
?- q("y3", Z)      QUERY 2
```

Answering this query would require the following steps:

1. Hash "y3" to the bit string "...011" from which we select just the last two bits since $d_1 = 2$, namely $Y_2Y_1 = 11$.

2. Since the second attribute is a variable, the bit $Z_1 = *$, where * represents an unknown bit.

3. Search the pages where $Y_1Z_1Y_2 = 1*1$ (namely pages 101 and 111) for tuples which match the query; this would retrieve the tuples:

    q("y3", "z2")

    q("y3", "z1").

Partial Match Joins

It is possible to apply these partial match schemes directly, for instance, in a PROLOG system which finds answers a tuple at a time (Naish and Thom [1983], Ramamohanarao and Shepherd [1986]. Consider Query 1 again.

```
?- p(X,Y), q(Y,Z)
```

p

page X_1Y_1	tuples p(X,Y)
0 0	p("x0", "y0") p("x2", "y2")
0 1	p("x0", "y1") p("x2", "y1")
1 0	p("x1", "y0")
1 1	p("x1", "y1")

r

page X_1Z_1	tuples r(X,Z)
0 0	r("x0", "z0") r("x2", "z2")
0 1	r("x0", "z1") r("x2", "z1")
1 0	r("x1", "z0")
1 1	r("x1", "z1")

q

page $Y_1Z_1Y_2$	tuples q(Y,Z)
0 0 0	q("y4", "z0") q("y4", "z2")
0 0 1	q("y2", "z2")
0 1 0	q("y4", "z1")
0 1 1	q("y2", "z1")
1 0 0	q("y1", "z2")
1 0 1	q("y3", "z2")
1 1 0	q("y1", "z1")
1 1 1	q("y3", "z1") q("y7", "z1")

s

page $X_1Y_1Y_2$	tuples s(X,Y)
0 0 0	s("x0", "y0") s("x2," "y4")
0 0 1	s("x0", "y0")
0 1 0	s("x0", "y1") s("x2", "y1")
0 1 1	s("x0", "y3")
1 0 0	s("x1", "y0")
1 0 1	s("x1", "y2")
1 1 0	s("x1", "y1")
1 1 1	s("x1", "y3")

Figure 1: "p", "q", "r" & "s" Predicates

In answering the query, a straightforward implementation in PROLOG would begin by reading the first page of "p"(page 00). PROLOG would get the first solution from this page, namely the tuple:

```
p("x0", "y0")
```

and try to find tuples from the second predicate that match. Since "y0" hashes to "...00," only pages 000 and 010 from "q" would need to be read. However, as there are no matching tuples, PROLOG would proceed with the second solution from the first page of "p" in a similar fashion. Thus, the second solution

```
p("x2", "y2")
```

would join with the tuples

```
q("y2", "z2")
q("y2", "z1")
```

This would require reading pages 001 and 011 from "q" since "y2" hashes to "...10." After exhausting all the tuples in the first page of "p," PROLOG would proceed in a similar fashion with subsequent pages of "p."

This scheme for implementing joins fits in naturally with other relational operators such as selection. Consider the query

```
?- p("x0",Y), q(Y,Z)      QUERY 3
```

This query performs a selection on "p" while performing the join, reducing the number of pages which need to be considered.

Using partial match retrieval to implement joins creates a workable system. However, there is one important inefficiency: For most queries, this approach requires that many pages need to be read more than once. For example in Query 1, each tuple in "p" causes a separate partial match query on "q" which results in two pages being read. All four pages of "p" are read and, since there are six tuples in "p," twelve page reads from "q" will occur (including some repeat reads) in the following sequence: 000, 010, 001, 011, 100, 110, 100, 110, 000, 010, 100, 110.

The Superjoin Algorithm

Multiple reading from pages of disc in the naive tuple at a time algorithm can be eliminated by keeping pages in main memory buffers. In Query 1 above, if we allocate twelve buffers (four for the "p" predicate and eight for the "q" predicate) then no page needs to be read from disc more than once. If buffers are allocated on demand, then only ten are needed because no Y values in "p" hash to "...11," so two pages of "q" are never read (101 and 111). This simple method, of buffering all pages which are read, is not feasible with large predicates. Available main memory is limited and, in large database systems, is usually much less than the total size of the predicates. Hence it is desirable to substantially reduce the number of buffers required in main memory.

If we use multi-key hashing and the join attributes have the same hash function, then it is possible to partition the join into several *sub-joins*. Each sub-join accesses only some of the tuples required for the full join. The result of the full join is simply the union of the results of all the sub-joins. The super-join algorithm partitions a join and orders the execution of the sub-joins so as to minimize the number of buffers required, while still only reading the pages of each predicate from disc at most once.

Marek and Rauszer [1986] also consider partitioning joins, partitioning the predicates such that a join on the predicates can be broken into sub-joins of disjoint sets of tuples. We consider a finer partitioning which does not have disjoint sets of tuples in each partition but which allows us to further reduce the number of buffers required.

Partitioning into Sub-Joins

A simple partitioning of Query 1 results in four sub-joins, each being the join of a different page of "p" with the relevant four pages of "q." Each sub-join only considers tuples with a particular hash value for Y_1 and X_1. If we read the pages of "p" sequentially, nine buffers are sufficient (one for the "p" predicate and eight for the "q" predicate). Only seven buffers are needed if they are allocated on demand.

By changing the order in which we access the pages of the "p" predicate we can reduce the number of buffers needed. Suppose, instead of accessing tuples from "p" in the order the pages are stored (00, 01, 10, 11), we read the pages in the order 00, 10, 01, 11. That is, we read all the pages in "p" such that Y_1 is 0 before reading the pages in "p" in which Y_1 is 1. While we are joining tuples from the pages 00 and 10 in "p," the tuples will all hash to $Y_1 = 0$, thus matching tuples will only appear in the pages 000, 001, 010, 011 from "q." Later, when we join tuples from the pages 01 and 11 in "p," the tuples will all hash to $Y_1 = 1$ and matching tuples will only appear in the pages 100, 101, 110, 111 from "q." When this is done, the number of buffers required is reduced to only five (one for the "p" predicate and four for the "q" predicate), whether or not buffers are allocated on demand.

It is possible to further reduce the number of buffers required by a more complex partitioning. In the optimal partitioning, each partition consists of tuples with particular hash values for Y_1, Y_2, and Z_1. This partitions the join into eight sub-joins. Each sub-join consists of all tuples in one page of the "q" predicate and, on average, half the tuples in two pages of the "p" predicate. For example, the sub-join where $Y_1 Z_1 Y_2 = 001$, consists of all tuples in page 001 of "q" and the tuples in pages 00 and 10 of "p" with hash value such that $Y_2 = 1$. If the sub-joins are done in increasing values of $Y_1 Z_1 Y_2$, then the number of buffers required is three (two for "p" and one for "q"). The same is true with increasing values of $Y_1Y_2Z_1$. However, with any other permutation of Y_1, Y_2, and Z_1, more than three buffers are required if no page is to be read from disc more than once (see the sub-section on "Superjoin Execution").

Sfb-Vector

Our use of bit strings, such as $Y_1Z_1Y_2$, in the previous section can be formalized by defining an *sfb-vector* (slow-fast bits vector). An sfb-vector is a string of elements of the form V_j where V is the name of variable in the query and j is an integer specifying a bit position in the hash value of V. Given an sfb-vector of length f, an *sfb-value* is a string of 0's and 1's of length f. The elements in the sfb-vector will define the partitioning of the join, and each sfb-value corresponds to a single partition. A partition consists of the sets of tuples from each predicate that *match* the sfb-value. A tuple matches an sfb-value when the hash bit values from the tuple which correspond to the elements of the sfb-vector are the same as the corresponding bits of the sfb-value. For example, given the sfb-vector for query 1 is $Y_1Y_2Z_1$ then the partition for the sfb-value of 001 is the sets {p("x0","y0"), p("x1","y0")} and {q("y4","z1")}. Sfb-values are generated in increasing order so the order of the elements of the sfb-vector defines the order in which the sub-joins are done.

Given an sfb-vector, an sfb-value and a choice vector for a file, a set of pages in that file is identified. For example, given the sfb-vector for query 1 is $Y_1Y_2Z_1$ and the choice vector for p is X_1Y_1, then the sfb-value 001 would identify the pages *0 in p (that is 00 and 10). The matching tuples of p for the partition 001 are a subset of the tuples in these pages.

The superjoin generates a sequence of sfb-values from 0 to $2^f - 1$ and performs a sub-join for each value. The sfb-vector and choice vectors are used to access the corresponding pages of the files. Only tuples that match with the sfb-value are considered. A set of tuples, one from each predicate in the query, with common values for the join variable(s) must appear in the same sub-join. Thus the union of the sub-joins is the same as the whole join.

Superjoin Execution

We now describe the execution mechanism in more detail, including the management of buffers. Associated with each predicate call is a pool of buffers. Consider a predicate P; let e be the maximum value such that the most significant e bits of the sfb-vector are also in the choice vector for P (that is, are used for indexing P). These are called the *slow bits* for this predicate.

Each sub-join is executed like a partial-match join. However, in answering the partial-match queries, we only consider tuples that match both the query and the sfb-value. If pages on disc need to be accessed, new buffers are allocated on demand. The pages remain buffered and may be accessed several more times until the current values of the slow bits change. However, when these bits change, the pages are never accessed again, since the sub-joins are done in order of increasing sfb-value. Therefore, the whole buffer pool for that call can be deallocated.

During execution of the superjoin, the addresses of the pages in the buffers always match the current value of the slow bits. Thus there is a maximum of 2^{c-e} buffers in the buffer pool of the relation at any one time, where c is the length of the choice vector. The number of buffer pages for an n-way join is the sum of those needed for each relation:

$$\text{nbufs} = \sum_{i=1}^{n} 2^{c_i - e_i}$$

c_i is the choice vector length of the ith predicate and

e_i is the number of slow bits for the ith predicate.

The sfb-vectors should be constructed so that this cost function is minimized.

An Algorithm to Construct Sfb-Vectors

A PROLOG program using a greedy algorithm to construct sfb-vectors is given in Appendix 1. The algorithm constructs the sfb-vector one element at a time. The element chosen at each stage optimizes the marginal cost. We will illustrate the algorithm with the following example.

$$?-\ q(Y,Z),\ r(X,Z),\ s(X,Y) \qquad \text{QUERY 4}$$

With a null sfb-vector the cost (number of buffer pages) for the join would be $2^3 + 2^2 + 2^3 = 20$ pages.

The bits for the sfb-vector can come from any of X, Y, or Z. If we chose X_1 for the first bit, this would reduce the cost to $2^3 + 2^1 + 2^2 = 14$ pages. Similarly, if we chose Z_1, this would reduce the cost to $2^2 + 2^1 + 2^3 = 14$ pages. However, if we chose Y_1, the cost would only be $2^2 + 2^2 + 2^2 = 12$ pages. The greedy algorithm chooses Y_1 as the first bit of the sfb-vector since that results in the greatest reduction in the number of buffer pages required.

The next bit to be chosen would again be from Y since the sfb-vector "Y_1Y_2" would mean the join only required $2^1 + 2^2 + 2^1 = 8$ pages. With the sfb-vector "Y_1X_1" we need $2^2 + 2^2 + 2^1 = 10$ pages, and with "Y_1Z_1" we need $2^1 + 2^2 + 2^2 = 10$ pages. Note that after choosing a Y bit, we cannot reduce the number of buffers required for the "r" predicate, since the number of slow bits of "r" has been fixed at zero.

The final bit to be chosen will be either X_1 or Z_1 since both the sfb-vectors "$Y_1Y_2X_1$" and "$Y_1Y_2Z_1$" would reduce the number of buffers required to $2^1 + 2^2 + 2^0 = 7$ pages and $2^0 + 2^2 + 2^1 = 7$ pages respectively. Any more X, Y, or Z bits will not further reduce the number of buffer pages required.

Some larger examples are given in Appendix 2. The algorithm guarantees that at least one predicate will only need one buffer and produces an optimal sfb-vector for all two-way joins. However, for multi-way joins, the algorithm may produce sub-optimal solutions.

Even using the minimal number of buffers, it is possible that there will be insufficient main memory for the superjoin algorithm. This can occur with multi-way joins where there are no common variables to all predicates in the join. This leads to buffering of all pages of one or more predicates (for example "r" in Query 4). Use of temporary relations can alleviate this problem. Insufficient main memory can occur also with two-way joins when there is only a small amount of main memory available, the relations themselves are extremely large, or there is inadequate indexing on the join variables. In such cases it is possible to resort to a secondary partitioning of the problem using the method described in Bratbergsengen [1984].

Superjoin and Deductive Databases

We show now how the superjoin algorithm is ideally suited to PROLOG-style deductive databases. It can be implemented with a few quite simple system predicates and can be made very flexible by incorporating more of the features of PROLOG. With these additions the superjoin can be applied to almost any query, including those containing ordinary PROLOG predicates as well as external database predicates. We outline an implementation of the superjoin using the external database facilities of NU-PROLOG (Thom and Zobel [1986]) and show how it can be used with other query optimizations. Initial experiments with the current implementation have shown improvement over a PROLOG partial match join with a naive buffering scheme. The interface between NU-PROLOG and the database is a major bottleneck in the present implementation. The overheads in the interface outweigh the cost of disc accesses in many cases, so we have no figures that accurately reflect the performance of the superjoin.

Implementation in PROLOG

The method of evaluating joins in PROLOG, a tuple at a time using backtracking, is very similar to the superjoin algorithm. Two additional features are needed. The first is the use of buffer pools associated with each predicate in the query; primitives are needed to allocate and deallocate buffer pools. Secondly, we need the ability to call a predicate using a buffer pool and only return answers matching the sfb-value. For this, we use the primitive db__call(Pool, Call, Sfb), which allocates new buffers on demand. Sfb is a data structure specifying the current sfb-value and the mapping between the sfb-vector and the choice vector.

A conjunction of calls to database relations in PROLOG is translated into a conjunction of calls to db__call, preceded by a call to db__sfbgenerate. Calls to other PROLOG tests in the conjunction are left unaltered. For example,

```
?- p(X,Y), q(Y,Z), Z @< "z2", r(X,Z)          QUERY 5
```

is translated into (approximately)

```
?- db__sfbgenerate([PPool, QPool, RPool], Sfb),
        db__call(PPool, p(X,Y), PSfb),
        db__call(QPool, q(Y,Z), QSfb),
        Z @< "z2",
        db__call(RPool, r(X,Z), RSfb)
```

The call to db__sfbgenerate generates the first sfb-value and on backtracking subsequent sfb-values. For each sfb-value generated it returns a value for Sfb. Sfb is a structure containing variables for the elements of the sfb-vector, these variables are the same as variables in the structures PSfb, QSfb, and RSfb. The predicate db__sfbgenerate should also allocate and deallocate the buffer pools at the appropriate times. Each call to db__call returns only those answers that match the given sfb-value. This requires modification to the low-level routines which implement the external database facility of NU-PROLOG. The set of answers to the query can then be found by PROLOG's normal backtracking mechanism.

Additional PROLOG Features

Since the join is implemented as a PROLOG conjunction, arbitrary constraints can be implemented by adding extra calls, such as Z @<"z2." Calls to procedures using the full power of PROLOG's recursion (at least for non-database predicates) and nondeterminism can be used. The superjoin algorithm can ignore all extra calls which do not bind any variables. Calls that generate bindings for variables can also be handled, by adding tests to check that hash values match the current sfb-value. There is also considerable flexibility in how calls to database relations are arranged. The method of partitioning works for disjunctions as well as conjunctions; the same sfb-vector can be used for both cases.

It is possible also to incorporate negation and an if-then-else construct. PROLOG uses the negation as failure rule Clark [1978], which is a weaker form of the closed world assumption Reiter [1978a] (see Shepherdson [1988]). Use of the partitioning scheme described in this paper and only negating ground calls ensures soundness of the negation as failure rule. Any ground call must match the current sfb-value, so the relevant facts in the relation are all considered. However, the use of some other partitioning schemes or negating non-ground calls could result in unsoundness.

Considerably more power can be provided, at very little cost, by allowing quantifiers (Naish [1986b]). Negations with quantified variables, for example $\forall X \; \neg p(X, Y)$, are implemented by calling the predicate with the quantified (local) variables uninstantiated. Soundness is still guaranteed providing these local variables do not appear in the sfb-vector. The insertion of existential quantifiers is particularly useful for optimization. For example, in Query 5, if only the values of X and Y are needed, Z can be existentially quantified:

```
?- p(X,Y), ∃Z (q(Y,Z), Z @< "z2", r(X,Z))
```

The effect of the existential quantifier is that if one value of Z is found for particular values of X and Y, then no more are sought. Subsequent backtracking skips over the calls to "q" and "r" entirely, potentially saving much computation and disc reading. If Z is included in the sfb-vector, the computation is sound, but for particular values of X and Y more than one value of Z may be found. Using the scheme we have outlined so far, it is most efficient to exclude the local variable from the sfb-vector (possibly increasing the number of buffers needed).

Another important higher level optimization is the creation of temporary predicates. This can be used for avoiding repeated computations, bottom up evaluation, and reducing buffer requirements for large multi-way joins. This can be implemented by allowing PROLOG's assert and retract primitives in superjoins. To avoid reading and writing pages more than once, they could be translated into primitives which use buffer pools: db__assert(Fact, Pool, Sfb) and db__retract(Fact, Pool, Sfb). The only type of goal we must avoid is one that modifies some of the relations we are reading; even when PROLOG does not include the superjoin, the result is not well defined. A partial solution to this problem using transactions is discussed in Naish et al. [1987].

When creating a temporary relation, the choice of indexing is a compromise between optimizing the creation and the use of the relation. It sometimes is useful to add extra dummy arguments which are used for indexing but not stored. The details of this are beyond the scope of this paper.

In summary, superjoins can be applied to any reasonable PROLOG goal containing calls to database predicates. This flexibility enables many higher level optimizations.

Query Optimization

Query optimization takes place at several levels. We briefly outline how the superjoin can be used with various higher level query optimization techniques, such as described in Grant and Minker [1981], Ullman [1985], and Jarke and Koch [1984]. Given an expression consisting of calls to database predicates, other PROLOG predicates and logical connectives, the following optimizations can be performed: removing redundant computations, eliminating common sub-expressions (Hall [1976]), creating temporary relations, distributing unions over joins, inserting existential quantifiers (equivalent to decomposition (Wong and Youssefi [1976]) and isolating independent sub-queries (Warren [1981]), and reordering of goals (Warren [1981], Naish [1986a]). Once these optimizations have been performed, the superjoin can be applied to the resulting expression(s). The present implementation includes some simple reordering.

Databases containing rules can use the superjoin in the following way. When there is no recursion involving database access, unfolding can be used to obtain a single expression which is equivalent to the query. This can be processed as outlined above.

To illustrate this, we use an example from Reiter [1987b]. Suppose the database contained the base relations "teaches," "course," and "enrolled," and the following rules:

```
teacher(S, T) :- enrolled(S, U), teach(T, U).

teach(teacher1, U) :- course(U, "calculus").
teach(teacher2, U) :- course(U, "databases").
teach(T, U) :- teaches(T, U).
```

Reiter [1978b] shows how the rule for "teacher" can be "compiled" by unfolding the definitions of "teacher" into it, with the following result:

```
teacher(S, T) :-
        (           teaches(T, U), enrolled(S, U)
        ;           enrolled(S, U), T = teacher1,
                        course(U, "calculus")
        ;           enrolled(S, U), T = teacher2,
                        course(U, "databases")
        ).
```

By applying the optimizations mentioned earlier, the following definition can be obtained (it could also be obtained more directly):

```
teacher(S, T) :-
        enrolled(S, U),
        (           teaches(T, U)
        ;           T = teacher1, course(U, "calculus")
        ;           T = teacher2, course(U, "databases")
        ).
```

Given the query

```
?- teacher(S, T)
```

the superjoin algorithm can be applied to the body of the rule for "teacher." Suppose the choice vector for "enrolled" is "$S_1S_2S_3S_4S_5U_1U_2U_3U_4U_5$," the choice vector for "teaches" is "$T_1T_2U_1U_2$," and the choice vector for "courses" is "$U_1U_2C_1C_2$"; then the sfb-vector "$U_1U_2U_3U_4U_5S_1S_2S_3S_4S_5$" would be used. This results in seven buffers being needed (one for "enrolled," four for "teaches," and one for each of the calls to "course"). The naive join algorithm would result in many pages being read more than once.

More complex queries involving "teacher" would use also the body of the definition, but further optimization would be done before applying the superjoin.

For recursive databases, unfolding is no longer possible in general, and we must use more elaborate program transformations with bottom-up computation (Rohmer et al. [1986], Balbin and Ramamohanarao [1986], Bancilhon and Ramakrishnan [1987], Bancilhon et al. [1985], Beeri and Ramakrishnan [1987], Sacca and Zaniolo [1986], McKay and Shapiro [1981]) or use methods similar to Earley deduction (Earley [1970], Vieille [1987]). Bottom-up methods are iterative and the superjoin can be used in each iteration to evaluate relational expressions. In Earley deduction methods, the superjoin can be used in the reduction step, which is similar to an iteration on a single relational expression in the bottom-up methods.

As an example, we show where the superjoin can be applied to the bottom-up evaluation of "ancestor," defined below ("parent" is assumed to be a base relation).

```
ancestor(A, B) :- parent(A, B).
ancestor(A, C) :- parent(A, B), ancestor(B, C).
```

The bottom-up method yields the following iterative program, which terminates when $\text{ancestor}_{i+1} = \text{ancestor}_i$.

```
ancestor₀(A, B) = parent(A, B)
ancestorᵢ₊₁(A, C) = ancestorᵢ(A, C) ; parent(A, B),
        ancestorᵢ(B, C)
```

The superjoin can be used to compute "parent(A, B), ancestor$_i$(B, C)" and insert the values of A and C into the "ancestor$_{i + 1}$" relation on each iteration. Dummy variables can be used to make insertion into the relation and its use (on the next iteration) efficient.

Analysis

In this section we analyze the performance of the superjoin. We use a similar analysis as Bratbergsengen [1984] and assume there are two relations ("p" and "q") and only one join attribute. The following parameters are used in the analysis:

P = size of relation "p" in pages

Q = size of relation "q" in pages

kp = number of attributes in relation "p"

kq = number of attributes in relation "q"

np = number of tuples in relation "p"

nq = number of tuples in relation "q"

p_n = number of bits allocated for the nth attribute of relation "p"

q_n = number of bits allocated for the nth attribute of relation "q"

ti = average insertion cost / tuple in the buffer pool

ts = average search cost / tuple

Storage requirements:
If the greedy algorithm is used to construct the sfb-vector then the larger predicate will only need one buffer. From the analysis in "Superjoin Execution," the maximum number of buffers required is therefore

$$nbufs = 1 + 2^{min(pp,qq)}$$

where

$$pp = (\sum_{n = 1}^{kp} p_n) - m$$

$$qq = (\sum_{n = 1}^{kq} q_n) - m$$

$$m = min(p_i, q_j)$$

where i and j are the join attributes of "p" and "q" respectively.

Input / Output cost:
Assuming sufficient buffers are available and ignoring any overhead of the operating system, the number of disc pages read during the superjoin is

disc reads $\leq$ P + Q pages

CPU cost:
If we assume that there is no indexing available within buffer pools, then we need to build some form of indexing in main memory for each buffer pool for efficiency. The CPU cost of the superjoin operation would then be

cpu cost = (np + nq).ti + np.ts

However, we can further reduce the join cost by having further indexing, such as superimposed coding, on the disc files. This eliminates the need for additional indexing in main memory and CPU cost is then reduced to

cpu cost = np.ts

Values for ts and ti depend on the indexing scheme used, the size of the relations and the distribution of join attribute values (the selectivity factor).

Comparison with Other Join Algorithms

The superjoin algorithm does not require the expensive sorting phase of the sort-merge join algorithm and the physical partitioning of the hash-join algorithm. Hence the scheme is very efficient with respect to input / output and CPU time requirements. Another feature of the scheme is that it has at least the efficiency of the nested-loop join algorithm. Other algorithms are much less efficient than nested loops for some joins, for example, when one of the relations is small compared with the other.

One drawback with the scheme is that it may require a large number of buffer pages. However, for binary relations, if we give equal number of bits to both attributes the number of buffers required will be

$$\sqrt{\min(P,Q)}$$

which is similar to the requirements of the hash-based join algorithms described in Shapiro [1986].

Another drawback with the scheme is that it suffers from the problems of any multikey hashing scheme, namely that storage requirements will be higher when the data is non-uniformly distributed and / or the attributes are highly correlated.

Interaction with Host Operating System

When one develops a database system on top of an existing file system provided by the host operating system it is important to control the way the pages are accessed from the files. For example, accessing pages sequentially will be more efficient than a random access. In Unix^{TM}, for small files (less than $k * 2^{10}$ pages, where k depends on the I/O buffers used in the operating system) both access methods require only one page access. However, accessing pages at random from a larger file containing up to 2^{20} pages of size 4096 bytes requires an average access of two pages, whereas a sequential access requires one page access.

Although the superjoin does not guarantee that the disc pages will be read in sequential order, pages in the disc file will be read in ascending order in one or more passes of the file, which is almost as good. This quasi-sequential access is achieved because the slow bits of the sfb-vector tend to come from the more significant bits of the choice vector.

Conclusions

Research into deductive database systems based on partial match retrieval motivated the development of the superjoin algorithm. Partitioning joins using the superjoin method described in this paper will also be very useful in relational database systems.

Some of the features of the superjoin algorithm which make it particularly attractive when sufficient memory is available are:

- each relation is read at most only once;

- the algorithm outperforms other join algorithms;

- it fits naturally into PROLOG's top-down computation; and

- arbitrary constraints, negation and quantifiers can easily be incorporated.

Further work needs to be done to integrate the superjoin with other optimizations, including the task of determining when to apply the superjoin (possibly using methods of Krishnamurthy and Zaniolo [1986] and integrating the superjoin with a recursive query evaluation scheme. Two other areas requiring further research are choice vector determination (Ramamohanarao et al. [1983]) and predicate reordering. We are currently investigating other algorithms for constructing sfb-vectors. Other methods for defining partitions and orderings are being considered also.

Acknowledgments

We would like to thank John Shepherd for implementing the underlying database system. We would like to thank Justin Zobel and other members of the Machine Intelligence Project for their careful reading of earlier drafts of this paper.

An earlier version of this paper was presented at the Twelfth International Conference on Very Large Databases in Kyoto, August 1986.

This work was performed as part of the Machine Intelligence Project at the University of Melbourne. It was supported by the Commonwealth of Australia, Department of Science and, during 1985, by Pyramid Technology, Australia.

Appendix 1

```
%
%          usage:   ?- sfb([v,...],[[b,...],...],
%                   [[x,...],...], [[n,...],...],Sfb,Cost).
%
%                   [v,...] is list of variables in the
%                        expression
%                   [[b,...],...] is list of hash bits
%                        (from choice vectors) for each
%                             variable v,
%                        each b is a variable
%                   [[x,...],...] is list of the variables
%                        occurring in each predicate call
%                             in the superjoin
%                   [[n,...],...] is list of sizes of
%                        attributes in choice vectors in
%                             each predicate
%                   Sfb is the resulting sfb-vector
%                   Cost is the resulting number of
%                        buffer pages
%
%           for example to calculate the sfb-vector
%                for QUERY 1:
%
%                ?- sfb([X,Y,Z],
%                     [[X1], [Y1, Y2], [Z1]],
%                     [[X, Y], [Y, Z]], [[1, 1], [2, 1]],
%                          Sfb, Cost).
%
```

```
%                       Sfb = [Y1, Y2, Y3],
%                       Cost = 3
%
%         description:    construct slow-fast bits
%              vector using greedy algorithm
%
%         authors:               James Thom
%                                Lee Naish
%


%
%         Calculate sfb-vector for superjoin
%              (greedy algorithm)
%
sfb(Vs, Bits, Preds, Sizes, Bit.Sfb, TotCost) :-
        choose(Vs, Preds, NewPreds, Sizes, NewSizes,
            Choice, FixedCost, FreeCost),
        allocbit(Vs, Bits, NewBits, Choice, Bit),
        length(NewPreds, L),
        (if FreeCost > L then
                sfb(Vs, NewBits, NewPreds, NewSizes,
                    Sfb, Cost),
                TotCost is FixedCost + Cost
        else
                Sfb = [],
                TotCost is FixedCost  + FreeCost
        ).
%
% allocate next bit from chosen variable
%
allocbit(V.Vs, [VBit|VBits].Bits, VBits.Bits, Choice,
    VBit):-
            V = = Choice.
allocbit(V.Vs, VBits.Bits, VBits.NewBits,
    Choice, XBit):-
            allocbit(Vs, Bits, NewBits, Choice, XBit).
%
% choose next bit for sfb-vector from list V.Vs so
    that cost is
            minimized
%         when that variable is used for partitioning
%
choose(V.[], Preds, NewPreds, Sizes, NewSizes, V,
        FixedCost, FreeCost) :-
```

```
            partition(V, Preds, NewPreds, Sizes, NewSizes,
                FixedCost, FreeCost).
    choose(V.Vs, Preds, NewPreds, Sizes, NewSizes, Choice,
                FixedCost, FreeCost) :-
            choose(Vs, Preds, XPreds, Sizes, XSizes, X,
                XFixedC, XFreeC),
            Xcost is XFixedC + XFreeC,
            partition(V, Preds, VPreds, Sizes, VSizes,
                VFixedC, VFreeC),
            Vcost is VFixedC + VFreeC,
            (if Vcost < Xcost; Vcost = Xcost,
                VFixedC = < XFixedC then
                    Choice = V,
                    NewPreds = VPreds,
                    NewSizes = VSizes,
                    FixedCost = VFixedC,
                    FreeCost = VFreeC
            else    % Vcost > Xcost;
                    % Vcost = Xcost, VFixedC > XFixedC
                    Choice = X,
                    NewPreds = XPreds,
                    NewSizes = XSizes,
                    FixedCost = XFixedC,
                    FreeCost = XFreeC
            ).

%
% partition join using V
%
partition(V, [], [], [], [], 0, 0).
partition(V, P.Preds, NewPreds, S.Sizes, NewSizes,
        FixedCost, FreeCost):-
        partition(V, Preds, NewPs, Sizes, NewSs,
                FixedC, FreeC),
        ( pred__partition(V, P, S, PartitionSize) ->
                NewPreds = P.NewPs,
                NewSizes = PartitionSize.NewSs,
                FixedCost = FixedC,
                sum(PartitionSize, Sum),
                FreeCost is FreeC + 1 << Sum
        ;
                /* no arguments of P match with V so
                    make P fixed and remove
```

```
                                from further partitioning */
                        NewPreds = NewPs,
                        NewSizes = NewSs,
                        sum(S, Sum),
                        FixedCost is FixedC + 1 << Sum,
                        FreeCost = FreeC
                ).
%
% partition a predicate using V
%
pred__partition(V, Arg.Args, Size.Sizes,
        NewSize.NewSizes) :-
            V = = Arg,
            /* this argument matches */
            Size > 0,
            NewSize is Size - 1,
            ( pred__partition(V, Args, Sizes,
                NewSizes1) ->
                    /* other arguments of this predicate
                        also match */
                    NewSizes = NewSizes1
            ;
                    /* no other arguments of this
                        predicate match */
                    NewSizes = Sizes
            ).
pred__partition(V, Arg.Args, Size.Sizes,
        Size.NewSizes) :-
            (
                    V \e= = Arg
            ;
                    Size = 0
            ),
            /* this argument doesn't match - see if any
                other matches */
            pred__partition(V, Args, Sizes, NewSizes).
%
%       Sum a list of integers
%
sum([], 0).
sum(L.List, Sum) :-
        sum(List, S)
        Sum is S + L.
```

Appendix 2

```
Examples of sfb-vector construction.
(1)
        XPreds = [[X, Y], [Y, Z]] % ?- p(X,Y), q(Y,Z)
        NBits = [[1, 1], [2, 1]] % number of bits on
                                            each attribute
        Sfb = [Y1, Y2, Z1] % sfb-vector Y₁Y₂Z₁
        Cost = 3 % number of buffers


(2)
        XPreds = [[X, Y], [Y, Z], [X, Y]]
        NBits = [[4, 4], [5, 3], [2, 3]]
        Sfb = [Y1, Y2, Y3, Y4, X1, X2, X3, X4]
        Cost = 21


(3)
        XPreds = [[A, B], [B, C], [A, B, C]]
        NBits = [[3, 2], [3, 2], [2, 2, 3]]
        Sfb = [B1, B2, A1, A2, C1, C2, C3]
        Cost = 11


(4)
        XPreds = [[B, D, A], [D, C], [A, B, C],
                  [A, B, C]]
        NBits = [[2, 1, 2], [5, 2], [3, 0, 3],
                 [3, 0, 3]]
        Sfb = [C1, C2, A1, A2, A3, C1]
        Cost = 66


(5)
        XPreds = [[Y, Z], [X, Y], [Z, Z1]]
        NBits = [[7, 5], [3, 6], [4, 7]]
        Sfb = [Z1, Z2, Z3, Z4, Y1, Y2, Y3, Y4, Y5, Y6,
               Y7, Z5]
        Cost = 641


(6)
        XPreds = [[X, Y, Z], [Y, Z1], [Y, Z, Z1]]
        NBits = [[7, 4, 3], [4, 7], [6, 4, 4]]
        Sfb = [Y1, Y2, Y3, Y4, Z1, Z2, Z3, X1, X2, X3,
               X4, X5, X5, X6]
        Cost = 257
```

(7)

```
XPreds = [[X, Y, X], [Y, X, Z]] % note repeated
                                        variable
NBits = [[3, 1, 4], [2, 3, 5]]
Sfb = [X1, X2, X3, Y1, Y2, Z1, Z2, Z3, Z4, Z5]
Cost = 3
```

References

1. Aho, A. V. and Ullman, J. D. [1979] Optimal Partial-Match Retrieval When Fields Are Independently Specified, *ACM Transactions on Database Systems* **4**(2):168–179.

2. Balbin, I. and Ramamohanarao, K. [1986] A Differential Approach to Query Optimisation in Recursive Deductive Databases, Technical Report 86/7, Department of Computer Science, University of Melbourne.

3. Bancilhon, F., Maier, D., Sagiv, Y., and Ullman, J. D. [1985] Magic Sets and Other Strange Ways to Implement Logic Programs, *Proceedings of the ACM SIGMOD Conference*, Washington, DC, 1–15.

4. Bancilhon, F. and Ramakrishnan, R. [1988] Performance Evaluation of Data Intensive Logic Programs, *Foundations of Deductive Databases and Logic Programming* (J. Minker, Ed.), Morgan Kaufmann Publishers, Los Altos, CA, 439–517.

5. Beeri, C and Ramakrishnan, R. [1987] On the Power of Magic, *Proceedings of the ACM Symposium on the Principles of Database Systems*, San Diego, CA, 269–283.

6. Bratbergsengen, K. [1984] Hashing Methods and Relational Algebra Operations, *Proceedings of the Tenth International Conference on Very Large Data Bases*, Singapore, 323–333.

7. Clark, K. L. [1978] Negation as Failure in *Logic and Data Bases* (H. Gallaire and J. Minker, Eds.), Plenum Press, New York, 293–322.

8. Clocksin, W. F. and Mellish, C. S. [1981] *Programming in PROLOG*, Springer-Verlag, Berlin.

9. DeWitt, D. J., Katz, R. H., Olken, F., Shapiro, L. D., Stonebraker, M. R. and Wood, D. [1984] Implementation Techniques for Main Memory Database Systems, *SIGMOD Conference on the Management of Data*, 1–8.

10. Earley, J. [1970] An Efficient Context-free Parsing Algorithm, *Communications of the ACM* **13**(2):94–102.

11. Grant, J. and Minker, J. [1981], Optimization in Deductive and Conventional Relational Database Systems, in *Advances in Data Base Theory, Volume 1* (H. Gallaire, J. Minker, and J. Nicolas, Eds.), Plenum Press, New York, 195–234.

12. Hall, P. A. V. Optimization of Single Expressions in a Relational Database System, *IBM Journal of Research and Development* **20**(3):167–183.

13. Jarke, M. and Koch, J. [1984] Query Optimization in Database Systems, *ACM Computing Surveys* **16**(2):111–152.

14. Krishnamurthy, R. and Zaniolo, C. [1986] Safety and Optimization of Horn Clause Queries, *Proceedings of the Workshop on Foundations of Deductive Databases and Logic Programming* (J. Minker, Ed.), Washington, DC, 518–543.

15. Lloyd, J. W. and Ramamohanarao, K. [1982] Partial-match Retrieval for Dynamic Files, *BIT* **22**:150–168.

16. Marek, W. and Rauszer, C. [1986] Query Optimization in Databases Distributed by Means of Product Equivalence Relations, *Preprints of the Workshop on Foundations of Deductive Databases and Logic Programming* (J. Minker, Ed.), Washington, DC, 315–337.

17. McKay, D. P. and Shapiro, S. [1981] Using Active Connection Graphs for Reasoning with Recursive Rules, *Proceedings of the Seventh IJCAI*, 368–374.

18. Naish, L. and Thom, J. A. [1983] The MU-Prolog Deductive Database, Technical Report 83/10, Department of Computer Science, University of Melbourne.

19. Naish, L. [1986a] *Negation and Control in Prolog*, Lecture Notes in Computer Science 238, Springer-Verlag.

20. Naish, L. [1986b] Negation and Quantifiers in NU-Prolog, *Proceedings of the Third International Conference on Logic Programming*, London, 624–634.

21. Naish, L., Thom, J. A., and Ramamohanarao, K. [1987] Concurrent Database Updates in Prolog, *Proceedings of the Fourth International Conference in Logic Programming*, Melbourne, Australia, 178–195.

22. Ramamohanarao, K., Lloyd, J. W., and Thom, J. A. [1983] Partial-match Retrieval Using Hashing and Descriptors, *ACM Transactions on Database Systems* **8**(4):552–576.

23. Ramamohanarao, K. and Shepherd, J. [1986] A Superimposed Codeword Indexing Scheme for Very Large Prolog Databases, *Proceedings of the Third International Conference on Logic Programming*, London, 569–576.

24. Reiter, R. [1978a] On Closed World Data Bases, in *Logic and Data Bases* (H. Gallaire and J. Minker, Eds.), Plenum Press, New York.

25. Reiter, R. [1978b] Deductive Question-Answering on Relational Data Bases, in *Logic and Databases* (H. Gallaire and J. Minker, Eds.), Plenum Press, New York.

26. Rivest, R. L. [1976] Partial Match Retrieval Algorithms, *SIAM Journal of Computing* **5**(1):19–50.

27. Rohmer, J. Lescoeur, R., and Kerisit, J. M. [1986] The Alexander Method—A Technique for the Processing of Recursive Axioms in Deductive Database Queries, *New Generation Computing* **4**:273–285.

28. Rothnie, J. B. and Lozano, T. [1974] Attribute Based File Organization in a Paged Memory Environment, *Communications of the ACM* **17**(2):63–69.

29. Saccà, D. and Zaniolo, C. [1986] Implementation of Recurisve Queries for a Data Language Based on Pure Horn Logic, Technical Report DB-092-86, MCC.

30. Shapiro, L. D. [1986] Join Processing in Database Systems with Large Main Memories, *ACM Transactions on Database Systems* **11**(3):239–264.

31. Shepherdson, J. C. [1988] Negation in Logic Programming, in *Foundations of Deductive Databases and Logic Programming* (J. Minker, Ed.), Morgan Kaufmann Publishers, Los Altos, CA, 19–88.

32. Thom, J. A. and Zobel, J. (Eds.) [1986] NU-Prolog Reference Manual, Version 1.1, Technical Report 86/10, Department of Computer Science, University of Melbourne.

33. Ullman, J. D. [1985] *Principles of Database Systems (2nd edition)*, Pitman, London.

34. Vieille, L. [1987] Recursive Axioms in Deductive Databases: The Query-subquery Approach, *Proceedings from the First International Conference on Expert Database Systems* (L. Kerschberg, Ed.), Benjamin/Cummings Publishing Co., Menlo Park, CA, 253–267.

35. Warren, D. H. D. [1981] Efficient Processing of Interactive Relational Database Queries Expressed in Logic, *Proceedings of the Seventh International Conference on Very Large Databases*, Cannes, France, 272–281.

36. Wong, E. and Youssefi, K. [1976] Decomposition—A Strategy for Query Processing, *ACM Transactions on Database Systems* **1**(3):223–241.

III

UNIFICATION AND LOGIC PROGRAMS

14

Logic Programming and Parallel Complexity

Paris C. Kanellakis
Department of Computer Science
Brown University, Providence, RI

Abstract

We survey the many applications of parallel algorithms and complexity to logic programming problems. The problems examined are related to the optimization of logical query programs, which are the most common deductive database formalism, and to the fast parallel execution of primitive operations in logic programming languages, such as term unification and term matching. Our presentation highlights the importance of the complexity class NC, as well as of the stage function s(n) associated with each logical query program (where n is the size of the relational database queried by the program). The stage function can be used to model the number of calls made by a program to a relational database and provides a means of distinguishing parallelizable from inherently sequential queries. Queries that are hard to evaluate in parallel are logspace-complete in PTIME and can only be expressed using programs with $s(n) = \Omega(\log^k n)$, for any k. Queries with a large amount of potential parallelism are in NC and can be expressed using programs with $s(n) = O(\log^k n)$, for some fixed k. In the context of stage functions we also derive two new results about parallelism and logical query programs. We show that:

1. There is a program that does not satisfy the superpolynomial fringe property of Van Gelder and Ullman but does define a parallelizable query. Our extension of derivation trees strengthens their parallel algorithm and allows us to evaluate this program in O(log n) stages.

2.   Given a linear single rule program, we show that it is NP-hard to decide whether its stage function is O(1). This complements the bounded recursion analysis of Ioannidis and Naughton.

Introduction

Programming in logic has been a fundamental theme in computer science theory and practice ever since their early days and is, in large part, motivated by the elegant and precise qualities of mathematical logic. The 1965 seminal paper, "A Machine Oriented Logic Based on the Resolution Principle," by J.A. Robinson, was a breakthrough in theorem proving and in the use of first-order predicate calculus as a programming language (Robinson [1965]). This theme was further developed in the 1970s and early part of this decade (Apt and van Emden [1982], Kowalski [1974,1979], van Emden and Kowalski [1976]), largely through the programming language PROLOG (Clocksin and Mellish [1981], Roussel [1975]). Another (seemingly unrelated) important development was the identification by E.F. Codd in 1970 of first-order relational calculus, with finite interpretations, as the natural formalism for database description and manipulation (Codd [1970]). The 1970s was both a decade of logic programming and of relational database systems, e.g., Ullman [1978, 1983].

The challenge of deductive databases and of knowledgebase systems is to combine the technology of artificial intelligence (exemplified by PROLOG, LISP, and other programming tools) with the efficiency of database technology. This would be a concrete step toward a new generation of computing; some already refer to it as the fifth generation. The technological advance driving this ambitious effort is, as so often happens in computer science, new hardware. Parallel computers, a reality of the 1980s, offer the new element which has made advances in logic programming and databases feasible. A thornier issue, as is also usual in computer science, is the development of efficient software for these multiprocessors.

Logic programming languages for parallel machines have been the object of much recent study (e.g., Clark and Gregory [1981], Shapiro [1983]). AND-parallelism and OR-parallelism have been the most celebrated qualitative measures of parallelism in logic programs. In this paper we would like to "complete the picture" through the use of the theory of parallel algorithms and complexity. We believe that this connection sheds much light on the algorithmic aspects of parallel logic programming. For example, one of the most fundamental contributions to complexity theory has been the concept of alternation (Chandra et al. [1981]). Alternating Turing Machines (ATMs) with simultaneous resource bounds capture the parallel complexity of derivation trees, rule-goal trees, and AND-OR trees, all familiar concepts in logic programming

(Kowalski [1974]). The importance of ATMs for analyzing logic programs has been stressed in Shapiro [1984].

The logic programming problems addressed in this paper are related to deductive database retrieval (Gallaire, Minker, and Nicolas [1984]) as well as to algorithms for operations of logic programming languages, i.e., term unification and term matching. Logical query programs (or DATALOG) is the "toy" formal language we use to illustrate the addition of recursion to first-order database queries. This survey can be viewed as complementing the exposition in Bancilhon and Ramakrishnan [1986, 1988]. Its theme is parallel computation, whereas Bancilhon and Ramakrishnan [1986, 1988] review advances in sequential algorithms for logical query program evaluation. Another important issue, which is outside the scope of our paper, is the use of negation (Apt and van Emden [1982], Chandra and Harel [1985], Clark [1978], Shepherdson [1988]).

Our exposition is divided into three sections: on algorithms and complexity, on unstructured data, and on structured data.

In "Parallel Algorithms and Complexity," we present the mathematical tools relevant to the analysis of parallel logic programs. These include: alternation, the complexity class NC (problems solvable in polylogarithmic time with a polynomial number of processing elements), and parallel algorithms using randomization and / or achieving optimal speed-ups. We stress the ATM model of parallel computation because of its natural connections with derivation trees for logic programs.

The complexity theory developed around the class NC, first defined in Pippenger [1979], accurately describes the problems that can be considerably sped-up through the use of polynomial-bounded hardware. Problems in NC are exactly those with a great deal of potential parallelism. In contrast, significant speed-ups cannot be achieved for logspace-complete problems in PTIME, unless PTIME = NC (Cook [1985]) (one more unlikely fact of complexity theory, such as, NP = PTIME, NP = co-NP, etc.). Logspace-complete problems in PTIME are, in a worst case sense, inherently sequential and represent the type of lower bounds that can be shown given the state of the art in computer science theory.

As with sequential computation and the class PTIME, polynomial (e.g., n^{100}) does not necessarily mean practical time or number of processors or processing elements. Moreover, even low degree polynomials, which are satisfactory time bounds for sequential algorithms, are sometimes unsatisfactory processor bounds. It is, however, widely accepted that PRAM algorithms (for the Parallel Random Access Machine model of computation) with "small" processor bounds are quite close to algorithms for "real" multiprocessor machines. Well, how small is "small"? For primitive combinatorial operations such as sorting or unification, PRAM algorithms using $O(n)$ processors are potentially useful. For database applications, where n is the database size, processor bounds beyond $O(\log n)$ are positively unrealistic. Optimal parallel algorithms and randomization have been developed to address precisely these concerns.

In "Parallelism and Unstructured Data," we review recent developments in the study of logic programs when these are used as database queries. Our presentation highlights that all of these results deal with the stage function $s_H(n)$ of a logical query program H, where n is the database size. We stress the definition of the stage function of a logical query program, first identified in a different context by Immerman [1981]. Intuitively this function corresponds to the number of calls the logical query program makes to the underlying relational database system and it seems to be the single relevant computational resource.

We start the section with some lower bounds. In Proposition 1, we present the simplest known program defining a query that is hard to evaluate in parallel; this result is from Kanellakis and Papadimitriou [1986]. This query is logspace-complete in PTIME. The stage function of any logical query program defining this query is $\Omega(\log^k n)$, for any k. This last strict lower bound can be derived because of the syntactic restrictions on logical query programs (Immerman [1981]) and does not depend on whether NC is a proper subset of PTIME. There are many other such programs; we list this one in detail because of its simplicity and the generality of the method used in identifying its complexity.

In the rest of the section we deal with programs that have potential parallelism. Here we describe derivation trees and sufficient conditions for parallelizability, such as the superpolynomial fringe property of Ullman and Van Gelder [1986], Proposition 2. The subject of Theorem 1 is a program that does not satisfy the superpolynomial fringe property but which defines a query in NC. We use the theorem to present and extend derivation trees from width one to constant width and thus properly strengthen the parallel algorithm of Ullman and Van Gelder [1986]. The new algorithm, which allows us to evaluate the counterexample program in O(log n) stages, is a simple extension of Ullman and Van Gelder [1986].

Finally we deal with bounded recursion, i.e., when the stage function is O(1). Proposition 3 summarizes two basic intuitions about bounded recursion. Namely, from Naughton [1986] and Naughton and Sagiv [1987], the observation that if a logical query program has a constant stage function any equivalent logical query program has a constant stage function as well. Also, from Cosmadakis and Kanellakis [1986], the observation that if stages are viewed as a resource there is a gap between O(1) and O(log n) stages. Theorem 2 complements the bounded recursion analysis of Ioannidis [1985] and Naughton [1986]. We show that, given a linear single rule program, it is NP-hard to decide whether its stage function is O(1). Upper bounds for this syntactically restricted case, even decidability, are still open. Theorems 1 and 2 are new.

In "Parallelism and Structured Data," our topic is unification of terms. This is the primitive operation of logic programming defined by Robinson

[1965]. Robinson's unification algorithm required time exponential in the size of terms. The following years saw a sequence of unification algorithms culminating with the linear-time algorithm of Paterson and Wegman [1978]. Unification can also be generalized to higher-order logics and equational theories (Huet and Oppen [1980]). These generalizations, although quite interesting, usually lead to hard computational questions outside PTIME. We concentrate on parallel (first-order uninterpreted) unification, and we review the lower and upper bounds appearing in Dwork et al. [1984, 1986] and in Verma et al. [1986], Vitter and Simons [1986], Yasuura [1983]. The lower bounds are summarized in Proposition 4 (for term unification) and the upper bounds in Propositions 5 (for term equivalence) and 6 (for term matching).

In order to complete the picture of the state of art, we include two subsections with open questions about unstructured and structured data, respectively. Finally, in "Conclusions" we comment on the potential impact of these theoretical results to practice.

Parallel Algorithms and Complexity

For sequential computation, we use the standard models of *Deterministic Turing Machines* (DTMs), *Nondeterministic Turing Machines* (NTMs), their *time* and *space* resource definitions as well as *logspace reducibility* (Hopcroft and Ullman [1979]). A decision problem is in the class LOGSPACE = DTM-space(log n) if it can be decided by a DTM, which uses $O(\log n)$ auxiliary space on inputs of size n. Similarly we define NLOGSPACE = NTM-space(log n). PTIME = DTM-time($n^{O(1)}$), that is, PTIME consists of those decision problems, which can be decided by some DTM using $O(n^k)$ time (for some constant k) on inputs of size n. We use *polynomial* for $n^{O(1)}$, *polylogarithmic* for $\log^{O(1)} n$, and *superpolynomial* for $2^{\log^{O(1)} n}$.

Many models have been proposed for parallel computation. One of the most common ways of expressing parallel algorithms is by using the model of *Parallel Random Access Machines* (PRAMs) of Fortune and Wyllie [1978]. The class NC, first defined in Pippenger [1979], is the class of problems solvable on a PRAM using simultaneously polylogarithmic PRAM-time and a polynomial number of PRAM-processors.

For the purposes of this survey it is very useful to describe NC in an equivalent way using Alternating Turing Machines (ATMs). These are generalizations of NTMs, defined in Chandra et al. [1981]. We assume that their input (of size n) is on an end-marked, read-only input tape. They can informally, but fairly intuitively, be described as follows.

The ATM states are partitioned into *existential* and *universal* states. As with a NTM, the transitions of an ATM on an input string determine a relation among *configurations* (IDs) (Hopcroft and Ullman [1979]), where (ID_i, ID_j) is in this relation if and only if the machine can move in one step from ID_i to ID_j. A *computation tree* of an ATM on an input string consists of a tree. The nodes of this tree are configurations of the ATM constrained so that: the children in a computation tree of any non-leaf configuration ID_i with a universal (resp. existential) state, include all (resp. one) of the configurations that are possible one step next moves from ID_i of the ATM. A computation tree is accepting if the root is the input string configuration and all leaves are accepting configurations. The input string is accepted if and only if there is an accepting computation tree. A NTM is an ATM all of whose states are existential.

An ATM uses (a) time $T(n)$, (b) space $S(n)$, (c) tree-size $Z(n)$, if for all accepted inputs of size n there is an accepting computation tree (a) whose longest path has at most $T(n)$ nodes, (b) each of whose nodes is a configuration using auxiliary space at most $S(n)$, (c) whose number of nodes is at most $Z(n)$. ATM-time($T(n)$) is the class of decision problems each of which can be decided by an ATM using time $O(T(n))$. Similarly, we define ATM-space($S(n)$), ATM-treesize($Z(n)$). The importance of the *tree-size* resource was demonstrated in Ruzzo [1980]. The following fundamental identity is shown in Chandra et al. [1981]:

PTIME = ATM-space(log n) (or ALOGSPACE)

Problems decided by ATMs using simultaneously space $O(S(n))$ and time $O(T(n))$, or simultaneously space $O(S(n))$ and tree-size $O(Z(n))$ form the complexity classes ATM-space-time($S(n)$, $T(n)$) and ATM-space-treesize($S(n)$, $Z(n)$). Complexity classes with simultaneous resource bounds have been used to make precise the notions of "problems with inherent parallelism" or "problems which can be solved very fast in parallel using a bounded amount of processing elements." The complexity class NC, described above using PRAMs, is such a class. It is largely independent of the choice of parallel computation model. We now provide two characterizations of NC based on ATMs (Ruzzo [1980, 1981]). Note its relationship to PTIME.

$$NC = \text{ATM-space-time}(\log n, \ \log^{O(1)} n) = \text{ATM-space-treesize}(\log n,$$
$$2^{\log^{O(1)} n})$$

$$PTIME = \text{ATM-space-time}(\log n, \ n^{O(1)}) = \text{ATM-space-treesize}(\log n,$$
$$2^{n^{O(1)}})$$

NC is a subset of PTIME = ALOGSPACE because of the additional simultaneous polylogarithmic time or superpolynomial tree-size restrictions. Refining the space-time bounds we have NC^k: $NC^k = \text{ATM-space-time}(\log n, \log^k n)$, for $k = 2,3,\dots$. Refining the space-treesize bounds we have the class LOGCFL, important for the study of context free languages as well as logic programs (Ruzzo [1980]): LOGCFL = ATM-space-treesize($\log n, n^{O(1)}$).

Let us further illustrate the robustness of NC. Another perhaps more fundamental model of parallel computation is *Uniform Circuits of bounded fan-in*, (UCs); see Cook [1985], Ruzzo [1981] for the technical uniformity conditions. Once again NC captures "parallel solutions in very fast time and bounded hardware" because it is equal to the class of problems solvable by UCs using simultaneously polylogarithmic circuit-depth and polynomial circuit-size. The classes NC^k k = 2,3,... can also be defined using UCs and are the same as the ones defined above. In addition, the standard definition of NC^1 is based on this (as opposed to the ATM) model: $NC^k = $ UC-size-depth($n^{O(1)}$, $\log^k n$), for k = 1,2,...

We can close our review of these complexity classes, all subsets of PTIME, with the following containements which are believed (but not yet proven) to be proper:

$$NC^1 \subseteq LOGSPACE \subseteq NLOGSPACE \subseteq LOGCFL \subseteq NC^2 \subseteq NC \subseteq ALOGSPACE.$$

A problem is *logspace-complete* in PTIME if it is in PTIME and every other problem in PTIME can be reduced to this problem by a DTM, which uses logarithmic auxiliary space. Since the containement NC $\subseteq$ PTIME = ALOGSPACE is strongly conjectured to be proper, a proof that a problem is logspace-complete in PTIME is evidence of its inherently sequential nature. On the other hand, membership in NC denotes the presence of a high degree of potential parallelism (Cook [1985]). Many natural problems are known to be logspace-complete in PTIME. Such problems that are also relevant to our exposition are: *path system accessibility*, the first such problem discovered (Cook [1974]); *monotone circuit value* (Goldschlager [1977]); *propositional Horn clause implication* (Jones and Laaser [1977]), the propositional formulation of deductive databases; *unification of terms* (Dwork et al. [1984, 1986], Yasuura [1983]), the fundamental operation of logic programming (Robinson [1965]).

The problems listed above are complete in PTIME under more strict notions of reducibility than logspace-reducibility. They are complete under *NC^1-reducibility* (Cook [1985]) and even *first-order-reducibility* (Immerman [1983]). This last reducibility is useful for proving less general but unconditional lower bounds (Immerman [1981]) for deductive database formalisms.

Optimal Parallel Algorithms are PRAM algorithms that use m processors and run in time O(Seq(n)/m), where Seq(n) is the best known sequential time bound for the problem solved. Optimal parallel algorithms achieve the greatest speed-up possible given m processors. In addition, most common PRAM algorithms using m processors and using T(n) time can be modified to use k processors, for $1 \leq k \leq m$, and run in time O(T(n)m/k), by having k machines simulate m machines. Therefore, an optimal parallel algorithm for m processors is a potentially useful algorithm for the entire range of 1 up to m processors.

Randomization can also play an important role, combined either with NC or with optimal parallel algorithms. Randomized algorithms are like PRAM algorithms, where each processor can at any step flip an unbiased coin and the coin flips of different processors are independent. Without any assumptions on the distribution of their inputs, randomized algorithms compute the correct answer with overwhelming probability, e.g., Karp et al. [1985], Rabin [1980], Schwartz [1980]. For example, the algorithm in Karp et al. [1985] is a randomized polylogarithmic time algorithm, which uses a polynomial number of processors for finding a maximum matching in a graph (this graph matching is not to be confused with the term matching problem). Without randomization, an algorithm with this running time and number of processors is not known. Processor requirements for certain problems can be substantially reduced using randomization (Dwork et al. [1986], Reif [1985], Vishkin [1984]).

Graph Accessibility Problems   Given a graph G and two distinguished nodes u and v in G the graph accessibility problem GAP is, "does there exist a path in G from u to v?" If G is undirected, we have u-GAP, and if G is *directed acyclic of bounded degree*, we have dag-GAP. GAP is in NLOGSPACE; in fact, dag-GAP is logspace-complete in this class (Hopcroft and Ullman [1979]), i.e., the existence of a logspace DTM for it would imply that LOGSPACE = NLOGSPACE.

For u-GAP there are optimal parallel algorithms; see Cole and Vishkin [1986] for the history and recent developments on this problem. For dag-GAP, it is easy to see that Seq(n) = O(n), using a graph search and the O(n) number of arcs, because of the bounded degree. However the known NC algorithms for dag-GAP use $M(n)/\log n$ processors to achieve $O(\log^2 n)$ time (Chandra [1976]). $M(n) = n^x$ is the best known sequential-time bound for n by n matrix multiplication (Coppersmith and Winograd [1982], [1987]). At present, x is greater than 2. Thus for m processors, the best known time bound is order $min(n, M(n)\log n/m)$ $1 \leq m \leq M(n)/\log n$. Therefore, for $m \leq n$ the best known solution effectively uses only one processor! The existence of an optimal parallel algorithm for dag-GAP is an important open question in parallel computation.

Parallelism and Unstructured Data

Databases, Data Complexity, and Logical Query Programs

Let our *universe* be a fixed, countably infinite set of constants. A *database* is a vector $B = (D, r_1, \ldots, r_p)$, where D is a finite subset of the universe called the *database domain*, and for each i, $1 \leq i \leq p$, $r_i \subseteq D^{k_i}$ (for some integer $k_i \geq 0$) is a *relation* of *arity* k_i. An element of a relation is called a *tuple*. Database B is said to have *sort* $(k_1,...,k_p)$. A *query* of sort $(k_1,...,k_p) \rightarrow (k)$ for some integer $k \geq 0$, is a function Q from databases of sort $(k_1,...,k_p)$ to databases of sort (k), such that, if $B = (D, r_1,...,r_p)$, then $Q(B) = (D, r)$ and $r \subseteq D^k$. Note that when $k = 0$ we have a *Boolean* query, which returns either $\emptyset$ (false) or D^0, which is the set containing the empty tuple (true). The tuples in relations represent unstructured data.

The *data complexity* of query Q (Chandra and Harel [1982], Vardi [1982]) is the computational complexity of testing membership in the set $\{(w,B) \mid$ tuple $w \in Q(B)\}$. With a slight abuse of notation, we say that query Q is in the class LOGSPACE, NC, PTIME, ... if the set $\{(w,B) \mid$ tuple $w \in Q(B)\}$ can be decided in LOGSPACE, NC, PTIME ... . Similarly query Q is logspace-complete in PTIME if the corresponding decision problem is logspace-complete in PTIME. For the purposes of measuring data complexity, the *size* of database B, $|B| = n$, is the length of the representation of B in some standard encoding. Note that the database size and not the size of a program for Q is the asymptotically growing parameter.

First-order queries are the queries expressible in first-order relational calculus with finite domains. First-order logic has been recognized as a powerful declarative language for expressing queries (Codd [1970]). The ability to translate first-order queries into relational algebra, a procedural language, and their low data complexity are the theoretical foundations of database theory (Aho and Ullman [1979], Codd [1970], Ullman [1983]). First-order queries are in LOGSPACE and thus contain a great deal of potential parallelism. Not all queries in LOGSPACE are first-order queries. This limitation of first-order logic is true even if we augment it with an order predicate $\leq$, or other interpreted predicates, or even weak monadic second order quantification. The finiteness of the domains makes these theorems nontrivial (Aho and Ullman [1979], Chandra and Harel [1982], deRougemont [1984], Fagin [1975], Gaifman and Vardi [1985], Immerman [1981, 1983]).

Fixpoint queries are obtained by augmenting first-order logic with the *fixpoint operator* μ. Detailed expositions of these queries and their expressive power can be found in Barwise and Moschovakis [1978], Moschovakis [1974] for finite and infinite domains and Chandra and Harel [1982] and Harel and Kozen [1984] for the finite case. For finite domains, which concern us here, fixpoint queries are in PTIME. However, in order to be able to express every PTIME query as a fixpoint query we need to add to the language an order predicate $\leq$ (see deRougemont [1984], Fagin [1974], Gurevich [1983], Immerman [1982], Papadimitriou [1985], Sazonov [1980], Vardi [1982]). This robust expressibility result linking PTIME to logic was first derived in Immerman [1982] and Vardi [1982]. We are interested in a subset of the fixpoint queries that does not contain negation. The expressive power of negation in fixpoint queries has been examined in Chandra and Harel [1982]. An important observation in Gurevich and Shelah [1985] and Immerman [1982] is that negation interacts differently with fixpoint operator μ in the finite case (the database case) than it does for infinite domains. For the finite case application of μ once on some first-order query can express any fixpoint query; for the infinite case this is not true.

An interesting subset of the fixpoint queries, without negation, can be expressed using function-free Horn clauses as a programming language (Chandra and Harel [1985], Gallaire, Minker, and Nicolas [1984]). These are the logical queries and are the heart of the programming language PROLOG whenever it is used to handle unstructured data.

Logical queries are queries expressible in the language of *logical query programs* (Ullman and Van Gelder [1986]). Logical query programs are also known as Horn clause query programs (Chandra and Harel [1985]), deductive database query programs (Gallaire, Minker, and Nicolas [1984]), or recursive rule query programs (Cosmadakis and Kanellakis [1986]). In order to make this paper self contained, we define their syntax and semantics. This "toy" language is often refered to as DATALOG (the term is due to David Maier).

Logical Query Program Syntax We assume we have a countably infinite set of variables $\{x,y,z,...\}$ and of predicate symbols of all arities $\{R,R_0,R_1,...\}$. A *rule* is an expression of the form: $A \leftarrow A_1,...,A_e.$ for $e \geq 0$, where $A,A_1,...,A_e$ are *atomic formulas* of the form $R_i(x_1,...,x_{k_i})$ and each x_j, $1 \leq j \leq k_i$, is a variable and $k_i \geq 0$ is the arity of R_i (for $k_i = 0$ there are no variables in the atomic formula). We call A the *consequence* and $A_1,...,A_e$ the *antecedents* of this rule (for $e = 0$ there are no antecedents in the rule). A *logical query program* (program for short) H is a finite set of rules. A predicate symbol in program H is said to be an *intensional database predicate* (IDB) iff it appears in the consequence of some rule; otherwise it is an *extensional database predicate* (EDB).

Note that a rule does not contain any instantiated variables or any interpreted predicates (e.g., order or inequality), and that equality is expressed using equal variables. The absence of inequality is a slight departure from Chandra and Harel [1985] that makes the syntax cleaner without affecting any of the results in this paper.

Logical Query Program Semantics Let $B = (D,r_1,...,r_q)$ be a database, and let program H have EDBs $R_1,...,R_q$ and IDBs $R_{q+1},...,R_p$.

A *valuation* ρ is a function from variables to the finite set D. If A is the atomic formula $R(x_1,...,x_k)$ then $A\rho$ is the tuple $(\rho(x_1),...,\rho(x_k))$. In addition, if predicate symbol R is interpreted as relation r in database $B = (D,...,r,...)$ then the notation $A\rho \in B$ means that tuple $(\rho(x_1),...,\rho(x_k)) \in r$. We define a sequence of databases $I_H^s(B)$ $(s = 0,1,...)$:

$I_H^s(B) = (D, r_1^s, \ldots, r_q^s, r_{q+1}^s, \ldots, r_p^s)$, where we have, $r_i^0 = r_i$, $1 \le i \le q$, $r_j^0 = \emptyset$, $q{+}1 \le j \le p$, and

$r_i^{s+1} = r_i^s \cup \{ A\rho \mid \rho$ is a valuation and there is a rule $A \leftarrow A_1, \ldots, A_e$. in H such that, the predicate symbol of A is R_i and each $A_j\rho$ is in $I_H^s(B)$, $1 \le j \le e\}$, $1 \le i \le p$.

Note that $r_i^s \subseteq r_i^{s+1} \subseteq D^{k_i}$, for all i, s. The EDB relations are not modified, $r_i^s = r_i$ for all i, s, $1 \le i \le q$.

$I_H^\omega(B) = (D, r_1^\omega, \ldots, r_q^\omega, r_{q+1}^\omega, \ldots, r_p^\omega)$, $r_i^\omega = \bigcup_{s \ge 0} r_i^s$, $1 \le i \le p$.

The *minimum model* of program H on database B is $I_H^\omega(B)$. This operational definition is equivalent to the fixpoint definition in Apt and van Emden [1982] and van Emden and Kowalski [1976]. The database $I_H^{s+1}(B)$ can be computed from the database $I_H^s(B)$ using only logarithmic auxiliary space, so this computation can be done with an NC algorithm. We call this computation the sth *naive iteration*. The *naive evaluation* of the minimum model $I_H^\omega(B)$ is to perform successive naive iterations until for some s we have $I_H^s(B) = I_H^{s+1}(B)$. Since D is finite such an s_0 exists and therefore for $s \ge s_0$ $I_H^\omega(B) = I_H^s(B)$.

Logical Queries A logical query program H can be used to define a query on a database by designating all the EDBs as inputs and a single special IDB as output. The input EDB relations, which form database B, are mapped to the output IDB relation of the minimum model of program H on B. When the output IDB is clear from the context we will refer to the query defined by H as Q_H. Logical queries are all those definable by some logical query program.

Logical queries form a strict subset of the fixpoint queries. This is because of the absence of negation, even of inequality. They are therefore in PTIME, although not necessarily in NC. Precise expressibility results are investigated in Chandra and Harel [1985] and Shmueli [1987]. Logical query programs define a natural class of queries. Important combinatorial problems can be defined using them, such as transitive closure and path system accessibility. Logical query programs combine recursion (a single application of fixpoint operator μ) with *a union of untyped, tagged, tableaux* (the most common first-order queries, Ullman [1983]). We now give two central definitions: of the stage function associated with each program and of the query complexity classes based on this function.

DEFINITION 1

The *stage function* $s_H(n)$ of logical query program H is the least s, such that, $I_H^\omega(B) = I_H^s(B)$ for all B with $|B| \le n$. ∎

DEFINITION 2

Query Q is in STAGE(f(n)) if there is a logical query program H, such that $Q = Q_H$ and $s_H(n) = O(f(n))$. ∎

As is shown in Chandra and Harel [1985], for each fixed H we have $s_H(n) = O(n^k)$, for some constant $k \geq 0$, which depends on the arities of predicates in H. Whenever $s_H(n) = O(\log^k n)$, for some constant $k \geq 0$, $I_H^\omega(B)$ can be computed in NC by performing $s_H(n)$ naive iterations. If $s_H = O(1)$ we will say that H is *bounded*, else it is *unbounded*.

A query in STAGE(f(n)) can be evaluated in O(f(n)) naive iterations, where each iteration is a first-order query. In fact each iteration is a union of untyped tagged tableaux queries. Also each bounded query is clearly in STAGE(1) and is easily seen to be a union of untyped tagged tableaux. These STAGE classes are similar to the iterated query classes of Immerman [1981,1982] without negation. Clearly, for each program H and any output choice the query Q_H is in STAGE[$s_H(n)$].

The following inclusions indicate the natural STAGE analogs of the classes NC^2, NC and PTIME.

$$STAGE(\log n) \subseteq NC^2,$$

$$STAGE(\log^{O(1)} n) \subseteq NC,$$

$$STAGE(n^{O(1)}) \subseteq PTIME, \text{ and}$$

$$STAGE(\log^{O(1)} n) \subseteq STAGE(n).$$

Because of the absence of interpreted predicates (e.g., order) in logical query programs, it is possible to demonstrate that these inclusions are *proper* (Immerman [1981]).

EXAMPLE 1

In addition to their other rules, let the following programs contain

$$R(x,y) \leftarrow R_0(x,y).$$

1. Transitive closure of R_0 is defined using rule, $R(x,y) \leftarrow R(x,z),R(z,y)$. We have $s(n) = \Theta(\log n)$.

2. This transitive closure is also defined using rule, $R(x,y) \leftarrow R(x,z),R_0(z,y)$. We have $s(n) = \Theta(n)$.

3. Undirected transitive closure is defined using rules, $R(x,y) \leftarrow R(x,z),R(z,y)$. and $R(x,y) \leftarrow R_0(y,x)$. With $s(n) = \Theta(\log n)$.

4. Bipartite transitive closure is defined using rule,
    $R(x,y) \leftarrow R(x,y_1),R(x_1,y),R(x_1,y_1)$. With $s(n) = \Theta(\log n)$.

5. If 0-ary IDB predicate R_c is true, directed graph R_0 has a cycle,
    $R_c \leftarrow R(x,x)$. and $R(x,y) \leftarrow R(x,z),R(z,y)$. With $s(n) = \Theta(\log n)$.

6. Context free language $\{a^n cb^n \mid n \geq 0\}$ is related to rule, $R(x,y) \leftarrow R_1(x,z),R(z,z_1),R_2(z_1,y)$. Here $s(n) = \Omega(n)$, but as we shall see this query is in STAGE($\log n$).

7. All tableaux queries can be trivially written in this language and are bounded. It is possible to write less trivial programs, which are also bounded. $R(x,y) \leftarrow R(z,z_1),R_1(x,y),R_1(z,z_1)$. is bounded with $s(n) = 1$. ∎

Logical Query Program Sublanguages There are various syntactically restricted subsets of logical query programs, which are of independent interest.

I. Some syntactic restrictions lead to queries with a great deal of potential parallelism.

    We say that program H is *linear* if the antecedents of each rule contain at most one IDB symbol. The programs in Example 1 (b, f, g) are linear.

    Linear programs can be generalized to piecewise linear programs. Let G_H be the directed labeled multigraph where,

    a. The set of nodes is $\{i \mid R_i$ is a predicate symbol in $H\}$.

    b. The multiset of labeled arcs is constructed as follows:
        for the j-th rule in H $R_i(\ldots) \leftarrow R_{i_1}(\ldots),R_{i_2}(\ldots),\ldots,R_{i_e}(\ldots)$ *add* the arcs $(i_1, i), (i_2, i),\ldots,(i_e, i)$ labeled j.

    The nodes of G_H can be partitioned uniquely into *strongly connected components*. Each labeled arc of G_H is either contained in a component or is between nodes in different components. We call H *piecewise linear* iff no strong component of G_H contains two arcs with the same label. All queries expressible by piecewise linear programs are in STAGE($\log n$).

    If G_H is acyclic, then H is piecewise linear. In this case we say that H is *nonrecursive*, else it is *recursive*. All queries expressible by nonrecursive programs are clearly in STAGE(1).

II. Some syntactic restrictions facilitate program analysis.

    One such class of programs is those consisting of *elementary chain rules*. A rule with consequence $R(x,y)$ is an elementary chain rule if the variables in its antecedents form a chain from x to y (see Ullman and Van Gelder [1986] for a precise definition). Example 1 (a, b, f) clearly illustrates such rules. The theory of context free grammars is useful in the analysis of elementary chain programs.

A logical query program with IDB predicates R, R',... is *uniform* if it contains *initialization* rules $R(x,y,...) \leftarrow R_0(x,y,...)$. and $R'(x,y,...) \leftarrow R'_0(x,y,...)$. ... and in addition the EDBs $R_0, R'_0,...$ appear in no other rules. The programs in Example 1 (a, d, f, g) are uniform. This restriction is equivalent to arbitrarily initializing every IDB. Homomorphism techniques from database dependency theory are useful in the analysis of uniform programs (Sagiv [1987]).

III.   The simplest recursive logical query programs are the *single rule programs* (sirups).

A sirup H is a uniform, recursive program with one IDB predicate R. In addition to the trivial initialization rule $R(x,y,...) \leftarrow R_0(x,y,...)$, program H has one nontrivial rule. Note that because H is uniform and recursive, therefore, the defining rule has consequence R, does not contain R_0, and contains R in its antecedents. A sirup can have one possible output IDB, predicate R.

The sirup is *pure* if R is the only predicate in the nontrivial rule. The sirup is *typed* if it is pure and there is a partition of the variables into k blocks such that if $R(x_1,...,x_k)$ appears in H then x_i is in the i-th block. Typed sirups and full template dependencies (Ullman [1983]) are identical. Examples 1 (a, d, f, g) are sirups: (a) is pure, (d) is typed, (f, g) are linear, (a, f) are elementary chains. When we refer to a sirup we need only describe its nontrivial rule.

Inherently Sequential Programs

Logical query programs express queries in PTIME. Despite the lack of features, such as, negation, order, and so on in the language, there are simple programs defining queries whose data complexity is as high as that of any PTIME query. These are typically nonlinear sirups. The most celebrated one is path system accessibility (Cook [1974]) $R(x) \leftarrow R(y), R(z), R_3(x,y,z)$.

We call this sirup *monadic* since R is 1-ary. Path system accessibility is logspace-complete in PTIME. In addition, Immerman [1981] has shown using a game argument that it is in $STAGE(n) \setminus STAGE(\log^{O(1)} n)$. This strict lower bound depends on the lack of an order predicate in logical query programs.

Interesting new insights involve syntactically constrained sirups that are logspace-complete in PTIME. Some such examples are elementary chain sirups, examined in Afrati and Papadimitriou [1987] and Ullman and Van

Gelder [1986], typed and pure sirups, examined in Cosmadakis and Kanellakis [1986], and monadic sirups, examined in Kanellakis and Papadimitriou [1986]. The following sirup is in a syntactic sense the simplest hard sirup known (from Kanellakis and Papadimitriou [1986]).

PROPOSITION 1
The query defined by sirup, $R(x) \leftarrow R(y), R(z), R_1(y,x), R_1(x,z)$. is logspace-complete in PTIME and in $STAGE(n) \backslash STAGE(\log^{O(1)} n)$. ∎

It is instructive to outline the proof technique for this proposition. The logspace-hardness in PTIME follows from a reduction from monotone circuit value. W.l.o.g. the circuit consists of alternating layers of AND and OR gates; AND gates have indegree 2 and outdegree 1; OR gates have indegree 2 and outdegree $k \geq 2$. Every wire w in the circuit is associated with a constant w in the EDB relations, such that, wire w has value 1 iff $R(w)$ is true in the minimum model. The 0,1 inputs to the circuit are encoded using the initialization rule $R(x) \leftarrow R_0(x)$ and EDB relation r_0. The AND and OR gates are simulated by patterns of tuples in EDB relations r_0 and r_1. These patterns are presented graphically in Figure 1a. Pairs in r_1 are arcs labeled r_1 and elements of r_0 are nodes labeled r_0. Some care has to be taken in showing that wire w has value 1 iff $R(w)$ is true. Simple reasoning about the constructions in Figure 1a shows that they do satisfy this last condition. The above argument works for most monadic sirups but the AND-OR constructs might depend on the syntax of the sirup.

The strict lower bound follows from the results in Immerman [1981] and from the nature of these reductions. These reductions are more constrained than logspace-reductions; they require only transformations that involve one database first-order query. Such transformations are known as first-order translations Immerman [1983].

EXAMPLE 2 (KANELLAKIS AND PAPADIMITRIOU [1986]).
The query defined by sirup,

$$R(x) \leftarrow R(y), R(z), R_1(y,x), R_1(x,z), R_1(z,y).$$

is logspace-complete in PTIME and in $STAGE(n) \backslash STAGE(\log^{O(1)} n)$. The proof scheme is like that of Proposition 1, but the AND-OR construction (in Figure 1b) is different. ∎

Parallelizable Programs

Let H be a program to be evaluated on database B. If D is the finite domain of B, then the finite *Herbrand Base* of H on B are all possible ground atomic formulas, *atoms*, which are instantiations of IDBs of H with elements of D. Note

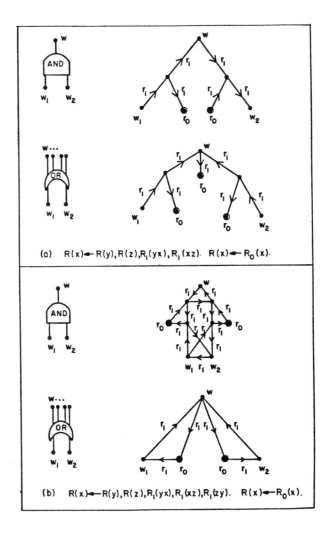

Figure 1: Logspace-complete Queries Defined by Sirups

that for EDBs the relevant atoms are the input tuples in B, and we define the Herbrand Base with only IDB atoms. A natural notion associated with the evaluation of H on B is the derivation tree.

DEFINITION 3

Let w be an element of the Herbrand Base of H on B. A *derivation tree of width* k for w is a tree, each of whose nodes is labeled with a subset of the Herbrand Base of size at most k, and such that:

1. If v is the root node, then w is its label;

2. If v is a leaf node, then its label is empty;

3. If v is an internal node, whose children are labeled by sets $V_1, \ldots, V_i$, then all elements of its label can be derived in *one naive iteration* of H on relations $B \cup V_1 \cup \ldots V_i$. ∎

DEFINITION 4
A program H has the polynomial (superpolynomial) tree-size property for width k, if for every database B and atom w in the minimum model of H on B, atom w has a derivation tree of width k and size polynomial (superpolynomial) in the size of B. ∎

Clearly w is in the minimum model of H on B iff there is a derivation tree for w (of some width). A derivation tree, which has a single path of length polynomial in n, but unfortunately of width polynomial in n is provided by naive evaluation (n is the size of B).

Consider the following monadic sirup from Example 2, that is:

$$R(x) \leftarrow R(y), R(z), R_1(y,x), R_1(x,z), R_1(z,y).$$

Database $B = (D, r_0, r_1)$ is represented pictorially in Figure 2a, using the obvious notation. R(7) is in the minimum model. A derivation tree for R(7) of width 2 is shown in Figure 2b and one of width 1 in Figure 2c. It is easy to see that the database in this example can be extended downwards, so that, the top node has a width 2 derivation tree that is a long path, but its best derivation tree of width 1 is exponential.

With every program H and constant k we can associate an Alternating Turing Machine $ATM_{H,k}$, that uses O(log n) space on inputs of size n. The inputs to this machine are pairs (w, B), where B is a database and w an element of the Herbrand Base of H on B. $ATM_{H,k}$ accepts (w, B) iff w is in the minimum model of H and B. The accepting computation trees of $ATM_{H,k}$ on input (w, B) are the derivation trees for w of width k. In an existential state the configuration of $ATM_{H,k}$ has, using only logarithmic auxiliary storage, a subset V of the Herbrand Base. The machine guesses sets $V_1, \ldots, V_i$ and verifies that condition (c) of the derivation tree definition holds. This brings it to a universal state, with i children existential states whose configurations are $V_1, \ldots, V_i$. From our review of parallel complexity it is clear that, if for some constant k $ATM_{H,k}$ uses polynomial (superpolynomial) tree-size, the queries defined by H are in LOGCFL (NC). $ATM_{H,k}$ is a natural machine to associate with a program H and justifies the use of the above definitions.

The *superpolynomial and polynomial fringe properties* of Ullman and Van Gelder [1986] are the superpolynomial and polynomial tree-size properties for

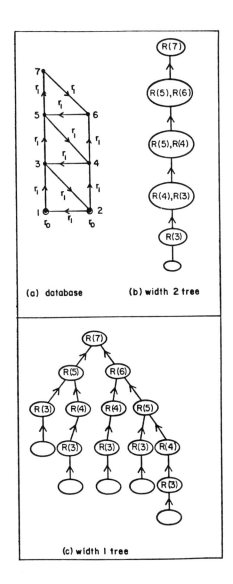

Figure 2: Derivation Tree Example

width 1. They can be used to characterize programs expressing NC queries. In fact Ullman and Van Gelder [1986] show something far more interesting related to the stage function.

Given such a parallelizable program H (Ullman and Van Gelder [1986]) provides a simple syntactic transformation of H into an equivalent program H'. The transformation is such that the naive evaluation of H' takes, at most, polylogarithmic naive iterations of H'. The method used has many other interesting applications in parallel computation, e.g., Miller and Reif [1985] and Valiant et al. [1983]. The following proposition is from Ullman and Van Gelder [1986].

PROPOSITION 2
Any query defined by a program H, which has the polynomial (superpolynomial) tree-size property for width 1, is in STAGE(log n) (STAGE($\log^{O(1)}$ n)). ∎

Part (a) of the following theorem extends this proposition to width k derivation trees. By part (b) this extension is strict.

THEOREM 1

1. Any query defined by a program H, which has the polynomial (superpolynomial) tree-size property for some fixed width, is in STAGE(log n) (STAGE($\log^{O(1)}$ n)).

2. There exists a program with the polynomial tree-size property for width 2, which does not satisfy the superpolynomial tree-size property for width 1.

Proof: (a) As in the proof of Ullman and Van Gelder [1986], each naive iteration is augmented by one step of a logarithmic transitive closure algorithm on an implication graph. The old naive iteration takes care of "bushy but short" derivation trees, the transitive closure of "skinny but long" derivation trees. This new *fast iteration* is the naive iteration of a new program H' and handles all derivation trees fast. H can be transformed into H' in a first-order fashion. The stage function of H' is logarithmic (polylogarithmic) if H has the polynomial (superpolynomial) tree-size property.

The only modification of the implication graph from the width 1 (Ullman and Van Gelder [1986]) to the width k case is that its nodes are all subsets of size k of the Herbrand base. An arc in the implication graph from V to V' denotes the syllogism that from a proof of V and the subset of the minimum model discovered up to this point one naive iteration of H would produce V'. Since the argument is a direct one we refer to Ullman and Van Gelder [1986] for the detailed correctness proof.

Each naive iteration of H' can be performed with polynomial in n (the size of B) number of PRAM-processors in O(log n) PRAM-time. The exponent, however, depends on the maximum arity c in H and on k, $O(n^{3ck})$. Since the implication graph might involve large parts of the Herbrand Base (in each iteration) this is the unrealistic part of the transformation.

(b) This part is based on the example of Figure 2 and the sirup H_1:

$$R(x) \leftarrow R(y),R(z),R_1(y,x),R_1(x,z),R_1(z,y).$$

The sirup H_1 cannot be used directly since it is logspace-complete in PTIME, i.e., there are more complex databases to evaluate it on than that of Figure 2a. It is possible to modify the example to produce another query expressed by a logical query program H_2 and in the class STAGE(log n) with the following property: "it does not always have derivation trees of width 1 of polynomial size, although it does have width 2 polynomial size derivation trees."

The basic intuition is to notice the "triangle" symmetry in the sirup and to create databases where recursion takes place only if two "triangles" share a side. For triangle adjacency we use transitive closure. Here is this logical query program H_2:

$$R_2(x,x_1,y_1,z_1) \leftarrow R_0(x), R_1(x_1,y_1),R_1(y_1,z_1),R_1(z_1,x_1).$$

$$R_3(x,y,z,x,y,z_1) \leftarrow R_1(x,y),R_1(y,z),R_1(z,x),R_1(y,z_1),R_1(z_1,x).$$

$$R_3(x,y,z,x_1,y_1,z_1) \leftarrow R_3(x,y,z,x_2,y_2,z_2), R_3(x_2,y_2,z_2,x_1,y_1,z_1).$$

$$R_2(x,x_1,y_1,z_1) \leftarrow R_2(y,x_1,y_1,z_1), R_2(z,x_1,y_1,z_1), R_3(x,y,z,x_1,y_1,z_1).$$

Let us explain these rules. The second and third rules express undirected transitive closure for "triangles" that share a side. So $R_3(x,y,z,x_1,y_1,z_1)$ expresses the fact that "triangle" xyz is reachable from "triangle" $x_1y_1z_1$ by a sequence of shared sides. The fourth rule is like H_1, only it makes sure that the recursion is performed on "triangles" reachable from "triangle" $x_1y_1z_1$. The first rule serves to initialize the fourth.

Because of the undirected reachability, this computation can be performed in NC, and polynomial size width 2 derivation trees exist (as in Figure 2b). However, there are no width 1 polynomial size derivation trees for databases, such as that of Figure 2a. ∎

The proof of Theorem 1a may be viewed as an abstract interpreter. This interpreter will, without testing for parallelizability, work in polylogarithmic iterations in the presence of the superpolynomial tree-size property and otherwise degenerate into naive evaluation. In order to utilize other, more realistic interpreters or compilers, one would like syntactic characterizations of parallelizability. Syntactic characterizations will be sufficient conditions because testing for parallelizability is undecidable (Ullman and Van Gelder [1986]).

All known syntactic sufficient conditions follow from Theorem 2 and involve the class STAGE(logn). For example, piecewise linear programs are in STAGE(log n) (Cosmadakis and Kanellakis [1986], Ullman and Van Gelder [1986], Vardi [1985]). Some elementary chain programs in STAGE(log n) are described in Ullman and Van Gelder [1986] and some typed sirups in this class are in Cosmadakis and Kanellakis [1986]. Bounded programs are also in STAGE(log n), but they deserve their own subsection.

Some of the most elegant combinatorial results in this area involve sirups and new insights into context free languages. For example, all elementary chain sirups are syntactically classified as in STAGE(log n) or logspace-complete in PTIME in Afrati and Papadimitriou [1987]. Another interesting observation is that there exists an inherently nonlinear sirup in STAGE(log n) (Ullman and Van Gelder [1986]).

Bounded vs Unbounded Programs

Recall that H is bounded if its stage function is bounded by a constant, $s_H = O(1)$. A program H may be used to define a set of queries, one for each choice of output IDB symbol. The queries defined by bounded programs are in STAGE(1). In database terminology they are first-order queries expressible using finite unions of untyped tagged tableaux.

The converse is also true. If the program H is unbounded, it defines a query which is not in STAGE(1). Or equivalently, if all the queries defined by a program are in STAGE(1), the program is bounded. This observation from Naughton and Sagiv [1987] is summarized in Proposition 3a (it has also been made independently by Stavros Cosmadakis, Phokion Kolaitis, and Moshe Vardi).

In addition, a gap theorem can be shown about unbounded programs. It is easy to extend the arguments used in Cosmadakis and Kanellakis [1986] for typed sirups and show that if the program is unbounded, the stage function is $\Omega(\log n)$. This is summarized in Proposition 3b.

PROPOSITION 3

1. Program H is bounded iff all queries defined using H are in STAGE(1).

2. Program H is unbounded iff $s_H = \Omega(\log n)$. ∎

Let us briefly comment on Proposition 3a. Boundedness is a property of the stage function of a particular program and thus a syntactic condition. Expressibility of a query by some bounded program is a semantic condition. If we were to allow infinite databases, then Proposition 3a would be a simple application of the compactness theorem of first-order logic. In fact the more general statement would hold: "program H is bounded iff all queries defined using H are first-order." For finite databases, compactness arguments fail. Even to show the less general statement in the finite case one must use the fact that STAGE(1) queries are first-order queries expressible using unions of tagged untyped tableaux.

The problem of deciding boundedness has received a fair amount of attention. The first sufficient condition for boundedness was formulated in Minker and Nicolas [1982]. Boundedness is decidable for elementary chain programs because it corresponds to context free language finiteness. It is also decidable for typed sirups (and sets of typed rules) (Sagiv [1985]), although it is NP-hard in the size of the sirup (Yannakakis [1986]).

For linear programs, sufficient conditions for boundedness appear in Ioannidis [1985], Naughton [1986], and Naughton and Sagiv [1987]. These lead to efficient decision procedures for certain subsets of the linear sirups. An example of such a subset from Naughton [1986] is "linear sirups with no repetitions of EDB symbols in the defining rule of the sirup."

Unfortunately, boundedness of programs is undecidable even for uniform linear programs with a single IDB (Gaifman et al. [1987]). Although the undecidability results in Gaifman et al. [1987] satisfy many syntactic restrictions, there are still a number of interesting open cases. In particular, the decidability of boundedness of sirups is still open even for pure or linear sirups.

We complete this review of the state of the art on boundedness with a new observation' about linear sirups. This theorem generalizes certain example sirups in Naughton [1986] not covered by known efficient criteria. It indicates that there is no structured characterization of boundedness, even in a very restricted class of rules.

THEOREM 2
Boundedness of linear sirups is NP-hard in the size of the sirups. This is true even for a linear sirup with IDB of arity 4 and one EDB of arity 2 in the defining rule.

Proof: The reduction is from three colorability of an undirected graph G (Hopcroft and Ullman [1979]). Given graph G construct the following sirup H(G):

$$R(x,y,z,v) \leftarrow R(x,y,z,w), R_1(x,v),R_1(y,v),R_1(z,v),R_2(w,x),R_2(w,y),$$
$$R_2(w,z), R_3(x,y),R_3(y,x),R_3(z,x),R_3(x,z), R_3(z,y),R_3(y,z),$$
$$...,R_1(x_i,v),R_2(w,x_i),... \text{ (where } x_i \text{ is a node in G)}$$
$$...,R_3(x_i,x_j),R_3(x_j,x_i),... \text{ (where } x_ix_j \text{ is an edge in G).}$$

The reduction is illustrated in Figure 3a. In this figure the nodes represent the variables and the labeled arcs the EDB symbol occurrences in the rule body. Note that the three EDB symbols R_1,R_2,R_3 can be encoded by a single EDB symbol. This involves the common technique of encoding labeled arcs in

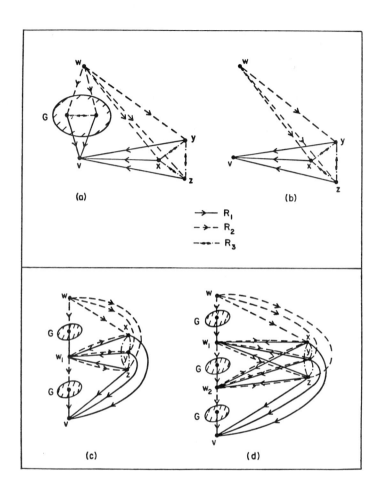

Figure 3: Illustrating the Proof of Theorem 2

Figure 3a by unique subgraphs, and will be omitted. One can show that H(G) is bounded iff G is three-colorable.

"If" Let G be three-colorable, then the above sirup is equivalent to the following sirup:

$$R(x,y,z,v) \leftarrow R(x,y,z,w), R_1(x,v),R_1(y,v),R_1(z,v),R_2(w,x),R_2(w,y),$$

$$R_2(w,z), R_3(x,y),R_3(y,x),R_3(z,x),R_3(x,z),R_3(z,y),R_3(y,z).$$

This is represented in Figure 3b. For this all one has to note is that Figure 3a (3b) can be homomorphically mapped in Figure 3b (3a), where x,y,z,v,w are mapped to x,y,z,v,w (Ullman [1983]). Now the sirup represented by Figure 3b is bounded because it satisfies the sufficient condition of Naughton [1986].

"Only if" Let H(G) be bounded. This will imply by Naughton [1986] that the first-order query corresponding to the $k + 1$rst naive iteration is contained in one of the previous naive iterations. In graph theoretic terms, this implies the existence of a certain homomorphism between graphs. These graphs are like the graphs of Figures 3c, 3d. They correspond to the i-th $(k + 1$rst) naive iteration and they contain i $(k + 1)$ copies of the graph H. Now consider the graph of Figure 3c (for iteration i, where i is less than $k + 1$) and the graph of Figure 3d (for iteration $k + 1$). Because of boundedness, there must be a homomorphism mapping nodes of Figure 3c to Figure 3d such that x,y,z,v,w are mapped to x,y,z,v,w. Because of their structure, each w_i node of Figure 3c must be mapped to a w_j node of Figure 3d. Thus, some copy of H must be mapped completely onto x,y,z (and be three-colorable). To be convinced of this, one only has to see that if this claim were not true there would exist a path of length i in Figure 3c mapped into a path of strictly greater length $k + 1$ in Figure 3d. This would be a contradiction. ∎

Open Questions

We are now going to outline a number of interesting open questions about these logical query programs.

ANALYSIS

1. First some concrete technical questions. Is boundedness decidable for linear sirups, for pure sirups, or under other syntactic restrictions that are weaker than the ones of Gaifman et al. [1987]?

2. Show that if a program is unbounded it defines a query that is not first-order expressible over finite databases. This has been shown for programs expressing specific queries such as transitive closure (Aho and Ullman [1979], Fagin [1975], and Gaifman and Vardi [1985]). It is true for programs consisting of elementary chain rules because it follows from the analysis in Beeri et al. [1987].

3. The fundamental question in this area is to develop techniques to estimate the stage function of a given program. Boundedness is a special case. For example, find sufficient conditions on typed sirups that guarantee $s(n) = O(\log n)$. Naive evaluation is a simple algorithm. Is it possible to use tools from the mathematical analysis of algorithms to compute expected time bounds for the stage function on random input databases?

EQUIVALENCE

4. A technical question here from Cosmadakis and Kanellakis [1986] is: Let H be a typed sirup and Q a tableau query, is $Q_H \subseteq Q$ decidable? Note that the containement $Q \subseteq Q_H$ is decidable.

5. The fundamental question here is to develop equivalence preserving transformations for use in query optimization. An interesting example is the *magic sets* of Bancilhon et al. [1986]. Theorem 1 is based on an equivalence preserving transformation. Unfortunately equivalence of programs is undecidable (Shmueli [1987]). One interesting feature of uniform programs, and of sirups in particular, is that their equivalence is decidable (Sagiv [1987]). These decidability results are based on database dependency techniques.

CLASSIFICATION

6. A technical question here is to syntactically classify typed sirups and monadic sirups with respect to their parallel complexity, as was done for elementary chain sirups in Afrati and Papadimitriou [1987].

7. The author knows of no NC problem that is expressible as a logical query and is not in STAGE(log n). Is Theorem 1a a necessary condition for parallelizability of logical query programs?

8. The STAGE complexity classes should be investigated for hierarchy and gap properties.

9. It would be interesting to study the expressibility of logical query programs when the arity of IDBs is restricted. Even for small arities there are hard open questions in this area (Chandra and Harel [1982]).

PARALLEL EVALUATION

10. Restricted fixpoint operators, such as transitive closure, undirected transitive closure, and so on, have interesting expressibility properties (Immerman [1983]). Study parallel algorithms for these operations on databases. A difference from conventional parallel algorithms for such problems as u-GAP is the emphasis on external storage costs (Ioannidis [1986], Valduriez and Boral [1986]).

11. The fundamental issue here is to study good top-down and bottom-up evaluation methods using m processors where m = O(log n). In the presence of "goals with bound arguments," top-down methods might be better than bottom-up ones. Much recent work in the area by Bancilhon

et al. [1986], Bancilhon and Ramakrishnan [1986], Henschen and Naqvi [1984], Sacca and Zaniolo [1986], and Ullman [1985] could be combined with parallel evaluation algorithms.

12. Is there an optimal parallel algorithm for the dag-GAP problem? This theoretical question is well motivated by the large PRAM processor bounds of Theorem 1.

Parallelism and Structured Data

Term Unification, Matching, and Equivalence

PROLOG and other logic programming languages, in addition to their recursive control structure exemplified by logical query programs, provide primitive operations for the definition and manipulation of structured data. The most important of primitive operations for symbolic computation is the operation of unification of terms (Martelli and Montanari [1982], Paterson and Wegman [1978], Robinson [1965]). A special case of unification is term matching with many applications in term rewriting, equational reasoning (Huet and Oppen [1980], Knuth and Bendix [1970]), and even in PROLOG compilation (Maluszynski and Komorowski [1985]).

We start with a countably infinite set of *variables* $\{x,y,z,\ldots\}$ and a disjoint countably infinite set of *function* symbols $\{f,g,\ldots\}$ of all *arities*. A *constant* is a function symbol of arity 0. The set of *terms* is the smallest set of finite strings, such that:

1. Every variable and constant is a term.

2. If f is a k-ary function symbol, $k \geq 1$, and $t_1,\ldots,t_k$ are terms then $ft_1\ldots t_k$ is a term.

A term t_v is usually represented by a labeled-directed, acyclic graph rooted at node v (dag v, for short). Every node is labeled by either a variable or a k-ary function symbol.

1. A node labeled by variable x has outdegree 0 and represents the term x.

2. A node labeled by constant g has outdegree 0 and represents the term g.

3. A node labeled by k-ary function symbol f with $k \geq 1$ has k outgoing arcs labeled 1 to k. The term represented by the dag rooted at this node is $ft_1\ldots t_k$, where t_i is represented by its subdag rooted at the head of the outgoing arc labeled i.

Since dag v is rooted at v, all of its nodes are reachable from v. A dag v could be a *tree* (with root v). A dag v is *compact* if for all pairs of different nodes w and w' of this dag t_w and $t_{w'}$ are different terms; that is, a compact dag contains no repeated subdags. Note that although each node of a dag v determines a single term, the converse is only true for compact dags. It is easy to see that the dag representation can be very concise; a dag v of size n may represent a term of (string) length 2^n. Since term representations are not unique, the first problem is one of equivalence of representations. We use = for syntactic equality of strings.

A *substitution* is a mapping σ from variables to terms. The action of substitution σ on a term t, written $\sigma(t)$, is the result of replacing each variable x in t by $\sigma(x)$, where these replacements take place simultaneously. A substitution σ is *more general* than a substitution τ if there exists a substitution ρ, such that, $\tau(t) = \rho(\sigma(t))$, for all terms t. Term matching and unification are defined in terms of substitutions.

> **THE INPUT:** Throughout our presentation we assume that the input consists of two *disjoint* dags respectively rooted at u and v. They represent terms t_u and t_v. Their size is n, and we explicitly state if one or both of them are trees or compact dags.
>
> **EQUAL:** (Term equivalence) Given dags u,v, is $t_u = t_v$?
>
> **MATCH:** (Term matching) Given dags u,v, is there a substitution σ, such that, $\sigma(t_u) = t_v$?
>
> **UNIFY:** (Term unification) Given dags u,v, is there a substitution σ, such that, $\sigma(t_u) = \sigma(t_v)$?

A basic fact about unification is that whenever two terms are unifiable there is a unifier that is more general than any other unifier, the mgu. The mgu is unique up to renaming of variables. For example, terms fxy and fgygz are unifiable with mgu $\sigma(x) = ggz$ $\sigma(y) = gz$ and $\sigma(z) = z$; after the substitution both terms become fggzgz. Two canonical examples of ununifiable terms are x and gx, as well as fxy and gz. Term matching of t_u and t_v is a subcase of unification where w.l.o.g. t_v contains no variables. Algorithms for UNIFY and MATCH typically produce the mgu. We now present a simple algorithm that can also serve as an operational definition of UNIFY and of the mgu.

Naive Unification First given the input dags u,v, for each variable x, identify all nodes with label x into a single node with label x. Let us call the resulting dag G. Let r be the smallest binary relation on the nodes of G such that:

1.   Tuple (u,v) is in r, i.e., r(u,v).

2.   Relation r is an equivalence relation.

3.   If nodes a_i and b_i are the i-th children of nodes a and b respectively, and r(a,b), then $r(a_i,b_i)$. This condition is known as propagation to children.

Given an instance of UNIFY, t_u and t_v are unifiable iff relation r defined above is *homogeneous* and *acyclic*. Relation r is homogeneous if whenever r(a,b) then nodes a and b are not labeled by different function symbols; that is, the nodes in each r-equivalence class are either labeled by variables or by a unique function symbol. Relation r is acyclic if the r-equivalence classes are partially ordered by the arcs of the input dags. If r is homogeneous and acyclic, then shrinking the r-equivalence classes to single nodes results in a rooted dag representing $\sigma(t_u) = \sigma(t_v)$ and σ is the mgu. A detailed example follows.

EXAMPLE 3
Let 0 be a constant and f a binary function symbol (e.g., "nil" and "cons"). The input terms $t_u = ff...f0x_k...x_2x_1$, $t_v = fx_1fx_2...fx_k0$ are represented by the (disjoint) dags u,v in Figure 4a. Note that t_u and t_v share variables. If we identify nodes labeled by the same variable we get Figure 4b. In this same figure the undirected edges represent r-equivalence classes of relation r of naive unification. If we shrink each r-equivalence class to a node we get the mgu σ. Note that $\sigma(t_u) = \sigma(t_v)$ is an exponentially long string in k represented by the compact dag of Figure 4c.

Let the structure of the terms in Example 3 be described in three EDB relations. r_0 contains the pair to be unified (u,v), r_i contains pairs of nodes (p,c)

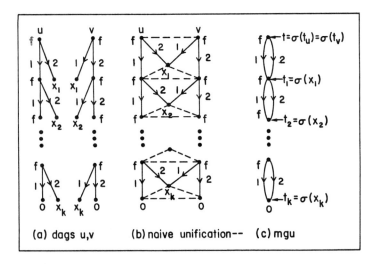

(a) dags u,v   (b) naive unification--   (c) mgu

Figure 4: Naive Unification for Example 3

where c is the i-th child of p, i = 1,2. r is the minimum model of the following program H on these relations.

initialization $R(x,y) \leftarrow R_0(x,y)$.

reflexivity $R(x,x) \leftarrow$.

symmetry $R(x,y) \leftarrow R(y,x)$.

transitivity $R(x,y) \leftarrow R(x,z),R(z,y)$.

propagation $R(x,y) \leftarrow R(x_1,y_1),R_1(x_1,x),R_1(y_1,y)$.

propagation $R(x,y) \leftarrow R(x_2,y_2),R_2(x_2,x),R_2(y_2,y)$.

For the above logical query program the stage function is linear, each naive iteration alternating between maintaining equivalence and propagating to children. This type of alternating behavior is the intuitive cause of the logspace-completeness of unification. ■

Inherently Sequential Operations

The operation of unification of terms is logspace-complete in PTIME (Dwork et al. [1984], Yasuura [1983]). Furthermore, as shown in Dwork et al. [1984], this lower bound does not depend on the conciseness of the dag representation; it holds for tree inputs. Clearly the lower bounds are tighter for inputs represented as trees, and the upper bounds are more general for inputs represented as dags.

If a variable appears in both input terms, we say that these terms *share variables*. Variable sharing is a major cause of difficulty of unification, as indicated by Example 3, and this is quantified in Dwork et al. [1986]. In a PROLOG interpreter, where each rule is really a local procedure, unification may be performed without any variable sharing.

We say that a term t is *linear* if no variable appears in (string) t twice. Nonlinearity of both input terms is the major difficulty of unification in PROLOG and this is quantified in Dwork et al. [1984].

We summarize the basic bounds of Dwork et al. [1984, 1986] in the following proposition. Note that MATCH is a special case of part (b), which refers to the most general case of unification known to be in NC.

PROPOSITION 4

1. For inputs represented by trees, UNIFY is logspace-complete in PTIME even if: both input terms are linear but share variables, or they do not share variables but are both nonlinear.

2.   For inputs represented by dags, UNIFY is in NC^2 provided the input terms do not share variables and one of them is linear. ∎

We would also like to add that the bounds above do not depend on having to test for acyclicity.

The parallel algorithms for UNIFY of case (b) involve a modification of the parallel algorithms for MATCH. This is in order to account for unifying a set of trees representing linear terms that do not share variables. In the next section we will concentrate on algorithms for MATCH. It is interesting to note that the acyclicity test of naive unification (i.e., the notorious "occur" check in PROLOG) may be omitted in case (b). The only possible ways for this case to fail involve inhomogeneity.

Apart from case (b), which we believe characterizes many unifications in the PROLOG interpreter, there has been work (in Vitter and Simons [1986]) on how limited parallelism can be used to give limited speed-ups for the general unification problem.

A different operation that has some operational similarities with unification is *congruence closure* (Downey et al. [1980] and Kozen [1977]). Congruence closure is also logspace-complete in PTIME (Kozen [1977]).

Parallelizable Operations

The complexity of MATCH is the critical part of the parallelizable case for UNIFY of Proposition 4. In order to solve MATCH efficiently, we must solve the more elementary problem EQUAL. We first reduce MATCH to EQUAL (steps M1-M4 below) and then summarize the known results about EQUAL (Proposition 5) and about MATCH (Proposition 6).

Recall that in MATCH w.l.o.g. we are given a dag u and a disjoint dag v with no variables. We want either to find a substitution of terms for the variables of u to make it syntactically equal to v or determine that no such substitution exists. Different results can be obtained depending on the form of dag v (e.g., tree or compact dag). It is instructive to present the four main steps M1-M4 of the algorithm from Dwork et al. [1986]. For the parallel implementation, which is the more technical part, we refer to Dwork et al. [1986].

M1 We can assume that each variable in dag u labels exactly one node. Multiple copies of variable x can be merged in one copy. A spanning tree T of dag u is formed by having each node of dag u arbitrarily choose one of the arcs that is directed into it. T is produced because the dag is rooted at u.

M2 T is embedded in dag v. Formally an embedding of T in dag v is a mapping ρ from the nodes of T to those of dag v (not necessarily a one-to-one mapping) such that:

1.   The root of T, node u, is mapped by ρ to v.

2.   For all nodes w of T, w and $\rho(w)$ are labeled by the same function, or w is labeled by a variable.

3.   For all nodes w and w' of T, if there is an arc in T labeled i from w to w' then there is an arc in dag v labeled i from $\rho(w)$ to $\rho(w')$.

If there is no embedding, then clearly t_u and t_v are not unifiable.

M3   The embedding ρ gives a substitution for all the variables of t_u. Specifically, if variable x is the label of (the unique) node w in dag u then the subdag rooted at $\rho(w)$ represents the term substituted for x. The substitution is performed by replacing all arcs in T of the form (w',w) by (w',$\rho(w)$). If terms t_u,t_v are unifiable, then clearly this substitution is the only one possible. However, this substitution is not necessarily a unifying substitution since spanning tree T may not contain all the edges of the dag u. There is one more thing to check.

M4   Let dag c be the dag without variables obtained from dag u by making the substitution defined in M3. Check whether dags c,v are equivalent, i.e., $t_c = t_v$. This is like the EQUAL problem, only the input dags are not necessarily disjoint. The answer to MATCH is yes iff $t_c = t_v$.

Steps M1-M3 can be implemented using $O(n^2)$ processors in NC^2. Step M4 can also be implemented using $O(n^2)$ processors in NC^2 provided dag v is compact or a tree (for the tree case the time bounds are logarithmic). The proofs use techniques from Tarjan and Vishkin [1985]. Step M4 is the only step that for general dag v seems to require M(n) processors. Recall from "Parallelism and Unstructured Data" that M(n) is the best sequential time for multiplying n by n matrices and for practical applications $O(n^3)$. In general, step M4 is the dominating step. In Dwork et al. [1986], it is implemented in NC^2 using $M(n^2)$ processors, and in random NC^2 using M(n) processors. The proofs for the randomized algorithm use techniques from Rabin [1980] and Schwartz [1980].

There is some "circumstantial" evidence that no deterministic NC^2 algorithm can improve on the M(n) processor bound of this randomized algorithm for MATCH. The dag-GAP problem reduces to EQUAL (Dwork et al. [1986]). As defined in the beginning of this section, the inputs to EQUAL in this reduction are disjoint dags rooted at u,v. The reduction is in constant time and using $O(n^2)$ processors. Thus an NC^2 algorithm with better than M(n) processor bounds for EQUAL would imply one for dag-GAP. We now summarize the results from Dwork et al. [1986] about EQUAL. $NC^i[n^j]$ denotes membership in NC^i using $O(n^j)$ processors.

PROPOSITION 5

For inputs represented by dags,

1. EQUAL is in $NC^2[M(n^2)]$ and in random $NC^2[M(n)]$.

2. The problem dag-GAP reduces in constant time to EQUAL using $O(n^2)$ processors. ∎

Use of $M(n)$ processors would also allow us to dispense with our disjoint and rooted character of input dags u,v. With $M(n)$ processors the input could be one labeled directed acyclic graph with two special nodes u,v.

The most general algorithm for MATCH uses EQUAL as a basic subroutine and the steps M1-M4 above, from Dwork et al. [1986] (Proposition 6a). If dag v is a tree or a compact dag there are almost optimal algorithms. For input trees Verma et al. [1986] has an NC^2 algorithm using $O(n)$ processors (Proposition 6d). As noted in Dwork et al. [1984], this special case of MATCH is in LOGSPACE, and in $NC^1[n^2]$ Dwork et al. [1986] (Propositions 6b, 6c).

PROPOSITION 6

For inputs represented by dags,

1. MATCH is in $NC^2[M(n^2)]$ and in random $NC^2[M(n)]$.

2. ¬ (MATCH) is in NLOGSPACE and for inputs represented by trees in LOGSPACE.

3. MATCH is in $NC^2[n^2]$ if dag v is compact, and in $NC^1[n^2]$ if dag v is a tree.

4. For inputs represented by trees, MATCH is in $NC^2[n]$. ∎

Open Questions

1. Improving the processor bounds for the dag-GAP problem or showing lower bounds is the most elegant and probably hardest open question. Interestingly this is also the last and probably most significant open question of the section on Unstructured Data.

2. Is it possible to improve Proposition 5 to $NC^2[M(n)]$, but without randomness?

3. For inputs represented as trees is MATCH in $NC^1[n]$? Some progress is reported in Ramesh et al. [1986].

4. A practical problem is how to incorporate the various algorithmic techniques for the special cases in the design of specialized hardware for unification.

5. What is the exact role of the acyclicity test? Surprisingly the fastest known algorithm to compute relation r of "naive unification" uses UNION-FIND and is slightly slower than linear-time. Acyclicity is an integral part of the linear-time algorithm of Paterson and Wegman [1978].

6. Which is the best expected time algorithm for unification? Some practical comparisons, using implementations and experimentation, appear in Trum and Winterstein [1987].

7. Rewrite rule systems (Huet and Oppen [1980], Knuth and Bendix [1970]) are a good example of the use of term matching as a primitive. More analysis is needed of the overall parallel complexity of these systems.

8. For trees unification of a single pair of nodes (u,v) is logspace-complete in PTIME. For trees the congruence closure of n pairs (as opposed to one pair) is logspace-complete in PTIME. In the operation of congruence closure, propagation to parents replaces propagation to children. Moreover in this operation the inputs could be directed graphs with cycles (i.e., not only dags). It is possible to show that congruence closure of a single pair (u,v) of a directed acyclic graph is in NC. What is the complexity of computing the congruence closure of a single pair of nodes (u,v) of a graph with cycles?

Conclusions

AND-parallelism and OR-parallelism have been the most investigated qualitative measures of parallelism in logic programming languages. We complete the intuition of these qualitative measures by focusing on parallel complexity. The complexity class NC is the quantitative criterion for identifying those computational problems in logic programming with large amounts of potential parallelism. Although evaluation of logical query programs and unification of terms in their full generality are inherently sequential tasks, many important parallelizable cases have been identified.

Lower bounds based on logspace-completeness in PTIME indicate some basic limitations, such as differences from arithmetic operations, but make no statements about average performance or constant factor speed-ups. They are worst-case asymptotic lower bounds. Therefore, from a practical point of view, much remains to be done both in developing algorithms for parallel evaluation of database queries and in building special hardware for primitive operations.

However, we believe that the theory of parallel computation, even if it does not provide all the answers, contributes to a better understanding of these "real world" problems.

Some of the theoretical results we reviewed here could be directly applicable to practice. Let us close our exposition with two such examples.

1. Piecewise linear programs are a class of parallelizable programs that is rich in expressive power and easy to use. They are the natural candidates for efficient database system extensions. Sufficient conditions such as Proposition 2 clearly identify this potential. From the point of view of parallel algorithms, more experimental work is required in order to identify how to use O(log n) processors to exploit this potential parallelism.

2. There are very good parallel algorithms for unification of arbitrary and linear PROLOG terms, given the appropriate representations. These could be incorporated in special hardware for unification. The reduction of MATCH to EQUAL is an efficient parallel reduction to a more elementary question. What are good hardware approaches for solving EQUAL?

Acknowledgments

The author would like to thank Stavros Cosmadakis, Phokion Kolaitis, Jeff Naughton, and Moshe Vardi for their many helpful comments.

This paper was supported partly by an IBM Faculty Development Award and partly by ONR-DARPA grant N00014-83-K-0146, ARPA Order No. 4786. A preliminary version of this paper has appeared, as an invited paper, in the Proceedings of the First International Conference on Database Theory, Rome, September 1986.

References

1. Afrati, F. and Papadimitriou, C. H. [1987] The Parallel Complexity of Simple Chain Queries, *Proceedings of the 6th PODS*, ACM, 210–214.

2. Aho, A. V. and Ullman, J. D. [1979] Universality of Data Retrieval Languages, *Proceedings of the 6th POPL*, ACM, 110–117.

3. Apt, K. R. and Emden M. H. van [1982] Contributions to the Theory of Logic Programming, *JACM* **29**(4):841–862.

4. Bancilhon, F. Maier D., Sagiv, Y., and Ullman, J. D. [1986] Magic Sets and Other Strange Ways to Implement Logic Programs, *Proceedings of the 5th PODS*, ACM, 1–14.

5. Bancilhon, F. and Ramakrishnan, R., [1986] An Amateur's Introduction to Recursive Query Processing Strategies, *Proceedings of the 86 SIGMOD*, ACM, 16–52.

6. Bancilhon, F. and Ramakrishnan, R. [1988] Performance Evaluation of Data Intensive Logic Programs, in *Foundations of Deductive Databases and Logic Programming* (J. Minker, Ed.), Morgan Kaufmann Publishers, Los Altos, CA, 439–517.

7. Barwise, J. and Moschovakis, Y. N. [1978] Global Inductive Definability, *Journal of Symbolic Logic* **43**(3):521–534.

8. Beeri, C., Kanellakis, P. C., Bancilhon, F., and Ramakrishnan, R. [1987] Bounds on the Propagation of Selection into Logic Programs, *Proceedings of the 6th PODS*, ACM, 214–227.

9. Chandra, A. K. [1976] Maximal Parallelism in Matrix Multiplication, RC 6193, IBM.

10. Chandra, A. K. and Harel, D. [1982] Structure and Complexity of Relational Queries, *JCSS* **25**(1):99–128.

11. Chandra, A. K. and Harel, D. [1985] Horn Clause Programs and Generalizations, *J. Logic Programming 2*, 1–15.

12. Chandra, A. K., Kozen, D. C., and Stockmeyer, L. J. [1981] Alteration, *JACM* **28**(1):114–133.

13. Clark, K. L. [1978] Negation as Failure, in *Logic and Databases* (H. Gallaire and J. Minker, Eds.), Plenum Press, New York, 293–324.

14. Clark, K. L. and Gregory, S. [1981] A Relational Language for Parallel Programming, *Proceedings of the ACM Conference on Functional Programming Languages and Computer Architecture*, ACM.

15. Clocksin, W. F. and Mellish, C. S. [1981] *Programming in Prolog*, Springer Verlag.

16. Codd, E. F. [1970] A Relational Model for Large Shared Data Banks, *CACM* **13**(6):377–387.

17. Cole, R. and Vishkin, U. [1986] Deterministic Coin Tossing and Accelerating Cascades: Micro and Macro Techniques for Designing Parallel Algorithms, *Proceedings of the 17th STOC*, ACM, 206–219.

18. Cook, S. A. [1974] An Observation on a Time-Storage Trade-off, *JCSS* **9**(3):308–316.

19. Cook, S. A. [1985] A Taxonomy of Problems with Fast Parallel Algorithms, *Information and Control 64*, 2–22.

20. Coppersmith, D. and Winograd, S. [1982] On the Asymptotic Complexity of Matrix Multiplication, *SIAM J. of Computing* **11**, 472–492.

21. Coppersmith, D. and Winograd, S. [1987] Matrix Multiplication via Behrend's Theorem, *Proceedings of the 19th STOC*, ACM (to appear).

22. Cosmadakis, S. S. and Kanellakis, P. C. [1986] Parallel Evaluation of Recursive Rule Queries, *Proceedings of the 5th PODS*, ACM, 280–293.

23. deRougemont, M. [1984] Uniform Definability of Finite Structures with Successor, *Proceedings of the 16th STOC*, ACM, 409–417.

24. Downey, P. J., Sethi, R., and Tarjan, R. E. [1980] Variations on the Common Subexpression Problem, *JACM* 27(4):758–771.

25. Dwork, C., Kanellakis, P. C., and Mitchell, J. C. [1984] On the Sequential Nature of Unification, *J. Logic Programming* 1(1):35–50.

26. Dwork, C., Kanellakis, P. C., and Stockmeyer, L. J. [1986] Parallel Algorithms for Term Matching, *Proceedings of the 8th International Conference on Automated Deduction*, Springer Verlag LNCS, 416–430.

27. Emden, M. H. van and Kowalski, R. A. [1976] The Semantics of Predicate Logic as a Programming Language, *JACM* 23(4):733–742.

28. Fagin, R. [1975] Monadic Generalized Spectra, *Zeitschr. f. math. logik 21*, 89–96.

29. Fagin, R. [1974] Generalized First-Order Spectra and Polynomial-Time Recognizable Sets, *SIAM-AMS Proc.* 7(1):43–73.

30. Fortune, S. and Wyllie, J. [1978] Parallelism in Random Access Machines, *Proceedings of the 10th STOC*, ACM, 114–118.

31. Gaifman, H., Mairson, H., Sagiv, Y., and Vardi, M. [1987] Undecidable Optimization Problems for Database Logic Programs, *Proceedings of the 2nd LICS*, IEEE.

32. Gaifman, H. and Vardi, M. Y. [1985] A Simple Proof that Connectivity of Finite Graphs Is Not First-Order Definable, *Bulletin of the EATCS* **26**, 44–45.

33. Gallaire, H., Minker, C., and Nicolas, J.-M. [1984] Logic and Databases: A Deductive Approach, *Computing Surveys* **16**, 153–185.

34. Goldschlager, L. M. [1977] The Monotone and Planar Circuit Value Problems are Logspace-Complete for P, *SIGACT News* **9**(2):25–29.

35. Gurevich, Y. [1983] Algebra of Feasible Functions, *Proceedings of the 24th FOCS*, IEEE, 210–214.

36. Gurevich, Y. and Shelah S. [1985] Fixed-Point Extensions of First-Order Logic, *Proceedings of the 26th FOCS*, IEEE, 346–353.

37. Harel, D. and Kozen, D. C. [1984] A Programming Language for the Inductive Sets, and Applications, *Information and Control* **63**, 118–139.

38. Henschen, L. J. and Naqvi, S. A. [1984] On Compiling Queries in Recursive First-Order Databases, *JACM* 31(1):47–85.

39. Hopcroft, J. E. and Ullman, J. D. [1979] *Introduction to Automata Theory, Languages, and Computation*, Addison-Wesley, Reading, MA.

40. Huet, G. and Oppen, D. [1980] Equations and Rewrite Rules: A Survey, in *Formal Languages: Perspectives and Open Problems* (R. Book, Ed.), Academic Press, 349–403.

41. Immerman, N. [1981] Number of Quantifiers Is Better than Number of Tape Cells, *JCSS* **22**(3):65–72.

42. Immerman, N. [1982] Relational Queries Computable in Polynomial Time, *Proceedings of the 14th STOC*, ACM, 147–152.

43. Immerman, N. [1983] Languages which Capture Complexity Classes, *Proceedings of the 15th STOC*, ACM, 347–354.

44. Ioannidis, Y. E. [1985] A Time Bound on the Materialization of Some Recursively Defined Views, *Proceedings of the 85 VLDB*, Stockholm.

45. Ioannidis, Y. E. [1986] On the Computation of the Transitive Closure of Relational Operators, *Proceedings of the 86 VLDB*, Tokyo.

46. Jones, N. D. and Laaser, W. T. [1977] Complete Problems for Deterministic Polynomial Time, *TCS* **3**(2):105–117.

47. Kanellakis, P. C. and Papadimitriou, C. H. [1986] Notes on Monadic Sirups—unpublished.

48. Karp, R. M., Upfal, E., and Wigderson, A. Constructing a Perfect Matching Is in Random NC, *Proceedings of the 17th STOC*, ACM, 22–32.

49. Knuth, D. E. and Bendix, P. B. [1970] Simple Word Problems in Universal Algebras, in *Computational Problems in Abstract Algebra*, (J. Leech, Ed.), Pergamon, Oxford, 263–297.

50. Kowalski, R. A. [1974] Predicate Logic as a Programming Language, *Proceedings IFIP 74*, Amsterdam, 569–574.

51. Kowalski, R. A. [1979] *Logic for Problem-Solving*, North Holland.

52. Kozen, D. [1977] Complexity of Finitely Presented Algebras, *Proceedings of the 9th STOC*, ACM, 164–177.

53. Maluszynski, J. and Komorowski, H. J. [1985] Unification-free Execution of Horn-clause Programs, *Proceedings of the 2nd Logic Programming Symposium*, IEEE.

54. Martelli, A. and Montanari, U. [1982] An Efficient Unification Algorithm, *ACM Trans. on Programming Languages and Systems* **4**(2):258–282.

55. Miller, G. L. and Reif, J. H. [1985] Parallel Tree Contraction and Its Applications, *Proceedings of the 26th FOCS*, IEEE, 478–489.

56. Minker, J. and Nicolas, J. M. [1982] On Recursive Axioms in Relational Databases, *Information Systems* **8**, 1–13.

57. Moschovakis, Y. N. [1974] *Elementary Induction on Abstract Structures*, North Holland.

58. Naughton, J. [1986] Data Independent Recursion in Deductive Databases, *Proceedings of the 5th PODS*, ACM, 267–279.

59. Naughton, J. and Sagiv, Y. [1987] A Decidable Class of Bounded Recursions, *Proceedings of the 6th PODS*, ACM, 227–237.

60. Papadimitriou, C. H. [1985] A Note on the Expressive Power of PROLOG, *Bulletin of the EATCS* **26**, 21–23.

61. Paterson, M. S. and Wegman, M. N. [1978] Linear Unification, *JCSS* **16**, 158–167.

62. Pippenger, N. [1979] On Simultaneous Resource Bounds, *Proceedings of the 20th FOCS*, IEEE, 307–331.

63. Rabin, M. O. [1980] Probabilistic Algorithm for Testing Primality, *J. Number Theory* **12**, 128–138.

64. Ramesh, R., Verma, R. M., Krishnaprasad, T., and Ramakrishnan, I. V. [1986] Term Matching on Parallel Computers, Tech Rep. 86/20, SUNY Stony Brook, NY.

65. Reif, J. [1985] Optimal Parallel Algorithms for Integer Sorting and Graph Connectivity, *Proceedings of the 26th FOCS*, IEEE, 496–503.

66. Robinson J. A. [1985] A Machine Oriented Logic Based on the Resolution Principle, *JACM* **12**, 23–41.

67. Roussel, P. [1975] PROLOG: Manuel de Reference et d' Utilisation, Groupe de IA, UER Luminy, Univ. d' Aix-Marseille, France.

68. Ruzzo, W. L. [1980] Tree-size Bounded Alternation, *JCSS* **21**(2):218–235.

69. Ruzzo, W. L. [1981] On Uniform Circuit Complexity, *JCSS* **22**(3):365–383.

70. Sacca. D. and Zaniolo C. [1986] On the Implementation of a Simple Class of Logic Queries for Databases, *Proceedings of the 5th PODS*, ACM, 16–23.

71. Sagiv, Y. [1985] On Computing Restricted Projections of Representative Instances, *Proceedings of the 4th PODS*, ACM, 171–180.

72. Sagiv, Y. [1987] Optimizing Datalog Programs, *Proceedings of the 6th PODS*, ACM, 349–362; also in *Foundations of Deductive Databases and Logic Programming* (J. Minker, Ed.), Morgan Kaufmann, Los Altos, CA, 659–698.

73. Sazonov, V. [1980] Polynomial Computability and Recursivity in Finite Domains, *Electronische Informationsverarbeitung and Kybernetik* **16**, 319–323.

74. Schwartz, J. T. [1980] Fast Probabilistic Algorithms for the Verification of Polynomial Identities, *JACM* **27**(4):701–717.

75. Shapiro, E. Y. [1983] A Subset of Concurrent PROLOG and its Interpreter, No. 3, ICOT, Tokyo.

76. Shapiro, E. Y. [1984] Alternation and the Computational Complexity of Logic Progams, *J. of Logic Programming* **1**(1):19–35.

77. Shepherdson, J. [1988] Negation in Logic Programming, in *Foundations of Deductive Databases and Logic Programming* (J. Minker, Ed.) Morgan Kaufmann Publishers, Los Altos, CA, 19–88.

78. Shmueli, O. [1987] Decidability and Expressiveness Aspects of Logic Queries, *Proceedings of the 6th PODS*, ACM, 237–249.

79. Tarjan, R. E. and Vishkin, U. [1985] An Efficient Parallel Biconnectivity Algorithm, *SIAM J. of Computing* **14**(4):862–874.

80. Trum, P., and Winterstein, G. [1987] Description, Implementation and Practical Comparison of Unification Algorithms, *Fachbereit Informatik*, U. Kaiserslautern.

81. Ullman, J. D. [1978, 1983] *Principles of Database Systems*, Computer Science Press, Rockville, MD.

82. Ullman, J. D. [1985] Implementation of Logical Query Languages for Databases, *ACM Trans. on Database Systems* **10**, 289–321.

83. Ullman, J. D. and Van Gelder, A. [1986] Parallel Complexity of Logical Query Programs, *Proceedings of the 27th FOCS*, 438–454.

84. Valduriez, P. and Boral, H. [1986] Evaluation of Recursive Queries Using Join Indices, *Proceedings of the 1st International Conference on Expert Database Systems*, Charleston, SC.

85. Valiant, L. G., Skyum, S., Berkowitz, S., and Rackoff, C. [1983] Fast Parallel Computation on Polynomials Using Few Processors, *SIAM J. of Computing* **12**(4):641–644.

86. Vardi, M. Y. [1982] Complexity of Relational Query Languages, *Proceedings of the 14th STOC*, ACM, 137–145.

87. Vardi, M. Y. [1985] Personal Communication.

88. Verma, R. M., Krishnaprasad, T., and Ramakrishnan, I. V. [1986] An Efficient Parallel Algorithm for Term Matching, Tech. Rep. 86/12, SUNY Stony Brook, NY.

89. Vishkin, U. [1984] Randomized Speed-ups in Parallel Computation, *Proceedings of the 16th STOC*, ACM, 230–239.

90. Vitter, J. S. and Simons, R. [1986] New Classes for Parallel Complexity: A Study of Unification and Other Complete Problems for P, *IEEE Trans. on Computers* C-**35** (5):406–418.

91. Yannakakis, M. [1986] Personal Communication.

92. Yasuura, H. [1983] On the Parallel Computational Complexity of Unification, ER 83-01, Yajima Lab.

15

Unification Revisited

J-L. Lassez
M.J. Maher
IBM Thomas J. Watson Research Center,
Yorktown Heights, NY

K. Marriott
Department of Computer Science,
University of Melbourne,
Parkville,
Australia

Abstract

In the literature, unification is often treated as a simple and straightforward matter, even though it is recognized as a deep and fundamental concept. However when a thorough presentation is attempted, it is realized then that the matter is fairly subtle and treacherous. For instance, the notion of most general unifier and its property of being unique up to renaming are open to different interpretations. In fact, there are several approaches to unification based on different mathematical concepts that are not equivalent. We present the alternatives and clarify their relationships. In the process, new results are obtained related to the notions of equation solving, most specific generalization, and constraint solving. This leads to a comprehensive presentation of an elementary theory of unification.

Introduction

Herbrand [1930] gave an algorithm to solve equations over what is now known as the Herbrand universe. This algorithm may be considered as the first unification algorithm. It is, however, with Robinson's seminal paper (Robinson [1965]) that a systematic treatment of unification was provided and its full significance recognized. Robinson provided an algorithm to compute a most general unifier (mgu) of two terms from which all unifiers of the terms can be derived. Because of its practical importance, a number of efficient algorithms have been proposed. Two classical algorithms are given in Paterson and Wegman [1978] and in Martelli and Montanari [1982].

The dual concept of anti-unification or most specific generalization was introduced independently and concurrently by Plotkin [1970] and by Reynolds [1970]. It was proposed as a formal basis for inductive inference (Plotkin [1971]) and has led to work on the automatic generation of production rules from examples (Vere [1975, 1977]). This concept is closely related also to Robinson's notion of "lifting."

The development of Prolog and other logic programming languages has led to new avenues of research into unification. For instance, Colmerauer [1984], following Herbrand, views unification as a process of rewriting a set of equations into a reduced form. He extends the treatment to include inequations and extends the domain to infinite trees. (This paper will not be concerned with the latter extension.)

Other important and relevant works are Manna and Waldinger's exposition of unification (Manna and Waldinger [1981], a more complete treatment will appear in their forthcoming book), Huet's presentation of anti-unification and his generalization to infinite trees (Huet [1976]), and Eder's work on substitutions and unifiers (Eder [1985]).

Our aim is to present a self-contained and comprehensive treatment of elementary unification, taking into account the previously cited works, and establish the relationships between the various points of view. This treatment forms a basis for lecture notes on unification. Much care has been given to provide natural and straightforward proofs whenever possible. This process led us to understand better the essence of even the most basic results and to make a number of interesting remarks and novel extensions.

There is some confusion in the literature concerning the definition of most general unifier and the property of being unique up to renaming. For instance, the definitions of most general unifier (mgu) to be found in Robinson [1965], Robinson [1979], Chang and Lee [1973], and Sterling and Shapiro [1986] are not equivalent. We will informally clarify these differences in the following section. The formal treatment will be given in later sections.

A brief second section contains preliminary definitions. In "Solving Equations," we give an algorithm to transform a solvable set of equations into a solved form. This algorithm is based upon Herbrand's original "unification" algorithm. We introduce the notions of dimension and rank of a set of equations. Exploiting further the analogy with linear algebra, we derive a number of elementary but fundamental results.

In "Most General Unifiers," we establish the relationships between mgus, idempotent mgus, and reduced sets of equations, formally clarifying the differences between the definitions of Herbrand, Robinson, and Chang and Lee.

In "Anti-unification and Most General Solutions," we show the existence of a most general solution (mgs) to a set of equations by using anti-unification. We also investigate the relationship between mgs and equations in solved form. As an application of the anti-unification algorithm, we give an algorithm to compute the most specific generalization of a collection of sets of equations.

In the last section, we consider systems consisting of a set of equations and a set of inequations. We address the problem of solvability of such systems and the problem of the finite representation of the set of solutions by substitutions. This section is not self contained. It makes use of and improves upon results of Lassez and Marriott [1986], which are too involved to be fully reproduced here. The results of this section are relevant to recent developments on negation in logic programs (Kunen [1987a], Naish [1986], and Sato [1986]), hierarchical databases (Kunen [1987b]), constraints logic programming (Jaffar and Lassez [1987] and Maher [1988]), and term rewriting systems (Kirchner and Lescanne [1987]).

On the Definitions of mgus

"All mgus are equal, but some mgus are more equal than others."

There is undoubtedly some confusion over what precisely is a most general unifier and what it means for it to be unique. The first definition, due to Robinson [1965], states that it is the substitution produced by the unification algorithm to be found in the same paper. Another definition given later by Robinson in his book Robinson [1979] is: μ is the most general unifier iff for every unifier θ, $\theta = \mu \circ \theta$. A third definition, to be found in Chang and Lee [1973], Lloyd [1984], and adopted in many other treatments as the "official" one, is: μ is the most general unifier iff for every unifier θ there is a substitution β such that $\theta = \mu \circ \beta$ A fourth more recent definition is to be found in the text Sterling and Shapiro [1986] which defines the most general unifier via a partial order on terms as the substitution that maps two terms to their most general common instance.

In general, in the literature it is assumed, and sometimes proved in some way, that the terminology "the" most general unifier is justified by the fact that all most general unifiers of a collection of terms are equal up to the "renaming" of variables. The confusion arises because all these definitions in fact define *different* objects, and the meaning of "renaming" is often assumed to be simpler than its formal definition implies. It is not even quite clear what the formal definition is. It is our experience that those who do not realize these points are often satisfied with a casual understanding, leading to formally wrong statements, incorrect proofs, or, when they suspect that there is a flaw somewhere in establishing a "simple" result, "the proof is left as an exercise for the reader."

Let us try to find (or guess) why the previously mentioned authors may have chosen their various definitions. We first make the following remark: A most general unifier is a substitution, and a substitution is a destructive assignment, akin to the $X = X + 1$ in FORTRAN. It is well known that the destructive assignment is a complex object to reason about, as occurrences of the same variable have different meanings. (Reading Manna and Waldinger [1980] should remove any doubts.) There is, however, a class of substitutions, the *idempotent* substitutions, where all occurrences of a variable in a substitution have the same meaning. The semantics of such substitutions is in fact the semantics of mathematical equality, as we will show later.

Now very clearly Robinson in Robinson [1965] wants to distinguish among all unifiers those provided by his algorithm. These unifiers possess the property of being more general than any other unifier. Later Robinson [1979] provided a declarative definition as a counterpart to his initial operational one. This new definition happens to restrict the class of most general unifiers to idempotent unifiers. It is appropriate since all the mgus produced by his algorithm and its variants are idempotent. They are also very similar, "isomorphic" in a sense we will make precise, justifying the terminology "the" most general unifier.

Chang and Lee and others following them are interested in the algebra of unifiers and the partial order induced by the operation of composition. In that context, they have a definition of most general unifier that is strictly more general than Robinson's as it does not require idempotence. Consequently, the proofs are more painful and tricky because we are now dealing with a destructive assignment. They are nevertheless justified as this definition is an appropriate one in the general study of unifiers. The restriction to idempotent unifiers would not be satisfactory as the composition of idempotent unifiers is not necessarily idempotent. However, the notion of similarity of all most general unifiers is much weaker: Two most general unifiers may differ arbitrarily in size and in the number of variables they instantiate.

Sterling and Shapiro give a definition that would come naturally to people familiar with Plotkin's notion of most specific generalization (Plotkin [1970]) or Reynolds' notion of anti-unification (Reynolds [1970]). This definition is not, however, equivalent to any of the preceding ones. The reason is that a unifier that maps two terms into their most general common instance in the algebra of terms is not necessarily most general in the algebra of unifiers. In fact, their definition is more closely related to the definition of most general solution that we will introduce later. Huet and Oppen [1980] consider unification in the more general context of equational theories. For the theory of the Herbrand universe their definition of mgu is very similar to the most general solution.

To each of these different definitions of mgu corresponds a different notion of variable renaming.

Herbrand [1930] initially provided a "unification" algorithm as an equation solving process. However he did not introduce the notion of most general unifier or even unifier and, consequently, did not study their properties, as Robinson did in his more systematic treatment. The relationship between equations in solved form and most general unifiers has to be clarified.

Preliminary Definitions

We assume we have disjoint sets of *variables* V and *function symbols* Σ. not containing the symbol "=". Each function symbol has an associated *arity*. Function symbols with arity 0 are called *constant symbols*. A *term* is a variable, a constant or of the form $f(t_1,\ldots,t_n)$ where f is a function symbol with arity n and $t_1,\ldots,t_n$ are terms. We use $\equiv$ to denote syntactic identity. A term is *ground* if it contains no variable symbols. The set of all ground terms is called the *Herbrand universe*. If the Herbrand universe contains none or only one element, it is *trivial*, otherwise it is *non-trivial*. This distinction is made because some results do not hold in the trivial case. An *equation* is of the form $s = t$ where s and t are terms. Throughout this paper we consider only finite sets of equations.

> $depth(x) = 1$. when x is a variable or a constant.
> $depth(f(t_1,\ldots,t_n)) = 1 + \max depth(t_i)$ when f is a n-ary function symbol.
> $size(t) =$ number of symbol occurrences in t $-$ number of variables appearing in t.
> *size* has the following properties:

> $size(t) \geq 0$

> $size(t\ \alpha) \geq size(t)$

$|X|$ denotes the cardinality of the set X.

The set of variables occurring in any syntactic object o is denoted by *vars(o)*. For example $vars(\{x \leftarrow f(a,y), y \leftarrow z\}) = \{x,y,z\}$.

A *substitution*, $\theta = \{v_1 \leftarrow t_1, v_2 \leftarrow t_2, \ldots, v_n \leftarrow t_n\}$ where $v_i \neq t_i$, assigns terms to variables. It is *applied* to a term, t, by simultaneously replacing all occurrences of each v_i in t by t_i. The term obtained, $t\theta$, is called an *instance* of t. It is easily verified that $\alpha = \beta$ iff $\forall t\ t\alpha \equiv t\beta$ iff $\forall v \in V\ v\alpha \equiv v\beta$. A substitution can be applied to other syntactic objects to form an instance in a similar way. The set of variables $\{v_1,\ldots v_n\}$ is denoted by *domain(θ)*, and *range(θ)* is the set of variables appearing in $t_1,\ldots,t_n$. An element $v_i \leftarrow t_i$ of a substitution is called a *binding*.

Substitution θ is a *grounding substitution* if its right hand side (rhs) consists of ground terms. It is a *grounding substitution for W* if its domain is W. For example, $\{x \leftarrow a, y \leftarrow f(a)\}$ is a grounding substitution for $\{x,y\}$.

A *solution*, θ, of equation set $E = \{s_1 = t_1,\ldots,s_n = t_n\}$ is a grounding substitution for V such that $s_1\theta \equiv t_1\theta,\ldots,s_n\theta \equiv t_n\theta$. For example, $\{x \leftarrow g(a), y \leftarrow g(a), z \leftarrow g(g(a))\}$ is a solution of $\{f(x, z) = f(y, g(y))\}$. The (possibly empty) set of solutions of equation set E is denoted by $soln(E)$. It is immediate that $soln(E_1 \cup E_2) = soln(E_1) \cap soln(E_2)$. An equation set E is *solvable* if it has a solution. An equation set E is *trivial* if every grounding substitution for V is a solution. One verifies easily that the empty equation set is trivial, as well as equation sets of the form $\{t_1 = t_1,\ldots,t_n = t_n\}$.

Equation sets E and E' are *equivalent*, written $E \approx E'$ if $soln(E) = soln(E')$. Clearly two sets which differ only by equations of the type $x = x$ are equivalent.

A *partial order* is a reflexive, transitive, anti-symmetric relation. A *partially ordered set* (or *poset*) $(S, \leq)$ is a set S with a partial order $\leq$. A *least upper bound* (*lub*) of a subset S' of a poset S is an element t of S such that $s \leq t \ \forall \ s \in S'$ and if $\forall \ s \in S' \ s \leq x$ then $t \leq x$. Dually a *greatest lower bound* (*glb*) can be defined. A *lattice* is a poset where every finite subset has a least upper bound and a greatest lower bound. A *complete lattice* is a poset where every subset (finite or infinite) has a least upper bound and a greatest lower bound. Equivalently, a poset is a complete lattice if every subset has a least upper bound and the poset has a least element.

Solving Equations

Throughout this section we assume that the Herbrand universe is non-trivial and the set of variables V is finite. An equation set (possibly empty) is *solved* if it has the form $\{v_1 = t_1,\ldots,v_n = t_n\}$ and the v_i's are distinct variables which do not occur in the right hand side of any equation. The variables $v_1,\ldots,v_n$ are said to be *eliminable*. The set $\{v_1,\ldots,v_n\}$ is denoted by $elim(E)$. The remaining variables of V are called *parameters* and the set of parameters is denoted by $param(E)$.

For example, if $V = \{w,x,y,z\}$, then $\{x = f(y), z = f(g(y))\}$ is in solved form with parameters w and y and eliminable variables x and z.

The justification for calling this form solved form comes from the easily verified fact that any assignment of ground terms to the parameters determines a *unique* solution, and conversely every solution can be obtained that way.

Now we present an algorithm based upon Herbrand's original unification algorithm (Herbrand [1930], p.124, Martelli and Montanari [1982]) which transforms any solvable equation set into an equivalent solved form equation set. For any unsolvable equation set, the algorithm halts with failure.

Solved Form Algorithm

Non-deterministically choose an equation from the equation set to which a numbered step applies. The action taken by the algorithm is determined by the form of the equation:

1. $f(t_1,\ldots,t_n) = f(s_1,\ldots,s_n)$
   replace by the equations $t_1 = s_1,\ldots,t_n = s_n$

2. $f(t_1,\ldots,t_n) = g(s_1,\ldots,s_m)$ *where* $f \not\equiv g$
   halt with failure

3. $x = x$ *delete the equation*

4. $t = x$ *where t is not a variable*
   replace by the equation $x = t$

5. $x = t$ *where* $t \not\equiv x$ *and x has another occurrence in the set of equations*
   if x appears in t then halt with failure
   otherwise replace x by t in every other equation ■

The algorithm terminates when no step can be applied or when failure has been returned.

As an example of this algorithm's operation consider the solvable equation set $\{g(x) = g(g(z)), f(a, z) = f(a, y)\}$. Choosing the first equation, step (1) applies and the new equation set is $\{x = g(z), f(a, z) = f(a, y)\}$. The second equation must be chosen now, since no step applies to the first equation, and by (1) we obtain $\{x = g(z), a = a, z = y\}$. (5) can be applied to the third equation to give $\{x = g(y), a = a, z = y\}$ and then the application of (1) to the second equation gives $\{x = g(y), z = y\}$. No step can be applied to this equation set and so the algorithm halts.

The following theorem is analogous to Robinson's unification theorem. It establishes the correctness of the solved form algorithm.

THEOREM 1
The solved form algorithm applied to a set of equations E will return an equivalent set of equations E' in solved form if and only if E is solvable. It will return failure otherwise.

Proof: Termination. Applications of steps (1) and (3) strictly diminish the total number of occurrences of variables and function symbols on the left hand sides of equations. Step (4) can be applied only a finite number of times before applying another step, and its application does not increase this total number.

After a finite number of applications of steps (1), (3), and (4), either the algorithm terminates or there is an application of step (5).

The application of step (5) leads to failure and termination or eliminates all occurrences of a variable on the right hand side of equations. Consequently, for a given variable, step (5) can be performed only once. As there are only a finite number of variables in E, step (5) can be performed only a finite number of times. Therefore the algorithm terminates for any input.

Correctness. Assume first that the algorithm has not failed and has returned a set E' of equations. It is easy to see that every step in the algorithm replaces a set of equations by a new set that has the same solutions as the preceding. This is because we are dealing with syntactic identity (so, for instance, $f(u) = f(v)$ has the same solutions as $u = v$) and mathematical equality (so when $x = t$ we can replace x by t in other equations without affecting the set of solutions). Consequently E' is equivalent to E.

All the left hand sides of equations in E' are variables since otherwise steps (1), (2), or (4) could be further applied. All these variables are different and do not appear on the right hand side of an equation, otherwise step (5) could be further applied. So E' is in solved form. As E is equivalent to E', E is solvable.

Assume now that the algorithm terminates with failure. The set of equations at the failure step is equivalent to E, since all previous steps have preserved equivalence. If failure occurred by application of step (2), the set is not solvable as no substitution to the variables can make terms with distinct outermost function symbols identical. If failure occurred by application of step (5), the set is not solvable as $x = t$ is not solvable. This is because any ground substitution to x will lead to a right hand side strictly larger than the left hand side, so syntactic identity is not possible. Therefore, when the algorithm returns failure, E is not solvable.

Since the algorithm either fails or returns E' in solved form equivalent to E, the proof is completed. ∎

We now establish a preliminary result that will enable us to exploit an analogy with equation solving in other algebras.

PROPOSITION 1
Two equivalent sets of equations E_1 and E_2 in solved form have the same number of parameters and the same number of eliminable variables.

Proof: It is sufficient to prove that E_1 and E_2 have the same number of eliminable variables as, by definition, they will then have the same number of parameters. We will establish a bijection between the two sets of eliminable variables.

If x belongs to both sets then x is assigned itself.

Let x be an eliminable variable of E_1 and a parameter of E_2. As x is an eliminable variable, there is an equation $x = t$ in E_1. As x is a parameter, t must be a variable y, since we must be able to assign any ground term to a parameter. Now y cannot be a parameter of E_2 since then E_2 would have two parameters, x and y, bound by $x = y$. This is not possible since we must be able to assign them distinct ground terms. So y is an eliminable variable of E_2. We assign y to x. The mapping so constructed is well-defined: A single value is assigned to every eliminable variable of E_1. This is because E_1 is in solved form and each eliminable variable appears only once. Since $y \notin elim(E_1)$, elements of $elim(E_1) - elim(E_2)$ are mapped to elements of $elim(E_2) - elim(E_1)$.

The mapping is one-to-one. It suffices to consider the restriction of the mapping to $elim(E_1) - elim(E_2)$. If different variables x and z were both assigned y we would have both $x = y$ and $z = y$ in E_1. Consequently x and z would be bound to take the same values. As both are parameters of E_2, this is impossible.

By symmetry there is a one-to-one mapping from $elim(E_2)$ into $elim(E_1)$. So there is a bijection between the sets of eliminable variables of E_1 and E_2; they have the same cardinality. ∎

This relationship between equivalent sets of equations in solved form will be strengthened in Theorem 4. The *rank* of a solvable set of equations E, $rank(E)$ is the number of equations in one of its solved forms. The *dimension* of the set of solutions of a solvable equation set E is the number of parameters in one of the solved forms of E. We will also define the dimension of a set of equations E, $dim(E)$, to be the dimension of its set of solutions. This slight abuse of terminology is justified as we can view E as a representation of its set of solutions. Clearly $rank(E) + dim(E) = |V|$.

We have the following consequences of the previous proposition.

PROPOSITION 2
The notions of rank of a set of equations and dimension of its set of solutions are well defined. ∎

PROPOSITION 3
All equivalent sets of equations have the same rank and dimension. ∎

PROPOSITION 4
Let E_1 and E_2 be two solvable sets of equations. If $soln(E_1) \supset soln(E_2)$ then $rank(E_1) < rank(E_2)$ and $dim(E_1) > dim(E_2)$. ∎

Proof: We can assume that E_1 and E_2 are both in solved form. Now $soln(E_1 \cup E_2) = soln(E_1) \cap soln(E_2) = soln(E_2)$. So $rank(E_1 \cup E_2) = rank(E_2)$. We apply the Solved Form Algorithm to the set $E_1 \cup E_2$ in the following way. For every equation $x = t$ in E_1 we replace x by t in E_2 (that is we apply step (5)) and proceed toward a solved form. If there is an equation $y = s$ in the solved form such that y is not an eliminable variable for E_1, then $rank(E_1 \cup E_2) = rank(E_2) > rank(E_1)$. If there is no such equation in the solved form, then the solved form is equal to E_1, so E_1 and E_2 have the same solutions, which contradicts the initial assumption. ∎

For an equation set E that is not in solved form, a set W is a *set of eliminable variables of E* if it is the set of eliminable variables of some equivalent solved form equation set. From the proof of the above proposition we can also obtain the following result, which is an instance of a result of Colmerauer [1984].

COROLLARY 1
Let E_1 and E_2 be solvable equation sets. If $soln(E_1) \supset soln(E_2)$ and W_1 is any eliminable variable set of E_1 then there is a set W_2 of eliminable variables of E_2 such that $W_1 \subset W_2$. ∎

COROLLARY 2
If $soln(E_1) \subseteq soln(E_2)$ and $dim(E_1) = dim\ (E_2)$ then $E_1 \approx E_2$. ∎

The following result and its corollary establish a relationship between the number of equations in a set, its rank, and the presence of redundant equations.

PROPOSITION 5
Let E be a solvable set of equations. Then E contains an equivalent subset E' such that $|E'| \leq rank(E)$.

Proof: Let $E = \{e_1, e_2, ..., e_n\}$ and for each i $1 \leq i \leq n$ let W_i be a set of eliminable variables of $\{e_1, e_2, ..., e_i\}$ chosen so that $W_0 = \emptyset \subseteq W_1 \subseteq W_2 \subseteq ... \subseteq W_n$. This is possible by Corollary 1. Let $E' = \{e_i : W_{i-1} \subset W_i\}$. Clearly $|E'| \leq |W_n| = rank(E)$. For every j, $soln(\{e_1, e_2, ..., e_{j-1}\}) \supseteq soln(\{e_1, e_2, ..., e_j\})$. Thus, by the contrapositive of Corollary 1, if $W_{j-1} = W_j$ then $\{e_1, e_2, ..., e_{j-1}\} \approx \{e_1, e_2, ..., e_j\}$. Consequently adding the remaining equations to E' to form E does not change the set of solutions and so $E' \approx E$. ∎

A subset E' of a set of equations E is *redundant* if $soln(E) = soln(E - E')$.

COROLLARY 3
If E is a solvable equation set then

1. If $|E| > rank(E)$ then E contains redundant equations.

2. If E contains no redundant equations and if $|E| = |V|$ then E has a unique solution. ∎

The following theorem further illustrates the usefulness of the notion of dimension. An interesting alternative view of this theorem will be found at the end of the section on anti-unification and most general solutions.

THEOREM 2
Suppose the Herbrand universe is infinite. Let E be a set of equations of dimension d and E_1, E_2 ,...,E_n be sets of equations of dimension strictly less than d. Then there is a solution of E which is not a solution of any E_i.

Proof: We can assume, without loss of generality, that E and the E_i are in solved form. Note that, since E has strictly greater dimension (and so strictly lesser rank) than the E_i, each E_i has an eliminable variable y_i which is a parameter of E, and which appears as $y_i = s_i$ in E_i. There are two cases to consider.

If there are no function symbols of arity 1 or greater then, as the Herbrand universe is infinite, there must be an infinite number of constant symbols. Consider the solution of E determined by assigning to the parameters x_1, x_2,...,x_k the distinct constant symbols a_1, a_2,...,a_k that do not appear in any E_i. Under this substitution, for each i, y_i and s_i receive different values. Thus this substitution is not a solution of any E_i.

Otherwise there is at least one function symbol and one constant. Let m be the maximum depth of any term in any E_i. Consider the solution of E determined by assigning to the parameters x_1, x_2,...,x_k terms of depth respectively $m, 2 \times m,...,k \times m$. In this substitution, for each i, the value assigned to y_i has depth $j \times m$ for some j and the value of s_i has depth $l + (p \times m)$ where $0 \leq l < m$ and $p \neq j$. Consequently this substitution is not a solution for any E_i. ∎

Theorem 2 does not hold if the Herbrand universe is finite. For example, if the Herbrand universe consists of constant symbols a and b, $E = \{x = y\}$, $E_1 = \{x = a, y = a\}$, and $E_2 = \{x = b, y = b\}$, then clearly every solution of E is either a solution of E_1 or E_2. However, the dimension of E is strictly greater than the dimensions of E_1 and E_2.

Disjunction of equation sets is defined by $soln(E_1 \vee ... \vee E_n) = soln(E_1) \cup ... \cup soln(E_n)$. An equation set disjunction E_1 is a *generalization* of equation set disjunction E_2, written $E_2 \leq E_1$, if $soln(E_2) \subseteq soln(E_1)$. A simple consequence of Theorem 2 is

THEOREM 3 (STRONG COMPACTNESS)
Let E and E_1,...,E_n be equation sets.

1.   If $E \approx E_1 \vee ... \vee E_n$ then, for some E_j, $E \approx E_j$.

2.   If $E \leq E_1 \vee ... \vee E_n$ then, for some E_j, $E \leq E_j$.

Proof: If, for every i, $soln(E_i) \subset soln(E)$ then $dim(E_i) < dim(E)$ for every i by proposition 3.5. But Theorem 2 gives a contradiction to the hypothesis. Thus, for some j, $E \approx E_j$.

The second part follows from the first by noting that the hypothesis implies that $E \approx (E_1 \cup E) \vee \ldots \vee (E_n \cup E)$. ∎

This result will have important corollaries in the section on systems of equations and inequations.

We will now make more precise the relationships between the syntactic structures of equivalent sets of equations in solved form. We first give a preliminary result.

LEMMA 1

Let E_1 and E_2 be two equivalent sets of equations in solved form. If E_1 and E_2 have the same set of parameters then E_1 and E_2 are identical.

Proof: As E_1 and E_2 have the same set of parameters, they have the same set of eliminable variables. Thus we can take $E_1 = \{x_1 = t_1, \ldots, x_n = t_n\}$ and $E_2 = \{x_1 = s_1, \ldots, x_n = s_n\}$. If $t_i \neq s_i$ for some i then there is a place where they differ. If the place where they differ corresponds to two occurrences of different function symbols, or an occurrence of a function symbol and a variable, E_1 and E_2 cannot have the same solutions. Suppose now that the place where they differ corresponds to two occurrences of different parameters x and y. Consider an assignment of ground terms to all parameters such that x and y are assigned different terms. This assignment should determine a unique solution. But x_i is assigned two different values. So t_i must be syntactically identical to s_i for every i. ∎

The following theorem makes the relationship explicit in the general case. We say that a solved form equation set E_1 is *isomorphic* to E_2 if there is a subset $\{x_1 = y_1, \ldots, x_k = y_k\}$ of E_1 where the y_i's are distinct variables such that $E_2 = E_1 \{x_1 \leftarrow y_1, \ldots, x_k \leftarrow y_k, y_1 \leftarrow x_1, \ldots, y_k \leftarrow x_k\}$. Clearly if E_1 is isomorphic to E_2 then E_2 is also in solved form and, by considering the solutions of E_1 and E_2, it is apparent that E_1 and E_2 are equivalent. Furthermore, if E_1 is isomorphic to E_2 then E_2 is isomorphic to E_1. Thus although the definition of isomorphism is not symmetric, the notion is symmetric.

As an example of isomorphism, consider $E_1 = \{w = f(v), x = u, y = u, z = v\}$. If we take the subset $\{y = u, z = v\}$ as the subset in the definition, we find that E_1 is isomorphic to $E_2 = \{w = f(z), x = y, u = y, v = z\}$. E_1 is isomorphic to $E_3 = \{w = f(v), u = x, y = x, z = v\}$ by taking the subset $\{x = u\}$.

THEOREM 4

Let E_1 be a set of equations in solved form. Then E_2 is an equivalent set of equations in solved form iff E_1 is isomorphic to E_2.

Proof We need only prove the "only if" direction. Let $x_1, x_2,...,x_k$ be the set of eliminable variables of E_1 which are parameters of E_2. From the proof of Proposition 1 we know that if $x_1 = y_1$ is an equation of E_1, then $y_1 = z$ is an equation of E_2 for some z. Dually, we know that $z = w$ is an equation of E_1 for some w. We have $x_1 = y_1 = z = w$, x_1 and z are parameters of E_2 and y_1 and w are parameters of E_1. Consequently $x_1 \equiv z$ and $y_1 \equiv w$. So for each equation $x_i = y_i$ in E_1 we have an equation $y_i = x_i$ in E_2. From the remark following the definition of isomorphic: E_1 $\{x_1 \leftarrow y_1,...,x_k \leftarrow y_k, y_1 \leftarrow x_1,...,y_k \leftarrow x_k\}$ is equivalent to E_1 and therefore to E_2. It also has the same set of parameters as E_2. By the previous lemma it is therefore identical to E_2. ∎

COROLLARY 4
If E_1 and E_2 are equivalent sets of equations in solved form then $vars(E_1) = vars(E_2)$. ∎

We conclude this section with an investigation of lattice-theoretic properties of classes of equation sets.

Recall that an equation set E_1 is a *generalization* of equation set E_2 ($E_2 \le E_1$) if $soln(E_2) \subseteq soln(E_1)$. $\le$ forms a partial order on equation sets modulo $\approx$. The poset has a least element, which is the equivalence class of unsolvable equation sets, and a greatest element, which is the equivalence class of trivial equation sets. We now show that this poset forms a complete lattice.

LEMMA 2
Any solvable equation set has a finite number of generalizations, modulo $\approx$.

Proof Let $E_1...E_n...$be the generalizations of E. We can assume that the E_i are in solved form. $soln(E_i) \supseteq soln(E) = soln(E \cup E_i)$. We apply the Solved Form Algorithm to $E \cup E_i$ in the following manner. For every equation $x = t$ in E_i we replace x by t in E (that is, we apply step (5)) and proceed toward a solved form. The solved form will contain the equation $x = t\alpha$ for some α. Thus the size of terms in E_i is bounded by the size of the corresponding terms in the solved form of E and only the function symbols of E can appear in E_i. Also we know that $rank(E_i) \le rank(E)$. It follows that there are only a finite number of generalizations of E in solved form and hence E has a finite, modulo $\approx$, number of generalizations. ∎

Equation set E is a *most specific generalization* (*msg*) of the non-empty, possibly infinite, equation set collection $\{E_1,...,E_n,...\}$ if

1. E is a generalization of each E_i

2. Every generalization of $\{E_1,...,E_n,...\}$ is also a generalization of E.

LEMMA 3

Any nonempty finite or infinite collection of solvable equation sets has only a finite number of generalizations, modulo $\approx$.

Proof: Let the collection be $\{E_1,\ldots, E_n,\ldots\}$. Let $[g_i]$ be the set of distinct generalizations of $\{E_1,\ldots, E_i\}$, modulo $\approx$. Clearly $[g_1] \supseteq [g_2] \supseteq \cdots \supseteq [g_n] \supseteq \ldots$. From the above lemma there are only a finite number of elements in $[g_1]$ and so this lemma follows. ∎

As a consequence of this lemma, the poset of equation sets modulo $\approx$ has no infinite, strictly increasing sequence.

THEOREM 5

Any nonempty, possibly infinite, collection of solvable equation sets has an msg which is unique modulo $\approx$.

Proof: Let $E_1,\ldots,E_n$ be the finite set of distinct, modulo $\approx$, generalizations of this collection. Clearly $E_1 \cup \ldots \cup E_n$ is the desired msg. It follows from the definition of msg that it is unique, modulo $\approx$. ∎

In a following section we will give an algorithm for computing the msg of an equation set collection.

Since every collection of equation sets has a least upper bound (the msg), and since the partial order $\leq$ on equation sets modulo $\approx$ has a least element, it follows that

COROLLARY 5

The equation sets modulo $\approx$ form a complete lattice under the ordering $\leq$. ∎

Most General Unifiers

We establish here the basic properties of mgus. In particular, we will see that the relationship between idempotent mgus is very strong, as it is essentially the relationship between solved forms. We will see also that a non-idempotent mgu is strictly more complex than an idempotent mgu, as its size and number of variables are strictly greater. In the general case, the renaming operation is weaker than in the idempotent case.

We expand now our set of variables V to an infinite set $V' \supseteq V$. The new variables are to be used in substitutions but not in equations. First, some preliminary definitions and lemmas.

Two terms t_1 and t_2 are *unifiable* iff there is a substitution α such that $t_1\alpha \equiv t_2\alpha$. α is a *unifier* for t_1 and t_2. Consequently t_1 and t_2 are unifiable iff the equation $t_1 = t_2$ is solvable.

A *unifier* of equation set $\{s_1 = t_1,\ldots,s_n = t_n\}$ is a substitution θ such that $\{s_1\theta \equiv t_1\theta,\ldots,s_n\theta \equiv t_n\theta\}$.

For example, the substitution $\theta = \{x \leftarrow g(u), y \leftarrow g(u), z \leftarrow g(g(u))\}$ is a unifier of $\{f(x, z) = f(y, g(y))\}$. Clearly every solution of an equation set is a unifier of that equation set.

The (possibly empty) set of unifiers of equation set E is denoted by *unif(E)*. E is said to be *unifiable* if $unif(E) \neq \emptyset$. The empty equation set is unifiable, with all substitutions as unifiers.

The difference between unification and equation solving is that the notion of unifier provides an alternative means of representation for sets of solutions.

The *composition* of substitutions $\theta_1 = \{x_1 \leftarrow t_1,\ldots,x_n \leftarrow t_n\}$ and $\theta_2 = \{y_1 \leftarrow s_1,\ldots,y_m \leftarrow s_m\}$, denoted by $\theta_1 \circ \theta_2$, is the substitution obtained by removing elements of the form $y_k \leftarrow s_k$ where $\exists x_j\ y_k \equiv x_j$ and those of the form $x_i \leftarrow x_i$ from the set $\{x_1 \leftarrow t_1\theta_2,\ldots,x_n \leftarrow t_n\theta_2, y_1 \leftarrow s_1,\ldots,y_m \leftarrow s_m\}$.

For example, $\{x \leftarrow y, y \leftarrow x\}\circ\{y \leftarrow x, x \leftarrow y\}$ is $\{\}$ and $\{x \leftarrow f(z)\}\circ\{z \leftarrow g(a, x), x \leftarrow b\}$ is $\{x \leftarrow f(g(a, x)), z \leftarrow g(a, x)\}$.

Substitution composition has been defined in this manner so that

PROPOSITION 6

For any term t, $t(\theta_1\circ\theta_2) \equiv (t\theta_1)\theta_2$.

Proof: Let $\theta_1 = \{x_1 \leftarrow t_1,\ldots,x_n \leftarrow t_n\}$ and $\theta_2 = \{y_1 \leftarrow s_1,\ldots,y_m \leftarrow s_m\}$. It suffices to show that for any variable, v, $v(\theta_1\circ\theta_2) \equiv (v\theta_1)\theta_2$. There are 3 cases to consider.

1. If $v \in domain(\theta_1)$, say $v \equiv x_i$, then $v(\theta_1\circ\theta_2) \equiv t_i\theta_2 \equiv (v\theta_1)\theta_2$.

2. If $v \notin domain(\theta_2) - domain(\theta_1)$, say $v \equiv y_i$, then $v(\theta_1\circ\theta_2) \equiv s_i \equiv v\theta_2 \equiv (v\theta_1)\theta_2$.

3. Finally, if $v \notin domain(\theta_1) \cup domain(\theta_2)$ then $v(\theta_1\circ\theta_2) \equiv v \equiv (v\theta_1)\theta_2$. ∎

COROLLARY 6

Substitution composition is associative.

Proof: It follows from the above proposition that if θ_1, θ_2, and θ_3 are substitutions, then for all variables x, $x(\theta_1\circ(\theta_2\circ\theta_3)) \equiv (x\theta_1)(\theta_2\circ\theta_3) \equiv ((x\theta_1)\theta_2)\theta_3 \equiv (x(\theta_1\circ\theta_2))\theta_3 \equiv x((\theta_1\circ\theta_2)\circ\theta_3)$. Thus, $\theta_1\circ(\theta_2\circ\theta_3) = (\theta_1\circ\theta_2)\circ\theta_3$. ∎

Consequently, we can denote $\theta_1\circ(\theta_2\circ\theta_3) = (\theta_1\circ\theta_2)\circ\theta_3$ by $\theta_1\circ\theta_2\circ\theta_3$ without ambiguity. These two results also justify the notation. $t\theta_1\theta_2\ldots\theta_n$ for $(\ldots((t\theta_1)\theta_2)\ldots)\theta_n = t(\theta_1\circ\theta_2\circ\ldots\circ\theta_n)$.

A substitution θ is *idempotent* if $\theta = \theta\circ\theta$.

PROPOSITION 7

A substitution θ is idempotent $\longleftrightarrow$ $domain(\theta) \cap range(\theta) = \emptyset$.

Proof:

($\Rightarrow$) (by contradiction)

Let $y \in domain(\theta) \cap range(\theta)$ and $(x - t) \in \theta$ for some term t containing y. Then θ cannot be idempotent as $x\theta \equiv t \not\equiv t\theta \equiv (x\theta)\theta$.

($\Leftarrow$)

It suffices to consider $v \in domain(\theta)$. Now as $vars(v\theta) \cap domain(\theta) = \emptyset$ then $v\theta = (v\theta)\theta$ and so $\theta = \theta \circ \theta$. ∎

We now introduce a partial order on unifiers. α is *more general than* β if E $\gamma \beta = \alpha \circ \gamma$.

A unifier μ is a *most general unifier* (*mgu*) (Chang and Lee [1973]) of equation set E if

$$\phi \in unif(E) \longleftrightarrow \exists \, \alpha \; \phi = \mu \circ \alpha$$

For example, $\{x \leftarrow g(z), y \leftarrow z\}$ and $\{x \leftarrow g(w), y \leftarrow w, z \leftarrow w, w \leftarrow y\}$ are both mgu of

$$g(x) = g(g(z)), f(a, z) = f(a, y)$$

In contrast to systems of equations in solved form, mgus can differ in size, as the example shows, and can be arbitrarily large. The following mgu of the above set of equations demonstrates this fact.

$$\{x \leftarrow g(z), y \leftarrow z, x_1 \leftarrow x_2, x_2 \leftarrow x_3, \dots, x_n \leftarrow x_1\}$$

PROPOSITION 8

If the Herbrand universe is non-trivial then

1. $unif(E_1) \subseteq unif(E_2) \longleftrightarrow soln(E_1) \subseteq soln(E_2)$

2. $unif(E_1) = unif(E_2) \longleftrightarrow soln(E_1) = soln(E_2)$.

Proof: We first prove (b). Since every solution is a unifier, one direction is trivial.

If E_1 and E_2 are both in solved form then, by Theorem 4, they are isomorphic, that is, there is a subset $\{x_1 = y_1, \dots, x_k = y_k\}$ of E_1 where the y_i's are distinct variables and $E_2 = E_1\theta$ where $\theta = \{x_1 \leftarrow y_1, \dots, x_k \leftarrow y_k, y_1 \leftarrow x_1, \dots, y_k \leftarrow x_k\}$. If α is a unifier of E_1 then $x_i\alpha \equiv y_i\alpha$. It follows that $\theta \circ \alpha = \alpha$ and so α is a unifier of E_2. By symmetry, $unif(E_1) = unif(E_2)$.

Any equivalent E_1 and E_2 have equivalent solved forms which, by the above, have the same set of unifiers. It is straightforward that if E_3 is computed by the Solved Form Algorithm to be a solved form of E_1, then E_1 and E_3 have the same set of unifiers and similarly for E_2. Thus for any equivalent E_1 and E_2, $unif(E_1) = unif(E_2)$.

(a) Since every solution is a unifier, one direction is trivial. If $soln(E_1) \subseteq soln(E_2)$ then $soln(E_1) = soln(E_1 \cup E_2)$. Thus $unif(E_1) = unif(E_1 \cup E_2) = unif(E_1) \cap unif(E_2)$ and so $unif(E_1) \subseteq unif(E_2)$. ∎

This is not true in the trivial case. With Herbrand universe $\{a\}$, $E_1 = \{x = y\}$ and $E_2 = \{x = a, y = a\}$ have the same set of solutions but different sets of unifiers.

The next two results follow directly from the definition of mgu and the above proposition.

COROLLARY 7
If E_1 and E_2 are unifiable equation sets with mgu μ_1 and μ_2 (respectively) then $soln(E_1) \supseteq soln(E_2) \longleftrightarrow \exists\, \alpha\ \mu_2 = \mu_1 \circ \alpha$. ∎

We say that mgus μ_1 and μ_2 are *equivalent* if they are mgus of the same equation set.

COROLLARY 8
Mgus μ_1 and μ_2 are equivalent iff $\exists\, \alpha, \beta\ \mu_2 = \mu_1 \circ \alpha$ and $\mu_1 = \mu_2 \circ \beta$. ∎

A characteristic property of idempotent mgus is that

PROPOSITION 9
If θ is an idempotent mgu of equation set E then $\phi \in unif(E) \longleftrightarrow \phi = \theta \circ \phi$

Proof:
$(\Rightarrow)$
Let $\phi = \theta \circ \alpha$. Then $\phi = \theta \circ \theta \circ \alpha$ since θ is idempotent, and so $\phi = \theta \circ \phi$.
$(\Leftarrow)$ By the definition of mgu $\phi = \theta \circ \phi$ is a unifier of E. ∎

Robinson [1979] has chosen this property as a definition of most general unifier.

Now we investigate the relationship between mgus and solved form equation sets. The crux of this relationship is the mapping between an idempotent substitution $\theta = \{v_1 \leftarrow t_1, \ldots, v_n \leftarrow t_n\}$ and the equation set $eqn(\theta) = \{v_1 = t_1, \ldots, v_n = t_n\}$.

The assignment $\leftarrow$, as is the case with := in conventional programming languages, is different from mathematical equality. In $x \leftarrow f(x)$ and $x := x + 1$ the x's on the left hand side do not have the same meaning as the x's on the right hand side. However, the assignment $\leftarrow$ in the case of idempotent unifiers has the semantics of mathematical equality, so that idempotent mgus and solved form equation sets are essentially the same objects, as we show in the next proposition.

THEOREM 6
Let θ be an idempotent substitution. θ is an mgu for equation set E iff $eqn(\theta)$ is an equivalent solved form equation set for E.

Proof:
($\Leftarrow$)

Let $\theta = \{v_1 \leftarrow t_1, \ldots, v_n \leftarrow t_n\}$, and let ϕ be a unifier for E and hence also for eqn(θ). Then, for every i, $v_i \phi \equiv t_i \phi$ and so $v_i \theta \phi \equiv t_i \phi \equiv v_i \phi$. And if $x \notin domain(\theta)$ then $x \theta \equiv x$ and $x \theta \phi \equiv x \phi$. Consequently $\phi = \theta \circ \phi$. So θ is a mgu for $eqn(\theta)$ and so is an mgu for E.

($\Rightarrow$)

As we saw in the first part, θ is an mgu for $eqn(\theta)$, which is clearly in solved form. θ is an mgu of both $eqn(\theta)$ and E. So $eqn(\theta)$ and E have the same set of unifiers and the same set of solutions. ∎

It follows from this theorem that the lattice on equation sets is isomorphic to the lattice on idempotent substitutions given in Eder [1985]. It follows also from this theorem and the results of Proposition 3, Theorem 4, and Corollary 4, that

PROPOSITION 10
If θ is an idempotent mgu for E then $|\theta| = rank(E)$. ∎

PROPOSITION 11
If θ_1 is an idempotent mgu then θ_2 is an idempotent mgu of the same equation set iff there is $\phi = \{x_1 \leftarrow y_1, \ldots, x_k \leftarrow y_k, y_1 \leftarrow x_1, \ldots, y_k - x_k\}$ such that $\{x_1 \leftarrow y_1, \ldots, x_k \leftarrow y_k\} \subseteq \theta_1$ and $\theta_2 = \theta_1 \circ \phi$. ∎

and

PROPOSITION 12
If θ_1 and θ_2 are idempotent mgus of the same equation set then

1. $vars(\theta_1) = vars(\theta_2)$

2. $|domain(\theta_1)| = |domain(\theta_2)|$

3. $|range(\theta_1)| = |range(\theta_2)|$. ∎

Proposition 11 allows the syntactic identification and generation of equivalent idempotent mgus. However mgus need not be idempotent, for example $\{x \leftarrow a, y \leftarrow x, z \leftarrow x\}$ is an mgu of $\{x = a, y = z\}$.

We now investigate such non-idempotent mgu. The remaining results in this section, except for the last corollary, have been presented in a similar way in the literature (see, for instance, Eder [1985]). First we will characterize how to generate all mgus from an idempotent mgu.

A substitution α is *invertible* if there is a substitution α^{-1} such that $\alpha \circ \alpha^{-1} = \alpha^{-1} \circ \alpha = \{\}$. Such an inverse must be unique if it exists. A substitution $\alpha = \{x_1 \leftarrow y_1, \ldots, x_n \leftarrow y_n\}$ is a *permutation of variables* if the y_i's are distinct variables and $domain(\alpha) = range(\alpha)$. Clearly every permutation of variables is invertible with inverse $\alpha^{-1} = \{y_1 \leftarrow x_1, \ldots, y_n \leftarrow x_n\}$. In fact

PROPOSITION 13

α is invertible iff α is a permutation of variables.

Proof: We need only prove the "only if" direction. Let α^{-1} be the inverse of α. If, for some variable x and function symbol f, $x \leftarrow f(t_1, \ldots, t_k) \in \alpha$ then we must have $x \equiv f(t_1, \ldots, t_k) \alpha^{-1}$, a contradiction. If $x \leftarrow z \in \alpha$ and $y \leftarrow z \in \alpha$ for $x \not\equiv y$, then we cannot have $z\alpha^{-1} \equiv x$ and $z\alpha^{-1} \equiv y$, so α is not_invertible. Thus α must take the form $\{x_1 \leftarrow y_1, \ldots, x_n \leftarrow y_n\}$ where the y_i's are distinct variables.

If $x \leftarrow y \in \alpha$ then $y \leftarrow x \in \alpha^{-1}$ and so we must have $y \in domain(\alpha)$ if α is invertible. Thus $range(\alpha) \subseteq domain(\alpha)$. But $|range(\alpha)| = |domain(\alpha)|$ and so $range(\alpha) = domain(\alpha)$. ■

PROPOSITION 14

Let μ and θ be mgus and suppose that θ is idempotent. μ is equivalent to θ iff $\mu = \theta \circ \alpha$ for some invertible substitution α.

Proof:

$(\Rightarrow)$

Let $\alpha' = \{x \leftarrow x\mu: x \in domain(\mu), x \notin domain(\theta)\} = \{x_1 \leftarrow y_1, \ldots, x_n \leftarrow y_n\}$. Because θ is idempotent $\mu = \theta \circ \mu = \theta \circ \alpha'$. By corollary 4.6 $E\gamma\theta = \mu \circ \gamma$, that is, $E\gamma \ \theta = \theta \circ \alpha' \circ \gamma$. Because $domain(\alpha') \cap domain(\theta) = \emptyset$ and $\gamma \supseteq \{y_1 \leftarrow x_1, \ldots, y_n \leftarrow x_n\}$, the y_i's must be distinct variables. Let ϕ be a bijection from $range(\alpha') - domain(\alpha')$ to $domain(\alpha') - range(\alpha')$ and let $\alpha = \alpha' \cup \{x \leftarrow \phi(x): x \in range(\alpha') - domain(\alpha')\}$. α is well-defined and, since $(range(\alpha') - domain(\alpha')) \subseteq domain(\theta)$, $\theta \circ \alpha = \theta \circ \alpha' = \mu$. By definition, α is a permutation of variables and so is invertible.

$(\Leftarrow)$

By Corollary 8, since $\mu = \theta \circ \alpha$ and $\theta = \mu \circ \alpha^{-1}$. ■

We can extract from the proof of this result the construction of a specific invertible α such that $\mu = \theta \circ \alpha$: first obtain $\alpha' = \{x \leftarrow x\mu: x \in domain(\mu), x \notin domain(\theta)\}$ and then complete this to a smallest permutation of variables.

COROLLARY 9

Let μ_1 and μ_2 be mgus. μ_1 and μ_2 are equivalent iff $\mu_1 = \mu_2 \circ \alpha$ for some invertible substitution α. ■

The following propositions allow us to determine which substitutions are mgus and of which equations they are mgus.

PROPOSITION 15

Substitution μ is an mgu iff $v \in domain(\mu) \cap range(\mu) \Rightarrow E(x \leftarrow v) \in \mu$.

Proof: Let θ be an equivalent idempotent mgu, then $\mu = \theta \circ \alpha$ where $\alpha = \{x \leftarrow x\mu : x \in domain(\mu), x \notin domain(\theta)\}$. Now, $v \in domain(\mu) \cap range(\mu)$ implies that $v \in range(\alpha)$. There are two cases: If $v \notin range(\theta)$ then, since $v \in domain(\mu)$, we must have $v \in domain(\alpha)$. Thus, the v in $range(\theta)$ does not contribute to μ, and so $v \in range(\alpha)$. If $v \notin range(\theta)$ then, since $v \in range(\mu)$, we must have $v \in range(\alpha)$. From the previous proposition, α has the form $\{x_1 \leftarrow v_1, \ldots, x_m \leftarrow v_m\}$ and so $\exists (x \leftarrow v) \in \alpha$ and hence $\exists (x \leftarrow v) \in \mu$. ∎

Consequently not all substitutions are mgus of an equation set. For example, $\{v \leftarrow f(v)\}$ does not contain a binding of the form $x \leftarrow v$ and so cannot be an mgu.

PROPOSITION 16

Let μ be an mgu and let $\{x_1 \leftarrow v_1, \ldots, x_n \leftarrow v_n\} \subseteq \mu$ be chosen so that $v_1, \ldots, v_n$ are distinct variables and $\{v_1, \ldots, v_n\} = domain(\mu) \cap range(\mu)$. Then $\mu \circ \{v_1 \leftarrow x_1, \ldots, v_n \leftarrow x_n\}$ is an idempotent mgu of the same equation set as μ.

Proof: It follows from the preceding proposition that such a $\{x_1 \leftarrow v_1, \ldots, x_n \leftarrow v_n\}$ exists. By construction $\theta = \mu \circ \{v_1 \leftarrow x_1, \ldots, v_n \leftarrow x_n\}$ is idempotent. Let E be the corresponding equation set. Then μ is an mgu of E as $\mu = \theta \circ \{x_1 \leftarrow v_1, \ldots, x_n \leftarrow v_n\}$. ∎

Thus, for example, the substitution $\{x \leftarrow g(w), y \leftarrow w, z \leftarrow w, w \leftarrow y\}$ is an mgu and is equivalent to the idempotent mgu $\{x \leftarrow g(w), y \leftarrow w, z \leftarrow w, w \leftarrow y\} \circ \{w \leftarrow z, y \leftarrow w\} = \{x \leftarrow g(z), y \leftarrow z\}$.

An important corollary of this proposition is that idempotent mgus are strictly smaller than other mgus of the same equation set.

COROLLARY 10

If μ is a non-idempotent mgu and θ is an idempotent mgu of the same equation set, then $|\mu| > |\theta|$. ∎

Even if an mgu θ of an equation set E contains only variables from E (i.e., $var(\theta) \subset var(E))$ θ is not necessarily idempotent. For example, $E = \{x = f(y)\}$ has as one mgu $\{x \leftarrow f(x), y \leftarrow x\}$.

Anti-unification and Most General Solutions

We now introduce a lattice on terms. This lattice has been studied as an entity in its own right by Huet [1976], Plotkin [1970], and Reynolds [1970].

A term t is regarded as representing its set of ground instances, $ground(t)$. For technical convenience, a term t is also regarded as representing the set of all its instances, $inst(t)$. Later we prove that if the Herbrand universe is non-trivial then

$$inst(t) = inst(t') \longleftrightarrow ground(t) = ground(t') \text{ and}$$

$$inst(t) \supseteq inst(t') \longleftrightarrow ground(t) \supseteq ground(t').$$

A term t is a *variable renaming* or *variant* of t' if there is an invertible substitution α such that $t = t' \, \alpha$. For example, $f(x, g(y))$ is a variable renaming of $f(y, g(z))$ with $\alpha = \{x \leftarrow z, y \leftarrow x, z \leftarrow y\}$. Clearly, variable renaming is an equivalence relationship.

Two terms t and t' are equivalent, written $t \approx t'$, if $inst(t) = inst(t')$.

PROPOSITION 17
Term t is a variable renaming of t' iff $t \sim t'$

Proof:
$(\Rightarrow)$
Suppose $t = t'\alpha$. If $s \in inst(t')$, say $s = t'\theta$, then $s = t \, \alpha^{-1}\theta$ and so $s \in inst(t)$. Thus $inst(t') \subseteq inst(t)$. Similarly $inst(t) \subseteq inst(t')$.

$(\Leftarrow)$
From the definition of variable renaming, $\exists \, \theta \, t = t'\theta$ and $\exists \, \theta' \, s.t. \, t' = t\theta' = t'\theta\theta'$. We can choose θ so that $domain(\theta) \subseteq vars(t')$. The existence of θ' implies that θ has the form $\{x_1 \leftarrow y_1, \dots, x_n \leftarrow y_n\}$ where the y_i's are distinct variables and $y_i \in vars(t')$ implies $y_i \in domain(\theta)$.

Let ϕ be a bijection from $range(\theta) - domain(\theta)$ to $domain(\theta) - range(\theta)$. Then $\alpha = \theta \cup \{y \leftarrow \phi \, (y) : y \in range(\theta) - domain(\theta)$ is a permutation of variables and $t = t'\alpha$. ∎

Term t is a *generalization* of term t', written $t \geq t'$, if $inst(t) \supseteq inst(t')$. It follows from the definition of instance that $t \geq t' \longleftrightarrow \exists \alpha \, t' = t\alpha$. Hence t is also said to be an *anti-instance* of t'.

We now show that $\geq$ gives a complete lattice on terms with an added least element, modulo variable renaming. First we note that the glb of the lattice, called the *greatest common instance* (*gci*), can be calculated using a unification algorithm. Consider terms t and t'. We can assume that $vars(t) \cap vars(t') = \emptyset$. Let μ be an mgu of $t = t'$, if it exists. If μ does not exist, then t and t' have no common instances. Otherwise their gci is $t\mu \equiv t'\mu$ as $inst(t) \cap inst(t') = inst(t\mu)$.

Sterling and Shapiro [1986] define as mgu of t and t' any idempotent substitution θ such that $t\theta \equiv t'\theta \equiv gci(t, t')$. Any idempotent mgu will have that property, but there are other substitutions that satisfy this definition but are not mgus according to any of the previous definitions. For example, for terms

$h(g(x), f(y, y))$ and $h(g(x), f(g(u), g(z)))$, $\theta = \{y \leftarrow g(v), z \leftarrow v, u \leftarrow v\}$ satisfies this definition but not the others. As we will see later in this section, their definition is more closely related to our definition of mgs.

Now we investigate the lub of the lattice called the *least common anti-instance (lca)*.

Term t is an *anti-instance* of the nonempty, possibly infinite, set of terms, $\{t_1,\ldots,t_n, \ldots\}$, if for all t_i, $t \geq t_i$.

Term t is a *least common anti-instance (lca)* of $\{t_1,\ldots,t_n,\ldots\}$, if

1. t is an anti-instance of $\{t_1,\ldots,t_n,\ldots\}$

2.   any anti-instance of $\{t_1,\ldots,t_n,\ldots\}$ is also an anti-instance of t.

For example, $f(x, g(x, b))$ is an lca of $\{f(a, g(a, b)), f(b, g(b, b)), f(g(x, a), g(g(x, a), b))\}$.

It follows from the definition that lca of the same term set are instances of each other. Hence, an lca is unique up to variable renaming and any variable renaming of an lca is an lca.

LEMMA 4

Let S_1 and S_2 be sets of terms. Then

$$lca\{lca\; S_1, lca\; S_2\} = lca\; (S_1 \cup S_2)$$

Proof: For $i = 1$ and $i = 2$, $lca\; S_i \leq lca\; S_1 \cup S_2$ so $lca\{lca\; S_1, lca\; S_2\} \leq lca\; (S_1 \cup S_2)$. For every $s \in S_1 \cup S_2$, $s \leq lca\; S_i \leq lca\{lca\; S_1, lca\; S_2\}$ for $i = 1$ or $i = 2$. Thus, $lca\; (S_1 \cup S_2) \leq lca\{lca\; S_1, lca\; S_2\}$. ∎

LEMMA 5 (BOOMERANG)

Any lca for $\{t\theta_1,\ldots,t\theta_n,\ldots\}$ is of the form $t\theta$ for some (possibly empty) substitution θ.

Proof: By definition t is an anti-instance of $\{t\theta_1,\ldots,t\theta_n,\ldots\}$ and so by definition any lca must be an instance of t. ∎

LEMMA 6

Any term t has only a finite number of anti-instances up to variable renaming.

Proof: If t' is an anti-instance of t, then $t = t'\alpha$ for some substitution α. So $size(t') \leq size(t)$ and t' can contain only the (finitely many) function symbols used in t. It follows that there are only a finite number of possible anti-instances t', modulo $\sim$. ∎

LEMMA 7

Any finite or infinite set of terms $\{t_1, t_2,\ldots\}$ has only a finite number of anti-instances up to variable renaming.

Proof: Let $[g_i]$ be the set of distinct anti-instances of $\{t_1,\ t_2,...,t_i\}$ modulo variable renaming. Clearly $[g_1] \supseteq [g_2] \supseteq ... \supseteq [g_i] \supseteq ....$ From the above lemma there are only a finite number of elements in $[g_1]$, and so this lemma follows. ∎

THEOREM 7 (ANTI-UNIFICATION)
Any nonempty, possibly infinite, set of terms, $\{t_1,\ t_2,...,t_n,...\}$ has an lca which is unique up to variable renaming.

Proof: Let $\{s_1,...,s_m\}$ be the (finite, by the previous lemma) set of anti-instances of $\{t_1,\ t_2,...,t_n,...\}$. The greatest common instance of the terms $s_1,...,s_m$ can be calculated using the unification algorithm. Clearly it is an lca. It follows from the definition of lca that it is unique modulo variable renaming. ∎

COROLLARY 11
$\geq$ forms a complete lattice on terms modulo variable renaming and an added least element. ∎

The following non-deterministic *Anti-unification Algorithm* is from Huet [1976]. It can be used to calculate the *lca* of a set of terms. Other more procedural algorithms are found in Plotkin [1970] and in Reynolds [1970].

Let ϕ be any bijection between $T \times T$ and V' where T is the set of terms and V' the set of variables. We define the recursive algorithm λ on $T \times T$ as follows:

Anti-unification Algorithm

$\lambda(f(s_1,...,s_m), f(t_1,...,t_m)) = f(\lambda(s_1,\ t_1),...,\lambda(s_m,\ t_m))$
                                    for every function or constant symbol f
$\lambda(s,\ t) = \phi(s,\ t)$ *otherwise.* ∎

Different choices of ϕ may result in different terms. However, these will be equivalent up to variable renaming. For example,

$$\lambda(f(x,\ f(x,\ f(a,\ b))),\ f(a,\ f(a,\ f(a,\ a)))) = f(x,\ f(x,\ f(a,\ y)))$$

when $\phi(x,\ a) = x$ and $\phi(b,\ a) = y$.

The proof of the following theorem is substantially simpler than the one in Huet [1976], as we make use of Theorem 7.

THEOREM 8 (CORRECTNESS OF THE ANTI-UNIFICATION ALGORITHM)
$\lambda(t_1,\ t_2)$ is well defined and is an lca of $\{t_1,\ t_2\}$.

Proof: Let #*sym*(*t*) be the number of symbol occurrences in term *t*. By induction, $\lambda(t_1, t_2)$ can only be recursively called $\min\{\#sym(t_1), \#sym(t_2)\}$ times and so the algorithm must terminate.

By the Anti-unification Theorem, $\{t_1, t_2\}$ has an lca *t* and $t_1 \equiv t\,\alpha_1$, $t_2 \equiv t\,\alpha_2$ for some α_1 and α_2. So $\lambda(t_1, t_2) = \lambda(t\alpha_1, t\alpha_2)$. Thus the only calls to the base case of the algorithm are of the form $\lambda(x\alpha_1, x\alpha_2) = \phi(x\alpha_1, x\alpha_2) = y$ where *x* is a variable of *t*. Let γ be the union of all substitutions $\{x \leftarrow y, y \leftarrow x\}$. Clearly, γ is an invertible substitution and $\lambda(x\alpha_1, x\alpha_2) = x\gamma$ for every *x* appearing in *t*. It follows that $\lambda(t_1, t_2) = t\gamma$. ∎

Now,

PROPOSITION 18

$lca\{lca\{t_1, t_2\}, t_3\} \sim lca\{t_1, lca\{t_2, t_3\}\} \sim lca\{t_1, t_2, t_3\}$.

Proof: $lca\{t_1, t_2, t_3\}$ is an anti-instance of both $lca\{t_1, t_2\}$ and t_3. Thus it is an instance of $lca\{lca\{t_1, t_2\}, t_3\}$. However, $lca\{lca\{t_1, t_2\}, t_3\}$ is an anti-instance of t_1, t_2 and t_3 and so it is an instance of $lca\{t_1, t_2, t_3\}$. Hence, $lca\{lca\{t_1, t_2\}, t_3\} \sim lca\{t_1, t_2, t_3\}$. Similarly, $lca\{t_1, lca\{t_2, t_3\}\} \sim lca\{t_1, t_2, t_3\}$. ∎

Thus, the lca for any finite set of terms can be calculated using the Anti-unification Algorithm as follows:

$$lca\{t_1, t_2, \ldots, t_n\} \sim \lambda(\lambda(\ldots\lambda(\lambda(t_1, t_2), t_3), \ldots), t_n)$$

From the previous propositions this will terminate with a correct result.

Now consider the lca for the infinite set of terms $\{t_1, t_2, \ldots, t_n, \ldots\}$. Recall that *size*(*t*) is the number of symbol occurrences in term *t* minus the number of distinct variables in *t*. It follows from *size*'s definition and that of substitution application that

1. $size(t) \geq 0$.

2. $size(lca\{t_1, \ldots, t_k\}) \geq size(lca\{t_1, \ldots, t_k, t_{k+1}\})$.

3. If $size(lca\{t_1, \ldots, t_k\}) = size(lca\{t_1, \ldots, t_k, t_{k+1}\})$,
    then, $lca\{t_1, \ldots, t_k\} \sim lca\{t_1, \ldots, t_k, t_{k+1}\}$.

Consider the sequence

$$size(lca\{t_1, t_2\}), \ size(lca\{t_1, t_2, t_3\}), \ldots$$

It follows from (1) and (2) that

$$\lim_{n \to \infty} size(lca\{t_1, t_2,...,t_n\})$$

exists and will be found after a finite time.

Thus from (3) it follows that, modulo $\sim$,

$$\lim_{n \to \infty} lca\{t_1, t_2,...,t_n\}$$

exists and will also be found after a finite time. Hence the lca for an infinite set can be found after a finite time using the Anti-unification Algorithm as

$$lca\{t_1, t_2,...,t_n,...\} = \lim_{n \to \infty} lca\{t_1, t_2,...,t_n\} = \lim_{n \to \infty} \lambda(\lambda(...\lambda(t_1, t_2),...),t_n)$$

LEMMA 8

If the Herbrand universe is non-trivial, then term t is an lca of its ground instances.

Proof: The proof is by induction on the number of variables n in t. For $n = 0$ the result is clear. Suppose the result holds for n and write t as $t(x_1,...,x_n, x_{n+1})$ where $x_1,...,x_n, x_{n+1}$ are the variables in t. Since the Herbrand universe is non-trivial, there are ground terms a and b with different principal function symbols.

$t(x_1,...,x_n,x_{n+1}) \geq lca\ ground(t(x_1,...,x_n,x_{n+1}))$

$\geq lca\ ground(t(x_1,...,x_n,a)) \cup ground(t(x_1,...,x_n,b))$

$\sim lca\{lca\ ground(t(x_1,...,x_n,a)), lca\ ground(t(x_1,...,x_n,b))\}$ by Lemma 4

$\sim lca\ \{t(x_1,...,x_n, a), t(x_1,...,x_n, b)\}$ by induction hypothesis

$\sim t(x_1,...,x_n,x_{n+1}).$ ∎

Hence,

COROLLARY 12

If the Herbrand universe is non-trivial, then

1. $ground(t) \supseteq ground(t') \longleftrightarrow t \geq t'$.

2. $ground(t) = ground(t') \longleftrightarrow t \sim t'$.

Proof: It suffices to prove (1). Consider $ground(t) \supseteq ground(t')$. From the Anti-unification Theorem both sets have an lca. Clearly all elements of $ground(t')$ are instances of the lca of $ground(t)$. Thus $lca\ ground(t) \geq lca\ ground(t')$ and so it follows from the preceding lemma that $t \geq t'$. ∎

Now we use anti-unification to introduce the notion of most general solution.

Consider the set of solutions to a solvable equation set E. All will have the form

$$\{v_1 \leftarrow g_1, \ldots, v_n \leftarrow g_n\}.$$

We can treat these substitutions as terms, treating the v_i's as constants, and calculate an lca for them. It will have the form

$$\{v_1 \leftarrow t_1, \ldots, v_n \leftarrow t_n\}.$$

We call such a substitution a *most general solution (mgs)*.

Although the notions of mgs and mgu appear to be similar, they should not be confused. In particular we will see in the section dealing with equations and inequations that they have very different properties.

It follows from the Anti-unification Theorem that every unifiable equation set has an mgs. Different mgss for E differ only by a variable renaming for the variables on the rhs, as they are lcas. We can always choose the variables so that the mgs is idempotent. It follows from the definition that all mgs have domain V.

Consider an equivalent solved form of E. The set of variables is then classified into parameters and eliminable variables. We will characterize the syntactic form of an idempotent mgs σ. using an argument similar to one used in Proposition 1. Let x be a parameter and $(x \leftarrow t) \in \sigma$. The term t must be a variable as a parameter can be assigned any value. Also, as an assignment to the parameters is sufficient to entirely determine a solution, all variables in the rhs of σ must be assigned to a parameter in σ. *Consequently all the variables introduced by the anti-unification process can be replaced by the parameters.* We then obtain an idempotent mgu of E.

The next results follow from these remarks.

PROPOSITION 19

For a non-trivial Herbrand universe, let σ be an idempotent mgs for equation set E and μ be an idempotent mgu for E. Then $\sigma = \mu \circ \beta$ where $\beta = \{(x \leftarrow y) \in \sigma : x \notin domain(\mu)\}$. ∎

It follows immediately that any mgs for an equation set is also a unifier for that equation set.

LEMMA 9

For a non-trivial Herbrand universe, let σ be an idempotent mgs for equation set E. Then for each $y \in range(\sigma)$ there is a binding $x \leftarrow y$ in σ. ∎

The variables on the rhs of an mgs act as parameters. Any grounding substitution applied to these gives a solution. Formally, let $\oplus$ denote *parameter assignment* which is defined by

$$\{v_1 \leftarrow t_1,\ldots,v_n \leftarrow t_n\}\oplus\beta = \{v_i \leftarrow t_i\beta : v_i \not\equiv t_i\beta\}$$

For example, $\{x \leftarrow y\}\oplus\{y \leftarrow x\}$ is $\{\}$ and $\{x \leftarrow f(z)\} \oplus \{z \leftarrow g(a, x), y \leftarrow g(a, b)\}$ is $\{x \leftarrow f(g(a, x))\}$.

PROPOSITION 20
Let E_1 and E_2 be equation sets over a non-trivial Herbrand universe. Then $soln(E_1) \supseteq soln(E_2)$ iff $\exists\alpha$ s.t. $\sigma_2 = \sigma_1\oplus\alpha$ where σ_i is an mgs of E_i.

Proof:
($\Rightarrow$)
Since $soln(E_1) \supseteq soln(E_2)$, σ_2 must be an instance of σ_1 (considering the substitutions as terms). Thus $\sigma_2 = \sigma_1 \oplus \alpha$ for some α.
($\Leftarrow$)
If $\sigma_2 = \sigma_1\oplus\alpha$ then, as terms, σ_2 is an instance of σ_1 and so the ground instances of σ_2, that is, the solutions of E_2, are contained in the ground instances of σ_1. ∎

Any substitution θ with domain V which is such that for each $y \in range(\theta)$ there is a binding $x \leftarrow y$ in θ that can be transformed into an idempotent mgu μ (containing only variables from V) by replacing the y's by the corresponding x's and deleting bindings of the form $x \leftarrow x$. Clearly, any solution of $eqn(\mu)$ can be obtained by a grounding of the variables in $range(\theta)$, and conversely, any such grounding must produce a solution of $eqn(\mu)$. If we take an lca of these groundings we will obtain an mgs. By Lemma 8, an lca of the ground instances of θ is θ. Thus θ is an mgs.

PROPOSITION 21
Let θ be a substitution such that $domain(\theta) = V$. Then θ is an mgs iff for each $y \in range(\theta)$ there is a binding $x \leftarrow y$ in θ. ∎

We now give another application of the notion of anti-unification. The following *Generalization Algorithm* can be used to calculate the most specific generalization (msg) of the equation set collection $\{E_1,\ldots,E_n\}$. It first calculates the lca σ of the corresponding mgs $\sigma_1,\ldots,\sigma_n$. For the sake of simplicity, we will assume that σ is idempotent. In general σ will not be an mgs and so must be carefully generalized until an mgs is reached. The corresponding set of equations is an msg for $\{E_1,\ldots,E_n\}$.

Generalization Algorithm

$\epsilon(E_1,\ldots,E_n)$

for each E_i do

$\sigma_i \leftarrow mgs(E_i)$

$\sigma \leftarrow lca(\{\sigma_1,\ldots,\sigma_n\})$

while $\exists u \in range(\sigma)$ s.t. $\exists (x \leftarrow u) \in \sigma$ do

let $t_1(u),\ldots,t_k(u)$ *be those terms on the rhs of σ containing u*

select $t_i(u)$ *s.t.* $\forall j\ size(t_i(u)) \leq size(t_j(u))$

$\sigma \leftarrow \sigma \oplus \{t_i(u) \leftarrow u'\}$

return(equ(σ)) ■

where $mgs(E)$ is an mgs of equation set E, $\sigma \oplus \{t_i(u) \leftarrow u'\}$ is the substitution obtained by replacing all occurrences of term $t_i(u)$ in the rhs of σ by the new variable u' and $equ(\sigma)$ is an equation set with mgs σ, obtained by transforming σ first into an idempotent mgu and the mgu into a corresponding solved form.

For example, consider $\epsilon(\{x = f(a),\ y = f(f(a))\},\ \{x = f(b),\ y = f(f(b))\})$. σ will initially be assigned $\{x \leftarrow f(z),\ y \leftarrow f(f(z))\}$. After one iteration of the while loop the algorithm will terminate with $\sigma = \{x \leftarrow z',\ y \leftarrow f(z'),\}$ and return the msg $\{y = f(x)\}$.

THEOREM 9 (CORRECTNESS OF THE GENERALIZATION ALGORITHM)
$\epsilon(E_1,\ldots,E_n)$ is well defined and is an msg for $\{E_1,\ldots,E_n\}$

Proof: Termination: Each iteration of the while loop reduces by one the number of occurrences of variables u such that $u \in range(\sigma)$ and $\exists (x \leftarrow u) \in \sigma$. As the loop terminates when this is 0, the algorithm is well defined.

Correctness: At each stage in the algorithm's execution, σ is a generalization of $\{\sigma_1,\ldots,\sigma_n\}$ because it is initially the lca and is then generalized.

We now show that at each stage if E, with mgs σ_E, is a generalization of $\{E_1,\ldots,E_n\}$ then $\exists \alpha$ s.t. $\sigma = \sigma_E \oplus \alpha$. We assume that the variables on the rhs of σ_E are different from those used in the algorithm. Initially $\sigma = \sigma_E \oplus \alpha$ by Proposition 20. Now assume it is true at some stage in the execution of the while loop and let $\sigma' = \sigma \oplus \{t_i(u) \leftarrow u'\}$ and $\alpha' = \alpha \oplus \{t_i(u) \leftarrow u'\}$. We show that $\sigma' = \sigma_E \oplus \alpha'$. It suffices to consider $(z \leftarrow t) \in \sigma$ where t contains $t_i(u)$. Let $(y \leftarrow s(u))$ be the binding in α that introduces the u in t. As σ_E is an mgs $\exists (x \leftarrow y) \in \sigma_E$ and so $(x - s(u)) \in \sigma$. Hence $s(u) \in \{t_1(u),\ldots,t_k(u)\}$ and so $size(s(u)) \geq size(t_i(u))$. Thus $t_i(u)$ is a subterm of $s(u)$ and will be replaced by u' in α'.

On termination of the while loop it follows from Proposition 21 that σ is an mgs. Thus $equ(\sigma)$ is well defined, the set of solutions of $equ(\sigma)$ is included in $soln(E)$ and contains $soln(E_i)$ for each i. Consequently it is an msg. ■

The rank of the msg of an equation collection has analogous properties to the size of the lca of a term set. That is, for equation sets $E_1, E_2, \ldots$

1. $rank(msg\{E_1,\ldots,E_k\}) \geq rank(msg\{E_1,\ldots,E_k, E_{k+1}\})$.

2.   If $rank(msg\{E_1,\ldots,E_k\}) = rank(msg\{E_1,\ldots,E_k, E_{k+1}\})$,
      then $msg\{E_1,\ldots,E_k\} \approx msg\{E_1,\ldots,E_k, E_{k+1}\}$.

It follows from an identical argument to that given in the case of terms (following Proposition 18) that the Generalization Algorithm will find an msg for an infinite equation set collection after some finite time.

The analogy between terms and sets of equations provides a new insight into Theorem 2: In general, when we generalize we generalize "strictly;" that is, there exist instances of the msg that are not instances of the initial set generalized.

Systems of Equations and Inequations

Now we investigate systems containing both equations and inequations on the Herbrand universe. We are interested in determining two things: Does the system have any solutions; and how can these solutions be finitely represented.

If the Herbrand universe is finite, it is clear that algorithms exist to determine a system's solvability and that a suitable representation is provided by the solutions themselves.

For the remainder of this section, the Herbrand universe is assumed to be infinite. It is also assumed that the variables of any system are from the finite set $V = \{v_1,\ldots,v_m\}$.

A *solution* α to a system S of equations E and inequations, $s_1 \neq t_1,\ldots,s_n \neq t_n$, is a grounding substitution for V which solves E and for which $s_1\alpha \neq t_1\alpha,\ldots,s_n\alpha \neq t_n\alpha$. For example, $\{x \leftarrow g(a), y \leftarrow g(a), z \leftarrow a\}$ is a solution of the system $\{x = g(z), x \neq g(y)\}$.

The set of all solutions to a system S of equations and inequations is denoted by $soln(S)$. A system S is *solvable* if $soln(S) \neq \emptyset$, otherwise it is *unsolvable*. Two systems, S and S', are equivalent, written $S \approx S'$, if $soln(S) = soln(S')$. System S is equivalent to the disjunction of systems $S_1,\ldots,S_n$, written $S \approx S_1 \vee \ldots \vee S_n$, if $soln(S) = soln(S_1) \cup \ldots \cup soln(S_n)$. An empty disjunction has the empty set of solutions and is equivalent to any unsolvable system.

The *complementary equation* to an inequation I_j, obtained by replacing $\neq$ by $=$, is denoted by E_j. For example, $x = f(y)$ is the complementary equation to $x \neq f(y)$.

The solutions of a system can be expressed in terms of those of its component equations and inequations. For a system S consisting of equation set E and inequations $I_1,...,I_n$

$$soln(S) \;=\; soln(\mathrm{E}) \cap \bigcap_{j=1}^{n} soln(I_j) \;=\; soln(E) - \bigcup_{j=1}^{n} soln(E_j)$$

$$=\; soln(E) - \bigcup_{j=1}^{n} soln(E \cup E_j)$$

Thus $E \approx S \vee (E \cup E_1) \vee ... \vee (E \cup E_n)$.

The next theorem, which is our first corollary of the Strong Compactness Theorem (Theorem 3), is an instance of Colmerauer's Independence of Inequations (Colmerauer [1984]). A related result in a more general setting is to be found in Makowsky [1984].

THEOREM 10 (INDEPENDENCE OF INEQUATIONS)
If system S consists of equation set E and inequations $I_1,...,I_n$ then S is solvable iff each $\{E \cup I_i\}$ is solvable.

Proof: From Theorem 3 it follows that

$soln(E \cup \{I_1,...,I_n\}) = \emptyset$

$\longleftrightarrow E \approx (E \cup E_1) \vee ... \vee (E \cup E_n)$

$\longleftrightarrow \exists I_j \; E \approx (E \cup E_j)$

$\longleftrightarrow \exists I_j \; soln(E \cup \{I_j\}) = \emptyset.$ ∎

Thus, to test whether the system consisting of equations E and inequations $I_1,...,I_n$ is solvable, one needs only to compute the mgu of E and check that it does not unify any E_j. Clearly these tests can be executed in parallel.

Inequation I is *redundant* in system S if $soln(S) = soln(S - \{I\})$. The collection of inequations of S is redundant iff $S \approx E$. A system which has no redundant inequations is *redundancy free*. For example, $f(x, y) \neq f(a, a)$ is redundant in the system $\{z = f(x, y), f(x, y) \neq f(a, a), x \neq a\}$. $y) \neq f(a, a), x \neq a\}$.

Any system with redundant inequations may be transformed into an equivalent redundancy free system by removing redundant inequations one at a time until a redundancy free system is reached. The test for redundancy of inequations can be obtained from the following consequence of the Strong Compactness Theorem.

PROPOSITION 21

Inequation I_j is redundant in the system of equations E and inequations $I_1,...,I_n$ iff $\exists I_k$ such that $(E \cup E_k) \geq (E \cup E_j)$ or $(E \cup E_j)$ is unsolvable. ■

A natural question to ask is whether a finite set of mgu can provide an explicit representation for a system of equations and inequations. That is, for system S when are there idempotent substitutions $\theta_1,...,\theta_n$ s.t. $\alpha \in soln(S) \longleftrightarrow \alpha$ is a grounding substitution for V and $\exists \theta_i, \beta$ such that $\alpha = \theta_i{\circ}\beta$. We assume here that the only variables appearing in the substitutions are from V. If S is unsolvable then the empty set of idempotent substitutions provides a representation.

The second important corollary to the Strong Compactness Theorem (Theorem 3) is that such a set of mgus exists only when its collection of inequations is redundant or the system has no solutions:

THEOREM 11

Apart from the trivial cases in which a system is unsolvable or its collection of inequations is redundant, no finite set of mgu can provide an explicit representation for its solutions.

Proof: Let $R_i = eqn(\theta_i)$. $\theta_1,...,\theta_m$ form an explicit representation for the solutions of a system S iff S has an equivalent disjunction $R_1 \vee ... \vee R_m$. Clearly an equivalent disjunction exists if the system is unsolvable or its collection of inequations is redundant. Now assume that $R_1 \vee ... \vee R_m$ is an equivalent disjunction to S. Let S consist of equation set E and inequations $\{I_1,...,I_n\}$. Now,

$$E \approx R_1 \vee ... \vee R_m \vee (E \cup E_1) \vee ... \vee (E \cup E_n)$$

Hence, either $\exists j\ E \approx R_j$ or $\exists k\ E \approx E \cup E_k$. Thus, either $S \approx E$ or S is unsolvable. ■

An approach akin to that of the mgs sometimes provides an explicit representation for the solutions to a system. When dealing just with equations, we saw that an mgs could be transformed into an mgu by replacing all variables on the rhs by variables from V. For systems of equations and inequations we now see that this is no longer possible. The introduction of auxiliary variables in the mgs gives it more expressive power than the mgu.

The substitutions $\{x \leftarrow f(a), y \leftarrow f(f(u))\}$ and $\{x \leftarrow f(a), y \leftarrow a\}$ represent the solutions of the system $\{x = f(a), y \neq x\}$ when there is one constant symbol a and one unary function symbol f. We see here that u cannot be eliminated.

The finite set of substitutions $\{\sigma_1,...,\sigma_n\}$ forms a *most general solution set* (*mgss*) for the system of equations and inequations S if

$\alpha \in soln(S) \longleftrightarrow \alpha$ is a grounding substitution for V and $\exists \sigma_i$, β such that $\alpha = \sigma_i \oplus \beta$.

If S is unsolvable then the empty mgss provides a representation of its solutions.

We now show that it is decidable whether or not a given system has an mgss and what this is. This is done by transforming this problem into the problem of deciding whether or not there exist terms $r_1, \ldots, r_m$ which are an equivalent finite disjunction for the term expression $t / \{t\theta_1 \vee \ldots \vee t\theta_n\}$. That is, are there $r_1, \ldots, r_m$ such that

$$ground(r_1) \cup \ldots \cup ground(r_m) = ground(t) - (ground(t\theta_1) \cup \ldots \cup ground(t\theta_n))$$

To illustrate the transformation consider the system,

$$y = f(x), \ x \neq f(f(a)), \ y \neq f(f(a))$$

This is transformed into the term expression

$$p(x, y)\{y \leftarrow f(x)\} / \{(p(x, y)\{y \leftarrow f(x)\}) \{x \leftarrow f(f(a))\}$$
$$\vee (p(x, y)\{y \leftarrow f(x) r\}) \{x \leftarrow f(a)\} \}$$
$$= p(x, f(x)) / \{p(f(f(a)), f(f(f(a)))) \vee p(f(z), f(f(a)))\}$$

If Σ contains one function symbol f and one constant symbol a then this is equivalent to $p(a, f(a)) \vee p(f(f(f(u))), f(f(f(f(u)))))$ and thus $\{x \leftarrow a, \ y \leftarrow f(a)\}$, $\{x \leftarrow f(f(f(u))), \ y \leftarrow f(f(f(f(u))))\}$ is an mgss for the original system.

In general, consider a system S of equations E and inequations $I_1, \ldots, I_n$. Let μ_E be an idempotent mgu of E and let μ_i be an idempotent mgu of $E_i \mu_E$. If μ_E does not exist, then the system has no solutions, and if any μ_i does not exist, then the inequation I_i can be removed as it is redundant. The term expression corresponding to S is

$$p(v_1, \ldots, v_m)\mu_E / \{p(v_1, \ldots, v_m) \ \mu_E\mu_1 \vee \ldots \vee p(v_1, \ldots, v_m)\mu_E\mu_n\}$$

where p is a dummy function symbol and $v_1, v_2, \ldots, v_m$ are the variables of V appearing in S.

PROPOSITION 22
Substitutions $\sigma_1, \ldots, \sigma_n$ with domain V are an mgss for the system S iff

$$p(v_1, \ldots, v_m)\sigma_1 \vee \ldots \vee p(v_1, \ldots, v_m)\sigma_n$$

is an equivalent disjunction to the term expression corresponding to S.

Proof: Let α be a solution of E. $\mu_E \circ \mu_j$ is an mgu of $E \cup E_j$.

Hence $\alpha \notin soln(E \cup \{I_j\})$

iff $\alpha \in soln(E \cup E_j)$

iff $\exists \gamma \ \alpha = \mu_E \circ \mu_j \circ \gamma$

iff $p(v_1,\ldots,v_m)\alpha$ is an instance of $p(v_1,\ldots,v_m) \ \mu_E \circ \mu_j$.

Thus $\alpha \in soln(S)$

iff $\forall j \ \alpha \in soln(E \cup \{I_j\})$

iff $\forall j \ p(v_1,\ldots,v_m)\alpha$ is not an instance of $p(v_1,\ldots,v_m) \ \mu_E \circ \mu_j$

iff $p(v_1,\ldots,v_m)\alpha \in p(v_1,\ldots,v_m)\mu_E / \{p(v_1,\ldots,v_m)\mu_E\mu_1 \vee \ldots$
$\vee \ p(v_1,\ldots,v_m)\mu_E\mu_n\}$. $\blacksquare$

It now follows directly from results in Lassez and Marriott [1986] about term expressions that

PROPOSITION 23
If there is an infinite number of function symbols in Σ, then a system has an mgss iff it is unsolvable or its collection of inequations is redundant. $\blacksquare$

and that

PROPOSITION 24
If there is a finite number of function symbols in Σ then there exists an algorithm that will produce an mgss for a system of equations and inequations if one exists. Otherwise it will halt with failure. $\blacksquare$

We now characterize those systems which have an mgss when there is a finite number of function symbols in Σ.

Instance $t\theta$ of t is *restricted w.r.t.* t if any variable appears more than once in the multiset $\{x\theta : x \in vars(t)\}$ and is *unrestricted w.r.t.* t otherwise. For example, $f(y, f(g(y), g(y)))$ is restricted w.r.t. $f(y, f(x, x))$ while $f(a, f(g(y), g(y)))$ is not. If θ is a grounding substitution, then $t\theta$ is unrestricted w.r.t. t.

Let a system contain equations E with idempotent mgu μ_E. The inequation I_j is *effectively ground* in this system if $E_j \ \mu_E$ has a grounding substitution as its idempotent mgu. For example, the inequation $x \neq y$ is effectively ground in the system with equations $\{z = f(y), x = a\}$.

LEMMA 10
Let the system consisting of equation set E and inequations $I_1,\ldots,I_n$ have the corresponding term expression $t / \{t\mu_1 \vee \ldots \vee t\mu_n\}$ where $(t = p(v_1,\ldots,v_m)\mu_E)$. Then I_j is effectively ground iff $t\mu_j$ is unrestricted w.r.t. t.

Proof:

$(\Rightarrow)$

If I_j is effectively ground, then μ_j is a grounding substitution and so $t\,\mu_j$ is unrestricted w.r.t. t.

$(\Leftarrow)$

If I_j is not effectively ground there exists $v \in range(\mu_j)$. As μ_j is an idempotent mgu, $v \notin domain(\mu_j)$ and $v \in vars(t)$. Thus, v appears more than once in $\{v_i\mu_j : v_i \in vars(t)\}$ and so $t\mu_j$ is restricted w.r.t. t.

LEMMA 11

Any inequation in a solvable system with an mgss is either effectively ground or redundant.

Proof: Let the system S consist of equation set E and inequations $I_1,\dots,I_n$. Let μ_E be an idempotent mgu of E and let μ_i be an idempotent mgu for $E'_i = E_i\mu_E$. Clearly $soln(E'_i) = soln(E \cup E_i)$. Let $t/\{t\mu_1 \vee \dots \vee t\mu_n\}$ be the corresponding term expression for S.

Without loss of generality, assume I_1 is not effectively ground. We prove that it is redundant. Now, from the previous lemma, $t\mu_1$ will be restricted w.r.t t. Thus, from Proposition 4.8 in Lassez and Marriott [1986] there are instances $t\mu_1\alpha_1,\dots,t\mu_1\alpha_k$ which are unrestricted w.r.t. t and for which

$$ground(t\mu_1) \subseteq ground(t\mu_2) \vee \dots \vee ground(t\mu_n) \vee ground(t\mu_1\alpha_1) \vee \dots \\ \vee ground(t\mu_1\alpha_k)$$

For $t\mu_1\alpha_j$ to be unrestricted w.r.t. t it must ground those variables $y_1,\dots,y_l$ that cause $t\mu_1$ to be restricted w.r.t. t. Hence, each $t\mu_1\alpha'_j = t\,\mu_1\{y_1 \leftarrow y_1\alpha_j \dots, y_l \leftarrow y_l\alpha_j\}$ will also be unrestricted w.r.t. t. Clearly

$$ground(t\mu_1) \subseteq ground(t\mu_2) \vee \dots \vee ground(t\mu_n) \vee ground(t\mu_1\,\alpha'_1) \vee \dots \\ \vee ground(t\mu_1\,\alpha'_k)$$

Now, $t\mu_1\alpha'_j$ has been constructed so that $\mu_1\alpha'_j$ is an mgu for the equation $R_j = E'_1 \cup \{y_1 = y_1\alpha_j,\dots,y_l = y_l\alpha_j\}$. Thus,

$$soln(E'_1) \subseteq soln(E'_2) \cup \dots \cup soln(E'_n) \cup soln(R_1) \cup \dots \cup soln(R_k)$$

Clearly, for all j, $soln(E'_1) \supset soln(R_j)$. By the Strong Compactness Theorem $\exists m\; soln(E'_1) \subseteq soln(E'_m)$ and so, by Proposition 21, I_1 is redundant. ∎

In Proposition 24 we mentioned the existence of an algorithm to decide the existence of an mgss. The following theorem provides a far simpler algorithmic characterization.

THEOREM 12

A redundancy free system has an mgss iff each inequation is effectively ground.

Proof:

($\Rightarrow$)

Follows directly from above lemma.

($\Leftarrow$)

It follows from Lemma 10 that if each inequation is effectively ground then each $t\mu_i$ in the system's corresponding term expression $t / \{t\mu_1 \vee \ldots \vee t\mu_n\}$ is unrestricted w.r.t. t. Hence, from proposition 4.7 in Lassez and Marriott [1986] the term expression has an equivalent finite disjunction of terms and so the original system has an mgss. ∎

In some applications, for example Naish [1986] and Kunen [1987a], universally quantified variables appear naturally in the inequations.

For example, consider the logic program

$P(g(x))$

$Q(g(y)) \leftarrow not\ P(\ y\ )$

$R(g(z)) \leftarrow not\ Q(\ z\ )$

The answer substitutions for $R(w)$ are just those assignments for w that satisfy the system $w = g(g(g(x)))$ or the system $w = g(z) \wedge \forall y\ z \neq g(y)$.

We now consider the problems of solvability and representability within this context. We assume that there is a finite set U of universally quantified variables that appear in any given system. This set is disjoint from the finite set of unquantified variables V. We will sometimes be dealing with equations on variables from $U \cup V$.

We now allow inequations of the form $I = \{\forall y_1, \ldots,\ y_k\ s_1 \neq t_1, \ldots, s_n \neq t_n\}$ to appear in a system S. A *solution* to a system S of equations E and inequations I is a grounding substitution α for V which solves E and is such that for all grounding substitutions β to U, $s_1(\alpha \cup \beta) \neq t_1(\alpha \cup \beta), \ldots, s_n(\alpha \cup \beta) \neq t_n(\alpha \cup \beta)$. For example, $\{w \leftarrow a,\ z \leftarrow a\}$ is a solution of the system $\{w = g(z),\ \forall y\ z \neq g(y)\}$.

As for systems without universally quantified variables, determining whether a system has an mgss may be transformed into determining whether a term expression has an equivalent disjunction of terms. We first illustrate this process with an example.

The system $y = f(x)$, $\forall z\ x \neq f(f(a))$, $y \neq f(f(z))$ may be translated into the term expression

$$p(x, y)\{y \leftarrow f(x)\} \,/\, \{(p(x, y)\{y \leftarrow f(x)\})\, \{x \leftarrow f(f(a))\}$$
$$\vee\, (p(x, y)\{y \leftarrow f(x)\})\, \{x \leftarrow f(z)\}\}$$
$$= p(x, f(x)) \,/\, \{p(f(f(a)), f(f(f(a)))) \vee p(f(z), f(f(z)))$$

If the universe contains one function symbol f and one constant symbol a, then this is equivalent to $p(a, f(a))$ and thus $\{x \leftarrow a, y \leftarrow f(a)\}$ is an mgss for the original system.

More precisely, consider a system S of equations E and inequations $\forall y_1,\ldots,y_k\, I_1,\ldots, I_n$. Let μ_E be an idempotent mgu of E and let μ_j be an idempotent mgu of $E_j\, \mu_E$. The corresponding term expression is

$$p(v_1,\ldots,v_m)\mu_E \,/\, \{p(v_1,\ldots,v_m)\, \mu_E\mu_1 \vee \ldots \vee p(v_1,\ldots,v_m)\mu_E\mu_n\}$$

where p is a dummy function symbol and v_1, $v_2,\ldots,v_m$ are the variables of V appearing in S.

PROPOSITION 25
Substitutions $\sigma_1,\ldots,\sigma_k$ with domain V are an mgss for the system S iff

$$p(v_1,\ldots,v_m)\sigma_1 \vee \ldots \vee p(v_1,\ldots,v_m)\sigma_n$$

is an equivalent disjunction for the term expression corresponding to S.

Proof: Let a be a solution of E and let β range over grounding substitutions on U. $\mu_E{\circ}\mu_j$ is an mgu of $E \cup E_j$.

Hence $\alpha \notin soln(E \cup \{\forall y_1,\ldots,y_k\, I_j\})$

iff $\exists \beta\, (\alpha \cup \beta) \notin soln(E \cup E_j)$

iff $\exists \beta, \gamma\, (\alpha \cup \beta) = \mu_E{\circ}\mu_j{\circ}\gamma$

iff $p(v_1,\ldots,v_m)\alpha$ is an instance of $p(v_1,\ldots,v_m)\, \mu_E{\circ}\mu_j$.

Thus $\alpha \in soln(S)$

iff $\forall j\, \alpha \in soln(E \cup \{\forall y_1,\ldots,y_k\, I_j\})$

iff $\forall j\, p(v_1,\ldots,v_m)\alpha$ is not an instance of $p(v_1,\ldots,v_m)\mu_E{\circ}\mu_j$

iff $p(v_1,\ldots,v_m)\alpha \in p(v_1,\ldots,v_m)\mu_E \,/\, \{p(v_1,\ldots,v_m)\mu_E\, \mu_1 \vee \ldots$
$\vee p(v_1,\ldots,v_m)\mu_E\mu_n\}$.   ∎

We now obtain two propositions, which are the counterparts of Propositions 23 and 24, as a direct consequence of results in Lassez and Marriott [1986] about term expressions.

PROPOSITION 26

If there is an infinite number of function symbols in Σ, then for system S with equations E and inequations $\forall y_1,\ldots,y_m\, I_1,\ldots,I_n$

1. S is solvable iff each $\{E \cup \forall y_1,\ldots,y_m\, I_j\}$ is solvable

2. S has an mgss iff its collection of inequations is redundant or it is unsolvable. ■

THEOREM 13

If there is a finite number of function symbols in Σ, then there exists an algorithm that will produce an mgss for a system of equations and universally quantified inequations if one exists. Otherwise it will halt with failure. ■

An unsolvable system has the empty disjunction as its mgss. Hence

COROLLARY 13

If there is a finite number of function symbols in Σ, then there exists an algorithm that decides solvability of a system of equations and universally quantified inequations. ■

Unlike the case when there are only unquantified variables, a redundancy free system may still have an mgss when it contains inequations that are not effectively ground. For example, if there is one constant symbol a and one binary function symbol f, then the system

$$\{\forall u, v, u', v'\, f(x, y) \neq f(u, u), f(x, y) \neq f(f(u, v), f(u', v'))\}$$

has an mgss of $\{x \leftarrow a,\, y \leftarrow f(x', y')\}$ and $\{x \leftarrow f(x', y'),\, y \leftarrow a\}$.

The addition of universally quantified variables means that when Σ is finite the Independence of Inequations does not hold. For example, if there is one constant symbol a and one unary function symbol g, then both of the inequations $\{x \neq a\}$ and $\{\forall y\, x \neq g(y)\}$ are solvable but the system $\{\forall y\, x \neq a, x \neq g(y)\}$ is not.

Thus, the method given by Theorem 12 is not applicable when there are universally quantified variables.

Acknowledgments

The authors would like to acknowledge discussions with Alain Colmerauer and Alan Robinson.

References

1. Chang, C. L. and Lee, R. [1973] *Symbolic Logic and Mechanical Theorem Proving*, Academic Press, New York.

2. Colmerauer, A. [1984] Equations and Inequations on Finite and Infinite Trees, *FGCS'84 Proceedings*, 85–99.

3. Eder, E. [1985] Properties of Substitutions and Unifications, *Journal of Symbolic Computation* **1**, 31–46.

4. Herbrand, J. [1930] Recherches sur la Theorie de la Demonstration (these), Universite de Paris. (In: Ecrits logiques de Jacques Herbrand, Paris, PUF, 1968.)

5. Huet, G. [1976] Resolution d'Equations Dans Des Langages D'Ordre 1, 2, ..., ω (these d'etat), Universite de Paris VII.

6. Huet, G. and Oppen, D. C. [1980] Equations and Rewrite Rules: A Survey, *Formal Languages: Perspectives and Open Problems* (R. Book, Ed.), Academic Press.

7. Jaffar, J. and Lassez, J-L. [1987] Constraint Logic Programming, *Proc. POPL'87*, 111–119.

8. Kirchner, C. and Lescanne, P. [1987] Solving Disequations, *Proc. Logic in Computer Science Conf.*

9. Kunen, K. [1987a] Negation in Logic Programming, *Journal of Logic Programming*.

10. Kunen, K. [1987b] Answer Sets and Negation as Failure, *Proc. ICLP* **4**, MIT Press, 219–228.

11. Lassez, J.-L. and Marriott, K. G. [1986] Explicit Representation of Terms Defined by Counter Examples, *Proc. FST & TCS Conference*, LNCS 241. Full version to appear in *Journal of Automated Reasoning*.

12. Lloyd, J. W. [1984] *Foundations of Logic Programming*, Springer-Verlag.

13. Maher, M. J. [1987] Logic Semantics for a Class of Committed-choice Programs, *Proc. ICLP* **4**, MIT Press, 858–876.

14. Makowsky, J. [1984] Model Theoretic Issues in Theoretical Computer Science Part 1: Relational Databases and Abstract Data Types, *Logic Colloquium* **82** (G. Lolli, G. Longo and A. Marcja, Eds.), Elsevier.

15. Martelli, A. and Montanari, U. [1982] An Efficient Unification Algorithm, *TOPLAS* **4**(2):258–282.

16. Manna, Z. and Waldinger, R. [1980] Problematic Features of Programming Languages: A Situational-Calculus Approach, Report No. STAN-CS-80-779, Stanford University.

17. Manna, Z. and Waldinger, R. [1981] Deductive Synthesis of the Unification Algorithm, *Science of Computer Programming* **1**, 5–48.

18. Naish, L. [1986] Negation & Quantifiers in NU-Prolog, *Proc. 3rd Conf. on Logic Programming*, LNCS 225, 624–634.

19. Paterson, M. and Wegman, M. [1978] Linear Unification, *Journal of Computer and System Sciences* **16**(2):158–167.

20. Plotkin, G. [1970] A Note on Inductive Generalization, *Machine Intelligence* **5** (B. Meltzer and D. Michie, Eds.), 153–163.

21. Plotkin, G. [1971] A Further Note on Inductive Generalization, *Machine Intelligence* **6** (B. Meltzer and D. Michie, Eds.), 101–124.

22. Reynolds, J. [1970] Transformational Systems and the Algebraic Structure of Atomic Formulas, *Machine Intelligence* **5** (B. Meltzer and D. Michie, Eds.), 135–152.

23. Robinson, J. A. [1965] A Machine-Oriented Logic Based on the Resolution Principle, *JACM* **12**(1):23–41.

24. Robinson, J. A. [1979] *Logic: Form and Function—The Mechanization of Deductive Reasoning*, North Holland, New York.

25. Sato, T. [1986] Declarative Logic Programming, Research Memo, Electrotechnical Laboratory.

26. Sterling, L. and Shapiro, E. Y. [1986] *The Art of PROLOG*, MIT Press.

27. Vere, S. A. [1975] Induction of Concepts in the Predicate Calculus, *IJCAI-75*, 281–287.

28. Vere, S. A. [1977] Induction of Relational Productions in the Presence of Background Information, *IJCAI-77*, 349–355.

16

Equivalences of Logic Programs

M. J. Maher
IBM T. J. Watson Research Center
Yorktown Heights, NY[1]

Abstract

One of the most important relationships between programs (in any program-ming language) is the equivalence of such programs. This relationship is at the basis of most, if not all, programming methodologies. This paper provides a systematic comparison of the relative strengths of various formulations of equivalence for logic programs. It also introduces the notion of subsumption-equivalence, which is used to give syntactic characterizations of the programs P for which the function T_P satisfies some continuity properties.

Introduction

One of the most important relationships between programs (in any program-ming language) is the equivalence of such programs. This relationship is at the basis of most, if not all, programming methodologies. Each method of giving a semantics to programs induces a, possibly different, equivalence relation on programs. Thus it is essential to investigate how these equivalences are re-lated, especially in logic programming where there are many methods of giving semantics to programs.

---

[1]Much of this work was carried out in the Dept. of Computer Science at the University of Melbourne. A preliminary version of this paper was given at the Third International Conference on Logic Programming.

So far, there has not been any systematic treatment of ideas of equivalence of logic programs. As a result, programs are described in the literature as "equivalent," but it is left to the reader to infer from the context the type of equivalence that is meant. For example, the programs P_1 and P_2 in Figure 1 might easily be said to be equivalent, yet in many senses they are not equivalent (for instance, P_1 and P_2 are not logically equivalent).

This paper provides a systematic comparison of the relative strengths of various formulations of equivalence. These formulations arise naturally from several well-known formal semantics for logic programs. Different formulations that define identical equivalences offer different frameworks in which to reason about programs, and hence greater flexibility. We can also use stronger equivalences to reason about programs and then be assured that the programs are also equivalent in an intended weaker sense, which might not be as suitable for reasoning.

Reasoning about programs concerns not only verification of correctness and termination of programs but also the correctness of ad hoc source-to-source transformations such as those occurring in program development. At a more abstract level, it also involves the establishment of the correctness and other properties of automated transformation systems that can be used in program development and as a pre-compilation optimization.

We begin by summarizing some formal semantics of logic programs. We then introduce a syntactic notion of equivalence, *subsumption-equivalence*, which is shown to correspond to the equality of functions T_P of programs. We use this fact to study continuity properties of T_P and characterize syntactically the programs with these properties. In "Equivalences of Logic Programs" we first formulate different notions of equivalence based upon different semantics of logic programs. We examine these equivalences and subsumption-equivalence and determine their relative strength (i.e., whether equivalence of two programs in one sense implies their equivalence, in another sense). In particular, we show that logical equivalence of programs ($P_1 \leftrightarrow P_2$) is identical to equality of the functional semantics of Lassez and Maher [1983, 1984] ($[\![P_1]\!] = [\![P_2]\!]$).

We then extend the work of the first part of the previous section to the important case where two programs employ different function or predicate symbols. In three examples, we determine which equivalences are preserved by two program transformations. One transformation is from Jaffar and Stuckey

P_1:   *Even(0)* P_2:   *Even(0)*

   Even($S^2(x)$) ← Even(x)   *Even(S(x)) ← Odd(x)*

   Odd(x) ← Even(S(x))   *Odd(S(x)) ← Even(x)*

Figure 1: Programs for Odd and Even

[1986]. The second transformation is of independent interest, since it answers two open problems of Sebelik and Stepanek [1980]. A third example gives the correctness of a transformation system similar to—but weaker than—the transformation system of Tamaki and Sato [1986].

Semantics Of Logic Programs

A *language* consists of three disjoint sets: the variables V, the function symbols Σ, and the predicate symbols Π. We take the approach that a language is fixed and that programs and queries can use only the variables of V, function symbols of Σ, and predicate symbols Π. We assume that the language contains enough variables, function symbols of a given arity, etc., to write a program and query it effectively. In particular, we assume that Σ contains at least one constant symbol (that is, a function symbol of arity 0). Terms are constructed as usual from V and Σ, and atoms are formed from an n-ary predicate symbol and n terms in the usual manner. A ground term (ground atom) is a term (atom) containing no variables. The Herbrand universe HU (the set of ground terms) and the Herbrand base HB (the set of ground atoms) are defined for a given language.

A *substitution* θ is a function mapping variables to terms, which is extended to map syntactic objects (such as terms, atoms or clauses) to syntactic objects by replacing all occurrences of variables x in the syntactic object by $x\theta$. A substitution α is said to be *more general than* the substitution β if $\beta = \alpha \circ \gamma$ for some substitution γ. A substitution θ is a *unifier* of syntactic objects A and H if $A\theta \equiv H\theta$. Syntactic objects which are unifiable have a *most general unifier (mgu)* which is unique up to variable renaming. Lassez et al. [1988] gives a thorough treatment of these concepts. A *variant* of a syntactic object is obtained by applying a variable renaming substitution to the object.

We use an over tilde ˜ to denote a list or sequence of objects. For example, $\tilde{x}$ may denote a list of variables, $\tilde{t}$ a list of terms, and $\tilde{x} = \tilde{t}$ a list or conjunction of equations.

A *logic program* is a collection of definite clauses. A *definite clause* takes the form

$$A \leftarrow B_1, B_2, \ldots, B_n$$

where A, B_1, B_2,...,B_n are atoms. In what follows we use the terminology *clause* only to refer to definite clauses. A is called the *head* of the clause and B_1, B_2,...,B_n is called the *body* of the clause. A *Datalog* program is a logic program which contains no function symbols of arity > 0. Such programs occur as deductive databases or as recursive queries to relational databases.

There are two well-known logical formulas associated with a logic program P. One straightforwardly considers the program to be a conjunction of the formulas

$$\forall \bar{x} \; A \lor \neg B_1 \lor \neg B_2 \lor \ldots \lor \neg B_n$$

corresponding to the clauses

$$A \leftarrow B_1, B_2, \ldots, B_n$$

in P where $\bar{x}$ denotes the list of all variables in the clause. We will also denote this conjunction by P. The second takes P to be shorthand for a *complete logic program* (or completion of P) (Clark [1978]), a collection P^* of predicate definitions, each of the form

$$p(\bar{x}) \longleftrightarrow \begin{bmatrix} \exists \bar{y}_1(\bar{x} = \bar{t}_1 \land B_1) \\ \lor \; \exists \bar{y}_2(\bar{x} = \bar{t}_2 \land B_2) \\ \ldots \\ \lor \; \exists \bar{y}_n(\bar{x} = \bar{t}_n \land B_n) \end{bmatrix}$$

corresponding to the collection of all clauses in P with p in the heads:

$$p(\bar{t}_1) \leftarrow B_1$$
$$p(\bar{t}_2) \leftarrow B_2$$
$$\ldots$$
$$p(\bar{t}_n) \leftarrow B_n$$

where $\bar{y}_i$ denotes the variables in the ith clause above and each B_i is a (possibly empty) conjunction of atoms. If p does not appear in the head of a clause then P^* contains

$$\neg p(\bar{x})$$

Note that, in general, P^* does not form a complete theory in the usual logical sense (Shoenfield [1967]). Figure 2 gives the completions of the programs of Figure 1.

One logical semantics of a program is given simply as the theory P. Logical consequence with regard to P is concerned with all models of P in all domains. However, the expected domain of logic programs is the Herbrand universe with the Herbrand interpretation of function symbols as term con-

P_1^* $Even(x) \longleftrightarrow x = 0 \lor \exists y \ x = S^2(y) \land Even(y)$

  $Odd(x) \longleftrightarrow Even(S(x))$

P_2^* $Even(x) \longleftrightarrow x = 0 \lor \exists y \ x = S(y) \land Odd(y)$

  $Odd(x) \longleftrightarrow \exists y \ x = S(y) \land Even(y)$

Figure 2: Completed Programs for Odd and Even

structors. Models of P or P^* with this domain are Herbrand models. Two more semantics arise by considering *Herbrand logical consequence*, denoted by $\models_{HU}$, for P and P^*, which is concerned only with Herbrand models. $P \models_{HU} F$ ($P^* \models_{HU} F$) if the formula F evaluates to True under every Herbrand model of P (P^*) and valuation.

Clark [1978] axiomatized the Herbrand domain with the following equality theory E^* (dependent only on Σ).

$x = x$

$x = y \leftarrow y = x$

$x = z \leftarrow x = y, y = z$

For every $f \in \Sigma$

$f(\bar{x}) = f(\bar{y}) \longleftrightarrow \bar{x} = \bar{y}$

For every $f, g \in \Sigma, f \not\equiv g$

$f(\bar{x}) \neq g(\bar{y})$

For every term $\tau(x)$ containing x except 'x'

$x \neq \tau(x)$

Herbrand then gave a semantics of logic programs as the theory $P^* \cup E^*$. Logical consequence for this theory is concerned with more than just the Herbrand models of P^*, but not with all models of P^*.

The function T_P, introduced by van Emden and Kowalski [1976], maps subsets of the Herbrand base to subsets of the Herbrand base and is defined by

$T_P(I) = \{A \in HB :$ there is a ground instance $A \leftarrow B_1, B_2, \ldots, B_n$

of a clause in P such that $\{B_1, B_2, \ldots, B_n\} \subseteq I\}$

Application of T_P corresponds to one-step deductions, using P, of ground atoms from ground atoms. The following sets (Apt and van Emden [1982]) are defined by transfinite induction:

$$T_P{\uparrow}0 = \emptyset$$

$$T_P{\uparrow}(\alpha + 1) = T_P(T_P \mid \alpha)$$

$$T_P{\uparrow}\alpha = \bigcup_{\beta<\alpha} T_P \mid \beta \text{ if } \alpha \text{ is a limit ordinal}$$

$$T_P{\downarrow}0 = HB$$

$$T_P{\downarrow}(\alpha + 1) = T_P(T_P \mid \alpha)$$

$$T_P{\downarrow}\alpha = \bigcap_{\beta<\alpha} T_P \mid \beta \text{ if } \alpha \text{ is a limit ordinal}$$

T_P is continuous on the complete lattice of subsets of HB ordered by set inclusion. It follows that $T_P{\uparrow}\omega = lfp(T_P)$, the least fixedpoint of T_P. However, in general we have $T_P{\downarrow}\omega \neq gfp(T_P)$, the greatest fixedpoint of T_P.

The function corresponding to deductions of any number of steps is denoted by $[\![P]\!]$ (Lassez and Maher [1983, 1984]). We define the addition of functions f and g by $(f + g)(X) = f(X) \cup g(X)$, an iteration operator $^\omega$ by $f^\omega(X) = \bigcup_{i=0}^{\infty} f^i(X)$ and denote the identity function by Id. $[\![P]\!]$ can be defined by $[\![P]\!](X) = (T_P + Id)^\omega(X)$. $[\![P]\!]$ is a closure operator, that is $[\![P]\!]$ is monotonic $(X \subseteq Y \to [\![P]\!](X) \subseteq [\![P]\!](Y))$, increasing $(X \subseteq [\![P]\!](X))$ and idempotent $([\![P]\!]([\![P]\!](X)) = [\![P]\!](X))$. A closure operator $[\![P]\!]$ maps each X to the least of the fixedpoints of $[\![P]\!]$ which contains X. Consequently, the fixedpoints of a closure operator determine (uniquely) the closure operator. There is a partial order on functions defined in the following manner: $f \leq g$ iff $\forall X f(X) \subseteq g(X)$.

A *goal* is a collection of atoms. A *derivation* for a program P and initial goal G_0 is a (finite or infinite) sequence of goals $\{G_i\}$. Consecutive goals are related in the following manner: for some $A \in G_i$ and some variant $H \leftarrow B_1,...,B_n$ of a clause of P containing only new variables, and where H and A have the same predicate symbol and θ is an mgu of A and H, $G_{i+1} = ((G_i - \{A\}) \cup \{B_1,...,B_n\})\theta$.) A is said to be *selected* at step i. This derivation step is called *SLD-resolution* (Apt and van Emden [1982]). A *computation rule* determines (uniquely) for every goal in a derivation which atom in that goal is selected.

A derivation is infinite unless, for some goal in the derivation, there is no next goal. There are two cases. A derivation is *successful* if some G_i is empty. The second case occurs when the derivation is finitely failed. A derivation is *finitely failed* if no (variant of the) head of a clause of P unifies with the selected atom. A derivation is *fair* if every atom that appears in the derivation is chosen at some step. A *ground* derivation is a derivation except that θ is a unifier of A and H such that G_{i+1} is ground. If the initial goal is ground, then it is equivalent to say that a ground derivation is a derivation using the ground instances of clauses of P. An *SLD tree* for a goal G is a tree with goals as nodes where G is at the root, each non-empty goal contains a selected atom, and the children of a node are the goals obtained in one derivation step using the selected atom of that node.

The operational model we will use is fair SLD-resolution (Lassez and Maher [1984]); that is, SLD-resolution where every branch of the SLD tree forms a fair derivation. We consider three sets of ground atoms that correspond to finitary computations: the success set $SS(P) = \{A : A$ has a successful derivation for $P\}$, the finite failure set $FF(P) = \{A : A$ has a finite failed SLD tree for $P\}$ and the ground finite failure set $GFF(P) = \{A :$ every fair ground derivation of A for P is finitely failed$\}$. Fair SLD-resolution guarantees that A is in $FF(P)$ exactly when the goal A terminates with failure, independent of the specific computation rule. Success or finite failure of an atom can be discovered finitely using fair SLD-resolution. Thus, $SS(P)$ and $FF(P)$ correspond to terminating computations. However, $GFF(P)$ does not represent only terminating computations; although every fair ground derivation of an atom in $GFF(P)$ is finitely failed, there may be infinitely many of them.

There are several significant relationships between the different things we have defined. We can express in many ways the set of successful ground atoms, $T_P \uparrow \omega = lfp(T_P) = [\![P]\!](\emptyset) = SS(P) = \{A \in HB : P \models A\} = \{A \in HB : P^*, E^* \models A\} =$ least Herbrand model of P (where we use the standard set representation of Herbrand interpretations), the set of failed ground atoms, $FF(P) = \overline{T_P \downarrow \omega} = \{A \in HB : P^*, E^* \models \neg A\}$ and the set of ground-failed ground atoms, $GFF(P) = \overline{gfp(T_P)} = \{A \in HB : P^*, E^* \models_{HU} \neg A\} =$ complement of greatest Herbrand model of P^*. Furthermore, it is easy to show that the fixedpoints of T_P are the Herbrand models of P^* and the fixedpoints of $[\![P]\!]$ are the Herbrand models of P.

Proofs of most of the above relationships can be found in Lloyd [1984], and the remainder are contained in Maher [1985]. Jaffar et al. [1986b] discusses the development of these results.

Subsumption-Equivalence

We introduce a form of equivalence based only on the syntactic form of definite clauses and a weaker variant and demonstrate their usefulness by employing them in the syntactic characterization of some continuity properties of T_P. But first we examine a technical point concerning the function symbols in a program.

The proofs of the results of this section assume the existence of a potentially unbounded number of constant symbols in Σ, which do not appear in the relevant program (called *new* constants). The same effect could be obtained with one new function symbol (of arity > 0) to obtain new ground terms with new outermost function symbol. Thus, this technical requirement could be satisfied without forcing Σ to be infinite. But if we are to consider all programs definable in the language and guarantee that a new function symbol always exists, then we are forced to have an infinite Σ. The assumption that a new function symbol exists closely reflects implementations of logic interpreters such as PROLOG: queries are permitted to use function symbols that are not used in the program. In this setting, the above assumption is more appropriate than the assumption, employed by many, that queries use only those function symbols that appear in the program. However, the results in this paper will still hold if we assume instead that no program exploits the finiteness of Σ.

The existence of new constants allows the application of the following simple result of logic (see, for example, Shoenfield [1967]):

THEOREM 1 (THEOREM ON CONSTANTS)
Let L' be a language obtained from L by the addition of new constants and let T be a theory axiomatized in L. Then for every formula A in L and every substitution θ of the form

$$\{x_1 \leftarrow c_1, \ldots, x_p \leftarrow c_p\}$$

where the x_i's are free variables of A and the c_i's are distinct new constants we have

$$(L)\ T \models A \text{ iff } (L')T \models A\theta \quad \blacksquare$$

where we place in parentheses the underlying language of the theory. (One interesting consequence of this result is that soundness and completeness results for ground atoms can be lifted to non-ground atoms, so that, for example, the least Herbrand model of a program determines which queries can succeed without instantiation.) We will also use a closely related technique in which new constants replace variables and the ground expressions are manipulated before replacing the constants by the original variables.

We use the notion of subsumption, which is well known in automated theorem proving. Let C_1 and C_2 be the definite clauses $A \leftarrow B_1, \ldots, B_n$ and $G \leftarrow D_1, \ldots, D_n$ respectively. C_1 is *subsumed* by C_2 if there is a substitution θ such that $A = G\theta$ and $\{D_1\theta, \ldots, D_m\theta\} \subseteq \{B_1, \ldots, B_n\}$. A subsumed clause is, in a sense, already encapsulated in the subsuming clause. Some subsumption algorithms (for general clauses) and an analysis of their complexity can be found in Gottlob and Leitsch [1985]. The following proposition gives a well-known link between subsumption and logical implication.

PROPOSITION 1

Let $\bar{x}$ be all the variables in clause C_1 and $\bar{y}$ be all the variables in clause C_2. If C_2 subsumes C_1 then $\models \forall \bar{y} \ C_2 \rightarrow \forall \bar{x} \ C_1$. ∎

We say that two clauses are *subsumption-equal* if each subsumes the other. By the proposition above, such clauses are logically equivalent. A *redundancy* in a clause occurs when there are two identical atoms in the body of the clause or a non-renaming instance of the clause subsumes the original clause. A clause without redundancy is said to be *reduced*. The definition of reduced clause here is different, although equivalent, to the one in Plotkin [1970].

If two atoms in the body of a clause C unify with most general unifier θ, then the clause obtained from $C\theta$ by retaining only one occurrence of duplicated atoms is called a *factor* of C. Part (a) of the following proposition shows that the reduced clauses are canonical representatives of the equivalence classes formed by subsumption-equality. Part (b) suggests a method to find the reduced form of a clause C: if C is not reduced, obtain a factor C' as in the proposition and apply this process to C' until a reduced clause is found. Since the body of a factor of C must contain fewer atoms than the body of C, the method suggested by (b) must terminate. This algorithm is essentially that of Plotkin.

PROPOSITION 2

1.   Every clause is subsumption-equal to a unique (up to variable renaming) reduced clause.

2.   A clause C is not reduced iff C has a factor C' which subsumes C. ∎

Any program P can be reduced to a more compact but logically equivalent program by partitioning the clauses of P according to subsumption-equality, choosing the reduced clause from each class, and then deleting those clauses which are subsumed by some other clause. The resulting set is called the *canonical program* or *canonical form* for P. The canonical form of a program is unique (up to variable renaming). Two programs are *subsumption-equivalent* if they have the same canonical form. It follows from the construction of the canonical form that P_1 is subsumption-equivalent to P_2 iff every clause of P_1 is subsumed by some clause of P_2 and vice versa.

EXAMPLE 1

We illustrate the previous definitions with a simple example. Consider the programs P_1

$$A(x) \leftarrow B(x, y), C(y) \tag{1}$$

and P_2

$$A(c) \leftarrow B(c, y), C(y) \tag{2}$$

$$A(x) \leftarrow B(x, y), C(y), B(z, y) \tag{3}$$

$$A(x) \leftarrow B(x, y), C(y), D(y, x) \tag{4}$$

Clauses (2) and (4) are subsumed by clause (3). Clause (3) is not reduced since application $\theta = \{z \leftarrow x\}$ produces a factor, which in this case is clause (1). Since also clause (1) subsumes (3), these clauses are subsumption-equal. Furthermore, clause (1) is reduced. Consequently P_1 is the canonical form of P_2, so P_1 and P_2 are subsumption-equivalent. ■

We now begin to investigate the link between the $\leq$ ordering on functions T_P derived from sets of clauses and subsumption. This will lead us to show the identity of the two notions: equality of functions T_P and subsumption-equivalence of sets of clauses.

LEMMA 1
If C_1 and C_2 are clauses and C_1 subsumes C_2, then $T_{C_1} \geq T_{C_2}$.

Proof: Let C_1 be $G \leftarrow D_1,...,D_m$, C_2 be $H \leftarrow B_1,..., B_n$, $X \subseteq HB$ and $A \in T_{C_2}(X)$. Then there is some substitution θ with $A = H\theta$ and $\{B_1\theta,...,B_n\theta\} \subseteq X$. If C_1 subsumes C_2, then there is a substitution ψ such that $H = G\psi$ and $\{D_1\psi,...,D_m\psi\} \subseteq \{B_1,...,B_n\}$. But then $A = G\psi\theta$ and $\{D_1\psi\theta,...,D_m\psi\theta\} \subseteq X$ so that $A \in T_{C_1}(X)$. Thus, $\forall X \, T_{C_1}(X) \supseteq T_{C_2}(X)$, that is, $T_{C_1} \geq T_{C_2}$. ■

COROLLARY 1
If every clause of P_2 is subsumed by some clause in P_1 then $T_{P_1} \geq T_{P_2}$. ■

We are now able to show that the syntactic notion of subsumption-equivalence of programs and the notion that programs P that define the same function T_P are "equal," are identical.

THEOREM 2
P_1 is subsumption-equivalent to P_2 iff $T_{P_1} = T_{P_2}$.

Proof:
(only if)
If P_1 and P_2 are subsumption-equivalent, then every clause of P_1 is subsumed by some clause of P_2 and vice versa. Two applications of the above corollary give the required result.
(if)
Consider a clause $C_1 = (A \leftarrow B_1,...,B_n)$ in P_1. Let $\theta = \{x_1 \leftarrow c_1,...,x_p \leftarrow c_p\}$ where $x_1,...,x_p$ are the variables in the clause and $c_1,...,c_p$ are distinct

new constant symbols (i.e., symbols which do not occur in P_1 or P_2) and let $\tilde{B}$ denote $\{B_1,\ldots,B_n\}$. Then $A\theta \in T_{P_1}(\tilde{B}\theta)$ and so $A\theta \in T_{P_2}(\tilde{B}\theta)$. Thus, there is a clause $C_2 = (G \leftarrow D_1,\ldots,D_m)$ in P_2 and a substitution α such that $A\theta = G\alpha$ and $\{D_1\alpha,\ldots,D_m\alpha\} \subseteq \tilde{B}\theta$. By replacing c_i's by x_i's in α and θ, we can see that C_2 subsumes C_1. Similarly there is a clause in P_1 which subsumes C_2. Hence P_1 is subsumption-equivalent to P_2. ∎

Observe that for a fixed program P the proof of this result requires only a finite number of constants. Thus, this result (and the other results of this section) also holds when Σ is finite, provided it is sufficiently large.

From the proof of the "if" part of the above theorem and the corollary preceding it, we can derive the following.

COROLLARY 2
Every clause of P_2 is subsumed by some clause in P_1 iff $T_{P_1} \geq T_{P_2}$. ∎

A consequence of these results is that, for finite sets of clauses P_1 and P_2, we can now determine whether or not $T_{P_1} = T_{P_2}$, $T_{P_1} \leq T_{P_2}$, etc., without dealing directly with the functions.

The canonical program may still contain tautologies. A *tautology* is a logic formula which always (i.e., under every interpretation and valuation) evaluates to True. A definite clause is a tautology only when an exact copy of the head appears in the body. By deleting all the tautologies from a canonical program we obtain the *weakly canonical program*, which gives rise to *weak subsumption-equivalence* between two programs that have the same weak canonical form.

The weak canonical form of a program can be regarded as the natural form of a program since a program that is not weak canonical may result in extra, useless computation or non-terminating behavior which would otherwise not occur. We can give a characterization of weakly subsumption-equivalent programs in terms of the function T_P. Let ID denote the set of clauses $\{Q(\tilde{x}) \leftarrow Q(\tilde{x}) : Q \in \Pi$ and $\tilde{x}$ is a sequence of distinct variables$\}$. Then $T_{ID} = Id$.

PROPOSITION 3
P_1 is weakly subsumption-equivalent to P_2 iff $T_{P_1} + Id = T_{P_2} + Id$.

Proof:
(only if)
If C is a tautology, it is of the form $P(\tilde{t}) \leftarrow B_1,\ldots,B_{i-1}, P(\tilde{t}), B_{i+1},\ldots,B_n$. This is subsumed by $P(\tilde{x}) \leftarrow P(\tilde{x})$. Thus $T_C \leq T_{ID} = Id$. Let P be the weak canonical form of P_1 and P_2. Then, by Corollary 2 and the construction of P from P_i, $T_P \leq T_{P_i} \leq T_{P \cup ID} = T_P + Id$, for $i = 1,2$. Hence $T_{P_1} + Id = T_{P_2} + Id = T_P + Id$.

(if)

From the "only if" part we can assume that P_1 and P_2 are weak canonical. $T_{P_i \cup ID} = T_{P_i} + Id$, $i = 1,2$. $T_{P_1} + Id = T_{P_2} + Id$ so $P_1 \cup ID$ and $P_2 \cup ID$ are subsumption-equivalent. No clause of ID can subsume a clause of P_i, so P_1 and P_2 are subsumption-equivalent and consequently equal. ∎

For some properties of the function T_P we are able to characterize syntactically those sets of clauses P such that the property holds. These results, when taken with the obvious algorithm for computing the canonical form of a program, will mean that the presence or absence of such properties can be determined simply and without the need to deal directly with the functions. Theorem 2 greatly simplifies the proofs of these results.

T_P is *distributive* if $T_P \left(\bigcup_{i \in I} X_i \right) = \bigcup_{i \in I} T_P(X_i)$ for every collection $\{X_i : i \in I\}$ of subsets of *HB*. But, since T_P is continuous, this condition is equivalent to $\forall X, Y \subseteq HB, T_P(X \cup Y) = T_P(X) \cup T_P(Y)$. Distributive programs correspond to Nilsson's ideas on decomposition of data bases of facts (Nilsson [1980]). For such programs, a data base of facts (ground atoms) can be divided arbitrarily and one-step bottom-up computations can be performed on the parts without loss of information.

A program is *binary* if the body of each clause in P contains at most one atom. Tarnlund [1977] has shown that every computable function is computable by a binary program. Binary programs have been further investigated in Sebelik and Stepanek [1980]. The transformational systems of Reynolds [1970], when restricted to definite clauses, are binary programs.

PROPOSITION 4

T_P is distributive iff P is subsumption-equivalent to a binary program.

Proof:

(if)

By Theorem 2, we can assume without loss of generality that P forms a binary program. It suffices to show that $T_P(X) = \bigcup_{x \in X} T_P(\{x\})$ for arbitrary $X \subseteq HB$.

$$\bigcup_{x \in X} T_P(\{x\})$$
$$= \bigcup_{x \in X} \{H : \text{there is a ground instance } H \leftarrow x \text{ of a clause in } P\}$$
$$= \{H : \text{there is a ground instance } H \leftarrow x \text{ of a clause in } P \text{ such that } x \in X\}$$
$$= T_P(X)$$

(only if)

It is easy to see that a program P is subsumption-equivalent to a binary program iff the canonical form of P is binary. By this fact and Theorem 2 we can assume that P is in canonical form. We prove the contrapositive. Suppose P has a clause C of the form $H \leftarrow B_1,...,B_n$ where $n > 1$. Let $\theta = \{x_1 \leftarrow c_1,...,x_p \leftarrow c_p\}$ where the x_i are the variables of C, the c_i are distinct new constants and let $X = \{B_1\theta,...,B_n\theta\}$. Now $\forall i \; H\theta \notin T_P(\{B_i\theta\})$ since otherwise there must be a clause $C' = (G \leftarrow D_1,...,D_m)$ in P and a substitution γ such that $G\gamma = H\theta$ and $\{D_1\gamma,...,D_m\gamma\} \subseteq \{B_i\theta\}$ for some i and consequently C is subsumed by C' — a contradiction. So $T_P(\{B_1\theta,...,B_n\theta\}) \neq \overset{n}{\underset{i=1}{\cup}} T_P(\{B_i\theta\})$. Thus T_P is not distributive. ∎

T_P is *down-continuous* if, for every decreasing chain $\{I_j\}$, $\underset{j \in J}{\cap} T_P(I_j) = T_P(\underset{j \in J}{\cap} I_j)$. Interest in down-continuous functions stems from an interest in when the greatest fixedpoint of T_P, $gfp(T_P)$, is equal to $T_P \downarrow \omega$. If T_P is down-continuous, then $gfp(T_P) = T_P \downarrow \omega$, and so $FF(P) = GFF(P)$. This property has important implications for inferring falsity from failure (in a finite time) to succeed (i.e., the negation-as-failure rule). In particular it implies that it is only necessary to consider Herbrand models when determining whether ground literals are logical consequences of the corresponding complete program.

A variable in a clause is said to be *local* if it appears only in the body of that clause.

THEOREM 3

Suppose the Herbrand universe is infinite. T_P is down-continuous iff P is subsumption-equivalent to a program such that no clause has local variables.

Proof:

(if)

By Theorem 2, it suffices to consider the case when P has no local variables. For a decreasing chain $I_1 \supseteq I_2 \supseteq ... \supseteq I_j \supseteq ...$, let $A \in \underset{j > 0}{\cap} T_P(I_j)$. Then for every j there is a ground instance $A \leftarrow B_{j,1},...,B_{j,n(j)}$ of a clause in P such that $\{B_{j,1},...,B_{j,\,n(j)}\} \subseteq I_j$. Since there are no local variables and only a finite number of clauses, there are only a finite number of possible ground instances of clauses with A as the head. Thus, some ground instance $A \leftarrow D_1,...,D_n$ of a clause is used in generating $T_P(I_j)$ for infinitely many j's. Consequently $\{D_1,...,D_n\} \subseteq I_j$ for every j since $\{I_j\}$ forms a decreasing chain, and hence $A \in T_P(\underset{j > 0}{\cap} I_j)$. Thus T_P is down-continuous.

(only if)

It suffices to show that a canonical down-continuous program has no clauses with local variables. The proof is by contradiction. Suppose P is canonical and there is a clause $C = (A \leftarrow B_1,...,B_n)$ with local variables. Let $\theta = \{x_1 \leftarrow c_1,...,x_m \leftarrow c_m\}$ where the x_i's are the non-local variables of C and the c_i's are distinct new constants. We will use the local variables to demonstrate that T_P is not down-continuous by constructing a decreasing chain $\{I_j\}$ such that $\forall j \ A\theta \in T_P(I_j)$ and $A\theta \notin T_P(\bigcap_{j>0} I_j)$. Let D be the (possibly empty) set of ground atoms of $\{B_1\theta,...,B_n\theta\}$ and let $J_\beta = \{B_i\theta\beta : 1 \leq i \leq n\} - D$. Divide $\{J_\beta : \beta$ is a ground substitution for the local variables$\}$ into a countably infinite number of finite non-empty classes (possible since the Herbrand universe is countably infinite) and for each class i, let K_i denote the union of its constituent J_β's. Then let $L_i = \bigcup_{j=1}^{i} K_j$, $L = \bigcup_\beta J_\beta$ and $I_i = D \cup L - L_i$. Clearly $\{I_j\}$ forms a decreasing chain and $\bigcap_{j>0} I_j = D$. By construction $\forall j \ A\theta \in T_P(I_j)$ and $A\theta \notin T_P(\bigcap_{j>0} I_j)$ since if it were otherwise, then either C is not reduced or C is subsumed by another clause of P, in either case violating the assumption that P is canonical. This contradicts the assumption that T_P is down-continuous and hence such a C does not exist. ∎

If the Herbrand universe is finite, then T_P is always down-continuous, since any infinite descending chain must stabilize for some finite k (i.e., $\exists k$ such that $\forall j \geq k \ I_j = I_k$).

The cases where T_P is down-continuous do not constitute all cases where $gfp(T_P) = T_P\!\downarrow\!\omega$. This topic is pursued further in the next section.

Fitting [1985] defined a class of general logic programs (i.e., allowing negated atoms in clause bodies) which he claims are the only acceptable programs. In particular, the only definite clause programs P he considers acceptable are those for which T_P is down-continuous. From the above theorem it would seem that this class is quite restrictive since, for example, transitivity cannot be expressed naturally. Blair [1986] has shown that every program can be transformed into a down-continuous program with a similar operational semantics. But it seems that the transformation does not aid in reasoning about failure using only Herbrand models.

A program P is *locally deterministic* if, for every ground atom, that atom unifies with the head of, at most, one clause. Equivalently, P is locally deterministic if no pair of heads of clauses in P unify.

T_P is *down-distributive* if $T_P(\bigcap_{i \in I} X_i) = \bigcap_{i \in I} T_P(X_i)$ for every collection $\{X_i : i \in I\}$ of subsets of HB. T_P is down-distributive iff T_P is down-continuous and $\forall X,Y \ T_P(X \cap Y) = T_P(X) \cap T_P(Y)$. We have the following sufficient condition on P for T_P to be down-distributive.

PROPOSITION 5

If P is subsumption-equivalent to a program that is locally deterministic and such that no clause has local variables, then T_P is down-distributive.

Proof: By Theorem 3 T_P is down-continuous. Thus, it suffices to prove that $T_P(X \cap Y) = T_P(X) \cap T_P(Y) \; \forall X, Y$. Further, by Theorem 2, it suffices to consider only the case where P is locally deterministic and such that no clause has local variables. Let $X, Y \subseteq HB$. Since T_P is monotonic, $\forall X, Y \; T_P(X \cap Y) \subseteq T_P(X) \cap T_P(Y)$. Suppose $A \in T_P(X) \cap T_P(Y)$. Then, since there is only one instance of a clause of the form $A \leftarrow B_1,...,B_n$, we have that $\{B_1,...,B_n\} \subseteq X$ and $\{B_1,...,B_n\} \subseteq Y$. Thus $\{B_1,...,B_n\} \subseteq X \cap Y$ and so $A \in T_P(X \cap Y)$. ∎

EXAMPLE 2

The converse of the above proposition does not hold, as the following program P shows:

$P(a) \leftarrow Q(a)$

$P(x) \leftarrow Q(x), R(x)$

Clearly P is not locally deterministic, but T_P is down-continuous. If $Q(a) \notin X \cap Y$, then clearly $T_P(X \cap Y) = T_P(X) \cap T_P(Y)$ and if $Q(a) \in X \cap Y$, then $T_P(X \cap Y) = T_P(X' \cap Y') \cup \{P(a)\} = (T_P(X') \cap T_P (Y')) \cup \{P(a)\} = T_P(X) \cap T_P(Y)$ where X' is $X - \{Q(a)\}$ and Y' is $Y - \{Q(a)\}$. Thus T_P is down-distributive. ∎

Subsumption-equivalence has also proved useful in characterizing syntactically some (but not all) programs P which can be decomposed into subprograms P_1 and P_2 such that $[\![P]\!] = [\![P_1]\!] + [\![P_2]\!]$ or $[\![P]\!] = [\![P_1]\!] \circ [\![P_2]\!]$ (Maher [1985], Lassez and Maher [1983, 1984]).

Equivalences of Logic Programs

We assume in this section that programs are all written with the same language L. We will consider a number of formulations of equivalence based on either the logical semantics, the operational semantics or the functional semantics. The latter named provides three forms of equivalence: programs having the same T_P function, programs having the same $(T_P + Id)$ function and programs having the same $[\![P]\!]$. The operational semantics also provides three: programs with the same success set, those with the same finite failure set, and those with the same ground finite failure set. Logical semantics contributes four: logical equivalence and programs having logically equivalent completions with respect to E^*, and the two corresponding equivalences when only Herbrand models are considered. Additionally, we have two notions of equivalence based on the syntax: subsumption-equivalence and weak subsumption-equivalence. (Note that there are other notions of equivalence which have not been included.)

We already know that some of these equivalences are the same in that they give the same equivalence classes of programs, and we also know that there are other different formulations for some of the equivalences. For example, the equalities $SS(P) = [\![P]\!](\emptyset) = lfp(T_P) = \{A \in HB: P \models A\}$ give rise to four different formulations of the same equivalence relation.

The following theorem shows that equality of the closure operators $[\![P]\!]$ and Herbrand logical equivalence of programs are identical relationships between logic programs. Thus, two programs have the same Herbrand logical consequences exactly when they always produce the same generated set from the same starting axioms. It also shows that the partial order $\leq$ on functions $[\![P]\!]$ and the ordering of programs by Herbrand logical implication are the same. This result has been shown for Datalog programs independently in Cosmadakis and Kanellakis [1986], and in Sagiv [1988] as part of a stronger result. Sagiv [1988] and Buntine [1986] give algorithms that can be used to decide $[\![P_1]\!] \leq [\![P_2]\!]$ (called uniform containment in Sagiv [1988]) for Datalog programs, and hence can also be used to decide the equivalence $[\![P_1]\!] = [\![P_2]\!]$ for Datalog programs. In general $[\![P_1]\!] = [\![P_2]\!]$ is not decidable.

THEOREM 4

1. $[\![P_1]\!] = [\![P_2]\!]$ iff $\models_{HU} P_1 \leftrightarrow P_2$

2. $[\![P_2]\!] \leq [\![P_1]\!]$ iff $\models_{HU} P_1 \rightarrow P_2$

Proof: First recall that, for any program P, the fixedpoints of $[\![P]\!]$ are the Herbrand models of P and that a closure operator is determined by its fixedpoints. We also use, in the proof of (2), the result from Lassez and Maher [1984] that $[\![P_1 \cup P_2]\!] = ([\![P_1]\!] + [\![P_2]\!])^\omega$.

1. $\models_{HU} P_1 \leftrightarrow P_2$ iff P_1 and P_2 have the same Herbrand models iff $[\![P_1]\!]$ and $[\![P_2]\!]$ have the same fixedpoints iff $[\![P_1]\!] = [\![P_2]\!]$.

2.   Using part (1) we have $\models_{HU} P_1 \rightarrow P_2$ iff $\models_{HU} P_1 \leftrightarrow P_1 \wedge P_2$ iff $[\![P_1]\!] = [\![P_1 \cup P_2]\!]$.

Now if $[\![P_2]\!] \leq [\![P_1]\!]$, then $[\![P_1]\!] = [\![P_1]\!] + [\![P_2]\!] = ([\![P_1]\!] + [\![P_2]\!])^\omega = [\![P_1 \cup P_2]\!]$. Conversely, if $[\![P_1]\!] = [\![P_1 \cup P_2]\!]$ then $[\![P_1]\!] \leq [\![P_1]\!] + [\![P_2]\!] \leq ([\![P_1]\!] + [\![P_2]\!])^\omega = [\![P_1 \cup P_2]\!] = [\![P_1]\!]$. Thus $[\![P_1]\!] + [\![P_2]\!] = [\![P_1]\!]$ and so $[\![P_2]\!] \leq [\![P_1]\!]$. ∎

The question arises: Why bother with both semantics if equivalence wrt $[\![P]\!]$ is the same as Herbrand logical equivalence? The answer is that the respective frameworks of the two semantics provide different operations and theoretical tools for manipulating and reasoning about programs: The logical framework has the logical connectives such as conjunction and implication, and the functional framework has composition and function addition. Thus, the logical framework can easily express union of programs (by conjunction) or conditional truth of atoms (using implication) while the functional framework can express relationships such as $[\![P]\!] = [\![P_1]\!] + [\![P_2]\!]$ or commutativity, $[\![P_1]\!] \circ [\![P_2]\!] = [\![P_2]\!] \circ [\![P_1]\!]$. Similarly, we can use model theory to reason about programs in one framework and exploit known algebraic properties of closure operators in the other. Furthermore, knowing that the two semantics are equivalent offers greater flexibility in reasoning about programs, since the advantages of both frameworks are available.

The following proposition shows that, when there are an infinite number of function symbols, logical equivalence in Herbrand models can be "lifted" to logical equivalence. Consequently, the characterizations of the previous theorem can also be lifted. A more direct proof that $[\![P_1]\!] = [\![P_2]\!]$ iff $\models P_1 \longleftrightarrow P_2$ was given in Maher [1985].

PROPOSITION 6

If Σ is infinite then

1. $\models P_1 \longleftrightarrow P_2$ iff $\models_{HU} P_1 \longleftrightarrow P_2$ iff $[\![P_1]\!] = [\![P_2]\!]$

2. $\models P_1 \longrightarrow P_2$ iff $\models_{HU} P_1 \longrightarrow P_2$ iff $[\![P_2]\!] \leq [\![P_1]\!]$

Proof: First note the fact, related to Herbrand's Theorem, that for every model M of a set of clauses P we can define a Herbrand model H by:

for every ground atom A, A is true in H iff A is true in M

It suffices to show that $P \models_{HU} \forall \bar{x} \, C$ implies $P \models \forall \bar{x} \, C$ where C is a single clause containing variables $\bar{x}$. The proof is by contradiction. By the Theorem on Constants $P \models \forall \bar{x} \, C$ iff $P \models C\theta$ where the substitution θ replaces the variables of C by distinct new constants. Now if $P \not\models C\theta$ then, for some model M of P, $M \not\models C\theta$. But then, from the previously noted fact, $H \not\models C\theta$. This contradicts $P \models_{HU} \forall \bar{x} \, C$. ∎

Intuitively, the hypothesis of the theorem arises from a need to disallow programs referring exhaustively to the entire Herbrand universe with a "case statement." For example, if $\Sigma = \{a, f\}$ and P_1 is the program

$P(a)$

$P(f(x))$

then P_1 implies that $P(t)$ is true for any ground term t and so $\models_{HU} P_1 \longleftrightarrow P_2$ where P_2 is the program

$P(x)$

An important relationship between two equivalences is their relative strength. We say $\sim_1$ is *(strictly) stronger* than $\sim_2$ if whenever $P \sim_1 Q$ then $P \sim_2 Q$ for all programs P and Q (and $\sim_2$ is not stronger than $\sim_1$). Thus the stronger the equivalence, the finer the partition induced. Two equivalences that are stronger than each other are the same in the sense that they define the same equivalence classes.

Clearly equivalence wrt T_P is stronger than equivalence wrt $(T_P + Id)$, which, by the definition of $[\![P]\!]$, must be stronger than equivalence wrt $[\![P]\!]$. Clearly also, equivalence wrt $[\![P]\!]$ is stronger than equality of success sets since $SS(P) = [\![P]\!](\emptyset)$. These relations can easily be seen to be strict. We know from the previous section that equivalence wrt T_P is the same as subsumption-equivalence, and equivalence wrt $(T_P + Id)$ is the same as weak subsumption-equivalence.

Clearly logical equivalence of the completions of two programs implies their Herbrand logical equivalence. And (Herbrand) logical equivalence of the completions of programs P_1 and P_2 implies that P_1^* and P_2^* have the same (Herbrand) models. Soundness and completeness results allow us to word some operational notions in terms of models of P^*: $SS(P)$ is the set of ground atoms which are true in all Herbrand models of P^*, $FF(P)$ is the set of ground atoms which are false in all models of P^*, and $GFF(P)$ is the set of ground atoms which are false in all Herbrand models of P^*. Thus, logical equivalence of completions is stronger than each of the operational equivalences.

In fact equivalence of completions is strictly stronger than the combination of these three equivalences (and so also of the equivalences individually). Consider the complete programs $\{A \longleftrightarrow B, B \longleftrightarrow B, D \longleftrightarrow D\}$ and $\{A \longleftrightarrow D, B \longleftrightarrow B, D \longleftrightarrow D\}$. For both programs $SS = FF = GFF = \emptyset$ and yet the interpretation that makes A and B true and D false is a model for the first complete program but not the second. Thus, it seems that some kind of trace information is necessary to distinguish between logically unequivalent complete programs by their operational behavior.

We can show that subsumption-equivalence is the most fundamental of the equivalences we consider here, if we can show that it is stronger than equivalence of completed programs. Suppose C_1 subsumes C_2. Then, using Proposition 1, $E^* \models D_1 \rightarrow D_2$ where D_i is the disjunct in P^* corresponding to C_i. So we can omit D_2 from P^* and retain a logically equivalent complete program. It follows that subsumption-equivalent sets of clauses give rise to logically equivalent complete logic programs.

In Figure 3, an arrow from $\sim_1$ to $\sim_2$ denotes that $\sim_1$ is stronger than $\sim_2$. The results of this section are summarized by the following theorem.

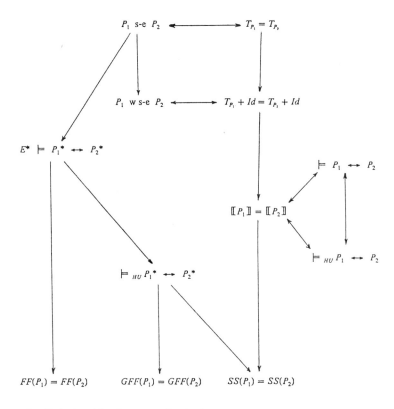

Figure 3: Relationships between Equivalences

THEOREM 5
Figure 3 exhibits the relative strengths of the formulations of equivalence we have considered. ∎

Maher [1985] has counter-examples to show that Figure 3 has not omitted any arrows. One counter-example of interest comes from the example of Figures 1 and 2. This shows that, although $P^* \to P$, logical equivalence of completions does not imply that the original programs were logically equivalent. This is seen by noting that, although $E^* \models P_1^* \leftrightarrow P_2^*$ in that example, $Even(S(0)) \in [\![P_2]\!](\{Odd(0)\}) - [\![P_1]\!](\{Odd(0)\})$ that is $P_2 \models Odd(0) \to Even(S(0))$ but $P_1 \models Odd(0) \to Even(S(0))$ does not hold. This example also demonstrates one advantage of Theorem 5. It is a simple matter to prove that $E^* \models P_1^* \leftrightarrow P_2^*$. We can conclude, by Theorem 5, that P_1 and P_2 have the same success and finite failure sets. This result would otherwise have required an induction argument.

On the other hand, logical equivalence of programs is not stronger than equivalence of completions: $\{A \leftarrow B\}$ and $\{A \leftarrow B; A \leftarrow A\}$ are logically equivalent but their completions are not.

Often we wish to use a program as part of a larger program. To express the fact that two programs will perform identically as subprograms we define, for each equivalence $\approx$ defined above, that two programs P_1 and P_2 are *equivalent as program segments* iff $P_1 \cup Q \sim P_2 \cup Q$ for every finite program Q. Clearly any equivalence as program segments is stronger than the corresponding equivalence (by taking $Q = \emptyset$). In some cases, the two concepts are the same. For example, since $T_{P \cup Q} = T_P + T_Q$ the two are the same for equivalence wrt T_P (i.e., subsumption-equivalence). The two are also the same for weak subsumption-equivalence.

The result for equivalence wrt $[\![P]\!]$ seems not so obvious. However, if we consider logical equivalence, then clearly $\models_{HU} P_1 \leftrightarrow P_2$ implies $\models_{HU} P_1 \wedge Q \leftrightarrow P_2 \wedge Q$ for any Q. Thus (Theorem 4) equivalence wrt $[\![P]\!]$ as program segments is the same as simple equivalence wrt $[\![P]\!]$. This illustrates one advantage, remarked upon earlier, of having different characterizations of the same equivalence. Demonstrating this fact wholly within the functional framework would be more difficult.

Consideration of the example of Figure 1 with $Odd(0)$ as Q shows that equivalences for success and finite failure and logical equivalence of completions are made strictly stronger when considering program segments rather than "stand-alone" programs.

Reasoning in the Herbrand Universe

There are important differences between logical equivalence of complete logic programs ($E^* \models P_1^* \leftrightarrow P_2^*$) and the corresponding Herbrand equivalence ($\models_{HU} P_1^* \leftrightarrow P_2^*$). Restricting to models with the Herbrand domain allows the use of techniques that exploit properties of the domain that are not shared by all models of E^*). One such technique is structural induction (that is, induction on the structure of the elements in the domain). This technique has proved very useful in the verification of functional programs (see, for example, Manna [1974]). However when non-Herbrand models are considered, this technique is, in general, not applicable since the domains may not be well founded.

Unfortunately it is not possible to "lift" from the Herbrand models to all models as in Proposition 6: Completed programs are not clauses. Thus, we can use structural induction to reason about one type of terminating computation (success) but not the other (finite failure). However, we can restrict to Herbrand models when dealing with ground finite failure. As discussed in Jaffar et al. [1986b], most programs occurring in practice satisfy $FF(P) = GFF(P)$ (or, equivalently, $gfp(T_P) = T_P \downarrow \omega$) and it is shown in Jaffar and Stuckey [1986] that every program has a counterpart that satisfies this condition. In this case we can use structural induction to determine that a ground goal is finitely failed.

It is not, in general, decidable whether $FF(P) = GFF(P)$ holds when given a program P. However, it is easy to find classes of programs for which this property holds. Theorem 3 gives one such class. Another example is the class of programs where non-constant function symbols appear only in clause bodies, and no clause head has repeated occurrences of a variable. To see this, first note that it is sufficient to show that every ground atom with an infinite derivation has an infinite ground derivation. Since the head of each clause contains only constants, or variables that occur only once there, the mgu computed in any derivation step can only bind variables in the goal to constants or other variables. Thus every variable occurring in an infinite derivation is either eventually bound to a constant, or else only to other variables. We can construct a ground derivation by using the ground instances of the original input clauses obtained by replacing variables that are eventually bound to a constant by that constant, and replacing all other variables by a fixed constant. This choice of ground input clauses ensures that the ground derivation does not fail, and so it must be infinite. Similarly, if Σ contains only constants, then every mgu will only bind the goal variables to constants or to other variables and the same argument applies. Thus we have

PROPOSITION 7
If either

1. Σ contains only constants, or

2. P is subsumption equivalent to a program such that

   a. non-constant function symbols appear only in clause bodies, and

   b. no clause head has repeated occurrences of a variable

then $gfp(T_P) = T_P\!\downarrow\!\omega$ ∎

The previous results characterize only a small proportion of the programs for that $gfp(T_P) = T_P\!\downarrow\!\omega$. There is a need for results characterizing more extensive classes of such programs. The following example presents a program that is representative of many programs that are not captured by the previous results.

EXAMPLE 3
Consider the program P:

   Plus(0, y, y)

   Plus(S(x), y, S(z)) ← Plus(x, y, z)

$Times(0, y, 0)$

$Times(S(x), y, z) \leftarrow Times(x, y, w), Plus(w, y, z)$

For this program $gfp(T_P) = T_P \downarrow \omega = \{Plus(x,y,z) : x + y \neq z\} \cup \{Times(x,y,z) : x \times y \neq z\}$, but the local variable in the fourth clause shows that T_P is not down-continuous, and clearly the previous proposition does not apply. ∎

When we want to extend this discussion to a non-ground goal G, we can simply form $P_G = \{Goal \leftarrow G\} \cup P$ where $Goal$ is a new 0-ary predicate symbol, and consider the goal $Goal$. Clearly $Goal$ is finitely failed for P_G iff G is finitely failed for P. So if $FF(P_G) = GFF(P_G)$, we can reason about the failure of G using techniques based on the Herbrand universe. If we wish to do the same for arbitrary goals, then we would like P to satisfy $\forall G \; FF(P_G) = GFF(P_G)$. It seems unlikely that the class of such programs is large, although Proposition 7 gives some examples. Programs as simple as those in Figure 1 do not fall into this class.

Another approach to the problem is to find a condition C on programs such that

$$\models_{HU} P_1^* \longleftrightarrow P_2^* \text{ and } C(P_1) \text{ and } C(P_2) \Rightarrow E^* \models P_1^* \longleftrightarrow P_2^* \qquad (*)$$

This would allow the determination of logical equivalence of completions by checking the condition C for the programs and determining Herbrand logical equivalence of completions (possibly by using structural induction). Such an approach would support more than simply reasoning about failure. One candidate condition $C(P)$ is that T_P be down-continuous, a fairly strong condition (see Theorem 3). However, the following program P_3 and the programs of Figures 1 and 2 give a counter-example.

P_3: $Even(0)$

$Even(S^2(x)) \leftarrow Even(x)$

$Odd(S(0))$

$Odd(S^2(x)) \leftarrow Odd(x)$

Clearly all the programs are down-continuous and have completions which are Herbrand logically equivalent (the completions have only one Herbrand model). However, P_3^* is not logically equivalent to P_1^* or P_2^* since P_3^*, E^* $\not\models Odd(x) \rightarrow Even(S(x))$. Of course there are trivial choices for C. But the problem of finding a non-trivial C remains open, and the first evidence is that only a very strong condition will satisfy $(*)$.

Ultimately it seems that the above approaches are too ambitious. Many programs occurring in practice do not exhibit the desired behavior for all goals.

It appears that a more piecemeal approach, treating only limited classes of goals, will prove more useful.

Equivalences of Logic Programs in Differing Languages

Often we wish to regard two programs as equivalent although they may use different predicate or function symbols. Some transformation systems find it useful to introduce auxiliary predicates (Tamaki and Sato [1984]), while others introduce new data structures, that is, new function symbols (Hansson and Tarnlund [1980]).

One of the simplest ways to define equivalence on programs written within different languages is to use the standard definitions of equivalence, but to restrict the ''input'' and ''output'' to a common sublanguage of the two languages. If, within this restriction, programs are equivalent by a standard definition of equivalence (for example, by an equivalence described in the previous section), then the extended definition makes them equivalent. This method of definition creates some anomalies since, for instance, any two programs written within disjoint languages would be equivalent. It is also important to note that the common sublanguage must be fixed as the programs vary, otherwise this method does not produce an equivalence relation. However, this method *is* appropriate where the difference in language of two programs arises from different definitions of the same predicates. For example, if P_1 is

$Sorted(x, y) \leftarrow Slowsorted(x, y)$

plus the definition of *Slowsorted*, and P_2 is

$Sorted(x, y) \leftarrow Quicksorted(x, y)$

plus the definition of *Quicksorted*, then this method would make the two equivalent if they agreed on *Sorted*. The derivation of a more efficient, ''equivalent'' program P_2 from a perhaps naive, but easy-to-prove-correct P_1, is a standard programming methodology. Hogger [1981] has applied this methodology to logic programming. It seems that the approach to extending definitions of equivalence described above is appropriate for this methodology.

Let L_1 and L_2 be two languages and let L denote a common sublanguage. We assume that L has the properties required from a language at the beginning of this paper, that is, enough variables, constants, etc. We redefine the equivalences used previously to allow for the fact that the programs may use languages larger than L. However these definitions will reduce to those used earlier when $L_1 = L_2 = L$.

Subsumption-Equivalence in L: The canonical forms of P_1 and P_2 are in L and are equal.

Weak Subsumption-Equivalence in L: The weak canonical forms of P_1 and P_2 are in L and are equal.

Equivalence wrt T_P in L: $T_{P_1}(X) \cap HB(L) = T_{P_2}(X) \cap HB(L)$ for every $X \subseteq HB(L)$

Equivalence wrt T_P + Id in L: $(T_{P_1} + Id)(X) \cap HB(L) = (T_{P_2} + Id)(X) \cap HB(L)$ for every $X \subseteq HB(L)$

Equivalence wrt $[\![P]\!]$ in L: $[\![P_1]\!](X) \cap HB(L) = [\![P_2]\!](X) \cap HB(L)$ for every $X \subseteq HB(L)$

Equality of Success Sets in L: $SS(P_1) \cap HB(L) = SS(P_2) \cap HB(L)$

Equality of Finite Failure Sets in L: $FF(P_1) \cap HB(L) = FF(P_2) \cap HB(L)$

Equality of Ground Finite Failure Sets in L: $GFF(P_1) \cap HB(L) = GFF(P_2) \cap HB(L)$

Logical Equivalence in L of Completions: For every logic formula A expressible in L, $P_1^*, E^* \models A$ iff $P_2^*, E^* \models A$

Herbrand Logical Equivalence in L of Completions: For every logic formula A expressible in L, $P_1^*, E^* \models_{HU(L_1)} A$ iff $P_2^*, E^* \models_{HU(L_2)} A$

Logical Equivalence in L: For every logic formula A expressible in L, $P_1 \models A$ iff $P_2 \models A$

Herbrand Logical Equivalence in L: For every logic formula A expressible in L, $P_1 \models_{HU(L_1)} A$ iff $P_2 \models_{HU(L_2)} A$

Many, though not all, of the relationships depicted in Figure 3 still hold for the more general case, and Figure 4 reflects this. The proofs are essentially the same as the simpler case and, of course, the counter-examples remain valid.

THEOREM 6

Figure 4 exhibits the relative strengths of the formulations of equivalence listed above. ∎

When two programs have different languages, they cannot have the same interpretations. Thus, for the (Herbrand) logical equivalence of completions, we lose the strong property that P_1^* and P_2^* have the same (Herbrand) models. As a result, the links between the operational equivalences and these logical equivalences must be characterized by logical consequence and Herbrand logical consequence for ground atoms. If A is a ground atom from $HB(L)$ then, for

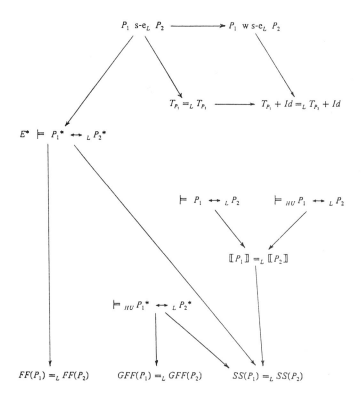

Figure 4: Relationships between Equivalences with Common Language L.

$i = 1, 2, A \in SS(P_i)$ iff $P_i^*, E^* \models A$ iff $P_i^*, E^* \models_{HU(P_i)} A,$ $A \in FF(P_i)$ iff $P_i^*, E^* \models \neg A$ and $A \in GFF(P_i)$ iff $P_i^*, E^* \models_{HU(P_i)} \neg A.$ Thus, logical consequence of completions in L preserves equality of success sets and finite failure sets in L while Herbrand logical consequence of completions in L preserves equality of success sets and ground failure sets in L.

However, logical equivalence of completions is no longer stronger than equality of ground failure sets. For example, consider the programs $P_1 = \{P(a) \leftarrow P(a)\}$ and $P_2 = \{P(a) \leftarrow Q(x); Q(S(x)) \leftarrow Q(x)\}$ where Q does not appear in L. $P(a) \in GFF(P_2) - GFF(P_1)$. However, their completions have the same logical consequences in L. Since Herbrand logical consequence of completions in L does preserve equality in L of ground failure, this example also shows that logical consequence of completions in L is not stronger than Herbrand logical consequence of completions in L.

Several other important relationships are lost. Logical equivalence is now strictly stronger than equivalence wrt $[\![P]\!]$. Strictness comes from considering the programs $P_1 = \varnothing$ and $P_2 = \{P(a)\}$ where a is not in L. We have $[\![P_1]\!](X)$ $\cap HB(L) = [\![P_2]\!](X) \cap HB(L) = X$ for every $X \subseteq HB(L)$ and $P_2 \models \exists x \, P(x)$ but $P_2 \models \exists x \, P(x)$ does not hold.

If P_1 and P_2 are (weakly) subsumption-equivalent in L, then the corresponding results of the previous section show directly that the programs are equivalent wrt T_P ($T_P + Id$) in L. The programs $\varnothing$ and $\{A \leftarrow B\}$, where A is in L and B is not, give a counter-example to the converses.

EXAMPLE 4

For the first example we consider a transformation that will transform any logic program into a program which is binary and stratifiable. A program P is *stratifiable* (Sebelik and Stepanek [1980]) if there is a function $\sigma : \Pi \rightarrow N$ (the natural numbers) and a predicate symbol Q (the *principal* predicate symbol) such that:

1. $\sigma(Q) = 0$

2.   if the clause $A(\tilde{x}) \leftarrow B_1 (\tilde{y}),...,B_n (\tilde{z})$ is in P, then $\sigma(B_i) = \sigma(A) + 1$ for $i = 2,3,...,n$

3.   for $i = 1$ either $B_1 = A$ or $\sigma(B_1) = \sigma(A) + 1$.

We assume that for each n-ary predicate symbol A we can choose an n-ary function symbol a (we represent it by the lower case of the predicate symbol) that does not appear in the language L_1 of the original program P. We also need a new binary predicate symbol, Q, a binary function symbol, ., which we write in infix form, and a constant symbol NIL. These are added to L_1 to form L_2. Thus, in this case L_1 is the greatest common sublanguage.

The clauses that are in the new program Q are determined as follows:
For every predicate symbol A in P include the clause

1. $A(\tilde{x}) \leftarrow Q(NIL, a(\tilde{x}).NIL)$

For every clause $A(\tilde{s}) \leftarrow B_1(\tilde{t}_1),...,B_n(\tilde{t}_n)$ in P with $n > 0$, include the clause

2a. $Q(u, a(\tilde{s}).v) \leftarrow Q(b_1(\tilde{t}_1). \ .... .b_n(\tilde{t}_n).u, v)$

If $n = 0$ then the new clause is

2b. $Q(u, a(\tilde{s}).v) \leftarrow Q(u, v)$

Also add the following two clauses

3. $Q(x.y, NIL) \leftarrow Q(NIL, x.y)$

4. $Q(NIL, NIL)$

The new program essentially implements SLD-resolution with two goal stacks rather than the one stack which is (conceptually) used in conventional PROLOG implementations. Clearly there is a fair SLD-resolution selection strategy for the original program that mimics the behavior of the new program for queries in L_1. This implies that the two programs have equivalent operational behavior in that $SS(P) = SS(Q) \cap HB(L_1)$, $FF(P) = FF(Q) \cap HB(L_1)$ and $GFF(P) = GFF(Q) \cap HB(L_1)$. Consequently, the transformation answers the two open problems in Sebelik and Stepanek [1980] in the affirmative: Every program has an operationally equivalent program that is binary and stratifiable.

Although the transformation preserves operational behavior, Q does not retain all the logical relationships of P. Consider the program $P = \{A \leftarrow B, B; B \leftarrow B\}$. The corresponding Q is

$A \leftarrow Q(NIL, a.NIL)$

$B \leftarrow Q(NIL, b.NIL)$

$Q(u, a.v) \leftarrow Q(b.b.u, v)$

$Q(u, b.v) \leftarrow Q(b.u, v)$

$Q(x.y, NIL) \leftarrow Q(NIL, x.y)$

$Q(NIL, NIL)$

Consider the Herbrand model of Q in which A is false, B is true, $Q(x, y)$ is true if $x = y = NIL$ or if $x = NIL$ and $y = b.NIL$ or if $x = b.NIL$ and $y = NIL$ and is false otherwise, and any other predicate is always false. $A \leftarrow B$ is not true in this model, even though this is logically equivalent to a clause of P. Since this model is also a model for the completion Q^* of Q, we find that the transformation does not preserve any of the equivalences based on the logical semantics. Clearly $A \in [\![P]\!] (\{B\})$ but $A \notin [\![Q]\!] (\{B\})$. Thus, of the equivalences we have considered, only the operational ones are preserved by the transformation. ∎

EXAMPLE 5
A second example is the (non-constructive) transformation in Jaffar and Stuckey [1986] of a program P_1 to another program P_2 such that $FF(P_2) = GFF(P_2)$. In this example, the language L_1 of P_1 is extended by the addition of

predicate and function symbols to form L_2. Again L_1 is the greatest common sublanguage. It is shown in that paper that, when restricting to L_1, P_1 and P_2 are equivalent for success and finite failure. For the transformation to be correct it cannot also preserve equivalence for ground failure. Consideration of the program

$$A \leftarrow B$$
$$B \leftarrow B$$

and its result under the transformation shows that none of the other equivalences we have considered apply to P_1 and P_2. ■

EXAMPLE 6

Finally, consider a transformation system like that of Tamaki and Sato [1986] (and also related to the transformation system in Tamaki and Sato [1984]) but somewhat weaker, which allows unfolding (except for direct recursion), reversible folding by clauses in the current program, application of replacement rules $M \Rightarrow N$ where $P_i^* E^* \models_{HU} M \leftrightarrow N$ (P_i is the initial program), provided none of the predicates in M and N is dependent on the predicate in the head of the target clause, and introduction of predicate symbols by definition (Maher [1987]). It is easily verified that unfolding (but not on direct recursion) and reversible folding preserve logical equivalence of completions, replacement preserves Herbrand logical equivalence of completions, and introduction preserves logical equivalence of completions with respect to any language omitting the introduced predicate symbol.

Thus, a final program P_f produced by this transformation system is Herbrand logically equivalent to the initial program P_i with respect to the initial language (assuming the introduced predicates are chosen to be disjoint from the initial language). It follows that, with respect to the initial language, the two programs have the same success set and the same ground finite failure set. Furthermore, if no replacement was used, they have the same finite failure set. When replacement is used, further work must be done to determine whether finite failure is preserved. ■

Discussion

A different approach to equivalence from that of the previous two sections for programs with (possibly) different languages could be based on a mapping, which preserved arity, of one language into the other. We could use this mapping to translate one program into the language of the other. This would provide us with a form of equivalence in which two programs that simply use different predicate names could be described as equivalent. This approach can be combined easily with the equivalences considered in this paper.

The results presented in this paper have been proved for untyped definite clause logic programs. They can be extended easily to definite clauses typed in the manner of Mycroft and O'Keefe [1984], but only provided the type system does not insist that, for example, an object of type $list(\alpha)$ must be of the form *NIL* or *x.y.* In this case, the technique of interchanging variables and new constants, and in particular the Theorem on Constants, cannot be applied. Similarly, the use of constraints other than equality in the programming language (Jaffar and Lassez [1987]) can invalidate this technique. Consequently, the results on subsumption-equivalence as stated would not hold. However, we can retain some of these results by generalizing the notion of subsumption to take into account the extra information about the expected domain implicit in the typing and the constraints.

The natural generalization of Proposition 6 to these languages does not hold in general. However, the semantics of logic programming languages using such types, constraints or "semantic unification" (i.e., a unification based on an equality theory) are somewhat similar to those for standard unification (Jaffar and Lassez [1987], Jaffar et al. [1984, 1986a, 1986b]), and apart from Proposition 6 the natural generalizations of Theorems 5 and 6 continue to hold (Maher [1985]).

Conclusion

For applications such as deductive databases employing the Open World Assumption, failed derivations have a lesser importance. In this case, use of the identical equivalences based upon the functional semantics $[\![P]\!]$ and the logical consequences of P allows the application of two different and powerful tools to reason about programs. We have seen that programs equivalent in this sense are also equivalent as program segments. This equivalence seems ideal for discussing the deductive structure of such deductive databases, independent of any particular state of the database of facts.

When negation-as-failure is used in evaluating queries, the equivalence and Herbrand equivalence of completed programs are more appropriate. These equivalences are stronger than some operational equivalences and the well-developed formalism of logic is available to facilitate reasoning about programs. Even when negation-as-failure is not relevant, these equivalences are useful for reasoning about termination of top-down computations. However, more work is needed in determining when it is sufficient to use only Herbrand models in reasoning about finite failure.

Acknowledgments

I thank Joxan Jaffar, Jean-Louis Lassez, and the referees for their comments on a previous version of this paper, which helped improve the presentation. This research was partially supported by the Australian Computer Research Board and the Australian Department of Science.

References

1. Apt., K. R. and Emden, M. H. van [1982] Contributions to the Theory of Logic Programming, *JACM* **29**(3):841–862.

2. Blair, H. [1986] Personal communication.

3. Buntine, W. [1986] Generalised Subsumption and Its Applications to Induction and Redundancy, *Artificial Intelligence*, to appear. Preliminary version appeared in *Proc. European Conference on Artificial Intelligence*, 23–31.

4. Clark, K. L. [1978] Negation as Failure, in *Logic and Databases* (H. Gallaire and J. Minker, Eds.), Plenum Press, New York, 293–322.

5. Cosmadakis, S. S. and Kanellakis, P. C. [1986] Parallel Evaluation of Recursive Rule Queries, *Proc. Conference on Principles of Database Systems*, 280–293.

6. Emden, M. H. van and Kowalski, R. A. [1976] The Semantics of Predicate Logic as a Programming Language, *ACM* **23**(4):733–742.

7. Fitting, M. [1985] A Kripke-Kleene Semantics for Logic Programs, *Journal of Logic Programming* **2**(4):295–312.

8. Gottlob, G. and Leitsch, A. [1985] On the Efficiency of Subsumption Algorithms, *ACM* **32**(2):280–295.

9. Hansson, A. and Tärnlund, S-A. [1980] Program Transformation by a Function that Maps Simple Lists into D-Lists, *Proc. Workshop on Logic Programming* (S-A. Tärnlund, Ed.), Debrecen, Hungary, 225–229.

10. Hogger, C. J. [1981] Derivation of Logic Programs, *JACM* **28**(2):372–392.

11. Jaffar, J. and Lassez, J-L. [1988] Constraint Logic Programming, *Proc. Conference on Principles of Programming Languages*, 111–119.

12. Jaffar, J., Lassez, J-L., and Maher, M. J. [1984] A Theory of Complete Logic Programs with Equality, *Journal of Logic Programming* **1**, 211–223.

13. Jaffar, J., Lassez, J-L., and Maher, M. J. [1986a] A Logic Programming Language Scheme, in *Logic Programming: Relations, Functions and Equations* (D. DeGroot and G. Lindstrom, Eds.), Prentice Hall, 441–267.

14. Jaffar, J., Lassez, J-L., and Maher, M. J. [1986b] Some Issues and Trends in the Semantics of Logic Programming, *Proc. 3rd International Conference on Logic Programming*, London, U.K., Lecture Notes in Computer Science 225 (E. Shapiro, Ed.), 223–241.

15. Jaffar, J. and Stuckey, P. J. [1986] Canonical Logic Programs, *Journal of Logic Programming* 3(2):143–155.

16. Lassez, J-L. and Maher, M. J. [1983] The Denotational Semantics of Horn Clauses as a Production System, *Proc. AAAI-83*, Washington DC, 229–231.

17. Lassez, J-L. and Maher, M. J. [1984] Closures and Fairness in the Semantics of Programming Logic, *Theoretical Computer Science* 29, 167–184.

18. Lassez, J-L., Maher, M. J., and Marriott, K. G. [1987] Unification Revisited, in *Foundations of Deductive Databases and Logic Programming* (J. Minker, Ed.), Morgan Kaufmann Publishers, Los Altos, CA, 587–625.

19. Lloyd, J. W. [1984] *Foundations of Logic Programming*, Springer-Verlag.

20. Maher, M. J. [1985] *Semantics of Logic Programs*, Ph.D. dissertation, University of Melbourne.

21. Maher, M. J. [1987] Correctness of a Logic Program Transformation System, *IBM Research Report*, T. J. Watson Research Center.

22. Manna, Z. [1974] *Mathematical Theory of Computation*, McGraw-Hill, New York.

23. Mycroft, A. and O'Keefe, R. A. [1984] A Polymorphic Type System for Prolog, *Artificial Intelligence* 23(3):295–307.

24. Nilsson, N. J. [1980] *Principles of Artificial Intelligence*, Morgan Kaufmann Publishers, Los Altos, CA.

25. Plotkin, G. D. [1970] A Note on Inductive Generalization, in *Machine Intelligence* 5 (B. Meltzer and D. Michie, Eds.), Edinburgh University Press, 153–165.

26. Reynolds, J. C. [1970] Transformational Systems and the Algebraic Structure of Atomic Formulas, in *Machine Intelligence* 5 (B. Meltzer and D. Michie, Eds.), Edinburgh University Press, 135–151.

27. Sagiv, Y. [1988] Optimizing Datalog Programs, in *Foundations of Deductive Databases and Logic Programming* (J. Minker, Ed.), Morgan Kaufmann Publishers, Los Altos, CA, 659–698.

28. Sebelik, J. and Stepanek, P. [1980] Horn Clause Programs Suggested by Recursive Function, *Proc. Workshop on Logic Programming* (S. A. Tärnlund, Ed.), Debrecen, Hungary.

29. Shoenfield, J. R. [1967] *Mathematical Logic*, Addison-Wesley, Reading, MA.

30. Tamaki, H. and Sato, T. [1984] Unfold/Fold Transformation of Logic Programs, *Proc. 2nd. Logic Programming Conference*, Uppsala, Sweden, 127–138.

31. Tamaki, H. and Sato, T. [1986] A Generalized Correctness Proof of the Unfold/Fold Logic Program Transformation, *Information Science Technical Report 86-4*, Ibaraki University.

32. Tärnlund, S-A. [1977] Horn Clause Computability, *BIT* **17**(2):215–226.

Chapter

17

Optimizing Datalog Programs

Yehoshua Sagiv
Department of Computer Science
The Hebrew University of Jerusalem,
Jerusalem, Israel

Abstract

Datalog programs, i.e, Prolog programs without function symbols, are considered. It is assumed that a variable appearing in the head of a rule must also appear in the body of the rule. The input to a program is a set of ground atoms (which are given in addition to the rules of the program) and, therefore, can be viewed as an assignment of relations to some predicates of the program. Two programs are equivalent if they produce the same result for all possible assignments of relations to the extensional predicates (i.e., the predicates that do not appear as heads of rules). Two programs are uniformly equivalent if they produce the same result for all possible assignments of initial relations to all the predicates (i.e., both extensional and intensional). The equivalence problem for Datalog programs is known to be undecidable. It is shown that uniform equivalence is decidable, and an algorithm is given for minimizing a Datalog program under uniform equivalence. A technique for removing parts of a program that are redundant under equivalence (but not under uniform equivalence) is described. A proof procedure for determining uniform equivalence is developed for the case that databases satisfy some constraints.

Introduction

Horn-clause programs without function symbols, also known as *Datalog* programs, are an important part of *deductive* (or *logical*) databases (Gallaire and Minker [1978]). Recent works have addressed the problem of finding efficient evaluation methods for queries expressed as Datalog programs[1] (e.g., Bancilhon et al. [1986a], Henschen and Naqvi [1984], Kifer and Lozinskii [1986], Lozinskii [1985], McKay and Shapiro [1981], Rohmer and Lescoeur [1985], Saccà and Zaniolo [1986], Ullman [1985], Van Gelder [1986]). It is important to remember that database applications usually require finding all answers to a query, and when there are no function symbols, it is possible to find all answers in finite time by a naive bottom-up computation. However, that requires retrieving all tuples of the relations specified in the program. Therefore, a common theme in many of the proposed methods for efficient query evaluation is to use the constants specified in the query in order to restrict the size of intermediate results as soon as possible.

In this paper we take a complementary approach to the one just mentioned and investigate the question of how to remove redundant parts from a Datalog program. A redundant part in a program is either a redundant rule or a redundant atom in the body of a rule. In most cases, removing redundant parts can only reduce the time needed to evaluate a query because it reduces the number of joins done during the evaluation. For example, if the query is going to be computed by the "magic set" method of Bancilhon et al. [1986a], then removing redundant parts can only speed up the computation. Some works (e.g., Chakravarthy et al. [1986,1988], Finger [1986], King [1981]) have also considered the opposite approach, namely, optimizing a program by adding more conjuncts to the body of a rule. This is usually useful when it is required to find only one answer to a query (as opposed to finding all answers). In some cases, it could be useful even if all answers are required. For example, if the intersection of two relations is to be computed and the database has a third relation that contains this intersection, then it may be better to compute the intersection of all three relations rather than just the original two (whether it is indeed better depends upon the sizes of the three relations, the size of their intersection, and the available indices). As already stated, in this paper we develop methods for finding redundant parts of a program and removing them. Our ideas, however, can also be used to determine when a redundant atom can be added to the body of a rule and, therefore, they can also be incorporated in the type of optimization that adds conjuncts rather than removes them.

Usually, a Datalog program receives, as an input, relations for the *extensional* predicates, namely, those predicates that do not appear as heads of rules, and the answer consists of relations for the *intensional* predicates, namely those that appear as heads of rules. The process of optimization re-

---

[1] See also Bancilhon and Ramakrishnan [1986b,1988] for a thorough review of this subject and a comparison of the performance of several evaluation strategies.

quires finding a program of least cost, which is *equivalent* to the original one, that is, for all possible inputs, the original and the optimized programs compute the same output. However, the equivalence problem for Datalog programs is undecidable (Shmueli [1986]).

We propose the notion of *uniform equivalence* which is defined as follows. Two programs are uniformly equivalent if they produce the same output for all inputs, where a possible input to a program is an assignment of initial relations to the extensional as well as the intensional predicates, and the program computes the final relations for the intensional predicates.[2] Clearly, uniform equivalence implies equivalence, but the converse is not true. We show how to minimize a program under uniform equivalence; that is, we give an algorithm that removes all redundant rules and all redundant atoms from the remaining rules while preserving uniform equivalence. The running time of the algorithm, in the worst case, is exponential in the size of the program. However, if the arity of predicates is bounded, then the running time is polynomial; and since the arity of predicates is typically small, this is a practically efficient algorithm. Moreover, the exponential part of the algorithm consists of applying the program being optimized to a "small" database, i.e., a database whose size is the same as the size of the program. Thus, programs that are hard to optimize are programs that are hard to compute in general. Therefore, minimizing a program is expected to reduce the total time spent on optimization and evaluation. As an example, given the rule

$$G(x,y,z) :- G(x,w,z), A(w,y), A(w,z), A(z,z), A(z,y).$$

our algorithm determines that the atom $A(w,y)$ is redundant and, consequently, the rule can be replaced with

$$G(x,y,z) :- G(x,w,z), A(w,z), A(z,z), A(z,y).$$

To fully appreciate the importance of the algorithm, one should realize that optimization under uniform equivalence is the only one that can be done locally. In comparison, if a subset of the rules of a program P is replaced with an equivalent (but not uniformly equivalent) subset of rules, then the resulting program is not necessarily equivalent to P.

We also give a technique for minimizing Datalog programs under equivalence. Since this is an undecidable problem, it is clear that our technique may not find all parts of a program that are redundant under equivalence. However, we believe that this technique is going to be useful in many prac-

---

[2]Clearly, for each intensional predicate, the final relation contains the initial one, and for each extensional predicate, the final relation is the same as the initial one.

tical situations. For example, our technique can easily show that in the program

$G(x,z) :- A(x,z).$

$G(x,z) :- G(x,y), G(y,z), A(y,w).$

the atom $A(y,w)$, in the second rule, is redundant and can be removed without changing the result.

Related Work

Maher [1988] has proposed independently the notion of uniform equivalence, as well as other notions of equivalences of logic programs, but has not given any algorithm for testing uniform equivalence or minimizing under uniform equivalence.

Subsumption of Horn clauses (Gottlob and Leitsch [1985], Plotkin [1970]) is a weak notion of equivalence of Horn-clause rules (Maher [1988]). Aho et al. [1979] and Chandra and Merlin [1976] have shown that subsumption captures the notion of equivalence of conjunctive queries, which are essentially nonrecursive Horn-clause rules. Sagiv and Yannakakis [1980] have extended this result to disjunctions of conjunctive queries, which are essentially non-recursive Datalog programs. When recursion is introduced, subsumption implies equivalence and uniform equivalence, but the converse is not always true.

Buntine [1986] has introduced independently the concept of generalized subsumption that can express uniform equivalence. He has also discussed redundant atoms and redundant rules, and has shown how to detect them using generalized subsumption. We show how to minimize a Datalog program by removing all redundant atoms and rules without having to consider any rule or atom more than once. Thus, our algorithm is more efficient than the one described by Buntine [1986].

An issue that arises in deductive databases (but does not appear among the notions of equivalences of logic programs discussed by Maher [1988] and Buntine [1986]) is the equivalence of programs in the presence of constraints that databases must satisfy. Two programs that are not uniformly equivalent may become uniformly equivalent when the set of all possible databases is restricted to those satisfying some constraints. We assume that constraints are formulated in terms of tuple-generating dependencies and give a proof procedure for determining uniform equivalence of Datalog programs when the allowed databases satisfy some constraints (although the proof procedure is not complete, we believe that it is useful in practical cases). Chakravarthy et al. [1986,1988] have investigated query optimization in deductive databases in the presence of constraints, but they assumed that both rules and constraints are nonrecursive. An interesting open question is whether our proof procedure can be used in order to extend the results of Chakravarthy et al. [1986,1988] to recursive rules and constraints. Other works on semantic query optimization are those of Finger [1986] and of King [1981].

Naughton [1986] has developed a method for optimizing Datalog programs by moving atoms from a recursive rule to nonrecursive rules (the method may create new nonrecursive rules). The atoms that are moved to nonrecursive rules may not be redundant and, hence, Naughton's method can further optimize a program that does not have any redundant part. This method, however, applies only to linear rules.

Preliminaries

Basic Definitions

We consider *Datalog* programs, i.e., Prolog programs having only predicates, variables and constants. Function symbols as well as other features of Prolog (e.g., lists, cuts, arithmetic operations) are not permitted. A Datalog *program* is a set of *rules* (also known as *Horn-clause rules*). Each rule has a *head*, appearing on the left-hand side of the symbol :-, and a *body*, appearing on the right-hand side of the symbol :-. The head of a rule is a single *atomic formula* or simply *atom*, that is, a *predicate*[3] with either a *variable* or a *constant* in each argument position. For example, $Q(x,y,3,10)$ is an atom, where Q is a predicate, x and y are variables and 3 and 10 are constants. The body of a rule is a (possibly empty) conjunction of atoms. A rule with an empty body is also called a *fact*. In this paper, we do not distinguish between rules with a nonempty body and rules with an empty body—we refer to all of them just as rules.

EXAMPLE 1
The following is a program with two rules.

$G(x,z) :- A(x,z)$.

$G(x,z) :- G(x,y), G(y,z)$.

The input to this program is A and the output, G, is the transitive closure of A. ∎

---

[3]In traditional database terminology, a predicate is called a *relation scheme*.

We conveniently denote a conjunction of atoms (e.g., in the body of the second rule) by separating the atoms with commas rather than with the "logical and" symbol $\wedge$.

We do not consider rules with an empty head; rules of these form are used in logical databases to express integrity constraints.

We assume that every variable in the head of a rule must appear also in the body (therefore, rules with an empty body are not allowed unless the head has only constants and no variables). Thus, if we want to write rules for the predicate $Anc(x,y)$, whose meaning is that x is an ancestor of y, we cannot write the rule $Anc(x,x) :-$, whose meaning is that everybody is his own ancestor. This does not present any real restriction, as far as databases are concerned, since in database applications each variable is assumed to be bound to some finite set of values from the database. For example, in the rule $Anc(x,x) :-$, variable x is bound to the set of all persons mentioned in the database. Thus, the rule $Anc(x,x) :-$ can be replaced with $Anc(x,x) :- Person(x)$.

The above restrictions imply that rules considered in this paper are always *domain independent* (Fagin [1982]) or *safe* (Ullman [1982]) formulas. Therefore, it is irrelevant how the set of constants that may appear in databases and programs is defined. We only assume that the set of constants is infinite, and usually use integers for constants in examples.

Computing Programs

A *relation q* for a predicate Q is a set of *ground* atoms of Q, i.e., atoms having only constants (and no variables), e.g., $Q(34,3,12,15)$. Unless otherwise stated, we assume that relations are finite. A collection of relations, such as a database, can be viewed as a single set consisting of all the ground atoms of these relations. If $q_1,...,q_n$ are relations for the predicates $Q_1,...,Q_n$, respectively, then $\langle q_1,...,q_n \rangle$ denotes their union,[4] namely, the set containing the ground atoms of all the q_i. The set $\langle q_1,...,q_n \rangle$ is also called an *interpretation* or a *structure*.

A predicate is *intensional*, in a given program P, if it appears as the head of some rule in P. An intensional predicate is supposed to be evaluated by the program P. A predicate is *extensional* if it does not appear in the head of any rule.

A program P has an associated directed graph, called the *dependence graph*, that has a node for each predicate of the program, and an edge from predicate Q to predicate R whenever predicate Q is in the body of some rule and predicate R is in the head of that same rule. Program P is *recursive* if its dependence graph has a cycle. A predicate Q is *recursive* in program P if

---

[4]Note that this definition of the union is more general than the definition of the union operator in relational algebra.

there is a path from Q to itself. Note that recursive predicates are intensional, but an intensional predicate is not necessarily recursive. Finally, a rule is *recursive* if the dependence graph has a cycle that includes the predicate from the head of the rule and a predicate from the body of the rule. In particular, a rule is recursive if the predicate in the head of the rule appears also in the body.

The *input* to a program P is a relation for each extensional predicate, and it is called the *extensional database* (EDB). The *output* computed by P is, in principle, a relation for each intensional predicate, and it is called the *intensional database* (IDB). To simplify notation, we formally define the output to be both the EDB and the IDB, and simply call it the *database* (DB). Note that the EDB-part of the output is the same as the input.

Now we are going to describe how the output can be computed. The ground atoms of the DB are known facts. Initially, the known facts are those in the EDB. A rule of a program states that if some facts are known, then another fact can be deduced from them. Newly deduced facts become ground atoms of the IDB (and hence of the DB) and, so, the rules can be used once again to deduce more new facts. Formally, a rule r is used to deduce a new fact by *instantiating* its variables to constants, i.e., substituting a constant for all occurrences of each variable. If under the instantiation, each atom in the body of rule r becomes a ground atom of the DB, then the instantiated head of the rule is added to the IDB.

EXAMPLE 2

Consider the program of Example 1 and suppose that the EDB is the following set of ground atoms: $\{A(1,2), A(1,4), A(4,1)\}$. Initially, the IDB is the empty set. If, in the first rule, we instantiate x to 1 and z to 2, then the body of the rule becomes $A(1,2)$, which is a ground atom of the EDB. Therefore, $G(1,2)$ is added to the IDB. Two similar instantiations of the first rule add $G(1,4)$ and $G(4,1)$ to the IDB. As for the second rule, the instantiation of x to 1, y to 4, and z to 1 produces the ground atoms $G(1,4)$ and $G(4,1)$ in the body of the rule. Since both are already in the DB, the instantiated head, $G(1,1)$, is added to the IDB. Similarly, instantiating both x and z to 4 and y to 1 yields $G(4,4)$. Finally, $G(4,2)$ is obtained when x is instantiated to 4, y to 1, and z to 2. No more ground atoms can be produced by any instantiation, and so, the DB

$$\{A(1,2), \ A(1,4), \ A(4,1), \ G(1,2), \ G(1,4), \ G(4,1), \ G(1,1), \ G(4,4),$$
$$G(4,2)\}$$

is the output computed by the program for the above EDB. ∎

Since we assume that the input to a program consists of finite relations, the output is also a set of finite relations. Computing the output by repeatedly instantiating rules, until no new ground atoms can be generated, is known as *bottom-up* computation. For a fixed program, this method runs in polynomial time in the size of the EDB.

Let P be a program with the extensional predicates $E_1,\ldots,E_n$ and the intensional predicates $I_1,\ldots,I_m$. Given an EDB $\langle e_1,\ldots,e_n \rangle$, where each e_k is a relation for E_k, the DB computed by P is denoted by $P(\langle e_1,\ldots,e_n \rangle)$. Recall that $P(\langle e_1,\ldots,e_n \rangle)$ is a set of ground atoms, and the EDB-part of $P(\langle e_1,\ldots,e_n \rangle)$ is the same as the input.

Sometimes we would like to view P as a program whose input is both an EDB and an IDB. The output is computed as defined earlier, i.e., by repeatedly instantiating rules until no new ground atoms can be added to the IDB. Clearly, the output is a DB that contains the input. When P is viewed as a program whose input is both an EDB $\langle e_1,\ldots,e_n \rangle$ and an IDB $\langle i_1,\ldots,i_m \rangle$, the output computed by P is denoted as $P(\langle e_1,\ldots,e_n,i_1,\ldots,i_m \rangle)$.

EXAMPLE 3
Let P be the program of Example 1. In Example 2, we have computed the output of P for the input $\{A(1,2), A(1,4), A(4,1)\}$. It is easy to see that the output of P for the input $\{A(1,2), A(1,4), G(4,1)\}$ is the same as the one computed in Example 2, but with the ground atom $A(4,1)$ omitted. ■

Note that if a program P has rules with an empty body, then, by our restrictions, these rules are just ground atoms, and these ground atoms are in every output of P, even if the input is empty.

Equivalence, Uniform Equivalence, and Models

Let P_1 and P_2 be programs with the same set of extensional predicates and the same set of intensional predicates. Program P_1 *contains* P_2, written $P_2 \subseteq P_1$, if for all EDBs $\langle e_1,\ldots,e_n \rangle$, the output of P_1 contains that of P_2, i.e., $P_2(\langle e_1,\ldots,e_n \rangle) \subseteq P_1(\langle e_1,\ldots,e_n \rangle)$. In traditional database terminology, it means that for each predicate Q, the relation for Q in the DB $P_2(\langle e_1,\ldots,e_n \rangle)$ is a subset of the relation for Q in the DB $P_1(\langle e_1,\ldots,e_n \rangle)$.

Programs P_1 and P_2 are *equivalent*, written $P_2 \equiv P_1$, if $P_2 \subseteq P_1$ and $P_1 \subseteq P_2$. Equivalence simply means that the two programs have the same output whenever they are given the same EDB as an input.

Programs P_1 *uniformly contains* P_2, written $P_2 \subseteq^u P_1$, if for all pairs of an EDB $\langle e_1,\ldots,e_n \rangle$ and an IDB $\langle i_1,\ldots,i_m \rangle$, the following containment holds:

$$P_2(\langle e_1,\ldots,e_n,i_1,\ldots,i_m \rangle) \subseteq P_1(\langle e_1,\ldots,e_n,i_1,\ldots,i_m \rangle)$$

Programs P_1 and P_2 are *uniformly equivalent*, written $P_2 \equiv^u P_1$, if $P_2 \subseteq^u P_1$ and $P_1 \subseteq^u P_2$. Uniform equivalence means that the two programs have the same output whenever they are given the same input, where the input may also include ground atoms for some intensional predicates.

PROPOSITION 1

Uniform containment implies containment.

Proof: If $P_2(\langle e_1,\ldots,e_n,i_1,\ldots,i_m\rangle) \subseteq P_1(\langle e_1,\ldots,e_n,i_1,\ldots,i_m\rangle)$ for all $\langle e_1,\ldots,e_n\rangle$ and $\langle i_1,\ldots,i_m\rangle$, then in particular, for all EDBs $\langle e_1,\ldots,e_n\rangle$

$$P_2(\langle e_1,\ldots,e_n,\emptyset,\ldots\emptyset\rangle) \subseteq P_1(\langle e_1,\ldots,e_n,\emptyset,\ldots,\emptyset\rangle)$$

where $\emptyset$ denotes the empty relation. Therefore, $P_2(\langle e_1,\ldots,e_n\rangle) \subseteq P_1(\langle e_1,\ldots,e_n\rangle)$ for all EDBs $\langle e_1,\ldots,e_n\rangle$ and, so, $P_2 \subseteq P_1$. ∎

EXAMPLE 4

This example shows that equivalence does not always imply uniform equivalence. Let P_1 be the program of Example 1, and let P_2 be the following program.

$G(x,z) :\!- A(x,z).$

$G(x,z) :\!- A(x,y),\, G(y,z).$

Both programs compute the transitive closure of A when the input has only ground atoms of A, i.e., they are equivalent. Moreover, as we shall see later, P_1 uniformly contains P_2. But P_2 does not uniformly contain P_1. To see this, suppose that the input is the empty relation for A and some nonempty relation g for G, such that g is not the transitive closure of itself. Then, the output of P_2 is the same as the input, i.e., g, while the output of P_1 is the transitive closure of g. Thus, containment does not always imply uniform containment. ∎

A DB $\langle e_1,\ldots,e_n,i_1,\ldots,i_m\rangle$ is a *model* of P if

$$\langle e_1,\ldots,e_n,i_1,\ldots,i_m\rangle = P(\langle e_1,\ldots,e_n,i_1,\ldots,i_m\rangle)$$

that is, no new ground atoms are generated when the program P is applied to the given DB. Let $M(P)$ denote the set of all models of P. It is well known that the set $M(P)$ is closed under intersection, and the output of P, given an input $\langle e_1,\ldots,e_n,i_1,\ldots,i_m\rangle$, is the minimal model of P that contains the input (van Emden and Kowalski [1976]).

The above results imply that two programs are equivalent if for all inputs $\langle e_1,\ldots,e_n\rangle$, the programs have the same minimal model that contains $\langle e_1,\ldots,e_n\rangle$. Uniform equivalence can also be characterized in terms of models.

Programs P_1 and P_2 are uniformly equivalent if they have the same set of models, i.e., $M(P_1) = M(P_2)$. The following proposition, whose proof is given in the appendix, is a characterization of uniform containment. Note that uniform containment means containment of the sets of models in the opposite direction.

PROPOSITION 2

$P_2 \subseteq^u P_1 \iff M(P_1) \subseteq M(P_2)$.

When discussing uniform containment of two programs P_1 and P_2, it is not necessary to assume that they have the same set of predicates, provided that an input is any set of ground atoms for the predicates appearing in either P_1 or P_2. It is even possible for an extensional predicate in one program to be an intensional predicate in the other program.

EXAMPLE 5

Let P_1 be the program of Example 1, and let P_2 be obtained from P_1 by adding the rule $A(x,z)$:- $A(x,y)$, $G(y,z)$. Note that program P_2 has only intensional predicates and, so, it is meaningful only if it may have a nonempty IDB as an input. Since every rule of P_1 is also a rule of P_2, it is easy to verify that $P_1(d) \subseteq P_2(d)$ for every DB d consisting of ground atoms for A and G. Therefore, there is uniform containment, i.e., $P_1 \subseteq^u P_2$. ∎

We conclude this section with a simple observation that further illustrates the relationship between containment and uniform containment, and shows that there is an important case in which equivalence implies uniform equivalence (recall that, by Proposition 1, the converse is always true). Given programs P_1 and P_2, we can construct programs P'_1 and P'_2 such that $P_2 \subseteq^u P_1$ if and only if $P'_2 \subseteq P'_1$. The programs P'_1 and P'_2 are obtained by adding rules that give arbitrary initial values to the intensional predicates. The rule added for an intensional predicate[5] $B(x_1,...,x_n)$ is simply $B(x_1,...,x_n)$:- $B_0(x_1,...,x_n)$, where B_0 is a predicate that does not appear in any other rule. Note that if P_1 and P_2 already have a rule of the form $B(x_1,...,x_n)$:- $G(x_1,...,x_n)$, where G appears only in this rule, then there is no need to add the rule for B. In particular, if for every intensional predicate B, both P_1 and P_2 already have a rule of the form $B(x_1,...,x_n)$:- $G(x_1,...,x_n)$, where G appears only in this rule, then $P_2 \subseteq^u P_1$ if and only if $P_2 \subseteq P_1$.

---

[5]If B is intensional only in one of the programs P_1 and P_2, then we still add the rule for B to both of them.

Optimizing Recursive Programs

In this paper we consider a particular type of optimization, namely, removing redundant atoms from the body of a rule and removing redundant rules from a program. This optimization is useful since it reduces the number of joins needed to compute the output. The problem of optimizing nonrecursive programs has been solved, both for the case of single-rule programs (Aho, Sagiv, and Ullman [1979], and Chandra and Merlin [1976]) and for the case of programs with many rules (Sagiv and Yannakakis [1980]). Essentially, it has been shown that a program consisting of nonrecursive rules has a unique equivalent program with a minimal number of rules and a minimal number of atoms in the body of each rule. Optimizing recursive programs, however, is considerably harder. In fact, there can be no algorithm for optimizing recursive programs, since equivalence of recursive programs is undecidable (Shmueli [1986]).

In the section "Minimizing Programs under Uniform Equivalence," we shall show that recursive programs can be optimized under uniform equivalence, i.e., we shall give an algorithm that finds redundant atoms in the body of a rule, as well as redundant rules in a program, and removes them while preserving uniform equivalence. The final result is a program with neither an atom nor a rule that can be deleted while preserving uniform equivalence. Unlike the nonrecursive case, however, the final result of this optimization is not necessarily unique (i.e., it may depend upon the order in which atoms and rules are considered for deletion).

In the section "Optimizing under Equivalence," we shall describe a more elaborate procedure that can remove redundant atoms while preserving equivalence, but not uniform equivalence. This procedure is not completely algorithmic, since it has to use some simple heuristics; and, of course, it cannot always remove all atoms that are redundant under equivalence. We believe, however, that this procedure is going to be an important tool for optimizing Datalog programs.

Testing Uniform Containment and Equivalence

Testing $M(P_1) \subseteq M(P_2)$ (and, by Proposition 2, testing $P_2 \subseteq^u P_1$) is conceptually simple and can be done by the *chase* process (Maier et al. [1979]). Originally the chase was used to test implications of database dependencies, and recently it has been noted by Cosmadakis and Kanellakis [1986] that the chase can also test uniform containment of Datalog programs with only one predicate symbol. It is easy to see, however, that the same is true for programs with many predicates.

Note that $M(P_1) \subseteq M(P_2)$ if and only if for all rules r of P_2, $M(P_1) \subseteq M(r)$, because a DB d is a model of P_2 if and only if it is a model of every rule r of P_2. Therefore, by Proposition 2, $P_2 \subseteq^u P_1$ if and only if for all rules r of P_2, $r \subseteq^u P_1$ (note that r is a single-rule program).

We will now show how to test $r \subseteq^u P_1$, where r is a single rule. Let r be the rule $h :- b$, i.e., h is the head and b is the body (recall that b may be empty and, if so, then h is a ground atom). In order to test whether $r \subseteq^u P_1$, we have to consider the atoms of b as an input DB to P_1. Technically, the atoms of b are converted into a DB by substituting distinct constants for the variables of r and, as a result, b becomes a set of ground atoms. The uniform containment $r \subseteq^u P_1$ holds if and only if $P_1(b\theta)$ contains the ground atom $h\theta$, where

1. θ is any one-to-one substitution that maps each variable of r to a distinct constant that is not already in r or P_1,

2. $b\theta$ is the set of ground atoms obtained from b by substituting according to θ, and

3. $h\theta$ is the ground atom obtained from h by substituting according to θ.

Note that the above conditions imply that if b is empty, then $r \subseteq^u P_1$ holds if and only if r is also a rule of P_1.

EXAMPLE 6
Consider again programs P_1 and P_2 of Examples 1 and 4. Recall that P_1 is

$G(x,z) :- A(x,z).$

$G(x,z) :- G(x,y), G(y,z).$

and P_2 is

$G(x,z) :- A(x,z).$

$G(x,z) :- A(x,y), G(y,z).$

We are now going to show that $P_2 \subseteq^u P_1$. First, the variables of P_2 have to be instantiated to distinct constants. In order that the instantiation be visible throughout the example, we use the subscript 0 to denote constants, that is, variable x is instantiated to a constant denoted by x_0, variable y is instantiated to the constant y_0, and z to z_0. The rules of P_2 must be considered one by one. So, consider the first rule of P_2, denoted r_1, i.e.,

$G(x,z) :- A(x,z).$

The instantiated body of r_1 is the DB $\{A(x_0,z_0)\}$. When P_1 is applied to this DB, the result is $\{G(x_0,z_0), A(x_0,z_0)\}$. Since the result contains the instantiated head of r_1, it follows that $r_1 \subseteq^u P_1$.

Now consider the second rule of P_2, denoted r_2, i.e.,

$G(x,z) :- A(x,y), G(y,z).$

The instantiated body of r_2 is the DB $\{A(x_0,y_0), G(y_0,z_0)\}$. The first rule of P_1 can be applied to $A(x_0,y_0)$ to produce $G(x_0,y_0)$, and then an application of the second rule gives $G(x_0,z_0)$. Thus, the instantiated head of r_2 (i.e., $G(x_0,z_0)$) is in the result, and so, $r_2 \subseteq^u P_1$. Since P_1 uniformly contains every rule of P_2, it follows that $P_2 \subseteq^u P_1$.

Next, we will show that $P_1 \not\subseteq^u P_2$. Consider the second rule of P_1, denoted s, i.e.,

$G(x,z) :- G(x,y), G(y,z).$

The instantiated body is the DB $\{G(x_0,y_0), G(y_0,z_0)\}$. No new ground atoms are produced when P_2 is applied to this DB. Therefore, $s \not\subseteq^u P_2$ and, so, $P_1 \not\subseteq^u P_2$. ∎

EXAMPLE 7

Let P_1 be the program

$G(x,y,z) :- G(x,w,z), A(w,y), A(w,z), A(z,z), A(z,y).$

and P_2 be the program

$G(x,y,z) :- G(x,w,z), A(w,z), A(z,z), A(z,y).$

Since the body of the rule of P_2 is a subset of the body of the rule of P_1, it is clear that $P_1 \subseteq^u P_2$. We will show that $P_2 \subseteq^u P_1$ and, hence, $P_1 \equiv^u P_2$. The instantiated body of the single rule of P_2 is the DB

$\{G(x_0,w_0,z_0), A(w_0,z_0), A(z_0,z_0), A(z_0,y_0)\}$

We first apply P_1 to this DB by instantiating the variables of P_1 as follows. Variable x is instantiated to x_0, variable w to w_0, and both z and y to z_0. It is easy to check that, under this instantiation, the body of the rule of P_1 becomes a subset of the DB and, therefore, the ground atom $G(x_0,z_0,z_0)$ is added to the DB. Now we apply P_1 again by instantiating x to x_0, both w and z to z_0, and y

to y_0, and the result is $G(x_0,y_0,z_0)$, which is the instantiated head of the rule of P_2. Therefore, $P_2 \subseteq^u P_1$. ∎

Minimizing Programs under Uniform Equivalence

Having an algorithm for testing uniform equivalence makes it possible to optimize Datalog programs in two ways. The first one has just been illustrated in Example 7, and it involves eliminating redundant atoms from the body of a rule in the following way. Consider a rule r and let $\hat{r}$ be the result of deleting one of the atoms in the body of r. If $\hat{r} \subseteq^u r$, then rule r can be replaced with $\hat{r}$, since it follows that $\hat{r} =^u r$ (note that $r \subseteq^u \hat{r}$ is trivially true). When r is replaced with $\hat{r}$, the process continues with $\hat{r}$, that is, another atom in the body of $\hat{r}$ is deleted and if the resulting rule is uniformly contained in $\hat{r}$, then $\hat{r}$ is replaced with that rule. The steps are summarized in the algorithm of Figure 1. The final result is a rule which is uniformly equivalent to the original one, but without any *redundant* atoms, i.e., atoms that can be deleted while preserving uniform equivalence. In proving the correctness of the algorithm, the only nontrivial point is to show that no atom has to be considered more than once. In other words, if some atom α is not redundant when it is considered for the first time, then subsequent deletions of other atoms cannot make α redundant. We shall formally prove this claim in the appendix. Generally, the final result of the algorithm is not unique and may depend upon the order in which atoms are considered. Finally, note that if $\hat{r}$ is obtained from r by deleting an atom α from the body, and some variable from the head of r appears in the body only in α, then $\hat{r}$ does not obey our restrictions on rules, i.e., it is not a domain independent formula. Clearly, the algorithm described in the previous section will determine in this case that $\hat{r} \not\subseteq^u r$, as it should (obviously, α cannot be redundant in this case).

begin
repeat
       let α be an atom in the body of r that has not yet been considered;
       let $\hat{r}$ be the rule obtained by deleting α from r;
       if $\hat{r} \subseteq^u r$ **then** replace r with $\hat{r}$;
until each atom has been considered once;
end.

Figure 1: Minimizing a Rule r

EXAMPLE 8

Consider programs P_1 and P_2 of Example 7. Each one of these programs has a single rule, and the rule of P_2 is obtained from that of P_1 by deleting the atom $A(w,y)$. In Example 7, it is shown that $P_2 \subseteq^u P_1$. Thus, if we execute the algorithm of Figure 1 with the rule of P_1 as an input, then it is going to be replaced with the rule of P_2. It is easy to show that the rule of P_2 does not have any redundant atom. Therefore, the algorithm terminates with the rule of P_2 as the minimal form of the rule of P_1. ∎

Redundant rules can be removed from a program P similarly to the elimination of redundant atoms from the body of a rule. A rule r is deleted from P to obtain a program $\hat{P}$, and if $r \subseteq^u \hat{P}$, then $P \equiv^u \hat{P}$ and, so, $\hat{P}$ can replace P. In order to minimize a program P, we first minimize each rule by removing its redundant atoms, and then remove all redundant rules. However, the following situation is possible. An atom in some rule r of P may not be redundant if r alone is considered, but it may be redundant if all the rules of P are considered. In other words, in order to minimize a rule r of P, we modify the algorithm of Figure 1 by replacing the test $\hat{r} \subseteq^u r$ in the **if** statement with $\hat{r} \subseteq^u P$. The complete algorithm for minimizing a program P is given in Figure 2. In the appendix, we prove that the final result of the algorithm has neither redundant rules nor redundant atoms. The only nontrivial part of the proof is showing that no rule or atom has to be considered more than once; the proof relies on the fact that at first each rule is minimized and only then redundant rules are removed. The final result of the algorithm is not necessarily unique.

begin
for each rule r **do**
    repeat
        let α be an atom in the body of r that has not yet been considered;
        let $\hat{r}$ be the rule obtained by deleting α from r;
        if $\hat{r} \subseteq^u P$ **then** replace r with $\hat{r}$;
    until each atom has been considered once;
repeat
    let r be a rule of P that has not yet been considered;
    let $\hat{P}$ be the program obtained by deleting rule r from P;
    if $r \subseteq^u \hat{P}$ **then** replace P with $\hat{P}$;
until each rule has been considered once;
end.

Figure 2: Minimizing a Program P

Tuple-Generating Dependencies

A *tuple-generating dependency* (tgd) (Beeri and Vardi [1984], Fagin [1982], Yannakakis and Papadimitriou [1982]) is a formula of the form $\forall \bar{x} \, \exists \bar{y} \, [\psi_1 (\bar{x})$ $\rightarrow \psi_2 (\bar{x}, \bar{y})]$, where $\bar{x}$ and $\bar{y}$ are vectors of variables and both ψ_1 and ψ_2 are conjunctions of atoms. We write a tgd without the quantifiers, e.g., $G(y,z) \rightarrow$ $G(y,w) \wedge C(w)$ instead of $\forall y \, \forall z \, \exists w \, [G(y,z) \rightarrow G(y,w) \wedge C(w)]$. Universally quantified variables are those appearing in the left-hand side of the formula (these variables can also appear in the right-hand side). Existentially quantified variables are those appearing only in the right-hand side of the tgd. Note that the tgds considered in this paper are untyped.

As usual, we say that a DB d *satisfies* a tgd τ if for every instantiation θ of the universally quantified variables, the following is true: If the left-hand side of τ is instantiated by θ to ground atoms of d, then the right-hand side of τ can also be instantiated to ground atoms of d by extending θ to an instantiation of all the variables of τ.

EXAMPLE 9
Consider the tgd $G(x,y) \rightarrow A(y,z) \wedge A(z,x)$, and the DB produced in Example 2. Recall that G is the transitive closure of A, and the DB is

$$\{A(1,2), \; A(1,4), \; A(4,1), \; G(1,2), \; G(1,4), \; G(4,1), \; G(1,1), \; G(4,4),$$
$$G(4,2)\}$$

If we instantiate both x and y to 4, then the instantiated left-hand side, $G(4,4)$, is a ground atom of the DB. We can now choose to instantiate z to 1, and as a result, the instantiated right-hand side consists of ground atoms, $A(4,1)$ and $A(1,4)$, that are in the DB. The DB, however, does not satisfy the tgd, since instantiating x to 4 and y to 2 converts the left-hand side to a ground atom of the DB, but there is no possible instantiation of z that also converts the right-hand side to ground atoms of the DB. The tgd $G(x,y) \rightarrow G(x,z) \wedge A(z,y)$, on the other hand, is satisfied by the DB. For example, if x is instantiated to 1 and y to 2, then instantiating z to 1 converts the right-hand side to ground atoms of the DB. ∎

Let S be a set of DBs. We say that program P_1 *uniformly contains* P_2 *over* S, written $P_2 \subseteq^u_S P_1$, if $P_2(d) \subseteq P_1(d)$ for all DBs $d \in S$. In most cases we assume that S is the set of all DBs satisfying a given set T of tgds, and we usually denote this set by $SAT(T)$.

Tuple-generating dependencies are important in Datalog, because in many cases optimizing a program requires looking only at DBs that satisfy some tgds. One case is when the EDB satisfies some constraints that can be expressed as tgds. Using constraints in order to optimize programs has already been investigated (e.g., Chakravarthy et al. [1986,1988]). We will show how to use tgds in a more general way. Essentially, we will give a proof procedure for showing $P_2 \subseteq^u_{SAT(T)} P_1$ and develop a technique for removing redundant atoms from a program P by doing the following steps. First, we have to show that $P_2 \subseteq^u_{SAT(T)} P_1$ for some suitable T, where P_2 is obtained from P_1 by deleting an atom α from some rule. Second, we have to show that $P_2 \subseteq^u_{SAT(T)} P_1$ implies $P_2 \subseteq P_1$. If we show both, then it follows that α is redundant in P_1, even if it is not redundant under uniform equivalence. This optimization technique will be described in detail later. In the remainder of this section, we will describe the first part of a procedure for determining whether $P_2 \subseteq^u_{SAT(T)} P_1$. The correctness of this procedure is proved in the appendix.

Considering Proposition 2, it comes as no surprise that in order to show $P_2 \subseteq^u_{SAT(T)} P_1$, we have to show $SAT(T) \cap M(P_1) \subseteq M(P_2)$, i.e., every model of P_1 that satisfies T is also a model of P_2. Moreover, the chase process can be easily modified to show that. As we shall see later, however, $SAT(T) \cap M(P_1) \subseteq M(P_2)$ alone does not imply $P_2 \subseteq^u_{SAT(T)} P_1$; and in the next section we shall describe a second step that is needed in order to conclude that $P_2 \subseteq^u_{SAT(T)} P_1$.

In order to test whether $SAT(T) \cap M(P_1) \subseteq M(P_2)$, we have to consider each rule r of P_2 and show that when both P_1 and T are applied to the body of r, the result includes the head of r. Applying the tgds of T to a DB is similar to the application of rules, since tgds are also Horn clauses.

We will now describe how to apply the tgds in greater detail. There are two types of tgds: *full* tgds, namely, tgds without existentially quantified variables, and *embedded* tgds, namely, tgds that have some existentially quantified variables. As illustrated by the following example, applying a full tgd to a DB is just the same as applying a rule.

EXAMPLE 10
The tgd $A(x,y,z) \wedge B(w,y,v) \rightarrow A(x,y,v) \wedge T(w,y,z)$ is full. Applying it to a DB is the same as applying the following two rules. Note that each of these rules has the left-hand side of the tgd as its body, and one of the atoms in the right-hand side of the tgd as its head.

$A(x,y,v) :- A(x,y,z), B(w,y,v).$

$T(w,y,z) :- A(x,y,z), B(w,y,v).$ ∎

An embedded tgd has existentially quantified variables and, therefore, in order to apply it we have to use Skolem functions. We follow the approach of database theory and view Skolem functions as *nulls*, i.e., unknown values. We denote nulls as $\delta_1,...,\delta_i,...$.

A tgd τ is applied to a DB as follows. Suppose that θ is an instantiation of the universally quantified variables of τ, such that θ shows that the DB violates τ. That is, θ converts the left-hand side of τ to ground atoms of the DB, and there is no extension of θ that also converts the right-hand side of τ to ground atoms of the DB. For each existentially quantified variable of τ, we choose a unique null δ_i (which is not already in the DB) and extend θ to an instantiation that maps each existentially quantified variable to its corresponding null. The instantiated atoms of the right-hand side of τ are added to the DB. For example, if τ is the tgd $G(x,y) \to A(x,w) \wedge G(w,y)$ and the atom $G(3,2)$ is in the DB, then we add $A(3,\delta_{23})$ and $G(\delta_{23},2)$ (provided, of course, that the DB contains neither δ_{23} nor a pair of atoms of the form $A(3,e)$ and $G(e,2)$, where e is either a constant or a null). The atoms $A(3,\delta_{23})$ and $G(\delta_{23},2)$ simply mean that there is some some unknown value c, such that $A(3,c)$ and $G(c,2)$ are in the DB.

The combined application of a program P and a set of tgds T is denoted $[P,T]$. We apply $[P,T]$ to a DB d until no new atoms can be added to the DB, and the final result is denoted $[P,T](d)$. Clearly, $[P,T](d)$ is both a model of P and a DB that satisfies T. Since the application of tgds may add nulls that are not already in the DB, some sets of tgds can be applied to an initial DB forever.[6] Note that once an atom with nulls is added to the DB, then it is viewed as a ground atom and nulls are viewed as constants, as far as applications of rules and tgds are concerned.

EXAMPLE 11

Let P_1 be the program

$G(x,z) :- A(x,z).$

$G(x,z) :- G(x,y), G(y,z), A(y,w).$

and let P_2 be the program

$G(x,z) :- A(x,z).$

$G(x,z) :- G(x,y), G(y,z).$

It is easy to show that $P_1 \subseteq^u P_2$. We will show that $SAT(T) \cap M(P_1) \subseteq M(P_2)$, where T consists of the single dependency:

$G(x,z) \to A(x,w)$

---

[6] When dealing with a nonterminating chase process, we have to consider also infinite databases in order to prove some of the results. This issue is discussed in the appendix, where all the proofs are given.

The rules of P_2 have to be considered one by one. We start by instantiating the first rule of P_2 and, so, its body becomes the DB $\{A(x_0,z_0)\}$. Now we have to apply $[P_1,T]$ to this DB, and the result is $\{A(x_0,z_0), G(x_0,z_0)\}$ (note that only the first rule of P_1 can be applied to this DB). This result contains the instantiated head of the first rule of P_2.

Next, consider the DB $\{G(x_0,y_0), G(y_0,z_0)\}$, which is the instantiated body of the second rule of P_2. At first, the only possible application of $[P_1,T]$ is to apply the tgd of T. If the left-hand side of the tgd is instantiated to $G(y_0,z_0)$, then this instantiation cannot be extended to any instantiation that converts the right-hand side to a ground atom of the DB and, therefore, $A(y_0,\delta_1)$ is added to the DB. Similarly, the left-hand side of the tgd can be instantiated to $G(x_0,y_0)$, which results in adding $A(x_0,\delta_2)$ to the DB. Now, the body of the second rule of P_1 can be instantiated to $G(x_0,y_0)$, $G(y_0,z_0)$, $A(y_0,\delta_1)$, and so $G(x_0,z_0)$ is added to the DB, thereby showing that the instantiated head of the second rule of P_2 is in the result. Thus, we have shown that $SAT(T) \cap M(P_1) \subseteq M(P_2)$. In the next section, we will use this fact in order to conclude that $P_2 \subseteq^u_{SAT(T)} P_1$.

Showing $P_2 \subseteq^u_{SAT(T)} P_1$ is useful, because it implies $P_2 \subseteq P_1$ by the following simple argument (the argument is given here informally, and will be given formally in the section ''Determining Equivalence''). Applying program P_1 (or P_2) to an EDB, which is given as an input, is the same as applying [7] P_1 (or P_2) to the *preliminary* DB, i.e., the DB consisting of the input and the ground atoms generated by the *initialization* rules (an initialization rule is a rule whose body has only extensional predicates). Since P_1 and P_2 have the same initialization rule, they have the same preliminary DB for every EDB; and it is easy to see that all preliminary DBs satisfy T. Therefore, $P_2 \subseteq^u_{SAT(T)} P_1$ implies $P_2 \subseteq P_1$. Clearly, $P_1 \subseteq P_2$ and, so, $P_1 \equiv P_2$. It thus follows that the atom $A(y,w)$ in the second rule of P_1 is redundant under equivalence, although it is not redundant under uniform equivalence. ∎

Preserving Tuple-Generating Dependencies

As stated earlier, $SAT(T) \cap M(P_1) \subseteq M(P_2)$ alone does not imply $P_2 \subseteq^u_{SAT(T)} P_1$. As shown in the appendix, however, if we also show that P_1 *preserves* T, then $P_2 \subseteq^u_{SAT(T)} P_1$ follows. We say that P_1 preserves T if $P_1(d) \in SAT(T)$ for all DBs $d \in SAT(T)$.

It is not known whether there is a proof procedure for showing that a program P preserves a set of tgds T. In this section we will describe a process that may efficiently show, in many practical cases, that P preserves T. The idea is to show that if we start with a DB $d \in SAT(T)$, then each iteration in

---

[7] When P_1 (or P_2) is applied to the preliminary DB, the initialization rules are redundant and can be ignored.

the bottom-up computation of $P(d)$ preserves T. To express the idea more formally, we need the following definitions. Applying P *nonrecursively* to a DB d means applying it only to ground atoms of d and not to ground atoms generated from d by previous applications. When P is applied nonrecursively, we denote it as P^n. Clearly, the result of applying P^n to a DB d, denoted $P^n(d)$, is

$\{h\theta \mid$ for some rule $h :- b$ of P and substitution θ, the atoms of $b\theta$ are in $d\}$

Note that by our previous definitions, the output $P(d)$ contains the input d. In comparison, $P^n(d)$ contains only the atoms generated by applying the rules nonrecursively to d but does not necessarily contain the atoms of d. This notation is just a matter of convenience and should not cause any confusion.

EXAMPLE 12
Let P be the program

$G(x,z) :- A(x,z).$

$G(x,z) :- G(x,y), G(y,z).$

and let $d = \{A(1,2), G(2,3), G(3,4)\}$. $P^n(d)$ is $\{G(1,2), G(2,4)\}$, whereas $P(d)$ is $\{A(1,2), G(2,3), G(3,4), G(1,2), G(1,3), G(2,4), G(1,4)\}$. ∎

Our idea is to show that P preserves T by showing that P *preserves* T *nonrecursively*, that is, $\langle d, P^n(d)\rangle \in SAT(T)$ for all $d \in SAT(T)$ (recall that $\langle d, P^n(d)\rangle$ is the union of d and $P^n(d)$). Note that if P preserves T nonrecursively, then P preserves T. The converse, however, is not necessarily true, that is, P may preserve T without preserving it nonrecursively.

Proving that P preserves T nonrecursively is done by a variant of the chase process that was originally proposed by Klug and Price [1982]. This process is complete for proving nonrecursive preservation of T, that is, it terminates with a positive answer if indeed P preserves T nonrecursively, but it may loop forever if T has embedded tgds and the answer is negative. Before fully defining this process, we illustrate it on a simple example.

EXAMPLE 13
Consider the following recursive rule, denoted r,

$G(x,z) :- G(x,y), G(y,z), A(y,w).$

and let τ be the tgd

$G(x,z) \rightarrow A(x,w)$

In order to show that r preserves τ nonrecursively, we will attempt to prove the opposite by trying to construct a counterexample, and if we fail to do so, then r preserves τ nonrecursively. A counterexample, in this particular case, is a DB $d \in SAT(\tau)$ such that $\langle d, r^n(d) \rangle$ violates τ. The DB $\langle d, r^n(d) \rangle$ violates τ if it has a ground atom $G(x_0, z_0)$ that *exhibits* a violation of τ, that is, a ground atom $G(x_0, z_0)$ such that for all w_0, the DB $\langle d, r^n(d) \rangle$ does not have a ground atom of the form $A(x_0, w_0)$. A ground atom $G(x_0, z_0)$ of $\langle d, r^n(d) \rangle$ that exhibits a violation of τ must be in $r^n(d)$ (it cannot be in d, since $d \in SAT(\tau)$). Therefore, we will try to build a counterexample by first assuming that $G(x_0, z_0)$ is in $r^n(d)$, and then adding atoms to d that are needed in order to

1. have the atom $G(x_0, z_0)$ in $r^n(d)$, and

2. make d satisfy τ.

The atom $G(x_0, z_0)$ can be in $r^n(d)$ only as a result of applying r^n to d. By unifying $G(x_0, z_0)$ with the head of r, we can determine which ground atoms must be in d in order to produce $G(x_0, z_0)$. In this particular case, the unification shows that d must have the following atoms:

$$G(x_0, y_0), \; G(y_0, z_0), \; A(y_0, w_0)$$

where y_0 and w_0 are some constants.

Since d satisfies τ, it is possible to apply the tgd τ to d. Applying τ to $G(x_0, y_0)$ yields $A(x_0, \delta_1)$, and applying it to $G(y_0, z_0)$ yields $A(y_0, \delta_2)$. Note that these applications result in ground atoms that must be in d (as opposed to applications of r^n that produce ground atoms in $r^n(d)$). Basically, the applications of τ correspond to inferences implied by the fact that d satisfies τ and by the fact that certain ground atoms are known to be in d. In principle, the tgd τ should be applied repeatedly to the atoms of d (both the atoms that have originally been in d and those added to d by previous applications of the tgd). In this particular case, the tgd can be applied only to the ground atoms originally known to be in d (i.e., those produced by unifying $G(x_0, z_0)$ with the head of r). Consequently, the ground atoms that must be in d are

$$G(x_0, y_0), \; G(y_0, z_0), \; A(y_0, w_0), \; A(x_0, \delta_1), \; A(y_0, \delta_2).$$

Among them there is $A(x_0, \delta_1)$, which shows that $G(x_0, z_0)$ does not exhibit a violation of τ. Therefore, there is no counterexample $\langle d, r^n(d) \rangle$ and, so, r preserves τ nonrecursively. ∎

We can now generalize the above example to an arbitrary P and T. In order to prove that P preserves T nonrecursively, we do the following for each $\tau \in T$. First, the left-hand side of τ is instantiated by replacing each variable with a distinct constant that is not already in P. The ground atoms of the instantiated left-hand side are treated according to one of the following two cases:

1.   Ground atoms of extensional predicates become part of d.

2.   Ground atoms of intensional predicates become part of $P^n(d)$.

For each ground atom α in $P^n(d)$, we should add to d some atoms that produce α when P is applied nonrecursively to d. In general, there are many ways to add atoms that produce α. Each possible way is determined by some rule with a head that can be unified with α. Thus, we should consider all possible combinations of unifying the ground atoms that have been added to $P^n(d)$ with heads of rules (if there are k ground atoms in $P^n(d)$ and }ieach can be unified with m rules, then there are m^k combinations to consider). Essentially, we have to show that for each possible combination, there is no violation of τ. So, consider one possible combination that unifies each ground atom α of an intensional predicate G (in the instantiated left-hand side of τ) with the head of some rule r for G. As a result of the unification, the variables of r that appear in the head are instantiated to constants. In order to convert the body of r to ground atoms, the rest of the variables of r are instantiated to new distinct constants, and the ground atoms of the body are added to d. In summary, d contains all the ground atoms that are either

1.   atoms of extensional predicates from the instantiated left-hand side of tgd τ, or

2.   atoms (extensional or intensional) from bodies of rules that have been unified with atoms of intensional predicates from the left-hand side of τ.

As for $P^n(d)$, it contains atoms of intensional predicates from the instantiated left-hand side of τ.

In the second step, the tgds of T (all of them—not just τ) are applied to d to produce more ground atoms that must be in d. The tgds are applied repeatedly, until no more ground atoms can be generated from existing ones (and, consequently, d becomes a DB that satisfies T).

In the third step,[8] the program P is applied nonrecursively to d to get $P^n(d)$.

In the final step, we should check whether $\langle d, P^n(d) \rangle$ satisfies τ. In order to check that, it is sufficient to consider the instantiated left-hand side of τ (which is part of $P^n(d)$), and check whether it *exhibits* a violation of τ in $\langle d, P^n(d) \rangle$. No violation is exhibited if the instantiation of the left-hand side can be extended to an instantiation that also includes the existentially quantified variables[9] of τ,

---

[8] In Example 13, this step is redundant and, hence, has been omitted.

[9] Recall that the existentially quantified variables of a tgd are those appearing only in the right-hand side.

such that the right-hand side of τ becomes a subset of $\langle d, P^n(d) \rangle$. In fact, it follows that there is no need to compute all of $P^n(d)$; instead, it is sufficient to determine whether $\langle d, P^n(d) \rangle$ contains ground atoms showing that the instantiated left-hand side of τ does not exhibit a violation. For clarity of presentation, however, we will continue to use the step that computes $P^n(d)$.

The program P preserves T nonrecursively, if for all $\tau \in T$ and for all combinations of unifying the instantiated left-hand side of τ with heads of rules of P, no violation of τ is exhibited.

In Example 13, the left-hand side of the tgd τ has only one atom and there is only one rule; therefore, there is only one combination to check, and as has been shown, it does not exhibit a violation. The steps for checking whether P preserves T nonrecursively are summarized in Figure 3. Finer details of the algorithm are explained in the next two paragraphs.

The step of applying T to d may not terminate if new nulls are repeatedly introduced. It is still possible, however, to terminate the inner loop in finite time (for any particular choice of $\tau \in T$ and any particular choice of rules for τ)

begin
repeat
    make d empty;
    choose a $\tau \in T$;
    let θ map the universally quantified variables of τ to distinct constants
        that are not already in P;
    instantiate the left-hand side of τ according to θ;
    add the instantiated atoms of extensional predicates to d;
    repeat
        choose a rule for each instantiated atom of an intensional
            predicate:
        unify each atom with the head of the rule chosen for it,
            and add the instantiated body to d;
        apply the tgds of T to d;
        compute $P^n(d)$;
        check whether the instantiated left-hand side
            exhibits a violation of τ in $\langle d, P^n(d) \rangle$;
    until a violation has been exhibited or
        all combinations of choosing rules have been examined;
until a violation has been exhibited or all $\tau \in T$ have been chosen;
if a violation has been exhibited
    then P does not preserve T nonrecursively
    else P preserves T nonrecursively
end.

Figure 3: Procedure for Testing Nonrecursive Preservation of T

if no violation of τ is exhibited. In order to achieve that, the last three steps of the inner loop should be interleaved as follows. First, T is applied to d to produce some more new atoms that must be in d. Next, $P^n(d)$ is computed again, since its value might have changed as a result of the new atoms that have just been added to d. The third step is to check whether the instantiated left-hand side of τ exhibits a violation in the current $\langle d, P^n(d) \rangle$. If no violation is exhibited, then τ is preserved and there is no need to continue. If a violation still exists, then the previous steps should be reiterated.

As already stated, each atom of an intensional predicate, in the instantiated left-hand side of τ, is unified with the head of some rule. This has the effect of testing whether τ is satisfied when atoms of intensional predicates in its left-hand side are restricted to be in $P^n(d)$. In Example 13, there is a single atom in the left-hand side of τ, and therefore, τ is satisfied in $\langle d, P^n(d) \rangle$ if the following is shown:

1. τ is satisfied in $\langle d, P^n(d) \rangle$ when the left-hand side is restricted to be in $P^n(d)$, and

2. τ is satisfied in $\langle d, P^n(d) \rangle$ when the left-hand side is restricted to be in d.

Part 1 has been shown in Example 13 by unifying the left-hand side with the head of r. Part 2 follows immediately from the fact that d satisfies τ. The situation, however, is not that simple if the left-hand side of τ has more than one atom of an intensional predicate. In this case, we have to check that τ is also satisfied when some atoms[10] are in $P^n(d)$, while others are in d. Thus, we should consider more combinations than stated earlier. The combinations are all those in which an atom of an intensional predicate in the left-hand side of τ is either unified with the head of some rule or is assumed to be in d (without, of course, being unified with any rule). If an atom is unified with the head of some rule, then the atom becomes part of $P^n(d)$, while the instantiated body of the rule becomes part of d. We can still use the old definition of the combinations to be considered if for each intensional predicate Q, we add a trivial rule of the form: $Q(x_1,\ldots,x_n) := Q(x_1,\ldots,x_n)$. From now on we will assume that each program is augmented with these trivial rules (although usually we do not explicitly write these rules as part of the program). Therefore, the combinations to be considered are the same as defined originally, that is, a combination unifies each atom of an intensional predicate with the head of some rule.

EXAMPLE 14
Consider again the program P_1 given in Example 11:

---

[10]The atoms referred to are, of course, the instantiated atoms of intensional predicates in the left-hand side of τ.

$G(x,z) :- A(x,z).$

$G(x,z) :- G(x,y), G(y,z), A(y,w).$

and the tgd τ:

$G(x,z) \rightarrow A(x,w)$

We will show that P_1 preserves $T = \{\tau\}$ nonrecursively, and hence it also preserves T. Combining this with the fact $SAT(T) \cap M(P_1) \subseteq M(P_2)$, which was shown in Example 11, implies that $P_2 \subseteq^u_{SAT(T)} P_1$. Let $G(x_0,z_0)$ be the instantiated left-hand side of τ. In Example 13, we have shown that no violation is exhibited when $G(x_0,z_0)$ is unified with the head of the second rule of P_1. Similarly, there can be no violation when $G(x_0,z_0)$ is unified with the trivial rule $G(x,z) :- G(x,z)$.[11] The last case to consider is unifying with the rule:

$G(x,z) :- A(x,z).$

As a result of unifying $G(x_0,z_0)$ with the head of the above rule, d becomes the DB $\{A(x_0,z_0)\}$. The tgds of T cannot be applied to d. Next, by applying P_1^n to d, we get that $P_1^n(d)$ is $\{G(x_0,z_0)\}$. Since $A(x_0,z_0)$ is in $\langle d, P_1^{\,n}(d)\rangle$, no violation of τ is exhibited and, therefore, P_1 preserves T, as was claimed. ∎

EXAMPLE 15
Let r be the same rule as in Example 13, that is

$G(x,z) :- G(x,y), G(y,z), A(y,w).$

and let the tgd τ be

$G(x,y) \wedge G(y,z) \rightarrow A(y,w)$

We will show that r (i.e., the program consisting of r) preserves τ nonrecursively. Recall that we should treat the program as if it also has the trivial rule

$G(x,z) :- G(x,z).$

---

[11] As a general rule, there can be no violation if the left-hand side of the tgd has only one atom of an intensional predicate and the unification is done with a trivial rule, because the whole instantiated left-hand side becomes part of d, which is assumed to satisfy T. The trivial rules have to be used only when we deal with a tgd that has more than one atom of an intensional predicate in its left-hand side (see Example 15).

and, hence, there are four possible combinations of unifying the atoms in the left-hand side of τ with heads of rules. So let

$$G(x_0,y_0), \; G(y_0,z_0)$$

be the instantiated left-hand side of τ, and consider the following four combinations.

Combination 1: $G(x_0,y_0)$ is unified with the head of r and, as a result, the following ground atoms (i.e., those from the body of r) are in d:

$$G(x_0,y_1), \; G(y_1,y_0), \; A(y_1,w_0)$$

and $G(y_0,z_0)$ is unified with the head of the trivial rule, which adds the following atom to d:

$$G(y_0,z_0)$$

Now $T = \{\tau\}$ should be applied to d and, actually, only the following application is possible. The left-hand side of τ is instantiated to the following ground atoms of d:

$$G(y_1,y_0), \; G(y_0,z_0)$$

Since this instantiation cannot be extended to one that also converts the right-hand side to ground atoms of d, the ground atom $A(y_0,\delta_1)$ is added to d. Note that no more applications of T are possible after this one. The atom $A(y_0,\delta_1)$ of d shows that no violation of τ is exhibited in $\langle d, r''(d) \rangle$ for the combination being considered.

Combination 2: $G(x_0,y_0)$ is unified with the head of the trivial rule and, as a result, the following ground atom is added to d:

$$G(x_0,y_0)$$

and $G(y_0,z_0)$ is unified with the head of r, and the following ground atoms are added to d:

$$G(y_0,y_1), \; G(y_1,z_0), \; A(y_1,w_0)$$

Now $T = \{\tau\}$ is applied to d. Again, there is only one possible application, which is obtained by instantiating the left-hand side of τ to the following ground atoms of d:

$$G(x_0,y_0), \; G(y_0,y_1)$$

This instantiation adds $A(y_0,\delta_1)$ to d, and this ground atom shows that no violation of τ is exhibited in $\langle d,r^n(d)\rangle$.

Combination 3: $G(x_0,y_0)$ is unified with the head of r, and the following ground atoms are added to d:

$$G(x_0,y_1), G(y_1,y_0), A(y_1,w_0)$$

and $G(y_0,z_0)$ is also unified with the head of r, and the following ground atoms are added to d:

$$G(y_0,y_2), G(y_2,z_0), A(y_2,w_1)$$

Now $T = \{\tau\}$ is applied to d by instantiating the left-hand side of τ to the following ground atoms of d:

$$G(y_1,y_0), G(y_0,y_2)$$

and, as result of this instantiation, $A(y_0,\delta_1)$ is added to d. The atom $A(y_0,\delta_1)$ shows that no violation of τ is exhibited in $\langle d,r^n(d)\rangle$ for the combination being considered.

Combination 4: Both $G(x_0,y_0)$ and $G(y_0,z_0)$ are unified with the head of the trivial rule and, therefore, become part of d. Clearly, there cannot be a violation in this case, since d satisfies T.

Since no combination exhibits a violation, r preserves τ. ∎

EXAMPLE 16
Consider the rule r

$$G(x,z) :- A(x,y), G(y,z), G(y,w), C(w).$$

and the following tgd, denoted τ

$$G(y,z) \rightarrow G(y,w) \wedge C(w)$$

To show that r preserves τ nonrecursively, we instantiate the left-hand side of τ to

$$G(y_0,z_0)$$

and unify it with the head of r. Consequently, the following ground atoms are in d:

$$A(y_0,y_1), G(y_1,z_0), G(y_1,w_0), C(w_0)$$

Note that in this case, the tgd τ cannot be applied to d to produce new atoms. But when r is applied nonrecursively to d, the DB $r^n(d)$ becomes equal to

$$G(y_0,z_0), G(y_0,w_0)$$

To see that $G(y_0,z_0)$ is in $r^n(d)$, note that this atom was unified with the head of r and the instantiated body became a part of d. To see that $G(y_0,w_0)$ is in $r^n(d)$, instantiate the variables of r as follows. Instantiate x to y_0, y to y_1, and both z and w to w_0.

The ground atoms $G(y_0,w_0)$ and $C(w_0)$ show that $\langle d,r^n(d,)\rangle$ does not violate τ when the left-hand side is instantiated to $G(y_0,z_0)$. Thus, r preserves τ. ∎

Determining Equivalence

In this section we will show how it is sometimes possible to infer that $P_2 \subseteq P_1$ from the fact that $P_2 \subseteq^u_{SAT(T)} P_1$. Later we will discuss how to use this technique in order to optimize programs. But first we need some definitions. A rule r of a program P is an *initialization* rule if the body of r has only extensional predicates. P^i is the program consisting of the initialization rules of P. Note that P^i is a nonrecursive program. Given an EDB d as an input to P, we define $P^i(d)$ to be the set of ground atoms generated by applying P^i to d (since P^i is a nonrecursive program, $P^i(d)$ is defined in the same way as applying a program nonrecursively, i.e., $P^i(d)$ does not include d). The *preliminary* DB for an EDB d is $\langle d,P^i(d)\rangle$.

EXAMPLE 17
Let P be the program

$$G(x,z) :- A(x,z).$$

$$G(x,z) :- G(x,y), G(y,z).$$

and let $d = \{A(1,2), A(2,3), A(3,4)\}$. $P^i(d)$ is $\{G(1,2), G(2,3), G(3,4)\}$, and the preliminary DB for d is $\{A(1,2), A(2,3), A(3,4), G(1,2), G(2,3), G(3,4)\}$. ∎

In the next example, we illustrate how to infer $P_2 \subseteq P_1$ from $P_2 \subseteq^u_{SAT(T)} P_1$.

EXAMPLE 18
Consider again the two programs of Example 11. Recall that P_1 is the program

$G(x,z) :- A(x,z)$.

$G(x,z) :- G(x,y), G(y,z), A(y,w)$.

and P_2 is the program

$G(x,z) :- A(x,z)$.

$G(x,z) :- G(x,y), G(y,z)$.

Clearly, $P_1 \subseteq^u P_2$. In Example 11 we have shown that $SAT(T) \cap M(P_1) \subseteq M(P_2)$, where T consists of the single tgd

$G(x,z) \rightarrow A(x,w)$

Consequently, $P_2 \subseteq^u_{SAT(T)} P_1$, since in Example 14 we have shown that P_1 preserves T. In this example, we will show that $P_2 \subseteq P_1$ and hence $P_1 \equiv P_2$, since $P_1 \subseteq^u P_2$ (and so $P_1 \subseteq P_2$).

First, we will show that for every EDB d, the preliminary DB, $\langle d, P_1^i(d) \rangle$, satisfies T. Recall that P_1^i consists of the rule

$G(x,z) :- A(x,z)$.

Essentially, the procedure of Figure 3 is used to show that $\langle d, P_1^i(d) \rangle$ satisfies T. There are, however, two important changes. First, we do not assume that d satisfies T and, therefore, we omit the step in which the tgds of T are applied to d. Second, d is an EDB given as an input to P_1 and, so, it does not have any ground atom of an intensional predicate. Therefore, we do not add to the program P_1^i the trivial rules (i.e., rules of the form $Q(x_1,\ldots,x_n) :- Q(x_1,\ldots,x_n)$) for the intensional predicates.

Thus, we start by instantiating the left-hand side of the only tgd in T, and the result is $G(x_0,z_0)$. There is only one rule in P_1^i and, hence, only one combination of unifying the instantiated left-hand side with heads of rules. This unification results in d being the DB $\{A(x_0,z_0)\}$. Since $A(x_0,z_0)$ has just been shown to be in $\langle d, P_1^i(d) \rangle$, no violation of the tgd is exhibited and, therefore, all the preliminary DBs of P_1 satisfy T.

P_1 and P_2 have the same initialization rule and, consequently, their preliminary DBs are the same (when given the same EDB as an input). Therefore $P_2 \subseteq^u_{SAT(T)} P_1$ implies $P_2 \subseteq P_1$, since all the preliminary DBs satisfy T. ∎

To sum up the approach illustrated in the above example, showing $P_2 \subseteq P_1$ entails showing the following:

1. $SAT(T) \cap M(P_1) \subseteq M(P_2)$.

2. P_1 preserves T.

3. For all EDBs d, programs P_1 and P_2 have the same preliminary DB.

4. All the preliminary DBs satisfy T.

Part 1 can be shown using the chase process described in the section "Tuple-Generating Dependencies." Part 2 may be shown using the process summarized in Figure 3. Part 3 requires showing that P_1^i and P_2^i are equivalent. Equivalence of nonrecursive programs is the same as uniform equivalence and, thus, there is an algorithm for showing that (i.e., the one described in the section "Testing Uniform Containment and Equivalence"). In fact, equivalence of nonrecursive programs is the same as equivalence of unions of tableaux (Sagiv and Yannakakis [1980]). Part 4 can be shown by the procedure of Figure 3 with the following modifications. First, the step of applying the tgds of T to d is removed. Second, the program (i.e, P_1^i) is not augmented with trivial rules for the intensional predicates.

The above recipe for showing $P_2 \subseteq P_1$ has some drawbacks that may limit its applicability. First, it is not always clear how to find a set of tgds T for which 1 – 4 hold. Moreover, the fact that $P_2 \subseteq P_1$ does not necessarily imply that there is such a T. Second, the procedure for testing 1 (or 2) terminates in finite time if the answer is positive but may loop forever if the answer is negative. Nevertheless, we believe that in many practical cases this approach is useful in optimizing programs.

We end this section with an important comment on conditions 1 – 4 above. Actually, it is not necessary to consider the preliminary DBs of both P_1 and P_2. Instead, it is sufficient to consider only the preliminary DBs of P_1 and show that they satisfy T. In other words, conditions 3 and 4 can be replaced with the following condition:

(3') For all EDBs d, the preliminary DB $\langle d, P_1^i(d) \rangle$ satisfies T.

The reason for that is as follows. We know that $P_2 \subseteq_{SAT(T)}^u P_1$ and we want to conclude that $P_2 \subseteq P_1$, that is, we want to show that if d is an EDB, then $P_2(d) \subseteq P_1(d)$. So, let d' be the preliminary DB of P_1 obtained from d, i.e., $d \subset d'$; and suppose that d' satisfies T. Since $P_2 \subseteq_{SAT(T)}^u P_1$ and d' satisfies T, it follows that

$$P_2(d') \subseteq P_1(d') \tag{A}$$

But Datalog programs are monotonic and, therefore,

$$P_2(d) \subseteq P_2(d') \tag{B}$$

because $d \subseteq d'$. Moreover, d' is the preliminary DB obtained by applying the initialization rules of P_1 to d and, hence,

$$P_1(d) = P_1(d') \tag{C}$$

From (A), (B), and (C) it follows that

$$P_2(d) \subseteq P_1(d)$$

Finally, another important comment. When defining the preliminary DB, it is not necessary to choose the one generated by the initialization rules. Instead, it is sufficient to consider any set of rules of P_1 and apply it a fixed number of times to the initial EDB given as an input. Applying a given set of rules a fixed number of times (even if the rules are recursive) can be expressed in terms of nonrecursive rules and, hence, testing whether the preliminary DB satisfies T can be done as described earlier (i.e., as described for a preliminary DB created by the initialization rules).

Optimizing under Equivalence

In Example 18, we have shown that the atom $A(y,w)$ is redundant in the recursive rule of P_1. Note that this cannot be shown using the algorithm of Figure 2, because $A(y,w)$ is not redundant under uniform equivalence. Compared to optimization under uniform equivalence, it is less clear how to carry out this type of optimization algorithmically. The problem is how to find a tgd that shows the redundancy of $A(y,w)$. In practice, the appropriate approach is to use some heuristics. In trying to generalize Example 18, note that the tgd used in that example, i.e., $G(x,z) \rightarrow A(x,w)$, has the property that the following (i.e., (1)) can be shown very easily.

$$SAT(T) \cap M(P_1) \subseteq M(P_2) \tag{1}$$

Recall that T consists of the above tgd and P_2 is obtained from P_1 by removing $A(y,w)$ (see Example 18 for more details). More specifically, a single application of T to the body of the recursive rule of P_2 makes that body identical to the body of the recursive rule of P_1 and, in effect, shows (1).

The above idea for choosing a tgd can be phrased in terms of the following syntactical properties. In order to make the following properties as clear as possible, recall that the rule that has been optimized in Example 18 is

$$G(x,z) :- G(x,y), G(y,z), A(y,w).$$

and the chosen tgd can also be written as $G(y,z) \rightarrow A(y,w)$, i.e., it consists of atoms appearing in the body of the above rule and having the following properties.

1.   The left-hand side of the tgd has the same predicate as the head of the rule being optimized.

2. If the tgd has a variable w that appears only in its right-hand side, then all the atoms (from the body of the rule) that contain w are in the right-hand side of the tgd.

3. All the variables of the tgd that appear only in its right-hand side are not in the head of the rule.

Once a tgd has been chosen, the next step is to test whether the atoms in the right-hand side of the tgd are redundant in the body of the rule.

It is not difficult to devise heuristics that look for a tgd satisfying the above properties. Once a tgd is found, it remains to check the conditions specified in the previous section. This is just a matter of syntactical manipulation, which is conceptually easy. The only problem is that it may not terminate. The common way of handling an optimization process that may run too long is to spend on optimization a predetermined amount of time. As a last example, we illustrate the above ideas.

EXAMPLE 19
Consider the following program.

$G(x,z) :- A(x,z), C(z).$

$G(x,z) :- A(x,y), G(y,z), G(y,w), C(w).$

Clearly, a candidate tgd for showing redundancy is

$G(y,z) \rightarrow G(y,w) \wedge C(w)$

which will be denoted by τ. Let P_1 be the original program, and let P_2 be the one obtained by deleting $G(y,w)$ and $C(w)$ from the body of the recursive rule of P_1. Clearly, $P_1 \subseteq^u P_2$. We will show that $P_2 \subseteq P_1$ by showing the following:

1. $SAT(T) \cap M(P_1) \subseteq M(P_2)$.

2. P_1 preserves τ.

3. For all EDBs d, the preliminary DB $\langle d, P_1^i(d) \rangle$ satisfies T.

It is easy to show that (1) holds. In Example 16, it was shown that the recursive rule of P_1 preserves T. Since T has a single tgd with only one atom in its left-hand side, (3') and the fact that the recursive rule of P_1 preserves T imply (2). Thus, it only remains to show that (3') holds. So let $G(y_0,z_0)$ be the instantiated left-hand side of the tgd τ. Unifying it with the head of the rule of P_1^i produces the DB $\{A(y_0,z_0), C(z_0)\}$. The ground atoms $G(y_0,z_0)$ and $C(z_0)$ show that there is no violation of τ, when its left-hand side is instantiated to

$G(y_0,z_0)$. Thus, all the preliminary DBs satisfy τ. We can, therefore, conclude that the atoms $G(y,w)$ and $C(w)$ are redundant in the recursive rule of P_1. ∎

Conclusion and Open Problems

We have given an algorithm for minimizing Datalog programs under uniform equivalence. This minimization reduces the number of joins needed to find all answers to a query. We have also given an algorithm for testing uniform containment (and hence also uniform equivalence) of programs, which may be useful when other types of optimizations are considered.

We have considered the problem of testing uniform containment when the DB satisfies some constraints that are expressed as tuple-generating dependencies. $P_2 \subseteq^u_{SAT(T)} P_1$ is implied by the following two conditions:

1. $SAT(T) \cap M(P_1) \subseteq M(P_2)$.

2. P_1 preserves T.

Condition 1 can be tested by the chase process described in the section "Tuple-Generating Dependencies." This process always terminates with the correct answer if there are only full tgds. If there are also embedded tgds, then the chase may not terminate when condition 1 is not true. As for condition 2, the procedure described in "Preserving Tuple-Generating Dependencies" can prove it in some, but not all, cases in which it is true. That procedure may not terminate if there are embedded tgds. There is, however, an important case in which condition 2 is obviously true, namely, when the tgds have only extensional predicates on the left-hand side (condition 2 is true in this case, because the evaluation of P_1 never adds new ground atoms of extensional predicates). In particular, if the tgds express constraints that the EDB satisfies, then they have only extensional predicates; and in this case, the chase process (for testing condition 1) can be used to transform a program to an equivalent one that may be more efficient, as done, for example, by Chakravarthy et al. [1986,1988].

We have also shown how to use the procedures for determining conditions 1 and 2 in order to optimize programs under equivalence. Some heuristics are needed to carry out this type of optimization, but we believe that this optimization technique can be applied easily and usefully in practice.

Some open problems remain. First, it is important to characterize cases in which the the procedures for testing conditions 1 and 2 are guaranteed to terminate. It is easy to give ad hoc generalizations based on examples shown in this paper. However, is it possible to find some nontrivial cases?

Another important open problem is to characterize cases that have algorithms for finding tgds that show redundancy whenever some atoms are redundant, or at least, whenever redundancy can be shown by some tgds. If no algorithms can be found, then more heuristics should be developed for finding tgds that may show redundancy.

Acknowledgments

The author thanks Jeff Finger, Georg Gottlob, Paris Kanellakis, Michael Kifer, Dave Maier, Oded Shmueli, Jeff Ullman, and Allen Van Gelder for helpful comments and discussions.

   This work was done when the author visited Stanford University, Stanford, California 94305-2085. It was supported by a grant from the AT&T Foundation, a grant from the IBM Corporation, and National Science Foundation grant 1ST-84-12791. At Hebrew University, this research was supported in part by grant 85-00082 from the United States-Israel Binational Science Foundation (BSF), Jerusalem, Israel.

Appendix

Correctness of Testing Uniform Containment

We first prove two lemmas about the relationship between uniform containment of two programs and containment of their sets of models. Proposition 2, which is stated in the section "Equivalence, Uniform Equivalence, and Models," follows as a special case of these lemmas. Similar lemmas, but for a very restricted class of rules, were proved by Beeri et al. [1981].

   Let S denote a set of DBs. Note that S can be any set, and not necessarily the set of DBs that satisfy some set T of tgds. For a program P, the set $P(S)$ consists of all outputs for inputs in S, that is, $P(S) = \{P(d) \mid d \in S\}$. Recall that $M(P)$ is the set of all models of P.

LEMMA 1
$P_2 \subseteq_S^u P_1 \Rightarrow S \cap M(P_1) \subseteq M(P_2)$.

Proof: Suppose that $P_2 \subseteq_S^u P_1$. Let $d \in S \cap M(P_1)$. We claim that the following is true:

$$d \subseteq P_2(d) \subseteq P_1(d) = d \tag{1}$$

In proof, the left containment holds, because the output of every program contains its input. The right containment holds, since $P_2 \subseteq_S^u P_1$ and $d \in S$. The equality holds, because $d \in M(P_1)$. Therefore, (1) implies that $d \in M(P_2)$. ∎

LEMMA 2

$$P_2 \subseteq_S^u P_1 \Leftarrow P_1(S) \cap M(P_1) \subseteq M(P_2).$$

Proof: Suppose that $P_1(S) \cap M(P_1) \subseteq M(P_2)$, and let $d \in S$ be an input to P_2 (d is not necessarily a model of P_2). Let $d_1 = P_1(d)$ and $d_2 = P_2(d)$. We have to show that $d_2 \subseteq d_1$. Since $d_1 \in P_1(S) \cap M(P_1)$, it follows that $d_1 \in M(P_2)$. Therefore, $d_2 \subseteq d_1$, since d_2 is the minimal model of P_2 that contains d and, as we have shown, d_1 is also a model of P_2 that contains d. ■

The previous two lemmas imply the following corollary. Proposition 2 is a special case of this corollary when S is the set of all DBs.

COROLLARY 1
Let P_1 be a program and S a set of DBs such that $P_1(S) \subseteq S$. Then

$$P_2 \subseteq_S^u P_1 \iff S \cap M(P_1) \subseteq M(P_2). \quad ■$$

Note that if S is the set of all DB satisfying the tgds of some T, i.e., $S = SAT(T)$, then $P_1(S) \subseteq S$ means that P_1 preserves T.

Clearly, $SAT(T) \cap M(P_1) \subseteq M(P_2)$ if and only if $SAT(T) \cap M(P_1) \subseteq M(r)$ for all rules r of P_2, because a DB is a model of P_2 if and only if it is a model of each rule r of P_2. The chase process, described in the section on Tuple-Generating Dependencies, tests $SAT(T) \cap M(P) \subseteq M(r)$, and the following theorem proves its correctness. Recall that in order to perform this process, the body of r has to be viewed as a DB, and this is accomplished by instantiating the variables of r to distinct constants, which are not already in r or P, according to some substitution θ. Also recall that the combined application of a program P and a set of tgds T, which is explained in the section on Tuple-Generating Dependencies, is denoted by $[P,T]$.

THEOREM 1
Let r be the rule $h :- b$, i.e., h is the head and b is the body, and let θ be a one-to-one mapping of the variables of r to constants that do not already appear in r or P. Then

$$h\theta \in [P,T](b\theta) \iff SAT(T) \cap M(P) \subseteq M(r)$$

Proof: The main idea of the proof is the same as in Maier et al. [1979]. First, we assume that $SAT(T) \cap M(P) \subseteq M(r)$ and will show that $h\theta \in [P,T](b\theta)$. So, consider the DBs $b\theta$ and $[P,T](b\theta)$. Clearly, $[P,T](b\theta) \in SAT(T) \cap M(P)$, since $[P,T](b\theta)$ is defined to be the DB obtained from $b\theta$ by applying the rules of P and tgds of T until no rule or tgd can be applied anymore. Therefore, $[P,T](b\theta) \in M(r)$, because we have assumed $SAT(T) \cap M(P) \subseteq M(r)$.

We will now show that $[P,T](b\theta) \in M(r)$ implies $h\theta \in [P,T](b\theta)$, which is what we have to prove. By definition, the DB $[P,T](b\theta)$ contains $b\theta$. If we apply r to $b\theta$, it is immediately clear that $h\theta \in r(b\theta)$, because when the body of r is instantiated according to θ, it becomes $b\theta$ and, therefore, $h\theta$ is in the output. But $[P,T](b\theta)$ is assumed to be a model of r and, so, applying r to $[P,T](b\theta)$ cannot generate any new atom. Therefore, $h\theta \in [P,T](b\theta)$, because applying r to $b\theta$, which is contained in $[P,T](b\theta)$, produces $h\theta$.

We will now prove the other direction, namely, we assume that $h\theta \in [P,T](b\theta)$, and will show that $SAT(T) \cap M(P) \subseteq M(r)$. So, let d be any DB in $SAT(T) \cap M(P)$. We have to show that $d \in M(r)$. Intuitively, the proof is by showing that any application of r to d can also be emulated by a sequence of applications of $[P,T]$, and since applications of $[P,T]$ to d cannot generate anything new, so do applications of r. To show that formally, we consider an arbitrary substitution ρ that instantiates the body of r (i.e., b) to ground atoms of d. Now, to complete the proof, we have to show that $h\rho$ is also in d. But $h\theta \in [P,T](b\theta)$ and, so, there is a sequence of substitutions $\varphi_1, \ldots, \varphi_n$ that shows $h\theta \in [P,T](b\theta)$, that is, for each i there is either a rule of P or a tgd of T, such that when the rule or tgd is instantiated according to φ_i, a new atom is generated, and the last application (i.e., the one for φ_n) generates $h\theta$. Thus, it follows that $\rho \circ \theta^{-1} \circ \varphi_1, \ldots, \rho \circ \theta^{-1} \circ \varphi_n$ is a sequence of instantiations that shows that $[P,T](d)$ contains $h\rho$. But $d \in SAT(T) \cap M(P)$ implies $d = [P,T](d)$ and, so, $h\rho$ is in d. ∎

Note that if rule r has an empty body (and, hence, its head is a ground atom), then Theorem 1 implies that $SAT(T) \cap M(P) \subseteq M(r)$ if and only if r is a rule of P. Also note that if T has embedded tgds, then the DB $[P,T](b\theta)$ may be infinite[12] and, therefore, there is no bound on the time it may take to discover that $[P,T](b\theta)$ contains $h\theta$ (although $h\theta$ will be discovered within a finite time if it is indeed in $[P,T](b\theta)$). Moreover, if $[P,T](b\theta)$ does not contain $h\theta$, then it may be impossible to determine this fact just by computing $[P,T](b\theta)$, since the computation may be infinite. Also note that if $[P,T](b\theta)$ does not contain $h\theta$, then it could be that the only DBs d, such that $d \in SAT(T) \cap M(P)$ and $d \notin M(r)$, are infinite. In other words, if T includes embedded tgds, then the direction $\Leftarrow$ in Theorem 1 is true provided that the set of all possible DBs (i.e., models) includes both finite and infinite DBs. Clearly, if there are no tgds at all, then we have the following important corollary to Theorem 1. This corollary is true when only finite DBs are considered, and it shows the correctness of the algorithm for testing uniform containment. Recall that this algorithm always terminates.

---

[12] This happens when repeated applications of embedded tgds create ground atoms with new nulls.

COROLLARY 2

Let r be a rule with head h and body b, and let θ be a one-to-one mapping of the variables of r to constants that do not already appear in r or P. Then

$$h\theta \in P(b\theta) \Longleftrightarrow M(P) \subseteq M(r). \quad \blacksquare$$

Correctness of Testing Nonrecursive Preservation of Tgds

The procedure described in "Preserving Tuple-Generating Dependencies" for testing whether a program P preserves nonrecursively a set T of tgds is based also on the chase. It is similar to the one described by Klug and Price [1982], and we shall not prove its correctness formally. It suffices to say that if the procedure either determines that P does not preserve nonrecursively some $\tau \in T$ or does not terminate, then it actually constructs a DB d such that d satisfies T and $\langle d, P^n(d) \rangle$ violates τ. Note that the procedure may not terminate only if T has embedded tgds, and in this case the counterexample d is infinite. If the procedure determines that P preserves T nonrecursively, then it essentially does that by constructing for each potential violation of some $\tau \in T$, a canonical DB in which that violation does not exist, and that canonical DB can be mapped homomorphically into any other DB that might exhibit the same violation. Therefore, no violation is possible.

Correctness of the Algorithm for Minimizing Programs

THEOREM 2

The algorithm for minimizing programs under uniform equivalence is correct.

Proof: Essentially, we have to show that no atom or rule has to be considered more than once. So, let P_f be the final program produced by the algorithm. We have to show that P_f has neither redundant rules nor redundant atoms. We will first show that P_f does not have any redundant rule.

Suppose that some rule r is redundant in P_f. Let P denote the program at the beginning of the iteration in which rule r was considered for deletion. Let $\hat{P}$ and $\hat{P}_f$ denote programs P and P_f, respectively, with r removed. Clearly, P and P_f are uniformly equivalent, since the algorithm deletes while preserving uniform equivalence. Since r has not been deleted permanently, $r \not\subseteq^u \hat{P}$. Let h and b be the head and (possibly empty) body, respectively, of rule r, and let θ be a one-to-one mapping of the variables of r to constants not already in r or P. We have $h\theta \notin \hat{P}(b\theta)$, since $r \not\subseteq^u \hat{P}$, and we also have $h\theta \in \hat{P}_f(b\theta)$, since r is redundant in P_f. But this is a contradiction to $\hat{P}_f(b\theta) \subseteq \hat{P}(b\theta)$, which follows from the fact that every rule of $\hat{P}_f$ is also a rule of $\hat{P}$ (note that here we have used the fact that redundant atoms are deleted before redundant rules and, therefore, a rule that appears in P_f has exactly the same body also in P; if some rule had appeared in P_f with some atoms deleted from its body, as compared to P, it would have been impossible to infer $\hat{P}_f(b\theta) \subseteq \hat{P}(b\theta)$). Thus, we have shown that P_f does not have any redundant rule.

Now suppose that some rule r of P_f (i.e., the final program) has a redundant atom α in its body. P denotes the program at the beginning of the iterations in which α was considered for deletion. Let h be the head of r, and let b and b_f be its bodies in P and P_f, respectively (note that every atom of b_f is also in b). The bodies $\hat{b}_f$ and $\hat{b}$ are obtained from b_f and b, respectively, by deleting α. Let θ be a one-to-one mapping of all the variables of r to constants not already in r or P. Since α has not been deleted permanently, $h\theta \notin P(\hat{b}\theta)$. Since α is redundant in P_f, it follows that $h\theta \in P_f(\hat{b}_f\theta)$. But this is a contradiction, since $P_f \equiv^u P$ and, therefore, $P_f(\hat{b}_f\theta) \subseteq P(\hat{b}\theta)$, because $\hat{b}_f\theta \subseteq \hat{b}\theta$, and Datalog programs are monotonic, that is, adding more atoms to the input does not remove any atom from the output. Thus, we have also shown that P_f does not have any redundant atom. ∎

References

1. Aho, A. V., Sagiv, Y., and Ullman, J. D. [1979] Equivalences among Relational Expressions, *SIAM J. Computing* **8**(2):218–246.

2. Bancilhon, F., Maier, D., Sagiv, Y., and Ullman, J. D. [1986a] Magic Sets and Other Strange Ways to Implement Logic Programs, *Proc. Fifth ACM SIGACT-SIGMOD Symp. on Principles of Database Systems*, Cambridge, MA, 1–15.

3. Bancilhon, F. and Ramakrishnan, R. [1986b] An Amateur's Introduction to Recursive Query Processing Strategies, *Proc. ACM SIGMOD Int. Conf. on Management of Data*, Washington, DC, 16–52.

4. Bancilhon, F. and Ramakrishnan, R. [1988] Performance Evaluation of Data Intensive Logic Programs, in *Foundations of Deductive Databases and Logic Programming* (J. Minker, Ed.), Morgan Kaufmann Publishers, Los Altos, CA, 439–517.

5. Beeri, C., Mendelzon, A. O., Sagiv, Y., and Ullman, J. D. [1981] Equivalence of Relational Database Schemes, *SIAM J. Computing* **10**(2):352–370.

6. Beeri, C. and Vardi, M. Y. [1984] A Proof Procedure for Data Dependencies, *J. ACM* **31**(4):718–741.

7. Buntine, W. [1986] Generalized Subsumption and Its Applications to Induction and Redundancy, manuscript, School of Computing Sciences, N. S. W. Institute of Technology, P. O. Box 123, Broadway, N. S. W., 2007, Australia.

8. Chakravarthy, U. S., Minker, J., and Grant, J. [1986] Semantic Query Optimization: Additional Constraints and Control Strategies, *Proc. First Int. Conf. on Expert Database Systems*, Charleston, SC, 259–269.

9. Chakravarthy, U. S., Grant, J., and Minker, J. [1988] Foundations of Semantic Query Optimization for Deductive Databases, in *Foundations of Deductive*

Databases and Logic Programming (J. Minker, Ed.), Morgan Kaufmann Publishers, Los Altos, CA, 243–273.

10. Chandra, A. K. and Merlin, P. M. [1976] Implementation of Conjunctive Queries in Relational Databases, *Proc. Ninth ACM SIGACT Symp. on Theory of Computing*, 77–90.

11. Cosmadakis, S. S. and Kanellakis, P. C.[1986] Parallel Evaluation of Recursive Rule Queries, *Proc. Fifth ACM SIGACT-SIGMOD Symp. on Principles of Database Systems*, Cambridge, MA, 280–293.

12. Emden, M. H. van and Kowalski, R. A. [1976] The Semantics of Predicate Logic as a Programming Language, *J. ACM* **23**(4):733–742.

13. Fagin, R. [1982] Horn Clauses and Database Dependencies, *J. ACM* **29**(4):952–983.

14. Finger, J. J. [1986] Exploiting Constraints in Design Synthesis, Ph.D. Thesis, Department of Computer Science, Stanford University, Stanford, CA.

15. Gallaire, H. and Minker, J. (Eds.) [1978] *Logic and Databases*, Plenum, New York.

16. Gottlob, G. and Leitsch, A. [1985] On the Efficiency of Subsumption Algorithms, *J. ACM* **32**(2):280–295.

17. Henschen, L. J. and Naqvi, S. A. [1984] On Compiling Queries in Recursive First-Order Databases, *J. ACM* **31**(1):47–85.

18. Kifer, M. and Lozinskii, E. L. [1986] Filtering Data Flow in Deductive Databases, *Proc. Int. Conf. on Database Theory*, Rome, Italy.

19. King, J. J. [1981] Query Optimization by Semantic Reasoning, Ph.D. Thesis (also Rept. No. STAN-CS-81-857), Department of Computer Science, Stanford University, Stanford, CA.

20. Klug, A. and Price, R.[1982] Determining View Dependencies Using Tableaux, *ACM Trans. on Database Systems* **7**(3):361–380.

21. Lozinskii, E. L. [1985] Evaluating Queries in Deductive Databases by Generating, *Proc. 9th IJCAI*, 173–177.

22. Maher, M. J. [1988] Equivalences of Logic Programs, in *Foundations of Deductive Databases and Logic Programming* (J. Minker, Ed.), Morgan Kaufmann Publishers, Los Altos, CA, 627–658.

23. Maier, D., Mendelzon, A. O., and Sagiv, Y. [1979] Testing Implications of Data Dependencies, *ACM Trans. on Database Systems* **4**(4):455–469.

24. McKay, D. and Shapiro, S. [1981] Using Active Connection Graphs for Reasoning with Recursive Rules, *Proc. 7th IJCAI*, 368–374.

25. Naughton, J. F. [1986] Redundancy in Function-Free Recursive Rules, *Proc. 1986 Symp. on Logic Programming*, Salt Lake City, UT, 236–245.

26. Plotkin, G. D. [1970] A Note on Inductive Generalization, in *Machine*

Intelligence, 5 (B. Meltzer and D. Michie, Eds.), Elsevier, North Holland, New York, 153–163.

27. Rohmer, J. and Lescoeur, R. [1985] The Alexander Method: A Technique for the Processing of Recursive Axioms in Deductive Databases, Bull Internal Report.

28. Saccà, D. and Zaniolo, C. [1986] On the Implementation of a Simple Class of Logic Queries for Databases, *Proc. Fifth ACM SIGACT-SIGMOD Symp. on Principles of Database Systems*, Cambridge, MA, 16–23.

29. Sagiv, Y. and Yannakakis, M. [1980] Equivalences among Relational Expressions with the Union and Difference Operators, *J. ACM* **27**(4):633–655.

30. Shmueli, O. [1986] Decidability and Expressiveness Aspects of Logic Queries, *Proc. Sixth ACM SIGACT-SIGMOD-SIGART Symp. on Principles of Database Systems*, San Diego, CA, 237–249.

31. Ullman, J. D. [1982]. *Principles of Database Systems*, Second Edition, Computer Science Press, Rockville, MA.

32. Ullman, J. D. [1985] Implementation of Logical Query Languages for Databases, *ACM Trans. on Database Systems* **10**(3):289–321.

33. Van Gelder, A. [1986] A Message Passing Framework for Logical Query Evaluation, *Proc. ACM SIGMOD Int. Conf. on Management of Data*, Washington, DC, 155–165.

34. Yannakakis, M. and Papadimitriou, C. H. [1982] Algebraic Dependencies, *J. Comput. Syst. Sci.* **25**, 2–41.

18

Converting AND-Control to OR-Control by Program Transformation

M. H. van Emden
University of Waterloo
Waterloo, Canada

P. Szeredi
Computer Research and Innovation Centre (SZKI)
Budapest, Hungary

Abstract

We show how AND-control of logic programs can be transformed to OR-control by the well-known program transformation of unfolding followed by folding. We demonstrate the technique by taking as starting point the logic specification of a dataflow network, which requires complex AND-control, so that it cannot be run by standard Prolog. After transformation, we supply the required OR-control, resulting in a program that can be run by a standard Prolog interpreter.

Introduction

The success of logic programming depends on how often it happens that a definition in logic can be transformed easily to an executable Prolog program. How easy it is to transform (or whether transformation has to done at all), depends on the power of Prolog's control mechanisms.

The control mechanisms of logic programming belong to two main categories. Goal selection determines the derivation tree when the query and the program are given. To find a successful derivation within this tree is the problem of *OR-control*. To select goals in such a way that the derivation tree as a whole is favorable is the problem of *AND-control*.

Prolog's AND-control is characterized by the fixed goal ordering where the leftmost goal is always selected. Thus, when the goals are $G_1, G_2, \ldots, G_n$, none of $G_2, \ldots, G_n$ will get any attention until G_1 is completely solved. This is not effective for an important class of logic definitions where co-routining between goals is required: A goal typically is not solved to completion, its execution being interrupted by work on other goals. Several variants of Prolog provide AND-control that is adequate for co-routining; see Clark and McCabe [1979], Colmerauer [1982], and Naish [1983].

Co-routining can be viewed as a way of running conceptually parallel cooperating processes on a single processor. Thus, it is not surprising that several variants of Prolog designed for parallel execution of goals also have more sophisticated AND-control than Prolog itself; see Clark and Gregory [1981], Clark and Gregory [1986], Gregory [1980, 1987], Shapiro [1983], and Ueda [1985]. In this paper we consider an alternative to providing such more sophisticated control, namely to transform a program requiring co-routining AND-control to one that can be run by plain Prolog. The elimination of the need for co-routining is obtained at the cost of additional OR-control.

In this paper, we demonstrate a transformation method applicable to logic definitions representing dataflow programs where each node in the dataflow network represents a perpetual cyclic process. This class is not executable by Prolog because co-routining AND-control is required.

Translation of Network Specifications

The type of network specification we translate here was proposed by Kahn and McQueen [1977]. Consider the dataflow network in Figure 1, which solves a

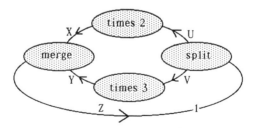

Figure 1: Dataflow Network for a Simplified Version of Hamming's Problem

version of Hamming's problem. This simplified version produces the sequence of integers containing no prime factors other than 2 and 3. Each node represents a processor; each arc, a communication channel. Each processor executes a cyclical computation and is activated as soon as its input channels contain enough data for one cycle of its computation.

The computation of the `merge` node is as follows. In case the first numbers in each of the input channels are equal, both are removed and one is written in the output channel. If the two first numbers are different, the smallest one is removed and output. The predicate `times2` outputs each input number multiplied by 2; analogously for `times3`; and `split` outputs a copy of each input number. The diagram in Figure 1 shows the initial state of the network, where all channels are empty except for the one between `merge` and `split`, which contains a 1.

According to van Emden and de Lucena [1979, 1982], a dataflow network is represented in logic in two parts. The logic program contains definitions of the individual nodes in the network as relations between lists of data items. Thus, the program contains no information about how the nodes are connected; this is done in the goal statement.

Here follow the definitions of the nodes in Figure 1:

```
merge (A.X, B.Y, A.Z)  if  lt (A, B) , merge (X, B.Y, Z) ;
merge (A.X, B.Y, B.Z)  if  lt (B, A) , merge (A.X, Y, Z) ;
merge (A.X, A.Y, A.Z)  if  merge (X, Y, Z) ;
times2 (A.U, B.X)  if  prod (A, 2, B) , times2 (U, X) ;
times3 (A.V, B.Y)  if  prod (A, 3, B) , times3 (V, Y) ;
split (A.Z, A.U, A.V)  if  split (Z, U, V)
```

The network is specified by the goal statement:

```
?  merge (X, Y, Z) , times2 (U, X) , times3 (V, Y) , split (1.Z, U, V)
```

Note how the shared variables represent the communication channels between the processors of the network. In cases where two goals have as argument just the shared variable itself, the corresponding channel is empty in the initial state. This is the case everywhere except for the channel connecting `merge` (where the argument is Z) and `split` (where the argument is 1.Z). The difference (in the sense of "difference lists") between these arguments is 1, just the content of the channel represented by the arguments.

Of course, if we ask the question

```
?  merge (X, Y, Z) , times2 (1.Z, X) , times3 (1.Z, Y)
```

obtained from the previous one by using, by the meaning of `split`, U and V both equal 1.Z, then we do not need the definition of `split` at all *and* we get a shorter question. This shorter question, however, has no corresponding dataflow network. This simplification is evidence for the greater power of logic programming compared to dataflow networks. In the sequel, we continue with the dataflow network because we need an instructive example rather than a most concise statement of Hamming's problem.

A Variant of the Dataflow Network Representation

For the purpose of the program transformation it is convenient to modify the dataflow network representation described in the previous section, where the network was represented directly by a question.

In this section we describe a network representation consisting of two parts. In the first part, consisting of an equivalence, we represent a conjunction of all nodes without specifying any connections.

For our example this equivalence is:

```
conj (X1,Y1,Z2,U1,X2,V1,Y2,Z1,U2,V2) iff
merge(X1,Y1,Z2) & times2(U1,X2) & times3(V1,Y2) &
    split(Z1,U2,V2)
```

Although this is not a clause, we have followed here the clausal convention of implicitly universally quantifying all variables. In the right-hand side we have named the variables in a way indicating how they are going to be "connected": $X1$ and $X2$ are now respectively the input and output ports of the same channel that was represented by X before; similarly for the other variables and channels. See Figure 2.

More helpfully, $X1$ and $X2$ can be regarded as lists: $X1$ is then the list of all items passing through the output port of X, while $X2$ is the list of all items passing through its input port. It follows that $X2$ must be a posterior sublist of $X1$ and that the (possibly empty) prefix of items in $X1$, which is not in $X2$, consists of the contents of the channel X. In other words, $X1$ and $X2$ are the two components of the *difference list* representation of channel X.

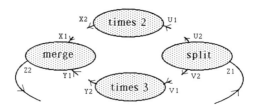

Figure 2: The Unconnected Conjunction of Nodes

In the second stage, we complete the network specification by a question. It is here that we use the difference list representation to specify the contents of each channel.

```
? conj (X, Y, Z, U, X, V, Y, 1. Z, U, V)
```

Although this representation will support our program transformation, it has the disadvantage that `conj` has a long list of arguments that hides a useful structure; the arguments can be partitioned into groups representing ports of the same node. We will therefore continue with a modification of the representation used before.

This modification is obtained by changing the predicates for the node computations to become, formally at least, unary by the use of a functor to package the input and output streams into a single term.

```
merge(m(A.X,B.Y,A.Z)) if lt(A,B),merge(m(X,B.Y,Z));
merge(m(A.X,B.Y,B.Z)) if lt(B,A),merge(m(A.X,Y,Z));
merge(m(A.X,A.Y,A.Z)) if merge(m(X,Y,Z));
times2(t2(A.U,B.X)) if prod(A,2 B),times2(t2(U,X));
times3(t3(A.V,B.Y)) if prod(A,3,B),times3(t3(V,Y));
split(s(A.Z,A.U,A.V)) if split(s(Z,U,V))
```

Now that each of the node relations has one argument, the definition of `conj` is simplified:

```
conj (M, T2, T3, S) iff merge (M) & times2 (T2) &
    times3 (T3) & split (S);
```

Finally, the network connections are specified by the question

```
? conj (m (X, Y, Z), t2 (U, X), t3 (V, Y), s (1. Z, U, V))
```

Deriving the Program

In this section we show how to apply the unfold/fold transformation due to Burstall and Darlington [1977] to obtain a logic program requiring OR-control where the original network specification required AND-control.

The key predicate in the derived program is `conj`. From the definition we use only the *if* part:

```
conj (M, T2, T3, S) if merge (M), times2 (T2), times3 (T3),
        split (S)
```

704 van Emden and Szeredi

Let us combine this definition with that of `merge`. As the first step, we obtain from the above implication the instance:

```
conj (m (A.X,B.Y,A.Z),T2,T3,S)
    if merge (m (A.X,B.Y,A.Z)),times2 (T2),times3 (T3),
        split (S)
```

We use the definition of `merge` to obtain by resolution ("unfolding" or "partial application"):

```
conj (m (A.X,B.Y,A.Z), T2,T3,S)
    if lt (A,B),merge (m (X,B.Y,Z)),times2 (T2),times3 (T3),
        split (S)
```

When we now use the *only if* part of the definition of `conj` on the right-hand side, we obtain (by "folding"):

```
conj (m (A.X,B.Y,A.Z),T2,T3,S)
    if lt (A,B),conj (m (X,B.Y,Z),T2,T3,S)
```

In a similar way, each of the clauses defining a node relation can be combined with the definition of `conj` to yield the following set of clauses:

```
conj (m (A.X,B.Y,A.Z),T2,T3,S)
    if lt (A,B),conj (m (X,B.Y,Z),T2,T3,S);
conj (m (A.X,B.Y,B.Z),T2,T3,S)
    if gt (A,B),conj (m (A.X,Y,Z),T2,T3,S);
conj (m (A.X,A.Y,A.Z),T2,T3,S)
    if conj (m (X,Y,Z),T2,T3,S);
conj (M,t2(A.U,B.X),T3,S)
    if not(var(A)),prod(A,2,B),conj(M,t2(U,X),T3,S);
conj (M,T2,t3(A.V,B.Y),S)
    if not(var(A)),prod(A,3,B),conj(M,T2,t3(V,Y),S);
conj (M,T2,T3,s(A.Z,A.U,A.V))
    if not(var(A)),conj(M,T2,T3,s(Z,U,V))
```

OR-Control of the Derived Program

The derived program is activated by the question:

```
? conj(m(X,Y,Z), t2(U,X), t3(V,Y), s(1.Z,U,V))
```

This call, and calls generated later by this call, are such that all clauses for
`conj` match. The required control is to select a suitable subset of clauses,
hence OR-control.

Just as with AND-control for the specification, the control is derived from
the computation rule for dataflow networks: *Any node is allowed to execute one
cycle whenever it has enough data in its input channels to execute this cycle.*

In this example, the computation rule translates to the condition that a
clause should only be selected when certain variables have become bound. A
straightforward approach is the following:

```
conj(m(A.X,B.Y,A.Z),T2,T3,S)
     if not(var(A)),not(var(B)),lt(A,B),
          conj(m(X,B.Y,Z),T2,T3,S);
conj(m(A.X,B.Y,B.Z),T2,T3,S)
     if not(var(A)),not(var(B)),gt(A,B),
          conj(m(A.X,Y,Z),T2,T3,S);
conj(m(A.X,A.Y,A.Z),T2,T3,S)
     if not(var(A)),conj(m(X,Y,Z),T2,T3,S);
conj(M,t2(A.U,B.X),T3,S)
     if not(var(A)),prod(A,2,B),conj(M,t2(U,X),T3,S);
conj(M,T2,t3(A.V,B.Y),S)
     if not(var(A)),prod(A,3,B),conj(M,T2,t3(V,Y),S);
conj(M,T2,T3,s(A.Z,A.U,A.V))
     if not(var(A)),conj(M,T2,T3,s(Z,U,V))
```

Each condition of the derived program has received its OR-control in the
form of ''guards'' on the conditions. In this way we intend to realize the requirement of the dataflow rule of computation that only those processes are allowed to be activated that have the required data in their input channels.

This example shows that just mechanically inserting guards of the form
`not(var(...))` does not always have the desired effect. In fact, the above
program does not solve Hamming's problem but generates, instead, an infinite
sequence of 2's. Why this happens may be seen as follows. Suppose the state
of the dataflow network is as represented in the question

```
?  conj(m(2.X,Y,Z),t2(U,X),t3(1.V,Y),s(Z,U,V))
```

Now the third clause

```
conj(m(A.X',A.Y',A.Z'),T2,T3,S)
     if not(var(A)),conj(m(X',Y',Z'),T2,T3,S)
```

will be used. But this clause represents an action by the `merge`-node, which
should only be allowed when *both* input channels are non-empty. Use of the
third clause results in the question

```
? conj (m (X, Y', Z') , t2 (U, X) , t3 (1. V, 2. Y') , s (2. Z', U, V) )
```

Not only has a 2 appeared in the output channel of merge, but the equivalent of pushing it into the empty input channel has also occurred.

The third clause should not be obtained by merely inserting the guard. Instead, it should be recognized that there is an implicit test for equality (the first two occurrences of A) and that this test should come *after* a guard ensuring that the input channels are nonempty, like this:

```
conj (m (A. X, B. Y, A. Z) , T2, T3, S)
    if not (var (A) ) , not (var (B) ) , eq (A, B) , conj (m (X, Y, Z) ,
        T2, T3, S)
```

An Alternative Route to the Transformed Program

The transformed program can also be obtained by considering the *state* of the dataflow network and regarding a computation by the network as a sequence of state transitions. And of course, we have to formulate a logic program having as a property that its execution by SLD-resolution somehow mimics the desired sequence of state transitions.

We first explain the general principle and then apply it to the dataflow situation. Consider a binary relation between states such that trans(State1, State2) iff the transition from State1 to State2 is possible.

Let us call a *computation* a sequence of states such that successive elements in the sequence are in the transition relation. If there is a last state in the computation, then it has to be a specially designated *halt state*. Let comp(State1, State2) be true iff there is a computation with State1 as first element and State2 as last element. The relation comp is then defined by:

```
comp(State,State) if halt(State);
comp(State1,State2) if trans(State1,State),
    comp(State,State2)
```

As we are interested in our dataflow example in computations without a halt state, the first clause is irrelevant. Moreover, in the second clause the second argument of comp becomes irrelevant. Hence we arrive at the predicate start which asserts of a state that it is the start state of a possibly infinite computation.

```
start(State1) if trans (State1, State2) , start (State2)
```

The state consists of the aggregation of the channel contents, represented as lists. We implement this aggregation by representing the state as a term with state as functor and with clusters of channels as arguments. Let us take as example one of the transitions possible when the merge node has nonempty input channels:

```
trans (state (m (A. X, B. Y, A. Z) , T2, T3, S) , state (m (X, B. Y, Z) ,
    T2, T3, S) )
    if lt (A, B)
```

When we do a resolution ("partial application") with the clause for start, we get:

```
start (state (m (A. X, B. Y, A. Z) , T2, T3, S) )
    if lt (A, B) , start (state (m (X, B. Y, Z) , T2, T3, S) )
```

Note that this is substantially the same as one of the clauses of the program obtained by the unfold / fold transformation and that the other clauses can be obtained in the same way from operational reasoning about state transitions.

Of course, we have to add the same OR-control as we did to the result of the unfold / fold transformation. We use the operational reasoning about state-transitions in the dataflow model to finish the incomplete control of the last version of the result of the unfold / fold transformation.

Opportunities for parallel computation arise in dataflow networks when more than one node has sufficient input. In our example it often happens that both multiplication nodes can operate in parallel. In the transformed program, this shows by more than one clause having its guard succeed. From the dataflow rule of computation it is apparent that one can commit on a choice to any clause for which the guard succeeds. Thus, the result of our transformation of dataflow programs can be made to exhibit the committed-choice nondeterminism typical of variants of Prolog for parallelism.

Taking this consideration into account, we find that we can place "cut" operators to obtain as our final program the one shown below. Of course, a Prolog hacker would have seen the opportunity for cuts right away; we prefer to conclude their permissibility from properties of the dataflow computation model.

```
conj(m(A.X,B.Y,A.Z),T2,T3,S)
    if not(var(A)),not(var(B)),lt(A,B), cut,
        conj(m(X,B.Y,Z),T2,T3,S);
conj(m(A.X,B.Y,B.Z),T2,T3,S)
    if not(var(A)),not(var(B)),gt(A,B), cut,
        conj(m(A.X,Y,Z),T2,T3,S);
```

```
conj(m(A.X,B.Y,A.Z),T2,T3,S)
    if not(var(A)),not(var(B)),eq(A,B),cut,
        conj(m(X,Y,Z),T2,T3,S);
conj(M,t2(A.U,B.X),T3,S)
    if not(var(A)),cut,prod(A,2,B),conj(M,t2(U,X),
        T3,S);
conj(M,T2,t3(A.V,B.Y),S)
    if not(var(A)),cut,prod(A,3,B),conj(M,T2,t3(V,Y),
        S);
conj(M,T2,T3,s(A.Z,A.U,A.V))
    if not(var(A)),cut,conj(M,T2,T3,s(Z,U,V))
```

Conclusions

We presented two ways of deriving Prolog-executable programs from logic specifications of dataflow diagrams. The first used the well-known unfold/fold transformation; it depended exclusively on declarative concepts. The second was based entirely on machine-oriented concepts: transitions allowed in the dataflow model of computation. It is surprising that a purely declarative approach can result in essentially the same Prolog program as a purely operational approach.

It is not surprising of course to find *some* connection with operational concepts. After all, the unfold transformation is a top-down computation step of a Prolog interpreter. But we found a close relation not directly to the action of the Prolog interpreter, but to the dataflow model of computation.

We have shown an example of conversion of AND-control to OR-control. AND-control is needed to exploit the potential for parallelism in the evaluation of the conditions of a clause. Our work raises the question: Have we also shown how to convert opportunities for AND-parallelism to opportunities for OR-parallelism?

The demonstration of this paper clearly applies to all static dataflow networks consisting of nodes executing nonterminating cyclic computations. An attractive area for further investigation is to expand our technique to a wider class of logic specifications.

Acknowledgments

We owe a debt of gratitude to Steve Gregory and two anonymous referees for their penetrating remarks, which made it possible for us to remedy some of the previous version's shortcomings. Our thanks also to Mantis H. M. Cheng for pointing out that the naive OR-control of the derived program is wrong, and why. Last, but not least, we gratefully acknowledge the role of the Digital Equipment Corporation of Canada and the National Science and Engineering Research Council of Canada in contributing to the research facilities used in the work reported here.

References

1. Burstall, R. and Darlington, J. [1977] A Transformation System for Developing Recursive Programs, *Journal of the ACM* **24**, 44–67.

2. Clark, K.L. and Gregory, S. [1981] A Relational Language for Parallel Programming, *Proceedings of the ACM Conference on Functional Languages and Computer Architecture*.

3. Clark, K.L. and Gregory, S. [1986] Parallel Programming in Logic, *ACM Transactions on Programming Languages and Systems* **8**, 1–49.

4. Clark, K.L. and McCabe, F.G. [1979] The Control Facilities of IC-Prolog, in *Expert Systems* (D. Michie, Ed.), Edinburgh University Press.

5. Colmerauer, A. [1982] Prolog II Reference Manual and Theoretical Model, Internal report, Groupe Intelligence Artificielle, Universite d'Aix Marseille II.

6. Emden, M.H. van, and Lucena, G.J. de [1979] Predicate Logic as a Language for Parallel Programming, Research Report CS-79-15, Computer Science Department, University of Waterloo.

7. Emden, M.H. van, and Lucena, G.J. de [1982] Predicate Logic as a Language for Parallel Programming, in *Logic Programming* (K. L. Clark and S.A. Tärnlund, Eds.), Academic Press, 189–198.

8. Gregory, S. [1980] Towards the Compilation of Annotated Logic Programs, Research Report DoC 80/16, Department of Computing, Imperial College, London.

9. Gregory, S. [1987] *Parallel Logic Programming in PARLOG*, Addison-Wesley.

10. Kahn, G. and McQueen, D.B. [1977] Co-routines and Networks of Parallel Processes, *Proceedings IFIP 1977*, 993–998.

11. Naish, L. [1983] The MU-Prolog 3.2 Reference Manual, Technical Report 85/11, Department of Computer Science, University of Melbourne.

12. Shapiro, E.Y. [1983] A Subset of Concurrent Prolog and Its Interpreter, *ICOT Technical Report TR-003*.

13. Ueda, K. [1985] Guarded Horn Clauses, *ICOT Technical report TR-103*.

Authors

Krzysztof R. Apt
Centre for Mathematics and
Computer Science
Kruislaan 413
1098 SJ Amsterdam
The Netherlands

Francois Bancilhon
INRIA
BP 105
78153 le Chesnay Cedex
France

Howard A. Blair
School of Computer and
Information Science
Syracuse University
Syracuse, NY 13244

Upen S. Chakravarthy
Computer Corporation of America
Four Cambridge Center
Cambridge, MA 02142

Maarten H. van Emden
Department of Computer Science
University of Victoria
Canada

John Grant
Department of Computer and
Information Sciences
Towson State University
Towson, MD 21204

Lawrence J. Henschen
Department of Computer Science
Northwestern University
Evanston, IL 60201

Tomasz Imielinski
Department of Computer Science
Rutgers University
New Brunswick, NJ 08903

Paris C. Kanellakis
Department of Computer Science
Brown University
P.O. Box 910
Providence, RI 02912

Robert Kowalski
Department of Computing
Imperial College of Science
and Technology
180 Queen's Gate
London SW7 2BZ
United Kingdom

Jean-Louis Lassez
IBM Thomas J. Watson Research
Center
P.O. Box 704
Yorktown Heights, NY 10598

Vladimir Lifschitz
Computer Science Department
Stanford University
Stanford, CA 94305-2085

Michael J. Maher
IBM Thomas J. Watson Research
Center
P.O. Box 704
Yorktown Heights, NY 10598

Sanjay Manchanda
Department of Computer Science
University of Arizona
Tuscon, AZ 85721

Kim Marriott
Department of Computer Science
University of Melbourne
Parkville, Victoria 3052
Australia

Jack Minker
Department of Computer Science
and
Institute for Advanced Computer
Studies
University of Maryland
College Park, MD 20742

Lee Naish
Department of Computer Science
University of Melbourne
Parkville, Victoria 3052
Australia

Hyung-sik Park
Department of Computer Science
Northwestern University
Evanston, IL 60201

Teodor C. Przymusinski
Department of Mathematical
Science
University of Texas at El Paso
El Paso, TX 79968-0514

Raghu Ramakrishnan
Computer Sciences Department
University of Wisconsin—Madison
Madison, WI 53706

Kotagiri Ramamohanarao
Department of Computer Science
University of Melbourne
Parkville, Victoria 3052
Australia

Fariba Sadri
Department of Computing
Imperial College of Science
and Technology
180 Queen's Gate
London SW7 2BZ
United Kingdom

Yehoshua Sagiv
Department of Computer Science
The Hebrew University of
Jerusalem
Givat-Ram 91904, Jerusalem
Israel

John C. Shepherdson
School of Mathematics
University of Bristol
University Walk
Bristol BS8 1TW
United Kingdom

Elizabeth A. Sonenberg
Department of Computer Science
University of Melbourne
Parkville, Victoria 3052
Australia

Peter Szeredi
Computer Research and Innovation
Center (SZKI)
Donati u. 35-45
Hungary

James A. Thom
Department of Computer Science
Royal Melbourne Institute
of Technology
Melbourne 3000
Australia

Rodney W. Topor
Department of Computer Science
University of Melbourne
Parkville, Victoria 3052
Australia

Allen Van Gelder
Department of Computer and
Information Sciences
University of California, Santa
Cruz
Santa Cruz, CA 95064

Adrian Walker
IBM Thomas J. Watson Research
Center
P.O. Box 704
Yorktown Heights, NY 10598

David S. Warren
Department of Computer Science
State University of New York at
Stony Brook
Stony Brook, NY 11794

Referees

Kryzsztof R. Apt, Centre for Mathematics and Computer Science, The Netherlands

Francois Bancilhon, Institut National de Recherche en Informatique et Automatique

Catriel Beeri, Hebrew University

Wolfgang Bibel, University of British Columbia

Howard A. Blair, Syracuse University

Kenneth Bowen, Syracuse University

Keith Clark, Imperial College of London

Martin Davis, Courant Institute

Umeshwar Dayal, Computer Corporation of America

Hendrik Decker, European Computer-Industry Research Center (ECRC)

Reinhard Enders, European Computer-Industry Research Center (ECRC)

Maarten van Emden, University of Waterloo

David Etherington, Bell Telephone Laboratories

Christos Faloutsos, University of Maryland

Hervé Gallaire, European Computer-Industry Research Center (ECRC)

Jean Gallier, University of Pennsylvania

Michael Gelfond, University of Texas at El Paso

Randy Goebel, University of Alberta

Joseph Goguen, Stanford Research Institute

John Grant, Towson State University

Steve Gregory, Imperial College of London

Lawrence J. Henschen, Northwestern University

Richard Hull, University of Southern California

Tomasz Imielinski, Rutgers University

Joseph Ja'Ja', University of Maryland

Joxan Jaffar, IBM Corporation, Yorktown Heights

Laxmikant Kale, University of Illinois

Michael Kifer, State University of New York at Stony Brook

Madhur Kohli, University of Maryland

Robert A. Kowalski, Imperial College of London

Jean-Louis Lassez, IBM Corporation, Yorktown Heights

Anne Litcher, University of Maryland

Vladimir Lifschitz, Stanford University

Jorge Lobo, University of Maryland

Michael Maher, IBM Corporation, Yorktown Heights

Witold Marek, University of Kentucky

Jack Minker, University of Maryland

Lee Naish, University of Melbourne

Shamim Naqvi, Microelectronics and Computer Technology Corporation (MCC)

Jeffrey F. Naughton, Stanford University

Stott Parker, University of California at Los Angeles

Luis Pereira, University of Lisboa

Donald Perlis, University of Maryland

Teodor Przymusinski, University of Texas at El Paso

Stan Raatz, University of Pennsylvania

I.V. Ramakrishnan, State Universiy of New York at Stony Brook

Kotagiri Ramamohanarao, University of Melbourne

Raymond Reiter, University of Toronto

Fariba Sadri, Imperial College of London

Yehoshua Sagiv, Hebrew University

Deepak Sherlekar, University of Maryland

Rick Stevens, Argonne National Laboratories

V.S. Subrahmanian, Syracuse University

Peter Szeredi, SZKI, Computer Research and Innovation Center

James Thom, University of Melbourne

Rodney W. Topor, University of Melbourne

Allen Van Gelder, Stanford University

Moshe Vardi, IBM San Jose

Laurent Vieille, European Computer-Industry Research Center (ECRC)

Clifford Walinsky, Oregon Graduate Center

David Scott Warren, State University of New York at Stony Brook

Larry Wos, Argonne National Laboratories

Keitaro Yukawa, University of Waterloo

Carlo Zaniolo, Microelectronics and Computer Technology Corporation

Author Index

717

Subject Index

Index Note: Page numbers in **boldface** indicate definitions.

Cost of recursive query evaluation strategies. *See* Performance evaluation of data intensive logic programs

Cost metrics for performance evaluation, 474

Counting, 440, **466**–468, 481, 485, 488, 498–507, 512–517

Counting sets, 466

Covering axiom, 143

Cuts in PROLOG, 707–708

CWA. *See* Closed World Assumption

Cyclic process, 700

Cylinder, 500

dag (directed acyclic graph), 554, 571–579

dag-GAP (directed acyclic graph-graph accessibility problem), **554**, 572, 577, 578

DARPA (Department of Defense Advanced Research Projects Agency), 191

Data complexity, 555

Data definition, DLP support of, 8

Data intensive logic programs. *See* Performance evaluation of data intensive logic programs

Database administrator (DBA), 382

Databases, **219**, **554–555**
  additions in. *See* Additions in databases
  allowed, **230**–231, 234
  binary relation on, 367
  CDB, 395, 398, 402
  completed, 6, **22**, 38–49
  completion of, **317**–318
  DEDB, 402
  deductive. *See* Deductive databases
  definite Horn, 195, **220**, 230, 231

deletions in. *See* Deletions in databases

description of, **368**, 374–378, 377

DIDB, 402

disjunctive, 72–73, **197**

domain independent. *See* Domain independent databases

domain of, 554–555

EDB, **249**–252, 269, 276, 279, 469–471, 503, 556–557, 568, 665–691

general, **230**

hierarchical, **220**, 230, 231, **339**

Horn, 396

IDB, **249**–253, 269–270, 276, 279, 395, 470–471, 556–557, 568, 571, 665–668

IEDB, 402

IIDB, 402

implicit deletions in, **335**

incomplete information, 380

language of, **219**

large, 8, 275

locally stratified, 193, **205**

logical. *See* Deductive databases

non-Horn, 8, 271–272, 396

with null values, 380

perfect model of, 6

positive, **194**

positive disjunctive, **196**, 209

positivistic, 197

preliminary, **686**

range-restricted, **316**

RDB, 4, 8, 395, 398, 402, 439

recursive, 250, 271–272, 532–533

recursive IDDB, 419–423

relational. *See* Relational databases

satisfying tgd, 674

semantics of, 193–194

standard model for, **221**

state of, 370, **371**

statements in, **219**

stratified. *See* Stratified databases

updates in. *See* Updates in databases

Dataflow networks, 699–708

DATALOG (function-free Horn clause) programs, 8, 549, 556, **629**, **663**
  application of Sagiv algorithm to, 12, 244
  equivalence of, 686–691
  optimization of. *See* Optimizing DATALOG programs
  uniformly equivalent, **9**, **666**–673

DBA (database administrator), 382

DCA (domain closure axiom), **28**–31, 46, 50, 70

Deadlock of goals, 150, 168

DEC (Digital Equipment Corporation) of Canada, 709

Decidable relation, 125

Decidable standard interpretation, 125

Decision problem, 224

Decker's algorithm, 348–351

Declarative meaning and procedural interpretations, 90–91

Declarative reading of clauses, 2

Declarative semantics, 3, 21–22, 193

Decomposition, modular, 292

DEDB (definite extensional database), 402

Deductive database query programs. *See* Logical query programs

Deductive databases, **316**, 659–670

T_p mapping, **98**–100, 108–110, **631**–633
Transactions with multiple updates, 338–341
Transfer ratio, **473**
Transformation systems, 628, 654
Transformations
of AND-control to OR-control, 699–708
of programs, 702–703
of rules. *See* Rule transformation
saturating, **290**, **296**–299
unfold / fold, 703–704, 707, 708
on view definitions, 387–391
Transitive closure operator, 172, 298, 508–509, 557–559, 565, 566, 570, 667
Translators
add, 366, **381**, 388–389
delete, 366, **381**, 389–391
semantically acceptable, **386**–391
semantically correct, **384**–391
view update, 363, 366, 381–391
Tree-oriented semantics, 159–171
Tree-size resource, 552
Tree structure, 500
Trivial Herbrand universe, **591**
True query, 399
Tuple-generating dependencies (tgd), **674**–686, 691–692
Tuples, 521
Twelfth International Conference on Very Large Databases, 536
2-valued Herbrand models, 79–84
2-valued models, 75–84
Typed rules, **279**
Typed single rule programs (sirups), **560**

UCs (uniform circuits of bounded fan-in), 553
u-GAP (undirected graph accessibility problem), **554**, 571
UMIACS (University of Maryland Institute for Advanced Computing Studies), 5, 14
Unbounded logical query programs, 558, 567–570
Undecidable conditions, 227
Undirected graph accessibility problem (u-GAP), **554**, 571
Unfold / fold transformation, 703–704, 707, 708
Unfolding, 9, 704, 707, 708
Unfolding axioms, 8
Unifiable terms, 152, **600**
Unification
and anti-unification, 588, 589, 606–615
best expected time algorithm for, 579
and congruence closure, 576, 579
future directions in, 12
and inherently sequential operations, 575–576
introduced, 572–573
and the mgs, 589, 606–615, **612**
and mgus. *See* Most general unifiers
naive, 573–575, 579
open questions about, 578–579
overview of, 8–9, 587–589
and parallelizable operations, 576–578
roots of, 9
semantic, 655
and systems of equations and inequations, 615–623
term (UNIFY), 9, 547, 549, **573**–576
Unification algorithm, 589, 591
Unification of terms

problem, 553
Unifiers, **600**, 604, **629**
Uniform circuits of bounded fan-in (UCs), 553
Uniform containment, 642, 669–672, 691, 692–695
Uniform equivalence, **661**, 669–673, 691, 692–696
Uniform logical query programs, **560**
Uniformly contains (defined), **666**–674, 692–695
Uniformly equivalent DATALOG programs, **9**, **666**–673
UNIFY (term unification), 9, 547, 549, **573**–576
Union, 280
of queries, 557
of relations, 664
UNION-FIND algortihm, 579
Unit clauses, 249
Unit queries, 419–423
United States-Israel Binational Science Foundation (BSF), 692
Universal quantifier, 271–272
Universal states, 551
Universally quantified (defined), 152
Universe, 554
University of Maryland Institute for Advanced Computing Studies (UMIACS), 5, 14
University of Melbourne, 536
Unix operating system, 535
Unrelated clusters, **114**
Unrestricted terms, **619**–620
Unsafe negation, 151–154
Untyped queries, 557, 567
U_p operator, **170**–171
Update queries, 364, 369–372
Update rules, 366, **368**, 373, 376, 388